at Global Knowledge Certif... W9-BNK-039

NETWORK+ TEST YOURSELF PERSONAL TESTING CENTER

Master the skills you need to pass the Network+ exam using the TEST YOURSELF Personal Testing Center on CD-ROM—the most effective MCSD exam simulator and knowledge building tool available. Choose the "Live Exam" mode for a timed exam or choose the "Practice Exam" mode, which lets you set the pace, displaying in-depth answers as needed. This CD-ROM features more than 300 interactive Network+ Practice questions, detailed score reports by exam topic, and a unique benchmarking tool that charts your progress. It's the closest you can get to having your own personal Network+ exam trainer!

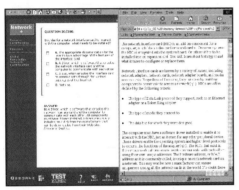

TEST YOURSELF
IN PRACTICE- OR LIVE-EXAM MODE

Experience realistic exams on your own computer with the interactive TEST YOURSELF software. Use the practice mode so you can pause the exam and link back to the text for more information, or use the live-exam mode—a timed exam that simulates the actual Network+ Test.

OTHER UNIQUE TESTING FEATURES

■ All exam questions randomly generated from a pool of 300 for a different test experience each time.

■ Hyperlinks to expertly written text for further explanations.

■ Written and prepared by professionals who have taken and passed the exams.

■ All CompTIA Network+ test objectives covered in detail.

■ Includes Internet Explorer 4.0 on CD-ROM.

ASSESS YOURSELF

Detailed score reports show which exam topics need further study and how your score compares to the required passing score.

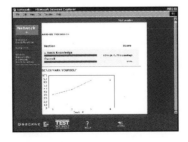

BENCHMARK YOURSELF

Chart your progress with the Benchmarking Tool—the scoring feature that records and graphs your exam scores over time.

SYSTEM REQUIREMENTS:

A PC running Internet Explorer version 4.0 or higher.

Network+ Certification

Study Guide

Syngress Media, Inc

Osborne/McGraw-Hill
Berkeley   New York   St. Louis   San Francisco
Auckland   Bogotá   Hamburg   London   Madrid
Mexico City   Milan   Montreal   New Delhi   Panama City
Paris   São Paulo   Singapore   Sydney
Tokyo   Toronto

Osborne/**McGraw-Hill**
2600 Tenth Street
Berkeley, California 94710
U.S.A.

For information on translations or book distributors outside the U.S.A., or to arrange bulk purchase discounts for sales promotions, premiums, or fund-raisers, please contact Osborne/**McGraw-Hill** at the above address.

Network+ Certification Study Guide

4567890 DOC DOC   01987654321

ISBN 0-07-211846-6

Publisher	**Technical Editors**	**Computer Designers**
Brandon A. Nordin	D. Lynn White	Roberta Steele
	Stace Cunningham	Michelle Galicia
Associate Publisher and		
Editor-in-Chief	**Series Editor**	**Illustrators**
Scott Rogers	D. Lynn White	Beth Young
		Robert Hansen
Acquisitions Editor	**Copy Editor**	
Gareth Hancock	Michelle Shaw	**Series Design**
		Roberta Steele
Project Editor	**Proofreader**	
Cynthia Douglas	Pat Mannion	
Editorial Assistant	**Indexer**	
Tara Davis	Claire Splan	

From Global Knowledge

At Global Knowledge we strive to support the multiplicity of learning styles required by our students to achieve success as technical professionals. In this series of books, it is our intention to offer the reader a valuable tool for successful completion of the Network+ Certification Exam.

As the world's largest IT training company, Global Knowledge Network is uniquely positioned to offer these books. The expertise gained each year from providing instructor-led training to hundreds of thousands of students worldwide has been captured in book form to enhance your learning experience. We hope that the quality of these books demonstrates our commitment to your lifelong learning success. Whether you choose to learn through the written word, computer-based training, Web delivery, or instructor-led training, Global Knowledge Network is committed to providing you the very best in each of those categories. For those of you who know Global Knowledge Network, or those of you who have just found us for the first time, our goal is to be your lifelong competency partner.

Thank you for the opportunity to serve you. We look forward to serving your needs again in the future.

Warmest regards,

Duncan Anderson
President and Chief Executive Officer, Global Knowledge

The Global Knowledge Advantage

Global Knowledge has a global delivery system for its products and services. The company has 28 subsidiaries, and offers its programs through a total of 60+ locations. No other vendor can provide consistent services across a geographic area this large. Global Knowledge is the largest independent information technology education provider, offering programs on a variety of platforms. This enables our multi-platform and multi-national customers to obtain all of their programs from a single vendor. The company has developed the unique CompetusTM Framework software tool and methodology which can quickly reconfigure courseware to the proficiency level of a student on an interactive basis. Combined with self-paced and on-line programs, this technology can reduce the time required for training by prescribing content in only the deficient skills areas. The company has fully automated every aspect of the education process, from registration and follow-up, to "just-in-time" production of courseware. Global Knowledge, through its Enterprise Services Consultancy, can customize programs and products to suit the needs of an individual customer.

Global Knowledge Classroom Education Programs

The backbone of our delivery options is classroom-based education. Our modern, well-equipped facilities staffed with the finest instructors offer programs in a wide variety of information technology topics, many of which lead to professional certifications.

Custom Learning Solutions

This delivery option has been created for companies and governments that value customized learning solutions. For them, our consultancy-based approach of developing targeted education solutions is most effective at helping them meet specific objectives.

Self-Paced and Multimedia Products

This delivery option offers self-paced program titles in interactive CD-ROM, videotape and audio tape programs. In addition, we offer custom development of interactive multimedia courseware to customers and partners. Call us at 1 (888) 427-4228.

Electronic Delivery of Training

Our network-based training service delivers efficient competency-based, interactive training via the World Wide Web and organizational intranets. This leading-edge delivery option provides a custom learning path and "just-in-time" training for maximum convenience to students.

ARG

American Research Group (ARG), a wholly-owned subsidiary of Global Knowledge, one of the largest worldwide training partners of Cisco Systems, offers a wide range of internetworking, LAN/WAN, Bay Networks, FORE Systems, IBM, and UNIX courses. ARG offers hands on network training in both instructor-led classes and self-paced PC-based training.

Global Knowledge Courses Available

Network Fundamentals
- Understanding Computer Networks
- Telecommunications Fundamentals I
- Telecommunications Fundamentals II
- Understanding Networking Fundamentals
- Implementing Computer Telephony Integration
- Introduction to Voice Over IP
- Introduction to Wide Area Networking
- Cabling Voice and Data Networks
- Introduction to LAN/WAN protocols
- Virtual Private Networks
- ATM Essentials

Network Security & Management
- Troubleshooting TCP/IP Networks
- Network Management
- Network Troubleshooting
- IP Address Management
- Network Security Administration
- Web Security
- Implementing UNIX Security
- Managing Cisco Network Security
- Windows NT 4.0 Security

IT Professional Skills
- Project Management for IT Professionals
- Advanced Project Management for IT Professionals
- Survival Skills for the New IT Manager
- Making IT Teams Work

LAN/WAN Internetworking
- Frame Relay Internetworking
- Implementing T1/T3 Services
- Understanding Digital Subscriber Line (xDSL)
- Internetworking with Routers and Switches
- Advanced Routing and Switching
- Multi-Layer Switching and Wire-Speed Routing
- Internetworking with TCP/IP
- ATM Internetworking
- OSPF Design and Configuration
- Border Gateway Protocol (BGP) Configuration

Authorized Vendor Training

Cisco Systems
- Introduction to Cisco Router Configuration
- Advanced Cisco Router Configuration
- Installation and Maintenance of Cisco Routers
- Cisco Internetwork Troubleshooting
- Cisco Internetwork Design
- Cisco Routers and LAN Switches
- Catalyst 5000 Series Configuration
- Cisco LAN Switch Configuration
- Managing Cisco Switched Internetworks
- Configuring, Monitoring, and Troubleshooting Dial-Up Services
- Cisco AS5200 Installation and Configuration
- Cisco Campus ATM Solutions

Bay Networks
- Bay Networks Accelerated Router Configuration
- Bay Networks Advanced IP Routing
- Bay Networks Hub Connectivity
- Bay Networks Accelar 1xxx Installation and Basic Configuration
- Bay Networks Centillion Switching

FORE Systems
- FORE ATM Enterprise Core Products
- FORE ATM Enterprise Edge Products
- FORE ATM Theory
- FORE LAN Certification

Operating Systems & Programming

Microsoft
- Introduction to Windows NT
- Microsoft Networking Essentials
- Windows NT 4.0 Workstation
- Windows NT 4.0 Server
- Advanced Windows NT 4.0 Server
- Windows NT Networking with TCP/IP
- Introduction to Microsoft Web Tools
- Windows NT Troubleshooting
- Windows Registry Configuration

UNIX
- UNIX Level I
- UNIX Level II
- Essentials of UNIX and NT Integration

Programming
- Introduction to JavaScript
- Java Programming
- PERL Programming
- Advanced PERL with CGI for the Web

Web Site Management & Development
- Building a Web Site
- Web Site Management and Performance
- Web Development Fundamentals

High Speed Networking
- Essentials of Wide Area Networking
- Integrating ISDN
- Fiber Optic Network Design
- Fiber Optic Network Installation
- Migrating to High Performance Ethernet

DIGITAL UNIX
- UNIX Utilities and Commands
- DIGITAL UNIX v4.0 System Administration
- DIGITAL UNIX v4.0 (TCP/IP) Network Management
- AdvFS, LSM, and RAID Configuration and Management
- DIGITAL UNIX TruCluster Software Configuration and Management
- UNIX Shell Programming Featuring Kornshell
- DIGITAL UNIX v4.0 Security Management
- DIGITAL UNIX v4.0 Performance Management
- DIGITAL UNIX v4.0 Intervals Overview

DIGITAL OpenVMS
- OpenVMS Skills for Users
- OpenVMS System and Network Node Management I
- OpenVMS System and Network Node Management II
- OpenVMS System and Network Node Management III
- OpenVMS System and Network Node Operations
- OpenVMS for Programmers
- OpenVMS System Troubleshooting for Systems Managers
- Configuring and Managing Complex VMScluster Systems
- Utilizing OpenVMS Features from C
- OpenVMS Performance Management
- Managing DEC TCP/IP Services for OpenVMS
- Programming in C

Hardware Courses
- AlphaServer 1000/1000A Installation, Configuration and Maintenance
- AlphaServer 2100 Server Maintenance
- AlphaServer 4100, Troubleshooting Techniques and Problem Solving

About Syngress Media

Syngress Media creates books and software for Information Technology professionals seeking skill enhancement and career advancement. Its products are designed to comply with vendor and industry standard course curricula, and are optimized for certification exam preparation. You can contact Syngress via the Web at www.syngress.com.

Contributors

Cameron Brandon (MCSE + Internet, CNE, A+, Network+) is a network engineer/administrator living in the Portland, Oregon area and working with Hicks Technology Services. His networking specialty is Windows NT with BackOffice Integration. Cameron participated in the Intel migration to Windows NT in Oregon, the largest migration of its kind in history. He completed his MCSE, CNE, CNA, MCPS: Internet Systems, and A+ certifications in just five months, and just received his Network+ certification.

Ralph Crump (MCSE, CNE3, CNE4, CNE5) is an architecture and design engineer in Atlanta, Georgia with a major telecommunications company. He specializes in Windows NT and BackOffice applications including Exchange and SMS and Novell NetWare solutions. He has been working in the IT industry for more than five years and is currently working toward his Cisco certifications. He could not have done this without the support of his wife and daughter.

Brian Frederick (MCSE, CNE4, CNE5, Compaq ASE) is a Systems Engineer with Entre Information Systems, Inc. in Iowa. He also holds his Network+ certification. Brian has been implementing and designing small and large networks for more than five years, with over 10 years general computer experience. He is married with two children and has written a variety of other titles for Syngress Media.

Mike Kendzierski (MCSE) Director of Internet Services at USWeb/CKS has extensive experience deploying complex client/server and Internet systems. Mike is also a regular speaker at technical conferences, such as Microsoft Explorer, on topics ranging from e-commerce systems to lowering the total cost of ownership.

Mike is a published technical author with several titles, including Windows NT and BackOffice technologies, such as Microsoft Site Server and Internet Information Server. When he's not deploying e-commerce systems, he can be found roaming Manhattan searching for a local Starbucks. Mike welcomes e-mail and can be reached at mkendzierski@att.net.

Technical Review by:

D. Lynn White (MCPS, MCSE, MCT, MCP+Internet) is president of Independent Network Consultants, Inc. Lynn has more than 14 years in programming and networking experience. She has been a system manager in the mainframe environment as well as a software developer for a process control company. She is a technical author, editor, trainer, and consultant in the field of networking and computer-related technologies. Lynn has been delivering mainframe, Microsoft-official curriculum and other networking courses in and outside the United States for more than 12 years.

Stace Cunningham (CCNA, MCSE, CLSE, COS/2E, CLSI, COS/2I, CLSA, MCPS, A+) is a Systems Engineer with SDC Consulting located in Biloxi, MS. SDC Consulting specializes in the design, engineering, and installation of networks. Stace received his MCSE in October 1996 and is also certified as an IBM Certified Lan Server Engineer, IBM Certified OS/2 Engineer, IBM Certified Lan Server Administrator, Microsoft Certified Product Specialist, IBM Certified Lan Server Instructor, IBM Certified OS/2 Instructor, Certified Cisco Network Associate, and also through the A+ Certification Program.

Stace has participated as a Technical Contributor for the IIS 3.0 exam, SMS 1.2 exam, Proxy Server 1.0 exam, Exchange Server 5.0 and 5.5 exams, Proxy Server 2.0 exam, IIS 4.0 exam, IEAK exam, and the revised Windows 95 exam.

ACKNOWLEDGMENTS

We would like to thank the following people:

- Richard Kristof of Global Knowledge for championing the series and providing us access to some great people and information. And to Patrick Von Schlag, Robin Yunker, David Mantica, Stacey Cannon, and Kevin Murray for all their cooperation.

- To all the incredibly hard-working folks at Osborne/McGraw-Hill: Brandon Nordin, Scott Rogers, and Gareth Hancock for their help in launching a great series and being solid team players. In addition, Cynthia Douglas, Anne Ellingsen, and Bernadette Jurich for their help in fine-tuning the book.

CONTENTS

12 Troubleshooting the Network **463**

This book's primary objective is to help you prepare for and pass the required Network+ exam so you can begin to reap the career benefits of certification. We believe that the only way to do this is to help you increase your knowledge and build your skills. After completing this book, you should feel confident that you have thoroughly reviewed all of the objectives that CompTIA has established for the exam.

In This Book

This book is organized around the actual structure of the Network+ exam administered at Sylvan Testing Centers. CompTIA has let us know all the topics we need to cover for the exam. We've followed their list carefully, so you can be assured you're not missing anything.

In Every Chapter

We've created a set of chapter components that call your attention to important items, reinforce important points, and provide helpful exam-taking hints. Take a look at what you'll find in every chapter:

- Every chapter begins with the **Certification Objectives**—what you need to know in order to pass the section of the exam dealing with the chapter topic. The Certification Objective headings identify the objectives within the chapter, so you'll always know an objective when you see it!

- **Exam Watch** notes call attention to information about, and potential pitfalls in, the exam. These helpful hints are written by authors who have taken the exams and received their certification—who better to tell you what to worry about? They know what you're about to go through!

- **Certification Exercises** are interspersed throughout the chapters. These are step-by-step exercises that mirror vendor-recommended labs. They help you master skills that are likely to be an area of focus on the exam. Don't just read through the exercises; they are hands-on practice that you should be comfortable completing. Learning by doing is an effective way to increase your competency with a product.

- **From the Field** sidebars describe the issues that come up most often in the training classroom setting. These sidebars give you a valuable perspective into certification- and product-related topics. They point out common mistakes and address questions that have arisen from classroom discussions.

- **Questions and Answers** sections lay out problems and solutions in a quick-read format:

QUESTIONS AND ANSWERS

My users cannot see World Wide Web servers on the Internet.	Check that your DNS settings on the client are configured properly. Also, verify that the DNS servers have access to Internet information.

- The **Certification Summary** is a succinct review of the chapter and a re-statement of salient points regarding the exam.

- The **Two-Minute Drill** at the end of every chapter is a checklist of the main points of the chapter. It can be used for last-minute review.

- The **Self Test** offers questions similar to those found on the certification exams, including multiple choice, true/false questions, and fill-in-the-blank. The answers to these questions, as well as explanations of the answers, can be found in Appendix A. By taking the Self Test after completing each chapter, you'll reinforce what you've learned from that chapter, while becoming familiar with the structure of the exam questions.

Some Pointers

Once you've finished reading this book, set aside some time to do a thorough review. You might want to return to the book several times and make use of all the methods it offers for reviewing the material:

1. *Re-read all the Two-Minute Drills*, or have someone quiz you. You also can use the drills as a way to do a quick cram before the exam.

2. *Re-read all the Exam Watch notes.* Remember that these are written by authors who have taken the exam and passed. They know what you should expect—and what you should be careful about.

3. *Review all the Q & A scenarios* for quick problem solving.

4. *Re-take the Self Tests.* Taking the tests right after you've read the chapter is a good idea, because it helps reinforce what you've just learned. However, it's an even better idea to go back later and do all the questions in the book in one sitting. Pretend you're taking the exam. (For this reason, you should mark your answers on a separate piece of paper when you go through the questions the first time.)

5. *Complete the exercises.* Did you do the exercises when you read through each chapter? If not, do them! These exercises are designed to cover exam topics, and there's no better way to get to know this material than by practicing.

6. *Check out the Web site.* Global Knowledge invites you to become an active member of the Access Global Web site. This site is an online mall and an information repository that you'll find invaluable. You can access many types of products to assist you in your preparation for the exams, and you'll be able to participate in forums, on-line discussions, and threaded discussions. No other book brings you unlimited access to such a resource. You'll find more information about this site in Appendix C.

Network+ Certification

Although you've obviously picked up this book to study for a specific exam, we'd like to spend some time covering what you need in order to attain

Network+ certification status. Because this information can be found on the CompTIA Web site, http://www.comptia.org/networkplus/index.htm, we've repeated only some of the more important information in the Introduction of this book, "How to Take a CompTIA Network+ Certification Examination."

The CD-ROM Resource

This book comes with a CD-ROM holding test preparation software and providing you with another method for studying. You will find more information on the testing software in Appendix B.

How to Take a CompTIA Network+ Certification Examination

Good News and Bad News

If you are new to certifications, we have some good news and some bad news. The good news, of course, is that a computer industry certification is one of the most valuable credentials you can earn. It sets you apart from the crowd and marks you as a valuable asset to your employer. You will gain the respect of your peers, and certification can have a wonderful effect on your income.

The bad news is that certification tests are not easy. You may think you will read through some study material, memorize a few facts, and pass the examinations. After all, these certification exams are just computer-based, multiple-choice tests, so they must be easy. If you believe this, you are wrong. Unlike many "multiple-guess" tests you have been exposed to in school, the questions on certification examinations go beyond simple factual knowledge.

The purpose of this introduction is to teach you how to take a computer certification examination. To be successful, you need to know something about the purpose and structure of these tests. We will also look at the latest innovations in computerized testing. Using *simulations* and *adaptive testing*, the computer industry is enhancing both the validity and security of the certification process. These factors have some important effects on how you should prepare for an exam, as well as your approach to each question during the test.

We will begin by looking at the purpose, focus, and structure of certification tests, and we will examine the effect these factors have on the kinds of questions you will face on your certification exams. We will define the structure of examination questions and investigate some common formats. Next, we will present a strategy for answering these questions. Finally, we will give some specific guidelines on what you should do on the day of your test.

Why Vendor Certification?

The CompTIA Network+ certification program, like the certification programs from Microsoft, Lotus, Novell, Oracle, and other software vendors, is maintained for the ultimate purpose of increasing the corporation's profits. A successful vendor certification program accomplishes this goal by helping to create a pool of experts in a company's software, and by "branding" these experts so that companies using the software can identify them.

Vendor certification has become increasingly popular in the past few years because it helps employers find qualified workers, and it helps software vendors, such as Microsoft, sell their products. But why vendor certification rather than a more traditional approach, such as a college degree in computer science? A college education is a broadening and enriching experience, but a degree in computer science does not prepare students for most jobs in the IT industry.

A common truism in our business states, "If you are out of the IT industry for three years and want to return, you have to start over." The problem, of course, is *timeliness*; a specific computer program that a first-year student learns about will probably no longer be in wide use when he or she graduates. Although some colleges are trying to integrate computer certification into their curriculum, the problem is not really a flaw in higher education, but a characteristic of the IT industry. Computer software is changing so rapidly that a four-year college just can't keep up.

A marked characteristic of the computer certification program is an emphasis on performing specific job tasks rather than merely gathering knowledge. It may come as a shock, but most potential employers do not care how much you know about the theory of operating systems, networking, or database design. As one IT manager put it, "I don't really care what my employees know about the theory of our network. We don't need someone to sit at a desk and think about it. We need people who can actually do something to make it work better."

You should not think that this attitude is some kind of anti-intellectual revolt against "book learning." Knowledge is a necessary prerequisite, but it is not enough. More than one company has hired a computer science graduate as a network administrator, only to learn that the new employee has no idea how to add users, assign permissions, or perform the other day-to-day tasks necessary to maintain a network. This brings us to the second major characteristic of computer certification that affects the questions you must be prepared to answer: real-world job skills.

The timeliness of CompTIA's Network+ certification program is obvious, and it is inherent in the fact that you will be tested on current network implementations in wide use today, including network-related hardware and software. The job task orientation of certification is almost as obvious, but testing real-world job skills using a computer-based test is not easy.

Computerized Testing

Considering the popularity of CompTIA's certification, and the fact that certification candidates are spread around the world, the only practical way to administer tests for the certification program is through Sylvan Prometric testing centers. Sylvan Prometric provides proctored testing services for Microsoft, Oracle, Novell, Lotus, and CompTIA's other certification, the A+ computer technician certification. Although the IT industry accounts for much of Sylvan's revenue, the company provides services for a number of other businesses and organizations, such as FAA pre-flight pilot tests. In fact, most companies that need secure test delivery over a wide geographic area use the services of Sylvan Prometric. In addition to delivery, Sylvan Prometric also scores the tests and provides statistical feedback on the performance on each test question to the companies and organizations that use their services.

Typically, several hundred questions are developed for the new CompTIA certification examination. The questions are first reviewed by a number of subject matter experts for technical accuracy, and then are presented in a beta test. The beta test may last for several hours, due to the large number of questions. After a few weeks, CompTIA uses the statistical feedback from Sylvan to check the performance on the beta questions.

Questions are discarded if most test takers get them right (too easy) or wrong (too difficult). A number of other statistical measures are taken of each question. Although the scope of our discussion precludes a rigorous treatment of question analysis, you should be aware that CompTIA and other vendors spend a great deal of time and effort making sure their examination questions are valid. In addition to the obvious desire for quality, the fairness of a vendor's certification program must be legally defensible.

The questions that survive statistical analysis form the pool of questions for the final certification examination.

Test Structure

The kind of test we are most familiar with is known as a *form* test. For the CompTIA certification, a form consists of 75 questions and takes 90–120 minutes to complete.

The questions in a CompTIA form test are equally weighted. This means they all count the same when the test is scored. An interesting and useful characteristic of a form test is that you can mark a question you have doubts about as you take the test. Assuming you have time left when you finish all the questions, you can return and spend more time on the questions you have marked as doubtful.

CompTIA, like Microsoft, may soon implement *adaptive* testing. To develop this interactive technique, a form test is first created and administered to several thousand certification candidates. The statistics generated are used to assign a weight, or difficulty level, for each question. For example, the questions in a form might be divided into levels one through five, with level one questions being the easiest and level five the hardest.

When an adaptive test begins, the candidate is first given a level three question. If he answers it correctly, he is given a question from the next higher level; if he answers it incorrectly, he is given a question from the next lower level. When 15–20 questions have been answered in this manner, the scoring algorithm is able to predict, with a high degree of statistical certainty, whether the candidate would pass or fail if all the questions in the form were answered. When the required degree of certainty is attained, the test ends and the candidate receives a pass/fail grade.

Adaptive testing has some definite advantages for everyone involved in the certification process. Adaptive tests enable Sylvan Prometric to deliver more tests with the same resources, because certification candidates often are in and out in 30 minutes or less. For CompTIA, adaptive testing means that fewer test questions are exposed to each candidate, which enhances the security, and therefore the validity, of certification tests.

One possible problem you may have with adaptive testing is that you are not allowed to mark and revisit questions. Because the adaptive algorithm is interactive, and all questions but the first are selected on the basis of your response to the previous question, it is not possible to skip a particular question or change an answer.

Question Types

Computerized test questions can be presented in a number of ways. Some of the possible formats are used on CompTIA certification examinations, and some are not.

True/False

We are all familiar with True/False questions, but because of the inherent 50 percent chance of guessing the correct answer, you will not see questions of this type on your Network+ certification exam.

Multiple Choice

The majority of Network+ certification questions are in the multiple-choice format, with either a single correct answer or multiple correct answers. One interesting variation on multiple-choice questions with multiple correct answers is whether or not the candidate is told how many answers are correct.

EXAMPLE:

Which networking protocols are routable? (Choose two.)

Or

Which networking protocols exist in the Network Layer of the OSI model? (Choose all that apply.)

You may see both variations on CompTIA certification examinations, but the trend seems to be toward the first type, where candidates are told explicitly how many answers are correct. During the beta exam I discovered around 18 questions of this type within the pool of 146 questions. Questions of the "choose all that apply" variety are more difficult and can be confusing.

Graphical Questions

One or more graphical elements are sometimes used as exhibits to help present or clarify an exam question. These elements may take the form of a network diagram or pictures of networking components on which you are being tested. It is often easier to present the concepts required for a complex performance-based scenario with a graphic than it is with words. Expect only a couple of graphical questions on your Network+ exam.

Test questions known as *hotspots* actually incorporate graphics as part of the answer. These questions ask the certification candidate to click a location or graphical element to answer the question. As an example, you might be shown the diagram of a network and asked to click on an appropriate location for a router. The answer is correct if the candidate clicks within the hotspot that defines the correct location. The Network+ exam has a few of these graphical hotspot questions, and most are asking you to identify network types, such as a bus or star network. As with the graphical questions, expect only a couple of hotspot questions during your exam.

Free Response Questions

Another kind of question you sometimes see on certification examinations requires a *free response* or type-in answer. This type of question might present a TCP/IP network scenario and ask the candidate to calculate and enter the correct subnet mask in dotted decimal notation. However, the CompTIA Network+ exam does not contain any free response questions.

Knowledge-Based and Performance-Based Questions

Psychometricians (psychologists who specialize in designing and analyzing tests) categorize test questions as knowledge based or performance based. As the names imply, knowledge-based questions are designed to test knowledge, and performance-based questions are designed to test performance.

Some objectives demand a knowledge-based question. For example, objectives that use verbs such as *list* and *identify* tend to test only what you know, not what you can do.

EXAMPLE:

Objective: Explain the following Transport Layer concepts.
Which two protocols are connectionless-oriented network protocols?
(Choose two.)

A. FTP

B. TCP

C. TFTP

D. UDP

Correct answers: C, D.

The Network+ exam consists of mostly knowledge-based multiple-choice questions that can be answered fairly quickly if you know your stuff. These questions are very straightforward, lacking a complex situation to confuse you.

Other objectives use action verbs such as *install, configure*, and *troubleshoot* to define job tasks. These objectives can often be tested with either a knowledge-based question or a performance-based question.

EXAMPLE:

Objective: Configure a Windows 98 workstation for NetBIOS name resolution.

Knowledge-based question:

Where do you configure a Windows 98 workstation to use a WINS server for NetBIOS name resolution?

A. Start | Settings | Control Panel | Network | WINS Configuration

B. Start | Settings | Control Panel | Network | TCP/IP | Properties | WINS Configuration

C. My Computer | Control Panel | Network | WINS Configuration

D. My Computer | Control Panel | Network | TCP/IP | Properties | WINS

Correct answer: B.

Performance-based question:

You want to ensure you have a reliable tape backup scheme that is not susceptible to fire and water hazards. You are backing up three Windows

NT servers and would like to completely back up the entire systems. Which of the following is the most reliable backup method?

A. Configure the backup program to back up the user files and operating system files; complete a test restore of the backup; and store the backup tapes offsite in a fireproof vault.

B. Configure the backup program to back up the entire hard drive of each server and store the backup tapes offsite in a fireproof vault.

C. Copy the user files to another server; configure the backup program to back up the operating system files; and store the backup tapes offsite in a fireproof vault.

D. Configure the backup program to back up the user files and operating system files and store the backup tapes offsite in fireproof vault.

Correct answer: A.

Even in this simple example, the superiority of the performance-based question is obvious. Whereas the knowledge-based question asks for a single fact, the performance-based question presents a real-life situation and requires that you make a decision based on this scenario. Thus, performance-based questions give more bang (validity) for the test author's buck (individual question).

The Network+ exam has plenty of performance-based questions that, compared to Microsoft exams, are less convoluted.

Testing Job Performance

We have said that CompTIA certification focuses on timeliness and the ability to perform job tasks. We have also introduced the concept of performance-based questions, but even performance-based multiple-choice questions do not really measure performance. Another strategy is needed to test job skills.

Given unlimited resources, it is not difficult to test job skills. In an ideal world, CompTIA would fly Network+ candidates to a test facility, place them in a controlled environment with a team of experts, and ask them to plan, install, maintain, and troubleshoot a network. In a few days at most, the experts could reach a valid decision as to whether each candidate should or should not be granted Network+ status. Needless to say, this is not likely to happen.

Closer to reality, another way to test performance is to use the actual software and create a testing program to present tasks and automatically grade a candidate's performance when the tasks are completed. This *cooperative* approach would be practical in some testing situations, but the same test that is presented to Network+ candidates in Boston must also be available in Bahrain and Botswana. Many Sylvan Prometric testing locations around the world cannot run 32-bit applications, much less provide the complex networked solutions required by cooperative testing applications.

The most workable solution for measuring performance in today's testing environment is a *simulation* program. When the program is launched during a test, the candidate sees a simulation of the actual software that looks, and behaves, just like the real thing. When the testing software presents a task, the simulation program is launched and the candidate performs the required task. The testing software then grades the candidate's performance on the required task and moves to the next question. In this way, a 16-bit simulation program can mimic the look and feel of 32-bit operating systems, a complicated network, or even the entire Internet.

Simulation questions provide many advantages over other testing methodologies, and simulations are expected to become increasingly important in the computer certification programs. For example, studies have shown that there is a very high correlation between the ability to perform simulated tasks on a computer-based test and the ability to perform the actual job tasks. Thus, simulations enhance the validity of the certification process.

Another truly wonderful benefit of simulations is in the area of test security. It is just not possible to cheat on a simulation question. In fact, you will be told exactly what tasks you are expected to perform on the test. How can a certification candidate cheat? By learning to perform the tasks? What a concept!

Study Strategies

There are appropriate ways to study for the different types of questions you will see on a CompTIA Network+ certification examination.

Knowledge-Based Questions

Knowledge-based questions require that you memorize facts. There are hundreds of facts inherent in every content area of every Network+ certification examination. There are several tricks to memorizing facts:

- **Repetition** The more times your brain is exposed to a fact, the more likely you are to remember it. Flash cards are a wonderful tool for repetition. Either make your own flash cards on paper or download a flash card program and develop your own questions.

- **Association** Connecting facts within a logical framework makes them easier to remember. Try using mnemonics, such as "All People Seem To Need Data Processing" to remember the seven layers of the OSI model in order.

- **Motor Association** It is often easier to remember something if you write it down or perform some other physical act, such as clicking on a practice test answer. You will find that hands-on experience with the product or concept being tested is a great way to develop motor association.

We have said that the emphasis of CompTIA certification is job performance, and that there are very few knowledge-based questions on CompTIA certification exams. Why should you waste a lot of time learning file names, IP address formulas, and other minutiae? Read on.

Performance-Based Questions

Most of the questions you will face on a CompTIA certification exam are performance-based scenario questions. We have discussed the superiority of these questions over simple knowledge-based questions, but you should remember that the job task orientation of CompTIA certification extends the knowledge you need to pass the exams; it does not replace this knowledge. Therefore, the first step in preparing for scenario questions is to absorb as many facts relating to the exam content areas as you can. In other words, go back to the previous section and follow the steps to prepare for an exam composed of knowledge-based questions.

The second step is to familiarize yourself with the format of the questions you are likely to see on the exam. You can do this by answering the questions in this study guide, or by using practice tests. The day of your test is not the time to be surprised by the complicated construction of some exam questions.

For example, one of CompTIA Certification's favorite formats of late takes the following form found on Microsoft exams:

Scenario: You have a network with…

Primary Objective: You want to…

Secondary Objective: You also want to…

Proposed Solution: Do this…

What does the proposed solution accomplish?

A. It achieves the primary and the secondary objective.

B. It achieves the primary but not the secondary objective.

C. It achieves the secondary but not the primary objective.

D. It achieves neither the primary nor the secondary objective.

This kind of question, with some variation, is seen on many Microsoft Certification examinations and will be present on your Network+ certification exam.

At best, these performance-based scenario questions really do test certification candidates at a higher cognitive level than knowledge-based questions do. At worst, these questions can test your reading comprehension and test-taking ability rather than your ability to administer networks. Be sure to get in the habit of reading the question carefully to determine what is being asked.

The third step in preparing for CompTIA scenario questions is to adopt the following attitude: Multiple-choice questions aren't really performance-based. It is all a cruel lie. These scenario questions are just knowledge-based questions with a little story wrapped around them.

To answer a scenario question, you have to sift through the story to the underlying facts of the situation and apply your knowledge to determine the correct answer. This may sound silly at first, but the process we go through in solving real-life problems is quite similar. The key concept is that every scenario question (and every real-life problem) has a fact at its center, and if we can identify that fact, we can answer the question.

Exam Blueprint

The Network+ exam is divided into two major categories: Knowledge of Networking Technology and Knowledge of Networking Practices. Each category is broken down into several exam objectives with a percentage applied reflecting the amount each objective relates to the entire Network+ exam.

Knowledge of Networking Technology	67%
Basic Knowledge	16%
Physical Layer	6%
Data Link Layer	5%
Network Layer	5%
Transport Layer	4%
TCP/IP Fundamentals	12%
TCP/IP Suite: Utilities	8%
Remote connectivity	5%
Security	6%

Knowledge of Networking Practices	33%
Implementing the Installation of the Network	6%
Administering the Change Control System	4%
Maintaining and Supporting the Network	6%
Identifying, Assessing, and Responding to Problems	6%
Troubleshooting the Network	11%

The following certification objectives are provided by CompTIA on their Web site, http://www.comptia.org/networkplus/index.htm:

Knowledge of Networking Technology

Basic Knowledge

- Demonstrate understanding of basic network structure, including:
    - The characteristics of star, bus, mesh, and ring topologies, their advantages and disadvantages
    - The characteristics of segments and backbones
- Identify the following:

- The major network operating systems, including Microsoft Windows NT, Novell NetWare, and Unix
- The clients that best serve specific network operating systems and their resources
- The directory services of the major network operating systems
- Associate IPX, IP, and NetBEUI with their functions.
- Define the following terms and explain how each relates to fault tolerance or high availabiRlity:
  - Mirroring
  - Duplexing
  - Striping (with and without parity)
  - Volumes
  - Tape backup
- Define the layers of the OSI model and identify the protocols, services, and functions that pertain to each layer.
- Recognize and describe the following characteristics of networking media and connectors:
  - The advantages and disadvantages of coax, Cat 3, Cat 5, fiber optic, UTP, and STP, and the conditions under which they are appropriate
  - The length and speed of 10Base2, 10BaseT, and 100BaseT
  - The length and speed of 10Base5, 100Base VGAnyLan, 100BaseTX
  - The visual appearance of RJ-24 and BNC and how they are crimped
- Identify the basic attributes, purpose, and function of the following network elements:
  - Full- and half-duplexing
  - WAN and LAN
  - Server, workstation, and host
  - Server-based networking and peer-to-peer networking
  - Cable, NIC, and router
  - Broadband and baseband
  - Gateway, as both a default IP router and as a method to connect dissimilar systems or protocols

Physical Layer

- Given an installation, configuration, or troubleshooting scenario, select an appropriate course of action if a client workstation does not connect to the network after installing or replacing a network interface card. Explain why a given action is warranted. The following issues may be covered:

- Knowledge of how the network card is usually configured, including EPROM, jumpers, and plug-and-play software
- Use of network card diagnostics, including the loopback test and vendor-supplied diagnostics
- The ability to resolve hardware resource conflicts, including IRQ, DMA, and I/O Base Address

- Identify the use of the following network components and the differences between them:
  - Hubs
  - MAUs
  - Switching hubs
  - Repeaters
  - Transceivers

Data Link Layer

- Describe the following data link layer concepts:
  - Bridges, what they are and why they are used
  - The 802 specs, including the topics covered in 802.2, 802.3, and 802.5
  - The function and characteristics of MAC addresses

Network Layer

- Explain the following routing and network layer concepts, including:
  - The fact that routing occurs at the network layer
  - The difference between a router and a brouter
  - The difference between routable and nonroutable protocols
  - The concept of default gateways and subnetworks
  - The reason for employing unique network IDs
  - The difference between static and dynamic routing

Transport Layer

- Explain the following transport layer concepts:
  - The distinction between connectionless and connection transport
  - The purpose of name resolution, either to an IP/IPX address or a network protocol

TCP/IP Fundamentals

- Demonstrate knowledge of the following TCP/IP fundamentals:
  - The concept of IP default gateways

- The purpose and use of DHCP, DNS, WINS, and host files
- The identity of the main protocols that make up the TCP/IP suite, including TCP, UDP, POP3, SMTP, SNMP, FTP, HTTP, and IP
- The idea that TCP/IP is supported by every operating system and millions of hosts worldwide
- The purpose and function of Internet domain name server hierarchies (how e-mail arrives in another country)

- Demonstrate knowledge of the fundamental concepts of TCP/IP addressing, including:
  - The A, B, and C classes of IP addresses and their default subnet mask numbers
  - The use of port number (HTTP, FTP, SMTP) and port numbers commonly assigned to a given service

- Demonstrate knowledge of TCP/IP configuration concepts, including:
  - The definition of IP proxy and why it is used
  - The identity of the normal configuration parameters for a workstation, including IP address, DNS, default gateway, IP proxy configuration, WINS, DHCP, host name, and Internet domain name

TCP/IP Suite: Utilities

- Explain how and when to use the following TCP/IP utilities to test, validate, and troubleshoot IP connectivity:
  - ARP
  - Telnet
  - NBTSTAT
  - Tracert
  - NETSTAT
  - ipconfig/winipcfg
  - FTP
  - ping

Remote Connectivity

- Explain the following remote connectivity concepts:
  - The distinction between PPP and SLIP
  - The purpose and function of PPTP and the conditions under which it is useful
  - The attributes, advantages, and disadvantages of ISDN and PSTN (POTS)

■ Specify the following elements of dial-up networking:
  ■ The modem configuration parameters that must be set, including serial port IRQ, I/O address and maximum port speed
  ■ The requirements for a remote connection

Security

■ Identify good practices to ensure network security, including:
  ■ Selection of a security model (user and share level)
  ■ Standard password practices and procedures
  ■ The need to employ data encryption to protect network data
  ■ The use of a firewall

Knowledge of Networking Practices

Implementing the Installation of the Network

■ Demonstrate awareness that administrative and test accounts, passwords, IP addresses, IP configurations, relevant SOPs, etc., must be obtained prior to network implementation.

■ Explain the impact of environmental factors on computer networks. Given a network installation scenario, identify unexpected or atypical conditions that could either cause problems for the network or signify that a problem condition already exists, including:
  ■ Room conditions (e.g., humidity, heat, etc.)
  ■ The placement of building contents and personal effects (e.g., space heaters, TVs, radios, etc.)
  ■ Computer equipment
  ■ Error messages

■ Recognize visually, or by description, common peripheral ports, external SCSI (especially DB-25 connectors), and common network componentry, including:
  ■ Print servers
  ■ Peripherals
  ■ Hubs
  ■ Routers
  ■ Brouters

■ Given an installation scenario, demonstrate awareness of the following compatibility and cabling issues:
  ■ The consequences of trying to install an analog modem in a digital jack

- That the uses of RJ-45 connectors may differ greatly depending on the cabling
- That patch cables contribute to the overall length of the cabling segment

Administering the Change Control System

- Demonstrate awareness of the need to document the current status and configuration of the workstation (i.e., providing a baseline) prior to making any changes.
- Given a configuration scenario, select a course of action that would allow the return of a system to its original state.
- Given a scenario involving workstation backups, select the appropriate backup technique from among the following:
  - Tape backup
  - Folder replication to a network drive
  - Removable media
  - Multi-generation
- Demonstrate awareness of the need to remove outdated or unused drivers, properties, etc. when an upgrade is successfully completed.
- Identify the possible adverse effects on the network caused by local changes (e.g., version conflicts, overwritten DLLs, etc.).
- Explain the purpose of drive mapping, and, given a scenario, identify the mapping that will produce the desired results using Universal Naming Convention (UNC) or an equivalent feature. Explain the purpose of printer port capturing and identify properly formed capture commands, given a scenario.
- Given a scenario where equipment is being moved or changed, decide when and how to verify the functionality of the network and critical applications.
- Given a scenario where equipment is being moved or changed, decide when and how to verify the functionality of that equipment.
- Demonstrate awareness of the need to obtain relevant permissions before adding, deleting, or modifying users.
- Identify the purpose and function of the following networking elements:
  - Profiles
  - Rights
  - Procedures/policies
  - Administrative utilities
  - Login accounts, groups, and passwords

Maintaining and Supporting the Network

■ Identify the kinds of test documentation that are usually available regarding a vendor's patches, fixes, upgrades, etc.

■ Given a network maintenance scenario, demonstrate awareness of the following issues:

   ■ Standard backup procedures and backup media storage practices

   ■ The need for periodic application of software patches and other fixes to the network

   ■ The need to install anti-virus software on the server and workstations

   ■ The need to frequently update virus signatures

Identifying, Assessing, and Responding to Problems

■ Given an apparent network problem, determine the nature of the action required (i.e., information transfer vs. handholding vs. technical service).

■ Given a scenario involving several network problems, prioritize them based on their seriousness.

Troubleshooting the Network

■ Identify the following steps as a systematic approach to identifying the extent of a network problem, and, given a problem scenario, select the appropriate next step based on this approach:

1. Determine whether the problem exists across the network.

2. Determine whether the problem is workstation, workgroup, LAN or WAN.

3. Determine whether the problem is consistent and replicable.

4. Use standard troubleshooting methods.

■ Identify the following steps as a systematic approach for troubleshooting network problems, and, given a problem scenario, select the appropriate next step based on this approach:

1. Identify the exact issue.

2. Recreate the problem.

3. Isolate the cause.

4. Formulate a correction.

5. Implement the correction.

6. Test.

7. Document the problem and the solution.

8. Give feedback.

■ Identify the following steps as a systematic approach to determining whether a problem is attributable to the operator or the system, and, given a problem scenario, select the appropriate next step based on this approach:

1. Have a second operator perform the same task on an equivalent workstation.

2. Have a second operator perform the same task on the original operator's workstation.

3. See whether operators are following standard operating procedure.

■ Given a network troubleshooting scenario, demonstrate awareness of the need to check for physical and logical indicators of trouble, including:

   ■ Link lights
   ■ Power lights
   ■ Error displays
   ■ Error logs and displays
   ■ Performance monitors

■ Identify common network troubleshooting resources, including:

   ■ Knowledge bases on the World Wide Web
   ■ Telephone technical support
   ■ Vendor CDs

■ Given a network problem scenario, including symptoms, determine the most likely cause or causes of the problem based on the available information. Select the most appropriate course of action based on this inference. Issues that may be covered include:

   ■ Recognizing abnormal physical conditions
   ■ Isolating and correcting problems in cases where there is a fault in the physical media (patch cable)
   ■ Checking the status of servers
   ■ Checking for configuration problems with DNS, WINS, HOST file
   ■ Checking for viruses

- ■ Checking the validity of the account name and password
- ■ Rechecking operator logon procedures
- ■ Selecting and running appropriate diagnostics

■ Specify the tools that are commonly used to resolve network equipment problems. Identify the purpose and function of common network tools, including:

- ■ Crossover cable
- ■ Hardware loopback
- ■ Tone generator
- ■ Tone locator (fox and hound)

■ Given a network problem scenario, select appropriate tools to help resolve the problem.

Signing Up

Signing up to take the CompTIA Network+ certification examination is easy. Sylvan operators in each country can schedule tests at any testing center. Contact Sylvan at 1-888-895-6116. Please check the CompTIA Web site for pricing information and further updates concerning the Network+ exam.

There are, however, a few things you should know:

1. If you call Sylvan during a busy time period, get a cup of coffee first, because you may be in for a long wait. Sylvan does an excellent job, but everyone in the world seems to want to sign up for a test on Monday morning.

2. You will need your social security number or some other unique identifier to sign up for a Sylvan test, so have it at hand.

3. Pay for your test by credit card if at all possible. This makes things easier, and you can even schedule tests for the same day you call, if space is available at your local testing center.

4. Know the number and title of the test you want to take before you call. This is not essential, and the Sylvan operators will help you if

they can. Having this information in advance, however, speeds up the registration process.

Taking the Test

Teachers have always told you not to try to cram for examinations, because it does no good. If you are faced with a knowledge-based test requiring only that you regurgitate facts, cramming can mean the difference between passing and failing. This is not the case, however, with many certification exams. If you don't know it the night before, don't bother to stay up and cram.

Instead, create a schedule and stick to it. Plan your study time carefully, and do not schedule your test until you think you are ready to succeed. Follow these guidelines on the day of your exam:

1. Start out with a good night's sleep. The scenario questions you will face on your Network+ certification examination require a clear head.

2. Remember to take two forms of identification—at least one with a picture. A driver's license with your picture, and social security or credit cards are acceptable.

3. Leave home in time to arrive at your testing center a few minutes early. It is not a good idea to feel rushed as you begin your exam.

4. Do not spend too much time on any one question. If you are taking a form test, take your best guess and mark the question so you can come back to it if you have time. You cannot mark and revisit questions on an adaptive test, so you must do your best on each question as you go.

5. If you do not know the answer to a question, try to eliminate the obviously wrong answers and guess from the rest. If you can eliminate two out of four options, you have a 50 percent chance of guessing the correct answer.

6. For scenario questions, follow the steps we outlined earlier. Read the question carefully and try to identify the facts at the center of the story.

Finally, I would advise anyone attempting to earn computer certifications to adopt a philosophical attitude. Even if you are the kind of person who never fails a test, you are likely to fail at least one certification test somewhere along the way. Do not get discouraged. If certifications were easy to obtain, more people would have them, and they would not be so respected and so valuable to your future in the IT industry.

Part I

Knowledge of Networking Technology

CERTIFICATION

I

Basic Knowledge

I n the world of computing today, the knowledge of how computers communicate in a network is very important to being a good network technician. In this chapter, we will introduce you to the basics of what makes a network tick.

You should refer to this chapter often as you read the rest of this book. We will look at the various topologies, different network operating systems, as well as common terminology. Some pieces of this chapter are very brief. That is because this chapter serves as the foundation for the following chapters. Be sure to get a basic understanding of the following sections. Once you understand this chapter, the following chapters will be easier to understand and learn.

CERTIFICATION OBJECTIVE 1.01

Understanding Basic Network Structure

Using computers in a professional setting without any kind of network is unthinkable these days. From the dial-up connection off a consultant's laptop to the company information distributed on an Intranet via the wide area network (WAN), networks are essential to a company's success. Network technicians have to know the essential ins and outs of how networks work since they can be responsible for maintaining and troubleshooting their own or a client's network.

A network is made up of two basic components: the entities that want to share information or resources and the medium that enables the entities to communicate. The entities are usually workstations and the medium is either a cable segment or a wireless medium such as an infrared signal.

There are different topologies that make up computer networks. Topology is the physical layout of computers, cables, and other components on a network. Many networks are a combination of the various topologies that we will look at:

- Bus
- Star

- Mesh
- Ring

Bus Topologies

A bus topology uses one cable to connect multiple computers. This may sound a little strange, but the fact is it is very easy to set up and install. The cable is also called a trunk, a backbone, and a segment. There are a couple of common ways a bus topology is configured. Most of the time, as seen in Figure 1-1, T-connectors are used to connect to the cabled segment. They are called T-connectors because they are shaped like the letter T. You will commonly see coaxial cable used in bus topologies.

Another key component of a bus topology is the need for termination. If a packet, which is an electronic signal, it bounces back on that cable. To prevent packets from bouncing up and down the cable, devices called *terminators* must be attached to both ends of the cable. A terminator absorbs an electronic signal and clears the cable so that other computers can send packets on the network. If there is no termination, the entire network fails.

Only one computer at a time can transmit a packet on a bus topology. Computers in a bus topology listen to all traffic on the network but accept only the packets that are addressed to them. Broadcast packets are an exception because all computers on the network accept them. When a computer sends out a packet, it travels in both directions from the computer. This means that the network is occupied until the destination

FIGURE 1-1   In a bus topology, all computers are connected on one linear cable

computer accepts the packet. The number of computers on a bus topology network has a major influence on the performance of the network.

A bus is a passive topology. The computers on a bus topology only listen or send data. They do not take data and send it on or regenerate it. So if one computer on the network fails, the network is still up.

If you are familiar with daisy chaining, then you will have no problem getting an idea of what the Bus topology is like. The Bus topology is really daisy chaining computers on a cable segment.

Advantages

One advantage of a bus topology is cost. The bus topology uses less cable than the star topology or the mesh topology. Another advantage is the ease of installation. With the bus topology, you simply connect the workstation to the cable segment, or backbone. You need only the amount of cable to connect the workstations you have. The ease of working with a bus topology and the minimum amount of cable make this the most economical choice for a network topology. If a computer fails, the network stays up.

Disadvantages

The main disadvantage of the bus topology is the difficulty of troubleshooting. When the network goes down, usually it is from a break in the cable segment. With a large network this can be tough to isolate. Figure 1-2 shows a cable

---

FIGURE 1-2

A bus topology with a break in the segment, which would take down the entire network

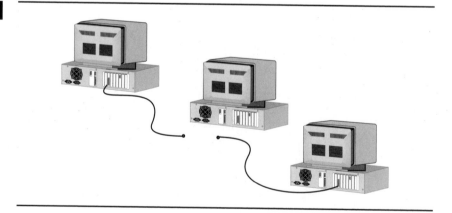

break between computers on a bus topology, which would take the entire network down. Another disadvantage of a bus topology is that the heavier the traffic, the slower the network.

Scalability is an important consideration with the dynamic world of networking. Being able to make changes easily within the size and layout of your network can be important in future productivity or downtime. The bus topology is not very scalable.

Star Topologies

In a star topology, all computers are connected through one central hub or switch, as illustrated in Figure 1-3. This is a very common network scenario.

A star topology actually comes from the days of the mainframe system. The mainframe system had a centralized point where the terminals connected.

Advantages

One advantage of a star topology is the centralization of cabling. With a hub, if one link fails, the remaining workstations are not affected like they are with other topologies, which we will look at in this chapter.

Centralizing network components can make an administrator's life much easier in the long run. Centralized management and monitoring of network traffic can be vital to network success. With this type of configuration, it is also easy to add or change configurations with all the connections coming to a central point.

FIGURE 1-3   Computers in a star topology are all connected to a central hub

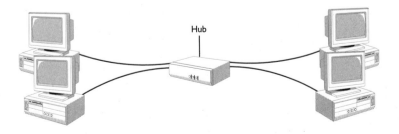

Disadvantages

On the flip side to this is the fact that if the hub fails, the entire network, or a good portion of the network, comes down. This is, of course, an easier fix than trying to find a break in a cable in a bus topology.

Another disadvantage of a star topology is cost: to connect each workstation to a centralized hub, you have to use much more cable than you do in a bus topology.

Mesh Topologies

A mesh topology is not very common in computer networking, but you will have to know it for the exam. The mesh topology is more commonly seen with something like the national phone network. With the mesh topology, every workstation has a connection to every other component of the network, as illustrated in Figure 1-4.

Advantages

The biggest advantage of a mesh topology is fault tolerance. If there is a break in a cable segment, traffic can be rerouted. This fault tolerance means that the network going down due to a cable fault is almost impossible. (I stress *almost* because with a network, no matter how many connections you have, it can crash.)

FIGURE 1-4

Computers in a mesh topology are all connected to every other component of the network

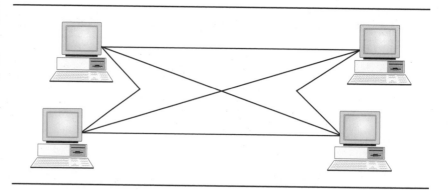

Disadvantages

A mesh topology is very hard to administer and manage because of the numerous connections. Another disadvantage is cost. With a large network, the amount of cable needed to connect and the interfaces on the workstations would be very expensive.

Ring Topologies

In a ring topology, all computers are connected with a cable that loops around. As shown in Figure 1-5, the ring topology is a circle that has no start and no end. Terminators are not necessary in a ring topology. Signals travel in one direction on a ring while they are passed from one computer to the next. Each computer checks the packet for its destination and passes it on as a repeater would. If one of the computers fails, the entire ring network goes down.

FIGURE 1-5

Signals travel in one direction on a ring topology

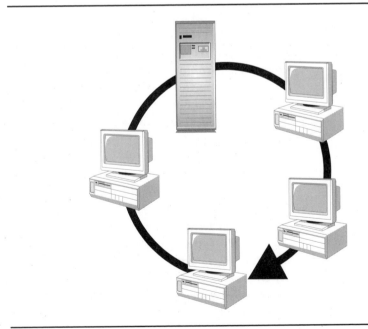

Advantages

The nice thing about a ring topology is that each computer has equal access to communicate on the network. (With bus and star topologies, only one workstation can communicate on the network at a time.) The ring topology provides good performance for each workstation. This means that busier computers who send out a lot of information do not inhibit other computers from communicating. Another advantage of the ring topology is that signal degeneration is low.

Disadvantages

The biggest problem with a ring topology is that if one computer fails or the cable link is broken the entire network could go down. With newer technology this isn't always the case. The concept of a ring topology is that the ring isn't broken and the signal hops from workstation to workstation, connection to connection.

Isolating a problem can be difficult in some configurations also. (With newer technologies a workstation or server will beacon if it notices a break in the ring.) Another disadvantage is that if you make a cabling change to the network or a workstation change, such as a move, the brief disconnection can interrupt or bring down the entire network.

on the
❶ o b

In many environments you will see a couple of these topologies integrated into the same network. One example of this I know of is a school that had both Token Ring and Ethernet segments. The server was running NetWare and had three network cards installed and was acting as a router for all of the segments.

The main thing about this scenario was that you had to make sure you understood how logical and physical cable segments work. We will look at segments and backbones shortly. Each network card determined a segment. There were two Token Ring and one Ethernet network card installed in the server. Not an ideal solution but they had the old Type 1 Token Ring along with the newer Token Ring using standard RJ-45 patch cables. This scenario made things complicated when moving equipment around. Thankfully they upgraded and eventually went to one topology and now are running all Ethernet.

Segments and Backbones

With the various topologies we've looked at you have seen the words *segment* and *backbone* mentioned a couple of times. To make clear what the word segment means we have to look at it two ways. The first is an actual physical cable segment. A physical cable segment can be a 6-foot piece of twisted-pair CAT5 cable. There is also a logical segment with networking. The logical segment contains all the computers interconnected on the same network. Figure 1-6 shows six different logical segments on a TCP/IP network. Even though they are physically connected, they are on six

| FIGURE 1-6 | Six different logical cable segments on a TCP/IP network |

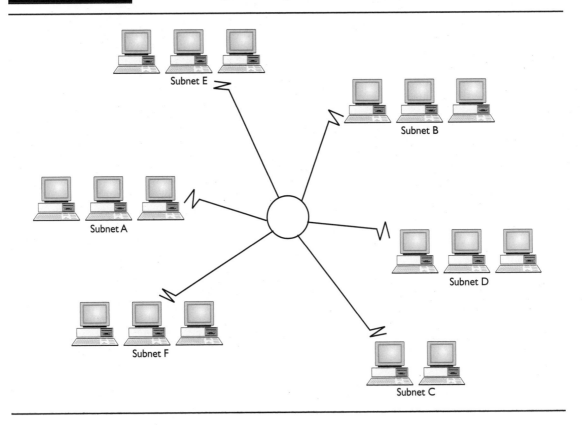

different logical segments due to the different addressing. Addressing determines your logical cable segment. The physical cable segment contains the physical cables connecting the various logical segments.

We also saw the word *backbone* mentioned a few times. A backbone is the main cable segment in the network. In a bus network you may see a cable that has smaller cables connected to it that connects the workstations at the other end. Figure 1-7 shows a Thick Ethernet backbone with Thin Ethernet drops coming off it.

Another example of a backbone in a global nature is a satellite linking geographically dispersed LANs making a WAN. This in an example of a wireless communications network, whereas the previous examples have all used cable as the medium.

FIGURE 1-7 A Thick Ethernet backbone with Thin Ethernet drops coming off it

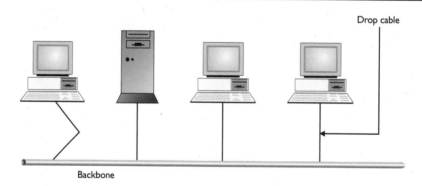

QUESTIONS AND ANSWERS

I am an engineer and I want to have a network with a single cable that all computers attach to with drop cables. Which type of network should I use?	Bus
I want to have a central hub that connects all the various computers via patch cables. Which topology should I use?	Star
As a network technician I want all of my computers to have multiple redundant links to ensure minimal downtime. Which topology would I use?	Mesh
I want to have a logically circular base for connecting all computers with no ending point. Which topology should I use?	Ring

CERTIFICATION OBJECTIVE 1.02

Network Operating Systems

Now that we have a general idea of the layout or topology of networks, we will look at the network operating system (NOS). We will focus on the three most widely used network operating systems available:

- Microsoft Windows NT
- Novell's NetWare
- UNIX

Network operating systems can operate in two fashions. In a *peer-to-peer* environment, each workstation on the network is equally responsible for managing resources. Each individual workstation can share its resources with other systems on the network. Configuring this type of network can be challenging, because nothing is centralized.

In a *client/server* environment, on the other hand, there is a centralized approach to the network operating system. If, as an administrator, you identify one machine as the network server, you can centralize network resource sharing. Clients then access the server. An example of a server operating system is Windows NT Server 4.0. Possible clients include Windows NT Workstation 4.0, Windows 95, Windows for Workgroups, Windows 3.1, and even MS-DOS Client.

Microsoft Windows NT

Developed from the VMS platform many years ago, Microsoft Windows NT has grown into a very popular network operating system with a new and different interface. The graphical interface and look and feel of the other operating systems in the Windows family made Windows NT very popular among users and network administrators. Figure 1-8 is a screen shot from Windows NT Server 4.0. The interface looks like that of Windows 95 or Windows 98 but has some differences in the utilities installed to manage the server.

Clients and Resources

With network operating systems, a major component of successful networking is the client software. Whether the workstations are in a workgroup environment (peer-to-peer), or a client/server relationship, the client software is needed. Client software has the proper drivers, software, and configuration to communicate with other computers across a network medium. Examples of client software include Windows NT Workstation 4.0, Windows 95, and Windows for Workgroups.

One reason Windows NT has been so successful is that it supports many different clients. Windows NT can communicate with MS-DOS Network Client 3.0, Windows 95, Windows 3.11 for Workgroups, Windows NT Workstation 4.0, OS/2, LAN Manager, Macintosh, NetWare, and UNIX clients.

FIGURE 1-8

Windows NT Server 4.0 enables you to manage your network operating system as a client/server environment

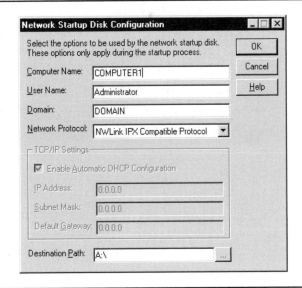

In a centralized environment, one computer has to be the master of the network. The computer that serves all other computers on the network is known as the server. The word "server" comes from the fact that it serves the needs of other computers on a centralized network.

Windows NT Server 4.0 and Windows NT Workstation 4.0 are very similar on the surface. Windows NT Server 4.0 is designed to be a powerful machine to serve other machines' needs, while Windows NT Workstation 4.0 is designed to run on a client machine on the network.

Windows NT Server 4.0 is geared to the server role. The software is designed to be a server that isn't used as a workstation but simply provides resource management and control to the network. Server software is really designed only for administrator use. The average user would not need to use even half the features included with server-side software. The main components of the server software are for network control, tracking, error control, and user management.

Directory Services

With Windows NT, the primary server that holds security account information is called a domain controller. A domain controller manages the access of users to the network. When users log on to a workstation on the network, the password is validated by one of the domain controllers. Domain controllers often serve as directory service servers as well. Directory services servers enable users to locate, store, and secure data on the network.

Novell NetWare

It started as a college project for one individual many years ago. Now Novell NetWare is in more businesses than any other network operating system in production today. NetWare has evolved into a very powerful network operating system. The major difference between Windows NT and NetWare is at the server. The server in NetWare, until NetWare 5, was truly a text-based network operating system with many of the administrative tasks being done at a client workstation. You could manage certain administrative items from the server console, but the main part of the user administration—file system administration—was done from a workstation while logged in to the server. Figure 1-9 shows a screen shot from a remote session with a Novell server.

FIGURE 1-9

With Novell NetWare, you can access the server remotely, from a workstation

```
MS-DOS Prompt - RCONSOLE                                    _ □ ×

  8 x 12                          A

    Version 5.00b    July 1, 1996
    (C) Copyright 1994-1995, Novell, Inc. All rights reserved.
    Patent Pending--Novell, Inc.
SPXS.NLM
    SPX/SPXII Protocol for NetWare 3.x & 4.x
    Version 5.00o    August 8, 1996
    (C) Copyright 1992-1995 Novell, Inc.
    All Rights Reserved.
SMDR.NLM
    NetWare SMS Data Requestor
    Version 4.10    July 2, 1996
    (C) Copyright 1991-1996 Novell, Inc. All Rights Reserved.
TSA410.NLM
    NetWare 4.10 Target Service Agent
    Version 4.14    July 23, 1996
    (C) Copyright 1990-1996 Novell, Inc.  All rights reserved.
AVENGINE.NLM
    Anti-Virus Scanning Engine Library v22.05
    Version 22.05    January 28, 1998
    (C) Copyright 1995-1997 Iris Software. All Rights Reserved.
TUI.NLM
    Textual User Interface MPR31A.PTF
    Version 1.04a    March 13, 1996
    Copyright 1992-1994 Novell, Inc.  All rights reserved.
NHCLCNWFS:_
```

Clients and Resources

NetWare 5 supports a wide variety of clients. The main ones, of course, are the Windows platform of operating systems. In the versions of NetWare prior to NetWare 5, you had to use IPX/SPX as your protocol. NetWare 5 gives you the capability to use pure IP on a NetWare network.

Directory Services

One of the driving features of NetWare since version 4 is the Novell Directory Services. The directory tree is a hierarchical grouping of objects that represent resources on the network, as shown in Figure 1-10. The objects on the tree can be users, printers, volumes, servers, as well as workstations.

The Directory Services built into NetWare makes administration easier because everything is organized and centralized within one utility. Maintenance and network upkeep are easier and more cost effective because less time is required to use one utility versus multiple utilities.

FIGURE 1-10

The NetWare Administrator directory tree shows resources on the network

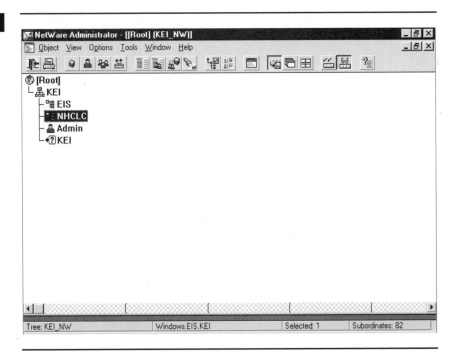

UNIX

Originally developed at the University of California, Berkeley, UNIX is becoming a very popular operating system for powerful networking and database management. UNIX boasts three key features that make it powerful: multitasking, multiusers, and networking capabilities.

UNIX is a very powerful multitasking operating system that can run many processes in the background while enabling users to work in the foreground on an application. The multiuser feature enables many users to use the same machine. The last feature, networking capability, is becoming standard in operating systems developed since 1995. UNIX has been the leader in several powerful and diverse utilities that have been ported over to other operating systems.

Clients and Resources

Most UNIX systems use a terminal to access the main computer. With a Windows 95 machine you can use a terminal emulation program to access a UNIX box. Most of what is done in UNIX is command-line driven. UNIX is one operating system that takes time to learn. The main thing to know is that UNIX is still accessed via terminal session, whether it is on a terminal itself or run through an operating system like Windows 95 or Windows NT with a terminal emulator.

Directory Services

The UNIX file system is similar to the DOS file system in that it has a directory structure. In UNIX, users are assigned permissions to directories and files enabling them to access certain parts of the Network File System (NFS). NFS drives the access and security of UNIX. We will look at NFS a little closer later in this chapter

CERTIFICATION OBJECTIVE 1.03

Network Protocols

Packets and protocols are the fundamental building blocks of data transmission over the network. All data that is transmitted across the network is put into packets containing information about the source and destination of the data. These packets are created using standards or protocols. Because there are many different network configurations, there are many different protocols. By having a variety of protocols, you can choose the one that best fulfills the needs of your network.

You can think of a protocol as a language your computer speaks to communicate with other computers on the network. Just as there are different languages in the real world, there are different protocols in the computer world. If two computers use different protocols to communicate on a network, they will not be able to communicate with each other. This is the same as two people who speak different languages trying to talk to each other. No real communication occurs. The information can be passed, but the receiving person or computer cannot understand that information due to the different language or protocol.

IPX

IPX/SPX (Internetwork Packet Exchange/Sequenced Packet Exchange) is the protocol most commonly used with Novell NetWare. IPX/SPX, a routable protocol, is a very fast and highly established protocol, but it is not used on the Internet. Novell developed IPX/SPX for use in NetWare. The protocol IPX/SPX/NWLink that is shipped with Windows 95 and Windows NT was written by Microsoft and is fully compatible with the Novell IPX/SPX protocol.

exam
Ⓦatch   *IPX/SPX is the fastest routable network protocol suite available.*

TCP/IP

TCP/IP (Transmission Control Protocol/Internet Protocol) is the most common protocol used today. TCP/IP, a routable protocol, is the protocol that the Internet is built upon. TCP/IP is very robust and is commonly associated with UNIX systems.

TCP/IP was originally designed in the 1970s to be used by the Defense Advanced Research Projects Agency (DARPA) and the Department of Defense (DOD) to connect systems across the country. This design required the capability to cope with unstable network conditions. Therefore, the design of TCP/IP included the capability to reroute packets.

The Network+ exam will focus on administering TCP/IP and knowing the protocol suite. We will look at how TCP/IP fits into the OSI model and how to configure and administer the IP addressing scheme. One thing you will definitely want to gain from this book is a clear understanding of TCP/IP. Not only will it prove vital for the exam, but you will need it for real life as well. Most networks today have some form of IP on them. TCP/IP drives the Internet and the Internet is driving computing.

NetBEUI

NetBEUI (NetBIOS Extended User Interface) is a transport protocol commonly found in smaller networks. NetBEUI was first implemented with LAN Manager products. It is not frequently used in large networks and will become even less frequently used in the future because it is not a routable protocol. A nonroutable protocol is unable to go across a router, which means it cannot be used in a Wide Area Network (WAN). NetBEUI is an extremely quick protocol with little overhead because of its inability to route packets.

exam
Ⓦatch   *NetBEUI is a nonroutable protocol.*

CERTIFICATION OBJECTIVE 1.04

Fault Tolerance (High Availability)

Possibly the biggest concern of any company today is ensuring that its data stays intact. Companies can lose millions upon millions of dollars if the data that drives their business is corrupted or gone.

A technology called Redundant Array of Inexpensive Disks (RAID) minimizes the loss of data when problems occur with accessing data on a hard disk. RAID is a fault-tolerant disk configuration in which part of the physical storage contains redundant information about data stored on the disks. Standardized strategies of fault tolerance are categorized in RAID levels 0–5. Each level offers various mixes of performance, reliability, and cost. The redundant information enables regeneration of data if a disk or sector on a disk fails, or if access to a disk fails. RAID 0 has no redundant information and therefore provides no fault tolerance. Table 1-1 shows the common RAID levels.

There are several ways to ensure that the integrity of data is kept intact. We will look at five of these to get a better understanding of how they work

TABLE 1-1	RAID Level	Description
RAID Levels	RAID 0	Disk striping
	RAID 1	Disk mirroring
	RAID 2	Disk striping across disks. Also maintains error correction codes across the disks.
	RAID 3	Same as level 2, except the error correction information is stored as parity information on one disk.
	RAID 4	Employs striping data in much larger blocks than in levels 2 and 3. Parity information is kept on a single disk.
	RAID 5	Disk striping with parity across multiple drives

and their advantages: mirroring, duplexing, striping, volumes, and tape backup. The most common of these is the tape backup system.

Mirroring

One of the more common ways to back up your data is to create a mirrored copy of the data on another disk. The mirroring system utilizes a code that duplicates everything written on one drive to another drive, making them identical. (As seen in Table 1-1, this is RAID level 1.) Figure 1-11 shows an example of two disks mirrored.

The best way to incorporate disk mirroring is at the hardware level with what is known as an array controller. An array controller is an interface card that connects to both drives via a SCSI cable and has the configuration information on the logical drive that is created. Today's network operating systems also allow for software level mirroring of two drives. Windows NT and Novell both offer a software level mirroring configuration.

Duplexing

Duplexing ensures fault tolerance not just with your data, but also with your disk controller. With traditional mirroring there is one disk controller. If the controller fails then the server is down until that component is replaced. Duplexing gives you a second controller. There can be a mirror with this type of configuration, but each drive is connected to its own

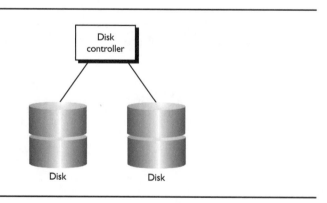

FIGURE 1-11

Disk mirroring writes everything to two separate disks

controller. If a controller fails, you still have an intact configuration. This can also speed up response time when writing to disk. Figure 1-12 shows an example of disk duplexing with the multiple controllers.

Striping (With and Without Parity)

Striping is becoming more and more popular. The striping of data is a way to spread the data out across the disks. This can improve performance. To do striping properly you need a minimum of three hard disks. Three or more different drives all acting to get a piece of the data will make the I/O (input/output) faster. Striping also gives you the option of adding parity to the drive set.

RAID 5, also known as disk striping with parity, provides the performance of RAID 0 but with fault tolerance. Disk striping consists of data being written in stripes across a volume that has been created from areas of free space. These areas are all the same size and spread over an array of 3 – 32 disks. The primary benefit of striping is that disk I/O is split between disks, improving performance, although improvements do not exceed the I/O capabilities of the disk controllers. Fault tolerance functionality is added to disk striping with the addition of parity information in one of the stripes. The parity stripe is the exclusive OR (XOR) of all the data values for the data stripes in the stripe. If no disks in the stripe set with parity have failed, the new parity for a write can be calculated without having to read the corresponding stripes from the other data disks.

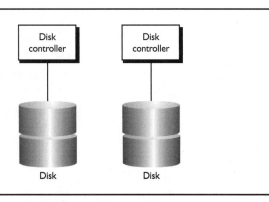

FIGURE 1-12

Disk duplexing provides fault protection with your data and your disk controller

With stripe set with parity, disk utilization increases as the number of disks increases, thus providing a lower cost per megabyte. Disk read operations can occur simultaneously, resulting in better disk performance. But the system or boot partition cannot be on a stripe set with parity. Also, if a disk that is part of the stripe set fails, read operations for data are substantially slower than that of a single disk. Because a stripe set with parity works with the operating system, it requires more memory than a mirror set.

Again, some vendors sell disk subsystems that implement RAID technology completely within the hardware. Some of these hardware implementations support hot swapping of disks, which enables you to replace a failed disk while the computer is still running.

Windows NT provides software support for two fault-tolerant disk configurations: mirroring and stripe sets with parity, as described above. The Disk Administrator utility configures mirror sets and stripe sets with parity and regenerates the volume when a disk fails. Here are some points to consider:

- Hardware fault tolerance is faster.
- Software fault tolerance is less expensive.
- The capability to swap a failed disk while the system still runs is only available with hardware fault-tolerant equipment.

Volumes

Most network servers are set up with various volume configurations. Usually you will see at least two volumes on a server: a System volume and a data volume, sometimes called VOL1. The System volume holds the network operating system files to make the server work. Separating the two helps ensure that the server does not run out of disk space on the System volume. If this were to happen, the server would probably crash.

Tape Backup

Tapes are a feasible means of storing data backups. Tapes are much less expensive than an array of disks and are reliable. A backup set is a group of files, directories, or disks selected for a single backup operation. A family set is a collection of related tapes containing several backup sets. Information describing the backup sets stored on the tape is called a catalog. A catalog for a family is located on the last tape.

Backup Strategies

A normal backup, also called full backup, copies all selected files and marks each file as having been backed up. With this type of backup, files can be restored easily because the most current files will be on the last tape.

An incremental backup backs up only files that have been created or changed since the last full or incremental backup and marks them as being backed up. To restore files when both full and incremental methods were used, start with the last full backup and then work through all the incremental tapes.

A differential backup copies files created or changed since the last full backup. It does not mark files as having been backed up. To restore files when both full and differential methods were used, only the last full backup and the last differential backup are needed. Note: Because in differential backups, files are not marked as backed up, if two differential backups are performed in a row, the files backed up during the first backup will be backed up again, regardless of whether or not the files have changed since the first differential backup.

A daily backup copies all selected files that have been modified the day the daily backup is performed and does not mark them as having been backed up.

Tape Logs

A log file of the backup operations can be generated, in the form of a text file, during the backup process. These are options available for logging:

- **Summary Only**   Logs only major operations such as loading a tape, starting a backup, etc.

- **Copy Full Detail**   Logs information for all operations, including the names of all the files and directories that are backed up.

- **Don't Log**   No information is logged.

The OSI Model

The OSI (Open Systems Interconnect) protocol suite is a group of standards for protocols that have been standardized into a logical structure for network operations. This structure contains seven layers that are commonly referred to as the OSI model. The seven layers of the OSI model from highest to lowest are: Application, Presentation, Session, Transport, Network, Data Link, and Physical. Network communication starts at the Application layer of the OSI Model and works its way down through the layers step by step to the Physical layer. The information then passes along the cable to the receiving computer, which starts the information at the Physical layer. From there it steps back up the OSI layers to the Application layer where the receiving computer finalizes the processing and sends back an acknowledgement if needed. Then the whole process starts over. Figure 1-13 shows an example of packets being transmitted down through the OSI layers, across the medium, and back up the OSI layers.

FIGURE 1-13

In an OSI Model, data is transmitted down through the layers, across the medium, and back up through the layers

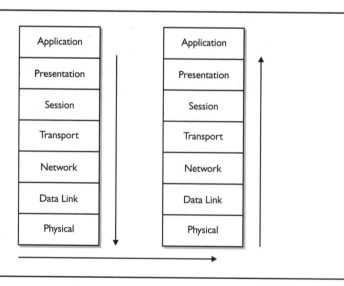

The OSI model is conceptual in nature, meaning that it is not followed exactly by every protocol. In fact, many protocols span layers, or can be associated with more than one layer. Table 1-2 shows the different layers and the protocols that reside at each.

Protocols

Different protocols work at different levels of the OSI model. Here, we will look at a few of the main protocols for this exam, apply them to the OSI model, and see how they fit in the OSI model's seven layers.

IPX

IPX is an extremely fast, streamlined protocol that is not connection oriented. IPX can be used for a Windows NT network and is fairly common because of its pre-existing widespread use on Novell NetWare. The primary responsibility of IPX is the handling of broadcast issues. IPX is a routable protocol that is located in the Network Layer of the OSI model. IPX is capable of being run over both Ethernet and Token Ring networks by using the appropriate network interface card (NIC) drivers, which are provided by the NIC manufacturer. For a number of years, IPX over Ethernet was the default use of NICs.

	OSI Layer	Protocols
TABLE 1-2 OSI Model Protocols and Layers	Application	AppleTalk, NFS
	Presentation	SMB, NCP
	Session	NCP, Telnet
	Transport	TCP, UDP, NetBEUI, SPX
	Network	IPX, IP
	Data Link	Ethernet, Token Ring
	Physical	Twisted Pair, Thinnet Coax, AUI, Network Interface Card

TCP/IP

TCP/IP is one of the most popular protocol suites. TCP/IP is actually a combination of two different protocols, TCP and IP, working together at different layers of the OSI model to build a foundation for other applications and protocols on the upper layers. Since TCP/IP is two different protocols, it is actually located in two different layers of the OSI model. TCP is located in the Transport Layer and IP is located in the Network Layer. TCP breaks the data into manageable packets, while IP tracks information such as the source and destination of the packets. TCP/IP is fully capable of running over either Token Ring or Ethernet networks, as long as an appropriate NIC is used. IP over Ethernet is the most common implementation in networking today because Ethernet is much less expensive than Token Ring and because TCP/IP is widely used on the Internet.

NFS

NFS (Network File System) is a protocol for file sharing that enables a user to use network disks as if they were connected to the local machine. NFS was created by Sun Microsystems for use on SOLARIS, Sun's version of UNIX. NFS is still frequently used in the UNIX world and is available for use with nearly all operating systems. NFS is a protocol that is universally used by the UNIX community. Vendor and third-party software products enable other operating systems to use NFS. It has gained acceptance with many different companies and can be added to nearly any operating system. In addition to file sharing, NFS enables you to share printers. NFS is located in the Application Layer of the OSI model and is considered to be a member of the TCP/IP protocol suite. The primary reason to use the NFS protocol is if you need to use resources that are located on a UNIX server or if you want to share resources with someone working on a UNIX workstation.

SMB and Novell NCP

SMB (server message block) and Novell NCP (NetWare Core Protocol) are protocols that are implemented in redirectors. A redirector is software that intercepts requests, formats them according to the protocol in use, and passes the message to a lower level protocol for delivery. Redirectors also intercept incoming messages, process the instructions, and pass them to the correct upper level application for additional processing.

SMB and NCP are primarily used for file and printer sharing in Microsoft and Novell networks, respectively.

SMTP

SMTP (Simple Mail Transport Protocol) is the protocol that defines the structure of Internet mail messages. SMTP uses a well-defined syntax for transferring messages. An SMTP session includes initializing the SMTP connection, sending the destination e-mail address, sending the sources email address, sending the subject, and sending the body of the e-mail message.

FTP and TFTP

FTP (File Transfer Protocol) is a standardized method of transferring files between two machines. FTP is a connection-oriented protocol, which means that the protocol verifies that packets successfully reach their destination.

TFTP (Trivial File Transfer Protocol) has the same purpose and function as FTP except that is not a connection-oriented protocol and does not verify that packets reach their destination. By not verifying that data is being successfully transferred to its destination, and therefore requiring less overhead to establish and maintain a connection, TFTP is able to operate faster than FTP.

DECnet

DECnet is a proprietary protocol developed by Digital Equipment Corporation for use primarily in wide area networks (WANs). You can run DECnet on an Ethernet network, but it is used infrequently. DECnet is a routable protocol.

DLC

DLC (Data Link Control) is not a commonly used protocol. DLC, a nonroutable protocol, is sometimes used to connect Windows NT servers to printers.

TCP/IP, IPX/SPX/NWLink, AppleTalk, and DECnet are routable protocols while NetBEUI and DLC are not.

Services

The NOS has a series of responsibilities to make sure that the workstation or server functions as needed. With Windows networking, there are many different services that run in the background and have key responsibilities of their own. One example of a service you will read about is the browser service, which controls the network browsing features in Windows NT. With Windows NT or Windows 95, you can use Network Neighborhood to find other computers on the network. The browser service enables this to function properly. There are other services within Windows NT that are responsible for certain actions. This information is covered in more depth in the book *Windows NT Server 4.0 in the Enterprise* (Osborne/McGraw-Hill).

Functions That Pertain to Each Layer

Each layer has specific functions that it defines. Some functions are defined in more than one layer (such as error control and flow control). While this seems redundant, it does not mean that these functions must be implemented at both layers. Don't forget that the OSI is a model. One designer may use error control at one layer, another may use it at a different layer. It all depends on the designer's goals.

While it is very easy to memorize the various layers of the OSI model from top to bottom, it is a bit easier to learn what these layers do by taking a bottom-to-top approach.

Physical

The bottom layer of the OSI hierarchy is concerned only with moving bits of data onto and off the network medium. The Physical Layer does not define what that medium is, but it must define how to access it. This includes the physical topology (or structure) of the network, the electrical and physical aspects of the medium used, and encoding and timing of bit transmission and reception.

Data Link

The Data Link Layer handles many issues for communicating on a simple network. (The Network Layer discussed in the next section performs the functions necessary to communicate beyond a single physical network.) This layer takes the frames generated by the upper layers and takes them apart for transmission. When receiving messages from the network, it reassembles this information back into frames to send to the upper layers. This layer actually does a lot more than just break apart and put together frames.

The 802 model (discussed later in this chapter) breaks the Data Link Layer into two sublayers: logical link control (LLC) and media access control (MAC). The LLC layer starts and maintains connections between devices. When sending data from your workstation to a server on the same network segment, it is the LLC sublayer that establishes a connection with that server. The MAC layer enables multiple devices to share the media. Most LANs have more than one computer (of course!), and the MAC sublayer determines who may speak and when.

Another important job of the Data Link Layer is addressing. The MAC sublayer maintains physical device addresses for communicating with other devices (commonly referred to as MAC addresses). Each device on the network must have a unique MAC address, otherwise the network will not know exactly where to send information when a node requests it. For example, how would the postal service know where to send your bills without your address?!

Most network interface cards (NICs) in a computer provide the MAC address as an address burned into the interface card. Some older network cards even required an administrator to set the address manually using switches. Even with a permanent MAC address burned into the card, some protocols enable you to define this address via software, although this is unusual.

The MAC address is used to communicate only on the local network. When transmitting to a server on the same LAN segment, the protocol uses the MAC addresses to communicate between the two computers. If the server is located on another network segment across a WAN, the MAC address of the nearest router (routers are discussed later in this chapter) is used to send the information, and it is up to the router to send the data further on.

Finally, the Data Link Layer manages flow control and error correction between devices in a simple network. In more complex internetworks, it is up to the Network Layer and other upper layers to perform these functions.

Network

The Network Layer is one of the most complex and important ones. The Network Layer manages addressing and delivering packets on a complex internetwork. Internetworks are joined by devices known as routers, which utilize routing tables and routing algorithms to determine how to send data from one network to another.

The most obvious example of an internetwork is the Internet. The Internet is very large, covering the entire globe, and consists of almost every conceivable type of computer, from palmtop to mainframe.

In order to operate on an internetwork, each network that participates must be assigned a network address. This address differentiates each network from every other network that forms the internetwork. When sending data from one network to another, the routers along the way use the network address to determine the next step in the journey.

The Network Layer also enables the option of specifying a service address on the destination computer. All modern operating systems, such as UNIX, Windows NT, and OS/2, run many programs at once. The service address enables the sender to specify which program on the destination the data being sent is for. Service addresses that are well defined (by networking standards, for example) are called well-known addresses. Service addresses are also called sockets or ports by various protocols.

Transport

The Transport Layer works hard to ensure reliable delivery of data to its destinations. The Transport Layer also helps the upper layers (Application, Presentation, and Session) to communicate with one another across the network while hiding the complexities of the network.

The Transport Layer also interacts with the Network Layer, taking on some of the responsibilities for connection services. One of the functions of the Transport Layer is segment sequencing. Sequence switching is a connection-oriented service that takes segments that are received out of order and resequences them in the right order.

Another function of the Transport Layer is error control. It commonly uses acknowledgments to manage the flow of data between devices. Some Transport Layer protocols can also request retransmission of recent segments to overcome errors.

Session

The Session Layer manages dialogs between computers. It does this by establishing, managing, and terminating communications between the two computers. There are three types of dialogs that the Session Layer uses.

Simplex dialogs enable data to flow in only one direction. Since the dialog is one way, information can be sent, but not responded to, or even acknowledged. An example of a simplex dialog is a Public Announcement (PA) system in a large building. Announcements can be made, but the PA system doesn't enable any response or acknowledgement.

Half-duplex dialogs enable data to flow in two directions, but only one direction at a time. With half-duplex dialogs, replies and acknowledgments are possible, but this isn't always the most efficient method. If an error is detected early in transmission, the receiver must wait for the sender to finish before any action can be taken. A CB radio is an excellent example of a half-duplex dialog.

Full-duplex dialogs enable data to flow in both directions simultaneously. This method provides more flexibility, but also requires more complex communication methods. A telephone is a prime example of full-duplex communication.

When a session is established, there are three distinct phases involved. Establishment is when the requestor initiates the service and the rules for communication are established. Once the rules are established, the data transfer phase may begin. Both sides know how to talk to each other, what the most efficient methods are, and how to detect errors, all because of the rules defined in the first phase. Finally, termination occurs when the session is complete and communication ends in an orderly fashion.

Presentation

It is up to the Presentation Layer to make sure that data sent by the Application Layer and received by the Session Layer is in a standard format. As discussed earlier, different types of computers can interpret identical data differently.

A network standard defines the proper format for any data as it is transmitted. When the Presentation Layer receives data from the Application Layer to be sent over the network, it makes sure that the data is in the proper format. If it is not, it converts the data. On the flip side, when the Presentation Layer receives data from the Session Layer from the network, it makes sure that the data is in the proper format and once again converts it if it is not.

Application

The Application Layer provides a consistent, neutral interface to the network. Many people confuse the Application Layer with an actual software package, such as a word processor. This is not the case. The Application Layer provides consistent ways for an application to save files to the network file server or print to a network printer.

An example of this is how Windows 95 makes it just as easy to print to a network printer as it is to print to a locally attached printer. This is the Application Layer in practice.

The Application Layer also advertises a computer's available resources to the rest of the network.

CERTIFICATION OBJECTIVE 1.06

Networking Media and Connectors

Cabling is the LAN's transmission medium. LANs can be connected together using a variety of cable types. Each cable type has its own advantages and disadvantages.

Cabling

There are three primary types of physical media that can be used at the Physical Layer: coaxial cable, twisted-pair cable, and fiber-optic cable. Transmission rates that can be supported on each of these physical media are measured in millions of bits per second (Mbps).

Coax

Coaxial (or coax) cable looks like the cable used to bring the cable TV signal to our television. One strand (a solid-core wire) runs down the middle of the cable. Around that strand is insulation. Covering that insulation is braided wire and metal foil, which shields against electromagnetic interference. A final layer of insulation covers the braided wire. Coaxial cable is resistant to the interference and signal weakening that other cabling, such as unshielded twisted-pair (UTP) cable, can experience. In general, coax is better than UTP cable is at connecting longer distances and for reliably supporting higher data rates with less sophisticated equipment.

Just because the TV cable is coax does not mean it will work with computer networks. Network coaxial cable has very specific requirements, such as the gauge, the impedance, and the attenuation.

Thinnet refers to RG-58 cabling, which is a flexible coaxial cable about ¼-inch thick. Thinnet is used for short-distance communication and is flexible enough to facilitate routing between workstations. Thinnet connects directly to a workstation's network adapter card using a BNC T-connector and uses the network adapter card's internal transceiver. 10Base2 refers to Ethernet LANs that use Thinnet cabling.

Thicknet coaxial cable can support data transfer over longer distances better than Thinnet can and is usually used as a backbone to connect several smaller Thinnet-based networks. The diameter of a Thicknet cable is about ½-inch and is harder to work with than a Thinnet cable. A transceiver is often connected directly to Thicknet cable using a connector known as a piercing tap. Connection from the transceiver to the network adapter card is made using a drop cable to connect to the adapter unit interface (AUI) port connector. 10Base5 refers to Ethernet LANs that use Thicknet cabling.

Cat 3

CAT3 is a grade of cable that enables networking, but CAT5 is the better way to go. The key thing about CAT3 is that it already exists in most office buildings and homes. CAT3 is a voice-grade cable used in phone networks. Again, it can be used for networking up to 10 Mbps.

Cat 5

Most UTP cable is CAT 5 in today's networks. CAT 5 is a standard that enables up to 100 Mbps data transmission. This is the standard UTP or STP cable type to use. CAT5 is the highest rating of the UTP cabling.

Fiber Optic

Optical fibers carry digital data signals in the form of modulated pulses of light. An optical fiber consists of an extremely thin cylinder of glass, called the core, surrounded by a concentric layer of glass, known as the cladding. There are two fibers per cable—one to transmit and one to receive. The cylinder can also be an optical quality plastic. The cladding can be made up of gel that reflects signals back into the fiber to reduce signal lost.

Fiber-optic cable supports up to 1000 stations and can carry the signal up to and beyond 50 miles. Fiber-optic cables are also highly secure from outside interference such as radio transmitters, arc welders, fluorescent lights, and other sources of electrical noise. On the other hand, fiber-optic cable is by far the most expensive of these cabling methods and a small network is unlikely to need these features. Depending on local labor rates and building codes, installing fiber-optic cable can cost as much as $500 per node.

Two electrical phenomena can disrupt your network: crosstalk and outside electrical noise. Crosstalk is caused by electrical fields in adjacent wires inducing false signals in each wire. Outside electrical noise comes from lights, motors, radio systems, and many other sources. Fiber-optic cabling is immune to these interferences.

UTP

Unshielded twisted-pair (UTP) cables are familiar to you if you have worked with telephone cable. Each pair of wires contained in the cable is twisted around each other. The typical twisted-pair cable for network use contains three or four pairs of wires. The twists in the wires help shield against electromagnetic interference. 10BaseT refers to Ethernet LANs that use UTP cabling.

UTP cable uses small plastic connectors designated as RJ-45. These are similar to the phone connectors except that instead of four wires found in the home system, the network RJ-45 contains eight contacts.

UTP cable is easier to install than coaxial because you can pull it around corners more easily. Twisted-pair cable is more susceptible to interference and should not be used in environments containing large electrical or electronic devices.

STP

Shielded twisted-pair cable differs from UTP in that it uses a much higher quality protective jacket for greater insulation. Thus, it is less subject to electrical interference and supports higher transmission speeds over longer distances than UTP.

Media Connectors

We've looked at some of the types of connectors that can be used in networking. With transmission types come distance limitations. In this section we will look at the different 10Mb (megabit) connection types, the different 100Mb connection types, and BNC connectivity.

10Base2, 10Base5, and 10BaseT

With 10Mb per second, or 10 million bits per second, there are three types of cabling schemes that give different distance limitations. The following table shows the differences between 10Base2, 10Base5 and 10BaseT. 10Base2 and 10Base5 are seen more in a coax environment and 10BaseT refers to twisted pair.

Cable Media	Maximum Distance per Segment
10Base2 (Thinnet)	185 meters
10Base5 (Thicknet)	500 meters
10BaseT (Twisted-Pair)	100 meters

100BaseT, 100VGAnyLan, 100Base TX

100Mb connectivity increases the performance of LANs and WANs. 100BaseT using CAT5 twisted pair to transmit at 100 Mbps. Another common term that relates to 100BaseT is Fast Ethernet. Distances are the same as 10BaseT. 100BaseTX cables use two sets of two pairs, or 8 wires. 8 wires are standard with CAT5. Distance on this is also around 100 meters, as with 10BaseT.

100VGAnyLAN is an Ethernet and Token Ring specification using 4 pairs of CAT3, CAT4, or CAT5. This technology was developed by Hewlett Packard.

BNC and RJ-45

The BNC connector is used to connect IEEE 802.3 10Base2 coaxial cable to a hub. The BNC connector looks like a connector you would plug into your television. The following illustration shows a T-connector that can connect to the workstation and join to physical cable segments.

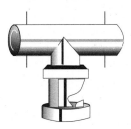

A special crimping tool is used to put the connector on the end of the wire. The actual wire runs down the middle and must make contact with the end of the connector shown in the middle.

The RJ-45 connector is used with twisted-pair cables. It looks like a telephone connector but wider. There are eight pins, hence eight wires. Ethernet can use only four of the wires or possibly all eight. If only four wires are used the pins to know are 1, 2, 3, and 6. The following illustration shows what an RJ-45 connector looks like. A special crimping tool is also needed to make contact between the pins and the cable inside.

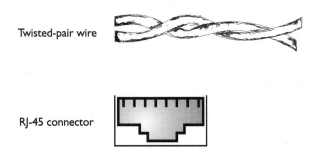

Twisted-pair wire

RJ-45 connector

FROM THE FIELD

The Role of Network Topology, Cabling, and Connectors

Just as network topology, cabling, and connectors are important in passing your Network+ exam, they also important in your role as a network professional. It is a very valuable skill set to have a strong understanding of how network topology, cabling, and connectors coexist. This is especially the case if you are a network engineer who must design and implement a network from the ground up. You must know the characteristics of each network topology and apply them in each unique situation you encounter. For example, you are designing a network for a small investment firm with 10 users and a minimal budget. Instantly you should be thinking bus topology, which is less expensive and the easiest to implement for smaller networks such as this one.

Your choice of network topology will also dictate your choice of cabling. In the above example we have implemented a bus topology, which is conducive to the coaxial cable.

Coaxial cables are connected from the network backbone, which is most likely another coaxial cable, to each workstation with a BNC T-connector, which leads us to our last specification: the network connector.

Just as the network topology dictated the choice of cabling, it also dictated our choice of connector. The BNC connector is the cornerstone of coaxial cabling.

Although the preceding demonstration seemed easy, the secret lies with understanding the limitations of each network, such as the maximum cable length and number of workstations per segment. What will truly set you apart as a network professional is your ability to understand the features and limitation of each network type. This will also come in handy during your Network+ exam, which will test your knowledge of these very rules.

—Cameron Brandon, MCSE+Internet,
CNE, A+, Network+

CERTIFICATION OBJECTIVE 1.07

Network Elements

In this section we want to review some of the common terminology that is used in networking environments. Some of these terms were used already and I want to make sure we have a clear understanding of each one for the exam. Any of these terms may be seen on the exam in different questions or scenarios.

Full- and Half-Duplexing

When data travels across the medium, it of course travels in a certain direction. With the newest of network adapters, hubs, and switches there is a term used to determine how the data travels in regards to direction. This term is duplex. There is either half duplex or full duplex. Half duplex means data travels both ways on the medium but in only one direction at a time. Full duplex means you can have data travel both directions simultaneously.

WAN and LAN

In case you aren't clear on the differences between a Wide Area Network (WAN) and a Local Area Network (LAN), a WAN spans multiple geographic locations and a LAN is confined to a single building, or a college campus, for example.

Server, Workstation, and Host

In networking today you have to have workstations. The workstation is what the terminal used to be. It is where the user accesses the applications and data. The user logs in and connects to various resources.

The user does not directly use the server. The server serves the workstations and users. Usually, the server is not directly used with its local keyboard or mouse. Administrators remotely manage the server from a workstation.

Server-Based Networking and Peer-to-Peer Networking

Different organization sizes, structures, and budgets need different types of networks. The local newspaper needs a different approach for its network than a multinational company. Networks can be divided into peer-to-peer and server-based networks. The difference between the two is explained in the following sections.

Peer-to-Peer Network

A peer-to-peer network has no dedicated servers. There are no hierarchical differences between the workstations in the network. The user at each workstation can decide which resources are shared on the network. In a peer-to-peer network, all workstations are clients and servers at the same time. Of course, this situation creates some restrictions for the properties of the network.

The size of a peer-to-peer network or workgroup is usually limited to 10 workstations. It is technically possible to connect more workstations and to let them share data. However, this is not advisable. Because there is no centralized administration in a workgroup, the security level is low and it is very hard to keep an overview of the shared resources on the network.

It is fairly simple to implement a peer-to-peer network. All users get a computer on their desks. The workstations are connected with a simple and visible cabling system. The users can then administer their own computers and the resources they want to share on the network. Because all users in a workgroup are administrators of their own computer, they need to be trained in order to function properly in the network.

Security is an issue on a peer-to-peer network. Anybody on the network can access any shared resource as long as they know the password for that resource. Too often, though, the resources don't have passwords. So if you have a network where a lot of sensitive data is stored and processed or you have other reasons to want high security, a peer-to-peer network is not the way to go.

Most of the modern operating systems for stand-alone computers already have built-in workgroup networking capabilities. Because there is no need for server-level security and performance, you can operate a peer-to-peer network on operating systems such as Windows for Workgroups, Windows NT Workstation 4.0, and Windows 95.

Server-Based Networks

When your network environment grows beyond 10 users, you may need a server-based network to ensure the security of your files and directories and to organize your resources efficiently. As your network traffic increases, you'll need more servers to spread their tasks so that they all can be performed in the most efficient way. That is when you introduce specialized servers such as the following:

- File and print servers
- Application servers
- Domain controllers
- Directory services

File and print servers control and share printers and large amounts of data. These servers are typically high-powered computers that are built specifically for the purpose of moving files between disk and network as quickly as possible. File servers often have the following characteristics:

- Large amounts of memory
- Fast hard disks
- Multiple CPUs
- Fast I/O buses

- High-capacity tape drives
- Fast network adapters
- Redundant power supplies
- Hot-swappable hard disks and power supplies

File and print servers also check the access control list (ACL) of each resource before enabling a user to access a file or use a printer. If the user, or a group to which the user belongs, is not listed in the ACL, the user is not allowed to use the resource. A good definition of a file and print server is that they can only send complete files to the client and cannot find or process data within those files.

Application servers enable users to access the server side of client/server applications. Application servers store vast amounts of data that is manipulated or extracted or otherwise used by the clients. For example, the salary administration of a large organization is typically on an application server. The server enables the users to do searches for people's names, add new data, and do calculations on it. These are some applications that you might find on an applications server:

- SQL Server
- Oracle
- Exchange Server
- Lotus Notes

A server can be both a file and print server as well as an application server. A good definition of an application server is when a client requests that the server find and/or manipulate data and return only the results.

Cable, NIC, and Router

Networking would not work without at least two of the following three items: cable, NIC, and router. The cable, of course, is the most common medium for connecting components in a computer network. The different types of cable that we have looked at in this chapter include untwisted pair, coaxial, and fiber.

The NIC, or Network Interface Card, is the key component that makes a workstation or computer communicate with the rest of the network. It is literally the interface to the network and how the workstation gets its information on the medium. A NIC has a transceiver of some sort to connect to the cable.

A router is a necessity in the WAN. It would not be possible to connect multiple sites if it were not for routers. Routers are what make the Internet what it is and bring all the various high speed backbones together in one large network. A router is a computer in and of itself that controls and routes the data on a large or small WAN-style communications solution.

Broadband and Baseband

Broadband LANs are the exception rather than the rule, although many cable companies are now offering Internet services at extraordinary transmission speeds. These networks differ from their baseband counterparts in that they use coaxial or fiber-optic cable to carry multiple channels of data. A single cable can carry five or six separate communications channels. A broadband network is analogous to cable TV: One cable brings in many TV channels as well as networking services.

Broadband systems use analog signaling and a range of frequencies. With analog transmission, the signals employed are continuous and nondiscrete. Signals flow across the physical medium in the form of electromagnetic or optical waves. Broadband technologies use amplifiers to bring analog signals back up to their original strength.

Most LANs are baseband. A baseband network uses only one channel on the cable to support digital transmission. Signals flow in the form of discrete pulses of electricity or light. With baseband transmission, the entire capacity of the communication channel is used to transmit a single data signal.

As the signal travels along the network cable, it gradually decreases in strength and can become distorted. If the cable length is too long, resulting in a signal that is weak or distorted, the received signal may be unrecognizable or misinterpreted. As a safeguard, baseband systems sometimes use repeaters to receive an incoming signal and retransmit it at its original strength and definition to increase the practical length of a cable segment.

Gateway

A gateway is used more and more in networking because of the internet. A gateway connects dissimilar systems. When UNIX wants to talk to NetWare there must be a gateway for the two to communicate. A gateway is like a translator between two systems that are different from each other. The most common example of this is the Internet. Everyone who connects to the Internet, whether through a dial-up connection or through a LAN, must have a default gateway that his workstation points to.

CERTIFICATION SUMMARY

This chapter plays a key part in this book. It serves as an introduction to all the various components of networking. Understanding the basic network structure takes a little knowledge of computing and information sharing. First, remember that for a network to exist we need to have two things that want to share information. To share the information we must have a medium to communicate across. This can be a cable, such as coaxial or unshielded twisted pair. We can also have a wireless network made up of infrared signals. In this chapter we looked at the different topologies that exist in networks: Bus, Star, Ring, and Mesh. These topologies each have their own strengths and weaknesses. We also looked at the difference between segments and backbones.

You learned about the different network operating systems: Windows NT, Novell's NetWare, and UNIX.

A network needs rules to govern how communicating will happen. These rules are known as protocols and we looked at some of the protocols that make network communication possible: IPX from Novell, TCP/IP, which drives the Internet today, and NetBEUI, which is a nonroutable protocol.

With networking we need to ensure we will not lose data and this takes fault tolerance. The more uptime and availability on a network, the better the return in investment a company receives. Some methods of fault tolerance are drive mirroring, disk striping with and without parity, disk duplexing, and tape backup.

With networking you will notice that there are standards that are followed throughout different operating systems. Many standards flow from one operating system to another. The OSI model is a seven-layer approach to a network operating system. We looked at each layer and what it does. An easy way to remember the layers (Application, Presentation, Session, Transport, Network, Data Link, and Physical) is with the sentence, "**A**ll **p**eople **s**eem **t**o **n**eed **d**ata **p**rocessing."

We also looked at the various networking media and connectors. The different grades of cable can be important for the exam, as well as knowing what a connector looks like. The most common are RJ-45 and coax connectors.

We reviewed some basic terminology in the last part of the chapter. From duplexing to WAN and LAN there are many terms to become familiar with for the exam. If there is one thing that networking gives you, it is acronyms, and you should know them for the exam.

✓ TWO-MINUTE DRILL

- ❏ A network is made up of two basic components: the entities that want to share information or resources and the medium that enables the entities to communicate.

- ❏ Topology is the physical layout of computers, cables, and other components on a network.

- ❏ Many networks are a combination of the various topologies:
    - ❏ Bus
    - ❏ Star
    - ❏ Mesh
    - ❏ Ring

- ❏ A bus topology uses one cable to connect multiple computers.

- ❏ In a star topology, all computers are connected through one central hub or switch.

❑ With the mesh topology, every workstation has a connection to every other component of the network. It is more commonly seen with something like the national phone network.

❑ In a ring topology, all computers are connected with a cable that loops around.

❑ The physical cable segment contains the physical cables connecting the various logical segments.

❑ A backbone is the main cable segment in the network.

❑ The three most widely used network operating systems available:

   ❑ Microsoft Windows NT

   ❑ Novell's NetWare

   ❑ UNIX

❑ Packets and protocols are the fundamental building blocks of data transmission over the network.

❑ IPX/SPX (Internetwork Packet Exchange/Sequenced Packet Exchange) is the protocol most commonly used with Novell NetWare.

❑ IPX/SPX is the fastest routable network protocol suite available.

❑ TCP/IP (Transmission Control Protocol/Internet Protocol) is the most common protocol used today. TCP/IP, a routable protocol, is the protocol that the Internet is built upon.

❑ NetBEUI (NetBIOS Extended User Interface) is a transport protocol commonly found in smaller networks.

❑ NetBEUI is a nonroutable protocol.

❑ RAID is a fault-tolerant disk configuration in which part of the physical storage contains redundant information about data stored on the disks.

❑ The mirroring system utilizes a code that duplicates everything written on one drive to another drive, making them identical.

❑ Duplexing ensures fault tolerance not just with your data, but also with your disk controller.

❑ The striping of data is a way to spread the data out across the disks.

❑ Usually you will see at least two volumes on a server: a System volume and a data volume, sometimes called VOL1.

❑ Tapes are a feasible means of storing data backups.

❑ The OSI (Open Systems Interconnect) protocol suite is a group of standards for protocols that have been standardized into a logical structure for network operations.

❑ The seven layers of the OSI model from highest to lowest are: Application, Presentation, Session, Transport, Network, Data Link, and Physical.

❑ Different protocols work at different levels of the OSI model.

❑ TCP/IP, IPX/SPX/NWLink, AppleTalk, and DECnet are routable protocols while NetBEUI and DLC are not.

❑ Cabling is the LAN's transmission medium.

❑ There are three primary types of physical media that can be used at the Physical Layer: coaxial cable, twisted-pair cable, and fiber-optic cable.

❑ Half duplex means data travels both ways on the medium but in only one direction at a time. Full duplex means you can have data travel both directions simultaneously

❑ Networks can be divided into peer-to-peer and server-based networks.

❑ The NIC, or Network Interface Card, is the key component that makes a workstation or computer communicate with the rest of the network.

❑ A router is a computer in and of itself that controls and routes the data on a large or small WAN-style communications solution.

❑ Broadband systems use analog signaling and a range of frequencies.

❑ A baseband network uses only one channel on the cable to support digital transmission.

❑ A gateway connects dissimilar systems.

SELF TEST

The following Self Test questions will help you measure your understanding of the material presented in this chapter. Read all the choices carefully, as there may be more than one correct answer. Choose all correct answers for each question.

1. Which of the following is an example of a network?

   A. A computer attached to a printer and a scanner to input and output information.

   B. A computer sharing a communication medium to communicate with peripherals or other computers to share information.

   C. Several printers connected to a switch box going to a single terminal.

   D. Several floppy disks holding information for one workstation.

2. The physical layout of computers, cables, and other components on a network is known as what?

   A. Segment

   B. Backbone

   C. Topology

   D. Protocol

3. Which topology uses one long cable segment and must terminate at each end to prevent signal bounce?

   A. Bus

   B. Start

   C. Mesh

   D. Ring

4. Which topology has a centralized location where all the cables come together to a central point, similar to a mainframe, and if this point fails, it will bring down the entire network?

   A. Bus

   B. Star

   C. Mesh

   D. Ring

5. Which topology has a layout where every workstation or peripheral has a direct connection to every other workstation or peripheral on the network?

   A. Bus

   B. Star

   C. Mesh

   D. Ring

6. Which topology is like a circle with a continuous loop connecting all computers without termination?

   A. Bus

   B. Star

   C. Mesh

   D. Ring

7. Which of the following are two logical segments of a computer network?

A. Two computers joined by a cable within the same IP subnet.

B. Several computers joined by several cables in a star topology within the same IP subnet.

C. Several computers joined by several cables in a star topology within different IP subnets.

D. Several computers joined by a backbone in a bus topology on or within the same IP subnet.

8. Which network operating system was developed from the VMS platform?

A. NetWare

B. UNIX

C. Windows 95

D. Windows NT

9. Which network operating system was developed originally as a college project and uses a popular directory services structure to organize the network management?

A. UNIX

B. NetWare

C. Windows NT

D. OS/3.90

10. Which operating system was originally developed at U.C. Berkeley and has multitasking, multiuser, and built-in networking?

A. UNIX

B. Windows NT

C. Windows 95

D. NetWare

11. What do networks use to communicate with each other that is sometimes known as a language that networked computers use?

A. NICs

B. Segment

C. Protocol

D. Cable

12. Which network protocol was developed by Novell for use in their network operating systems?

A. IPX

B. TCP/IP

C. NetBEUI

D. DLC

13. Which protocol is used on the Internet to give each computer a unique address?

A. IPX

B. TCP/IP

C. NetBEUI

D. DLC

14. Which of the following is not a routable protocol and cannot be used on the Internet?

A. IPX

B. TCP/IP

C. NetBEUI

D. DECnet

15. Which of the following are methods of ensuring fault tolerance with data on a network? (Choose all that apply.)

    A. Disk mirroring

    B. Disk striping without parity

    C. Disk striping with parity

    D. Tape backup

    E. Disk duplexing

16. Which of the following is not a layer in the OSI Model?

    A. Physical

    B. Transport

    C. Network

    D. Data Transmission

17. Which of the following is not a common type of media used in networking?

    A. coaxial

    B. twisted-pair

    C. fiber-optic

    D. RJ-45

18. What is the distance limitation on 10Base2 or Thinnet?

    A. 100 meters

    B. 185 meters

    C. 250 meters

    D. 500 meters

19. When data is able to travel in both directions on a cable this is known as what?

    A. Fault Tolerance

    B. Half Duplex

    C. Bi-Duplex

    D. Full Duplex

20. In what type of network is there no dedicated server and each node on the network is an equal resource for sharing and receiving information?

    A. Client/Server

    B. Peer-to-Peer

    C. Windows NT Server 4.0

    D. Novell IntraNetWare 4.x

21. In order for differing networks to communicate with each other we need to use a _____ to translate between the networks.

    A. Protocol

    B. Medium

    C. Gateway

    D. Bridge

22. When troubleshooting your network you know the following: the topology is a bus network, the entire network is down, and there is no cable break through the backbone. What could be a possible cause of the network being down?

    A. A bad network card

    B. Terminators missing from cable segment ends

    C. One PC turned off and not logged in

    D. User error with workstation that worked previously.

23. In which topology does each device on the network have equal access to communicate on the network?

    A. Bus

    B. Star

    C. Ring

    D. Mesh

24. Which of the following are network operating systems and not just operating systems that will communicate on a network? (Choose all that apply.)

    A. Novell NetWare

    B. Microsoft Windows 3.1

    C. Microsoft Windows 9X

    D. Microsoft Windows NT

25. When multiple disk controllers are used in a drive mirroring scenario it is known as what?

    A. Disk multiplexing

    B. Disk duplobuilding

    C. Bidirectional disking

    D. Disk Duplexing

2

Physical Layer

In Chapter 1 you learned the basic components of networking. A computer needs to have some sort of interface to the rest of the network. This is accomplished through the use of a network interface card (NIC). A NIC may be integrated into the system at purchase time or it may be installed at a later time. The NIC takes information from the computer and prepares for transmission across the network medium. It also takes signals from the network medium and translates them into information the computer can use. This involves converting the data stream on the computer bus, which is a parallel data stream, to a serial data stream that can travel along the network medium. Of course this is reversed when the communication is reversed.

In this chapter you will learn about the NIC, from installation, to configuration, to troubleshooting. You will learn the specifics of the different types of network interface cards, including features that some cards have and others do not. You will look at IRQs, diagnostics, EPROM, and other things you will need to know for the exam. You will learn how NICs communicate with each other using their unique MAC or hardware addresses.

You will also learn in more detail about other components that were introduced in Chapter 1, including hubs, switches, repeaters, and transceivers. These are networking components that directly interact with the network interface card.

CERTIFICATION OBJECTIVE 2.01

Network Interface Cards (NICs)

The network interface card (NIC) is an add-on component for a computer, much like a video card or sound card is. On some systems the NIC is integrated into the system board. On others it has to be installed into an expansion slot. You will learn about both types and what it takes to configure or replace them.

Network interface cards are known by a variety of names, including network adapters, network cards, network adapter boards, and media access cards.

Regardless of the name, they function by enabling computers to communicate across a network. NICs are often defined by the following criteria:

- The type of Data Link protocol they support, such as an Ethernet adapter or a Token Ring adapter
- The type of media they connect to
- The data bus for which they were designed

The computer must have a software driver installed to enable it to interact with the NIC, just as it must for any other peripheral device. These drivers enable the operating system and higher-level protocols to control the functions of the adapter. The NICs that exist in the various workstations on a network communicate with each other using their own unique addresses. The hardware address, or MAC address as it is commonly called, is unique on each network card on a network. You may wonder how a manufacturer can ensure uniqueness among all the network cards in the world. No doubt there are network cards that have the same address, but each manufacturer is assigned a range by the various network standards organizations, and they use only that range. Within the range, a manufacturer may have duplicates, but the duplicates are so spread out that it is almost impossible for a network, small or large, to have the same network address on two network cards.

The MAC (Media Access Layer) address, or hardware address, is a 12-digit number consisting of digits 0-9 and letters A-F. It is basically a hexadecimal number assigned to the card. The MAC address consists of two pieces: the first signifies which vendor it comes from, the second is the serial number unique to that manufacturer. For the exam you will not need to know how this breaks down; you just need to know what the MAC address is. You will learn more about MAC addresses later in this book.

The NIC performs the following functions:

- It translates data from the parallel data bus to a serial bit stream for transmission across the network.
- It formats packets of data in accordance with protocol.
- It transmits and receives data based on the hardware address of the card.

The Computer Bus

A computer bus is the term used for the speed and type of interface the computer uses with different types of interface cards and equipment. It is actually the combination of wires, chips, and components that enable all of the individual pieces to interact and make a computer what it is. The computer bus is the internal communication channel the computer uses to communicate between devices. Different computers have different bus types. Now that you are completely confused, let's look at two of the more common bus types in computers today: ISA and PCI.

ISA

ISA (Industry Standard Architecture) was implemented on the earliest of computers. The ISA bus started in the IBM PC/XT and PC/AT models in the early 1990s. Almost every computer today has ISA expansion slots in it. The ISA architecture is a 16-bit interface.

PCI

The PCI bus on the other hand is a 64-bit bus, but it is implemented as a 32-bit bus, making it faster when it comes to communicating between the system and the interface cards. PCI (Peripheral Component Interconnect) was developed by Intel. Most newer personal computers have a combination PCI/ISA bus in them, meaning they have both kinds of slots. PCI slots are shorter and usually the connectors on the motherboard are white or ivory in color. The 16-bit ISA bus on the other hand has a longer slot, which is brown in color on the system board. The interface cards come ready to fit these slots. The PCI cards are shorter and not sectioned like an ISA card could be.

MCA

Recognizing the speed limitations of the 16-bit bus, both IBM and other companies released new bus architectures in 1988. IBM's 32-bit data bus was called MCA (Microchannel Architecture). It was released with IBM's

PS/2 product line and was a totally new architecture that was not backward compatible with ISA cards. MCA adapters were predictably more expensive and offered higher performance than the ISA adapters. IBM has since phased out MCA and these types of adapters have become increasingly difficult to obtain.

EISA

EISA (Extended Industry Standard Architecture) is an alternate 32-bit bus architecture that was designed by a consortium of companies, including Hewlett-Packard and Compaq. It was designed to be backward compatible with ISA devices and is the data bus of choice for PC servers in non-IBM environments for high performance and throughput. They are also higher in terms of cost and performance than ISA cards.

PC Card (PCMCIA)

The PC card bus, formerly known as PCMCIA, is an architecture designed primarily for laptops and other portable computers. Adapters for this bus are sometimes called credit card adapters after their size and shape, which is roughly equal to the size of a credit card. Because of their small size, most have a receptacle to which an external adapter must be connected for attachment to the media. These NICs are also sometimes combined with a modem in a single card called a combo card.

Installing a NIC

Installing a NIC is like installing any other interface card in a computer. You have to determine the slot it will go in and have the right tools to remove the expansion slot cover and to remove and insert screws. Newer computers do not require any tools, even screwdrivers. The ability to work on a computer with your hands free of tools is making technician jobs easier. The Network+ exam will challenge you to know what to do in certain situations. In this section you will learn several troubleshooting techniques and how to recognize the common issues that you will face with network interface cards.

The Installation Process

Before you begin the physical installation of the NIC, or network adapter, be sure to address the following issues:

- Ensure that the adapter is compatible with the data bus, the protocol, the media, and the network operating system. In the case of Windows NT, the hardware compatibility list (HCL) lists adapters that have been verified for use with NT.

- Ensure that there is an open bus slot on the machine in which you want to install the adapter.

- Ensure that there are system resources, including an IRQ level, base I/O address, and DMA channel, available to be assigned to the adapter. Choose and record parameters from available settings, unless the adapter is configured automatically through Plug and Play.

- Ensure that the adapter includes all items necessary for installation, including external transceivers or adapters, a T-connector for a thinwire Ethernet adapter, and product documentation.

- Ensure that the software, including the network driver and utilities for testing and configuring the adapter, is included. If a software driver is not provided, a driver may be included with operating system installation media. If not, drivers and driver updates may be available for download from the adapter manufacturer via the Internet or a bulletin board service.

- Remember that the NIC cannot do any useful work until high-level protocols and network services have also been installed and configured.

The installation process is really straightforward. If you have never installed an interface card in a computer before, you need to get some hands-on experience before you go much further. Exercise 2-1 takes you through the process of installation.

Installing a Network Interface Card

In this exercise you will learn how to remove the cover, assign a slot, and install a network interface card. To help ensure no electrostatic damage is done to the computer, be sure to wear an anti-static strap on your wrist or ankle, or use an anti-static floor mat to ground yourself. Disconnect any power cables to the computer.

1. Review the installation instructions included in the documentation. This can help you avoid unnecessary problems and make the installation more efficient.

2. If necessary, configure selected settings on the network adapter, using either jumper plugs or DIP switches. If this is required, make sure that all settings are completed before installing the card or it will have to be removed again. With a software-configurable adapter, this configuration occurs after the physical adapter is installed.

3. Put the computer on a work surface that is at a good working height and with enough room to rotate the computer. Refer to the manufacturer's instructions and remove the case of the unit. This may require removal of screws or simply pressing a couple release levers or buttons.

4. Locate the expansion slots and on the rear of the computer you should see corresponding openings. Do the slots have covers on them? If yes, go to step 5. If no, go to step 6.

5. You must remove the covers from the expansion slots before you can install the interface card. Determine which slot you want to install the interface card in. (Remember that there is a difference between PCI cards and ISA cards, so take this into consideration before choosing a slot.) You may need a screwdriver to remove the slot cover, or you may just need to flip up a holder to remove the cover. Refer to your manufacture's documentation to see how yours are removed.

6. You are ready to install the card. Grasp the card only on the edges. (Touching the components on the interface card could cause damage to them.) Hold the card next to the slot cover and the upper-front

corner, and with even pressure insert the card into the slot. The card will not click, but there should be a noticeable insertion feeling.

7. Secure the card in its slot by replacing the screw or putting the holder back into place. This completes the physical installation of an interface card.

Installing Drivers

When you install a new device in a computer system, you must also install the corresponding software driver for that device. The following paragraphs describe the steps necessary to complete the network adapter driver installation. They also explain the parameters that you need to set on the driver software.

To install the network adapter driver, you need to copy files to the appropriate location on the system hard disk and make the operating system aware of the adapter and its drivers. You may accomplish this by using a setup utility provided by the adapter manufacturer, or you may use the operating system configuration utilities, such as the Network applet on the Control Panel in Windows 95 and Windows NT.

If a vendor-provided setup program is used, it is normally invoked from a command line. The setup program goes through various steps to prompt for parameter input, to check the card, and to load the required files.

To manually install a network driver in Windows 95/98 or Windows NT, open the Control Panel and double-click the Networks icon. The Network dialog box opens. At this point, the dialog boxes diverge for the different operating systems. In Window 95/98, click the Add button and then select Adapter from the list. The Select Network Adapters dialog box appears, as shown in Figure 2-1. Select the appropriate manufacturer from the Manufacturers list and then select the appropriate network adapter from the Network Adapters list.

Adding an adapter in Windows NT 4.0 is a little different even though the main GUI is the same as Windows 95 and Windows 98. You go to the same initial place to configure the networking components; however, the window is different since each component of the network is on a separate tab. In Windows 95 and Windows 98 the protocols, adapters, and other

FIGURE 2-1

Select the appropriate
manufacturer and network
adapter from the lists to
add a network adapter in
Windows 98

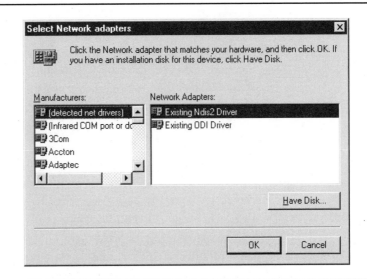

components are shown in one area. The Windows NT Network Properties
window is shown next.

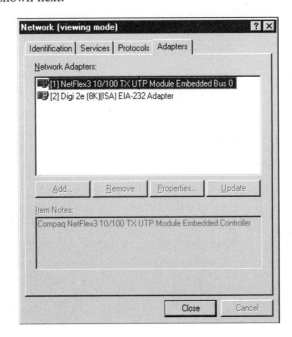

Testing

If there is one thing you will do a lot of, it is testing to be sure any updates or changes you made are working properly. Once your network card is installed you have to connect the cable to it. Some network cards will have multiple transceivers on them. Connect the appropriate cable for the network.

Once the cable is connected there are a couple of things you can check to see if the card is operating properly. The first of these is the link light on the back of the card. Some network interface cards do not have this feature, but if yours does you should see a light next to the transceiver. Some 10 Mbps cards have an activity light and a connection light. Some 10/100 Mbps cards have both a 10 Mbps and 100 Mbps light along with the activity light. This of course tells you what speed you are connected at.

The second thing you need to do to determine if there is connectivity is the most important. When the card is completely configured, try logging into the server and accessing various network resources. With Windows 95 and Windows 98 you will not see the same login screen when you are connected to the network as you do when you are not connected to the network. When you are not connected to the network you will simply get the Windows login screen, which asks you for a username and password. The username and password do not authenticate you, they simply determine your Start Menu icons and desktop layout if you have user profiles in place.

Drivers

When you install a network card in a Windows 95 or Windows 98 machine, usually Plug and Play will recognize and configure the hardware by loading the appropriate driver. The driver is a piece of the operating system that enables the operating system to communicate with the device. There are different types of drivers for modems, sound cards, and just about any other component in a computer.

The manufacturer provides the driver, and usually the driver has its own configuration program to set up and install the network adapter. This is usually a setup.exe or install.exe or install.bat file. If this isn't the case, and Plug and Play finds the network adapter but no default driver exists, you will have the opportunity to change to the appropriate drive and directory and update the driver.

From time to time, you may want to update the drivers for your various devices. Manufacturers will update their drivers if there are problems found in the current version. There are a couple of ways you can update the driver for your network card. Since most workstations have Windows 95 or 98 on them, we will look at some screen shots from those operating systems.

The easiest way to update your driver in Windows 95 or 98 is to find your device on the Device Manager page of the System Properties dialog box. Either right-click on the My Computer icon on your desktop and select Properties from the popup menu, or select Start | Programs | Control Panel and double-click the System icon. The System Properties dialog box appears. Click the Device Manager tab to bring it to the front. The Device Manager page lists all the devices installed on your machine. Select your network adapter from the list and then click the Properties button. A screen similar to the one shown next is displayed.

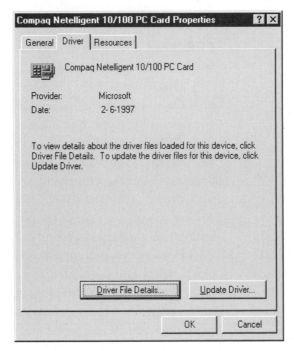

Click the Update Driver button to install the new driver. The driver can usually be downloaded from the manufacturer's Web site. There should be some information on what to do to install the driver, or at least what directory holds the appropriate files for your operating system. A good rule of thumb is always check out the readme file on the update. Even though it takes time to review the file, it will save time down the road.

Configuring a NIC

Depending on the network operating system or the workstation you may have some configuration to do with the network interface card. This is a definite if you have a DOS or Windows 3.1 workstation. The DOS level drivers have either a configuration file (CFG) or an initialization file (INI) that determines how the card functions.

Other components involved in configuration include software that is in the chips on the interface card. This is known as an EPROM. There may also be jumpers that determine settings for the card.

EPROM

Every interface card, whether it is a network card, a video card, or a sound card, comes with an EPROM. EPROM stands for Erasable Programmable Read Only Memory and is a set of software instructions built into the interface card to perform its functions.

An EPROM is sometimes *flashable*. This means that the software in the EPROM can be upgraded. This is done by downloading an update from the manufacturer and then using a utility to write the update out to the flash memory. Different EPROMs do different things. The most common of these on a network card is the boot PROM. The boot PROM boots the workstation if there is not a hard drive or disk to boot from.

The diskless workstation is a concept that has been around for some time. Designed for use in fairly large environments, it originally had two goals. The first was to enhance security on the network by removing local storage from the end user and requiring that all data and applications are stored on servers. By managing user access to this information via server permissions, the LAN administrator can more effectively control the environment. The second goal of diskless workstations was the cost of mass storage. By removing the cost of local storage, particularly as workstation populations increased, companies could save money. This has become less of an issue as the cost of mass storage has declined.

The challenge of using diskless workstations is booting them. Normally, a system at startup looks for a hard disk that is bootable in order to start the operating system. This specifically involves looking for a Master Boot Record that tells the system where to find the boot files. In the case of a diskless workstation, there is no disk available to perform this function, because all storage is accessed through the network adapter.

A remote boot PROM can be added to a network adapter to enable the system to boot using files stored on the network. An adapter capable of booting remotely has an empty socket that can be populated with a boot PROM. Once installed and configured, this boot PROM directs the system to the network location of the boot files.

on the **!** **(j)** o b

In some cases you will work with very old equipment when your clients have a small budget. If you are forced to work with workstations that have no hard disks, you will not only have to configure the workstations but you will also have to configure the server appropriately.

A client of mine was at school in a small town. They were holding off until the following school year to upgrade their computers. They had 30 or so diskless workstations with old IBM Token Ring network cards with a boot PROM. I had to configure the server to enable the network cards to connect to the server and to use a file that was a copy of a boot disk to load the appropriate DOS files as if the workstation were booting up. Then the workstation went through the normal login process.

Because these were legacy machines, I had to research the proper configuration. This was a Novell environment and it took some time to get everything to work properly. The thing I learned from this is that research sometimes is required to properly implement a solution for a client when unusual circumstances are involved. Once the appropriate research is done, the solution has to be implemented and tested, and tested again. As a network savvy person, you will learn to test yet again to make triple-sure everything is working as it should be.

Jumpers

Some network cards have jumpers on them to change the configuration. A jumper is a plastic piece that connects two metal posts on the card. Figure 2-2 shows an example of jumper blocks; the black areas represent where the jumpers are.

The jumpers on an interface card can do many different things. The most common things that they do are set the IRQ and the I/O addresses. If you are not familiar with what these are right now, don't worry—we will look at these two things later in this chapter. Jumpers configure a card that is not software configurable.

Jumpers may also determine which transceiver is being used on the network interface. Some network interface cards have multiple connection options, so setting the jumpers will determine which transceiver to hook the cable up to. Some network interface cards have jumpers to set the speed of the card if it handles multiple speeds. The point here for exam purposes is of course that jumpers can configure just about any setting for an interface card. Different network interface cards have different jumper settings and

| FIGURE 2-2 | Interface card and jumpers |

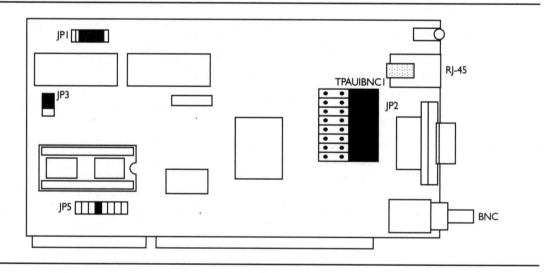

different jumper configurations, so refer to the documentation supplied by the manufacturer.

Plug and Play Software

With the introduction of Windows 95 came the Plug and Play operating system. Plug and Play has been around for a while. Windows 95 was the first operating system to take advantage of it. The Plug and Play operating system and the Plug and Play BIOS work hand in hand to configure expansion components such as network interface cards. The premise behind Plug and Play software is to make configuration by the end user minimal if not non-existent.

FROM THE FIELD

Installing and Configuring Network Interface Cards

From experience, I can tell you to please verify that you have installed and configured your network adapters correctly. These settings are easy to overlook if you are in a hurry. However, it is in your best interest to make sure you have these NICs configured correctly, or havoc may ensue. I would hate to see you learn the hard way as I did at my first networking job several years ago.

I was building a new Windows NT Server. We were in the process of upgrading the hubs from 10 Mbps to switched 100 Mbps, so we were installing new network cards in the servers. These network cards were capable of 100Mb per second; however, they needed to be configured for 10 Mbps, which is what our hubs were currently set to. After I installed the

network card, I began installing Windows NT Server as usual. I was talking with the other network administrator when my phone rang. A user said he no longer had access to a database. I asked him a few questions and then thought it would be better to just visit his workstation and fix the problem. On the way there, I saw that a lot of users were standing outside their cubicles wondering what was going on. By this time I knew that it was not an isolated incident. I retreated to the server room, and sure enough, the hub was not responding. This was not the only hub in the company, but it was the most important hub. Every Windows NT database, application, and file server in the server room was connected directly to this hub. The primary domain

FROM THE FIELD

controller and all backup domain controllers were also connected to this hub. We got the documentation out for the hub to find out why it was locked up. We reset it and powered it off and on, but nothing was working. This was panic time, because everything had come to a complete stop. The other network administrator asked what I did, and I told him I didn't do anything. Luckily, he asked me what I was doing before the crash, and I said, "just configuring this server." "What were you configuring?" he asked me, and I told him the network card. Of course, he realized what had happened. He pulled the network cable off the server and the hub lights began flickering with

activity and when he plugged it back in the network activity ceased. He loaded up the network card diagnostics, and sure enough, the network card was set for 100 Mbps.

One false move had rendered the entire company's network useless. This is a great example of how fragile networks can be. You need to understand what you are working on, and make sure you spend the time to do the job correctly. I would hate for the same thing to happen to you. Watch those network card settings!

—Cameron Brandon, MCSE+Internet, CNE,
A+, Network+

Troubleshooting NICs

If there is one thing a network administrator spends time doing, it is troubleshooting. Troubleshooting can seem like a difficult task. Networks can seem overwhelming sometimes. But if you take a structured approach to troubleshooting, it will be very easy to solve problems you encounter on a daily basis.

When you are troubleshooting network problems, it is important to follow a logical troubleshooting methodology. The first step is to determine which areas of the network are affected. For example, you need to determine if the problem is with one protocol, if it is with everything on one side of a router, or if all the machines are connected to the same cable. No matter what, the affected areas will always have something in common. This could, of course, be your entire network, but that is something that they have in common.

Second, identify any differences between the affected areas and the unaffected areas. For example, if you are unable to get a network connection with all of your workstations that are connected to a thinwire coax cable, but all other workstations are functioning, more than likely your problem resides in that thinwire coax cable.

Third, restart affected hardware. This is probably the most common solution to network outages. By restarting all affected hubs, routers, and switches, you can often clear up the problem.

Fourth, segment the affected area—divide the area in half. The best example of this is in thinwire coax. Determine the midpoint of the cable and place a terminator on each end. One-half of the cable should now be working and is obviously not your problem. Repeat this step until you find the problem.

Fifth, if you are still unable to find the problem, it's time to get some tools out. Tools can range from technical databases to diagnostics. We will focus on the diagnostic side of troubleshooting for purposes of this exam.

Network Card Diagnostics

One other option is to use a diagnostic program to run a series of tests on the network adapter. You can get a generic diagnostics program or you can get vendor-supplied diagnostics. Many diagnostics have to be run without the network drivers loaded. Figure 2-3 shows a diagnostic and testing program for a 3Com card.

Different diagnostic programs run different tests. Some test communication, others test communication in and out of the card with the use of a loopback plug.

Loopback Test

The loopback test is one that tests communication in and out of the card. A stream of data is sent out and loops back around into the card and is compared to see if the data received is the same as the data that was sent.

Some cards can run an internal loopback test. Others have to have a loopback adapter that plugs into the card. This way the data is actually sent out of the card and loops around and comes back into the card as if it were

FIGURE 2-3

Use a diagnostic program, such as this 3Com diagnostic, to troubleshoot a NIC

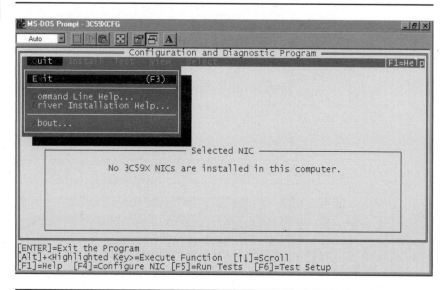

received from another device. Sometimes this is a more accurate and realistic test of the card.

Vendor-Supplied Diagnostics

If you use the general diagnostic programs, you should take a look at the vendor-supplied diagnostics that are available. The manufacturer designs specific tests that can be better than the generic tests run by the general diagnostic applications. All the major manufacturers have diagnostic programs available. Try the manufacturer's Web site for the latest programs.

Resolving Hardware Resource Conflicts

Today's computers have many different devices installed. Each device has to be able to communicate with the processor or other components within the computer. Sometimes you will see that two or more devices are trying to communicate across the same channels or the same link.

There are three main ways for a device to communicate with components in a computer: The first and most commonly configured is the IRQ, or interrupt request. The second is the DMA, or Direct Memory Access. The third is the I/O Address, which is a specific memory address. We will look briefly at each of these so you will know the basics for the exam.

IRQ

The IRQ (interrupt request) is used by the device to interrupt the processor and request service. There are sixteen IRQ lines, many of which are routinely committed to devices such as the disk controllers and serial and parallel ports. A common configuration for a network card may use IRQ 3, which is also used by the serial port COM2, IRQ 5, or IRQ 10. Like the I/O address, the IRQ must be chosen so the card does not conflict with another device. Table 2-1 lists some common IRQ settings.

TABLE 2-1 Common IRQ Settings	IRQ	Common Usage
	1	Keyboard
	2	Cascaded Controller with IRQ 9/commonly used for VGA display
	3	Com 2 or Com 4
	4	Com 1 or Com 3
	5	Sound/Parallel Port 2
	6	Floppy
	7	Parallel Port/LPT1
	8	Real-time Clock
	9	Redirected IRQ 2/sometimes available
	10	Open
	11	Open/SCSI
	12	Open/PS/2 port
	13	Coprocessor/Math Processor
	14	Primary IDE
	15	Secondary IDE

DMA

DMA (direct memory access) is a process whereby some devices can directly access memory on the system without the intervention of the CPU. This offloads the processor from having to handle these data transfers and speeds the transfer process. Any device with DMA capability is a DMA channel, which it uses to control direct memory access. Since many hardware devices do not use this feature, there is more flexibility in configuring this setting.

I/O Base Address

The I/O base address refers to the starting address for a series of registers used to control the card. A common I/O address for a network card is 300h. Care must be taken to ensure that this address in not already in use by another device or the adapter will fail.

Transceiver Type

The transceiver type setting is required for network adapters that are capable of attaching to more than one media type. Typical cards of this nature include Ethernet cards that have both twisted-pair and coaxial connectors. This is one of the more common oversights in configuring a network interface card and renders the card nonfunctional if configured for the wrong media connection. To alleviate this problem, some cards of this type have an auto setting that causes the card to search for the transceiver that has media connected to it. We will look at this in more detail later in this chapter.

CERTIFICATION OBJECTIVE 2.02

Network Components

Network interface cards must interact with other devices on the network. You were briefly introduced to some of the common network devices in Chapter 1. Here you will learn in more detail some of the common network components.

There are various connectivity devices that link computers. These include hubs, MAUs, switches, repeaters, and transceivers.

Hubs

Hubs are one of the most important components of a network. They are the central location that all cabling must connect to in most topologies. You can easily remember the layout of a hub if you think of a wheel and picture how the spokes go to the hub of the wheel. Each spoke is a connection and the hub of the wheel is the hub of the network where all the cables come together.

The Role of Hubs in Topologies

Most network topologies can use a hub in one way or another. Figure 2-4 shows an example of a hub with five workstations attached to it. This will help you to visualize where the hub fits into the network. The most prominent user of hubs is the 10BaseT topology. 10BaseT is entirely dependent on hubs for the infrastructure of the topology.

FIGURE 2-4   A network hub is like the hub of a wheel—the spokes are the connections to the workstations

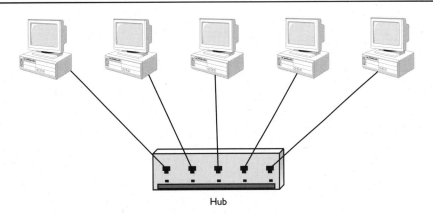

Hub

Passive

The function of a passive hub is simply to receive data from one port of the hub and send it out to the other ports. For example, an 8-port hub receives data from port 3 and then resends that data to ports 1, 2, 4, 5, 6, 7, and 8. It is as simple as that.

A passive hub contains no power source or electrical components. There is no signal processing. It simply attaches the ports internally and enables communication to flow through the network.

Active (Multi-Port Repeaters)

An active hub provides the same functionality that a passive hub does, with an additional feature. Active hubs repeat the data while resending it to all of the ports. By using active hubs you can increase the length of your network. It is important to remember that UTP (unshielded twisted pair) Category 5 cabling can be run a maximum of 100 meters. With an active hub, you can run Category 5 UTP 100 meters on each side of the hub. An active hub has a power source and built-in repeaters to boost the signal. There are extra electronics built into an active hub that allow for signal regeneration.

exam
ⓦatch

When exam time comes, remember the difference between an active and passive hub: an active hub contains electronic components to boost the signal; a passive hub contains no power source or electronic components.

Hybrid

A hybrid hub is a hub that can use many different types of cables in addition to UTP cabling. A hybrid hub is usually cabled using thinwire or thickwire Ethernet, which is discussed later in this chapter. A hybrid hub is the most common type of hub. Hybrid hubs are used to interconnect hubs that are farther than the 100-meter limitation of 10BaseT.

MAUs

A MAU (Multistation Access Unit) is a device that multiple workstations are connected to in order to communicate on a Token Ring network.

Sometimes a MAU is also referred to as a hub. Be careful not to confuse this with a UTP hub; their actual functions are quite different.

A MAU is typically eight ports and uses either UDC or RJ-45 connections. A MAU looks a lot like a hub at a glance, but it will say MAU or Token Ring or something like that on it. A MAU is typically nonpowered, but I have seen them powered with various lights for connectivity and activity.

Switching Hubs

Switches have become an increasingly important part of our networks today. As network usage increases, so do traffic problems. As a systems engineer, you will be faced with this problem on an almost continuous basis. A common solution to traffic problems is to implement switches. Figure 2-5 shows how traffic travels in a switched environment.

Multiport Bridging

Switches, also referred to as multiport bridges, automatically determine the MAC addresses of the devices connected to each port of the switch. The switch then examines each packet it receives to determine its destination MAC address. The switch then determines which port the packet is destined for and sends it out to that port only.

FIGURE 2-5

Network with switching hub

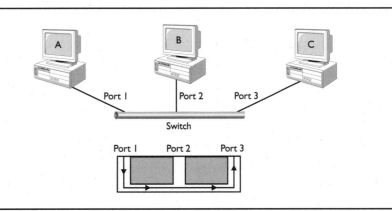

Network Performance Improvement with Switching

The primary benefit of implementing switching technology is to improve network performance. It is important to note that if you are not having traffic problems on your network, adding a switch will probably not change your network's performance. If your network is having traffic problems, switching, when implemented properly, can greatly increase your performance.

Switching is a fairly involved process. Computer A transmits a packet to Computer C. The packet enters the switch from Port 1 and then travels a direct route to Port 3. From Port 3 the packet is transmitted to Computer C. During this process, Computer B is unaware of the traffic between Computer A and C because there is a direct path within the switch and no shared bandwidth.

Repeaters

Repeaters can be used in the Ethernet coaxial cable environment just the same as they are used for UTP. Thickwire can normally transmit a distance of 500 meters, which can be extended by introducing repeaters. Thinwire can normally transmit a distance of 185 meters, and can also be extended by using a repeater. This, of course, is the advantage to using a repeater. If your network layout exceeds the normal specifications of cable you can use repeaters to build your network. This will allow for greater lengths when planning your cabling scheme.

Transceivers

Transceivers are that portion of the network interface that actually transmits and receives electrical signals across the transmission media. They are also the part of the interface that actually connects to the media. Transceiver types can be classified as being either on-board or external.

On-Board Transceivers

On-board transceivers are built onto the network interface card. With these types of transceivers, the media connector is built right on the back of the

NIC. Common examples of this include RJ-45 receptacles for twisted-pair and BNC connectors for thinwire coaxial cable.

External Transceivers

With an external transceiver, the actual media connection is made external to the network interface card using a small device that attaches via an extension cable to the network interface card. These types of connections use an AUI (adapter unit interface) connector, also called a DIX (Digital-Intel-Xerox) connector, on the back of the network interface card. The AUI connector is a female 15-pin D connector that looks very much like a joystick port. An AUI connector enables a network card to be used with multiple types of media. A common implementation is to use this configuration for an Ethernet card that can be attached to twisted-pair, thickwire, or thinwire coax by just changing the external transceiver type. The following illustration shows what an AUI connector looks like.

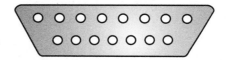

The types of transceivers and media that can be served by a network interface card determine the appropriate connector. Each media type has a typical connector type or connection method.

Thickwire Coax

Thickwire, or standard Ethernet coax, uses a connection method that typically involves an external transceiver connected to the adapter's AUI port. This external transceiver has a connection called a vampire tap. To attach a thickwire transceiver to the media, you must drill a hole in the cable using a special drilling jig that controls the depth of the hole. This jig prevents the drill from drilling through and severing the center conductor.

The vampire tap consists of a pin that is inserted into the hole drilled in the cable, and a clamp that holds the tap onto the cable. One of the challenges of this type of connection is to position the tap so it contacts the center conductor without shorting to the shield surrounding it. These difficulties, as well as the cost and size of thickwire cable, have rendered it largely obsolete, although it may occasionally be found in existing installations.

Thinwire Coax

Thinwire coax can be attached directly to an adapter if an on-board transceiver is used. In this case, a connector called a BNC or barrel connector on the network card attaches to a T-connector. The T-connector has a female fitting that attaches to the card, as well as two additional male fittings that attach to cable segments or a terminator.

Each end of a thinwire Ethernet segment must be terminated, so the last node on each end may have a terminator attached to the side of the T-connector opposite the inbound cable. All other nodes use T-connectors with cable segments attached to both sides, just like Christmas tree lights. A thinwire segment cannot be attached directly to the BNC connector on the network adapter; it must use a T-connector.

An alternative connection method can use the AUI connector with an external thinwire transceiver. In this case, the cable attachment to the transceiver is still made through a T-connector.

Twisted-Pair Wiring

The typical connector for a twisted-pair connection is called an RJ-45 connector. The RJ-45 connector looks like an oversized phone connector. The reason for the difference in size is that a phone connector has either a 4-wire connector or a 6-wire connector. RJ-45 has an 8-wire connector.

An RJ-45 patch cable can be plugged directly into the back of a twisted-pair network adapter or, less commonly, it can be attached to an external transceiver. The patch cable usually runs to a wall receptacle, which is wired back to a patch panel and ultimately back to a wiring hub.

Fiber-Optic Cabling

Fiber-optic adapters generally have two connectors, one each for incoming and outgoing fiber cables. The mechanical connectors that join the cable are called ST-connectors, and are designed to pass light seamlessly across the joined fiber segments. For this reason, these connectors must be made with great precision. Fiber-optic runs are generally made back to a concentrator that performs a hub function.

In many situations, fiber-optic cabling is used to connect high-speed computers, and to provide a high-speed backbone to which slower speed LANs are attached. The LANs might connect copper media, such as twisted-pair or coaxial cable, to a set of hubs that are then bridged to the fiber-optic backbone for high-speed data transfer between LANs.

Configuration

The transceiver type configuration is set using jumpers, DIP switches, or configuration software, in the same way that the I/O base address and other parameters are set on the card. Most cards have at most two types of transceivers. During configuration, these may be referred to in the following ways:

- **Internal vs. External**   The card has an AUI port and an onboard twisted-pair or coaxial connector.

- **DIX or AUI**   The card uses an external transceiver.

- **Coax, 10Base2, or BNC**   The card has an onboard thinwire Ethernet connection.

- **TP, UTP, or 10BaseT**   The card has an on-board twisted-pair connection.

The auto setting may be available if the card can autosense the connected media.

QUESTIONS AND ANSWERS

I have to explain how the network adapter converts the data for transmission on the network medium. What are the two types of data streams used in conjunction with the computer bus and the network medium?	Parallel, serial
I am troubleshooting a communication problem and I have to know the address of the network card that was assigned at the factory when it was made. What address am I looking for?	MAC or hardware
I am configuring my network adapter in a non-Plug and Play environment. What four things do I need to know to configure the adapter and ensure I can communicate on the network medium and not conflict with any other device in the system?	I/O base, IRQ, DMA, transceiver type
I have a new network adapter and need to know which type of slot it will go in. Knowing what I know, what are the three possible bus types?	MCA, EISA, PCI
I am finalizing configuration of my network adapter. What has to connect to the transceiver on the network adapter to connect the medium or cable to it?	Connector
I am configuring a network adapter. What does the connector connect to in order to make the link from network adapter to the rest of the network?	Transceiver
I am connecting a network card that has an external transceiver. What type of connector will I be connecting to?	AUI or DIX

CERTIFICATION SUMMARY

In this chapter you learned about the Physical layer, specifically the NIC, or network interface card. The NIC performs the following functions:

- It translates data from the parallel data bus to a serial bit stream for transmission across the network.

- It formats packets of data in accordance with protocol.

- It transmits and receives data based on the hardware address of the card.

There are many pieces to successful implementation of network interface cards. You learned what defines and differentiates the various network interface cards available on the market, all of which are important when determining the appropriate NIC to use:

■ The type of Data Link protocol they support, such as an Ethernet adapter or a Token Ring adapter

■ The type of media they connect to

■ The data bus for which they were designed

The data bus is the internal communication channel the computer uses to communicate between devices. The different types of buses include ISA, EISA, MCA, PCI, and PC Card. Each has its own distinct features. The EISA, MCA, and PCI are all 32-bit bus types. For the exam, the two to know are ISA and PCI. Most network interface cards today are designed to fit either the ISA bus or the PCI bus.

The ISA (Industry Standard Architecture) bus is a 16-bit interface and was implemented on the earliest computers. Almost every computer today has ISA expansion slots in it. The PCI (Peripheral Component Interconnect) bus, on the other hand, is a 64-bit bus, but it is implemented as a 32-bit bus, making it faster at communicating between the system and the interface cards. Most newer personal computers have a combination PCI/ISA bus in them, meaning they have both kinds of slots.

You learned how to install a network interface card. To prepare for the installation you have to ensure that the following things are in place first:

1. The card is compatible with the machine it is going in, including the bus, media, protocol, and operating system.

2. There is a slot available to install the card.

3. System resources are available to assign to the card, including IRQ, I/O base address, and DMA channel.

4. You have the drivers you need for the operating system you are installing to.

When all of this is accounted for, you can go through the process of physically installing the card and configuring it.

Configuring a NIC is different depending on the vendor and model of the NIC. Some NICs are software configurable for all settings; others have jumpers to set to determine the configuration. Some cards have a flashable EPROM chip that may even boot to the network if the workstation does not have a floppy or hard drive.

Troubleshooting NICs can seem challenging, but if a structured approach is taken the process is really pretty easy. The first thing to remember is to determine the problem and then isolate where the problem is occurring. The more you can narrow, the better off you will be when it comes to solving the problem. You can use different kinds of diagnostics to aid in the troubleshooting process. There are generic diagnostic programs and vendor-supplied diagnostic programs. One common test you learned about is the loopback test.

You learned about the types of resource conflicts that can occur when you are configuring a network card. There are three main ways for a device to communicate with components in a computer: the IRQ (interrupt request), the DMA (Direct Memory Access), and the I/O Address. You have to be concerned with the settings for each of these when you are configuring a NIC. Plug and Play can assist in the configuration piece, but if you don't have a Plug and Play board you will have to do some configuring of these resources first.

Network interface cards must interact with other devices on the network. The various connectivity devices that link computers include hubs, MAUs, switches, repeaters, and transceivers.

If your network layout exceeds the normal specifications of cable you can use repeaters to build your network. This will allow for greater lengths when planning your cabling scheme.

Transceivers are that portion of the network interface that actually transmits and receives electrical signals across the transmission media and connects to the media. Transceiver types can be classified as being either on-board or external; DIX or AUI; Coax, 10Base2, or BNC; and TP, UTP, or 10BaseT.

TWO-MINUTE DRILL

❑ Network interface cards (NIC) function by enabling computers to communicate across a network.

❑ The computer must have a software driver installed to enable it to interact with the NIC, just as it must for any other peripheral device.

❑ The MAC (Media Access Layer) address, or hardware address, is a 12-digit number consisting of digits 0-9 and letters A-F.

❑ A computer bus is the term used for the speed and type of interface the computer uses with different types of interface cards and equipment.

❑ The Network+ exam will challenge you to know troubleshooting techniques and how to recognize the common issues that you will face with network interface cards.

❑ Depending on the network operating system or the workstation you may have some configuration to do with the network interface card.

❑ EPROM stands for Erasable Programmable Read Only Memory and is a set of software instructions built into the interface card to perform its functions.

❑ Some network cards have jumpers on them to change the configuration.

❑ The premise behind Plug and Play software is to make configuration by the end user minimal if not non-existent.

❑ When you are troubleshooting network problems, it is important to follow a logical troubleshooting methodology.

❑ There are three main ways for a device to communicate with components in a computer: The first and most commonly configured is the IRQ, or interrupt request. The second is the DMA, or Direct Memory Access. The third is the I/O Address, which is a specific memory address.

❑ Hubs are the central location that all cabling must connect to in most topologies.

❏ When exam time comes, remember the difference between an active and passive hub: an active hub contains electronic components to boost the signal; a passive hub contains no power source or electronic components.

❏ A MAU (Multistation Access Unit) is a device that multiple workstations are connected to in order to communicate on a Token Ring network.

❏ A common solution to traffic problems is to implement switches.

❏ Repeaters can be used in the Ethernet coaxial cable environment just the same as they are used for UTP.

❏ Transceivers are that portion of the network interface that actually transmits and receives electrical signals across the transmission media.

SELF TEST

The following Self Test questions will help you measure your understanding of the material presented in this chapter. Read all the choices carefully, as there may be more than one correct answer. Choose all correct answers for each question.

1. What does a network interface card add to a computer functionality?

   A. It provides faster communication between the CPU and the hard disk.

   B. It provides the capability to communicate across a phone line to another computer.

   C. It provides the capability to communicate with other computers across a medium like a CAT5 cable, with an RJ-45 connector connecting the computer to a hub.

   D. It provides the capability to save more information on a floppy than normal.

2. In order for a network interface card to interact with the computer, what needs to be installed?

   A. The appropriate documentation for the user to take advantage of the features of the interface card.

   B. A driver, which is software that enables the network interface card and the computer to communicate with each other.

   C. A bus, which enables the interface card to communicate through the various topologies of the Internet.

   D. Nothing.

3. Which of the following is NOT a function of a network interface card?

   A. To translate data from the parallel data bus to a serial bit stream for transmission across the network

   B. To format packets of data in accordance with protocol

   C. To transmit and receive data based on the hardware address of the card

   D. To send data from the CPU to the various expansion slots within the computer

4. Which of the following is a 16-bit computer bus?

   A. ISA
   B. EISA
   C. PCI
   D. MCA

5. Which of the following is a 32-bit computer bus? (Choose all that apply.)

   A. ISA
   B. EISA
   C. PCI
   D. MCA

6. Which of the following is a 64-bit computer bus?

 A. ISA

 B. EISA

 C. PCI

 D. MCA

7. Which of the following are methods that you can use to prevent electrostatic discharge when installing a network interface card? (Choose all that apply.)

 A. Wear an anti-static wrist strap.

 B. Wear an anti-static ankle strap.

 C. Use anti-static spray on all components.

 D. Use an anti-static floor mat.

8. If the network interface card is not software configurable, what is the most likely method of configuring the NIC with the appropriate IRQ?

 A. Diagnostics supplied by manufacturer

 B. Jumpers on the interface card itself

 C. Setup utility by manufacturer

 D. Plug and Play will automatically set the IRQ

9. What determines that a device can interrupt the process and request service?

 A. I/O Address

 B. DMA

 C. IRC

 D. IRQ

10. What has to be set to enable a device to directly access memory on the system without the intervention of the CPU?

 A. I/O Address

 B. DMA

 C. IRC

 D. IRQ

11. In addition to the IRQ, what other configuration setting must not conflict with other devices?

 A. IRA

 B. I/O base address

 C. IDE

 D. PCI

12. If a card has the capability to connect to more than one kind of media, you may have to set which of the following in order to ensure connectivity?

 A. IRQ setting

 B. Link light on/off setting

 C. Transceiver type setting

 D. PCI setting

13. Which of the following is not a network component that connects multiple computers on a network?

 A. Bus

 B. Hub

 C. Switch

 D. MAU

14. Which of the following types of hubs does not regenerate the signal and therefore is not a repeater?

    A. Active

    B. Hybrid

    C. Passive

    D. Switching Hub

15. What network component is used to extend the distance of the signal when transmitting over the normal specified distance?

    A. Passive Hub

    B. NIC

    C. IRQ

    D. Repeater

16. Which types of transceivers are built into the network interface card?

    A. External

    B. Internal

    C. On-board

    D. T-connector

17. What is the fourth step in troubleshooting, using the logical step-by-step plan presented in this chapter?

    A. Restart affected hardware.

    B. Segment the affected area.

    C. Identify any differences between affected and unaffected areas.

    D. Get additional tools out, such as technical databases or diagnostics.

18. What does EPROM stand for?

    A. Enhanced Programmable Read Only Memory

    B. Erasable Programmable Read Out Memory

    C. Enhanced Permanent Read Only Memory

    D. Erasable Programmable Read Only Memory

19. If you are configuring a network interface card in DOS, what is the most likely extension for the file that determines the settings for the interface card?

    A. INF

    B. CON

    C. CFG

    D. DOS

20. If you have a workstation that has no floppy drive or hard drive and you want to put it on your network, what do you have to do?

    A. Simply add any network card.

    B. Add a network card that has a mini-hard disk on it.

    C. Add a network card that has an external connector for a floppy disk drive.

    D. Add a network card that has a remote boot PROM chip.

21. What type of connector does a twisted-pair cable use?

    A. RJ-45

    B. T-connector

C. RJ-11

D. BNC connector

22. What is an AUI connector?

A. A 9-pin DB male connector

B. A 15-pin D female connector

C. A 25-pin D female connector

D. Same as an RJ-45 connector

23. What type of network component enables each device to have the full bandwidth of the medium when transmitting?

A. Hub

B. Repeater

C. Switching Hub

D. Transceiver

24. What does MAU stand for?

A. Multisensing Action Unit

B. Multistation Access Unit

C. Multisplit Addtransmission Unit

D. Multistation Action Unit

25. What type of hub enables more than one type of cable or media to connect to it?

A. Passive

B. Active

C. Hybrid

D. Multi-station access unit

Network+

CERTIFICATION

3

Data Link, Network, and Transport Layers

This chapter covers the intricacies of the three layers that reside north of the Physical Layer of the OSI Model: the Data Link Layer, the Network Layer, and the Transport Layer. We begin with the Data Link Layer, which packages data into smaller frames for easier routing across the network. Next, we cover the Network Layer, which addresses these frames with the source and destinations, so the frames know where they are going. And finally, we cover the Transport Layer, which has the function of making sure these frames are reordered correctly and that an acknowledgement is sent to the source computer confirming that the frame was received. Each of these layers performs a unique function, and work together, one continuing where the other layer left off.

This chapter will also present you with the network devices that are located within these layers, such as the bridge and router. This information is crucial for your exam. Also of equal importance is the concept of routing. We discuss the topic in detail, including the differences between routable and non-routable protocols, and when to choose one over another.

CERTIFICATION OBJECTIVE 3.01

Data Link Layer Concepts

The Data Link Layer handles many issues for communicating on a simple network (the Network Layer discussed in the next section performs the functions necessary to communicate beyond a single physical network). This layer takes the frames generated by the upper layers and disassembles the frame into bits for transmission. When receiving messages from the network, it reassembles this information back into frames to send to the upper layers. This layer actually does a lot more than just break apart and put together frames.

The IEEE 802 model (discussed later in this chapter) breaks the Data Link Layer into two sublayers: *logical link control* (LLC) and *media access control* (MAC). The LLC layer starts and maintains connections between devices. When you send data from your workstation to a server on the same network segment, it is the LLC sublayer that establishes a connection with that server. The MAC Layer enables multiple devices to share the media.

Most LANs have more than one computer (of course!), and the MAC sublayer determines who may speak and when.

Another important job of the Data Link Layer is *addressing*. The MAC sublayer maintains *physical device addresses* for communicating with other devices (commonly referred to as *MAC addresses*). Each device on the network must have a unique MAC address, otherwise the network will not know exactly where to send information when a node requests it. For example, how would the postal service know where to send your bills without your address?

Finally, the Data Link Layer manages *flow control* and *error correction* between devices in a simple network. In more complex internetworks, it is up to the Network Layer and other upper layers to perform these functions.

MAC Addresses

Most network interface cards (NICs) in a computer provide the MAC address as an address burned into the interface card. Some older network cards even required an administrator to set the address manually using switches. Even with a permanent MAC address burned into the card, some protocols enable you to define this address via software, although this is unusual.

The MAC address is used to communicate only on the local network. When transmitting to a server on the same LAN segment, the protocol uses the MAC addresses to communicate between the two computers. If the server is located on another network segment across a WAN, the MAC address of the nearest router (routers are discussed later in this chapter) is used to send the information, and it is up to the router to send the data further on.

EXERCISE 3-1

Determining Your Local Machine's MAC Address

In this exercise you will learn how to determine the MAC address of your computer. This can be helpful if you are having address resolution problems and need to investigate MAC address and IP address issues.

 1. Open up a command prompt window. In Windows 95/98 you can select Run from the Start menu and enter **COMMAND** in the space provided and then click OK. In Windows NT, you can also

select Run from the Start menu, but instead you can issue the CMD command in the space provided.

2. When the command prompt appears, type **WINIPCFG** and press ENTER if you are using a Windows 95 or Windows 98 machine. If you are using Windows NT, type **IPCONFIG /ALL.**

The following illustration shows the dialog box that appears when you are using Windows 95 or Windows 98.

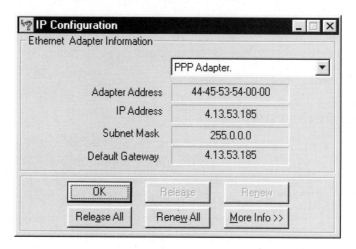

You can see that the adapter address, known as the MAC address, is present, as well as the IP address.

The following is the output from a Windows NT machine when the IPCONFIG /ALL command is issued:

```
Windows NT IP Configuration
    Host Name . . . . . . . . . : nevermore.dreamingneonblack.com
    DNS Servers . . . . . . . . : 172.18.160.224
    Node Type . . . . . . . . . : Broadcast
    NetBIOS Scope ID. . . . . . :
    IP Routing Enabled. . . . . : No
    WINS Proxy Enabled. . . . . : No
    NetBIOS Resolution Uses DNS : Yes
Token Ring adapter IBMTRP1:
    Description . . . . . . . . : IBM PCI Token-Ring Adapter
    Physical Address. . . . . . : 00-20-35-29-C5-29
```

```
   DHCP Enabled. . . . . . . . : Yes
   IP Address. . . . . . . . . : 172.18.193.104
   Subnet Mask . . . . . . . . : 255.255.252.0
   Default Gateway . . . . . . : 172.18.192.254
   DHCP Server . . . . . . . . : 172.18.160.242
   Lease Obtained. . . . . . . : Tuesday, January 19, 1999 7:29:32 AM
   Lease Expires . . . . . . . : Tuesday, January 19, 1999 7:29:32 PM
Ethernet adapter NdisWan5:
   Description . . . . . . . . : NdisWan Adapter
   Physical Address. . . . . . : 00-00-00-00-00-00
   DHCP Enabled. . . . . . . . : No
   IP Address. . . . . . . . . : 0.0.0.0
   Subnet Mask . . . . . . . . : 0.0.0.0
   Default Gateway . . . . . . :
```

As you can see, there is much more information with the IPCONFIG /ALL command than with the WINIPCFG command.

There is another little known way to get the MAC address from a Windows computer: the ARP command. ARP is an acronym for Address Resolution Protocol, which is the portion of the TCP/IP protocol that resolves an IP address to a MAC address. In order to send packets on a TCP/IP network, you need to resolve the IP address to a MAC address. A special packet will be broadcast on the network from the source computer that is trying to determine the destination computer's MAC address. Each host on the network will respond, indicating whether the address in question belongs to it or not. Every computer that doesn't match the address in question will disregard the message. The destination host will recognize its IP address in the request and send back a response to the source host that contains the destination host's MAC address. When the source host receives the news, it will use the newly attained physical address to send the packet directly to the destination host.

You can view, add, or delete entries that are located in your ARP cache. You will not find much use for this utility; however, you should be aware of its existence. The –a switch is used to view the contents of the ARP cache. Before I initiated the ARP command on my machine, I verified that there were no entries in the cache. I then browsed through Network Neighborhood on a Windows NT machine and clicked on a couple of servers. I went back to the command prompt and typed the ARP –a command. The output from the command is illustrated here:

```
C:\arp -a
Interface: 172.18.193.104 on Interface 2
  Internet Address      Physical Address      Type
  172.18.192.249        00-06-29-87-d3-48     dynamic
  172.18.194.209        00-20-35-29-c5-d2     dynamic
```

A few minutes later, I did the same command and the ARP cache was empty. This is because on Windows NT, the entries in the ARP cache are purged if they are not used within two minutes; if they are used, the entries remain there for ten minutes.

Now view the contents of the ARP command with the –g switch:

```
Interface: 172.18.193.104 on Interface 2
  Internet Address      Physical Address      Type
  172.18.192.249        00-06-29-87-d3-48     dynamic
  172.18.194.209        00-20-35-29-c5-d2     dynamic
```

Look familiar? That's because the output from the ARP –a and ARP –g commands are identical; you use both commands to view the contents of the ARP cache.

Bridges

A bridge is a network connectivity device that connects two different networks and makes them appear to be one network. The bridge filters local traffic between the two networks and copies all other traffic to the other side of the bridge. Bridges operate at the Data Link Layer. Bridges use the Data Link Layer and its physical addressing to join several networks into a single network efficiently.

Network Segmentation

A bridge is a simple way to accomplish network segmentation. Placing a bridge between two different segments of the network decreases the amount of traffic on each of the local networks. Although this does accomplish network segmentation, most network administrators opt to use routers or switches, which are discussed later in the chapter.

Bridges segment the network by MAC addresses. When one of the workstations connected to Network 1 transmits a packet, the packet is copied across the bridge as long as the packet's destination is not on Network 1. A bridge uses a bridge routing table to calculate which MAC addresses are on which network.

Source Routing and Spanning Tree Bridges

Of the two primary types of bridges, source routing and spanning tree bridges, there is no major difference except for their applications. The end result of both types of bridges is the same, even though the mediums that they are used on are different. Spanning tree bridges are used to connect rings in a Token Ring network and source routing bridges are used for Ethernet networks.

Building a Bridge Routing Table

Most bridges maintain their own bridge routing table dynamically and do not require that the administrator manage it unless he wishes to make a manual change to the table. To make a manual change to your bridge routing table, refer to the instructions that accompanied your bridge. Figure 3-1 illustrates a bridge with a bridge routing table.

OSI Data Link Layer

A bridge is constantly tracking the destination MAC addresses of all packets that it receives. If the bridge determines that the packets should cross the bridge, it passes them across the bridge. Since the only information the bridge knows about the packet is the MAC address of the destination, the bridge is said to reside in the Data Link Layer of the OSI Model.

802 Project Model

The *Institute of Electrical and Electronics Engineers* (IEEE) is a large and respected professional organization that is also active in defining standards. The 802 committee of the IEEE defines one set of standards dear to the

A bridge connects two local networks

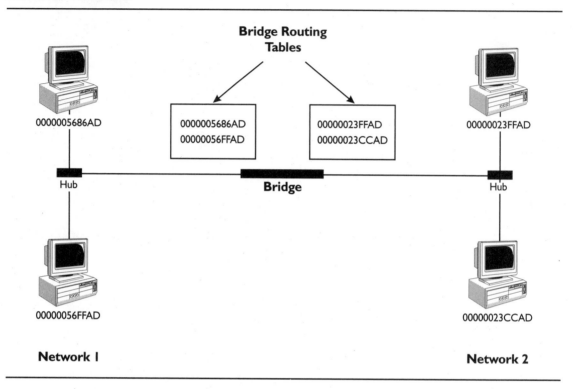

hearts of most network professionals. Twelve subcommittees of the 802 committee define low-level LAN and WAN access protocols. Most of the protocols that the 802 committee has defined reside in the Physical and Data Link Layers of the OSI Model.

IEEE 802 Categories

As the use of local area networks began to increase, standards had to be developed to define consistency and compatibility. The Institute of Electrical and Electronic Engineers (IEEE) began a project in February of 1980, known as Project 802, for the year and month it began. IEEE 802 is a set of standards given to the various LAN architectures such as Ethernet,

Token Ring, and ARCnet by the LAN standards committee. The goal of the committee was to define more of the OSI's Data Link Layer, which already contained the Logical Link Control and the Media Access Control sublayers.

There are several 802 subcommittee protocols that are the heart of PC networking.

802.2

The *logical link control* (LLC) sublayer is used by other protocols defined by the 802 committee. This LLC sublayer allows Network Layer protocols to be designed separately from the low-level Physical Layer and MAC sublayer protocols.

The LLC adds header information that identifies the upper layer protocols sending the frame. The header can also specify destination processes for the data (the *service address* discussed earlier).

802.3

Based on the original Ethernet network from *DIX (Digital-Intel-Xerox)*, 802.3 is *the* standard for popular Ethernet networks today. The only difference between 802.3 Ethernet and DIX Ethernet V.2 is frame type. The two Ethernet networks can use the same physical network, but devices on one standard cannot communicate with devices on the other standard.

The MAC sublayer uses *Carrier Sense Multiple Access with Collision Detection (CSMA/CD)* for access to the physical medium. CSMA/CD keeps devices on the network from interfering with one another when trying to transmit; when they do interfere with each other, a *collision* has occurred. To reduce collisions, CSMA/CD devices listen to the network before transmitting. If the network is "quiet" (no other devices are transmitting), the device can send its data. Since two devices can think the network is clear and start transmitting at the same time, resulting in a collision, all devices listen as they transmit. If a device detects another device transmitting at the same time, a collision has occurred. The device stops transmitting and sends a signal to alert other nodes to the collision. Then all the nodes stop transmitting and wait a random amount of time before they begin the process again.

CSMA/CD doesn't stop collisions from happening, but it helps manage the situations when collisions occur. In fact, collisions are a very normal part of Ethernet operation. It's only when collisions begin to occur frequently that you need to become concerned.

exam
ⓌatchThe exam leans quite heavily on Ethernet technology, due to the fact of Ethernet's dominance in the marketplace. Pay special attention to special characteristics of the various media types of Ethernet.*

Ethernet has evolved over the years to include a number of popular specifications. These specifications are due in part to the media variety they employ, such as coaxial, twisted-pair, and fiber-optic cabling.

■ The 10Base5 specification, commonly referred to as Thicknet, was the original Ethernet specification and has a maximum distance of 500 meters (about 1640 feet) with a maximum speed of 2.94 - 10 Mbps.

■ The 10Base2 specification, commonly referred to as Thinnet, uses a thinner coaxial cable than 10Base5 and has a maximum distance of 185 meters (about 607 feet) with a maximum speed of 10 Mbps.

■ The 10BaseT specification uses twisted-pair cabling with a maximum distance of 100 meters (about 328 feet) with a speed of 10 - 100 Mbps.

802.5

Although the first Token Ring design was made in the late sixties, IBM's token passing implementation did not become a standard until 1985. It became IEEE standard 802.5 under the IEEE Project 802. The 802.5 standard was actually modeled after the IBM Token Ring network, which had been in use for many years before the standard was even developed.

The 802.5 network introduced a unique access method: token passing. The Token Ring IEEE 802.5 standard passes a special frame known as the "token" around the network. This token is generated by the first computer that comes online on the Token Ring network. When a workstation wants to transmit data, it grabs the token and then begins transmitting. This computer will send a data frame on the network with the address of the destination computer. The destination computer receives the data frame, modifies it, and sends it on to the network and back to the destination computer, indicating that the transmission of data was successful. When the workstation is done transmitting, the token is released back onto the network. This ensures workstations will not simultaneously communicate on the network, as in the CSMA/CD access method.

exam
ⓦatch

It's pretty much a guarantee you will be asked about the IEEE standards, especially the three listed here. For example, know which 802 standard maps to Ethernet, and which IEEE standard number Token Ring maps to. Don't expect any questions on the less common IEEE standards; they have been omitted here for that very reason.

CERTIFICATION OBJECTIVE 3.02

Network Layer Concepts

The Network Layer is one of the most complex and important ones. The Network Layer manages addressing and delivering packets on a complex *internetwork*. This layer must determine a route in which to route the packet from the source to the destination computer. This route to the destination computer through the internetwork is determined by factors such as network conditions, speed of the network, and priority of the packet. Internetworks are joined by devices known as *routers*, which utilize *routing tables* and *routing algorithms* to determine how to send data from one network to another.

The most obvious example of an internetwork is the Internet. The Internet is very large, covering the entire globe, and consists of almost every conceivable type of computer, from palmtops to mainframes.

The Network Layer must also take large packets and break them down into smaller units that are more conducive to travelling over many different complex routes than one big chunk of data. The packets must be broken into smaller pieces by the sending computer, and then reassembled by the Network Layer of the destination computer once the packets arrive.

Unique Network IDs

In order to operate on an internetwork, each network that participates must be assigned a network ID. This address differentiates each network from every other network that forms the internetwork. When sending data from one network to another, the routers along the way use the network ID to determine the next step in the journey. Each host within this network ID uses the same network ID, much like each person or business within a zip code area uses the same zip code. The Postal Service sends your letter to the post office for your zip code first, and then your local post office uses your unique street address to determine where you are located within that zip code. In Chapter 4 you will see how the network ID portion of the IP address is crucial to routing IP packets effectively.

Routing

Routing protocols are quite different from bridging protocols. Bridging is designed to combine packets from multiple physical networks and consolidate them into one virtual network. Routing is designed to separate a physical network into multiple virtual networks..

The manner in which bridging and routing protocols operate also varies. A bridging protocol enables all traffic to cross that is not destined for the local network. A routing protocol enables traffic to cross that is destined for networks on the other side of the router.

Routing also requires intelligent devices that can determine the most effective path to the destination computer through a complex web of subnetworks. Routers can also remember the addresses of each segment, ensuring quicker delivery time without the need to "ask" other routers the address to a remote network.

Routers are also very popular because they filter unwanted traffic such as broadcasts from other network segments. Traffic is also isolated so that one extremely busy segment, such as a high-bandwidth CAD department, will not overcome the users in another segment.

Figure 3-2 illustrates the concept of two distinct networks separated by a router or gateway. The central host has two network cards, each with an address for its respective subnets. As you learned earlier, each network must have a unique ID. In Figure 3-3, the network on the left has a network ID of 223.4.5, and the network on the right has a network ID of 223.4.6. On this TCP/IP network, the subnet mask is 255.255.255.0. Don't worry if you don't understand exactly what a subnet mask is; after Chapter 4 you will be versed in subnet masking!

FIGURE 3-2   Subnetworks connected by a router or a gateway

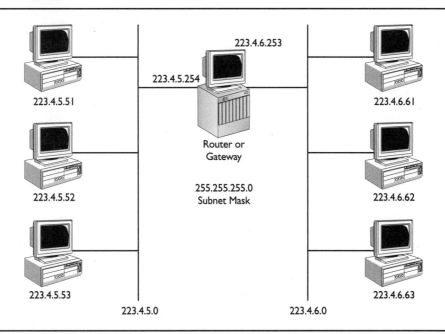

Router and Brouter Differences

A brouter is a hybrid of both a bridge and a router and has a connection to more than two networks. When the brouter receives a packet from one segment of the network, it must first determine what the destination IP address is. If the packet is not destined for a port of the brouter, it sends it to the gateway address. If the packet is destined for a port of the brouter, it bridges the packet to the other port instead of routing it.

Remember, when you are making the decision to use either a bridge or a router on a network, you must consider whether you need to "isolate" or "consolidate" segments of the network. Routers are much more popular (and more expensive) than bridges because the most common network protocol is TCP/IP, which is used to create many "logical" networks out of one physical network. A bridge is incapable of taking advantage of subnetting networks with the complex TCP/IP protocol, which requires a tremendous amount of routing. However, you can use a brouter when your network consists of both routable and non-routable protocols, such as TCP/IP and NetBEUI. Brouting may provide a more cost-effective means of bridging and routing in one unit, rather than using two individual components.

Figure 3-3 illustrates the placement in the OSI model for both the router and the bridge.

Remember, the higher the network device is within the OSI layer, the more intelligent the device is. A router can make more intelligent decisions based on the address of the packet than the bridge can; therefore, a router is used for more complex protocols, such as TCP/IP, which employs subnetting a network extensively.

FIGURE 3-3

Where bridges and routers are located within the OSI model.

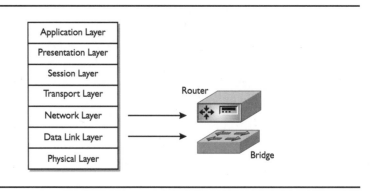

Routable and Nonroutable Protocols within the Network Layer

An important difference between some protocols is their ability to be routed. A protocol that is *routable* is a protocol that can have packets transferred across a router. This section will discuss exactly which packets are routable and which ones are not. It might seem like a routable protocol is the best solution for your network, but routable protocols require that additional information be included in the packet header for routing purposes: for example, a time to live field.

If your company wants to route packets to remote networks, you will be dealing with routers to route these packets. You can see that the choice of protocol often makes the decision for you regarding which network device you will use to isolate or consolidate your network.

TCP/IP

TCP/IP (Transmission Control Protocol/Internet Protocol) is the most common protocol used today. TCP/IP, a routable protocol, is very robust and is commonly associated with UNIX systems. TCP/IP was originally designed in the 1970s to be used by the Defense Advanced Research Projects Agency (DARPA) and the Department of Defense (DOD) to connect systems across the country. This design required the capability to cope with unstable network conditions. Therefore, the design of TCP/IP included the capability to reroute packets. You will learn much more about the TCP/IP protocol and routing in Chapter 4.

Note: Only IP of the TCP/IP protocol resides in the Network Layer. The TCP portion of the protocol is part of the Transport Layer.

IPX/SPX/NWLink

IPX/SPX (Internetwork Packet Exchange/Sequenced Packet Exchange) is the protocol most commonly used with Novell NetWare. IPX/SPX, a routable protocol, is a very fast and highly established protocol, but it is not used on the Internet. Novell developed IPX/SPX for use in NetWare. The protocol IPX/SPX/NWLink that is shipped with Windows 95 and Windows NT was written by Microsoft and is fully compatible with the Novell IPX/SPX protocol.

Note: Only IPX of the IPX/SPX protocol resides in the Network Layer. The SPX portion of the protocol is part of the Transport Layer.

AppleTalk

AppleTalk is the proprietary protocol developed by Apple Computer. AppleTalk is rarely found in network environments where Apple Computers are not present. AppleTalk is a routable protocol.

NetBEUI

NetBEUI (NetBios Extended User Interface) is a transport protocol commonly found in smaller networks. NetBEUI is not frequently used in large networks and will become less used in the future because it is not a routable protocol. NetBEUI is an extremely quick protocol with little overhead because of its inability to route packets. NetBEUI is also very easy to configure, and actually, you don't need to configure anything once you have the NetBEUI protocol installed and bound to the network adapter.

on the
ⓘ o b

On the first day of work at a new job, I sat down and attempted to log on with my newly created Windows NT account. After I entered my user name and password, my workstation took what I thought was way too much time authenticating me. I had never seen a Windows NT computer take so long. I commented on what I saw to a coworker, and he told me the network is very slow, and keeps getting worse. Later that day, I noticed that it was a company standard to use TCP/IP and to continue to use NetBEUI (a broadcast intensive protocol) as a means of fault tolerance in case of a problem with TCP/IP. Having both of these protocols on every machine and bound to every adapter was saturating the network. Management knew this, but a standard is a standard. To solve this problem, eventually every workstation will have to have the NetBEUI protocol removed, which will minimize broadcasts and increase performance.

Now that you have seen the differences between the network devices, here is a quick reference of possible scenario questions on the choice of one device over another, and the appropriate answer.

QUESTIONS AND ANSWERS

I need to minimize broadcast storms…	Don't use a bridge. They pass all broadcasts to the other network.
I use a routable protocol…	Don't use a bridge. Use a brouter or a router, which can route the protocol appropriately.
I only use NetBEUI…	There's your answer; NetBEUI is not routable, so you cannot use a brouter or router.
I need to separate or segment…	Use a brouter or a router. Routers isolate networks, not consolidate them.
I use a routing protocol and a non-routing protocol…	Use a brouter. The brouter can route a routable protocol while it passes a non-routable protocol.

exam
ⓦatch

It's a guarantee you will have a question or two on your exam regarding the appropriate use of a bridge, brouter, or router. With the information we provided here, you should do just fine. Bear in mind that they will give you a long, complex scenario with tons of information to confuse you.

Static and Dynamic Routing

When it comes to routing, there is a huge difference between the two types of routing: static and dynamic. Early routers had to be programmed with exactly which networks they could route between which interfaces, especially if there were many network interfaces. This is called static routing, which consists of adding, maintaining, and deleting routes of the network routing devices by the network administrator. In a small company this may not be much of a chore, but for medium to large networks, this can be nearly impossible. These larger networks almost always employ many logical subnets, which requires you to update the route tables on each routing device. If these remote subnets are connected by routers with static route tables, you have to add the exact static route in order to communicate between the two subnets.

Table 3-1 gives you an example of what is contained in the routing table.

In this table you can see how you only specify the router to be used to reach your destination, not the actual destination itself. Also notice the column for Hops. This is what determines which route is the most efficient, similar to "Name That Tune." If a route claims it can reach the destination in one fewer hop than the next router, then let him prove it. If there are two identical routes to the same destination, the route with the fewest hops will be used.

One change to a network address means visiting every routing device that employs static routing and updating the entry. What do we do if our network is fairly large and complex? We must then use routing devices capable of dynamically updating the route tables.

Dynamic routing does not require the network administrator to edit complex routing tables in order to communicate with other networks or segments. These routers communicate with each other using a powerful routing protocol such as Routing Information Protocol (RIP) or Open Shortest Path First (OSPF). They can also query other routers for updated route information, which can create more efficient paths for sending packets or locate an alternative route if the original route fails. The routers can broadcast the routes they have discovered to neighboring routers, and, in turn, accept routes from other neighboring routers. The Internet is comprised

TABLE 3-1	Destination	Adjacent Router	Hops
An Example of a Routing Table	Network 1	Router A	1
	Network 1	Router B	2
	Network 2	Router B	2
	Network 2	Router C	3
	Network 3	Router D	3

of many dynamic routers. Could you imaging having to update a static routing table on thousands of static routers? I don't think so.

These dynamic routers, however, cannot update the route tables of static routers or non-dynamic routers. There are a few situations in which integrating static and dynamic routers is acceptable:

- **When you have a router at either end of a slow WAN link**
  This router will not increase traffic by broadcasting updated route information to the router on the other end of the link.

- **When you require a packet to travel the same path each time to a remote network**   Add the path you would like the packet to take in order to reach the destination network. You cannot enter the entire path over several routers, only the path to the first router.

- **When you want to configure a static router to point towards a dynamic router to take advantage of the dynamic router** *indirectly*   This is the next best thing to using a dynamic router. You can hand off the packet to the dynamic router and let this router determine the most efficient path to the destination based on the paths it has learned from neighboring dynamic routers.

Of course, dynamic routers cost much more. Although you can add static paths to a newer dynamic router, you cannot enable dynamic routing on an older static router. Also, dynamic routing generates continuous traffic from the routers with route update information.

Comparing Static and Dynamic Routing

With just two networks, the static routing setup is the more appropriate. If your network has three or four parallel networks, then static routing may still be useful, although dynamic routing would be easier to set up.

However, the actual setup is far more complex. You cannot simply have the routers route to the other network by assigning the gateway addresses to the other network interface card. This simply moves the packet to the other side when in actual fact the router needs to send the packet on to the specific gateway from that network to the next network.

Default Gateways and Subnetworks

Although we will be discussing the default gateway and subnetworks in much greater detail in Chapter 4, it is appropriate to discuss the role of both of these concepts while we are on the subject of routing.

We have learned that packets are routed to their destination through a web of routers. We have discussed how these routers are updated: either statically or dynamically. What gets the whole process rolling when we are routing packets to remote subnetworks, or subnets for short, is the use of the default gateway. The default gateway is specified on each computer, and is what initially sends the packet on its way to the first router. When the packet hits this first router, the router must determine if the destination computer is on the local network, or send the packet to the next router that will get the packet to its destination. The default gateway is very important to the routing process, so expect to hear much more about it.

on the **!** ***j***ob   *When I was at one company, one of my coworkers was sent out to reconfigure the printers. These printers had their own IP addresses, which is what he was reconfiguring. He successfully entered the new IP address, but he couldn't get the printer to print on the network. I took a look, asked him what he configured, and he said just the IP address and subnet mask. I asked him if he configured the default gateway. He said no. Once we entered the default gateway, the printer took off and started printing. We had forgotten that the printers were located on a different subnet than the rest of the computers, and without the default gateway the printers had no idea of how to get information to the other subnet.*

You have to be on your toes when you are administering a network with subnets, which is quite common today. Without that default gateway, you are stuck on the local network. The subnet mask, which you will learn about in the next chapter, is also very important. Without a properly configured subnet mask to determine which subnet your computer is on, you aren't going to be talking to anyone!

Since TCP/IP is so popular in the real world, you can expect your exam to lean heavily towards configuring TCP/IP—more specifically, the IP address, subnet mask, and default gateway: the three essential TCP/IP configuration parameters.

The IP address and subnet mask of a Windows 98 computer are shown in Figure 3-4 . To get to this point, open the Network applet in the Control Panel, double-click on TCP/IP on the Configuration tab (or select the TCP/IP protocol and then click Properties), and select the IP Address tab if it is not already selected.

FIGURE 3-4

Configuring the IP address and subnet mask on a Windows 98 computer

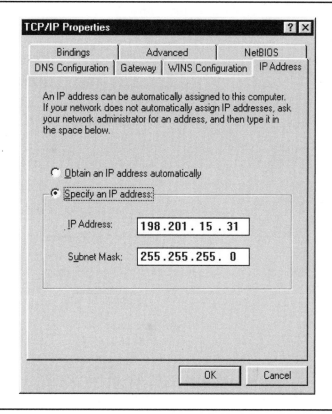

Figure 3-5 illustrates configuring a Windows 98 computer with the default gateway. This tab is also in the TCP/IP properties dialog box and can be reached by clicking the Gateway tab.

Figure 3-6 illustrates configuring a Windows NT computer with all of the critical TCP/IP information on one tab, also located in the Network applet of the Control Panel. This is also in the TCP/IP properties dialog box and can be reached by clicking the Gateway tab.

exam
ⓦatch

Make sure you have the IP address, subnet mask, and default gateway for your exam. You will thank me later, because this knowledge will help you each and every day of your networking career! Want to know more about TCP/IP? The next chapter will give you everything you need to prepare for the exam.

FIGURE 3-5

Configuring the default gateway on a Windows 95 computer

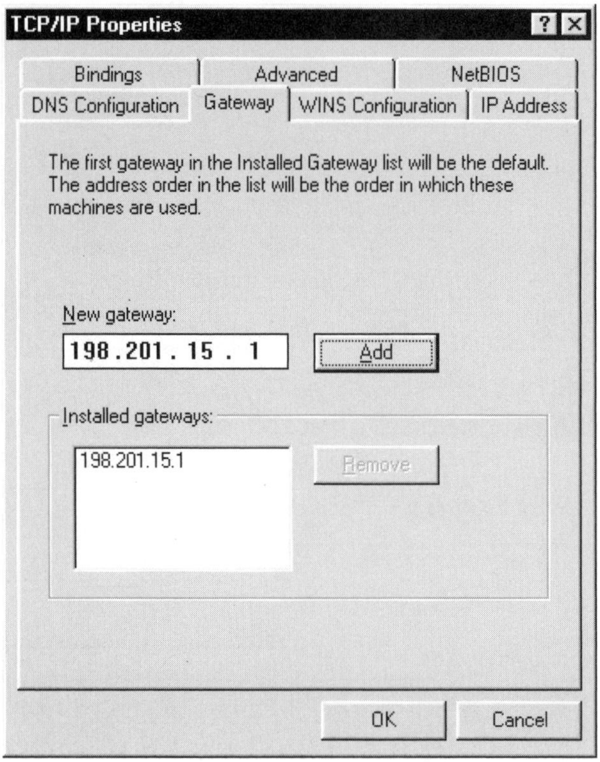

FIGURE 3-6

Configuring the IP address, subnet mask, and default gateway on a Windows NT computer

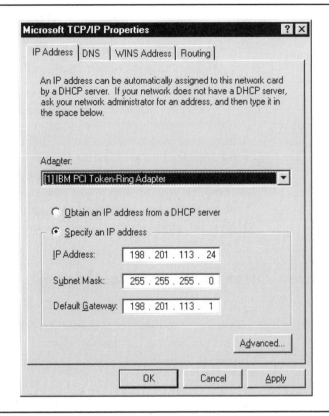

CERTIFICATION OBJECTIVE 3.03

Transport Layer Concepts

The Transport Layer works hard to ensure reliable delivery of data to its destinations. The Transport Layer also helps the upper layers (Application, Presentation, and Session) communicate with one another across the network while hiding the complexities of the network.

The Transport Layer also interacts with the Network Layer, taking on some of the responsibilities for connection services.

One of the functions of the Transport Layer is *segment sequencing*. Sequence switching is a connection-oriented service that takes segments that are received out of order and resequences them in the right order.

Another function of the Transport Layer is *error control*. It commonly uses acknowledgments to manage the flow of data between devices. Some Transport Layer protocols can also request retransmission of recent segments to overcome errors.

exam
ⓌＡtch

Be prepared on your exam for a few questions about what each of the layers of the OSI model is responsible for. These can be quite tricky, so you have to know your stuff. Make sure you understand the order of the layers; I found that helps when trying to memorize each layer, because each layer begins where the other layer left off.

Connection-Oriented Communication

Connection-oriented communication ensures reliable delivery of data from the sender to the receiver, without intervention required by the sender or receiver. Error correction and flow control are provided at various points from the source to the destination.

Handshaking and Data Reliability

Connection-oriented services must ensure that data is sent reliably across the network. When establishing these services, the protocol must perform some sort of *handshaking* function. Handshaking takes place at the beginning of a communication session. During handshaking, the two computers determine the rules for communication, such as transmission speed, and which ports to use.

Handshaking also determines the proper way to terminate the session when done. This ensures that communication ends in an orderly manner.

Sessions

A *session* is a reliable dialog between two computers. Because connection-oriented services can provide reliable communication, they are used when two computers need to communicate in a session. Sessions are maintained until the two computers decide that they are done communicating.

A session is just like a phone call. You set up a phone call by dialing (handshaking), you speak to the other person (exchange data), and finally say "Goodbye," and hang up when done.

Virtual Circuits

Virtual circuits establish formal communication between two computers on an internetwork using a well-defined path. This enables two computers to act as though there is a dedicated circuit between the two, even though there is not.

The path the data takes while being exchanged between the two computers may vary, but the computers do not know this. They do not need to. Since the virtual circuit uses connection-oriented communication, all the points that make up the circuit ensure that the data gets through unharmed, even if those points change while the virtual circuit is in place.

Connection-Oriented Protocols

Most network protocols have connection-oriented services. These protocols ensure a reliable connection across the network. They can handle errors on their own, independently of any higher level protocols or applications.

The Internet's TCP/IP protocol provides this capability with the *transmission control protocol* (TCP). In Novell's IPX/SPX protocol, the *sequenced packet exchange* (SPX) protocol provides connection-oriented services.

Connectionless Communication

Connectionless communication is a form of communication in which the destination computer does not notify the source when the information is received. This type of communication can be unreliable because there is no notification to guarantee delivery. Connectionless communication can be faster than connection-oriented communication due to the fact that after information is sent there is no second step to ensure proper receipt of information.

Datagrams

Datagrams, used by the UDP protocol, are self-contained, independent pieces of data that contain enough information to be routed from the source computer to the destination computer without any help from the source or destination. The network uses the self-contained information of the data to determine how to send the datagram along.

A datagram is just like a piece of postal mail. You drop mail in the slot, and the stamp and address are enough for the postal service to route the mail to your recipient. However, the post office may lose a piece of mail and there is no way to track when or where the mail was lost.

exam
⚐atch

Remember, connectionless protocols in TCP/IP use the UDP protocol. TFTP is one example of a connectionless-oriented protocol that uses UDP.

Mailslots

Mailslots are an easy way for one computer to send information to many clients. A server can open a mailslot and can only write data to it. Other computers on the network may connect to the mailslot and read from it. The server sends the information out from the mailslot, but cannot be sure who is listening.

A mailslot is much like a bulletin board. Anyone can post a note to it and walk away. A few people, everybody, or nobody, may actually read the note. You just don't know how many people may have seen it.

Lack of Reliable Delivery

Because all the nodes between the source and destination computers don't check to see that the data is unharmed, these computers must manage this function. A higher layer such as the Transport Layer usually handles this, since it has error control, sequencing, and flow control capabilities.

Expanding the bulletin board example above, you could ask people if they saw your message. This is one way to determine if your note was read, without actually having the note tell you. The Transport Layer of the OSI model can act in this role, enabling even connectionless communication to have some degree of reliability.

exam
Watch

It is important for the Network+ test that you understand the difference between connection-oriented and connectionless communication, and in what situations each one is appropriate.

Name Resolution

In order to make it easier for humans, not computers, to remember things, we use friendly names for computers. In TPC/IP, these friendly names are resolved to an IP address, where they are then resolved to a MAC address by the computer. We, as humans, can still use the IP address, or, in some instances, the MAC address, when communicating with other computers, but it is much easier to remember and utilize the friendly name.

There are two potential types of names that have to be resolved when using a Windows-based computer: the NetBIOS name and the host name.

NetBIOS Name Resolution

The NetBIOS name is the computer name you specify in the Networking applet of the Control Panel in Windows 95/98, or Windows NT. NetBIOS is a Microsoft solution only present in Windows-based operating systems. Now, since we are using NetBIOS names on the network, we need a way to resolve these NetBIOS names to IP addresses. There are two methods for resolving a NetBIOS name: LMHOSTS or WINS. LMHOSTS is a text file located on each computer (sometimes located on a central server), containing a list of NetBIOS name-to-IP address mappings. The LMHOSTS file is parsed when a NetBIOS name needs to be resolved to an IP address. The following is an example of the default LMHOSTS file sample provided by Microsoft:

```
# Copyright (c) 1993-1995 Microsoft Corp.
#
# This is a sample LMHOSTS file used by the Microsoft TCP/IP for Windows
# NT.
#
# This file contains the mappings of IP addresses to NT computernames
# (NetBIOS) names. Each entry should be kept on an individual line.
# The IP address should be placed in the first column followed by the
# corresponding computername. The address and the comptername
# should be separated by at least one space or tab. The "#" character
```

```
# is generally used to denote the start of a comment (see the exceptions
# below).
#
# This file is compatible with Microsoft LAN Manager 2.x TCP/IP lmhosts
# files and offers the following extensions:
#
# #PRE
# #DOM:<domain>
# #INCLUDE <filename>
# #BEGIN_ALTERNATE
# #END_ALTERNATE
# \0xnn (non-printing character support)
#
# Following any entry in the file with the characters "#PRE" will cause
# the entry to be preloaded into the name cache. By default, entries are
# not preloaded, but are parsed only after dynamic name resolution fails.
#
# Following an entry with the "#DOM:<domain>" tag will associate the
# entry with the domain specified by <domain>. This affects how the
# browser and logon services behave in TCP/IP environments. To preload
# the host name associated with #DOM entry, it is necessary to also add a
# #PRE to the line. The <domain> is always preloaded although it will not
# be shown when the name cache is viewed.
#
# Specifying "#INCLUDE <filename>" will force the RFC NetBIOS (NBT)
# software to seek the specified <filename> and parse it as if it were
# local. <filename> is generally a UNC-based name, allowing a
# centralized lmhosts file to be maintained on a server.
# It is ALWAYS necessary to provide a mapping for the IP address of the
# server prior to the #INCLUDE. This mapping must use the #PRE directive.
# In addition the share "public" in the example below must be in the
# LanManServer list of "NullSessionShares" in order for client machines to
# be able to read the lmhosts file successfully. This key is under
# \machine\system\currentcontrolset\services\lanmanserver\parameters\nullsessionshares
# in the registry. Simply add "public" to the list found there.
#
# The #BEGIN_ and #END_ALTERNATE keywords allow multiple #INCLUDE
# statements to be grouped together. Any single successful include
# will cause the group to succeed.
#
# Finally, non-printing characters can be embedded in mappings by
# first surrounding the NetBIOS name in quotations, then using the
# \0xnn notation to specify a hex value for a non-printing character.
#
```

```
# The following example illustrates all of these extensions:
#
# 102.54.94.97 rhino #PRE #DOM:networking #net group's DC
# 102.54.94.102 "appname \0x14" #special app server
# 102.54.94.123 popular #PRE #source server
# 102.54.94.117 localsrv #PRE #needed for the include
#
# #BEGIN_ALTERNATE
# #INCLUDE \\localsrv\public\lmhosts
# #INCLUDE \\rhino\public\lmhosts
# #END_ALTERNATE
#
# In the above example, the "appname" server contains a special
# character in its name, the "popular" and "localsrv" server names are
# preloaded, and the "rhino" server name is specified so it can be used
# to later #INCLUDE a centrally maintained lmhosts file if the "localsrv"
# system is unavailable.
#
# Note that the whole file is parsed including comments on each lookup,
# so keeping the number of comments to a minimum will improve performance.
# Therefore it is not advisable to simply add lmhosts file entries onto the
# end of this file.
```

You can see a NetBIOS name-to-IP address mapping example in the following line:

102.54.94.97   rhino

First of all, this line is commented out (a line preceded by a # will not be parsed); therefore, the mapping will not work. If we removed the # sign from the line, we would effectively be telling the computer that the NetBIOS name of rhino maps to an IP address of 102.54.94.97. If the NetBIOS name were to change to kangaroo, we would have to visit each computer that uses an LMHOSTS file for name resolution and change the name from rhino to kangaroo. There has to be an easier way than updating a static LMHOSTS on every computer! Well, there is, and it's called WINS (Windows Internet Naming Service).

exam
Ⓦatch

Remember, a UNIX machine can use an LMHOSTS file to resolve machine names.

Using the WINS service on a Windows NT server eliminates the need for many network broadcasts, and therefore reduces network usage. Also, the need for manually updating tons of LMHOSTS files on every computer is eliminated. Enabling WINS on a Windows-based client uses a directed, or point-to-point, transmission for name resolution. WINS is dynamic, and is updated when machines are started or stopped, or when replicated with other WINS servers. When a name is registered, it will be reserved for that one computer, further simplifying naming schemes. Each computer will always have its own unique name. When a computer in a WINS-enabled network is started, it will automatically register all its NetBIOS names with the WINS Server. If the computer's IP address has changed, the WINS Server will know immediately. This is WINS' strength: its ability to keep an accurate IP mapping database in an ever-changing network environment. It is the best choice for NetBIOS name resolution in a routed network because it is designed to solve the problems that occur with name resolution.

When your computer is configured to use WINS for NetBIOS name resolution, you will query the WINS server directly when your computer is trying to determine the IP address of a computer you are communicating with. Since WINS is dynamic, it will have up-to-date information on the current mapping for the computer you are trying to locate.

Host Name Resolution

Remember, NetBIOS name resolution is not the only form of name resolution. We also have host name resolution. The Internet is full of host names, such as microsoft.com. Also note that NetBIOS names are specific to Windows-based computers, whereas host names can be any type of operating system, from UNIX to Macintosh. As with NetBIOS name resolution, host name resolution can also use a static text file located on each computer. This file is called the HOSTS file, not to be confused with the LMHOSTS file for NetBIOS resolution. The premise is exactly the same for the HOSTS file; it contains a list of host name-to-IP address mappings that are parsed in order when your computer is trying to resolve a host name to an IP address.

FROM THE FIELD

Just What Is NetBIOS?

You may be asking yourself, "What is NetBIOS? It's not a protocol. So what is it?" Well, in the working world you will hear a lot of myths and rumors about what NetBIOS actually is and what it does for networking. The following is a listing of the several aspects associated with NetBIOS that I have found helpful in understand what NetBIOS means to your Windows NT networking career.

- You may have heard that NetBIOS is the same thing as NetBEUI, but it is not.

- NetBIOS is not a protocol or protocol stack.

- When you install TCP/IP on Windows NT, you automatically get NetBIOS; there is no separating the two.

- Since NetBIOS is not a transport protocol, it does not directly support routing, but it depends on one of three transport protocols it can run on Windows NT: TCP/IP, NWLink IPX/SPX, or NetBEUI.

- NetBIOS names can be a maximum of 16 bytes long. 15 bytes for the name and one byte for the control character at the end.

- NetBIOS is used for all the NET commands, such as NET USE.

- The NBTSTAT command examines the contents of the NetBIOS name cache.

- NetBIOS names can be resolved through broadcast, an LMHOSTS file, or a WINS server.

What does all this mean to you? If you don't thoroughly understand NetBIOS, you may also have a difficult time understanding important concepts that rely on NetBIOS, such as WINS, LMHOSTS, and NetBIOS name resolution. It's very common for modern Windows NT networks to use WINS for NetBIOS resolution. If you are a Windows NT network administrator, you will be responsible for supporting, maintaining, and troubleshooting WINS. This can be a daunting task if you don't understand NetBIOS, because I believe WINS is one of the most difficult concepts to understand in Windows NT networking. I have a very experienced Windows NT network engineer sitting at the WINS server for hours trying to solve a WINS issue. Make sure you have an understanding of NetBIOS and you can use this to solve any NetBIOS-related problems on your network.

—Cameron Brandon, MCSE+Internet,
CNE, A+, Network+

The following is an example of the HOSTS sample file provided by Microsoft:

```
# Copyright (c) 1998 Microsoft Corp.
#
# This is a sample HOSTS file used by Microsoft TCP/IP stack for Windows98
#
# This file contains the mappings of IP addresses to host names. Each
# entry should be kept on an individual line. The IP address should
# be placed in the first column followed by the corresponding host name.
# The IP address and the host name should be separated by at least one
# space.
#
# Additionally, comments (such as these) may be inserted on individual
# lines or following the machine name denoted by a '#' symbol.
#
# For example:
#
#      102.54.94.97      rhino.acme.com          # source server
#       38.25.63.10      x.acme.com              # x client host
127.0.0.1          localhost
```

As with the LMHOSTS file, the lines are commented out with a #, meaning they will not be processed. The only line that will be processed in the HOSTS sample file is the mapping for the localhost. If you needed to add an entry in this file, you would begin with the IP address, followed by a space or tab, and then the host name, such as:

143.67.119.31   gorilla

Does using the HOSTS file sound just as troublesome as the LMHOSTS file for maintenance? Yes, and like NetBIOS name resolution, there is also another way to resolve a host name. This method is by using a DNS (Domain Name System), which is a server that provides a database and search algorithm for resolving the host name to an IP address. DNS is the service that takes a domain name and resolves it to an IP address for the TCP/IP hosts. The DNS server eliminates the need for the HOSTS file, but DNS is still not dynamic, like WINS. Therefore, all changes must be made manually. However, instead of manually updating 492 hosts with a new HOSTS file, you need to manually update the DNS server and have the 492 hosts point to the DNS server to resolve the host names. Please understand that DNS is only used for the TCP/IP protocol; WINS was not tied to the TCP/IP protocol and can also be used with NetBEUI.

IP/IPX Addresses

There are a few differences between IP and IPX addresses. Chapter 4 will focus heavily on the IP address and many more aspects of the TCP/IP protocol, which is dominating the network industry.

Both the IP and IPX addresses are used to uniquely identify a host on a network. If this address is duplicated on the network, the packet will be confused about which computer is the actual destination for the packet. This is, of course, much like the real-world dilemma if you and your neighbor have the exact same address. This is remedied through using a Dynamic Host Configuration Protocol (DHCP) server to hand out addresses to clients when you are using the TCP/IP protocol. You will learn more about DHCP in Chapter 4. With Windows NT, if the system detects a duplicate IP address on the network, TCP/IP will refuse to initialize on this computer and an error will be generated. You must find the offending computer and determine who is at fault. Why did this second computer use an IP address that was already taken?

on the Ojob

At one place I worked, we would get duplicate IP address conflicts every week, sometimes a few times a week. We were using TCP/IP with addresses assigned via a DHCP server. I would have to free the IP addresses (using the IPCONFIG or WINIPCFG command) on both computers, release the IP address lease on the DHCP server, and then reboot the offending machines. We haven't figure out to this day what caused the storm of duplicate addresses. We did discover that although the IP address lease process is dynamic, the IP address was written into the Registry. We had to delete the Registry key that contained this IP address and reboot the computer to obtain a new address.

The second most common protocol is IPX, which is due in part to Novell NetWare's wide install base. With NetWare, you must also be sure you are not using duplicate IPX addresses. When you are installing your NetWare server, you will be asked for a one- to eight-digit IPX *internal network number*. This number will uniquely identify this server on the network. Most people accept the randomly generated IPX number. However, you should write this number down for future reference, or use a predetermined IPX number for this server to keep in line with company standards.

on the
Job

When I was installing NetWare servers at Intel, we could not accept the default IPX number that was generated during system installation. We needed to acquire a predetermined IPX address before we began the installation process. If Intel does it, then so should your company. Then again, your company may not have a zillion servers like Intel does.

Protocols Within the Transport Layer

Just as the Network Layer contained routable and non-routable protocols such as TCP/IP and IPX, the Transport Layer also contains its very own protocols. As you discovered in the Network Layer discussion, IP and IPX are located in the Network Layer, and the other components of these protocols, TCP and SPX, are located within the Transport Layer. The protocols in this layer provide for communications sessions between computers to move data reliably.

exam
Watch

I found it helpful to remember that the protocols that begin with I (IP and IPX) are located in the Network Layer.

TCP

The TCP portion of the TCP/IP protocol is responsible for guaranteed delivery of data. The TCP protocol is a reliable, connection-oriented protocol that reorders the packets of information between two communicating devices for sending and receiving data. Note how the IP portion of the TCP/IP protocol works at a lower layer, forwarding and routing packets across the network.

SPX

The SPX portion of the IPX/SPX protocol is responsible for the sequencing of data during the communication session between two computers. Note that the IPX portion of the IPX/SPX protocol works at a lower level, just like IP does for the TCP/IP protocol, forwarding and routing packets across the network.

NetBEUI

NetBEUI was present in the Network Layer, but is also considered a Transport Layer protocol. NetBEUI is considered a Transport protocol because it establishes sessions between computers with the use of NetBIOS, and also provides the data transport services.

CERTIFICATION SUMMARY

In this chapter, you learned about the three important layers of the OSI model for addressing and forwarding packets of information: The Data Link Layer, the Network Layer, and the Transport Layer. First, you learned how the Data Link Layer packages data into smaller frames for routing across the network and about the two sublayers of the Data Link Layer: *logical link control* (LLC) and *media access control* (MAC). You discovered the importance of the MAC address, or hardware address, and how to retrieve the MAC address from a Windows 95/98 or Windows NT machine. You learned about the bridge, which resides in the Data Link Layer and is used for consolidating networks. And finally for the Data Link Layer, you learned the IEEE 802 standards 802.2, 802.3, and 802.5.

You learned how the Network Layer addresses frames of information with the source and destinations so the frames know where they are going. Routing is very important in this layer, and you can expect more than a few questions about routing on your exam, so we spent plenty of time on routable vs. non-routable protocols, the default gateway, subnets, and the difference between bridges, brouters, and routers.

Finally, you learned about the Transport Layer, which has the function of making sure these frames are reordered correctly and an acknowledgement is sent to the source computer confirming that the frame was received. You learned about connectionless and connection-oriented transport, which describes the two methods in which two computers transfer data. You discovered the need for name resolution, which makes it easier for us humans to use friendly names and not have to memorize IP or MAC addresses. Finally, you learned about the protocols within the Transport Layer, such as TCP, SPX, and NetBEUI. These protocols create and maintain the session between two computers while the data is being transferred.

In the next chapter, you will learn the TCP/IP protocol and everything you will need to know to ace any TCP/IP questions on your Network+ exam, but first read through the Two-Minute Drill and finish by taking the Self Test to see just how well you learned the information presented in this chapter.

TWO-MINUTE DRILL

- ❑ The Data Link Layer handles many issues for communicating on a simple network.

- ❑ The Data Link Layer is divided into two sublayers: *logical link control* (LLC) and *media access control* (MAC).). The LLC layer starts and maintains connections between devices. The MAC Layer enables multiple devices to share the media.

- ❑ Another important job of the Data Link Layer is *addressing*.

- ❑ The Data Link Layer manages *flow control* and *error correction* between devices in a simple network.

- ❑ The MAC address is used to communicate only on the local network.

- ❑ A bridge is a network connectivity device that connects two different networks and makes them appear to be one network.

- ❑ Most of the protocols that the 802 committee has defined reside in the Physical and Data Link Layers of the OSI Model.

- ❑ *Carrier Sense Multiple Access with Collision Detection (CSMA/CD)* keeps devices on the network from interfering with one another when trying to transmit; when they do interfere with each other, a *collision* has occurred.

- ❑ The exam leans quite heavily on Ethernet technology, due to the fact of Ethernet's dominance in the marketplace. Pay special attention to special characteristics of the various media types of Ethernet.

❑ It's pretty much a guarantee you will be asked about the IEEE standards, especially the three listed in this chapter. For example, know which 802 standard maps to Ethernet, and which IEEE standard number Token Ring maps to. Don't expect any questions on the less common IEEE standards; they have been omitted here for that very reason.

❑ The Network Layer manages addressing and delivering packets on a complex *internetwork*.

❑ The Network Layer also enables the option of specifying a *service address* on the destination computer.

❑ In order to operate on an internetwork, each network that participates must be assigned a *network ID*.

❑ Routing protocols are designed to separate a physical network into multiple virtual networks.

❑ A brouter is a hybrid of both a bridge and a router and has a connection to more than two networks.

❑ A protocol that is *routable* is a protocol that can have packets transferred across a router.

❑ *TCP/IP (Transmission Control Protocol/Internet Protocol)* is the most common protocol used today. TCP/IP, a routable protocol, is very robust and is commonly associated with UNIX systems.

❑ It's a guarantee you will have a question or two on your exam regarding the appropriate use of a bridge, brouter, or router. With the information we provided here, you should do just fine. Bear in mind that they will give you a long, complex scenario with tons of information to confuse you.

❑ When it comes to routing, there is a huge difference between the two types of routing: static and dynamic.

❑ The default gateway is specified on each computer, and is what initially sends the packet on its way to the first router.

❑ Without a properly configured subnet mask to determine which subnet your computer is on, you aren't going to be talking to anyone!

❑ Since TCP/IP is so popular in the real world, you can expect your exam to lean heavily towards configuring TCP/IP—more specifically, the IP address, subnet mask, and default gateway: the three essential TCP/IP configuration parameters.

❑ Make sure you have the IP address, subnet mask, and default gateway for your exam.

❑ The Transport Layer works hard to ensure reliable delivery of data to its destinations.

❑ Be prepared on your exam for a few questions about what each of the layers of the OSI model is responsible for. These can be quite tricky, so you have to know your stuff. Make sure you understand the order of the layers; I found that helps when trying to memorize each layer, because each layer begins where the other layer left off.

❑ Connection-oriented communication ensures reliable delivery of data from the sender to the receiver, without intervention required by the sender or receiver.

❑ Connectionless communication is a form of communication in which the destination computer does not notify the source when the information is received.

❑ Remember, connectionless protocols in TCP/IP use the UDP protocol. TFTP is one example of a connectionless oriented protocol that uses UDP.

❑ There are two potential types of names that have to be resolved when using a Windows-based computer: the NetBIOS name and the host name.

❑ Remember, a UNIX machine can use an LMHOSTS file to resolve machine names.

❑ I found it helpful to remember that the protocols that begin with I (IP and IPX) are located in the Network Layer.

SELF TEST

The following Self Test questions will help you measure your understanding of the material presented in this chapter. Read all the choices carefully, as there may be more than one correct answer. Choose all correct answers for each question.

1. Which network layer has the important job of addressing?

    A. Network Layer

    B. Physical Layer

    C. Data Link Layer

    D. Transport Layer

2. What happens when a server you are trying to reach is located on another segment of the network?

    A. You don't need the MAC address of this server.

    B. You still need the MAC address of this server.

    C. You need the MAC address of the nearest bridge.

    D. You need the MAC address of the nearest router.

3. Which of the following is not displayed when you issue the WINIPCFG command on a Windows 98 machine?

    A. MAC address

    B. Default gateway

    C. DNS server

    D. Subnet mask

4. What layer of the OSI model does a bridge function in?

    A. Data Link Layer

    B. Network Layer

    C. Transport Layer

    D. Physical Layer

5. Which IEEE 802 category uses *Carrier Sense Multiple Access with Collision Detection (CSMA/CD)* for access to the physical medium?

    A. 802

    B. 802.2

    C. 802.3

    D. 802.5

6. Which network topology does the IEEE 802 standard 802.5 map to?

    A. ARCnet

    B. Token Ring

    C. Ethernet

    D. Twisted Pair

7. In order to operate on an internetwork, each network that participates must be assigned what?

    A. An IP address

    B. A network address

    C. A IPX address

    D. A default gateway

8. What is a bridging protocol designed to do?

    A. Combine several networks into one virtual network

B. Combine several protocols into one distinct protocol

C. Separate a physical network into multiple virtual networks

D. Separate a number of physical networks into smaller subnetworks

9. When should you use a brouter?

A. When you are only using one protocol on the network

B. When you are using a routable and non-routable protocol

C. When you have to subnet the network with the TCP/IP protocol

D. When you need to make other network segments visible to the entire network with a non-routable protocol such as NetBEUI

10. You have just migrated your small company from Novell NetWare to Windows NT. Since you are very familiar with the IPX/SPX protocol, you decide to use this protocol on your Windows NT network and not TCP/IP. What limitations will you have as your company network grows larger and requires access to the Internet?

A. You will not be able to route the IPX/SPX protocol.

B. Your network will become saturated due to the large broadcast traffic associated with the IPX/SPX protocol.

C. You will have to eventually install TCP/IP for access to the Internet or use an Internet gateway.

D. None. IPX/SPX is a very logical choice for ease of configuration, speed, routing, and access to the Internet.

11. What will happen if we have a routing table with the same route to the same destination network?

A. You cannot have the same route listed twice.

B. You cannot have the same destination listed twice.

C. The route with the closest router will be used.

D. The route with the fewest number of hops will be used.

12. Which of the following is not true regarding a dynamic router?

A. It can choose the most efficient path to a destination network

B. It can communicate and share information with neighboring routers

C. It cannot be configured with static routes

D. It can communicate with other routers using RIP and OSPF.

13. What will happen if the default gateway is not specified on your computer and you are trying to reach another network?

A. The packet will ask every router if they know the path to reach the destination.

B. The packet will broadcast for the IP address of the nearest router.

C. The packet will be forwarded to the DNS server.

D. The packet will not be sent.

14. Which of the following is not true of the Transport Layer of the OSI model?

    A. It is responsible for error control.

    B. It is responsible for encrypting session information.

    C. It interacts with the Network Layer.

    D. It is responsible for segment sequencing.

15. Virtual circuits are examples of what?

    A. Mailslots

    B. Connectionless-oriented delivery

    C. Datagrams

    D. Connection-oriented delivery

16. What of the following is not a characteristic of connection-oriented communication?

    A. Datagrams

    B. Handshaking

    C. Virtual Circuits

    D. Sessions

17. Why is connection-oriented data delivery faster?

    A. Because a session between the two computers is maintained for the entire duration of the transfer of data.

    B. Because you can quickly resend data if it becomes lost or corrupt.

    C. Because the packets already know where they are going and don't have to find alternate routes.

    D. Connection-oriented data transfer is not quicker than connectionless-oriented data transfer.

18. Which is the best example of a mailslot?

    A. A two-way telephone conversation

    B. A bulletin board

    C. An answering machine

    D. A specific port on a computer used for sending and receiving mail

19. The LMHOSTS file is a static file to resolve what types of names?

    A. UNIX

    B. NetBEUI

    C. Host

    D. NetBIOS

20. What does DNS stand for?

    A. Directory Name Structure

    B. Domain Name System

    C. Domain Naming System

    D. Directory Naming System

21. What will happen on a Windows NT Workstation if a duplicate IP address is detected during the boot process?

    A. An error will be issued and you can continue, just don't forget to fix the problem before it gets worse.

    B. An error will be generated and TCP/IP will not be working on your machine.

    C. You will be prompted to change your IP address to avoid an address conflict.

D. Nothing will happen, at least until the first computer attempts to access the network.

22. Which of the following is a valid IPX internal network address?

    A. 00EE2210FF

    B. 112233ZZ

    C. ABACAB

    D. 1EF332001

23. Which two protocols are located in the Network Layer?

    A. IPX and NetBEUI

    B. IP and SPX

    C. IPX and SPX

    D. IP and IPX

24. In which layer of the OSI model is the SPX protocol present?

    A. Network

    B. Internet

    C. Data Link

    D. Transport

25. NetBEUI is considered a protocol at what layer of the OSI model?

    A. Network

    B. Data Link

    C. Transport

    D. Physical

4

TCP/IP
Fundamentals

CERTIFICATION OBJECTIVES

T he most popular protocol in use today is the TCP/IP protocol. The Internet and most company intranets are currently using the TCP/IP protocol because of its popularity, flexibility, compatibility, and capability to perform in both small and large network implementations. The TCP/IP protocol can connect a diverse range of hosts, from mainframes to palmtop computers. The popularity of this protocol makes it a likely culprit to appear many times throughout your Network+ exam. Although TCP/IP is the most commonly used protocol, it is not the easiest to configure, or even to understand. This chapter will give you a great understanding of the TCP/IP protocol, including the architecture, addressing issues, and configuration involved. The Network+ exam will test your knowledge of the protocol, but most importantly it will test your ability to configure the protocol on workstations. Real world experience, in addition to this chapter on TCP/IP, will ensure that you can easily answer any TCP/IP-related questions thrown at you on your exam.

CERTIFICATION OBJECTIVE 4.01

TCP/IP Fundamentals

TCP/IP stands for *Transmission Control Protocol (TCP) / Internet Protocol (IP)*. Don't let its name fool you; TCP/IP is a *suite* of protocols, not just the two represented in the name.

As you'll learn in this chapter, each protocol in the suite has a specific purpose and function. It is not important for the Network+ exam for you to understand the evolution of the TCP/IP protocol, so you will get the details of the TCP/IP protocol that you will likely be tested on.

IP Address

TCP/IP's unique addressing mechanism provides for over 4.2 billion addresses. Each host is referred to by its unique 32-bit address. These unique addresses are made up of network and host identification.

Four-Octet Address

The 32-bit IP address is broken into four octets that can be represented in decimal or binary format:

```
11010100 00001111 10000100 01110101 Binary Representation of Address
212.15.132.117 Dotted-Decimal Representation of the Address
```

Network ID

The IP address is further fragmented into the network ID and the host ID. The Internet is one large communication network that consists of multiple networks. Each machine uses part of the IP address to identify the network it belongs to and the rest of the address to identify its host or local computer address.

DHCP

Configuring IP addressing on a large TCP/IP-based network can be a nightmare, especially if users move machines from one subnet to another without consulting you. The Dynamic Host Configuration Protocol (DHCP) can help with configuration problems in these, as well as in other, situations.

Manual or Automatic Address Assignment

There are two methods of assigning an IP address to a client computer: An individual can configure the client manually, or a server computer can configure the client automatically.

Assigning Multiple Addresses

Suppose your boss tells you that 240 computers on your TCP/IP-based network were recently moved from one building to another and that you must reconfigure them all to work properly on the new subnet. This is a tedious process if you are using manual IP addressing. You will have to go to each machine and enter the correct IP address, subnet mask, and default gateway, along with the WINS and DNS addresses if you are using those services on your network.

Errors in Manual Entry

Not only is manually entering all of this information time consuming, it is also vulnerable to human error. If the same IP address is configured for two or more computer systems, then network problems will occur and they can be difficult to trace. Also, an error in entering any of the numbers for the IP address, subnet mask, or default gateway can lead to problems communicating through TCP/IP.

Looking back at the situation with the 240 computers, you are probably groaning, thinking of how long it will take you to accomplish this task manually. Fortunately, there is a better way to handle this situation: by using DHCP. DHCP, as described in RFC 1541, provides a dependable, flexible option to manual TCP/IP configuration.

The DHCP server can assign all items normally configured manually to the client system. At a minimum, a DHCP server provides the DHCP client with the IP address, subnet mask, and usually a default gateway.

IP Address

The DHCP server issues an IP address to each DHCP client system on the network. Each system connected to a TCP/IP-based network is identified by a unique IP address. The IP address consists of four 8-bit octets separated by periods. The IP address is normally shown in dotted-decimal notation: for example, 127.10.24.62.

Subnet Mask

The IP address actually consists of two parts: the network ID and the host ID. The subnet mask is used to identify the part of the IP address that is the network ID and the part that is the host ID. Subnet masks assign 1s to the network ID bits and 0s to the host ID bits of the IP address.

Default Gateway

A default gateway is required when the client system needs to communicate outside its own subnet. Normally, the default gateway is a router connected to the local subnet, which enables IP packets to be passed to other network segments. If the default gateway is not configured in the DHCP server, then it defaults to 0.0.0.0.

FROM THE FIELD

Understanding DHCP

You will find that nearly every site that uses Windows NT and TCP/IP in the real world will also use DHCP to automatically assign TCP/IP information to clients. This doesn't mean that you don't have to understand the fundamentals of TCP/IP. You still need to be knowledgeable with IP addressing, subnet masking, and default gateways for several reasons:

- Not every workstation or server on the network will be a DHCP client.

- You may have to manually configure TCP/IP on a workstation or server.

- You may have to evaluate the current DHCP settings and possibly modify them.

- You may have to configure TCP/IP on routers and hubs, which are not recommended DHCP clients.

- You may also have to coexist with a non-DHCP operating system or server, such as a mainframe or standalone server or workstation.

It is imperative that you understand DHCP, both from the client side and the server side. Configuring the clients with DHCP is a no-brainer, but setting up the DHCP server with an address scope, subnet mask, default gateway, and other entries, such as DNS and WINS, can be very challenging. One incorrect setting and you may affect the entire network.

If you are in charge of a DHCP rollout, make sure you spend the time planning to ensure that the settings are correct from the onset. Ask yourself the following questions:

- Is the scope of IP addresses large enough to support our network's future growth?

- Do we also assign settings for WINS and DNS servers in the process?

- Will we be assigning DHCP information to clients across a subnet or segment?

- Do we need a backup DHCP server?

Answering these questions *before* the rollout will minimize growing pains during the life of your DHCP network.

If you are a new network administrator at a site with DHCP already implemented, make sure you spend the time to take note of the following information:

- The range of IP addresses your company uses

FROM THE FIELD

- The subnet mask

- The default gateway

- Whether you are also assigning addresses for DNS or WINS servers

- Which servers and workstations are not DHCP clients

Understanding Dynamic Host Configuration Protocol means that you understand how a TCP/IP network functions, and you will be ready to troubleshoot any DHCP-related problem with ease, whether it be server-based or client-based.

—Cameron Brandon, MCSE+Internet, CNE, A+, Network+

Scope Options

A DHCP *scope* is a managerial arrangement that identifies the configuration parameters for all of the DHCP clients on a physical subnet. As previously mentioned, the IP address and subnet mask are required items that the DHCP scope must include. Another requirement in the scope is the *lease duration*. It specifies how long a DHCP client can use an IP address before it must renew it with the DHCP server. It can be set for an unlimited time period or for a predetermined time period. You have the option of configuring a scope to reserve a specific IP address for a DHCP client or even for a system on the network that is not DHCP-enabled.

In addition, there are many DHCP options that can be configured by an administrator. You will learn DHCP options in more detail later in this chapter.

DHCP Server and Client Requirements

To successfully use DHCP on your network, your servers and clients must be able to support the protocol. In this section, our discussion centers on Microsoft products. To see if another product supports DHCP, refer to the documentation that comes with the product.

Server

Several versions of Windows NT Server can act as a DHCP server on your network, including versions 3.5, 3.51, and 4.0. But is it necessary to set up each of the servers on your network to support DHCP? Actually, the answer depends on the layout and the needs of your network. If your network is small, then a single DHCP server may be adequate. The main item to consider if you have multiple subnets is that your routers must comply with RFC 1542 so that the broadcast for an IP address from the DHCP client can be received by the single DHCP server. It is wise to keep in mind that if your single DHCP server goes down and your DHCP clients cannot renew their lease, then the clients will cease to function when their leases expire! Of course, this is assuming that TCP/IP is the only protocol used on your network.

One of the benefits of using multiple DHCP servers is redundancy. Redundancy can prevent your network from going down. If you decide to use multiple DHCP servers, you should place them on different subnets to achieve a higher degree of fault tolerance in case one of the subnets becomes unavailable. You can manage multiple servers on different subnets with the DHCP Manager, the graphical utility used to maintain and configure DHCP servers.

Supported Clients

The following Microsoft operating systems can perform as DHCP clients on your network:

- Windows NT Server, versions 3.5, 3.51, and 4.0
- Windows NT Workstation, versions 3.5, 3.51, and 4.0
- Windows 95
- Windows for Workgroups, versions 3.11, 3.11a, and 3.11b, when using TCP/IP-32
- Microsoft Network Client, version 3.0 for MS-DOS
- Microsoft LAN Manager Client, version 2.2c for MS-DOS

Of course, DHCP clients are not limited to Microsoft operating systems. Any system that conforms to RFC 1541 can be a DHCP client.

DNS

One service that is used throughout the Internet is the Domain Name System (DNS) Service. All IP-based traffic requires the IP address of the destination. DNS is one method of resolving a host name to a given IP address. As you learned in Chapter 3, when you are using friendly host names, such as eng001.engineering.microsoft.com, you need to resolve those host names to IP addresses. You also learned in Chapter 3 that the static HOSTS file was used before the advent of DNS. DNS is much more robust and reliable. Every domain name, such as microsoft.com, could represent a DNS Service zone containing the local hosts and their associated IP addresses. DNS provides a segmented service of small local databases that can pass, along a hierarchical chain, any requests for host name resolution that cannot be resolved locally.

The hierarchical design of DNS is similar to a file tree structure. The root servers provide resolution to the same layer and the next below. Any further layers provide localized data zone authorities. In a private intranet, the domain servers can have any names. In the Internet, the root server names have been around a long time and are expanded all the time to allow for the exponential growth seen in the past few years.

exam
ⓦatch

DNS is not a dynamic service like WINS and DHCP are.

Domain Names in a Nutshell

A DNS host record consists of a name, record type, and an IP address. A set of these records can be associated with a grouping called a *domain*. The Fully Qualified Domain Name (FQDN) is the name of the host suffixed by a period, followed by the domain name.

An FQDN, such as engineering.microsoft.com, can be interpreted to mean there is a root server somewhere that manages the .com root zone. The next layer of zones is microsoft.com. The next layer represents a zone within microsoft.com, in this case engineering, which is the left-most part in the FQDN, representing the host. Note that the names are delimited by periods similar to the format in a file system. All the host names are grouped into smaller, locally managed databases. Each of these databases knows about the parent servers above them, called *root servers*.

All clients will automatically use DNS when they request a host name for an IP address that is not known locally. The host name request is passed to DNS, which will use all known resources to try to resolve the host name to an IP address. Optionally, you can configure the NT version of DNS to query any configured WINS servers. You will learn more about WINS in the next section.

Figure 4-1 shows the three basic levels of DNS. The root servers are named A, B, C, etc. The top-level domains are .com, .edu, .gov, and there are many more.

The second level, or layer, represents the distributed DNS servers for each zone. Each zone maintains its own set of local host records. These are just the registered host records and may or may not be separate physical machines. These records are maintained on the DNS server that manages the microsoft.com zone.

DNS Server Location

The DNS server and the domain are not necessarily on one machine. A DNS server may support multiple domains or zones. The DNS hierarchy is just the structure of how the data is supported. The actual DNS server machine is not indicated within the DNS hierarchy. Any machine could provide this DNS domain service for one or more zones.

FIGURE 4-1

Small selected DNS hierarchical structure from the Internet

DNS Search Pattern

This hierarchical design for DNS provides an indexed search pattern that does not require looking at every host record. Each domain or zone database has records that point to at least the named root server and possibly other root servers. The local server provides an indexed search of its cached records or its database of records and passes the request up the hierarchy only if needed.

Internet Domain Name Server Hierarchies

Root domains represent the upper-indexed pointers to other DNS servers. These root domains represent the highest level of the DNS hierarchy and are the first to be consulted in the name resolution process. For example, if you are trying to connect to microsoft.com, the .com root domain DNS server will check its database for an entry for microsoft. Once the entry is found, the root domain server will pass your request to the microsoft.com DNS server.

The following is a description of the most popular DNS root domains found on the Internet:

- **.com** This is the commercial organizations group and is by far the largest group. Almost everyone wants to be here because it is the first default extension for all commercial organizations such as DEC, SUN, IBM, and Microsoft.

- **.org** This is for non-commercial organizations.

- **.net** This is for networking organizations such as island.net and nfs.net, and Internet Service Providers such as netzero.net.

- **.mil** This is for military organizations such as army.mil and navy.mil.

- **.gov** This is for the government offices of the U.S. only.

- **.edu** This is for educational organizations.

COUNTRIES' DOMAIN NAMES The Internet started in the U.S. and as such, the organizations normally are located in this country. For the rest of the world, country servers are based on a two-letter shortcut. Every country has one, including the U.S. Here are a few of the most common country domain names:

- .ca   Canada
- .ie   Ireland
- .uk   United Kingdom
- .us   Unites States

Top-Level Domain Servers

The root servers are used to route the request to the next correct server. The root server for Canada, .ca, has another root server or subdomain for each province. A provincial server may or may not have further nested subdomain servers, as required. In other countries, the root servers may have city-based nested subdomains.

Within the .us and .ca root servers are another set of servers for each state/province/region and from there, possibly many cities. For example, dallas.tx.us for Dallas, Texas, United States, and vancouver.bc.ca for Vancouver, British Columbia, Canada. The host names are appended to these domain names. For example, a host called info in the city of Vancouver in British Columbia, Canada could be reached with info.vancouver.bc.ca or www.vancouver.bc.ca. Normally, DNS names are displayed in lowercase. However, most DNS Services are not case sensitive.

Root Servers

There are many root servers, but the .com server is by far the largest and most overloaded. The other root servers offer local access with faster response for local users and make it easier to get a domain name that is not already used by another DNS service.

The root servers provide addresses to the domain servers associated with that root. For example, the .com root server maintains IP address pointer records for all the *name*.com DNS servers. In turn, each of these *name*.com domains contains records for all of their local machines only. The root DNS database is maintained locally by a specific authority.

The .com root server knows the .edu, .mil, and all the other root server addresses. When a host name request comes in to a root server, it simply looks at the root portion of the name and passes the name off to this root server. This second root server then looks up the domain name in its database and sends the packet on to that specific domain name service. This specific domain name then provides an answer, or an error if nothing is found.

Resolving Host and Domain Names

When a program requests a host by a single name, such as sunsite, the network protocol provides a sequence of steps to resolve the name. If the client is DNS-aware, then the DNS Service request appends the local domain name to the end of the requested host name and tries to resolve this within its database. If this first domain name fails and there are other suffix names configured within DNS, then the name is appended to each of them successively and tried within the specified DNS Service again.

If a Fully Qualified Domain Name (FQDN) is supplied, then the DNS Service is queried directly first.

Primary DNS Server

The primary DNS server for arg.com first tries to resolve the request locally by checking its own records. The DNS server may have more than one zone database. If so, the TCP/IP protocol properties for alternate suffix search names must reflect these alternate domain names.

Some specialized servers are configured to maintain a cache of previous hits so that common requests may not have to repeat the longer full-request process.

Search DNS Servers

If the local DNS Service cannot provide an address resolution for an FQDN, then it passes the request "up the ladder" to the .com server, which looks in its local databases. If it does not find the IP address for the host, it passes the record on to the root server of the remote host name.

Return to Resolver

The .edu server passes the request on to the unc.edu DNS zone server, which hopefully has the IP address. The found IP address then passes back through the same chain to the original host. At this point, the original host is finally able to send packets directly to the remote host.

DNS Files

All DNS information that is maintained in the registry can also be maintained in text file format, if you select Update Data Files from the DNS Menu of DNS Manager. If you are using files from a UNIX BIND version of DNS, you can force the DNS server to not read the registry and just use the files ported over from UNIX. Be aware that the UNIX BIND files may contain some commands that NT DNS will not understand.

The files are located in

%systemroot%\system32\DNS

WINS

The Windows Internet Naming Service (WINS) provides tools that enhance Windows NT to manage the NetBIOS names of servers and workstations in a TCP/IP networking environment. In order to understand WINS, it is necessary to understand the precursor to it, NetBIOS. NetBIOS names are 16 characters in length. The NetBIOS name space is flat, meaning that names may be used only once within a network. These names are registered dynamically when computers boot, services start, or users log on. NetBIOS names can be registered as unique or as group names. All Windows NT network commands, such as Explorer, use NetBIOS names to access services.

Unique names have one address associated with a name. Group names have more than one address mapped to a name. NetBIOS is responsible for establishing logical names on the network, establishing sessions between two logical names on the network, and supporting reliable data transfer between computers that have established a session.

Before WINS, the LMHOSTS file was used to assist with remote NetBIOS name resolution. The LMHOSTS file is a static file that maps NetBIOS names to IP addresses. This is similar to the HOSTS file in functionality; the only difference is that the HOSTS file is used for mapping host names to IP addresses.

If you are at a site that currently uses a WINS server, but has used an LMHOSTS file in the past, make sure the LMHOSTS file doesn't contain entries that are not updated. Some sites use the LMHOSTS file as a backup to WINS, but forget to update the LMHOSTS file. I spent hours with another technician troubleshooting one computer that wouldn't connect to an application server. We finally figured out that the LMHOSTS file was still active with an incorrect entry for that server.

WINS Features

WINS includes many features that provide simpler networking. By enabling computers to register NetBIOS names in one location, the maintenance and management become easier. A WINS Service eliminates the need for many network broadcasts, therefore reducing network usage. This is accomplished by using directed, or point-to-point, transmissions for name resolution. WINS is dynamic, and is updated when machines are started or stopped, or by replication with other WINS Services. When a name is registered, it will be reserved for that one computer, further simplifying naming schemes. Each computer will always have its own unique name.

Requirements for WINS

The WINS Service is any Windows NT server on a TCP/IP network. This server should also have a static IP address, not one obtained dynamically from a Dynamic Host Configuration Protocol (DHCP) server. The WINS Service maintains a database of mappings for IP addresses to NetBIOS names. When a WINS Client requests an IP address, the WINS Service will check its database and return the address to the client. It is not required, but a secondary WINS Service can be implemented for larger networks.

Dynamic Registration

WINS provides a distributed database for registering and querying dynamic NetBIOS names to IP address mappings in a routed network environment. When a computer in a WINS-enabled network is started, it automatically registers all its NetBIOS names with the WINS Server. If the computer's IP address is changed, the WINS Server knows immediately. This is WINS' strength: its ability to keep an accurate IP mapping database in an ever-changing network environment. It is the best choice for NetBIOS name resolution in a routed network because it is designed to solve the problems that occur with name resolution.

Table 4-1 will help you to understand the differences between WINS and DNS.

HOSTS Files

In early TCP/IP networks, all known host names and their associated IP addresses were stored in a simple text file called *HOSTS*. In most UNIX installations, the HOSTS file is located in the /etc directory and is also commonly referred to as /etc/HOSTS.

The HOSTS file contained one line for each IP address and at least one associated name. The HOSTS file design allowed for multiple names for the same IP address, all on one line as shown in the following HOSTS file example:

```
206.197.150.11 bigsun BIGSUN ftp www
206.197.150.51 host51 HOST51 nevermore
206.197.150.52 host52 HOST52 icedearth
206.197.150.53 host53 HOST53 justinharvey
206.197.150.54 host54 HOST54 sanctuary
206.197.150.55 host55 HOST55 warrel
```

TABLE 4-1   The Differences Between WINS and DNS

Feature	WINS	DNS
Purpose	Resolves NetBIOS names to IP addresses	Resolves host names to IP addresses
Names	Flat in structure and limited to 15 characters	Hierarchical structure and limited to 255 characters
Name Registration	Dynamic and happens automatically	Static and must be done manually
Replication	Replicates changes	Replicates whole database

The HOSTS file provides a static lookup of a host name for the associated IP address. Notice also that the HOSTS file is flexible, in that multiple names can be associated with one IP address. In the first line of the HOSTS file example there are four names associated with the one IP address on the left. This enables a network user the option of using bigsun, BIGSUN, ftp, or www as reference host names to reach the machine with the IP address 206.197.150.11.

To illustrate the design and functionality of DNS, let's look at the largest public network in the world: the Internet.

Sharing the HOSTS File

Each isolated TCP/IP network has to maintain its own HOSTS file and make it available, by some copy method, to every other host on the network. In a small network of less than a hundred, this can be managed centrally by paper and pencil. This design becomes cumbersome if the network is larger than a few hundred. You could not change a host name or IP address without updating the HOSTS file on every other host in the network.

Limitation of HOSTS File

As networks became more and more complex, not only topologically and geographically, there was a corresponding need to simplify name resolution. In small offices, a host name might reflect the name of the user; the server may reflect the name of the company. But when there are hundreds of servers, spread out in many office locations, and thousands of users pressing the need for central management, the hosts file system reveals its limitations.

Internet Growth

As the Internet grew, every time a host was added, every other machine had to add that name to its host file. When this became too cumbersome, the host files were trimmed down to directly reachable hosts. These hosts would then pass the requests on, if they were not destined locally, to the remote hosts of all the other networks that could possibly get the packet to the eventual host. This was like a drop on water, creating a wave of packets heading out in all directions from the server. Because some hosts knew about others who knew about them, the packets sometimes ended up in a circle, routing. This routing loop was controlled with a Time To Live (TTL) value included in each packet.

The Main Protocols of the TCP/IP Suite

Contained within the TCP/IP model are several protocols that direct how computers connect and communicate using TCP/IP. Even though the protocol suite is called TCP/IP, many other protocols are available besides the TCP and IP protocols.

TCP

Transmission Control Protocol (TCP) is one of the protocols that the TCP/IP suite is named for. TCP provides a reliable, connection-based delivery service. Successful delivery of packets is guaranteed by the TCP protocol. It uses a checksum to ensure that data is sequenced correctly. If a TCP packet is lost or corrupted during transmission, TCP resends a good packet. The reliability of TCP is necessary for critical services, such as electronic mail. However, the reliability does not come cheaply, because TCP headers have additional overhead added to them. The overhead is necessary to guarantee successful delivery of the data. Another factor to remember about TCP is that the protocol requires the recipient to acknowledge the successful receipt of data. Of course, all the acknowledgments, known as ACKs, generate additional traffic on the network, which causes a reduction in the amount of data that is passed for a given time frame.

UDP

User Datagram Protocol (UDP) offers a connectionless datagram service that is an unreliable "best effort" delivery. UDP does not guarantee the arrival of datagrams, nor does it promise that the delivered packets are in the correct sequence. Applications that don't require an acknowledgment of receipt of data use UDP.

ICMP

Internet Control Message Protocol (ICMP) enables systems on a TCP/IP network to share status and error information. You can use the status information to detect network trouble. ICMP messages are encapsulated within IP datagrams, so they may be routed throughout an internetwork. Two of the most common usages of ICMP messages are *ping* and *tracert.*

You can use ping to send *ICMP Echo Requests* to an IP address and wait for ICMP Echo Responses. Ping reports the time interval between sending the request and receiving the response. With ping you can determine whether a particular IP system on your network is functioning correctly. There are many different options that can be used with the ping utility.

Tracert traces the path taken to a particular host. It can be very useful when troubleshooting internetworks. Tracert sends ICMP echo requests to an IP address while it increments the TTL field in the IP header by a count of one after starting at one and then analyzing the ICMP errors that get returned. Each succeeding echo request should get one further into the network before the TTL field reaches 0 and an *ICMP Time Exceeded* error is returned by the router attempting to forward it.

ARP

ARP is used to provide IP-address-to-physical-address resolution for IP packets. To accomplish this feat, ARP sends out a broadcast message with an *ARP request packet* in it that contains the IP address of the system it is trying to find. All systems on the local network detect the broadcast message and the system that owns the IP address ARP is looking for replies by sending its physical address to the originating system in an *ARP reply packet.* The physical/IP address combo is then stored in the ARP cache of the originating system for future use.

All systems maintain an ARP cache that includes their own IP-address-to-physical-address mapping. The ARP cache is always checked for an IP-address-to-physical-address mapping before initiating a broadcast.

You can see the contents of your ARP cache by using the ARP utility you learned in Chapter 3.

SMTP

Simple Mail Transfer Protocol (SMTP) is a protocol used to send and receive mail over the Internet. In the days of mainframes and terminals, workstations had continuous connections to the mainframe; therefore, electronic mail could be sent and received with great assurance. Because most computers are stand-alone workstations, and no longer terminal based, SMTP cannot provide a high degree of reliability between the non-permanent connections.

POP3

Post Office Protocol (POP) was designed to overcome the problem encountered with SMTP in which workstations were not confined to permanent terminal-based connections to a mainframe. A POP3 mail server holds the mail in a maildrop until the workstation is ready to receive the mail. When you set up a mail account with your Internet Service Provider (ISP), your ISP gives you the name of the POP3 server to which you can log in, with the correct username and password, to obtain your mail. (POP is on its third iteration, so now it's POP3.)

SNMP

Simple Network Management Protocol (SNMP) is an Internet standard that provides a simple method for remotely managing virtually any network device. A network device could be a network card in a server, a program or service running on a server, or a standalone network device such as a hub or router.

The SNMP standard defines a two-tiered approach to network device management: a central *management system* and the *management information base* (MIB) located on the managed device. The management system can monitor one or many MIBs, allowing for centralized management of a network. From a management system you can see valuable performance and operation statistics from network devices, enabling you to diagnose network health without leaving your office.

The goal for a management system is to provide centralized network management. Any computer running SNMP management software is referred to as a management system. For a management system to be able to perform centralized network management, it must be able to collect and analyze many things, including the following:

- Network protocol identification and statistics
- Dynamic identification of computers attached to the network (referred to as *discovery*)
- Hardware and software configuration data
- Computer performance and usage statistics
- Computer event and error messages
- Program and application usage statistics

FTP

File Transfer Protocol (FTP) is a TCP/IP utility that exists solely to copy files from one computer to another. Like Telnet and ping, FTP can establish a connection to a remote computer using either the host name or IP address, and must resolve host names to IP addresses to establish communication with the remote computer. As you read in Chapter 1, Windows NT includes an FTP server in its Internet Information Services (IIS) software. Windows NT and Windows 95 computers each include a command-line FTP client with their TCP/IP protocol software. Although it is not widely known, the Windows FTP client supports scripting, which enables users to automate repetitive FTP tasks.

There are a number of third-party graphical user interface (GUI) FTP clients for all versions of Windows computers. If you use FTP a lot, a GUI FTP client may save you a lot of time and frustration.

IP

IP is the other protocol that the suite is named for. It is a vital link in the suite because all information that is sent using the TCP/IP protocol suite must use it.

IP provides packet delivery for all other protocols within the suite. It is a connectionless delivery system that makes a "best-effort" attempt to deliver the packets to the correct destination. IP does not guarantee delivery, nor does it promise that the IP packets will be received in the order they were sent.
IP does use a checksum, but it confirms only the integrity of the IP header. Confirmation of the integrity of data contained within an IP packet can be accomplished only through higher level protocols.

Now that you have seen some of the more confusing aspects of TCP/IP, here is a quick reference of possible scenario questions involving TCP/IP protocols and services, and the appropriate answer:

QUESTIONS AND ANSWERS

I need to send e-mail from one server to another.	Use SMTP. The key to using SMTP is when servers are passing mail back and forth to each other, not involving a client.
I need to download e-mail from my mail server.	Use POP3. The POP3 protocol was designed to store electronic messages for later retrieval by e-mail clients.
I need to resolve a hardware address.	Use ARP. Whenever you see hardware address and resolve in the same question, you are most likely talking about the Address Resolution Protocol (ARP).
I need to resolve a machine name.	Use LMHOSTS or WINS. These services are designed to resolve NetBIOS (machine) names to IP addresses. Note that a UNIX host uses the LMHOSTS file, not the WINS service.
I need to resolve a host name.	Use HOSTS or DNS. These services are designed to resolve host names to IP addresses. Remember that the HOSTS file is located on each workstation and server, and the DNS service provides a central HOSTS file located on a server.
I need a connectionless-oriented protocol.	Use IP or UDP. UDP and IP are connectionless protocols, meaning they don't establish connections between two computers. These protocols don't guarantee data will arrive at all, but they are very fast.
I need a connection-oriented protocol.	Use TCP. This protocol establishes a connection between the sending and receiving computer. Although slower than UDP, it can guarantee that data will arrive.

CERTIFICATION OBJECTIVE 4.02

TCP/IP Addressing

Many of the questions on the Network+ exam regarding TCP/IP will cover configuring TCP/IP, the architecture of TCP/IP, and TCP/IP addressing, which you learn in this section. The following TCP/IP addressing topics are covered here:

- The IP address
- The address classes
- Subnetting and the subnet Mask

You learned a lot about the IP address in this chapter and in Chapter 3, so here we will focus on the address classes and the subnet mask.

A, B, and C Classes of IP Addresses and Their Default Subnet Masks

A subnet mask is used to determine which part of the IP address is used for the network ID and which part is for the host ID. There are two required parameters you must supply to initialize TCP/IP:

- **IP address** 4-octet address
- **Subnet mask** 4-octet value

Every IP address belongs to a distinct class. The Internet community defined these classes to accommodate networks of various sizes. The class that the IP address belongs to initially determines the network ID and host ID portions of the address. The classes range from Class A to Class E; however, Microsoft TCP/IP supports only Class A, B, and C addresses assigned to hosts. In this section you will learn each class of addresses.

As you just learned, the IP addressing scheme can build fairly large networks. The following Table lists the three types of network addresses, called network classes, that are assigned to a company or an organization.

Network Class	Number of Hosts
Class A	Approximately 16,000,000
Class B	Approximately 65,000
Class C	254

Class A

As you can see in the preceding table, Class A addresses are assigned to networks with a very large number of hosts. The next table illustrates the most important features of a Class A address, which you need to memorize for the exam.

Class A Range	Number of Class A Networks	Default Subnet Mask
Class A addresses range from 1.0.0.0 to 126.0.0.0.	The Class A range has the possibility of 126 networks, with each network having the capability of 16,777,214 unique hosts when using the default subnet mask.	The default subnet mask for a Class A network is 255.0.0.0 or in binary representation 11111111 00000000 00000000 00000000.

Managing a Class A Network Address

When addressing classes first came about, companies that received a Class A address had over 16 million host addresses at their disposal. With only 126 allocated Class A networks, there was a very large waste of prime host addresses.

This is where subnetting comes in. Breaking down one Class A network address into multiple subnetworks makes for better use of the available IP address pool.

Class B

Class B addresses are assigned to medium-sized networks. The following table illustrates the most important features of a Class B address, which you need to memorize for the exam.

Class B Range	Number of Class B Networks	Default Subnet Mask
Class B addresses range from 128.0.0.0 to 191.255.0.0.	The Class B range has the possibility of 16,384 networks, with each network having the capability of 65,534 unique hosts when using the default subnet mask.	The default subnet mask for a Class B network is 255.255.0.0 or in binary representation 11111111 11111111 00000000 00000000.

Class C

Class C addresses are usually assigned to small Local Area Networks (LANs) and comprise most of the Internet and intranet sites available. Even the Class C addresses are quickly being used up, due to the overwhelming popularity of the Internet. The next table illustrates the most important features of a Class C address, which you need to memorize for the exam.

Class C Ranges	Number of Class C Networks	Default Subnet Mask
Class C addresses range from 192.0.1.0 to 223.255.255.0.	The Class C range has the possibility of 2,097,152 networks, with each network having the capability of 254 unique hosts when using the default subnet mask.	The default subnet mask for a Class C network is 255.255.255.0 or in binary representation 11111111 11111111 11111111 00000000.

Class D

Class D addresses are used for multicasting to a number of different hosts. Data is passed to one, two, three, or more users on a network. Only those hosts registered for the multicast address will receive the data.

Class D Ranges

Class D addresses range from 224.0.0.0 to 239.255.255.255. Class D has the potential for 268,435,456 unique multicast groups.

Broadcast Examples

Currently, Class D addresses are used mainly for experimentation. Membership in an IP multicast group is dynamic. A host can join or leave a group at any time. You may see Class D addressing used for audio news multicasting, video presentations, or a music multicast.

Class E

Class E is an experimental address block that is reserved for future use.

Class E Ranges

Class E addresses range from 240.0.0.0 to 247.255.255.255.

exam
ⓌatchWatch

It's a guarantee you will see a question or two on the address classes. Make sure you know the ranges for each address class, as well as the default subnet mask for each class.

Special Internet Addresses

Now you need to learn some special Internet addresses. You may wonder why a Class C address can have only 254 hosts and not 256 as it would seem, since an 8-bit number can have 256 different values. The reason for this is that two addresses are lost from the available host pool. The first is an address that has all 0s in the host ID, which signifies "this host" and is normally used in a BOOTP process when a host doesn't yet know its IP address. The second is an address that has all 1s in the host ID, which signifies a broadcast address. So, for example, in the Class C network 200.158.157.x, the addresses 200.158.157.0 and 200.158.157.255 are not available to hosts, which reduces the available number from 256 to 254.

A network ID that is all 1s is used for limited broadcasts. A network ID that is all 0s signifies "this network." The number of Class A networks is reduced by one for this situation.

Loopback Addresses

Network IDs cannot start with 127 because this address is reserved for loopback and is used mainly for testing TCP/IP and internal loopback functions on the local system. If a program uses the loopback address as a destination, then the protocol software in the system returns the data without sending traffic across the network. 127 is technically a Class A address because the high-order bit has a value of 0. But remember that 127 is reserved and is not in use for live networks.

Port Numbers (HTTP, FTP, SMTP)

When you are using the TCP/IP protocol, it is very common to hear the term *port*. A TCP/IP port is what an application or process uses when communicating between a client and server computer. *Port numbers*, often called "well-known ports" are preassigned TCP/IP port numbers on the server that do not change (although they can be changed), and are preassigned so they can expect traffic on a corresponding port relating to the service that is using that port. For example, FTP uses two ports: 20 and 21. The server has the preassigned ports of 20 and 21 set aside for FTP traffic, and nothing else. Clients, however, do not have to use the preassigned well-known port numbers when they are connecting to a server with an application or process; clients can use any dynamically assigned port to connect to the server. It's sort of like a telephone. You (the client) can pick up a telephone anywhere in the world and dial your friend's number (the server), and they will pick up the phone.

Table 4-2 is a list of well-known port numbers that remain constant on all TCP/IP-based operating systems.

exam
ⓦatch

You don't have to memorize the entire table for the exam. The most popular, and therefore most likely, exam choices to remember are the FTP ports (20 and 21), SMTP port (25), and HTTP port (80).

TABLE 4-2	Port number	Process	Description
	20	FTP-DATA	File Transfer Protocol—Data
Well-known TCP/IP Port Numbers	21	FTP	File Transfer Protocol—Control
	23	TELNET	Telnet
	25	SMTP	Simple Mail Transfer Protocol
	69	TFTP	Trivial File Transfer Protocol
	70	GOPHER	Gopher
	80	HTTP	HTTP
	110	POP3	Post Office Protocol, version 3

CERTIFICATION OBJECTIVE 4.03

TCP/IP Configuration Concepts

Configuring TCP/IP on a workstation is a topic that will surely make its way on to your Network+ exam. Now that you have a good understanding of the main TCP/IP properties that must be configured for each workstation, we can go about configuring these workstations. The following sections involve configuring TCP/IP on the most popular client operating systems: Windows 95/98 and Windows NT Workstation.

Configuration Parameters for a Workstation

As we have indicated before, you have two options for configuring a workstation: manually, or through the use of a DHCP server. Configuring the DHCP server is beyond the scope of the Network+ exam, so we will exclude coverage of the server-side of DHCP configuration and focus more on manually configuring each workstation. Although you are more likely to encounter a TCP/IP network using DHCP for the workstations at a company, the servers will not be DHCP clients and will require manual configuration. Manually configuring TCP/IP properties for a Windows NT server is identical to configuring Windows NT workstation properties. In addition, the knowledge gained here will benefit you when you will be the administrator that must install and configure the DHCP scope of IP addresses, and the additional TCP/IP settings, such as the default gateway and address of the WINS servers.

IP Address and Subnet Mask

The single most important piece of information required for a TCP/IP-based workstation to operate is the IP address. This address must be unique on the network. If you are using DHCP to assign the workstation's IP address, the DHCP server will assign the workstation an IP address that is not in use. When you are manually assigning an IP address to a workstation, it is imperative that you do not duplicate IP addresses on the network. This can be avoided by using a spreadsheet that contains workstation and server names and the corresponding IP addresses. This spreadsheet should also contain all static IP address, such as routers and printers, and should specify which range of IP addresses are in the DHCP scope of addresses, and which addresses are currently not being used. You must update this information frequently.

The second most important piece of information is the subnet mask. With an improperly configured subnet mask, you won't be communicating with anyone on a TCP/IP-based network. As you learned earlier, the subnet mask performs double duty by determining the host ID and network ID from the IP address.

exam
ⓦatch

Expect more than a few questions on your exam regarding TCP/IP, especially the IP address and subnet mask. These two are the most important settings of any TCP/IP implementation and are guaranteed to find their way into your Network+ exam.

In Windows 95, 98, and NT, you can specify an IP address and subnet mask, or specify the use of a DHCP Service. From the Control Panel, double-click the Network applet, click the Properties button, and select

TCP/IP Protocol. On the TCP/IP Properties dialog box, click the IP Address tab to bring it to the front. Select the Specify an IP address option button, as shown in Figure 4-2, to manually assign an IP address and subnet mask.

If you use DHCP, simply select the Obtain an IP address automatically option button.

DNS

To configure a client to use DNS, you need to configure your TCP/IP protocol settings to point to the DNS Service and to indicate the domain name that this DNS Service provides.

From the Control Panel, double-click the Network applet, click the Properties button, and select TCP/IP Protocol. On the Microsoft TCP/IP Properties dialog box, click the DNS tab to bring it to the front. If you are a client only of the DNS service, you need to enter the Internet domain name and the IP address of the DNS service. Click in the Domain text box and enter your domain name, for example, arg.com, as shown in Figure 4-3.

FIGURE 4-2

Use the IP Address page of the TCP/IP Properties dialog box to specify DHCP or manually assign an IP address and subnet mask

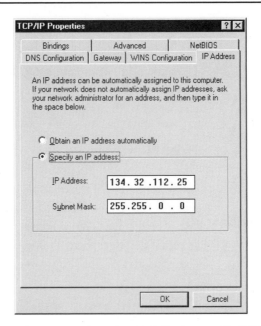

FIGURE 4-3

Use the DNS page on the TCP/IP Properties dialog box to configure a client to use DNS

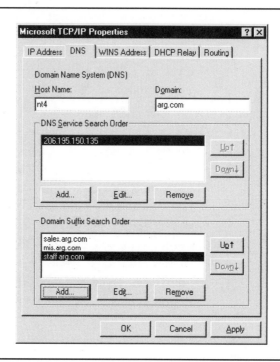

Click the Add button and enter the IP address of this service in the DNS Service Search Order box. These are the minimum requirements to be a client of a DNS Service.

Host Name

By default, your DNS host name on a Windows-based machine is your computer name. In the example in Figure 4-3 the host name is nt4. You can override this default by specifying a new host name in the Host Name text box. There is a difference between the host name and the NetBIOS name, so please don't get them confused. You will learn how to change your computer name (NetBIOS name) later in this chapter.

DNS Client Setup with Secondary Server

A secondary DNS server is a backup server with a copy of the zone information from the master server. If there are one or more secondary

DNS servers for this domain, you need to enter one or more additional IP addresses in the DNS Service Search Order box (the same way you did for the primary DNS Service IP address). Press the Add button within this box, and then add the IP address of the secondary DNS server.

The DNS Service Search Order is a fail-over list, not an additional location. Only if the first one fails to respond after a nominal timeout period, is the next DNS Service list tried with the same request, and so on. These secondary servers must have a valid domain zone file for this to work.

For the client, you need to add the domain name and IP address for the server that is running the DNS Service.

In the example in Figure 4-3, the arg.com domain is being managed. The IP address of the server managing arg.com is 206.195.150.135, the same IP address as the current host.

If your DNS Service will be splitting up the domain information into subdomains, such as sales.arg.com, mis.arg.com, and staff.arg.com, then you need to add these additional domain suffixes to this list. The request for a single host name with no domain qualification, no periods in the name, will iterate through the main domain suffix and then try each of these additional suffixes to try to resolve the name to an IP address.

To add each additional domain suffix to the list, click the Add button in the Domain Suffix Search Order box on the DNS page. Enter each path with the full domain name structure. No leading period is required; the period will be supplied when the suffix is appended after the host name.

exam
ⓦatch

There are way too many details associated with configuring a DNS server, so don't expect detailed questions in this area. Focusing on configuring client workstations to use DNS is much more important.

Default Gateway

The default gateway is needed only for systems that are part of an internetwork. Data packets with a destination IP address not on the local subnet, nor elsewhere in the route table, are automatically forwarded to the default gateway. The default gateway is normally a computer system or router connected to the local subnet and other networks that knows the network IDs for other networks in the internetwork and the best path to reach them. Because the default gateway knows the network IDs of the other networks in the internetwork, it can forward the data packet to other gateways until the packet is ultimately delivered to a gateway connected to the intended destination. However, if the default gateway becomes unavailable, the system cannot communicate outside its own subnet.

Multiple Gateways

If the default gateway becomes unavailable, data packets cannot reach their destination. Multiple gateways can be used to prevent this from happening. When a system is configured with multiple gateways, data transmission problems result in the system trying to use the other configured gateways, enabling internetworking communications capabilities to continue uninterrupted.

To configure the default gateway for a client, click the Gateway tab on the TCP/IP Properties dialog box. Figure 4-4 illustrates configuring the default gateway for a Windows 98 machine.

FIGURE 4-4

Use the Gateway page on the TCP/IP Properties dialog box to configure the default gateway for a client

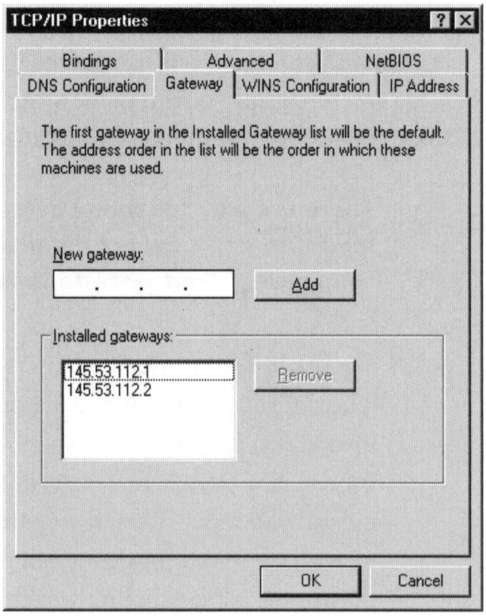

WINS

A WINS client is the machine that requests a NetBIOS mapping. This computer can use one of several operating systems. In addition to an acceptable operating system, a WINS client must also be configured with the address of the WINS Service. On computers running Windows 95 or Windows NT, this is entered on the WINS Address page on the Microsoft TCP/IP Properties dialog box. (From the Control Panel, double-click the Network applet, click the Properties button, and select TCP/IP Protocol. Then click the WINS Address tab to bring it to the front.) In Windows 98, the WINS information is entered on the WINS Configuration page, as shown in Figure 4-5.

The address of the WINS Service may be obtained dynamically from a DHCP server. In Windows 98, you can specify this by selecting the Use DHCP for WINS Resolution option button. This sends the address of the

Use the WINS Configuration page to configure the WINS Service on a Windows 98 machine

WINS server down to the DHCP client, along with the vital TCP/IP information, such as the IP address, subnet mask, and default gateway.

Computer Name

The computer name, or NetBIOS name, is the name of the machine that you specified during the installation of the Windows-based operating system. NetBIOS names are used only with Windows-based machines. The NetBIOS name is specified in the Control Panel Network applet, but not on the TCP/IP Properties dialog box. On a Windows 98 machine, click on the Identification tab on the Network dialog box to change the NetBIOS name, as illustrated in Figure 4-6.

Having the same computer name and DNS host name eliminates confusion. Changing the NetBIOS name won't override your host name if you have manually specified one.

FIGURE 4-6

Use the Identification page to specify the NetBIOS name for the computer

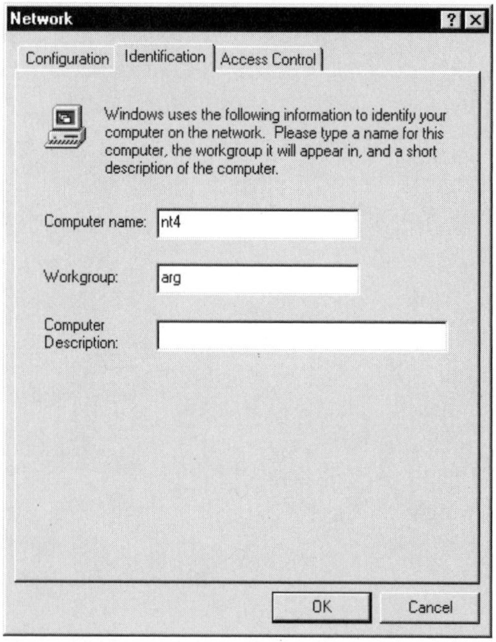

CERTIFICATION SUMMARY

In this chapter you learned the fundamentals of the TCP/IP protocol and what makes this protocol so common in the networking market today. The following list sums up what you learned about TCP/IP:

■ The IP address and subnet mask are the most important configuration settings and must be specified correctly in order to communicate on the TCP/IP-based network. Next in importance is the default gateway that specifies where to route packets if you are communicating outside the local network.

■ Dynamic Host Configuration Protocol (DHCP) automatically configures a workstation with the correct TCP/IP settings, relieving the burden of manually configuring every workstation.

■ Domain Name System (DNS) is essential for Internet-based machines and company intranets that use the DNS Service for host name resolution. You learned the host name, domain name, resolution, and Internet domain name server hierarchies.

■ The Windows Internet Naming System (WINS) Service, which ironically has little to do with the Internet as the name implies, enables workstations to resolve NetBIOS names to IP addresses, rather than using a static LMHOSTS file on each machine.

■ HOSTS files, the predecessor to the DNS Service, is a means of host name resolution. HOSTS files are difficult to maintain in medium-to large-sized networks. This is where DNS is much more common; however, DNS is still not dynamic at this time.

■ TCP/IP is a suite of protocols, the most popular being TCP, UDP, IP, and ARP. (Your Network+ exam will definitely have a couple questions on some of these TCP/IP protocol suite members.)

■ TCP/IP addressing involves a strong knowledge of the IP address, subnet mask, network classes, and the special reserved addresses. (Each network class should be memorized for the exam.)

■ The most important portion of TCP/IP as it relates to your Network+ exam is the TCP/IP Configuration Concepts. You will need these to configure workstations with TCP/IP. They include the IP address, subnet mask, DHCP, DNS, WINS, the Default Gateway, host name, and NetBIOS name.

With a strong understanding of the material presented in this chapter, you will have no problems with any TCP/IP-related questions on your exam. Not only is the material presented here important for the exam, but it is also important for when you ace the exam and continue on a career as a networking professional.

TWO-MINUTE DRILL

❑ The popularity of the TCP/IP protocol makes it a likely culprit to appear many times throughout your Network+ exam.

❑ TCP/IP is a *suite* of protocols.

❑ TCP/IP's unique addressing mechanism provides for over 4.2 billion addresses.

❑ The Dynamic Host Configuration Protocol (DHCP) can help with configuring IP addressing on a large TCP/IP-based network.

❑ One service that is used throughout the Internet is the Domain Name System (DNS) Service.

❑ DNS is one method of resolving a host name to a given IP address.

❑ DNS is not a dynamic service like WINS or DHCP are.

❑ The Fully Qualified Domain Name (FQDN) is the name of the host suffixed by a period, followed by the domain name.

❑ Root domains represent the upper-indexed pointers to other DNS servers.

❑ When a program requests a host by a single name, such as sunsite, the network protocol provides a sequence of steps to resolve the name.

❏ The Windows Internet Naming Service (WINS) provides tools that enhance Windows NT to manage the NetBIOS names of servers and workstations in a TCP/IP networking environment.

❏ Before WINS, the LMHOSTS file was used to assist with remote NetBIOS name resolution.

❏ The LMHOSTS file is a static file that maps NetBIOS names to IP addresses.

❏ In early TCP/IP networks, all known host names and their associated IP addresses were stored in a simple text file called *HOSTS.*

❏ Even though the protocol suite is called TCP/IP, many other protocols are available besides the TCP and IP protocols.

❏ TCP provides a reliable, connection-based delivery service.

❏ *User Datagram Protocol* (UDP) offers a connectionless datagram service that is an unreliable "best effort" delivery.

❏ *Internet Control Message Protocol* (ICMP) enables systems on a TCP/IP network to share status and error information.

❏ ARP is used to provide IP-address-to-physical-address resolution for IP packets.

❏ *Simple Mail Transfer Protocol* (SMTP) is a protocol used to send and receive mail over the Internet.

❏ *Post Office Protocol* (POP) was designed to overcome the problem encountered with SMTP in which workstations were not confined to permanent terminal-based connections to a mainframe.

❏ *Simple Network Management Protocol* (SNMP) is an Internet standard that provides a simple method for remotely managing virtually any network device.

❏ File Transfer Protocol (FTP) is a TCP/IP utility that exists solely to copy files from one computer to another.

❏ IP provides packet delivery for all other protocols within the suite.

❏ Many of the questions on the Network+ exam regarding TCP/IP will cover configuring TCP/IP, the architecture of TCP/IP, and TCP/IP addressing.

❑ A subnet mask is used to determine which part of the IP address is used for the network ID and which part is for the host ID.

❑ Class A addresses are assigned to networks with a very large number of hosts.

❑ Class B addresses are assigned to medium-sized networks.

❑ Class C addresses are usually assigned to small Local Area Networks (LANs) and comprise most of the Internet and intranet sites available.

❑ Class D addresses are used for multicasting to a number of different hosts.

❑ Class E is an experimental address block that is reserved for future use.

❑ A TCP/IP port is what an application or process uses when communicating between a client and server computer.

❑ The most popular, and therefore most likely, exam choices to remember are the FTP ports (20 and 21), SMTP port (25), and HTTP port (80).

❑ Configuring TCP/IP on a workstation is a topic that will surely make its way on to your Network+ exam.

❑ You have two options for configuring a workstation: manually, or through the use of a DHCP server.

❑ Expect more than a few questions on your exam regarding TCP/IP, especially the IP address and subnet mask. These two are the most important settings of any TCP/IP implementation and are guaranteed to find their way into your Network+ exam.

❑ There are way too many details associated with configuring a DNS server, so don't expect detailed questions in this area. Focusing on configuring client workstations to use DNS is much more important.

SELF TEST

The following Self Test questions will help you measure your understanding of the material presented in this chapter. Read all the choices carefully, as there may be more than one correct answer. Choose all correct answers for each question.

1. TCP/IP's unique addressing mechanism provides for more than how many IP addresses?

   A. 3.5 billion addresses

   B. 5.2 billion addresses

   C. 4.2 billion addresses

   D. 6.6 billion addresses

2. What if the default gateway is not configured in the DHCP server for a client that is configured to use DHCP?

   A. An error will be issued.

   B. The default gateway defaults to 0.0.0.0.

   C. The default gateway defaults to 255.255.255.255.

   D. You must specify the IP address, subnet mask, and default gateway as a minimum for DHCP configured clients.

3. Which of the following is not true regarding DNS servers?

   A. Any machine can provide this DNS domain service for one or more zones.

   B. The DNS server and the domain are not necessarily one machine.

   C. The DNS server for the domain must be indicated by the top-level domain server.

   D. The actual DNS server machine is not indicated within the DNS hierarchy.

4. Which of the following is not true regarding DNS root servers?

   A. DNS root servers are not required.

   B. The root DNS database is maintained locally by a specific authority.

   C. The root servers are used to route the request to the next correct server.

   D. The root servers provide addresses to the domain servers associated with that root.

5. Where is DNS information stored?

   A. unix/bin/etc/DNS

   B. %systemroot%\system32\DNS

   C. unix/etc/bin

   D. %systemroot%\system32\etc\DNS

6. How are name registration and replication implemented in WINS?

   A. Name resolution is static, and replication is done manually.

   B. Name resolution is dynamic, and the whole database is replicated.

   C. Name resolution is static, and changes are replicated.

   D. Name resolution is dynamic, and changes are replicated.

7. How can you stop name resolution packets from looping around the network endlessly?

    A. Specify a lower TTL value.

    B. Specify a maximum number of hops in the HOSTS file.

    C. Specify a higher TTL in the HOSTS file.

    D. Specify a lower TTL in the DNS cache file.

8. What does ICMP stand for?

    A. Internal Control Message Protocol

    B. Internet Control Mail Protocol

    C. Internet Control Message Protocol

    D. Internal Control Mail Protocol

9. Which of the following is not associated with the SNMP implementation?

    A. Network protocol identification and statistics

    B. Management system

    C. Packet routing

    D. Management Information Base

10. Which of the following is true regarding the IP protocol?

    A. The IP protocol guarantees timely and error-free delivery.

    B. The TCP protocol can be used to send information if the IP protocol is not configured correctly.

    C. The IP protocol is a connectionless delivery system.

    D. The IP protocol requires that the TCP protocol provide routing information.

11. Which network address class supports more than 70,000 hosts?

    A. Class A

    B. Class B

    C. Class C

    D. Class D

12. The Class C address range is from 192.0.1.0 to what?

    A. 221.255.255.0

    B. 223.255.255.0

    C. 223.255.0.0

    D. 225.255.255.0

13. What is the default subnet mask for a Class C network?

    A. 255.255.0.0

    B. 225.225.225.0

    C. 255.255.255.0

    D. 225.255.255.0

14. Which host is normally used in a BOOTP process?

    A. The local host

    B. The DHCP server

    C. 255.255.255.255

    D. 0.0.0.0

15. Which address is reserved for internal loopback functions?

    A. 0.0.0.0

    B. 1.0.0.0

C. 121.0.0.0

D. 127.0.0.0

16. What is the well-known port number for the HTTP service?

A. 20

B. 21

C. 80

D. 70

17. Which of the following methods would not be helpful when you are trying to stop the assignment of duplicate IP addresses on your network?

A. Using two DHCP servers on the same network

B. Using a spreadsheet to track in-use IP addresses

C. Using ping to test for connectivity before you assign an IP address

D. Using a DHCP server

18. On a Windows 98 machine, which page of the TCP/IP properties dialog box would you use to configure your workstation to use a DHCP server?

A. Identification

B. DHCP

C. IP Address

D. WINS

19. Which of the following is not on the DNS page of the TCP/IP Properties dialog box?

A. DNS Service Search Order

B. Domain Suffix Search Order

C. Use WINS for DNS Resolution

D. Domain name

20. Where can you specify a second DNS Service for faster host and domain name resolution?

A. DNS Service Search Order

B. Domain Suffix Search Order

C. Domain Name

D. You can't specify a second DNS Service for faster host and domain name resolution.

21. You are having problems communicating with a remote network via the default gateway. Which of the following will not ensure fault tolerance if you have specified an incorrect default gateway on a client computer?

A. Obtain the default gateway entry from a DHCP Service.

B. Configure the workstation to use the WINS Service instead.

C. Implement a route table, which can be used to route packets to known networks before the default gateway entry is used.

D. Specify multiple gateways.

22. Which tab would you click on a Windows 98 machine to configure the gateway?

A. IP Address

B. NetBIOS

C. Advanced

D. Gateway

23. Which is not an available option on the WINS Configuration page of the TCP/IP Properties dialog box on a Windows 98 machine?

    A. WINS Suffix Search Order

    B. Scope ID

    C. Use DHCP For WINS Resolution

    D. WINS Server Search Order

24. How do you automatically configure a Windows 98 client to point to a specific WINS server?

    A. Enter the IP address on the WINS Configuration page of TCP/IP Properties dialog box.

    B. Select the Enable WINS Lookup option button on the WINS Configuration page of the TCP/IP Properties dialog box.

    C. Select the Use DHCP for WINS Resolution option button on the WINS Configuration page of the TCP/IP Properties dialog box.

    D. Enter the NetBIOS name of the WINS server on the WINS Configuration page of the TCP/IP Properties dialog box.

25. Where can you specify a new computer name on a Windows 95 machine?

    A. The TCP/IP Properties dialog box

    B. The IP Address page

    C. The Identification page

    D. The DNS page

5

TCP/IP Suite Utilities

CERTIFICATION OBJECTIVES

Many utilities are available to troubleshoot TCP/IP connectivity problems. Most utilities are public domain and are included with the TCP/IP protocol stack provided with the operating system. This also means that they vary slightly depending upon the implementation of these programs by the vendor. Although these utilities generally provide very basic functions, a proper understanding of the usage of these tools will enable you to effectively troubleshoot most problems.

The most commonly used TCP/IP troubleshooting tools are discussed within this chapter. Individual sections are further organized by tool. The final section identifies common problems and how the different tools can be used to troubleshoot and resolve these problems. The following list provides a brief description of each utility discussed in this chapter and its core functions.

- **Arp**   Displays and modifies local ARP cache
- **Telnet**   Remote Terminal Emulation, administration, and troubleshooting
- **NBTSTAT**   Checks the state of NetBIOS over TCP/IP connections
- **Tracert**   Traces and reports on the route to a remote computer
- **Netstat**   Displays statistics for current TCP/IP connections
- **IPCONFIG/WINIPCFG**   Displays current IP configuration information
- **Ftp**   Enables file transfers between remote computers
- **Ping**   Verifies host name, host IP address, and physical connectivity to a remote TCP/IP computer

ARP

As discussed in Chapter 3, network interface cards (NICs) each have a hardware address or MAC address associated with them. Applications understand TCP/IP addressing, but network hardware devices, such as NICs, do not. For example, when two Ethernet cards are communicating, they have no knowledge of the IP address being used. Instead, they use the MAC addresses assigned to each card to address data frames. The *Address Resolution Protocol (ARP)* was designed to provide a mapping from the logical 32-bit TCP/IP addresses to the physical 48-bit MAC addresses.

Address resolution is the process of finding the address of a host within a network. In this case, the address is resolved by using a protocol to request information via a form of broadcast to locate a remote host. The remote host receives the packet and forwards it with the appropriate address information included. The address resolution process is complete once the original computer has received the address information.

ARP maintains the protocol rules for making this translation and providing address conversion in both directions within the OSI layers, as illustrated in the following illustration. A utility by the same name is available for Windows 95, Windows 98, and Windows NT. This utility is used to display and modify entries within the ARP table.

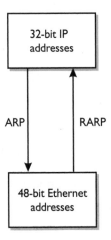

exam
ⓦatch

ARP is discussed in-depth in RFC 826.

Remember that ARP translates IP addresses into MAC addresses. The Reverse Address Resolution Protocol, or RARP, is used to find a TCP/IP address from a MAC address.

How ARP Works

When a data packet destined for a computer on a particular local area network arrives at a host or gateway, the ARP protocol is tasked to find a MAC address that matches the IP address for the destination computer. The ARP protocol then looks inside its cache table for the appropriate address. If the address is found, the destination address is then added in the date packet and forwarded on. If no entry exists for the IP address, ARP broadcasts a request packet to all the machines on the local area network to determine which machine maintains that IP address. If found, the host with that IP address will send an ARP reply with its own MAC address. If the destination is on a remote subnet, the address of the router or gateway used to reach that subnet is placed in the packet and forwarded on. If the ARP cache does not contain an IP address for the router or gateway, it will use the same methods to resolve the address. The ARP cache is then updated for future reference and the original data packets are then forwarded to the correct host.

As protocols go, ARP provides a very basic function. Only four types of messages can be sent out by the ARP protocol on any machine:

- ARP request
- ARP reply
- RARP request
- RARP reply

ARP Cache

To reduce the number of address resolution requests, thereby minimizing network utilization, a client caches resolved addresses for a short time. This table, known as the ARP cache, is used to maintain the mappings between each MAC address and its corresponding IP address locally. This is the most important part of this protocol. Since the size of the ARP cache is limited, entries need to be cleaned out periodically. Without purging entries from the cache, it could continually grow to become huge in size and could contain quite a few obsolete entries. Therefore, ARP cache entries are removed at predefined intervals. This process also removes any unsuccessful attempts to contact computers which are not currently running.

Entries in the ARP cache can be viewed, added, or deleted by using the ARP utility. Entries that are added with this utility manually are static and will not age out of the cache like the dynamic entries. This can be helpful when trying to resolve address resolution problems. By displaying the current cache, you can determine whether a remote host MAC address is being resolved correctly.

Type the following command and press ENTER to view the ARP cache:

ARP -a

Figure 5-1 shows an example of an ARP cache.

CUSTOMIZING THE ARP CACHE   Additional options are available to customize the information found in the ARP cache. For example, you can filter the entries displayed when you list them with ARP. By appending the appropriate IP address after the –a switch, the table will list entries only for that particular IP address, as shown in Figure 5-2. This can be useful when trying to isolate specific entries in a large table.

FIGURE 5-1	

Use the ARP –a command to view the ARP cache

```
C:\>arp -a
Interface: 207.222.234.73
    Internet Address        Physical Address        Type
    10.37.14.92             00-60-08-72-43-d6       static
    198.70.146.70           20-53-52-43-00-00       dynamic
    199.182.120.2           20-53-52-43-00-00       dynamic
    199.182.120.202         20-53-52-43-00-00       dynamic
    206.246.150.88          20-53-52-43-00-00       dynamic
    207.211.106.40          20-53-52-43-00-00       dynamic
    207.211.106.90          20-53-52-43-00-00       dynamic
    208.223.32.77           20-53-52-43-00-00       dynamic
```

```
C:\>arp -a 10.37.14.92

Interface: 207.222.234.73
  Internet Address         Physical Address      Type
    10.37.14.92            00-60-08-72-43-d6     static
```

Type the following command and press ENTER to view the ARP cache for a specific IP address:

ARP –a <*IP address*>

Computers that contain multiple NICs, or multi-homed computers, have more than one network interface listed. The ARP cache maintains addresses for each interface within its tables. By using the ARP –a option, all interfaces will be listed. To filter the display address listing based upon a specific interface, use the –n option. This enables you to specify which interface to display addresses for, as shown in Figure 5-3.

Type the following command and press ENTER to view the ARP cache for a specific interface:

ARP –a –n <*interface*>

ADDING STATIC ENTRIES   Static entries can be added manually when necessary. This can be especially helpful when you have a computer that transfers large amounts of data to a remote host continually. By adding a static entry for the remote host into the computer's ARP cache table, updates do not need to constantly occur. This option can also be used to test whether the local computer is receiving updates correctly.

```
C:\>arp -a -n 207.222.234.73

Interface: 207.222.234.73
  Internet Address         Physical Address      Type
    10.37.14.92            00-60-08-72-43-d6     static
    32.97.105.123          20-53-52-43-00-00     dynamic
    198.70.146.70          20-53-52-43-00-00     dynamic
    199.182.120.2          20-53-52-43-00-00     dynamic
    207.211.106.40         20-53-52-43-00-00     dynamic
    207.211.106.90         20-53-52-43-00-00     dynamic
```

Suppose that you are trying to connect to another computer on the same network. You are unable to find the remote computer; however, the other machines around you seem to work fine. First, display the local ARP cache to determine if the remote host has an entry present. If not, you can add a static entry into the ARP cache to allow you to determine whether the computer is properly receiving updates. With the entry in place, you notice that you can locate the remote computer now. It is safe to say that the cache did not get updated correctly with the appropriate MAC address and by adding a static entry, this bypassed that problem.

You can manually add entries by using the following command:

ARP –s <IP address> <MAC address>

DELETING STATIC ENTRIES   You may need to delete any entries you have manually added. You also may need to manually remove any entries that have been dynamically added to the ARP cache. Use the following command to delete entries from the ARP cache:

ARP –d <IP Address>

ARP CACHE AGING   Unlike static addresses, which never age out, dynamic addresses remain for only a predetermined amount of time. Windows NT adjusts the size of the ARP cache automatically. Entries not used after two minutes are removed. If entries are in use, they remain for ten minutes before they are removed. A registry parameter within Windows NT is also available to allow for more control over the aging parameters. The registry parameter is located in the following directory:

Hkey_Local_Machine\System\CurrentControlSet\Services\ Tcpip\Parameters\ArpCacheLife

RARP

A little-known protocol exists to facilitate the reverse function of ARP. *Reverse Address Resolution Protocol (RARP)* enables a machine to learn its own IP address by broadcasting to resolve its own MAC address. A RARP server containing these mappings can respond with the IP address for the requesting host. In most cases, a machine knows its own IP address; therefore,

RARP is primarily used for situations such as diskless workstations, or machines without hard disks. Dumb terminals and NetPCs are good examples of diskless workstations.

Troubleshooting Duplicate IP Address Problems

During system startup and as the IP protocol initializes, an ARP request is broadcast containing its own MAC and IP addresses. This is done so that other computers can update their ARP caches with this information. If a computer already has this IP address, it will respond with an *ARP reply* containing its own MAC and IP addresses, indicating a conflict. Other computers will have already updated their own ARP caches, though. By having two computers with the same IP address, you can potentially cause problems with many different computers.

In the event a duplicate address is found, the Windows NT 4.0 Service Pack 3 TCP/IP stack is written to send out a new ARP broadcast to re-map the ARP cache on all affected computers. The MAC and IP addresses of the original computer will be contained within this new ARP. Once this ARP has been broadcast, the TCP/IP protocol stack will shut down and the computer will log the address conflict.

Although ARP is simple compared to most other protocols, it is just as important to TCP/IP for proper functionality. The utility included with this protocol will enable you to display and modify the ARP cache as needed. This enables you to effectively troubleshoot any issues that may arise with ARP.

CERTIFICATION OBJECTIVE 5.02

Telnet

Another utility commonly used is Telnet (telecommunications network). This utility was designed to provide a virtual terminal or remote login across the network. This enables the user to execute commands on a remote machine anywhere on the network as if he were sitting in front of the console. The term Telnet refers to both the protocol and application used for remote logins.

Telnet was originally designed to allow for a single universal interface in a world that was very diverse. It was an efficient method of simulating a console session when very little else was available. It is still widely used today for remotely administering devices such as network equipment and UNIX servers. It can also be a great troubleshooting tool when used correctly.

How Telnet Works

The Telnet service uses TCP port 23 and is defined in-depth in RFC 854. It is connection based and handles its own session negotiation. This is what makes it so efficient and effective. By maintaining its own protocol, it can set up its own sessions and manage them accordingly. This keeps the remote host from spending too much time processing requests and enables it to concentrate on its own processes. Usually a client-based program is used to connect to the remote server. The remote server must also be running a Telnet service to enable the client to connect.

Telnet uses a concept known as network virtual terminal (NVT) to define both ends of a Telnet connection. Each end of the connection maintains a logical keyboard and printer. The logical keyboard generates characters and the logical printer displays them. The logical printer is usually a terminal screen and the logical keyboard is the user's keyboard.

Using Telnet

A Telnet client utility is included with Windows 9x and Windows NT. To use Telnet you must be connected to the network. You can run this utility by typing TELNET.EXE at a command prompt, or by selecting Start | Programs | Accessories | Telnet. Select Connect | Remote System. The Connect dialog box appears, as shown here.

Connect	☒
Host Name: 10.1.1.1	▼
Port: telnet	▼
TermType: vt100	▼
Connect	Cancel

You can enter either an IP address or a host name. To connect via a host name, the client must be able to resolve the name to an IP address. You must also specify the port to connect to and the terminal emulation type. By default, this Telnet will try to connect to the Telnet port (port 23) on the remote server. VT100 is the default terminal emulation used for Telnet.

Telnet requires a username and password on the server to log in. Different functions and applications are available to assist you in performing remote administration. These are dependent upon what services are being offered by the remote host. Many external devices also offer Telnet capability, such as Uninterruptible Power Supplies, Remote Control Server administration cards, and most networking equipment.

Customizing Telnet Settings

Due to the different environments that exist, TELNET offers multiple types of terminal emulation. Options include setting the terminal emulation, command buffer size, screen fonts, and cursor behavior. Some of these options are required to work on different types of remote hosts, but others are purely cosmetic. The following illustration shows the available options for customization.

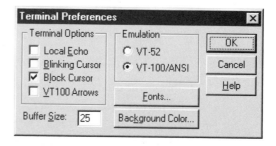

You can change screen fonts and cursor behavior to fit the screen output to your needs. These settings will not affect the server-based process. Some Telnet applications will not function correctly without particular cursor or font settings. The Local Echo option displays all of your keyboard input. The VT100 Arrows option specifies how cursor movement is handled. The Blinking Cursor and Block Cursor options adjust how the cursor is displayed on screen.

The Buffer Size enables you to customize the amount of history that remains in memory. You can scroll through to see what commands or output have already been processed. The default is 25 lines, but you can set this value as high as 399. The Telnet application will not enable you to specify fewer than 25 lines.

The terminal emulation option defines what type of remote terminal to use. This controls how commands are interpreted and displayed by the remote server. VT-52 is an older standard not commonly used anymore. VT100 is the default standard emulation used today.

Another function of Telnet is logging. It logs the console display to keep a record of all activity. To start or stop logging, select Terminal from the menu bar and select Start Logging or Stop Logging from the menu. When you select Start Logging, the Open Log File window appears. You need to select the folder that you want Telnet to save the log files to. The log files are saved as telnet.log and are readable by any standard text editor.

Troubleshooting with Telnet

The primary use of telnet is remote administration. If you are unable to connect to a remote server by other methods, depending upon the problem, Telnet may still work. This will enable you to troubleshoot and work with a remote server without being in front of it. If a server is inaccessible, you may still be able to contact its peripherals.

Suppose an NT Server has crashed and is displaying a Blue Screen. Some servers include an option to have remote administration cards plugged in. In this case, you could Telnet to this card and possibly determine if there is a hardware failure or reboot the server. Suppose you have a UPS attached to the server. This peripheral may have Telnet capability to enable you to power cycle the server. Both cases enable you to remotely troubleshoot the server without local interaction.

Another example of troubleshooting with Telnet is to connect to an applications service to verify that it is functioning properly. As discussed earlier, every TCP/IP service uses a specific TCP or UDP port. You can specify a particular port to connect to and test the connectivity and functionality of a service. For example, you can connect to a Windows NT server running Microsoft Exchange to verify that the Internet Mail Connector is transferring mail properly. Exercise 5-1 shows a trick to troubleshooting the Exchange Internet Mail Service.

EXERCISE 5-1

Connecting to an Exchange Internet Mail Service

1. Connect to the IP Address of the Exchange server Internet Mail Service. Specify port 25 to connect to.

2. Type **HELO test.company.com**.

3. Type the following to list who the message is from: **MAIL FROM** *<admin@test.company.com>*.

4. Type the following to list who the message is to: **RCPT TO:** *<user@hi.company.com>*.

5. Type the following command to tell the connector that you are ready to send data: **DATA**. You should now see the following: `"354 Send data. End with CRLF.CRLF"`

6. Type the following command to add a subject: **Subject: test**. Press ENTER twice.

7. Enter the following as the message body: **This is a test message.** Press ENTER and add a period to the next line and press ENTER again. This will end the data portion.

8. Type **QUIT** to end the connection.

When you have finished this exercise, you can check to see if the message was delivered. If the message arrives, the Internet Mail Connector is functioning properly.

exam
ⓦatch

Make sure you can recognize the output from each of the TCP/IP utilities listed in this chapter. On your Network+ exam you will be presented with output from a command and asked which command produced the output.

NBTSTAT

The Microsoft TCP/IP stack uses an additional sub-protocol for its services, NetBIOS over TCP/IP (NetBT). This provides additional functionality, but it can make troubleshooting much more difficult. You must fully understand how it works and when it can be a factor in any issues that may arise. Because this is a Microsoft addition to the TCP/IP protocol, Microsoft created this utility to troubleshoot the problems that can arise.

How NetBIOS over TCP/IP Works

NetBIOS is a software interface and naming convention. It was used in the early days of local area networking in a communication protocol, known as NetBEUI. It was designed for use in small local environments, so it has no routing functions built into it. It also primarily relied upon broadcast-based name resolution. This design does not port well to today's expanded wide area networks. Microsoft has taken this protocol and incorporated it into TCP/IP to enable it to be used in today's expanded environments. This helps to take advantage of the WAN environment while allowing for interoperability with other operating systems.

NetBT Naming

The NetBIOS namespace is a flat structure, meaning that all names within its network must be unique. This means that all computers within a workgroup or domain must have a unique name. Names are made up of 16 hexadecimal characters. The first 15 can be set by the administrator or user and the 16th specifies a resource type. This resource type is used to determine what services are available from a computer. The following table shows some common resource types.

Suffix	Usage
00	Workstation Service
06	Remote Access Server
20	File Server Service
87	Microsoft Exchange Message Transfer Agent

NetBT Sessions

Because NetBT travels through TCP/IP, sessions are set up the same way. There is an additional overhead associated with this, but it is usually very small. When a service using NetBT attempts to access a resource, it first resolves the name to an IP address. Next, a TCP connection is established to port 139, designated for the NetBIOS Datagram service. When connected, the computer sends a NetBIOS session request to the server name over the TCP connection. If the server is listening, it will respond with the requested information.

When the session is established, the two computers negotiate a higher-level protocol to use over the connection. Microsoft networking uses only one session between two computers at any time. Additional services required between the two machines will travel through the same connection.

Using NBTSTAT

NBTSTAT is used to troubleshoot connectivity between two computers trying to communicate via NetBT. It displays the protocol statistics and the current connections to each remote host. You can also display the information about a remote host and the names stored in its local name cache.

Displaying the Local Cache

Every connection made via NetBIOS keeps the name in cache for a short period of time. You can display the local cache by using the NBTSTAT –c option. By using this option, each machine that remains in cache will be displayed. This listing will also include the type of connection, TCP/IP address of the remote connection, and the time the connection will be kept for.

By using the –n option, you can display the services the local machine is advertising. This lists the registered names for the local machine as well. You can also reload the local name cache with the –R option. This will enable you to reload the LMHOSTS file after the name cache is cleared out.

Connecting to Remote Machines

You can also display the cache of registered services on a remote machine by using the –a or –A option. The –a option enables you to specify a remote host by host name and the –A option specifies it by IP address. These options will enable you to determine what services the remote machine is offering. Core operating system services such as the Server service or Browse services are listed here. Applications such as Microsoft Exchange or Microsoft Internet Information Server may also list entries here as well. Figure 5-4 shows an example of a remote machine's cache table.

Displaying Registration Statistics

Services can register in two ways, via broadcast or with a WINS service. You can display the statistics of how many times you have registered and with what method. You can also display information on how remote NetBIOS names are being resolved. This can help you to determine if you are using a WINS service correctly or are broadcasting for services. Broadcasting can consume a lot of bandwidth and is generally not recommended except in the smallest networks. To view the registration statistics, use the –r option with NBTSTAT.

FIGURE 5-4

Use the –A option to display a remote machine's name table

```
C:\>nbtstat -A 10.10.10.1

      NetBIOS Remote Machine Name Table

    Name               Type         Status
  ---------------------------------------------
  WORKSTATION1    <00>  UNIQUE    Registered
  WORKSTATION1    <20>  UNIQUE    Registered
  WORKGROUP       <00>  GROUP     Registered
  WORKSTATION1    <03>  UNIQUE    Registered
  WORKGROUP       <1E>  GROUP     Registered
  WORKGROUP       <1D>  UNIQUE    Registered
  ..__MSBROWSE__.<01>  GROUP     Registered
  ADMINISTRATOR   <03>  UNIQUE    Registered

  MAC Address = 00-60-97-E4-D7-CB

  C:\>
```

on the
()ob

The NBTSTAT utility can be crucial in defining problems with Microsoft computers. Since they use the NetBIOS naming standard, this utility is good at finding and isolating connectivity problems. It provides the extra information on NetBIOS statistics that you can't get out of regular TCP/IP utilities such as tracert.

Displaying Session Information

Another option with NBTSTAT is to list the sessions that are currently open. You can not only see what you are connected to, but also list the open sessions that other computers have with your machine. Use the –s option to list names by IP address only. When you use the –s option, NBTSTAT will attempt to resolve the IP addresses to host names.

Statistics available with this option include number of bytes in, number of bytes out, current state, and whether the connection is inbound or outbound. Figure 5-5 shows an example of the sessions displayed with this option.

exam
⦿atch

Make sure you know the options available with the NBTSTAT command, such as NBTSTAT –R and NBTSTAT –a. I was surprised when I received a question asking which option to use to accomplish a certain goal.

FIGURE 5-5

Local NetBIOS sessions listing. The lowercase –s option resolves the IP address to its host name

```
C:\>nbtstat -s

                   NetBIOS Connection Table

Local Name              State     In/Out  Remote Host        Input    Output
----------------------------------------------------------------------------
WORKSTATION2    <03>  Listening
WORKSTATION2          Listening
ADMINISTRATOR   <03>  Listening

C:\>
```

Tracert

Network routing can quickly become a very complicated beast. This can be the case even in the smallest networks. There is an arsenal of public utilities and third-party products to help troubleshoot and isolate network-related problems. Many of these utilities require at least a moderate level of knowledge to understand how to use these tools and interpret the results of using them. A good example is a network sniffer. Using a network sniffer can become complicated quickly.

Tracert is a command-line utility that was designed to provide a very basic task: to determine the path taken by a data packet to reach its destination. This can be very helpful in determining at what point a network connection is no longer active. It can also be helpful in troubleshooting issues around network response times.

How Tracert Works

Tracert functions by sending out ICMP (Internet Control Message Protocol) echo packets to the destination specified by either an IP address or host name. These packets are sent with varying IP Time To Live (TTL) values. Each router along the path is required to decrement the TTL on a packet by at least one before forwarding it, so the TTL is effectively a hop count. When the TTL on a packet reaches zero, the router should send an ICMP Time Exceeded message back to the source computer.

Tracert then determines the route by sending the first echo packet with a TTL of one and incrementing by one on each subsequent transmission. This is done until the target responds or the maximum TTL is reached. The route is actually determined by looking at the ICMP Time Exceeded messages sent back by intermediate routers. Tracert then displays a list of the routers in the path that returned the ICMP Time Exceeded message.

When using the utility, you will notice several numbers in the display. Figure 5-6 shows an example of the tracert command.

Although a tracert may look rather confusing at first, it is fairly easy to understand. Each row gathers information about that hop three times. The first column shows the number of hops. The next three columns show the response time it took for the router or gateway to respond for each attempt. The last column lists the router name and router address.

Using Tracert

Let's say that you notice that you cannot access a particular web site on the Internet. Your company is directly connected to the Internet via an ISDN line, which is used by approximately 35 people. You are able to hit certain web sites consistently, but others are available only sporadically. Other users begin to notice that they are unable to connect to the same web sites that you are seeing a problem with.

Tracert fits in well here to begin isolating where the problem is. Although you may have a good idea of what network equipment and options are used within your company, once packets enter the Internet, there is no telling what they may come across. Because routes can be so dynamic, this is a great tool for figuring out where the data is traveling to reach its destination.

You can begin troubleshooting this problem by typing one of the following commands:

TRACERT <*hostname*>

or

TRACERT <*ipaddress*>

FIGURE 5-6

A tracert to a local workstation

```
C:\>tracert 10.10.10.1
Tracing route to WORKSTATION1    [10.10.10.1]
over a maximum of 30 hops:
  1    1 ms    1 ms    1 ms  WORKSTATION1    [10.10.10.1]
Trace complete.
C:\>
```

After the utility has run, you may notice the following entry show up on one of the routers along the way:

Destination Net Unreachable

Although this utility is unable to determine why the error is occurring, it has effectively found at what point the problem is being caused. Armed with this information, that router or link can then be looked at by the owner to help him resolve the issue.

In the event a name resolution method is not available for remote hosts, you can specify the –d option to prohibit the utility from trying to resolve host names as it runs. Without this switch the program will still work, but it will attempt to translate every hop's host name, thereby slowing the process.

Maximum Number of Hops

One function of the tracert utility is to provide the number of hops, or networks, the data is crossing. Because each network can use different devices and have varying bandwidth, this function can be very helpful. There are instances, however, in which you will need to limit the number of hops the program will make to search for the remote host. This means that a tracert will continue for 30 hops by default if it cannot reach its destination. This can be very time-consuming if you are working with a device four or five hops away. In the unusual case that you must surpass more than 30 hops, you can also specify a greater interval.

By using the –h option with tracert, you can specify the maximum number of hops to trace a route to. An example of this option is shown in Figure 5-7.

Adjusting Timeout Values

Another option associated with tracert is to adjust the timeout value. This value determines the amount of time in milliseconds the program will wait for a response before moving on. Using this option will enable you to possibly understand a little more about the problem that is occurring. For example, if you notice that many responses are timing out, you can raise this value. If you notice that after raising this value that remote devices are responding, this could be a good indication that you have a bandwidth problem.

FIGURE 5-7

An example of a tracert
with the –d and –h options

```
C:\>tracert -d -h 15 www.syngress.com
Tracing route to www.syngress.com [146.115.28.75]
over a maximum of 15 hops:
  1      *   ms      *   ms      *   ms  Request timed out.
  2    312  ms    325  ms    381  ms  165.236.51.1
  3    383  ms    272  ms    354  ms  163.179.232.194
  4    396  ms    354  ms    408  ms  163.179.220.182
  5    301  ms    354  ms    258  ms  192.41.177.74
  6    384  ms    325  ms      *   ms  204.152.42.2
  7    366  ms    422  ms    353  ms  207.152.148.41
  8    301  ms    272  ms    299  ms  207.152.148.30
  9    268  ms    270  ms    268  ms  207.152.148.34
 10    383  ms   2030  ms    409  ms  207.152.148.37
 11    410  ms    382  ms    271  ms  198.32.178.13
 12    439  ms    272  ms    368  ms  146.115.17.125
 13    384  ms    381  ms    410  ms  199.232.56.39
 14    274  ms    382  ms    271  ms  146.115.28.75
Trace complete.

C:\>_
```

Loose Source Routing Options

An additional option is to use what is known as *loose source routing*. The -j
option can be used to force the outbound datagram to pass through a
specific router and back. This enables you to trace the round-trip route
for a destination. A normal Tracert follows the route until it reaches its
destination or times out. When you specify this option, tracert follows the
path to the router specified and returns to your computer. To use loose
source routing, enter the following command:

TRACERT –j <router name> <local computer>

Tracert can be a useful tool in determining why a remote host can't be
reached. It can also be a good tool to notice other issues, such as bandwidth
utilization problems. Its additional options and functionality make it a
powerful tool.

CERTIFICATION OBJECTIVE 5.05

Netstat

Now that you've learned how to trace data packets throughout the network,
another utility similar to NBTSTAT is available for troubleshooting

TCP/IP specific issues. Netstat displays protocol statistics and current TCP/IP network connections. TCP/IP can be a complicated protocol to understand and therefore very difficult to troubleshoot. This utility can be used to display in-depth detail about protocol status and statistics for the different network interfaces as well as the current routing tables.

How Netstat Works

TCP-based connections use a three-step handshake method for establishing and disconnecting sessions. This forms the basis for TCP and its reliable data transfer methodology. This enables it to act as a message-validation protocol to provide reliable communications between two hosts. A virtual circuit is created via this handshake to appropriately handle the transport messages. Netstat displays information about these virtual circuits, the network interfaces, and how they are being used.

By default, netstat lists the protocol type, local address and port information, remote address and port information, and current state. The information provided explains what connections are open or in progress, through what ports, and what their current state is. Figure 5-8 shows an example of the netstat utility.

The State column dislpays the current status of TCP connections only. You can determine from the status in this column whether the connection

---

FIGURE 5-8

Output from the netstat command

```
C:\>netstat

Active Connections

   Proto  Local Address      Foreign Address       State
   TCP    workstation2:1192  207.211.106.40:80     TIME_WI
   TCP    workstation2:1201  207.211.106.90:80     TIME_WI
   TCP    workstation2:1218  www.syngress.com:80   ESTABL
```

is properly functioning. For example, if the connection stays at a form of wait state for a long period of time, you may need to look at the connection between the two hosts and verify that a network problem does not exist. Table 5-1 lists the states that are available.

Netstat Options

Different types of statistics are available depending upon the utility options that you use. You can display all connections and listening ports because server connections are not displayed in the standard output. You can also display Ethernet statistics and per protocol statistics. The routing table can also be displayed with this command.

You can use the –n option to display addresses and port numbers without resolving the names. This could take additional overhead if the listing is long and it may not work properly if you have no form of name resolution set up. Suppose you want the information that is displayed to continually update. By default, the information is displayed once. You can

TABLE 5-1	State	Explanation
TCP Connection States	SYN_SEND	Indicates an active open
	SYN_RECEIVED	Server just received a SYN from the remote client
	ESTABLISHED	Client received SYN and connection is complete
	LISTEN	Server is awaiting a connection
	FIN_WAIT_1	Indicates an active close
	TIMED_WAIT	Clients enter this state after an active close
	CLOSE_WAIT	Indicates a passive close. The server has just received the first FIN from client
	FIN_WAIT_2	Client just received acknowledgement of its first FIN from the server
	LAST+ACK	Server enters this state when it sends its own FIN
	CLOSED	Server received the ACK from client and the connection is closed

specify an interval in seconds appended to the end of the command to have the utility update itself. The following is an example of the command line:

NETSTAT –a 5

This command will display the active connections every five seconds. Use CTRL-C to stop this program. This can be helpful when trying to actively monitor connections and their statistics.

Displaying Server Connections and Listening Ports

From the standard output, netstat does not display the server-based connections and listening ports. This information may be necessary to understand who the computer is communicating with and what its current status is. Therefore, this information can be obtained by using the –a option with netstat. This listing contains all local server services that are currently active or communicating.

Displaying Ethernet Statistics

Another option available enables you to display the Ethernet interface statistics. The information available with the -e option includes the number of bytes received and sent, the number of discards and errors, and unknown protocols. By understanding what this information means, you can monitor the amount of traffic that is being used in communications. Since this option also displays error, you can check here to see if there are communication-related problems occurring. Figure 5-9 shows an example of the netstat utility with this option.

FIGURE 5-9

The -e option displays the Ethernet interface statistics

```
C:\>netstat -e
Interface Statistics

                           Received           Sent
Bytes                      1242591          302546
Unicast packets               2406            2568
Non-unicast packets            252             262
Discards                         0               0
Errors                           0             144
Unknown protocols               64

C:\>
```

Displaying per-Protocol Statistics

While the previous option shows Ethernet interface-specific information, protocol-specific information is also available. With the –s option, you can display statistics for the communications protocols and how they are being used. The protocols include TCP, UDP, ICMP (Internet Control Message Protocol), and IP. Detailed information can be obtained with this option that can help you to isolate TCP/IP communications issues.

You can also filter by protocol to drill down to specific areas. The –p option can be used alone to filter the standard netstat output by TCP or UDP or you can use it with the protocol statistics option to filter by TCP, UDP, ICMP, or IP. An example of this filtering is shown in Figure 5-10.

Displaying the Current Route Table

Netstat offers another option that enables you to display the current route table. This enables you to see what routes are used as well as display the active sessions and their addresses. Because routing tables are constantly updating, this can be a good reference as you troubleshoot with this utility to understand how the data is traveling across the network. For every route, it displays the network address, the net mask, the gateway address and interface, and the number of hops away the host is.

FIGURE 5-10

Use the -s option and the –p option together to display specific information about a protocol

```
C:\>netstat -s -p IP

IP Statistics

    Packets Received                    = 2564
    Received Header Errors              = 0
    Received Address Errors             = 28
    Datagrams Forwarded                 = 0
    Unknown Protocols Received          = 0
    Received Packets Discarded          = 0
    Received Packets Delivered          = 2564
    Output Requests                     = 2801
    Routing Discards                    = 4194332
    Discarded Output Packets            = 0
    Output Packet No Route              = 0
    Reassembly Required                 = 0
    Reassembly Successful               = 0
    Reassembly Failures                 = 0
    Datagrams Successfully Fragmented   = 0
    Datagrams Failing Fragmentation     = 0
    Fragments Created                   = 0

C:\>_
```

Troubleshooting with Netstat

Using netstat to monitor TCP protocol activity can enable you to troubleshoot TCP/IP based connections. Netstat can be used in a variety of ways.

You can use the –a option to monitor active connections. The state of a good TCP connection is usually established with 0 bytes in the send and receive queues. If the state is irregular or the data is blocked in either queue, there is probably a problem with the connection. If not, you are probably experiencing network or application delay.

You can also monitor the error counts for protocols and the Ethernet interface. These are a good indication that a problem may be occurring. Also, monitor the route tables. If there is a network routing problem, you may be able to spot something here as well.

CERTIFICATION OBJECTIVE 5.06

IPCONFIG/WINIPCFG

IPCONFIG and WINIPCFG are utilities used to display the current TCP/IP configurations on the local workstations and to modify the DHCP addresses assigned to each interface. IPCONFIG is a command-line based utility for WINDOWS NT. WINIPCFG is a graphical interface used in Windows 95 and Windows 98. By default, they both display the IP address, the subnet mask, and the default gateway.

Table 5-2 lists the information available from these utilities.

IPCONFIG

IPCONFIG is used in Windows NT to display TCP/IP information from a command prompt. With this utility, you can also display other related IP settings, such as DNS servers, WINS servers, and the network interface's physical MAC address. If you have more than one network interface, statistics are displayed about each one individually or can be filtered to a particular one.

TABLE 5-2	Item Displayed	Description
Parameters Displayed with IPCONFIG or WINIPCFG	Host Name	TCP/IP-based host name
	DNS Servers	Configured IP addresses for DNS servers
	Node Type	NetBIOS node type
	NetBIOS Scope ID	Scope ID used to segment NetBIOS networks
	IP Routing Enabled	Displays if NT is set up as a TCP/IP router
	WINS proxy enabled	An advanced WINS feature
	NetBIOS resolution uses DNS	Enables NetBIOS name requests to query DNS for resolution
	Description	Network interface description
	Physical Address	MAC address of adapter
	DHCP Enabled	States whether the configured IP address was assigned via DHCP
	IP Address	TCP/IP address assigned
	Subnet Mask	Network subnet mask
	Default Gateway	Default router to send through
	Lease Obtained	Time and date DHCP address was obtained
	Lease Expires	Time and date DHCP address expires

You can append /ALL to this command to display all TCP/IP information available. Figure 5-11 shows an example of IPCONFIG /ALL.

IPCONFIG DHCP Parameters

The IPCONFIC command-line utility enables you to control DHCP functions. Two switches are available to release and renew the addresses assigned to an interface. You can specify a particular adapter for these options, or allow it to work for all adapters that have DHCP-assigned addresses.

The /Release option removes the assigned IP address from all adapters configured for DCHP use. By specifying the adapter name after the switch, only it will be affected by the command. This can be useful if your are

FIGURE 5-11

The IPCONFIG /all command displays all TCP/IP information available

```
C:\>ipconfig /all

Windows NT IP Configuration

        Host Name . . . . . . . . . : workstation1
        DNS Servers . . . . . . . . :
        Node Type . . . . . . . . . : Broadcast
        NetBIOS Scope ID. . . . . . :
        IP Routing Enabled. . . . . : No
        WINS Proxy Enabled. . . . . : No
        NetBIOS Resolution Uses DNS : Yes

Ethernet adapter E190x1:

        Description . . . . . . . . : 3Com 3C90x Ethernet Adapter
        Physical Address. . . . . . : 00-60-97-E4-D7-CB
        DHCP Enabled. . . . . . . . : No
        IP Address. . . . . . . . . : 10.10.10.1
        Subnet Mask . . . . . . . . : 255.0.0.0
        Default Gateway . . . . . . : 10.10.1.1

C:\>
```

experiencing problems associated with DHCP. It can also be used to release the address if an IP conflict occurs.

The /Renew option sends a request to the DHCP server asking for an address. It takes the last address DHCP assigned if it is available. If not, the computer is given the next available addresses in the pool. As with the /Release option, you can specify a particular adapter after the switch to renew the address. This will only work if the adapter has been set up to receive its IP address from a DHCP server.

WINIPCFG

WINIPCFG is the Windows 95/98-based graphical utility used to display TCP/IP information. The information displayed is the same as that in the Windows NT IPCONFIG utility. Microsoft has added a graphical interface for ease of use, but it can still be run from the command line with specific options.

WINIPCFG Options

As with the IPCONFIG utility, several features are available from a command-line prompt in the WINIPCFG utility. When you open

WINIPCFG, the only information displayed is the TCP/IP address, the subnet mask, and the default gateway. There is a button at the bottom for more information, or you can use the WINIPCFG /ALL switch. Both present the same interface. A drop-down box is included to enable you to specify a specific adapter. WINIPCFG is shown in Figure 5-12.

DHCP Options

The WINIPCFG utility includes buttons for releasing and renewing IP addresses for DHCP. It also contains information pertaining to the time and date the lease was obtained and expires. WINIPCFG does not, however, enable you to specify specific adapters for a particular function such as releasing an address through the graphical interface. You can,

---

FIGURE 5-12

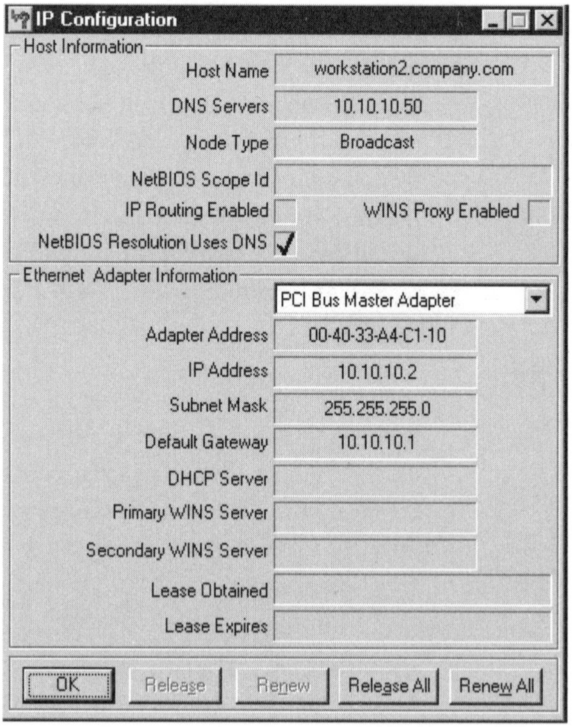

WINIPCFG /ALL displays all of the TCP/IP information available

however, use command-line options to specify certain or all adapters. The available options are listed below:

- ■ **\Renew_All**   Renew all adapters
- ■ **\Release_All**   Release all adapters
- ■ **\Renew** *<adapter>*   Renew a specified adapter
- ■ **\Release** *<adapter>*   Release a specified adapter

Batch Option

An additional option included with WINIPCFG is the /Batch switch. This enables you to forward the information in this utility to a text file. Be default, output is placed in the WINIPCFG.OUT file in the %WINDIR% directory. By appending a path and filename to the end of this switch, you can place this information wherever you prefer. The batch option can be used with any command-line option available for this utility.

CERTIFICATION OBJECTIVE 5.07

FTP

FTP (File Transfer Protocol) is designed primarily for transferring data across a network. FTP denotes both a protocol and a utility used for this purpose. It was created to quickly and efficiently transfer data files from one host to another without impacting the remote hosts' resources. You can also manage remote directories and even access e-mail; however, this program does not enable you to execute remote commands such as the Telnet utility.

How FTP Works

FTP is unusual in that it uses two TCP channels to operate. It uses TCP port 20 as the data transfer channel and TCP port 21 for commands. The data transfer channel is known as the DTP, or Data Transfer Process, and the command channel is known as the PI, or Protocol Interpreter. The two channels enable you to transfer data and execute commands at the same time and provide a more efficient and faster data transfer. FTP also works in real time. It does not queue up requests like most other utilities do; it transfers data while you watch.

Like Telnet, FTP requires a server-based program to facilitate client requests. The remote host FTP server application performs FTP processing and hands the data back to the client.

FTP enables file transfers in several formats based upon the type of remote system. Most systems have two modes of transfer, text and binary. Text transfers are ASCII based and use characters separated by carriage returns and newline characters. The binary format uses a transfer method that requires no form of conversion. Because it requires no conversion or formatting, binary mode is faster. Most systems default to text mode, although many systems still use binary transfers. FTP is unable to transfer file permissions because they are not part of the protocol. An example of an FTP session is shown in Figure 5-13.

Using FTP

A command-line client utility is included with Windows NT and Windows 95/98. Quite a few third-party FTP server and client applications are available. Some add a graphical interface while others add add-ons and functionality.

FTP is started by typing FTP at a command prompt followed by the name or address of the target machine. As with Telnet, the computer must be able to resolve the remote computer's name into an IP address for the command to succeed. Once logged on, users can transfer files, manage directories, and log in or log out.

FIGURE 5-13

An example of an
FTP session

```
C:\>ftp
ftp> open 10.10.10.2
> ftp: connect:10061
ftp> ls
Not connected.
ftp>
```

There is a wide array of commands available in the FTP utility. These commands are used to control the FTP application and its functions. Some of the more common commands are included in Table 5-3.

Configuring FTP

Users require a login ID to access FTP services. Most systems today enable an anonymous login, but you do not want to allow these users to have full rights to the system. A common problem with connecting via FTP is an invalid login or insufficient access rights. If you are having problems connecting to an FTP server, contact your FTP server administrator to verify that your ID is set up correctly.

FTP Options

Several switches are available for the command-line FTP utility. These options enable you to further customize the use of FTP to meet your needs. The –v option suppresses the display of remote server responses. This provides a more user-friendly interface to the utility. By default, when you start FTP it attempts to log in automatically. You can disable this function by using the –n option.

The –I option turns off the interactive prompting that occurs during multiple transfers. This makes for a more automated approach to FTP. The –d option enables you to turn on the debugging functions. This feature displays all FTP commands that are passed between the client and server.

TABLE 5-3

Common FTP Commands

Command	Description
CD	Change working directory
DELETE	Delete File
LS	List current directory contents
BYE	Log out
GET	Download a file
PUT	Upload a file
VERBOSE	Turns on and off verbose mode

The –g option turns off filename globbing. By disabling these functions, you able to use wildcard characters in local filenames and directories.

Another option included with the FTP command-line utility is the capability to run a script of commands after the program is started. The script file is used instead of redirection and can include any standard command. You must append the –s: switch followed by the path and filename of the script.

Troubleshooting with FTP

One of the most common forms of troubleshooting with FTP is to use online services to obtain patches and documentation. For example, Microsoft provides an online FTP server from which you can obtain any public updates and fixes. You can find the information you need much faster this way; then you can contact Microsoft support. Most vendors supply online sites such as this for the same type of updates for their own products. Many companies also set up internal FTP sites to enable remote users to quickly access information.

If you need a way to efficiently get updates to your servers when a new patch is available, you can set up FTP services on each machine to copy the updates to. You can use the –s option to automate most of this process. Because FTP is much faster than a traditional file copy, it can save you a lot of time.

TFTP

The Trivial File Transfer Protocol (TFTP) is a slight variation of FTP. TFTP differs from FTP in two ways: it uses the User Datagram Protocol (UDP) connectionless transport instead of TCP, and you do not log on to the remote machine. Because it uses UDP, TFTP does not provide error-correcting services like TCP does. This has advantages, but it does have to use more complex algorithms to guarantee data integrity. Because users do not log in, user access and file permission problems are avoided.

TFTP is generally not used for file transfers as FTP is; instead, it is used in scenarios such as diskless terminals or workstations. Typically, TFTP is

FROM THE FIELD

The TCP/IP Suite of Utilities

I cannot stress enough how the TCP/IP suite of utilities presented here will help you in the field. I use these utilities almost daily in maintaining and troubleshooting the network. You will find yourself biased towards the most helpful utilities, such as ping and IPCONFIG/WINIPCFG, but I recommend you learn when and how to use each utility. You never know when you will be placed in a situation where one of these lesser-used utilities can come in really handy. For example, FTP has been decreasing in popularity, so administrators don't get a chance to use it as much as we used to. My FTP skills had dwindled, like many other administrators. One day, I received a call from another branch of the corporation that needed immediate access to a few spreadsheets that were temporarily unavailable because the WINS server was currently not replicating to remote sites. We figured the quickest way we could get these files to the remote site was through the FTP service. I placed the spreadsheets in the correct FTP drop box, and the remote administrator loaded up the FTP utility and downloaded the spreadsheets minutes later.

You can even enhance the effects of the TCP/IP utilities through batch files and programming languages. I recently worked on an automated ping utility that would ping key servers on the network and report their status, in addition to the time required for the ping, and display the results in a spreadsheet or network diagram. Each network link to a key server would appear as a green line if the ping was successful and a red line if the ping was unsuccessful. With a click of a button, any user on the network could determine if there was a network problem affecting their workstation. A user could call you and say "The link to the database server from my workstation appears to be down," rather than, "My computer is broken. Can you come and fix it?" This proactive approach on the user's part can save you time and effort when troubleshooting problems.

So, make sure you have these TCP/IP utilities committed to memory for the exam, and for real life get practice using them. I wish I had a nickel for every time I used the ping command!

—Cameron Brandon, MCSE+Internet,
CNE, A+, Network+

used to load applications or for bootstrapping. Because the operating systems are not loaded at this point, the diskless machines cannot execute FTP. TFTP handles access and file permissions by imposing restraints from within the host operating system. For example, by setting the file permissions on the TFTP server, you can limit the security to areas inside the TFTP server.

exam
ⓦatch

Make sure you know what each TCP/IP utility is used for. For example, ARP is used to view and modify hardware (MAC) addresses. You will definitely receive a couple questions testing your knowledge of this.

CERTIFICATION OBJECTIVE 5.08

Ping

The ping (Packet Internet Groper) command is the most basic TCP/IP troubleshooting tool available. This command is used to test a machine's connectivity to the network and to verify that it is active. Usually, using this command is the first step to any troubleshooting if a connectivity problem is occurring between two computers. This can quickly help you to determine if a remote host is available and responsive.

How Ping Works

Ping uses the Internet Control Message Protocol (ICMP) to verify connections to remote hosts by sending echo packets and listening for reply packets. Ping waits for up to one second for each packet sent and prints the number of packets sent and received. Each packet is then validated against the transmitted message. By default, four packets are transmitted containing 64 bytes of data. Figure 5-14 shows an example of a ping.

FIGURE 5-14

Ping uses ICMP to
verify connections to
remote hosts

```
C:\>ping 10.10.10.1

Pinging 10.10.10.1 with 32 bytes of data:

Reply from 10.10.10.1: bytes=32 time=1ms TTL=128
Reply from 10.10.10.1: bytes=32 time=1ms TTL=128
Reply from 10.10.10.1: bytes=32 time=1ms TTL=128
Reply from 10.10.10.1: bytes=32 time<10ms TTL=128

C:\>
```

Ping Options

Additional options are available to customize the output that ping provides.
Options include changing packet length, type of service, and TTL (Time
To Live) settings. You can append the –a option to resolve IP addresses to
its host name. The –f option will not enable the packets to be fragmented
by a router or gateway. This can be used to further stress connections to see
if they are failing.

The TTL settings can be specified with the –I option. Also, the type of
service option is available via the –v switch.

SETTING THE LENGTH OPTION   By default, packets are sent in
64-byte chunks. You can modify the packet size to further test the response
time. When larger packets are involved, you can see what larger loads will
do to response time as well as responsiveness. To change the packet size, use
the –l option followed by the packet length. The maximum packet length
that can be specified is 8192 bytes.

SETTING THE NUMBER OF ECHO PACKETS   You can specify
the number of packets to send to the remote host. By default, only four
packets are sent. You can specify any number of packets to send with the –n
option. You can also use the –t option to specify a continuous stream of
packets. This functionality is useful in monitoring trends in data transfers.

TIMEOUT INTERVALS   Timeout intervals are used to interpret
the time to travel between hops. A normal local area network usually lists

devices as being less than 10 milliseconds away. By default, two seconds is the timeout before a reply timed out message is generated. You can use the –w option to raise this value for troubleshooting.

LOOSE SOURCE ROUTING   Use ping to specify intermediate gateways to test against. You can route packets through particular IP addresses or host names specified. The –j option enables you to specify the hosts to route through. The –k option enables you to exclude hosts from this route list. The maximum number of hosts you can specify with both options is nine.

Troubleshooting with Ping

Use the ping utility to verify connectivity by IP address or host name. You must be able to resolve the host name to use this functionality. If you are unable to ping by host name but you can ping by IP address, you may have a name resolution problem.

If you are receiving reply timed out messages, you may try to bump up the timeout value with the –w option. Maybe the packets are arriving but are timing out before two seconds. After bumping up the value, if the replies are returning, a bandwidth problem may be present. Contact the network administrator where the numbers seem to rise.

Troubleshooting with TCP/IP Utilities

The two most common TCP/IP problems are network connectivity problems and name resolution problems. In this section, you will learn how to troubleshoot these problems and how to determine where the problems truly reside.

Given the following scenario, how do you know how to troubleshoot the problem?

You are trying to use a third-party application to access a remote computer via TCP/IP. You are unable to connect to the remote server at all.

To properly troubleshoot this problem, you must know where to begin. A scenario like this is very common in the TCP/IP world and could be categorized by one of the following problems:

- Basic network connectivity problem
- Name Resolution problem

It is very easy to determine which problem is occurring in a given situation. Start by trying to access the resource via the IP address rather than the host name. For example, if the problem is related to name resolution, **PING** *<hostname>* may not work but **PING** *<ipaddress>* will. This indicates that because the name cannot be resolved, the application does not know what the IP address is and therefore cannot access the remote host. If you cannot access the local resource via the IP address, this indicates a connectivity problem.

QUESTIONS AND ANSWERS

My users cannot see World Wide Web servers on the Internet.	Check that your DNS settings on the client are configured properly. Also, verify that the DNS servers have access to Internet information.
I don't know what my DNS client settings are.	Use the WINIPCFG or IPCONFIG command with the /All option.
I can ping a server, but the NBTSTAT utility shows its tables are empty.	The appropriate services on the remote computer are not started. The services broadcast are dependent upon items such as the Server or Workstation services.
If I ping a remote server, it does not respond; however, every now and then I can connect.	Try upping the timeout value for Ping. This may be an indication of a network problem between the client and remote server.
I need to find my computer MAC address.	Use the WINIPCFG or IPCONFIG command.

Connectivity Problems

Connectivity problems can be tough to isolate and resolve quickly, especially in complex networks. Let's use some of the tools you've learned about to troubleshoot the earlier problem of using a third-party application to access a remote computer via TCP/IP and being unable to connect to the remote server. You cannot ping the remote host by its IP address.

Check Your TCP/IP Configuration

Start by checking your TCP/IP configuration. TCP/IP requires several settings to be complete and accurate. When you use TCP/IP as your network protocol, an incorrect setting such as a mistyped subnet mask can keep your computer from talking with other hosts on the network. For example, if you have an incorrect default gateway setup, you may not be able to communicate with anyone on a remote network.

Use the IPCONFIG or WINIPCFG utility to determine your computer's basic TCP/IP settings. Verify that the IP address and subnet mask displayed by the IPCONFIG/WINIPCFG command are the correct values for your computer. Verify that your default gateway is set up with the correct address.

Ping the Loopback Address

Try pinging the loopback address. You can use the ping command to verify that TCP/IP is working properly. By pinging the loopback address, which is 127.0.0.1, you are actually verifying that the protocol stack is functioning properly. You should receive a reply like the one shown in Figure 5-15.

An error while pinging the loopback address usually indicates a problem with the TCP/IP protocol installed locally. If you do receive an error at this point, you should try uninstalling and reinstalling TCP/IP. You can remove and install TCP/IP from within the Control Panel.

Ping the Local IP Address

If you can successfully ping the loopback address, try pinging your local computer's IP address. If you do not know what you IP address is, remember that IPCONFIG/WINIPCFG will display this information for you. By typing the following at a command prompt, you should receive a response similar to the one shown in Figure 5-15.

PING *local IP address*

If an error occurs at this point, there may be a problem communicating with the Network Interface Card. You can first try reinstalling the adapter driver for the card. If that doesn't work, trying removing and reseating the card. This error may only be resolved by completely replacing the NIC.

Clear the ARP Cache Table

If the local IP address responds correctly, try clearing the ARP cache. If an IP address was errantly stored here, it could cause the client to attempt to contact the wrong computer.

Start by displaying the ARP cache. You can then see if there is an entry located for the remote IP address. If an entry exists, try deleting it with the –d option.

Verify the Default Gateway

When you have removed any errant entries, the next step is to ping the default gateway. This will only be involved if the host is on a remote subnet. When trying to ping a host, if it is not located on the local subnet, the request is automatically forwarded to the appropriate route. If a route does not exist, then the packet is forwarded to the default gateway. If the gateway does not respond, the packets will not be able to get to the remote host.

You can use IPCONFIG/WINIPCFG to display your default gateway. Once you have that address, try pinging that address or host name.

FIGURE 5-15

Ping the loopback address to test local connectivity

```
C:\>ping loopback
Pinging workstation2.company.com [127.0.0.1] with 32 bytes of data:
Reply from 127.0.0.1: bytes=32 time<10ms TTL=128
Reply from 127.0.0.1: bytes=32 time=1ms TTL=128
Reply from 127.0.0.1: bytes=32 time<10ms TTL=128
Reply from 127.0.0.1: bytes=32 time<10ms TTL=128

C:\>
```

Trace the Route to the Remote Host

After a packet leaves the default gateway, any route can be taken to reach a remote computer. The next step is to try to trace the route to the remote computer. Figure 5-16 shows a tracert in action.

A wide array of problems could show up here. You may notice that when the utility gets to a certain point, it responds with "Request timed out." If this occurs, it could indicate a route problem or a device failure. It could also indicate bandwidth issues. Try raising the timeout value. If it responds, but with high values, your data transfers could be failing because the application does not wait long enough. Try reconfiguring your application or adding more bandwidth to your network.

Another error you may receive is "Destination Net Unreachable." This usually indicates a network routing problem. Contact the network administrator responsible for that network segment.

Check IP Security on the Server

The next thing to try is to verify the security and settings on the remote computer. Port settings for services on the other computer may be different from the port settings you are trying to use to connect. Table 5-4 lists the standard port settings for commonly used protocols.

You can use the Telnet tool to verify that the other computer is configured to permit connections on the same port you are using. If you do not receive an error message, the other computer is configured to enable connections. If you do receive an error, try looking at the settings on the remote computer to verify that they are set up properly.

Use tracert to help you troubleshoot this problem

```
C:\>tracert 10.10.10.1

Tracing route to WORKSTATION1      [10.10.10.1]
over a maximum of 30 hops:

  1    1 ms     1 ms     1 ms   WORKSTATION1     [10.10.10.1]

Trace complete.

C:\>
```

PORT	PROTOCOL
80	HTTP
20	FTP
21	FTP
23	TELNET
25	SMTP
110	POP3

TABLE 5-4

Standard Port Settings for Common Protocols

Name Resolution Problems

Suppose you are able to connect to a remote host but are unable to connect via its host name. This indicates a name resolution problem. In the Microsoft world, there are two types of computer names: TCP/IP-based host names and NetBIOS names. These names can be resolved in several ways, including Domain Name System (DNS), Windows Internet Naming Service (WINS), a HOSTS file, or an LMHOSTS file. Each method has its advantages and disadvantages.

Name Resolution Order

The two types of Microsoft hosts each work a little differently. They can use the other's services; however, they use their own resolution methods first. TCP/IP-based hosts use the following resolution method:

1. Check local name
2. Check local HOSTS file
3. Check DNS servers
4. Check local NetBIOS cache
5. Check WINS servers
6. Broadcasts

NetBIOS resolution works in a very similar way. Name resolution for these services work in the following method:

1. Check its local NetBIOS cache

2. Check the WINS server

3. Broadcast for computer

4. Check LMHOSTS file

5. Check local host name (if Enable DNS for Windows Resolution is checked in TCP/IP properties)

6. Check TCP/IP HOSTS file

7. Check DNS servers

By knowing the order of name resolution, you can better understand how these services work and effectively troubleshoot them.

Check the HOSTS File

You can start by checking the HOSTS file. A HOSTS file is a text file that can be configured with any standard text editor. It contains static mappings for remote TCP/IP hosts. Each computer has its own host file, HOSTS.SAM, located in %windir% for Windows 95\98, and HOSTS, located in %SystemRoot%\System32\Drivers\Etc for Windows NT 4.0.

Because every machine maintains its own HOSTS file, they are not generally used in medium or large environments. If a modification or addition had to be made, each machine would have to receive this update. When you are talking about four or five machines, it's not that bad. When you have to modify 150 machines, it can become very difficult. Figure 5-17 shows an example of a HOSTS file.

To check your HOSTS file, open it and scan for the entry of the remote host. If this file is the method by which your computer is resolving addresses, verify that the entry exists and that it contains the correct information. If this is not the resolution method you are using, try checking your DNS configuration.

FIGURE 5-17

An example of a
HOSTS file

```
# This file contains the mappings of IP addresses to host names. Each
# entry should be kept on an individual line. The IP address should
# be placed in the first column followed by the corresponding host name.
# The IP address and the host name should be separated by at least one
# space.
#
# Additionally, comments (such as these) may be inserted on individual
# lines or following the machine name denoted by a '#' symbol.
#
# For example:
#
#      102.54.94.97      rhino.acme.com          # source server
#      38.25.63.10       x.acme.com              # x client host

127.0.0.1         localhost
10.10.10.1        workstation1
```

Check Your Domain Name System (DNS) Configuration

A Domain Name System (DNS) provides TCP/IP name resolution services.
This is a central server that computers can use to query for name resolution.
The advantage over the host file here is that you only have to make the
change on your server; all clients querying it will receive the update. This is
much easier to administer than 150 or more workstations.

If you use DNS for name resolution, first verify that you have the DNS
client set up correctly on the workstation. From a command prompt, type
IPCONFIG /ALL or **WINIPCFG /ALL** to list the DNS servers. If they
exist and are correct, try pinging the DNS server to see if it is online. If it
responds, try changing your DNS server to another server. It is possible that
one DNS server may have different information than another one does. You
also may need to contact your DNS administrator to verify that the name
exists in DNS and has the correct information.

Check the LMHOSTS File

The LMHOSTS file is similar to the HOSTS file, but is primarily used for
NetBIOS-based host name resolution. It can be used to handle TCP/IP
host name resolution, but it is not recommended because it is low in the
resolution order.

Like the HOSTS file, LMHOSTS is a text file that can be edited with any standard text editor. If your network uses LMHOSTS files for NetBIOS-based name resolution and you cannot connect to the remote computer using its NetBIOS name, there could be an invalid entry in your LMHOSTS file. Try scanning this file for the name of the remote machine. Verify that it exists and that it contains the correct information. If you are not using LMHOSTS, try checking your WINS server configuration settings.

Check Your Windows Internet Naming Service (WINS)Configuration

A WINS (Windows Internet Naming Service) server provides NetBIOS name resolution much like DNS servers provide TCP/IP host name resolution. If you use WINS for NetBIOS name resolution and you cannot connect to the other machine with its NetBIOS name, there may be a problem with your computer's WINS configuration.

Start by verifying your WINS configuration. From a command prompt, type **IPCONFIG /ALL** or **WINIPCFG /ALL**. This will display the current WINS servers configured for your computer. If the correct servers are listed, try pinging the primary WINS server. This is the first server that your requests will go to. If the host name is not located here, your computer will not try to get to the secondary WINS server. This second WINS server is used only in the event the primary cannot be reached.

If you cannot ping the primary WINS server address, try switching your primary with the secondary in the Control Panel. If you are able to resolve the name now, contact your WINS administrator to correct the problem. You may also need to verify that the remote host is registered with WINS correctly.

exam

ⓦatch

Make sure you understand the differences between host name resolution and NetBIOS (machine) name resolution. The exam will quiz you on both name resolution scenarios.

CERTIFICATION SUMMARY

The ARP utility is used to display and modify the Address Resolution Protocol name cache. This protocol maintains the mappings between the 32-bit TCP/IP addresses and the 48-bit Ethernet addresses. Each time you access a remote computer, its entry is updated in the ARP cache. Entries can also be manually added and deleted. By default, the ARP cache maintains unused entries for two minutes and entries in use for 10 minutes. RARP works in reverse to provide 48-bit Ethernet addresses to 32-bit TCP/IP address mappings.

The Telnet utility provides a virtual terminal to execute remote console commands. Telnet uses a TCP protocol connection to port 23. Telnet can also be used to connect to other port's set up to be interactive. The default line buffer size is 25 and can be configured to a maximum of 399 lines. The default terminal emulation for Telnet is VT100.

NBTSTAT displays NetBIOS over TCP/IP (NetBT) protocol statistics and connections. NetBT is a software standard and naming convention. Each workstation in a domain or workgroup must have a unique name. NetBIOS names are 16 characters with the last reserved for a hexadecimal number used as a resource type identifier. You can display remote statistics, registration information, and session information.

Tracert is used to determine the route data travels to reach its destination. It uses the ICMP protocol to display information such as hop count and timeout values. You can specify the maximum number of hops and timeout values to further customize the utility.

Netstat displays TCP/IP protocol statistics and session information. You can also display the local IP route table. Netstat can display Ethernet-specific statistics, sub-protocol statistics, and session information including listening ports.

IPCONFIG displays the current TCP/IP configuration for a Windows NT computer. WINIPCFG is a graphical interface used on Windows 95/98 computers to display this information. Information includes DNS servers, WINS servers, default gateway, subnet mask, IP address, and DHCP lease information. These utilities can be used to release or renew DHCP addresses assigned to an interface.

FTP (File Transfer Protocol) is used for file transfers between two computers. FTP requires two TCP port connections, port 20 for data and port 21 for commands. This allows for higher rate of transfer speeds. A server-based FTP program is used to store files and process commands. Additional features include debugging, disabling auto-logons, and suppressing screen output.

Ping is used to verify a remote computer's connectivity to the network. Additional options for troubleshooting include setting packet lengths, changing the TTL values, and specifying host lists to return routing statistics for.

TWO-MINUTE DRILL

- ❏ The most commonly used TCP/IP troubleshooting tools are:
    - ❏ **Arp** Displays and modifies local ARP cache
    - ❏ **Telnet** Remote Terminal Emulation, administration, and troubleshooting
    - ❏ **NBTSTAT** Checks the state of NetBIOS over TCP/IP connections
    - ❏ **Tracert** Traces and reports on the route to a remote computer
    - ❏ **Netstat** Displays statistics for current TCP/IP connections
    - ❏ **IPCONFIG/WINIPCFG** Displays current IP configuration information
    - ❏ **Ftp** Enables file transfers between remote computers
    - ❏ **Ping** Verifies host name, host IP address, and physical connectivity to a remote TCP/IP computer
- ❏ The *Address Resolution Protocol (ARP)* was designed to provide a mapping from the logical 32-bit TCP/IP addresses to the physical 48-bit MAC addresses.
- ❏ *Address resolution* is the process of finding the address of a host within a network.

❑ Remember that ARP translates IP addresses into MAC addresses. The Reverse Address Resolution Protocol, or RARP, is used to find a TCP/IP address from a MAC address.

❑ Only four types of messages can be sent out by the ARP protocol on any machine:

   ❑ ARP request

   ❑ ARP reply

   ❑ RARP request

   ❑ RARP reply

❑ *Reverse Address Resolution Protocol (RARP)* enables a machine to learn its own IP address by broadcasting to resolve its own MAC address.

❑ Telnet was designed to provide a virtual terminal or remote login across the network. It is connection based and handles its own session negotiation.

❑ The primary use of telnet is remote administration.

❑ Make sure you can recognize the output from each of the TCP/IP utilities listed in this chapter. On your Network+ exam you will be presented with output from a command and asked which command produced the output.

❑ The Microsoft TCP/IP stack uses an additional sub-protocol for its services, NetBIOS over TCP/IP (NetBT).

❑ NBTSTAT is used to troubleshoot connectivity between two computers trying to communicate via NetBT.

❑ Make sure you know the options available with the NBTSTAT command, such as NBTSTAT –R and NBTSTAT –a. I was surprised when I received a question asking which option to use to accomplish a certain goal.

❑ Tracert is a command-line utility that was designed to provide a very basic task: to determine the path taken by a data packet to reach its destination.

❑ Netstat displays protocol statistics and current TCP/IP network connections.

❏ Using netstat to monitor TCP protocol activity can enable you to troubleshoot TCP/IP based connections.

❏ IPCONFIG and WINIPCFG are utilities used to display the current TCP/IP configurations on the local workstations and to modify the DHCP addresses assigned to each interface.

❏ IPCONFIG is used in Windows NT to display TCP/IP information from a command prompt.

❏ WINIPCFG is the Windows 95/98-based graphical utility used to display TCP/IP information.

❏ FTP (File Transfer Protocol) is designed primarily for transferring data across a network.

❏ One of the most common forms of troubleshooting with FTP is to use online services to obtain patches and documentation.

❏ TFTP differs from FTP in two ways: it uses the User Datagram Protocol (UDP) connectionless transport instead of TCP, and you do not log on to the remote machine.

❏ Make sure you know what each TCP/IP utility is used for. For example, ARP is used to view and modify hardware (MAC) addresses. You will definitely receive a couple questions testing your knowledge of this.

❏ The Ping command is used to test a machine's connectivity to the network and to verify that it is active.

❏ Ping uses the Internet Control Message Protocol (ICMP) to verify connections to remote hosts by sending echo packets and listening for reply packets.

❏ Use the ping utility to verify connectivity by IP address or host name.

❏ The two most common TCP/IP problems are network connectivity problems and name resolution problems.

❏ Make sure you understand the differences between host name resolution and NetBIOS (machine) name resolution. The exam will quiz you on both name resolution scenarios.

SELF TEST

The following Self Test questions will help you measure your understanding of the material presented in this chapter. Read all the choices carefully, as there may be more than one correct answer. Choose all correct answers for each question.

1. Which utility can be used to display and modify the table that maintains the TCP/IP address to MAC address translation?

   A. NBTSTAT

   B. TELNET

   C. ARP

   D. SNMP

2. Which format types are not valid for ARP? (Choose all that apply.)

   A. ARP reply

   B. ARP decline

   C. ARP response

   D. ARP request

3. Which command uses the proper syntax for adding a static entry to the ARP cache?

   A. ARP -s 137.21.19.211 00-1A-0B-1C-32-11

   B. ARP –add 137.21.19.211

   C. ARP –s 00-1A-0B-1C-32-11 137.21.19.211

   D. ARP –s 137.21.19.211

4. How long will a dynamic ARP entry remain in cache if it is not in use?

   A. 10 minutes

   B. 5 minutes

   C. 2 minutes

   D. None of the above

5. Which utility enables you to execute console commands remotely at a virtual terminal?

   A. FTP

   B. Ping

   C. Telnet

   D. NBTSTAT

6. Which protocol is defined to use TCP port 23?

   A. Telnet

   B. FTP

   C. HTTP

   D. SMTP

7. What is the default terminal emulation type for Telnet?

   A. DEC

   B. ANSI

   C. VT52

   D. VT100

8. Which protocol uses a 16-character name with the last digit reserved as a resource identifier?

A. TCP/IP

B. IPX

C. NetBT

D. NBTSTAT

9. Which utility can be used to troubleshoot NetBIOS over TCP/IP connectivity issues?

A. NetBT

B. NetBEUI

C. NBTSTAT

D. NetBIOS

10. Which NBTSTAT switch enables you to display the computer's local NetBT name cache?

A. –R

B. –c

C. –a

D. –A

11. In what ways can a computer with a NetBIOS name register its services on the network?

A. Broadcast

B. HOSTS file

C. WINS server

D. Both A and C

12. Which NBTSTAT option will display statistics such as number of bytes inbound?

A. –s

B. –r

C. –n

D. –a

13. Which utility is used to determine the path data is taking during transport to a remote host?

A. NBTSTAT

B. ARP

C. FTP

D. Tracert

14. What is the default HOP count used by tracert?

A. 5

B. 16

C. 30

D. 32

15. Which utility is used to display TCP/IP specific protocol and interface statistics?

A. NBTSTAT

B. ARP

C. Netstat

D. None of the above

16. Which netstat option continually updates the displayed output based upon a time interval?

A. –p

B. –r

C. <interval>

D. –e

17. Which option is used with netstat to display server-based connections and listening ports?

A. –r

B. –k

C. −s

D. None of the above

18. Which protocols do not have statistics available with the netstat utility?

A. TCP

B. ICMP

C. ARP

D. IP

19. Which utility is used to display TCP/IP address information in Windows 95?

A. IPCONFIG

B. NBTSTAT

C. WINIPCFG

D. None of the above

20. Which items are not available for display in IPCONFIG?

A. TCP/IP address

B. MAC address

C. DHCP Lease information

D. None of the above

21. Which option listed is not available with WINIPCFG?

A. /ALL

B. /Release

C. /Obtain

D. /Renew

22. Which utility is used to facilitate file transfers between two remote hosts?

A. FTP

B. Telnet

C. Ping

D. None of the above

23. What TCP ports are used by FTP services?

A. TCP port 20

B. TCP port 25

C. TPC port 21

D. Both A and C

24. Which FTP command line option is used to turn on debugging?

A. −r

B. −d

C. −debug

D. −v

25. Which utility is used to verify network connectivity of a remote host?

A. Route

B. ARP

C. Ping

D. None of the above

6

Remote Connectivity

Due to the expansion of networks in the world today, user demands are increasing dramatically. They require additional functionality that has not existed before and the industry is challenged with making this happen. Many new advancements in the computing industry have come about this way. A very common example is remote connectivity. Remote connectivity came about as the need to interconnect networks and users became more and more prevalent.

As companies expanded and the world became a global market, the need to interconnect offices became crucial to their operation. The Internet is now based upon this entire concept, to enable information to be accessible to anyone in the world from any location. The government, to enable remote installations to communicate with each other and to provide redundancy in case of war, created the first truly remote network—ARPANET. As ARPANET began its transformation into what is now known as the Internet, universities began using the Internet to interconnect them to share information and resources. Now, a large portion of the world population uses the Internet for information exchange and research.

Today, companies use networks to interconnect remote sites. They also provide dial-up access to their users to enable them to connect from home or the road. This helps to increase productivity and allows for additional communication channels to be used. Many technologies we take for granted today use these concepts. For example, telephone systems use complex networks to enable us to call almost anyone in the world. E-mail is used to send messages and files through the Internet to reach anyone who has access to these services. As with any technology that we come to depend upon, remote connectivity has become a part of our everyday lives.

CERTIFICATION OBJECTIVE 6.01

Remote Connectivity Concepts

Many different technologies and functions are used for remote connectivity. One of the first networks created is still used today by almost everyone in the world: the telephone system. This concept was based upon the idea of enabling two people in different physical locations to speak with each other. The same basic idea is used today for many different applications. Global networks have been created by corporations and institutions alike to enable communicating remotely and sharing information.

The basic functionality that remote connectivity uses is available in many different protocols and devices. For example, companies use network links such as Frame Relay and ATM today that encompass many different technologies. More common applications include PPP dialup and the Public Switched Telephone Network (PSTN), which are used by the general public.

As technology has progressed, additional features have been added that allow for a more seamless and better remote connection. Higher bandwidths and better media have made remote networking an effective tool in today's global market. Additionally, as more and more features are added, the new technologies must provide support or they will not be as effective. For example, the Serial Line Internet Protocol (SLIP) was designed to enable users to connect remotely to a TCP/IP network through a standard phone line. Some networks require additional protocols to function. PPP has replaced SLIP because it enables you to pass multiple protocols over a single connection.

Each type of technology has its uses and advantages over others; however, you must first understand how these things work and the functionality they offer.

SLIP and PPP

SLIP and PPP are two communication protocols that are used to connect a computer to a remote network through a serial connection using a device such as a modem. When attaching to the remote network, it treats the computer as an actual node. This enables you to run network applications from home as if you were on the network. The most common use of these protocols is to connect to the Internet.

SLIP and PPP are fairly similar. They both use some of the same underlying technologies, but PPP is newer and better suited for today's expanding networks. The following sections will discuss what each protocol is, how it works, and some of its advantages.

SLIP

The Serial Line Internet Protocol, or SLIP, is a communications protocol used for making a TCP/IP connection over a serial interface to a remote network. SLIP was designed for connecting to remote UNIX servers across a standard phone line. This protocol was one of the first of its kind, enabling a remote network connection to be established over a standard phone line.

SLIP was designed when TCP/IP was the only network protocol commonly used by all UNIX platforms. TCP/IP was the protocol used to interconnect UNIX servers with the Internet and on a private network. It only made sense to design a dial-up method that would use the same network layer. Although it is still in use today, it has primarily been replaced by the Point-to-Point protocol. SLIP services are still available with Windows 95 and Windows NT.

USING SLIP TO CONNECT TO A REMOTE HOST   To set up SLIP, you must first set up a Dial-Up networking connection. Once a profile is set up, you can configure the dialup protocol to use from within the properties of the connection. Figure 6-1 shows an example of the Properties available for configuring a SLIP connection.

You may notice that many of the fields are grayed out. This is because SLIP provides no support for advanced features such as software compression, password encryption, or multiple network protocols. Click the TCP/IP Settings button to configure parameters such as the TCP/IP address, DNS server addresses, default gateway, and IP header compression.

SLIP is a very simple serial-based protocol. It does not provide the complexity that others do, such as the Point-to-Point Protocol. Although this can be an advantage, unfortunately it does not include the feature set that other protocols do. For example, it does not support option negotiation or error detection during the session setup. It cannot be assigned a DHCP address. It also cannot negotiate the authentication method. Issues such as these have helped define the new protocols that are emerging, because the functionality does not exist in SLIP.

SLIP is an older technology that is really no longer in use. Many Internet Service Providers (ISPs) still provide support for SLIP, but SLIP is quickly

FIGURE 6-1

Configure the dial-up
protocol for your SLIP
connection

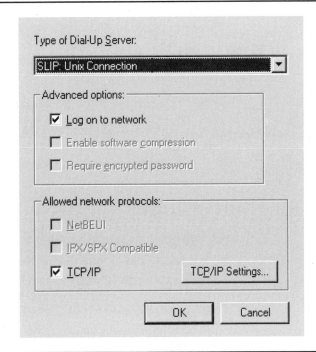

being replaced by protocols with much more functionality, such as PPP or
PPTP.

PPP

The Point-to-Point Protocol, or PPP, is a Data Link Layer protocol used
to encapsulate higher network layer protocols to pass over synchronous
and asynchronous communication lines. It was originally designed as an
encapsulation protocol for transporting multiple network layer traffic over
point-to-point links. PPP also established other standards, including
asynchronous and bit-orientated synchronous encapsulation, network
protocol multiplexing, session negotiation, and data-compression
negotiation. PPP also supports protocols other than TCP/IP, such as
IPX/SPX and DECnet.

To enable PPP to transmit data over a serial point-to-point link, three
components are used. Each component has its own separate function but

requires the use of the other two to complete its tasks. The following list explains the three components and their purpose:

- PPP uses the High-Level Data-Link Control (HDLC) protocol as the basis to encapsulate its data during transmission.

- PPP uses Link Control Protocol (LCP) to establish, test, and configure the data link connection.

- Different Network Control Protocols (NCPs) are used to configure the different communications protocols. This enables you to use different protocols such as TCP/IP and IPX over the same line simultaneously.

NETWORK CONTROL PROTOCOLS   Although multiple NCPs are available, Microsoft products use three main protocols for PPP. Each NCP is specific to a particular Network Layer protocol such as IP or IPX/SPX.

- The Internet Protocol Control Protocol (IPCP) is the NCP used to configure, enable, and disable the IP protocol modules at each end of the link.

- The Internet Packet eXchange Control Protocol (IPXCP) is used to enable, configure, and disable IPX protocol modules at each end of the link. There are multiple versions of this NCP available; however, IPXCP is the most common and is overtaking the other IPX NCPs out there.

- The NetBIOS Frames Control Protocol (NBFCP) is used to enable, configure, and disable NetBEUI protocol modules at each end of the link. This NCP is a Microsoft-proposed protocol and is in draft status with the IETF (Internet Engineering Task Force).

HOW PPP WORKS   PPP uses each of these three components together to enable it to communicate. It starts by sending LCP frames to test and configure the data link. This establishes the link and negotiates any additional options required to facilitate the connection. Next, the authentication protocols are negotiated. There are multiple types of authentication protocols available to use; however, the most common are CHAP and PAP. This determines what type of validation is performed for security. The client then sends NCP frames to configure and set up the network layer protocols to be used during this session. When this step is complete, each network protocol can pass data through this connection. HDLC is used to encapsulate the data stream as it passes through the PPP connection. The link remains active until an LCP or NCP frame closes the link or until an error or external event occurs, such as a user disconnecting the link.

A control mechanism is included in PPP to enable protocols to communicate with each other. The Finite-State Automation (FSA) processes status messages between each layer to coordinate communications. The FSA does not actually participate in data flows, but works with the other protocols to keep then in sync and enable them to concentrate on their own jobs.

PPP FRAMING   PPP Framing defines the format in which data is encapsulated before it crosses the network. PPP offers a standard framing solution to enable connections to any standard PPP server because all of these vendors use the same format. PPP uses HDLC as the basis for its encapsulation framing for serial connections. HDLC is widely used in other implementations and has been slightly modified for use with PPP. The modifications were made to facilitate multiplexing Network Control Protocol layers.

PPP DEVICES   PPP is capable of operating across any DTE/DCE device. There are many examples of these devices available, including the most common, EIA/TIA 232 standard, better known as a modem. PPP is able to use any DTE/DCE devices as long as they support duplex circuits. These can be dedicated or switched and can operate in an asynchronous or synchronous bit-serial mode. Also, the limit on transmission rates is specified by the interfaces and is not controlled by the PPP protocol.

AUTHENTICATION PROTOCOLS   With PPP, each system may be required to authenticate itself. This can be done by using an authentication protocol. The most common authentication protocols include Password Authentication Protocol (PAP), the Challenge Handshake Authentication Protocol (CHAP), and the Microsoft adaptation of CHAP—MS-CHAP. When a connection is being established, either end node can require the other to authenticate itself, whether it is the remote host or the originator of the call. The LCP can be used to send information to the other node to specify the authentication type. By using the authentication protocols, you enable the capability to offer a level of security by requiring authentication to make a remote connection as well as have control over the level of security used.

PAP works very similar to a regular network login. The client authenticates itself to a server by passing the username and password to it. The server then compares this information to its password store. Because the password is passed in clear text, this would not work well in an environment where security concerns are an issue. This opens the doors for anyone listening to the line, such as with a network sniffer, and to brute force password-cracking attacks.

CHAP uses an encryption algorithm to pass the authentication data to protect it from hackers. The server sends a randomly generated challenge request with its hostname to the client. The client then uses the hostname to look up the appropriate secret and returns a response using a one-way hash with the client's hostname. The host now compares the result and acknowledges the client if it matches. CHAP also sends challenges at regular intervals to verify that the correct client is still using this connection. The challenge values change during each interval. Because CHAP is so much more secure than PAP, it is used widely today on the Internet. PAP is usually used only in public FTP sites or other public areas.

MS-CHAP is a Microsoft adaptation of CHAP. It uses the same type of encryption methodology but is slightly more secure. The server sends a challenge to the originating host, which must return the user name and an MD-4 hash of the challenge string, the session ID, and the MD-4 hashed password. This enables the authenticator to store the passwords in an encrypted format instead of plain text. MS-CHAP also provides expanded functionality, such as more error codes and additional services.

EXERCISE 6-1

Creating a PPP Dial-Up Connection in Windows 95

1. To install dial-up networking for Windows 95, select Start | Settings | Control Panel. The Control Panel folder opens.

2. Double-click Add/Remove Programs. The Add/Remove Programs Properties dialog box appears.

3. Click the Windows Setup tab to bring it to the front. Highlight Communications in the Components box and click the Details button. The Communications dialog box appears.

4. Place a checkmark in the Dial-Up Networking check box in the Components box, and then click the OK button. OK out of the remaining dialog boxes and close the Control Panel. (If the Dial-Up Networking option is already selected, click the Cancel button, close the other dialog boxes, and go to Step 5.)

5. Select Start | Programs | Accessories | Dial-Up Networking. The Dial-Up Networking folder opens.

6. Double-click the Make New Connection icon. The Make New Connection dialog box appears. (If you do not have a modem installed, you will have to set one up prior to continuing.)

7. The connection wizard takes you through choosing the appropriate modem (if necessary) and entering the remote phone number to be used. When complete, an icon for the new PPP connection appears in the Dial-Up Networking window.

8. To connect with the new PPP connection, double-click the connection icon in the Dial-Up Networking folder and click the Connect button.

TROUBLESHOOTING PPP   When you use PPP to connect to a remote network, you may encounter problems. These problems can range from no dial tone to a modem misconfiguration to connectivity problems with the remote PPP server. A log is included with PPP to enable you to monitor the steps in opening a PPP connection and troubleshooting where the breakdown may have occurred. Exercise 6-2 shows how to set up a dial-up networking connection to enable the PPP log file.

Enabling the Log File for a PPP Dial-Up Networking Connection

1. Select Start | Settings | Control Panel. The Control Panel folder opens.

2. Double click the Network icon. The Network dialog box appears.

3. On the Configuration page, highlight Dial-Up Adapter and click Properties. The Dial-Up Adapter dialog box appears.

4. Click the Advanced tab to bring it to the front.

5. In the Properties box, select Record a log file; in the Value box, select Yes, and then click OK.

6. Click OK in the Network dialog box. You are prompted to reboot. Click Yes. Your system reboots.

When logging has been enabled, you can see the log file after the next attempt to connect to a PPP server. The log file, PPPLOG.TXT, is stored in the Windows directory by default. It can be viewed by any standard text editor and is appended to each time a new connection is attempted.

Figure 6-2 shows the beginning of a PPP connection to a remote network. It demonstrates the layout of the log file and how detailed it can

FIGURE 6-2

An example of the log file available for troubleshooting PPP connections

```
05-18-1998 20:10:30.83 - Remote access driver log opened.
05-18-1998 20:10:30.83 - Installable CP VxD SPAP      is loaded
05-18-1998 20:10:30.83 - Server type is  PPP (Point to Point
Protocol).
05-18-1998 20:10:30.83 - FSA : Adding Control Protocol 80fd (CCP) to
control protocol chain.
05-18-1998 20:10:30.83 - FSA : Protocol not bound - skipping control
protocol 803f (NBFCP).
05-18-1998 20:10:30.83 - FSA : Adding Control Protocol 8021 (IPCP) to
control protocol chain.
05-18-1998 20:10:30.83 - FSA : Protocol not bound - skipping control
protocol 802b (IPXCP).
05-18-1998 20:10:30.83 - FSA : Adding Control Protocol c029
(CallbackCP) to control protocol chain.
05-18-1998 20:10:30.83 - FSA : Adding Control Protocol c027 (no
description) to control protocol chain.
05-18-1998 20:10:30.83 - FSA : Adding Control Protocol c023 (PAP) to
control protocol chain.
```

become. Understanding how to read these log files will enable you to troubleshoot almost any PPP problem that may occur.

Advantages of PPP over SLIP

PPP offers several advantages over SLIP. First, PPP offers multi-network protocol support. SLIP can only be used with TCP/IP. PPP can use a myriad of different protocols through one session, such as TCP/IP, IPX, AppleTalk, and DECnet. You do not have to use TCP/IP with PPP. Any of these protocols can be used. This enables you to connect to multiple types of systems on the remote network. The addition of NCPs allows for this functionality in PPP.

In addition, PPP offers the capability to negotiate IP addresses during the session setup. In other words, you can specify that PPP uses DHCP and not have to manually set up an IP address during each connection. The addition of LCP made options such as this available to PPP. PPP also handles higher speed links better than SLIP does. This is due to the error-checking capability within the protocol. SLIP does not check datagrams as they pass through the connection for errors.

QUESTIONS AND ANSWERS

I want to use serial-based dial-up access with TCP/IP and IPX.	You should use PPP, because SLIP will not support anything except TCP/IP.
I only need TCP/IP; should I use SLIP instead of PPP?	Most ISPs do not provide support for SLIP. PPP has replaced SLIP in most cases, the exception being UNIX servers.
Can PPP be used for server data replication services?	Yes; however, if you plan on having much data, PPP through serial connection speeds can only reach 56 Kbps. You should consider a faster solution, such as ISDN.
I need to have 50 users connect to the internal network from their laptops.	PPP can facilitate that, but a modem bank to support it could be costly. You might consider PPTP if the internal network is connected to the Internet or other public TCP/IP network.

PPTP

The Point-to-Point Tunneling Protocol (PPTP) is a network protocol that provides for the secure transfer of data from a remote client to a private server by creating a multi-protocol virtual private network, or VPN. PPTP is used in TCP/IP networks as an alternative to conventional dial-up networking methods. This enables multi-protocol secure communications over a public TCP/IP network such as the Internet. PPTP takes advantage of an additional level of security that is not currently available in other standard implementations.

PPTP is actually an extension of PPP. It encapsulates PPP packets into IP datagrams for transmission across the network. This enables the functionality of PPP while using the VPN technology for security. By using both options tied into one protocol, you get the best of both worlds.

Brief History of PPTP

PPTP became recognized by the IETF in June of 1996. Many tunneling protocols have been created and implemented; however, this was the first standard tunneling protocol to become available. Since this time, many vendors have adopted it in an attempt to provide a secure method to connect across the public Internet into a corporate internal network.

How PPTP Works

Virtual private networks (VPNs) are used to provide tunneling through a public network with a secure communications channel. It can be used by normal users to dial into a public network, such as PSTN, to use the Internet to connect to their corporate offices. This enables you to use the network infrastructure that is already in place and replace the need for dedicated modem banks for your users.

PPTP tunneling can be defined as routing packets through an intermediate public network to reach a private network. Only the PPTP-enabled client can access the remote network; other clients on the same segment cannot. The interesting thing about this process is that you can dial into a standard PPP server and use it to establish a PPTP connection to the remote network. No additional setup or options are required of your ISP; most offer PPP access already. You could also set up a PPTP server to dial in to; this would enable you to only require PPP to be set up on the clients.

Once the PPTP server receives the packet from the client connection, it routes the data on to the appropriate resource. This occurs by stripping off the PPTP and PPP overhead to obtain the addressing information originally applied to it. The PPTP server must be configured with the TCP/IP protocol to communicate with PPTP and whatever other protocols are being passed through this VPN tunnel.

A VPN works by encapsulating the data within IP packets to transport it through PPP. This enables the data to pass through the Internet and use the standards already in place. No configuration changes are required to your existing network stacks; they can be used as-is over the PPTP connection. Other protocols, such as NetBEUI and IPX, can also pass through this secure connection.

VPNs are virtual devices set up as if they were regular devices such as a modem. In addition, PPTP must be set up on the client and server. Host computers in the route between these two computers do not need to be PPTP aware. They only need to provide an IP route to the remote server. Figure 6-3 shows the PPTP connection sequence.

FIGURE 6-3	PPTP connection methodology

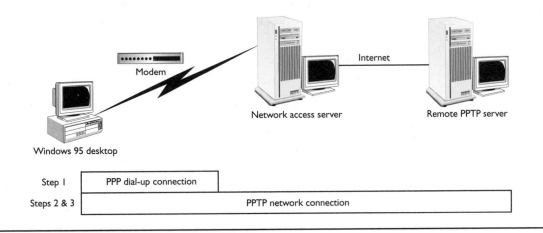

PPTP mainly involves three processes to set up a secure communications channel. Each process must be completed prior to beginning the next process. The following list identifies the process involved:

- **PPP Connection and Communication**   PPTP uses the PPP protocol to connect to a remote network. When connected, the PPP protocol is also used to encrypt the data packets being passed between the remote host and the local machine.

- **PPTP Control Connection**   When the PPP session is established, PPTP creates a control connection between the client and the remote PPTP server. This process is referred to as *tunneling*.

- **PPTP Data Tunneling**   PPTP creates the IP datagrams for PPP to send. The packets are encrypted by PPP and sent through the tunnel to the PPTP server. The PPTP server is then used to decrypt the PPP-encrypted packets, disassemble the IP datagram, and route to the appropriate host.

exam
ⓦatch

Be sure to know the three processes involved with PPTP and how PPP applies to each one.

PPTP relies heavily on PPP to perform its job. PPP is used to enable multiple network layer protocols to be used within the connection. PPP is also used to perform other functions such as establishing and maintaining a connection, authenticating users, and encrypting data packets.

Setting up PPTP

There are three main components when setting up a PPTP connection. Each is equally important and must be configured properly to enable a user to access resources on a remote network:

- PPTP Client
- PPTP Server
- Network Access Server (NAS)

Each component has its specified functions and requirements. Today, Windows 95 and Windows NT can both be used as a PPTP client. Windows NT Server also supports PPTP server services through Remote Access Service (RAS). Exercise 6-3 explains how to set up Windows NT as a PPTP client. The exercise demonstrates using Windows NT as a PPTP client dialing into an ISP to access a remote PPTP server.

EXERCISE 6-3

Setting Up Windows NT as a PPTP Client

1. Verify that the following are installed and configured:

   ■ TCP/IP

   ■ RAS with dial-Up networking

   ■ Analog modem or ISDN connection

   ■ ISP-based PPP account

2. Select Start | Settings | Control Panel, and then double-click the Network icon.

3. Click the Protocols tab to bring it to the front, and then click Add.

4. Select Point to Point Tunneling Protocol from the Network Protocol box, as shown next, and then click OK.

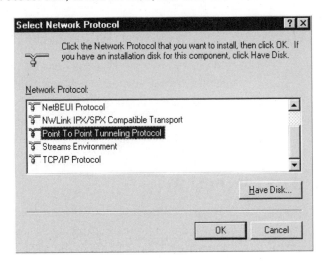

5. Type the drive and path to the Windows NT source files. The appropriate files will then be copied to the local hard drive.

6. The setup wizard asks you to define the number of VPNs to use. For the client, typically this should be the default setting of 1. By default, Windows NT server supports 256 VPNs. Choose 1 and click OK.

7. You must configure a VPN device for RAS in the Add RAS Device dialog box, as shown next. By default, the RAS-capable device is shown. Click OK to accept this device.

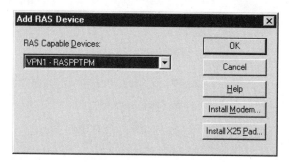

8. To configure VPN settings, use the Remote Access Setup applet. Click the Network button to assign protocols. Click the Configure button to set up dial-in and dial-up settings.

9. When finished, close all applets and applications and reboot the computer.

Because of the popularity of PPP and the Internet, a more secure dial-in solution was needed. PPTP grants you the capability to have a user log in to a remote private corporate network via any ISP and maintain a secure, encrypted connection. This concept is being implemented by more and more companies every year and its popularity has exploded since its first draft was proposed in 1996.

ISDN and PSTN (POTS)

In the past, the phone network consisted of an interconnection of wires that connected telephone users directly by an analog-based system. This system was very inefficient because it did not work well for long distance connections and was very prone to noise. In the 1960s, the telephone companies began converting this system to a packet-based, digital switching network. Today, nearly all voice switching in the United States is digital; however, the customer connection to the switching office is primarily still analog.

ISDN

Integrated Services Digital Network (ISDN) is a system of digital telephone connections that enables data to be transmitted simultaneously end to end. This technology has been available for more than a decade and is designed to enable faster, clearer communications for small offices and home users. It came about as the standard telephone system began its migration from an analog format to digital. ISDN is the format portions of the digital telephone system now used to replace analog systems.

HISTORY OF ISDN   In the 1950s, the phone companies began looking at ways to improve communications. They began by sampling the analog signals that were passed during a phone conversation and attempted to convert them to digital signals. From this analog sampling, they determined that 64 Kbps would enable a digital signal to properly handle voice communications through the telephone network. This became the foundation of ISDN.

Because a standard did not exist between the different phone companies, the Consultative Committee for International Telephony and Telegraph (CCITT) began working on the Integrated Digital Network (IDN) in the late 1960s. IDN combined the functions of switching and transmission into one piece of hardware that could be set as the standard for all telephone companies to use. This initiative not only moved telephony services towards a standard, but also made the network much more efficient. It wasn't perfect, but was a step in the right direction.

The concept of ISDN was introduced in 1972. The concept was based upon moving the analog-digital conversion equipment onto the customer premises to enable voice and data services to be sent through a single line. Telephone companies also began using a new kind of digital communications link between each central office. A T1 link could carry twenty-four of these 64

Kbps voice channels, and it used the same amount of copper wire as only two analog voice calls. Throughout the 1970s the telephone companies continued to upgrade their switching offices. They began rolling out T1 links directly to customers to provide high-speed access. The need for an efficient solution was greater than ever.

When ISDN was recognized by the ITU (International Telecommunications Union), an initiative was begun to define its standards. The initial recommendations were published in CCITT Recommendation I.120 (1984) and described some initial guidelines for implementing ISDN. In the early 1990s, an effort was begun to establish a standard implementation for ISDN in the United States. The NI-1 (National ISDN 1) standard was defined by the industry so that users would not have to know the type of switch they are connected to in order to buy equipment and software compatible with it.

Because some major office switches were incompatible with this standard, some major telephone companies had trouble switching to the NI-1 standard. This caused some problems when trying to communicate between these nonstandard systems and everyone else. Eventually, all of the systems were brought up to standards. A set of core services was defined in all BRI interfaces of the NI-1 standard. The services include data call services, voice call services, call forwarding, and call waiting. Most devices today conform to the NI-1 standard.

A more comprehensive standardization initiative, NI-2 (National ISDN 2) was recently adopted. Now, several major manufacturers of networking equipment have become involved to help set the standard and make ISDN a more economical solution. The NI-2 standard had two goals: standardize the PRI interface as NI-1 did for the BRI, and simplify the identification process. Until this point, PRIs were mainly vendor-dependent and made it difficult to interconnect these together. Also, a standard was created for NI-2 for identifiers.

ISDN CHANNELS An ISDN transmission circuit consists of a logical grouping of data channels. With ISDN, voice and data are carried by these channels. Two types of channels are used for a single ISDN connection, a B channel and a D channel. Each channel has a specific function and bandwidth associated with it. The bearer channels (B channels) transfer data. They offer a bandwidth of 64 Kbps (kilobytes per second) per each channel. In ISDN terminology, kilobytes refer to 1000 bytes. Many other computer-related functions using this term refer to 1024 bytes instead. Therefore, ISDN B channels operate at 64000 bytes. A hardware limitation in some switches limits the B channels to 56 Kbps, or 56000 bytes.

The data channel (D channel) handles signaling at 16 Kbps or 64 Kbps. This includes the session setup and teardown using a communications language known as DSS1. The purpose of this channel is to enable the B channels to strictly pass data. You remove the administrative overhead from them by using the D channel. The bandwidth available for the D channel is dependent upon the type of service—BRIs usually require 16 Kbps and PRIs use 64 Kbps. Typically, ISDN service contains two B channels and a single D channel.

H channels are used to specify a number of B channels. The following list shows the implementations:

- **H0** 384 Kbps (6 B channels)
- **H10** 1472 Kbps (23 B channels)
- **H11** 1536 Kbps (24 B channels)
- **H12** 1920 Kbps (30 B channels)—Europe

ISDN INTERFACES Although B channels and D channels can be combined in any number of ways, the phone companies created two standard configurations. There are two basic types of ISDN service: Basic Rate Interface (BRI) and Primary Rate Interface (PRI). BRI consists of two 64 Kbps B channels and one 16 Kbps D channel for a total of 144 Kbps. Only 128 Kbps is used for user data transfers. BRIs were designed to enable customers to use their existing wiring. This provided a low-cost solution for customers and is why it is the most basic type of service today intended for small business or home use.

PRI is intended for users with greater bandwidth requirements. It requires T1 carriers to facilitate communications. Normally, the channel structure contains 23 B channels plus one 64 Kbps D channel for a total of 1536 Kbps. This standard is used only in North America and Japan. European countries support a different kind of ISDN standard for PRI. It consists of 30 B

Channels and one 64 Kbps D channel for a total of 1984 Kbps. A technology known as Non-Facility Associated Signaling (NFAS) is available to enable you to support multiple PRI lines with one 64 Kbps D channel.

To use BRI services, you must subscribe to ISDN services through a local telephone company or provider. By default, you must be within 18,000 feet (about 3.4 miles) of the telephone company central office for BRI services. Repeater devices are available for ISDN service to extend this distance, but these devices can be very expensive. Special types of equipment are required to communicate with the ISDN provider switch and with other ISDN devices. You must have an ISDN Terminal Adapter and an ISDN Router.

ISDN DEVICES The ISDN standard refers to the devices that are required to connect the end node to the network. Although some vendors provide devices that have several functions included, a separate device defines each function within the standard. The protocols that each device uses are also defined and are associated with a specific letter. Also known as reference points, these letters are R, S, T, and U. ISDN standards also define the device types. They are NT1, NT2, TE1, TE2, and TA. The architecture for these devices and the reference points can be seen in Figure 6-4.

exam
ⓦatch

Be sure to know the device types and where each type is used. Also, know the number of channels and speeds associated with a BRI and a PRI.

FIGURE 6-4

ISDN device architecture

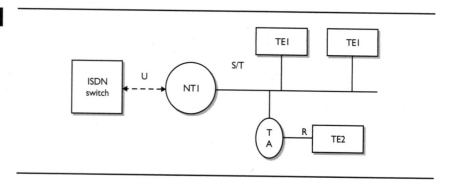

ISDN REFERENCE POINTS   Reference points are used to define logical interfaces. They are in effect a type of protocol used in communications. The following list contains the reference points:

- **R**   Defines reference point between a TE2 device and a TA device.
- **S**   Defines reference point between TE1 devices and NT1 or NT2 devices.
- **T**   Defines reference point between NT1 and NT2 devices.
- **U**   Defines reference point between NT1 devices and line termination equipment. This is usually the central switch.

Network Terminator 1 (NT1) is the device that communicates directly with the Central Office switch. The NT1 receives a U interface connection from the telephone company and puts out a T interface connection for the NT2. NT1 handles the physical layer portions of the connection, such as physical and electrical termination, line monitoring, and multiplexing.

Network Terminator 2 (NT2) is placed between an NT1 device and any adapters or terminal equipment. Many devices provide the NT1 and NT2 device in the same physical hardware. Larger installations generally separate these devices. An example of an NT2 device is a digital PBX or ISDN network router. An NT2 device provides an S interface and accepts a T interface from an NT1. NT2 usually handles data link and network layer functions in network with multiple devices such as contention monitoring and routing.

Terminal Equipment 1 (TE1) is a local device that speaks via an S interface. It can be directly connected to the NT1 or NT2 devices. An ISDN telephone or ISDN fax are good examples of TE1 devices.

Terminal Equipment 2 (TE2) devices are common everyday devices that can be used for ISDN connectivity. Any telecommunications device that is not in the TE1 category is classified as a TE2 device. A terminal adapter is used to connect these devices to an ISDN network and attaches through an R interface. Examples of TE2 devices include standard fax machines, PCs, and regular telephones.

A *terminal adapter (TA)* connects TE2 devices to an ISDN network. It connects through the R interface to the TE2 device and through the S interface to the ISDN network. The peripheral required for personal computers often includes an NT1 device. These are better known as ISDN modems.

on the job

ISDN modems are used in PCs to connect them to an ISDN network. The term modem *is used incorrectly here. ISDN passes data in a digital format. Conventional modems convert analog to digital and vice versa.*

IDENTIFIERS   Standard telephone lines use a ten-digit identifier that is permanently assigned. This is the telephone number. ISDN uses similar types of identifiers; however, they are not as easily used as a telephone number. ISDN uses five separate identifiers when making a connection. The provider assigns two of these when the connection is first set up: the Service Profile Identifier (SPID) and the directory number (DN). These are the most common numbers used because the other three are dynamically set up each time a connection is made. The three dynamic identifiers are TEI, BC, and SAPI.

The *Service Profile Identifier (SPID)* is the most important number needed when using ISDN. The provider statically assigns this number when the ISDN service is set up. It usually includes the Directory number plus a few extra digits. The SPID usually contains between 10 and 14 characters and varies from region to region. SPIDs can be assigned for every ISDN device, for the entire line, or for each B channel.

The SPID is unique throughout the entire switch and must be set up correctly. If it is incorrect, it is like dialing the wrong phone number—you will not be able to contact the person you were trying to reach. When an ISDN device is connected to the network, it sends the SPID to the switch. If the SPID is correct, the switch uses the stored information about your service profile to set up the data link. The ISDN device will not send the SPID again unless the device is disconnected from the network.

The *directory number (DN)* is the ten-digit phone number the telephone company assigns to any analog line. ISDN services enable greater flexibility in using this number than analog services do. Unlike with an analog line where a one-to-one relationship exists, the DN is only a logical mapping. A single DN can be used for multiple channels or devices. Also, up to eight

DNs can be assigned to one device. Because a single BRI can have up to eight devices, it can support up to 64 directory numbers. This is how offices are able to have multiple numbers assigned to their office. Most standard BRI installations include only two directory numbers, one for each B channel.

A *Terminal Endpoint Identifier (TEI)* identifies the particular ISDN device to the switch. This identifier changes each time a device is connected to the ISDN network. Unlike the SPID or directory number, it is dynamically allocated by the central switch.

The *Service Address Point Identifier (SAPI)* identifies the particular interface on the switch that your devices are connected to. This identifier is used by the switch and is also dynamically updated each time a device connects to the network.

The *bearer code (BC)* is an identifier made up of the combination of TEI and SAPI. It is used as the call reference and is dynamic like the two identifiers included within it. It changes each time a connection is established.

ADVANTAGES OF ISDN   ISDN offers several major advantages over conventional analog methods. First, it has a speed advantage over normal dial-up lines. Normal dial-up lines use a modem to convert the digital signals from a PC into analog. This enables data to be transferred over public phone lines. This technology does, however, have speed limitations. The fastest standard modem connection that is currently available is 56 Kbps. Because this is an analog connection, many modems cannot reach this speed because they are limited by the quality of the connection. This accounts for your connecting at different speeds each time you dial in to a remote network. Because phone lines cannot actually transmit at 56 Kbps, a special kind of compression is used to enable these speeds to be possible. Two standards currently exist. For Internet Service Providers to appease everyone, they must support both standards, which gets expensive quickly.

ISDN enables you to use multiple digital channels at the same time to pass data through regular phone lines. The difference is that the connection being made from your computer is completely digital instead of converting to analog. You can also use other protocols that enable you to bind channels together to get a higher bandwidth rate. In addition, ISDN takes half the time an analog line takes to make a connection.

In addition to speed, ISDN supports multiple devices set up in one link. In an analog system, a single line is required for each device attached. For example, a separate phone line is needed for a normal phone, a fax machine, or a computer modem. Since ISDN supports multiple devices, you can use each one of these items on a single line. It will also be clearer due to the fact that the data is being passed in a digital format.

Because ISDN uses a separate channel, the D channel for signaling, it removes the administrative overhead required. This means that the data is not hindered by the sessions setups and the communications required by the devices. The D channel keeps all of this information off the data streams. Because of the separation, the setup and takedown of each session are much faster. In addition, ISDN equipment is able to handle calls more intelligently.

PSTN (POTS)

Almost everyone in the world has used a telephone at least once. Today, you can call anywhere in the world and get a direct connection almost instantly by using this technology. The Public Switched Telephone Network (PSTN) was originally designed as an analog switching system for routing voice calls. Because it has existed for several decades and used by so many, it has come to be known as the Plain Old Telephone System (POTS). Because this is considered the first wide area network, it was the basis for many of the WAN technologies that exist today and has been instrumental in their evolution.

HISTORY OF PSTN During the initial years that PSTN was around, digital technologies had not even been considered yet. The telephone network was based purely upon analog signals traveling across copper wire to transport a human voice. The only repetitions of the signal that may have occurred were through one or two repeater devices. The term *Via Net Loss (VNL)* was coined to calculate the signal degradation that occurred. This was measured in *decibels (dB)*. The only metering equipment needed to test connections were test tones, decibel meters, or volume unit (VU) meters. Volume meters were used to measure complex signals such as the human voice. These meters simply measure the loss or gain of a specific circuit.

Prior to the 1960s, PSTN lines could not handle anything more than what they were originally designed for—voice communication. Since then, many great technology leaps have helped it progress. The beginning of this era was marked by the advent of the Bell T1 transmission system. As T1s became more steadily used in the telephone network, bandwidth and quality increased. This advent also began the true migration from using human operators to route calls to switching these functions electronically.

In the 1970s and 80s, the phone companies began to invest more resources in improving the quality of the PSTN backbone. This backbone, also known as the *Digital Access Cross-Connect System (DACCS)* was the combination of all of the T1 and T3 lines. Although many problems were associated during this time with the DACCS, it provided a technology upgrade to help improve services all the way around. Soon companies started looking at PSTN lines as an alternative to the dedicated point-to-point links they currently used.

As the industry started to move in this direction, manufacturers began to market modems for this purpose. As modems became more commonplace, the manufacturers began mass marketing them for everyday users. Today, using a modem to dial in to a remote network is quickly becoming as common as having a telephone in your house. More and more people are getting online, which has played a large part in the popularity of the Internet. Companies use PSTN lines today to enable remote users to dial in to private networks as well as back up data links for computer systems that require remote connectivity.

HOW PSTN WORKS   The POTS network originally began with human operators sitting at a switch manually routing calls. The original concept of the Bell system was a series of PSTN trunks connecting the major US cities. This was an analog-based system that met its requirements at the time—human voice transmissions. Since the inception of the telephone, a lot has changed. PSTN systems still use analog from the end node to the first switch. Once received, the switch converts the signal to a digital format and then routes the call on. Once the call is received on the other end, the last switch in the loop converts the signal back to analog, and the call is initiated. Because the end node is still analog, modems are used in most homes to facilitate dial-up access. Faster technologies such as ISDN or T1s use a dedicated point-to-point link through a completely digital path. This is how the higher bandwidths are reachable. Currently, analog lines can only reach a maximum speed of 56 Kbps. Using digital lines, speeds in excess of 2GB per second can be reached.

exam
Watch

Remember that the maximum available speed with an analog modem is 56 Kbps.

The telephone network works very similar to the TCP transport protocol. It is connection based and the connection is maintained until the call is terminated. This enables you to hear the other person almost instantaneously. Telephone networks also still use two wire coppers run into most homes. The switching media, however, is mainly fiber. This allows for the high speed switching in the backend, but slow response when using data communications methods because they generally attach to the end node.

MODEM TYPES   Analog modems are used to connect via a PSTN line to a remote network. Although there are many different types and makes of modems, they can be categorized into three areas: single external, single internal, and multiline rack or shelf mounted.

The external modem is the most common modem in use today. Many ISPs use pools of external modems to enable dial-in access. They are also common in server hardware. Many IT personnel include modems in production systems to allow for a backup communications link or for remote access.

The internal modem conforms to the same type as the external modem. The only real difference is the fact that it is located inside the computer chassis. Most companies do not use these anymore, because externals are easier to replace and troubleshoot. For example, internal modems do not have the LEDs that external modems do. This translates into a headache if you have to figure out why the modem won't connect to a remote host via the dial-up connection. Some modem manufacturers provide software interface; however, these generally are not as full featured as for the external modem. A common use for internal modems is in laptop computers. Many laptop vendors still integrate phone jacks into the chassis of the computer. Also, PCMCIA cards can technically be classified as an internal modem.

These are used widely and do not include the LEDs or lamps an external modem offers.

These types of solutions are becoming more and more popular every day. Many vendors are offering a solution that is a single chassis containing x number of modem cards that can be connected directly to the network. Its modularity and its size are much more efficient than trying to maintain a shelf with a stack of external modems sitting on it. These have also been included in some new networking equipment. Manufacturers place analog modems in their equipment to facilitate redundancy features such as a backup network link.

PSTN was one of the first true networks of our time. It provided the foundation on which the digital age has flourished and exploded. It was a huge contributor to the popularity of public online networks such as the Internet. We use this network for many different functions today, because it has evolved into a truly global communications network.

CERTIFICATION OBJECTIVE 6.02

Dial-Up Networking

Remote connectivity has had a huge impact on the world. It is used by many businesses around the world to interconnect sites to a single network. It is also used to connect users to the public Internet and to private corporate networks. Windows NT and Windows 95 include a dial-up networking client. This client supports all the major flavors of dial-up connectivity and network protocols. Although it is not installed by default, it is included with the operating systems. Exercise 6-4 explains the process of installing dial-up networking on a Windows 95 desktop.

EXERCISE 6-4

Installing Dial-Up Networking

1. Select Start | Settings | Control Panel, and then double-click the Add/Remove Programs icon.

2. Click the Windows Setup tab to bring it to the front, and then select Communications from the Components box and click the Details button.

3. Place a checkmark in the Dial-Up Networking check box, and then click OK. The appropriate files will be installed. If this is the first time dial-up networking has been installed, you will be prompted to fill in the location information. Otherwise click Make a New Connection to start the wizard.

Dial-up networking provides support for four types of line protocols. Each protocol can be used to connect to a subset of services on remote hosts. The line protocols available include the following:

- **NetWare Connect (NRN)**   Used to connect to NetWare services via IPX/SPX

- **Remote Access Services (RAS)**   Used to connect to Windows NT Remote Access Service

- **Serial Line Internet Protocol (SLIP)**   Used to connect to a SLIP server via TCP/IP

- **Point-to-Point Protocol (PPP)**   Used to connect to a PPP server. Multiple protocols can be utilized including TCP/IP, IPX, and NetBEUI

To use dial-up networking, you can invoke the process with one of three methods. Each method can be done by a regular user.

- **Explicit**   A user can manually initiate a connection.

- **Implicit**   In some events, if Windows 95 cannot find a connection, it will prompt you to try a dial-up connection.

- **Application invoked**   Some applications will try to establish a dial-up connection when connecting to server resources. Outlook trying to contact an exchange server can be set up to dial into the exchange server.

FROM THE FIELD

Establishing Foolproof Remote Access

Nearly every computer that has a Windows NT network also has some sort of remote access. Many employees have laptops that are configured to dial in to the network to download e-mail and upload information. Travelling salesmen are notorious for requiring a solid dial-in capability to perform their duties while they are out on the road.

Accessing a network through dial-up networking is usually much slower than accessing the network from the inside, so users tend to complain more about the amount of time it takes to achieve everyday activities such as retrieving e-mail. They do not tolerate when their computer cannot dial in correctly. Rest assured, you will be called when a user is having problems dialing in.

Many users work from home at night, and if their dial-up networking configuration is not working correctly 100% of the time, they cannot get their work done. You are causing them to miss deadlines and fall behind in their work. This is not a good thing. I was at a job interview once with the owners of the company and they were complaining that they just got back from Hawaii and could not dial in for a week. The previous administrator

assured them it would work correctly. Is it any wonder why they were interviewing new administrators?

To ensure that you have configured the user's laptops correctly, find an analog phone line inside the building and test the dial-up networking connection while the user is standing there. Demonstrate exactly how to access the network via the modem and what to do when they are dialed in. This seems like second nature to you, but to a user it is another new computer task they are unfamiliar with. After you have showed the user how to dial in once or twice, have them do it. Don't take their word that they know how to do it, because they don't. Why would they be calling you with problems if they knew how to do it? By testing the dial-up connection from inside the building, you are simulating a remote location. If it doesn't work in this situation, it probably won't work at the user's house. If there are problems, you will see them for yourself first hand during this test.

I have had users bring in their home computers for me to configure for remote access. If you give them a detailed list of instructions with the intent of them

FROM THE FIELD

configuring remote access, they will most likely not be successful.

There is nothing more rewarding than a happy user, so you will feel good about getting the job done right. Maybe the user will get a promotion for all the hard work they have been accomplishing at night!

—Cameron Brandon, MCSE+Internet, CNE, A+, Network+

Modem Configuration Parameters

Modems are defined as data communication devices that are used to pass data through the PSTN from node to node. A modem, which stands for Modulators/Demodulators, is used to convert a digital signal to an analog format to transmit across the network. It reverses the conversion process on the other end node to receive the data. Typically, the EIA/TIA-232 serial standard is used to connect the modem to a computer.

Modems are asynchronous, synchronous, or both. *Asynchronous communication* is sending all data separately and relying upon the node on the other end to translate the packet order. *Synchronous communications* sends all data in a steady stream and uses a clock signal to interpret the beginning and end of a packet. Regular users today use synchronous communication in the modems that they buy.

Various system parameters must be set up properly to enable a modem to work. These parameters define the system resources for the modem device to use during its operations. Common parameters include serial ports, IRQs, I/O Addresses, and baud rates.

Serial Port

Serial communications send signals across a point-to-point link. Bits are transmitted one after another in a continuous data stream. Serial ports are the common method for connecting modems to personal computers. They are based on 9-pin (DB-9) and 25-pin (DB-25) connectors commonly known as COM1, COM2, COM3, and COM4. The computer side of the connection is known as the *data terminal equipment (DTE)* and the modem is known as the *data circuit-terminating equipment (DCE)*. Various pins are used for different functions inside these connectors. Some are used for transmitting data, others for receiving data, and the remaining for control signals.

You must specify the appropriate serial port when setting up a modem. Most modems attempt to use COM1 by default. Each COM port is assigned a specific set of address variables by default when setting up connections. To change the modem COM port after the setup is complete, select Start | Settings | Control Panel, and then double-click the Modems icon. Highlight the appropriate modem and click the Properties button. Select the appropriate port from the Port box, as shown in the following illustration.

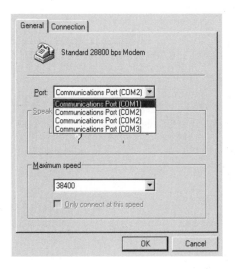

IRQ and I/O Address

Interrupt Request Levels (IRQs) are hardware lines over which devices send interrupt signals to the microprocessor. IRQs are used to provide a communications channel to the computer architecture to request processing power. Every time a command is sent to the computer by the device, an interrupt is used to interpret the signal. IRQs are an integral part of the modem setup.

Input/Output addresses (I/O addresses) are spaces in memory designated for the memory's own use. The address spaces are used to exchange information between the memory's and the rest of the computer. This concept is known as "memory mapped I/O" and uses a hexadecimal notation to define the locations. You may notice that some of these addresses overlap each other. You can have multiple devices set up with different IRQ's used such as COM1 and COM3 with the default settings. They cannot, however, be used at the same time. The exceptions to this rule are if plug-n-play is enabled and you cannot share I/O addresses for a device at any time.

The following table shows default IRQs and I/O addresses, and the illustration after it displays an example of IRQ 3 and I/O address 2F8 set up in a configuration for COM2.

COM port	IRQ	I/O Address
COM1	04	03F8 – 03FF
COM2	03	02F8 – 02FF
COM3	04	03E8-03EF
COM4	03	02E8-02EF

Maximum Port Speed

The *maximum port speed* is defined by the kilobytes per second that the modem can support. Maximum rates are defined primarily by the modem hardware, however, the current pubic telephone network has an upper limit of 56 Kbps through an analog modem. Port speeds are defined by standards and features available to them.

on the
Job

Note that the terms baud *and* port speed *do not truly match. Port speeds define how fast data is traveling and baud measures the signal change per second. With encoding, 2 bits look like 1; therefore they will not match.*

Multiple modem standards exist to define the different features and bandwidths available. Various models provide different standards levels. Verify before you purchase any modem that it fits your current needs and meets the appropriate standard. Table 6-1 illustrates the standards used.

To configure the port speed in Windows 95 or Window NT, select Start | Settings | Control Panel, and then double-click the Modems icon. Select

TABLE 6-1		
Modem Standards that Define Speeds or Feature Sets	**Standard**	**Feature Set**
	V.22	1200 bps, full-duplex
	V.22bis	2400 bps full-duplex
	V.32	Asynch/Sync 4800 bps/9600 bps
	V.32bis	Asynch/Sync 14,400bps
	V.35	Defines high transfer rates over dedicated circuits
	V.42	Defines error checking standards
	V.42bis	Defines modem compression
	V.34	28,800 bps
	V.34+	33,600 bps

your modem and click the Properties button. Select the appropriate port speed from the Maximum Speed list, as shown next.

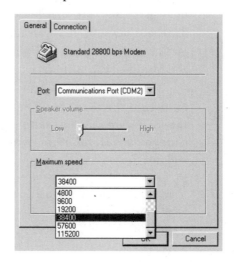

Unimodem

With Windows 95, an additional subsystem is available to simplify dial-up networking. Unimodem provides an easy, centralized mechanism for installing and configuring modems, as shown next.

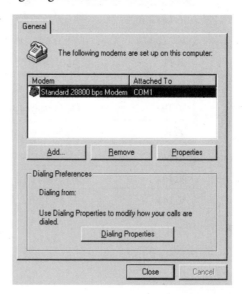

When installing the modem, the wizard enables you to specify configurations included with Windows 95 or to obtain the configuration from disk. Windows 95 ships with over 600 modem configurations included. The information obtained by this process is then accessible to any other applications. Many applications written today to run on Windows 95 specifically request information from this process if the modem is required.

Telephony API

The Microsoft Telephony API (TAPI) is an application interface used for accessing communications features such as connection monitoring. This API is used to provide services such as these without relying upon the hardware to set them up. It ties in heavily to the unimodem mechanism. It functions completely independently from the device hardware. It is now used for modem data transfers; the COMM.API is used for these operations.

When modems were first becoming popular, they could be difficult to configure. You had to understand the different settings to use such as which com port to set up; the system resources, such as IRQs and DMA channels; as well as modem baud rates. Each application that was to use this device had to be set up separately. This could take a lot of time and get complex quickly when attempting to use advanced modem initialization strings. TAPI replaced this requirement by providing a standard interface the modem would communicate with. This meant that the interface could be set up once, and all applications could use it.

TAPI also provides other features, such as having multiple calling locations. You can set up different connection profiles for different dial-up access numbers. You can also customize how the number is dialed. For example, you set up two separate connection profiles, one with call waiting enabled and the second without it. This enabled you to manage multiple connections without having to reconfigure your modem setup every time you needed a variation.

To access the TAPI options, Select Start | Control Panel | Modems. Click the Dialing Properties button. The following illustration displays some of the options available for customization.

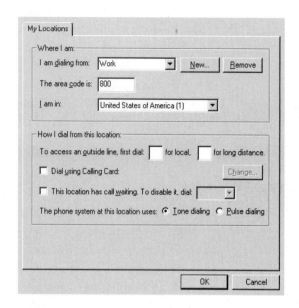

Requirements for a Remote Connection

Over the course of this chapter, several different types of remote connectivity technologies have been addressed. Each has its strength and weaknesses as well as its core functions. Some technologies provide features or functionality that other individuals may not need or want. Understanding how each one works and its benefits and disadvantages will enable you to recommend solutions to fit business needs. It is now time to pull all of the information together to figure out what is required to make it work.

To provide access to a remote server or network, several items must be set up and configured properly. Each item is dependent upon other items and this connection will not work without them. The following list contains the common components required to connect to remote resources.

- **Dial-up networking client**   This must be set up with the appropriate parameters defined.
- **Remote server**   You must have a remote server to dial in to reach a remote network.

- ■ **User account (PPP, SLIP, RAS)** You must maintain a valid ID and password on the remote server or network.

- ■ **Modem/ISDN** You must have a hardware device that will enable you to communicate with the remote host.

- ■ **Access protocol** A network layer protocol must be set up and configured properly to access resources on the remote server or network. Examples include TCP/IP, IPX, and NetBEUI.

CERTIFICATION SUMMARY

The concept of remote connectivity is to provide access to a network from a remote location. Networks have drastically expanded over the past several decades. The United States government used the ARPANET to connect remote sites. Many technologies have been spawned from the need for remote access.

The Point-to-Point Protocol (PPP) and the Serial Line Internet Protocol (SLIP) are communications protocols used to communicate with remote networks through the use of a serial device such as an analog modem. SLIP was originally designed for connecting to remote UNIX boxes. SLIP only supports the TCP/IP network layer protocol. It is quickly being replaced by PPP.

PPP is a more robust protocol than SLIP is. PPP was designed to handle multiple network layer protocols, such as TCP/IP, IPX, and NetBEUI. It includes additional features such as encapsulation, network protocol multiplexing, session negotiation, and data compression negotiation. PPP uses three sub-protocols to function: High-Level Data Link Control (HDLC) protocol, Network Control Protocol (NCP), and Link Control Protocol (LCP). HDLC handles data encapsulation, NCP handles Network Layer protocols, and LCP handles connection maintenance and testing. PPP uses three different NCPs: IPCP for TCP/IP, IPXCP for IPX, and NBFCP for NetBEUI. PPP uses authentication protocols such as CHAP, PAP, and MS-CHAP. PPPLOG.TXT is located in C:\Windows and is used for troubleshooting PPP issues.

Point-to-Point Tunneling Protocol (PPTP) provides a secure communications channel through a public TCP/IP network such as the Internet. PPTP provides multiple network layer support by using PPP as the underlying structure. PPTP uses a technology called Virtual Private Networks (VPN) to create the channel to tunnel through. You can use a PPTP client to connect to a standard PPP server and to create a tunnel to another PPTP server across the network. You can also use a PPP client to connect to a PPTP server and enable it to handle the tunneling. Virtual VPN devices are created to facilitate PPTP connectivity. A three-step process is followed: PPP connection and communication, PPTP control connection, and PPTP data tunneling.

Integrated Services Digital Network (ISDN) is a system of digital telephone connections that enables data to be transmitted simultaneously end to end. ISDN developed as the standard telephone network progressed. ISDN uses channels to make up a logical circuit. Two types of channels are used: a B channel for data transfer and a D channel for circuit control functions. Each B channel equals 64 Kbps and each D channel represents either 16 Kbps or 64 Kbps. H channels are used to specify a number of B channels. Basic Rate Interface consists of two B channels and one 16 Kbps D channel totaling 144 Kbps. A Primary Rate Interface (PRI) consists of 23 B channels and one 64 Kbps D channel totaling 1536 Kbps. Different ISDN device types define the type of hardware used and include NT1, NT2, TE1, TE2, and TA. Reference points are used to define logical interfaces. Identifiers are used to label the connection. Identifiers include Service Profile Identifier (SPID), directory number (DN), TEI, BC, and SAPI.

The Public Switched Telephone Network (PSTN) is used to facilitate voice communications globally. Also known as the Plain Old Telephone System (POTS) it was the first telecommunications network of its size in existence. Wide area network technologies were all based to some degree on this network. Different analog device types are available to enable data communications, including external modems, internal modems, and multilane modem banks.

Dial-up networking functionality is included with Windows 95 and Windows NT. It enables users to connect to their internal network or the

Internet from a remote location. Dial-up networking supports four line protocols: NetWare Connect (NRN), Remote Access Service (RAS), Serial Line Internet Protocol (SLIP), and Point-to-Point Protocol (PPP). Three methods exist to invoke a dial-up session: explicit, implicit, or application invoked. Because modems are used to connect to remote networks, you must know how to configure them. IRQs, I/O addresses, and serial ports all must be configured properly. Modems have a maximum port speed defined by the standard it meets. The unimodem subsystem provides one interface for all applications to tie into the modem. The Telephony API (TAPI) provides additional features such as connection monitoring and multiple location support. Specific items are required to use dial-up networking; you must have the appropriate network protocol set up, a line protocol set up, a server to dial in to, and a modem set up properly.

✓ TWO-MINUTE DRILL

- ❑ The basic functionality that remote connectivity uses is available in many different protocols and devices.

- ❑ Companies use network links such as Frame Relay and ATM today that encompass many different technologies.

- ❑ More common applications include PPP dial-up and the Public Switched Telephone Network (PSTN).

- ❑ SLIP and PPP are two communication protocols that are used to connect a computer to a remote network through a serial connection using a device such as a modem.

- ❑ The Serial Line Internet Protocol, or SLIP, is a communications protocol used for making a TCP/IP connection over a serial interface to a remote network.

- ❑ The Point-to-Point Protocol, or PPP, is a Data Link Layer protocol used to encapsulate higher Network Layer protocols to pass over synchronous and asynchronous communication lines.

- ❑ The most common authentication protocols include Password Authentication Protocol (PAP), the Challenge Handshake Authentication Protocol (CHAP), and the Microsoft adaptation of CHAP—MS-CHAP.

❑ The Point-to-Point Tunneling Protocol (PPTP) is a network protocol that provides for the secure transfer of data from a remote client to a private server by creating a multi-protocol virtual private network, or VPN. PPTP is used in TCP/IP networks as an alternative to conventional dial-up networking methods.

❑ A VPN works by encapsulating the data within IP packets to transport it through PPP. VPNs are virtual devices set up as if they were regular devices such as a modem.

❑ Be sure to know the three processes involved with PPTP and how PPP applies to each one.

❑ Integrated Services Digital Network (ISDN) is a system of digital telephone connections that enables data to be transmitted simultaneously end to end.

❑ There are two basic types of ISDN service: Basic Rate Interface (BRI) and Primary Rate Interface (PRI).

❑ Be sure to know the device types and where each type is used. Also, know the number of channels and speeds associated with a BRI and a PRI.

❑ *Network Terminator 1 (NT1)* is the device that communicates directly with the Central Office switch.

❑ *Network Terminator 2 (NT2)* is placed between an NT1 device and any adapters or terminal equipment.

❑ *Terminal Equipment 1 (TE1)* is a local device that speaks via an S interface.

❑ *Terminal Equipment 2 (TE2)* devices are common everyday devices that can be used for ISDN connectivity.

❑ The *Service Profile Identifier (SPID)* is the most important number needed when using ISDN.

❑ The *directory number (DN)* is the ten-digit phone number the telephone company assigns to any analog line.

❑ A *Terminal Endpoint Identifier (TEI)* identifies the particular ISDN device to the switch.

❑ The *Service Address Point Identifier (SAPI)* identifies the particular interface on the switch that your devices are connected to.

❑ The *bearer code (BC)* is an identifier made up of the combination of TEI and SAPI.

❑ The Public Switched Telephone Network (PSTN) was originally designed as an analog switching system for routing voice calls.

❑ Remember that the maximum available speed with an analog modem is 56 Kbps.

❑ Windows NT and Windows 95 include a dial-up networking client.

❑ Dial-up networking provides support for four types of line protocols.

❑ Modems are asynchronous, synchronous, or both.

❑ The computer side of the connection is known as the *data terminal equipment (DTE)* and the modem is known as the *data circuit-terminating equipment (DCE)*.

❑ *Interrupt Request Levels (IRQs)* are hardware lines over which devices send interrupt signals to the microprocessor.

❑ *Input/Output addresses (I/O addresses)* are spaces in memory designated for its own use.

❑ Unimodem provides an easy, centralized mechanism for installing and configuring modems.

❑ The Microsoft Telephony API (TAPI) is an application interface used for accessing communications features such as connection monitoring.

SELF TEST

The following Self Test questions will help you measure your understanding of the material presented in this chapter. Read all the choices carefully, as there may be more than one correct answer. Choose all correct answers for each question.

1. Which network layer protocols can the Serial Line Internet Protocol use during a dial-up session?

    A. TCP/IP

    B. IPX

    C. SLP

    D. None of the above

2. Which protocol supports multiple Network Layer protocols over a serial link?

    A. SLIP

    B. PPP

    C. IPX

    D. NetBEUI

3. Which components are part of the Point-to-Point Protocol?

    A. Network Control Protocol

    B. Link Control Protocol

    C. Internet Protocol

    D. Internet Packet eXchange Protocol

4. Which Network Control Protocol is used in PPP to facilitate the transport of TCP/IP?

    A. IPNP

    B. IPCP

    C. IPXCP

    D. None of the above

5. Which forms of validation can PPP use to authenticate users against a remote server? (Choose all that apply.)

    A. CHAP

    B. Domain Account

    C. PAP

    D. KPA

6. Where is the connection information for a PPP dial-up session stored?

    A. C:\Windows\ppp\PPPLOG.TXT

    B. C:\Windows\PPP.LOG

    C. C:\Windows\PPPLOG.TXT

    D. C:\PPP.TXT

7. What technology does Virtual Private Networks (VPNs) offer to provide a more secure communications channel?

    A. IP header compression

    B. Tunneling

    C. Multiple network protocol support

    D. None of the above

8. Virtual Private Networks use what kind of devices as if they were modems inside the computer?

    A. Network Interface Cards

    B. Virtual Devices

C. Non-Virtual Devices

D. Modems

9. What is the process called for setting up a "tunnel" for the PPTP protocol?

A. PPP Connection and Communication

B. PPTP Control Connection

C. PPTP Data Tunneling

D. PPTP Data Transfer

10. What is the maximum number of virtual devices a Windows NT 4.0 server can have set up?

A. 10

B. 50

C. 256

D. 1024

11. What was the first Integrated Services Digital Network standard to be published by the ITU?

A. ISDN-1

B. ISDN-NI

C. NI

D. NI-1

12. What is the standard bandwidth that is available with an ISDN B channel?

A. 4 Kbps

B. 64 Kbps

C. 64 Mbps

D. 128 Kbps

13. How many B channels are available in a typical ISDN PRI?

A. 2

B. 20

C. 23

D. 30

14. What category of ISDN devices would peripherals such as a standard telephone, a fax machine, or a personal computer fit into?

A. TE1

B. I1

C. NT1

D. None of the above

15. What ISDN identifier includes the directory number plus additional numbers used to identify an ISDN channel?

A. Bearer ID

B. SPID

C. SAPI

D. None of the above

16. What network did wide area network technologies originate from?

A. ISDN

B. PSTN

C. PKB

D. None of the above

17. What is the maximum speed current analog modems can reach?

A. 33.6 Kbps

B. 56 Kbps

C. 128 Kbps

D. 1.5 mbps

18. Which modem type is not a valid category for the Public Switched Telephone Network?

    A. Single internal modem

    B. Single external modem

    C. Multiline rack mount modems

    D. None of the above

19. What line protocols are available with Microsoft's dial-up networking?

    A. NetWare Connect

    B. Point-to-Point Protocol

    C. Serial Line Internet Protocol

    D. All of the above

20. What serial standard is typically used to connect a modem to a computer?

    A. IRQ

    B. EIA/TIA-232

    C. 232

    D. None of the above

21. What COM port is used by default when setting up a modem?

    A. 2

    B. 4

    C. 1

    D. 3

22. What is the default IRQ setting for COM2?

    A. 2

    B. 14

    C. 4

    D. 3

23. Which modem standard defines error-checking standards?

    A. V.42

    B. V.34

    C. V.52

    D. V.100

24. Which application programming interface is used to include features such as call monitoring and multiple localities?

    A. Unimodem

    B. COMM

    C. TAPI

    D. None of the above

25. Which items listed are required for a dial-up connection to a remote host?

    A. Modem device

    B. Line protocol setup

    C. Valid user ID and password

    D. All of the above

7

Network Security

In today's world of ever-changing technology, information has become an essential asset for any corporation. As computers have become the standard for storing and manipulating this information, the need has arisen to share this information and make it available to the appropriate parties. Networks have become commonplace to facilitate this need. The Internet has grown tremendously as more people and corporations harness the amount of information that this system provides. As a down side, if someone were able to obtain or modify this information, depending upon the content, it could be disastrous. Organizations such as the New York Stock Exchange or the United States Department of Defense (DOD) are interconnected with other networks to facilitate today's growing needs. If the information stored within these systems became accessible to the public, who knows what might happen. For example, the economy could be drastically altered if the New York Stock Exchange became infiltrated. Even though the DOD only has unclassified systems accessible via the Internet, if certain sensitive unclassified documents were accessible to the wrong people then it could be detrimental to the nation.

The need for security in today's networks has become a requirement for any size organization. Many different products, processes, and policies can be used to maintain the information and its validity. Security is more of a mind set or way of thinking. It is important to understand that many things can be done to maintain a secure environment, but being 100% secure is not possible. The best any organization can do is to understand the security threats that may exist and how to best control and react to them. In this chapter you will learn what you can do to help prevent security breaches.

When designing a network, be sure to take into consideration the available options and the security impacts of each. When securing information, make sure to understand the default permissions created and how to modify those in the most secure manner. Understand the utilities available and create processes and procedures around these for users to follow. Be sure to enforce these standards, or else the tools in place provide no value. Understand what can be done to protect the individual data and how it is stored. Lastly, protect the network itself from outside intrusion. Connecting to the Internet is quickly becoming a necessity for companies today. Make sure that access from across this huge global network is monitored and locked down.

CERTIFICATION OBJECTIVE 7.01

Selecting a Security Model (User-Level and Share-Level)

When you begin thinking about the security of your organization, you must first look at the security models you have in place or will use in the future. A security model is a generic term that describes methodologies used to secure a system. These can be anything from file versus share security or the underlying subsystem used by an operating system. Each model adds to the overall security architecture. Defining the model that you will use and deciding how it will be incorporated is important in any organization.

To understand the security mechanisms available for Windows NT and other operating systems, you must first understand the security available. First, you will learn about security subsystems and file and directory permissions. Then you will learn about the workgroup and domain model. Then we will discuss the share-level security model available in other operating systems.

Windows NT Security Subsystem

It is important to understand the underlying security subsystem used by Windows NT. This subsystem ties into every other form of security available within the operating system. The Department of Defense class C2 security rating was a major influence in the security design that Microsoft put forth. They wanted Windows NT to be able to achieve this certification. Windows NT 3.5 with U.S. Service Pack 3 did finally meet the certification requirements; however, you could not network the server or have access to a floppy drive.

There are four parts to the security subsystem in Windows NT. Each plays an integral part in the security functions provided. Table 7-1 lists the security subsystems and gives a brief description.

Security Subsystem Component	Description
Local Security Authority (LSA)	Handles local security policies and user authentication and generates audit log messages.
Security Accounts Manager (SAM)	Handles authentication services for LSA. Database of user, group, and machine accounts.
Security Reference Monitor	Verifies that a user has the appropriate permissions to access an object. It also enforces the audit generation policy provided by the LSA.
Logon Processes	User interface provided for interactive logon. Also provides interface for administrative tools.

The logon process uses each one of these four components. The following is the logon process for a domain user:

1. Press CTRL | ALT | DELETE. The username and password dialog are displayed.

2. Enter a valid domain userid and password and press ENTER.

3. The LSA makes a call to an authentication package. This requires that a secure RPC connection be established with a domain controller's NETLOGON service from the client.

4. The authentication package then compares the userid and password to the domain SAM database. The process of comparing these is known as NT Challenge and Response.

5. Once complete, the NETLOGON service returns the user's Security Identifier (SID) and the global SID obtained from the SAM. NETLOGON services on the client return the user SID and global SID to the LSA.

6. The local LSA accesses the local SAM to generate a local SID. All three SIDs are then used to generate an "access token."

7. The access token is assigned and the explorer interface is started. The access token is used for any process that is started by this user.

Access Tokens

When the Security Accounts Manager validates a user, an access token is created. This token is used in the future for all access validations that occur when a user tries to open a resource. The token is used until the user logs out and then it is permanently destroyed. The token maintains all of the information required for resource validation. The access token includes the following information:

- User Security Identifier (SID)
- Primary Group Security Identifier
- Group Security Identifier
- Access Permissions

Security Descriptors and Access Control Lists (ACL)

The security model is based upon objects. Every named object has security-related attributes associated with it that can be modified. The term used to describe these attributes is a *security descriptor,* which includes the access control list, or ACL, and the information about the object. The ACL is a list that provides the users and/or groups allowed to access the object as well as the level of permissions applied. Multiple groups or users can be associated to an object with the ACL. For example, a directory may be set up to allow the Sales team read-only access while the Marketing group may have read-write access. A user, John Doe, could be a member of both groups. Rules are set up within Windows NT to compare these and apply the appropriate set of permissions.

Security Descriptors are broken down into several components: the system access-control list (SACL), the discretionary access-control list (DACL), an owner, and a primary group. Each term is listed in Table 7-2 with a brief description.

Security Descriptor	Description
System Access-Control List (SACL)	Controls the security auditing for the Windows NT object.
Discretionary Access-Control List (DACL)	Determines which users and groups have rights to this object.
Owner	Maintains a record of the user who owns the resource.
Primary Group	Each user must be a member of a primary group. This is required for Macintosh support as well as the POSIX subsystem and is ignored by Windows NT.

ACCESS CONTROL ENTRIES   Every access control list is broken down into access control entries, or ACEs. ACEs specify the access or auditing permissions assigned for a specific user or group. Three types of ACEs exist: one for system security and two for discretionary access control. The system access control is used to maintain and generate the security audit log messages that appear. This ACE is called "SystemAudit." The discretionary ACEs are known as "AccessAllowed" and "AccessDenied." These are used to specifically deny or grant access for a specific user or group.

User-Level Security

One method of security that is available for use is file and directory level permissions. These permissions are based upon user or group accounts. Effectively combining these two types of permissions enables you to delineate what access a particular user will have when working in Windows NT. You must understand the permissions available and how to apply them.

File and directory permissions are available on NTFS formatted partitions only. Other file systems available with Windows NT, such as FAT, do not provide a mechanism to support permissions. In FAT file systems, only file attributes are available and any user can modify these.

In addition to the predefined permissions, you can custom specify certain access to a file or directory. Using individual permissions enables you to customize the files and directories to meet your security requirements. Predefined permissions use a combination of individual permissions to provide standard templates. Table 7-3 lists the predefined permissions available. These include the individual permissions given by default. The first parentheses define the individual permissions on the existing files and directories and the second illustrate the permissions given to new files or directories. It is important to note that both parentheses apply for directories but only the first parentheses apply for file permissions. You will also notice that an additional category exists for directory permissions, labeled "Not Specified." By having this permission setup, users and groups do not have access to those files or directories unless it is applied through something else, for example a group membership. A good example is the List permission, which enables users to list the contents; however, they will not be able to see new files added. Table 7-4 lists the individual permissions available and their uses. The following illustration shows an example of a security configuration for the D:\Data directory.

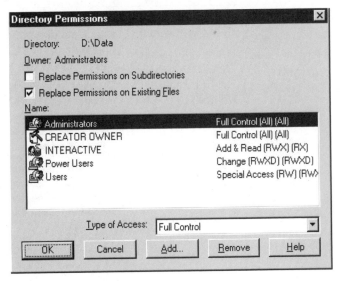

TABLE 7-3

File and Directory
Permissions Available

Access Permission	Description
No Access (None)(None)	Directory and File permission. This provides a user with no access at all.
List (RX)(Not Specified)	Directory permission. Enables users to display contents of directory along with permissions and attributes. This can include listing subdirectories if this permission is applied to all subdirectories as well.
Read(RX)(RX)	Directory and File permission. Enables a user to open and read files and directories and to run executable files. This also includes permissions granted by List.
Add(WX) (Not Specified)	Directory permission. Enables a user to add files to a directory and to create folders but they cannot view the contents of the folders.
Add & Read (RWX)(RX)	Directory permission. Enables a user to open and add files to directory. This also includes displaying directory contents and information and executing files.
Change (RWXD)(RWXD)	Directory permission. Enables users to open, modify, and delete directories and files. This also includes displaying contents, navigating subdirectories, and executing and viewing files.
Full Control (All)(All)	Directory and File permission. Grants full rights to a file or directory. This gives a user all the permissions that are available by using or combining the previous items as well as the right of taking ownership of the directory or file.
Special File Access	File permission. This can be used to customize file permissions. By using this access, you are creating individual permissions rather than using the predefined permissions.
Special Directory Access	Directory permission. This can be used to customize the directory permissions. By using this access, you are creating individual permissions rather than using the predefined permissions.

TABLE 7-4	Individual Permission Abbreviation	Description
Individual Permissions and Their Abbreviations	(R)	Read
	(W)	Write
	(X)	Execute
	(D)	Delete
	(P)	Change Permissions
	(O)	Take Ownership

Users and Groups

Windows NT uses user and group objects, more commonly known as accounts, to delineate access permissions. Two types of user accounts exist: global accounts that are used throughout a domain and local accounts that are used on a single Windows NT computer. During installation of a Windows NT system or domain, several group objects and two user objects are created by default. Some domain implementations can contain thousands of groups and tens of thousands of user IDs. By properly designing a strategy, you can use these to provide effective security levels without getting too complex. Windows NT creates two user objects by default for a server, workstation, or domain: Administrator and Guest. The Administrator account is given full control access to the entire system or domain. This account acts as the equivalent of "root" on a UNIX system. The Guest account is created with no password. This account is granted limited access permissions and is disabled by default. Most organizations leave this account disabled so users cannot gain access to any computers.

Windows NT creates several groups by default. Each group is used to provide access for specific types of users. Two types of groups exist: local groups and global groups. Global groups are used only in domain environments, but local groups can be used in domain, server, or workstation environments. Each group provides a method for delineating common groups of tasks to users. For example, an individual may be responsible for performing backups for a server. You can make this user a member of the Backup Operator group to give him permissions to perform this task. Table 7-5 lists the available groups and their primary functions and permissions:

TABLE 7-5   Default User and Groups Created During Installation of a Windows NT

NT Group	Description	Default Contents
Administrators	Local group found on servers, workstations, and domains. Provides full access to entire Windows NT computer or domain.	Domain Administrators (global group) and Administrator (user account)
Account Operators	Local group found in domains. This group is used to manage users and groups within a domain. It can only modify users or groups that have lesser security permissions.	None
Backup Operators	Local group found on servers, workstations, and domains. This provides privileges to perform functions of a backup operator, such as log on locally, shut down system, and back up and restore files.	None
Domain Admins	Global group found in domains. This group is set up in the Administrators local group on all member servers and workstations in a domain.	Administrator (user account)
Domain Guests	Global group found in domains. Provides guest privileges to a domain.	Guest (user account)
Domain Users	Global group found in domains. This provides access for a normal user.	Administrator (user account) and all new users created by default
Guests	Local group found on servers, workstations, and domains. This is used to provide limited guest access.	Domain Guests (in domains)
Print Operators	Local group found in domains. This privilege provides the capability to control printer resources, log on locally, and shut down the server.	None
Power Users	Local group found on workstations and servers. This group provides additional access to install applications, manage printers and local users, and modify file permissions.	None

TABLE 7-5	Default User and Groups Created During Installation of a Windows NT *(continued)*	
NT Group	**Description**	**Default Contents**
Replicator	Local group found on servers, workstations, and domains. These members can manage replication services for files and directories.	None
Server Operators	Local group found in domains. This privilege provides the capability to shut down the system, control shared resources, back up and restore files, and log on locally.	None
Users	Local group found on servers, workstations, and domains. On domains, the Domain Users global group is a member of the domain local Users group. This is set up for normal users.	Domain Users (in domains)

Computer or Domain Different groups are created based upon whether they reside on a server or workstation or in a domain. A domain group list includes Administrators, Account Operators, Backup Operators, Guests, Print Operators, Replicator, Server Operators, and Users. A server or workstation group list includes Administrators, Backup Operators, Guests, Power Users, Replicator, and Users. By using a combination of global groups within a domain and local groups on computers, you can create a good strategy that enables access permissions to flow down to the servers or workstations in a domain. Figure 7-1 shows the User Manager screen which displays the standard users and groups created for a member server.

When you are adding users to multiple groups, you may have groups set up for different permission levels to a resource. Although Windows NT handles the rules for how these permissions are applied, they vary depending upon the type of resource. A few rules need to be noted:

- File permissions override directory permissions.

- Permissions are cumulative; however, the No Access permission will always override the others that are set.

- When creating files, by default they inherit the permissions granted to the directory.

FIGURE 7-1

The User Manager screen shows the local users and groups available by default for a Windows NT member server

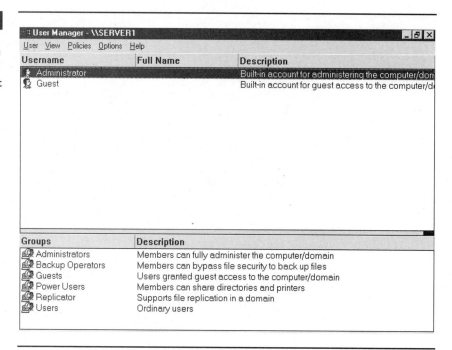

- When creating a file, that user is set as the owner. The owner always has control over permissions for a file. Administrators always have the capability to take ownership of any files.

Now that we have discussed the different permissions available in Windows NT it's time for an exercise. Exercise 7-1 explains how to set up a share and to apply user-level security to it.

Creating a New Share Using User-Level Security

1. Log on to the computer with a user ID that has Administrator group membership.

2. Open Windows Explorer by selecting Start | Programs | Windows NT Explorer.

3. Create a new directory on your local hard drive called "Data." Highlight the drive and select File | New | Folder. Type Data as the name and press ENTER.

4. Highlight the Data folder and select File | Sharing. The Data Properties dialog box appears, as shown in the following illustration. By default, the option is set to Not Shared.

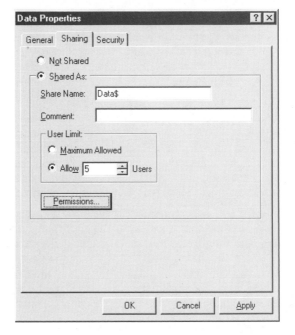

5. Select the Shared As option and type Data$ in the Share Name text box. (Appending the $ symbol hides the share from the browse listing.)

6. In the User Limit box, select the Allow option and enter 5 for the number of users. (The default is 10.)

7. Click the Permissions button to modify the permissions for this share. By default Everyone has Full Control. Change Everyone to Read and add Administrators as Full Control.

8. When complete, click OK to set the permissions and then click OK to create the share.

QUESTIONS AND ANSWERS

I need to give the data center operators rights to monitor and modify backup jobs but not permit them to perform domain or server administration.	Make them members of the Backup Operators group.
I want a group to have rights to add computer accounts to the domain, but I do not want them to have access to shut down any NT system.	You have two choices: give a global group on the domain the advanced right "Add workstations to Domain," or make them a member of the server operators group and remove the "Shutdown system" advanced right from this group.
I need to give the HR group list, read, and delete rights to a directory.	These rights are not available in a normal permission setup. You will have to give the directory special directory permissions to reach this level of granularity. This uses individual permissions rather than the predefined.
Users are connecting to a share and their NTFS permissions are set to Everyone Full Control. They still cannot delete files.	Check the share security. If the share permissions are set up for read-only access, they will be unable to delete any files found regardless of the file and directory permissions. This is because the share permission is more restrictive and overrides the NTFS permissions.
I changed the Everyone group to No Access and I have Full Control as an administrator. I get an "access denied" error message whenever I try to access that directory.	If you are a member of the Everyone group, the No Access permission overrides all others.

Several shares are created by default whenever a Windows NT workstation or server is installed. These include Admin$ for the <systemroot>, Repl$ for directory replication, and <drive>$ for every logical drive, such as C$ and D$. The $ sign appended to these makes these shares hidden. When creating a new share, this can be used to keep the share from appearing in the browse list of available resources. Effectively combining share permissions with NTFS permissions can provide a secure computing environment. User-level security is much more secure than the share-level security we discuss in the next section.

Share-Level Security

It is important to not become confused between share permissions which we just discussed and share-level security as they are two totally different items. Share-level security is available on client operating systems such as Windows 95 and Windows 98 as shown in the following illustration.

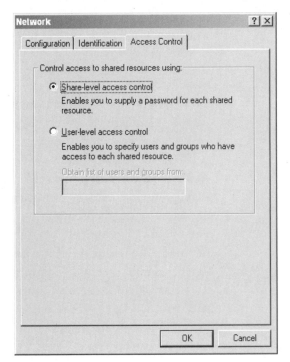

Access to a resource is determined by a password assigned to the resource and is not based on a user account or group membership. Any user that knows the share password can utilize the resource. Share-level security is easy to implement and maintain on small peer-to-peer networks; however, users must remember the password for each resource that is shared (unless password caching is in use). Access is very hard to control since anyone who knows the password can gain access. This is one reason that user-level access is much more secure than share-level access.

Domains and Workgroups

In addition to its underlying security model, Windows NT provides an additional type of security model. If you have ever installed Windows NT with networking, you have noticed that it always requires that you specify a workgroup or domain to make it a member of. Each type of implementation has its advantages. You need to understand the fundamental differences between each and the security architecture defined.

Workgroups

A workgroup can be defined as an organizational unit, or a way to organize a group of computers. Workgroups are primarily used in very small environments where users need to share information but do not have an NT server. A good example of this is a small office with a collection of Windows 98 computers that need to share information. Each computer in a workgroup maintains its own account information and these accounts are not shared or accessible elsewhere on the network. To access a remote resource on a Windows 98 computer, a share is created with a generic password. By entering this password, you have whatever permissions have been defined for everyone. This method does not enable you to audit to determine which users are accessing which resources. Anyone with the one password has access to the resource. In addition, these installations can be dangerous because the authentication methods used are less secure than other environments.

Domains

A domain is used to share common user accounts and policies. It consists of one or more Windows NT servers acting as domain controllers. Each domain consists of one primary domain controller and any number of backup domain controllers. The primary domain controller maintains the centralized accounts database and provides authentication services. The backup domain controllers provide authentication services and redundancy for the primary. In addition, member servers can be used to provide services such as file and print or application support while using this centralized database for authentication. Any Windows NT computer maintains a local SAM database and can use the domain accounts as well. The domain model also provides redundancy. The user account database is synchronized and other functions, such as the logon scripts, can be replicated to other Windows NT computers.

You can also link multiple domains to create an enterprise environment. This concept is known as "trust relationships." From these trusts, different domain models can be created to fit almost any environment. Because a single user account can be used to access any resource, auditing can be used to monitor what every user is doing; however, file and directory permission can only be audited on NTFS partitions. This additional level of security is used to meet the industry standards that the Windows NT security architecture was based upon.

Securing the Registry

You must secure the registry for any Windows NT computer. The registry contains the control parameters for the entire operating system. If this information were accessible to a malicious user, the results could be disastrous. Because of the risk involved in accessing the registry, Microsoft does not even list the utilities provided to do so with the rest of the administrative tools. These utilities, REGEDIT.EXE and REGEDT32.EXE, are located in the <systemroot>\system32 directory. Although both are included, only REGEDT32 contains the capability to modify the appropriate ACLs for the registry to make it secure.

There are two parts to securing the registry. First, the files that the registry information is stored in are located in <systemroot>\system32\config. This directory must have only the permissions required to enable the system to perform its job. If the partition that this directory is located on was created as NTFS, this is done by default. In addition, if you create an Emergency Repair Disk with the –S option, the files are updated and placed in the <systemroot>\repair directory. Although tampering with these files will not impact the registry, it will mess with the ERD process. This directory also contains the information that an intruder can use to compromise your system. For example, a copy of the SAM database is stored here that could be used to back out of a problem.

The second part to securing the registry includes applying permission directly to particular keys. The registry editor has the built-in functionality to connect to a remote computer and enable modification of certain keys. If these keys are not secured, you may find someone hacking away at your registry without you knowing. Be sure to test your security configuration carefully when modifying the registry because it can have some very adverse effects.

CERTIFICATION OBJECTIVE 7.02

Password Practices and Procedures

The most basic security mechanism is the password. We use passwords every day to access automated teller machines, to place calling card calls, and to access voice mail systems. Because it is such a basic concept, many implementations use this method to provide a form of security for accessing systems or resources. This widespread use is a concern, because passwords are noted as one of the poorest forms of protection available. According to the Computer Emergency Response Team (CERT), more security breaches result from poorly used passwords than from all other methods combined.

A password is a series of characters that can be used to lock down anything from an operating system to an individual file or directory. The purpose of this technique is to ensure that the user trying to access this resource is authorized to do so. If the user does not know the password, he is not allowed to access the resource. However, if a super-user account is compromised, then the other passwords stored in the same database can be at risk. In addition, someone can use one system as a starting point to reach other systems on the same network.

Password Policies

Setting up password authentication is a good start; however, it will be useless against a knowledgeable intruder without solid policies and processes defined. Each environment will be different and should be studied carefully to determine what policies would work best in that organization. Some organizations, such as the Department of Defense, may require a very stringent security setup, while others may require very little security. Most network operating systems provide these policies as a part of their implementation. For example, Windows NT enables you to specify required security settings, such as the number of characters required for a password, the number of tries before an account is locked out, and the maximum password age.

RFC 1244 is a security guidelines handbook and can be a good start as well as offer some basic guidelines to use when implementing password policies. This document provides some standard options and can be used to start creating a security policy for any environment. This is only provided as a starting point; additional policies and process will need to be defined to create an effective security guideline for an organization. Some security guidelines from the handbook are listed here:

- Do not use your login name as your password. This includes reversing it, changing the case of the name, or any other variable.

- Do not use a familiar name such as your child's name, your spouse's name, or your pet's name.

- Do not use your first, middle, or last name. This includes any nicknames as well.

- Do not use a password of all single digits or the same letter. For example: 1111111 or AAAAAAA.

- Do not use easily obtainable information about yourself, such as birth date, house number, or social security number.

- Do not use a word that can be found in a dictionary in any language.

- Use more than six characters in your password.

- Use a password with mixed-case characters. Use uppercase and lowercase randomly.

- Include non-alphanumeric characters, such as &#$@*.

- Do not write your password anywhere and do not give it to someone else for any reason.

In addition to these guidelines, you can implement other policies to secure your installation. Require that users change their passwords at defined intervals. In addition, administrators need to understand that other systems can be used to compromise another installation. Most users will use the same password for multiple accounts. For example, if one network is compromised, the intruder can use the same ID and password to log on to another network if it exists. This is a common attack method. For example, if a user sets the same password for two different e-mail accounts or uses his network password to log on to an FTP site, a hacker can trace this activity and use the password to access more secure systems. This enables an intruder to start with one system and hop to others.

Many organizations set stricter password policies for Administrator accounts than for normal user accounts, due to the security level. For example, a user account may require a password with six characters and a password change every 60 days. Administrator accounts may require passwords with eight characters and password changes every 30 days. Although this cannot be defined within Windows NT, you can set up a process to help enforce this as a standard. This higher security is due to the amount of access Administrator accounts retain. You also may want to set up two accounts for an administrator: the main account would have limited permissions for normal day-to-day activity, and the second would have full administrator access. Most installations also include a single main account with full access privileges. On a Windows NT server, the account is labeled Administrator. You should rename this account to make it a little more difficult to hack into since every hacker knows that Administrator is the default name for the most powerful account in Windows NT. Do not use this account once an administrative equivalent has been set up, unless absolutely necessary.

You may also use special accounts that are not assigned to normal users. For example, you may have an application service account or backup account that requires a great deal of access to a server or even multiple systems. Be sure to require a strict standard policy for these accounts, such as ten-character passwords and a combination of alphanumeric and other characters. Remember that you cannot set up multiple policies within a single account database and these policies need to be implemented as part of your environment security handbook. In addition to administrator accounts, many systems create a guest level account by default. This account usually has minimal permissions; however, you may want to disable this account outright.

Username and Password Guidelines

Policies and processes only begin to make an environment secure. Good guidelines should be developed around the username and password. Many people use a common word, name, or number as their password. With a little investigation, someone could quickly figure out many things that users might use as their passwords. In many cases, it would not take long to get a password for a regular user. Although this would provide limited access, administrators commonly use similar words or phrases as their own passwords. This can lead to a greater amount of access, even super-user access.

Many resources are available to help create guidelines to use when creating passwords. In addition, mechanisms have already been defined that will help you develop these guidelines.

Mechanisms for Creating Secure Usernames and Passwords

There are many different ways for creating usernames and passwords. Applications exist that will create a random series of characters based upon the guidelines you set; however, these usernames or passwords can be difficult to remember. This may work well for system accounts; however, a normal user needs something that can be easily remembered. This means that users must write the username and password down so they won't forget them, which creates another security problem. The trick to providing effective security is to create a username and password that is cryptic, but easily remembered by an everyday user.

Because usernames are more easily obtainable, most organizations tend to use basic names for user login and rely more heavily on password security. A common strategy is to use the first initial, last name or the first name, last initial. For example, Joe Smith would by Jsmith or JoeS. These are easily remembered and can be identified quickly by an administrator.

Another common strategy for usernames is to create a more cryptic name by using some combination of information. For example, you may choose to use the user's first initial, last initial, and the last four digits of his social security number. For example, Joe Smith with a social security number of 123-45-6789 would have a username of JS6789. More control is available when specifying usernames. These are created for the user; therefore, you can make sure that they meet the criteria set. There are many different methodologies available; however, you should evaluate your specific needs to determine what will work best.

When working with passwords, organizations tend to rely more heavily on securing their environment by requiring strict password policies. In most organizations, they generally rely upon the users to set up their own password. Here it is more difficult to maintain policies since not every user can be monitored. Few organizations set up passwords for users and force them to keep these passwords. This does not work well, because if the passwords are cryptic, users have to write them down to remember them and the administrator who set up the password also has access to that account. Generally, companies set up policies that are controllable and rely upon the user to use a cryptic password.

There are many different tactics to creating passwords. You might suggest taking a well-known dialogue or phrase and deriving the first letter from each word. Try to use one that would use a myriad of alphanumeric characters intermingled to create a secure password. Try creating your own word that sounds like rubbish but is pronounceable. This makes it a little easier to remember. Consider taking several words and using different

1. Backlit LED Display
2. Bandwidth Utilization Meter
3. Activity LEDs
4. Hexadecimal Key Pad

A portable Fluke LANMeter WAN/LAN testing tool for network troubleshooting and management. Can be used to test 10/100 Mbps Ethernet and Token Ring networks, including ISDN, T1, and frame-relay connections. Can detect duplicate IP addresses, generate test traffic, display the protocols in use on the network, and calculate the current bandwidth utilization. The exam will test your knowledge of when to implement tools such as network monitors and protocol analyzers.

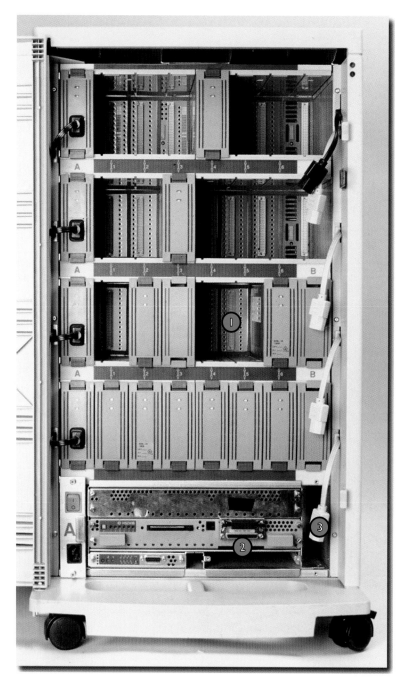

A Redundant Array of Inexpensive Disks (RAID) server. A hardware-based RAID solution—as opposed to a software-based RAID solution, such as Windows NT—is much quicker because the hardware-based solution does not calculate as much parity as the software-based solution does. Some of these hardware implementations support hot swapping of disks, which enables you to replace a failed disk while the computer is still running. However, hardware-based RAID solutions cost much more than their software-based counterparts. For the exam, you should understand the various levels of RAID support, such as RAID level 0, level 1, and level 5.

1. Hard Disk Drive Bays
2. SCSI Connector
3. Power Connectors

A notebook computer combination cable with support for twisted-pair and coaxial cable. This unit plugs into the PCMCIA network interface card located inside the PC card bay of the notebook computer (not shown). As a travelling network technician, it's a good idea to have a combination cable like the one shown so you can connect to both a coaxial or twisted-pair network with the same PCMCIA network card. For the exam, you should know what interfaces are available in a network adapter such as this.

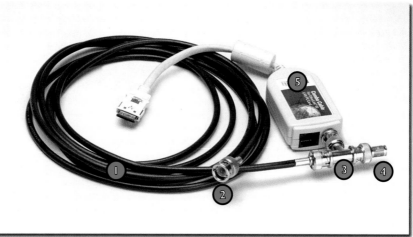

1. Thinwire 10Base2 Coaxial Cable
2. BNC Connector
3. BNC Connector
4. Terminator
5. Combination Twisted-Pair/ Coaxial Dongle

PCMCIA Ethernet Combo Network Interface Card, with Twisted-Pair and Coax Support

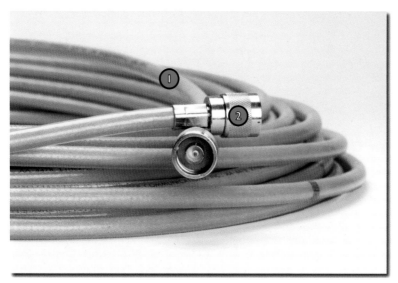

1. Thickwire (10Base5) Coaxial Cable
2. BNC Connector

A thickwire (10Base5) cable with a BNC connector. Thicknet is extremely bulky and difficult to work with, therefore it is rarely used. Thickwire cabling is used as a network backbone or a connection between two different hubs or routers. The major advantage of using thickwire rather than UTP for your network backbone is that data can be transmitted a greater distance than the 100-meter length supported by UTP. For the exam, you should know the maximum distance of thickwire coaxial cable and when it is appropriate to choose thicknet over the other types of cabling.

Thickwire Coaxial Cable and the Corresponding BNC Connector

Twisted-pair coaxial cabling with RJ-45 connector. Coaxial cable is resistant to the interference and signal weakening that other cabling, such as unshielded twisted-pair (UTP) cable, can experience. In general, coax is better than UTP for connecting longer distances and for reliably supporting higher data rates with less sophisticated equipment. For the exam, you should know the characteristics of UTP cabling, such as the maximum distance supported, the data rates, and the connectors used with UTP cabling.

1. Twisted-Pair Cabling
2. RJ-45 Connector

Twisted-Pair Cabling with RJ-45 Connector

An Ethernet twisted-pair transceiver for connecting 10BaseT stations to a coaxial-based network. A transceiver such as this can be used to connect a station with a network card equipped with a UTP port to the coaxial-based network via this transceiver, equipped with an adapter unit interface (AUI) port connector. For the exam, you should understand that AUI port connectors are usually associated with a thicknet 10Base5 backbone and connect via the vampire tap.

1. Twisted-Pair Connector
2. Link, Power, and Activity Lights
3. AUI Drop Cable

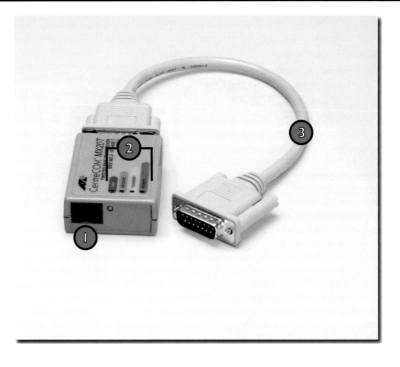

Ethernet Twisted-Pair Transceiver for Connecting 10BaseT Stations to a Coaxial-Based Network

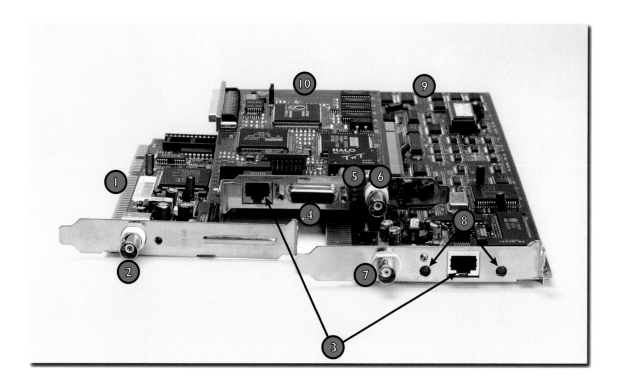

Various network interface cards with support for coax, twisted-pair, and AUI. The network interface card on the left has only one interface for a coax BNC connector. The network interface card on top has an interface for a coax BNC connector, an AUI connector, and a UTP RJ-45 connector. The network interface card on the right has an interface for a coax BNC connector and a UTP RJ-45 connector. Both the top and right network interface cards have power and link lights also. For the exam, you should know how to troubleshoot network interface cards, what interfaces are available on network interface cards, and the common resources, such as IRQ and I/O address, used for network cards.

1. Coaxial Network Interface Card
2. Coaxial Connector
3. Twisted-Pair Connectors
4. AUI Connector
5. Link and Power Lights
6. Coaxial Connector
7. Coaxial Connector
8. Link and Power Lights
9. Combo Network Card with Twisted-Pair and Coaxial Support
10. Combo Network Card with Twisted-Pair, Coaxial, and AUI Support

Various Network Interface Cards with Coaxial, Twisted-Pair, and AUI Support

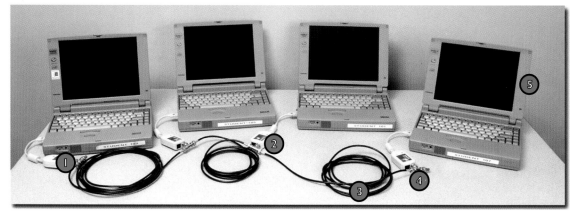

A small network consisting of four notebook computers connected using a thinwire coaxial backbone. Each notebook computer connects the PCMCIA network interface card to the network through a combination UTP/coaxial dongle. Each dongle connects to the network via a BNC T-connector. The notebook computers on the ends of the thinwire coaxial backbone are terminated with a 50-ohm terminator. The exam will test your knowledge of the coaxial network components, such as thinwire and thickwire cable, BNC connectors, and termination.

1. 50-ohm Terminator
2. Combination UTP/Coax Dongle
3. Thinwire Coaxial Backbone
4. 50-ohm Terminator
5. Notebook Computers

Bus Topology

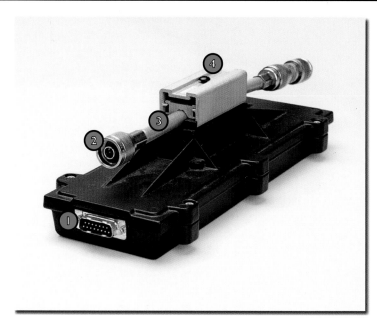

An Ethernet thicknet (10Base5) vampire tap connector with an AUI external transceiver. The vampire tap pierces the thicknet backbone to make a connection. A drop cable is used from the external transceiver to connect the workstations. These drop cables can be up to 50 meters (164 feet) long and are connected to the workstations using an AUI interface. The exam will test your knowledge of the purpose of a vampire tap, what networks make use of the vampire tap, and the types of cable and connectors associated with the vampire tap.

1. AUI Adapter
2. BNC Connector
3. Thicknet Coaxial Backbone
4. Vampire Tap

A Transceiver (AUI)

A Tone Generator used to perform tests on phone and network lines by clipping to a wire, terminal panel, or standard modular jack. A Tone Generator aids in the identification of wires during the wire-tracing process. Attach the Fox to the cable, jack, or panel you want to trace and then attach the Hound to the other end of the cable to find the Fox's tone. For the exam you need to know the types of situations that require the use of a Tone Generator.

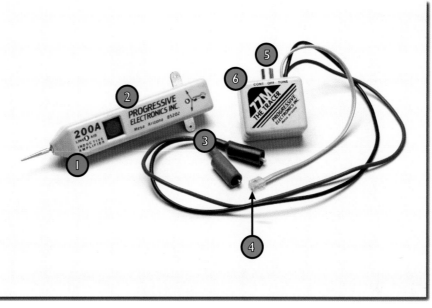

1. Inductive Amplifier
2. Hound
3. Standard Wire Connectors
4. RJ-11 Connector
5. Coaxial Connector
6. Fox

On the left is a DB-25 serial loopback adapter for testing ports on a system without having to connect to an external device. You can use a serial loopback adapter to verify that a transmitted signal is leaving your serial port and returning through the loopback adapter, ensuring that your serial port is working correctly. On the right is a twisted-pair RJ-45 loopback adapter for testing the network card for sending and receiving without having to connect to a network device. As with the serial loopback adapter, you test the port to verify that a transmitted signal is leaving your network port and returning through the loopback adapter, ensuring that your network port is working correctly. For the exam, you should know that you can troubleshoot network interface cards using an RJ-45 loopback adapter on a UTP network.

1. DB-25 Serial Loopback Adapter
2. Twisted-Pair RJ-45 Loopback Adapter

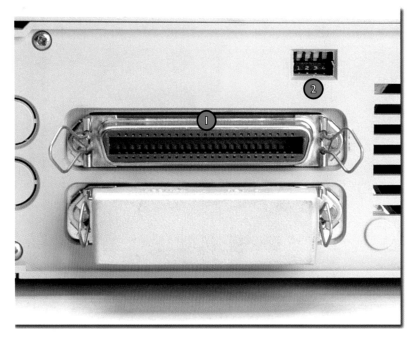

A device with external SCSI interfaces. This particular device uses a 50-pin Centronics SCSI connector, which is nearly identical to the Centronics printer cable connector. Also visible is the SCSI address ID jumper, which enables you to configure a SCSI device for a particular SCSI ID from 1–4. There are eight available addresses for SCSI IDs, with seven usually being reserved for the SCSI adapter itself. The exam will test your knowledge of the various SCSI connectors that are available.

1. Centronics 50-Pin
   SCSI Connector
2. SCSI Address ID Jumpers

The types of Small Computer Systems Interface (SCSI) connectors available. The top SCSI connector is a 50-pin high-density connector. The middle SCSI connector is a 68-pin high-density connector. The bottom connector is a Centronics 50-pin connector, not to be confused with a Centronics printer connector, which looks almost identical. For the exam, you need to know the types of SCSI connectors presented here.

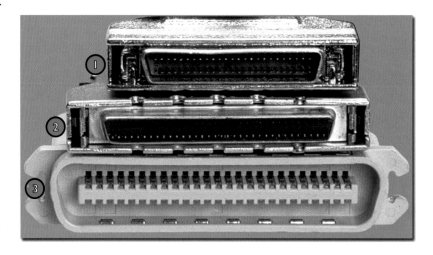

1. 50-Pin High-Density SCSI
2. 68-Pin High-Density SCSI
3. Centronics 50-Pin SCSI

An internal modem, which has visible jumpers in red for configuring COM port assignments. The illustration also shows a sticker on a chip, which details the various jumper settings to configure the COM port settings. The modem also includes RJ-11 connectors for connecting to the phone line and to the telephone. The exam will test your knowledge of the standard COM ports and IRQs for configuring modems.

1. Com Port Setting Jumpers
2. Jumper Diagram
3. Telephone and Phone Line Connectors

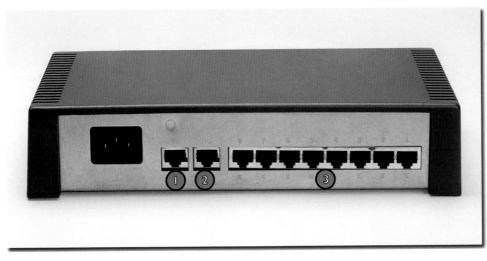

A Token Ring Media Access Unit (MAU). Most Token Ring networks use a star topology with MAUs as central access points. The token traverses a logical ring by visiting each port on the MAU. Any unused ports and ports that have non-functioning computers on the MAU can be bypassed. When multiple MAUs are used, it is important that they are configured to maintain the ring topology. This is made possible by the use of Ring In and Ring Out ports on the MAU. For the exam, you should know where MAUs are used and how you can connect multiple MAUs to each other.

1. Ring In Port
2. Ring Out Port
3. Twisted-Pair Ports

| 1. Coaxial BNC Interface | 2. Twisted-Pair RJ-45 Interface | 3. Parallel Printer Port |

A Hewlett Packard JetDirect external print device that enables printers to be strategically located throughout the network. The JetDirect print server connects a printer to a twisted-pair-based network through a 10BaseT connector, or to a coaxial-based network using a BNC connector, and then connects the printer using a standard parallel connector. The exam will test your knowledge of the purpose of the print server on a network.

HP JetDirect

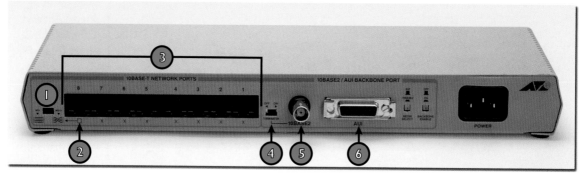

1. Eight Port Crossover Selector
2. Optional Port for Cascading Hubs
3. Eight Twisted-Pair RJ-45 Ports

4. 10Base2 Termination Switch
5. Thinwire 10Base2 Connector
6. AUI Connector

A small Ethernet hub for connecting up to eight twisted-pair network devices using an RJ-45 jack to a thinwire or thickwire network backbone. The 10Base2 connection is made to the hub using a BNC connector, and the thicknet connection is made to the hub using an AUI connector. Eight UTP ports are available for workstations or servers, or you can have seven available UTP ports with an eighth port available for cascading another Ethernet hub. The exam will test your knowledge of the purpose of hubs, what network implementations make use of the hub, and troubleshooting the hub.

Eight Port Ethernet Workgroup Hub

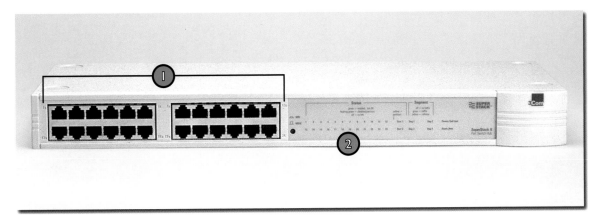

1. Twisted-Pair Ports
2. Status LEDs

A front and back view of a 3Com 24-port Ethernet 10BaseT switching hub. Most network topologies can use a hub in one way or another. The most prominent use of hubs is the 10BaseT topology, which depends on the hubs for the infrastructure of the topology. A switching hub is much faster and provides a direct path from each port in the switch to each of its other ports, creating a virtual connection that does not create traffic for every other port connected to the hub. For the exam, you should know the differences between a hub and a switching hub, and how the switching hub can improve network performance.

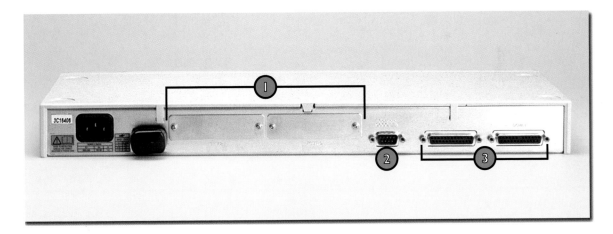

1. Hub Expansion Connectors
2. Serial Connection
3. Tranceiver Interface Module Connectors

Front (top) and Back (bottom) View of 3Com 24-Port Ethernet 10BaseT Switching Hub

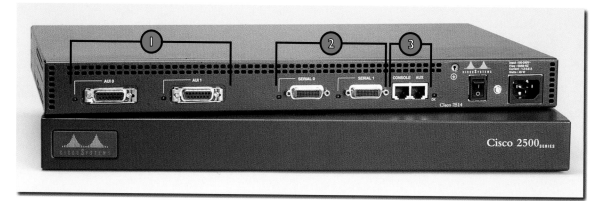

1. AUI Ethernet Ports
2. DB-60 Serial Ports
3. RJ-45 Connection

A front and back view of a Cisco router, which is a hybrid of both a bridge and a router and has a connection to more than two networks. The brouter can intelligently route packets between two separate networks just as a router can, but the brouter can also function as a bridge, which connects two different networks and makes them appear to be one network. For the exam, you should know when to choose a router over a brouter, and know at what layers of the OSI model both of these devices operate.

Cisco 2514 Dual Ethernet Serial Router Lets Remote Offices Communicate Between Two Ethernet LANs

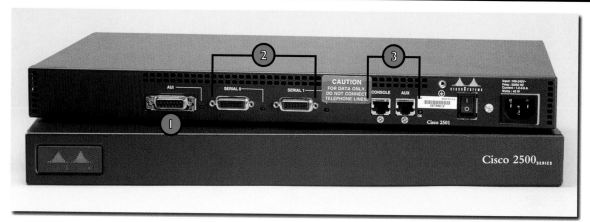

1. AUI Ethernet Port
2. DB-60 Serial Ports
3. RJ-45 Connection

A front and back view of a Cisco router, which receives packets from one side of the router and determines if the destination is on the other side of the router. If the destination is on the other side of the router, the packet will be forwarded. If the destination is not on the other side of the router, the packet will be forwarded to the next router. For the exam, you should know at what level of the OSI model the router operates, and that the router is used to connect remote networks.

Cisco 2501 Ethernet Dual Serial Router for LAN and WAN Connectivity

The Cisco Catalyst 5000 Ethernet switching hub, which supports 10/100 Mbps switching technology, creates "virtual circuits" between ports on the switch. A switching hub can deliver dedicated bandwidth when two devices on the switch are communicating with each other. This does not decrease the available network bandwidth on the switch because other ports are isolated from the data being delivered between the two communicating devices. The exam will test your knowledge of the purpose of hubs and switching hubs, and your ability to determine which networking implementations make use of the hub.

1. Modules
2. Power Supplies
3. Intellicom Office Stak Ethernet Switching Hub
4. AUI Ports
5. Fiber-Optic Cabling

1. Twisted-Pair Cabling
2. Patch Panels
3. Switching Hubs

A typical Ethernet wiring closet with twisted-pair switches, hubs, and patch panels. Cables connecting the computers and devices on the network are fed into the wiring rack and into their respective ports on the patch panels, which are numbered identically to the wall jacks at each network drop throughout the establishment. A connection is then made from the patch panel to an available port on the hub. For the exam, you should have an understanding of the connection from the computer to the network drop, into the patch panel, and then into a respective port on a hub or switch in an Ethernet 10BaseT implementation.

A Typical Wiring Closet with Ethernet Twisted-Pair Switches and Hubs

1. Fiber-Optic Transmit ST
   ST Connector
2. Fiber-Optic Receive ST
   Connector

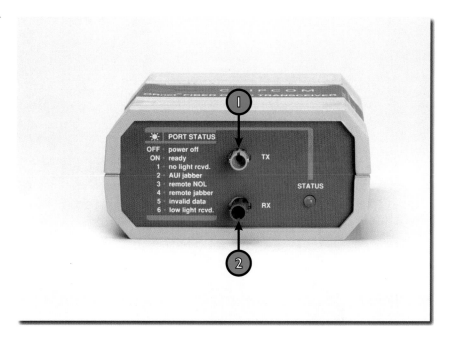

1. AUI Connector
2. Disable/Enable Jumper

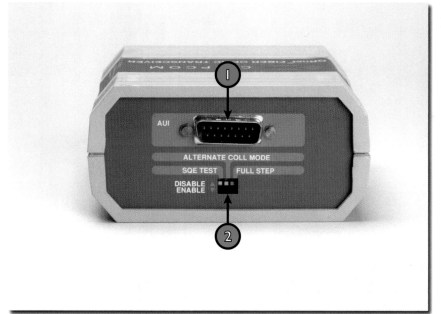

A fiber-optic transceiver that lets you transmit (TX) and receive (RX) Ethernet 10 Mbps traffic over fiber-optic cable. A transceiver such as this can be used as a means of connecting one device, such as a hub or bridge, to the fiber-optic network with an AUI connector. When more devices are required, you should use a hub or switch, which enables more ports and functionality than a transceiver does. For the exam, you should understand the purpose of a transceiver and how it connects two distinct network technologies.

Front (top) and Back (bottom) View of a Fiber-Optic Transceiver

1. Fiber-Optic Cable
2. Connector Caps to Prevent Injury to Eyes

A wall-mounted fiber-optic cable distribution box. This unit is a central station, similar to a hub, that receives fiber-optic cabling from numerous sources. The distribution box is located in areas such as server rooms and wiring closets where a number of centrally located fiber-based network devices are found. The exam will test your knowledge of the characteristics and use of fiber-optic cabling.

portions of each separated by a non-alphanumeric character. For example, you may take *Eat at Joe's* and turn it into *et$a#j's.*

These mechanisms can be used to design a method for creating passwords and usernames, but are useless if they are not followed and enforced.

Windows NT Security Policies

Because Windows NT provides an authentication method, it provides quite a few policies to help enforce password security. These can be set up to enforce that users are maintaining a secure environment. Several of these policies are listed in this chapter and are included in RFC 1244. To set up policies, you must run the User Manager application. The policies can be set up differently depending upon whether you are using Windows NT Workstation, a domain controller, or a member server to fit your environment. To access User Manager, choose Start | Programs | Administrative Tools | User Manager for Domains. The User Manager window opens. Select Policies | Account. The Account Policy dialog box appears. Use the Account Policy dialog box to set security policies for passwords and accounts in Windows NT.

Depending upon what policies you want to change, User Manager must be run differently or connected to a specific computer. If you want to set up policies on Windows NT Workstation, you must open User Manager on the individual workstation or type the command MUSRMGR.EXE. To access a domain policy, you must run User Manager for Domains (USRMGR.EXE). To access a specific member server, run User Manager for Domains on that server and when choosing a domain, type in the server name.

In addition to the password policies available, additional security can be defined through User Manager. Specific rights are delineated to users and groups when a domain is installed; however, these options may need to be modified from time to time. Options such as "Log on locally" might be required by specific users. These options are available from User Manager by choosing the Policies | User Rights option. Security for some of the more common tasks that can be defined include "Shutdown system," "Access this computer from network," "Log on locally," Change the system time," and "Back up files and directories." In addition, an advanced user rights option is available to control some of the more complex operations. The following illustration shows the users set up for Shutdown system privileges by default.

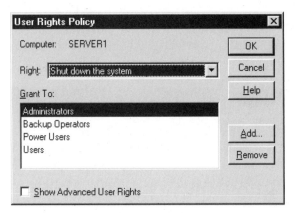

Select an option from the Right drop-down menu to set specific rights. Check the Show Advanced User Rights check box to include more complex operations.

Auditing Password Usage

After you have set up password policies, you must audit the systems being accessed to ensure that the policies are being enforced. With these policies set up, if someone is attempting to violate the password security, you will see evidence in the computer security event logs. This information can be used to track down what accounts are being hacked against. In addition, you can audit what resources are successfully being accessed or modified. This information is vital to ensuring the security of your Windows NT systems. Auditing is set up with User Manager also. Exercise 7-2 walks you through setting up auditing within Windows NT. The illustration within the exercise shows an example of an auditing configuration for a Domain.

EXERCISE 7-2

Auditing Setup

1. Select Start | Programs | Administrative Tools | User Manager for Domains. The User Manager window opens.

2. Select Policies | Audit. The Audit Policy dialog box, shown next, appears.

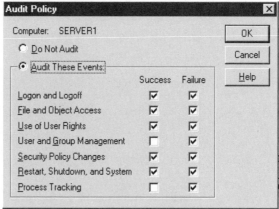

3. Select the Audit These Events option. (By default, no objects are selected.)

4. Place a check in the Failure column for the following objects: Logon and Logoff; File and Object Access; Use of User Rights; User and Group Management; Security Policy Changes; Restart, Shutdown, and System; and Process Tracking.

5. Place a check box under the success category for the following objects: Logon and Logoff; File and Object Access; Use of User Rights; Security Policy Changes; and Restart, Shutdown, and System.

6. Click the OK button. The policies take effect immediately.

Each object has its own use and purpose. You must understand what each object shown in the Audit Policy dialog box does and how it is used to tighten security. Table 7-6 displays each object and provides a brief description.

When setting up audit policies, the File and Object Access settings are dependent upon other portions of Windows NT. You can only use this function if the drive that data is stored on is on an NTFS-formatted partition. In addition, you must set the auditing attributes for specific files from within the Windows NT Explorer.

Auditing Object	Description
Logon and Logoff	Maintains a record of local and remote resource logins.
File and Object Access	Maintains listing of all file, directory, and printer access.
Use of User Rights	User rights are monitored, excluding logon and logoff.
User and Group Management	Maintains record of changes made to any user or group, including additions. Password changes are also monitored here.
Security Policy Changes	Monitors changes made to auditing, policies, or trust relationships.
Restart, Shutdown, and System	Monitors events around system startup, shutdown, and the security log itself.
Process Tracking	Monitors application execution, process access, and process termination.

After you've set auditing up, you can monitor the server security event logs to ensure that no one is trying to compromise your system. It will display the information you have specified in your audit policy, such as file access, logon and logoff, and security policy changes. You can access the events logs by selecting Start | Programs | Administrative Tools | Event Viewer. The Event Viewer window opens. Select Log | Security. Figure 7-2 shows the Event Viewer with entries from the security event log.

Passwords are the most common security authentication method used today. It can quickly become a point of access to an intruder if not set up and monitored properly. Be sure to set up strict guidelines and policies to secure your users' usernames and passwords. Several methods are available to help enforce and audit password policies. By applying these techniques, you can effectively tighten the security of your network.

FIGURE 7-2

The security event log is used to monitor usage and activity of your users. The information displayed is based upon the level of auditing set up by an administrator.

Date	Time	Source	Category	Event	User
1/1/90	1:29:29 PM	Security	Logon/Logoff	538	Administrato
1/1/90	1:29:28 PM	Security	Privilege Use	576	Administrato
1/1/90	1:29:28 PM	Security	Logon/Logoff	528	Administrato
1/1/90	1:29:28 PM	Security	Privilege Use	576	Administrato
1/1/90	1:29:28 PM	Security	Logon/Logoff	528	Administrato
1/1/90	1:29:17 PM	Security	Privilege Use	578	USER2
1/1/90	1:28:51 PM	Security	Logon/Logoff	538	Administrato
1/1/90	1:28:50 PM	Security	Logon/Logoff	538	USER2
1/1/90	1:28:50 PM	Security	Privilege Use	576	USER2
1/1/90	1:28:50 PM	Security	Logon/Logoff	528	USER2
1/1/90	1:28:50 PM	Security	Privilege Use	576	USER2
1/1/90	1:28:50 PM	Security	Logon/Logoff	528	USER2
1/1/90	1:28:42 PM	Security	Privilege Use	578	Administrato
1/1/90	1:28:30 PM	Security	Privilege Use	577	Administrato
1/1/90	1:28:30 PM	Security	Privilege Use	577	Administrato
1/1/90	1:28:27 PM	Security	Privilege Use	577	Administrato

FROM THE FIELD

Don't Expect a User to Know as Much as an Administrator

When it comes to users, groups, rights, and permissions, it can get very confusing. It's even confusing sometimes for administrators who study this stuff and use it on a daily basis. Imagine what users with little experience are going through when they have to manage files, shares, rights, or permissions. When dealing with security issues such as assigning permissions to a directory tree, users must know exactly what they are doing. If they do not, they can give access to private information that is not intended for all users. This is especially the case when users assign rights or permissions. Many times I have had users call me and say they accidentally checked the Replace Permissions on Subdirectories dialog box, which modified the rights on every subdirectory below the specified directory. It can take hours to restore the permissions that were wiped out in seconds.

FROM THE FIELD

In a small workgroup, it is imperative that everyone knows how to share and access files and directories on another person's computer. This sounds easy for administrators, but it can be quite difficult for a novice user. They need to share the directory, select share level security, enter the share name, determine a user limit, and then assign permissions to the share. There are too many chances for a user to make a mistake.

If you are an administrator in an organization where users are expected to take part in the daily administration of files, directories, and shares, then you should spend the time to make sure they are adequately trained. Spending a few minutes in advance can save headaches later when a user makes a costly mistake. Many users won't ask for help, so by training them beforehand, you will ensure they have the necessary skills to handle these administrative tasks. It may be more convenient for you to visit each user on an individual basis; however, you should consider a classroom environment if many users require training at once.

Ensuring that users are thoroughly trained can make your job easier. Having many users fulfill small tasks that you would normally be required to do can free you up for higher-level projects that require your training and dedication.

—Cameron Brandon, MCSE+Internet, CNE, A+, Network+

CERTIFICATION OBJECTIVE 7.03

Data Encryption and Protecting Network Data

As more companies go online with the Internet, the need to protect data becomes more prevalent. The industry has strived to provide a more secure data transfer mechanism. The idea is to protect the data during a transfer and guarantee that it makes it to its recipient unread and unmodified. From this need, encryption services have grown in popularity. Multiple encryption implementations have been published and are now available to the public. Several standards have also come about as the industry has grown.

To understand encryption, you must first learn how it works. You will also be introduced to some specific methods and algorithms used for encryption services. In addition, the main standards that have been defined will be explained, as well as a few other data protection methods.

Defining Data Encryption

Many different types of data encryption are available. Each methodology provides advantages and has a varying level of security. To date, some encryption standards have not been broken yet. Other more simple methods have been broken, but can still provide a level of security if used appropriately. Encryption can be defined as the process of taking plain text data and converting it to a meaningless format that is unreadable, better known as ciphertext. Once the data has been transferred, a mechanism exists to decrypt the data back to its original format.

A key of sorts is used during the encryption and decryption process to handle the data. This key is the algorithm that the data can be compared against. Only the persons who have obtained this key can encrypt or decrypt the data. Generally, a symmetric key contains a random number of bits that are used to encrypt the data. The longer the key, the more complex the encryption algorithm.

The most basic form of encryption is the *private-key encryption* or *symmetric algorithm*. This requires that each individual must possess a copy of the key. The problem is that you must have a secure way to transport the key to other people. If you do not, someone may intercept the key, which makes encryption useless. In addition, if you are using encryption techniques for multiple people, you may not want one person to have access to another's data. Now you must keep multiple single keys per person and this can get very cumbersome.

A second form of encryption available is the *public-key* or *asymmetric algorithm*. This system requires two related but separate keys. You freely publish one key, the public key, to anyone you choose. You could even post it in public places for anyone. The second key, the private key, is kept in a secure location and is used only by you. Both keys are required to pass data with this encryption technique. For example, say you want to send data to a coworker. You would retrieve his public key and encrypt the data. Once done, nothing but the private key can decrypt the message, not even the public key you have. Your coworker could then reply by using your public key and you would be the only person able to decrypt that message. This system works well because it enables you to send the public key over an insecure communications channel and still maintain the level of security. You could even publish your public key on the Internet. Rivest, Shamir, and Adleman created the standard for how this method is used. It is known as the RSA standard and is discussed later in this chapter.

Encryption Methods

When encrypting data, different methods can be used. Each method provides advantages and drawbacks. Some methods work in cooperation with others to provide an overall solution. Some common methods are discussed and explained here.

STREAM CIPHER   Stream cipher algorithms encrypt data one bit at a time. Plain text bits are converted into encrypted cipher text. This method is usually not as secure as block cipher techniques; however, stream cipher algorithms generally execute faster. In addition, the ciphertext is always the same size as the original plain text. This technique is also less prone to errors. If an error occurs during the encryption process, usually this only affects a single bit instead of the whole string. When block ciphers contain errors, at a minimum the entire block is garbage.

BLOCK CIPHER   Instead of encrypting a bit at a time, block cipher algorithms encrypt data in blocks. Block ciphers have more overhead than stream ciphers. The additional overhead is provided separately, depending upon the implementation, and the block size can be modified, but the most common size is 64 bits. Because it handles encryption at a higher level, it is generally more secure. The downside is that the execution time takes longer. Additional cipher options are available when using block cipher algorithms, such as Electronic Codebook (ECB), Cipher Block Chaining (CBC), and Output Feedback Mode (OFB). Each mode is displayed and explained in Table 7-7.

Block Cipher Mode	Description
Electronic Codebook (ECB)	Each block is encrypted individually. If information reappears in the same text, such as a common word, it is encrypted the same way.
Cipher Block Chaining (CBC)	Feedback is inserted into each cipher block before it is encrypted. It includes information from the block that proceeded it. This ensures that repetitive information is encrypted differently.
Cipher Feedback Mode (CFB)	This enables you to encrypt portions of a block instead of an entire block.
Output Feedback Mode (OFB)	This works very similarly to CFB. The underlying shift registers are used slightly differently.

PADDING   When encrypting data, plain text messages usually do not take up an even number of blocks. Many times, padding must be added to the last block to complete the data stream. The data added can contain all ones, all zeros, or a combination of ones and zeros. The encryption algorithm used is responsible for determining the padding that will be applied. Multiple padding techniques are available and used depending upon the algorithm implementation.

Encryption Standards

As encryption has become more popular, the need for industry standards has arisen. Standards for different implementations and algorithms have been defined to move the industry in the same direction. The most popular standards are discussed here with a brief history and explanation.

DES   The Data Encryption Standard (DES) was created by IBM and made into a standard in 1977. It is a 64-bit block symmetric algorithm and is specified in the ANSI X3.92 and X3.106 standards. The algorithm described in this standard specifies both enciphering and deciphering operations, which are based on a binary number. It has been stated as the standard by the National Security Agency (NSA) for use in government organizations. There currently exist 72 quadrillion (72,000,000,000,000,000) encryption keys for DES; a key is chosen at random. DES uses a block cipher methodology to apply a 56-bit symmetric key to each 64-bit block. An additional form of DES, known as triple DES, applies three keys in succession to each block. The United States government has banned DES's export to areas outside of the U.S. because of the algorithm's security value.

RSA   Ron Rivest, Adi Shamir, and Leonard Adleman (RSA) were the individuals responsible for creating the RSA standard at MIT. This standard defines the mathematical properties in using the public-key encryption methodology. The algorithm randomly generates a very large prime number that is used for the public key. The public key is then used to derive another prime number for the private key via mathematical computations. Many forms of RSA encryption are in use today, including the popular PGP. PGP, or Pretty Good Privacy, has worked well in the past. Some vendors have included implementations of RSA in their core application code. Novell NetWare, versions 4.1x and 5.0 have RSA encryption built into the client and server to provide a secure communications channel.

Digital Signatures

Digital signatures are used to verify that a message that was sent is from the appropriate sender and that it has not been tampered with. When using digital signatures, the message is not altered, but a signature string is attached to verify its validity. Digital signatures usually use a public-key algorithm. A public key is used to verify the message and the private key is used to create the signature. A trusted application is usually present on a secure computer somewhere on the network that is used to validate the signature provided. This computer is known as a *certificate authority* and stores the public key of every user on the system. Certificates are released containing the public key of the user in question. When these are dispensed, the certificate authority signs each package with its own private key. Several vendors offer commercial products that provide certificate authority services. For example, Microsoft Exchange Server can be set up to provide certificates to mail clients for using digital signatures. By using this methodology, you are not protecting your data completely; however, you will know if it has been tampered with.

Common Encryption Programs

Due to the popularity of encryption, several vendors and organizations have written and published cryptographic programs to provide security. Each works a little different from the others and can be applied in different ways. The most popular program in circulation is PGP. In addition, Microsoft provides an application-programming interface for encryption services, called CryptoAPI.

Pretty Good Privacy

A common implementation for encryption services is *Pretty Good Privacy*, or PGP. PGP is available for Windows, DOS, Amiga, UNIX, VAX, VMS, and Macintosh systems. It includes a full-featured tool set for encryption, digital signatures, and file compression. PGP includes multiple encryption methodologies, including symmetric keys, asymmetric keys, and a random number generator. PGP is available for anyone to use and works well with most security implementations.

CryptoAPI

Microsoft foresaw the need to provide encryption services within applications. PGP and other implementations cannot work at the API level to provide these services to custom applications. Therefore, Microsoft created an API that enables you to add cryptographic services to your programs. This API contains a set of modules known as cryptographic service providers, or CSRs. CryptoAPI was included in Windows NT 4.0 Service Pack 3, Windows 95 OEM 2, and Internet Explorer 3.02. The API is used in a very similar method as PGP; however, the encryption and decryption processes happen within the application.

CERTIFICATION OBJECTIVE 7.04

Uses of a Firewall

As the disadvantages of non-secure networks have become more apparent in today's business world, additional forms of protection have been devised. Because it seems to be a requirement today to connect to public networks such as the Internet, some form of protection from hackers must be provided at the network level. A *firewall* protects a secure internal network from outside influence from a public insecure network. It can also be used to provide protection to a secure portion of a private network, such as Human Resources physical network.

Although many vendors label products as firewalls, it is more of a network security strategy than it is a single product. A firewall is a collection of concepts used to protect one network from another. The most common implementation today is the use of a firewall between an organization's internal network and the Internet. Firewalls can be very complex, because they provide more features that just packet filtering. They can also provide multiple layers of protection, including actually scanning the information stored in the packets for malicious data as they pass through. They use advanced techniques to monitor connections, to log potential intrusions, and to act upon these incidents.

Firewall Architecture

As mentioned earlier, a firewall is a combination of techniques and technologies that are used to control the flow of data between networks. A firewall enables all traffic to pass through to each network; however, it compares the traffic to a set of rules that determine how the traffic will be managed. If the traffic matches the rules for acceptable data, the traffic is passed on to the network. If the rule specifies that the data be denied, the traffic cannot continue and will be bounced back. Although some implementations may do this differently, the same basic functionality is used.

Dual-Homed Host Firewalls

A *dual-homed firewall* consists of a single computer with two physical network interfaces. This computer acts as a gateway between two networks. The server's routing capability is disabled so that the firewall can handle all traffic management. Either an application-level proxy or circuit level firewall software is run to provide data transfer capability. You must be careful not to enable routing within the network operating system or you will bypass your firewall software. Figure 7-3 shows an illustration of a dual-homed host firewall configuration.

Screened Host Firewalls

Screened host firewall configurations are considered by many to be more secure than the dual-homed firewall. In this configuration, you place a screening router between the gateway host and the public network. This enables you to provide packet filtering before reaching the host computer. The host computer could then run a proxy to provide additional security to this configuration. As packets travel into the internal network, they only know of the computer host that exists. Figure 7-4 shows an illustration of a screened-host configuration.

Screened Subnet Firewalls

A screened subnet firewall configuration takes security to the next level by further isolating the internal network from the public network. An

FIGURE 7-3   An example of a basic firewall configuration to the Internet

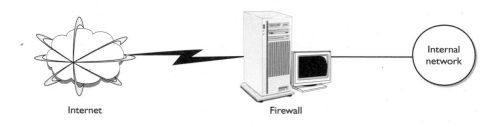

Internet   Firewall

FIGURE 7-4   An example of a screened host firewall configuration

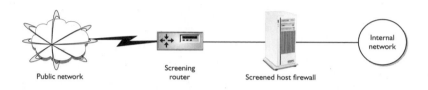

Public network — Screening router — Screened host firewall — Internal network

additional screening router is placed between the internal network and the firewall proxy server. The internal router handles local traffic while the external router handles inbound and outbound traffic to the public network. This provides two additional levels of security. First, by adding a link internally, you can protect the firewall host from an attack by an internal source. Second, it makes an external attack much more difficult because the number of links is increased. Figure 7-5 shows the screened subnet firewall configuration.

Firewall Types

There are three types of firewalls that can be used: Packet Level firewall, Application Level firewall, and Circuit Level firewall. Each uses different security approaches, thus providing advantages over the others. One additional feature that was discussed earlier is encryption services. Most firewalls provide some sort of cryptographic services for data transfers.

FIGURE 7-5   An example of the screened subnet firewall configuration

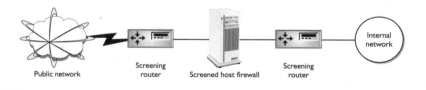

Public network — Screening router — Screened host firewall — Screening router — Internal network

When you have a complete understanding of the features and type of security that are needed from a firewall, you can then determine the implementation that bests fits the environment.

PACKET LEVEL FIREWALL   A packet level firewall is usually a form of screening router that examines packets based upon filters that are set up at the network and transport layers. You can block incoming or outgoing transfers based upon a TCP/IP address or other rules. For example, you may choose to not enable any incoming IP connections but to enable any outgoing IP connections. You can set up rules that will enable certain types of requests to pass while other are denied. The information that rules can be based on includes source address, destination address, session protocol type, and the source and destination port. Because this works at only three layers, it is a very basic form of protection and is only a type of implementation. To properly provide security to another network, all seven layers must be protected by a full-featured conventional firewall.

APPLICATION LEVEL FIREWALL   The application level firewall understands the data at the application level. Application layer firewalls operate at the application, presentation, and session layers. Data at the application level can actually be understood and monitored to verify that no harmful information is included. An example of an application level firewall is an Internet proxy or mail server. Many uses are available through some form of proxy; however, these functions are usually very intensive to provide security at that level. In addition, often clients must be configured to pass through the proxy to use it. Proxy servers are also used to mask the original origin of a packet. For example, an Internet proxy will pass the request on; however, the source listed in the packet is the proxy server address. The overall server doesn't just filter the packets, it actually takes in the original and retransmits a new packet through a different network interface.

CIRCUIT LEVEL FIREWALL   A circuit level firewall is similar to an application proxy except that the security mechanisms are applied at the time the connection is established. From then on, the packets flow between the hosts without any further checking from the firewall. Circuit level firewalls operate at the transport layer.

Firewall Features

As firewalls have evolved, additional feature sets have grown out of or been added to these implementations. They are used to provide faster access and better security mechanisms. As encryption techniques have improved, they are being incorporated more into firewall implementations. Also, caching is being provided for services such as the World Wide Web. This enables pages to be cached for a period of time, which can dramatically speed up the user experience. New management techniques and technologies such as Virtual Private Networks (VPNs) are now being included as well.

CERTIFICATION SUMMARY

Information has increasingly become more important for organizations, hence, the security of this information has become more of a priority. Organizations are using public communications channels such as the Internet to transfer data that must be secure.

Windows NT includes several different kinds of security models. The security subsystem consists of four components: the Local Security Authority (LSA), Security Accounts Manager (SAM), Security Reference Monitor, and the logon process. After the Security Accounts Manager validates a user, an access token is created that includes the User Security Identifier (SID), Primary Group Security Identifier, Group Security Identifier, Default Access Control List, Access Permissions, and the Owner. Every named object includes a security descriptor including information about the object and the access control list (ACL). The ACL is a list that provides the users and groups allowed to access the object as well as the level of permissions applied. The Security Descriptor is broken into four components: the system access-control list (SACL), the discretionary access-control list (DACL), an owner, and a primary group. Access Control Entries specify the access or auditing permissions assigned for a specific user or group. Windows NT file and directory permissions are available on NTFS-formatted partitions. Various levels of security are available based upon your environment's requirements.

Two users, Administrator and Guest, are created by default for a server, workstation, or domain. In addition, functional groups are created that have varying rights levels. Shares are required to connect to remote directories on an NT computer. You can also append a $ symbol to the end of a share name to prevent its being listed in the browse list. A workgroup is an organizational unit, or a way to organize a group of computers. In Windows 95/98 environments, accounts are not shared and resources are protected based upon a single password. In a Windows NT workgroup, user IDs and passwords are still used but are not shared among other computers. A domain is used to share common user accounts and policies and consists of one or more NT servers. The registry needs to be secured in two ways: set permissions on the registry keys themselves and set up file and directory permissions for the directory in which it is stored.

A password is a series of characters used to authenticate a user's access permissions. Creating an effective password policy is critical to any organization sharing or protecting resources. Administrative accounts generally require a greater level of security than normal user accounts. Guidelines can be adopted to create secure passwords and usernames. Most organizations use a common scheme for creating usernames while depending upon the password to protect the resources. Windows NT includes several built-in policies that enforce password standards. In addition, auditing can be set up within User Manager to monitor usage and activity. You use Event Viewer to read the logs generated.

Data security has become more important as networks are becoming interconnected. Data encryption provides a way to ensure that the data is kept secure. Encryption is the process of taking plain text data and converting it into a meaningless format that is unreadable. A key is used to decipher the encryption code to return the data to a readable format. Two types of encryption types exist: symmetric or private-key and asymmetric or public-key. Two common encryption methods include Stream Cipher and Block Cipher. Two standards for encryption have been accepted: the Digital Encryption Standard (DES) and RSA. Both use different methodologies and are in wide use today. Digital signatures can be used to verify that a message arrived without being tampered with. Digital signatures do not encrypt a message; they just attach a signature that can be verified against a certificate authority. Two common encryption-based products include PGP and Microsoft's CryptoAPI.

A firewall is a collection of methodologies for protecting one network from a second interconnected network such as the Internet. Firewalls compare the data passing through them to rules set up to allow or deny access. There are several architectures for firewalls, three of them are: dual-homed host, screened host, and screened subnet. A dual-homed host has two network interfaces and acts as a gateway between the two networks. A screened host firewall has a screening router placed between the public network and the host. This provides an addition level of security against outside intrusion. A screened subnet firewall puts a screening router on both sides of the firewall host. This provides protection on both sides of the host.

Three firewall types exist: packet level firewall, application level firewall, and circuit level firewall. The packet level firewall controls data at the network and transport layers. The application level type acts as a proxy and controls the top three layers of the OSI model. A circuit level firewall works similarly to an application level firewall but operates at the transport layer. Additional security features have been added to firewalls to provide better service such as support for VPNs and caching and better management tools.

 # TWO-MINUTE DRILL

- ❑ When designing a network, be sure to take into consideration the available options and the security impacts of each.

- ❑ A security model is a generic term that describes methodologies used to secure a system.

- ❑ There are four parts to the security subsystem in Windows NT. Each plays an integral part of the security functions provided.

- ❑ When the Security Accounts Manager validates a user, an access token is created.

- ❑ The ACL is a list that provides the users and/or groups allowed to access the object as well as the level of permissions applied.

- ❑ Security Descriptors are broken down into several components: the system access-control list (SACL), the discretionary access-control list (DACL), an owner, and a primary group.

❑ One method of security that is available for use is file and directory level permissions.

❑ Windows NT uses user and group objects, more commonly known as accounts, to delineate access permissions.

❑ Two types of user accounts exist: global accounts that are used throughout a domain and local accounts that are used on a single Windows NT computer.

❑ A domain group list includes Administrators, Account Operators, Backup Operators, Guests, Print Operators, Replicator, Server Operators, and Users.

❑ A server or workstation group list includes Administrators, Backup Operators, Guests, Power Users, Replicator, and Users.

❑ Share-level security is available on client operating systems such as Windows 95 and Windows 98.

❑ Share-level security is easy to implement and maintain on small peer-to-peer networks; however, users must remember the password for each resource that is shared (unless password caching is in use).

❑ Windows NT provides an additional type of security model. You need to understand the fundamental differences between domains and workgroups and the security architecture defined.

❑ You must secure the registry for any Windows NT computer. The registry contains the control parameters for the entire operating system.

❑ The most basic security mechanism is the password.

❑ Setting up password authentication is a good start; however, it will be useless against a knowledgeable intruder without solid policies and processes defined.

❑ Good guidelines should be developed around the username and password.

❑ Because Windows NT provides an authentication method, it provides quite a few policies to help enforce password security.

❑ As more companies go online with the Internet, the need to protect data becomes more prevalent.

❑ Multiple encryption implementations have been published and are now available to the public.

❑ Encryption can be defined as the process of taking plain text data and converting it to a meaningless format that is unreadable, better known as ciphertext.

❑ Due to the popularity of encryption, several vendors and organizations have written and published cryptographic programs to provide security.

❑ A *firewall* protects a secure internal network from outside influence from a public insecure network.

❑ A firewall enables all traffic to pass through to each network; however, it compares the traffic to a set of rules that determine how the traffic will be managed.

SELF TEST

The following Self Test questions will help you measure your understanding of the material presented in this chapter. Read all the choices carefully, as there may be more than one correct answer. Choose all correct answers for each question.

1. What portion of the Windows NT security subsystem handles local security policies and user authentication and generates audit log messages?

    A. Local Security Authority (LSA)

    B. Security Accounts Manager (SAM)

    C. Security Reference Monitor

    D. None of the above

2. What portion of the security reference model maintains the database used for storing user and group account information?

    A. Local Security Authority (LSA)

    B. Logon Process

    C. Security Reference Monitor

    D. Security Accounts Manager (SAM)

3. When an access token is created for a user, which information is included?

    A. User Security Identifier (SID)

    B. Primary Group Security Identifier

    C. Group Security Identifier

    D. All of the above

4. What access control list object determines what users and groups have permissions to this object?

    A. System Access-Control List (SACL)

    B. Discretionary Access-Control List (DACL)

    C. Owner

    D. User

5. Which of the following are valid, predefined file permission types? (Choose all that apply.)

    A. No access

    B. List

    C. Add

    D. Change

6. Which groups are created by default for a standalone Windows NT server and workstation? (Choose all that apply.)

    A. Administrators

    B. Account Operators

    C. Backup Operators

    D. Print Operators

7. What identifier is used in conjunction with a share name to make them hidden?

    A. #<share name>

    B. <share name>#

    C. <share name>$

    D. None of the above

8. Which of these is a common rule for creating a secure password?

    A. Do not use a familiar name such as your child's name, your spouse's name, or your pet's name.

    B. Do not use your first, middle, or last name or nickname.

    C. Do not use a password of all single digits or the same letter. For example: 1111111 or AAAAAAA.

    D. All of the above.

9. Which of the following is a common mechanism for creating passwords? (Choose all that apply.)

    A. Create a password that uses a myriad of intermingled alphanumeric characters.

    B. Take several words and use different portions of each, separated by a non-alphanumeric character.

    C. Uses a four-character password of non-alphanumeric characters.

    D. All of the above.

10. What policies are not available from within User Manager for Windows NT?

    A. Minimum password length

    B. Maximum password length

    C. Minimum password age

    D. Maximum password age

11. Within User Manager, what menu option lists additional user rights that can be added?

    A. Policies | Audit

    B. Users | Audit

    C. Policies | User Rights

    D. Users | User Rights

12. Which of the following options are available when setting up auditing?

    A. Interactive Logon

    B. Remote Resource Access

    C. Logon and Logoff

    D. System Process

13. After auditing has been set up, what utility is used to monitor the activity and the events generated?

    A. User Manager

    B. Server Manager

    C. Event Viewer

    D. Performance Monitor

14. What is the symmetric encryption algorithm better known as?

    A. Digital Encryption Standard (DES)

    B. RSA standard

    C. Private-key algorithm

    D. Public-key algorithm

15. Which of the following is classified as an encryption method? (Choose all that apply.)

    A. Stream Cipher

    B. Data Cipher

    C. Byte Cipher

    D. Block Cipher

16. What Block Cipher Mode encrypts each block individually during the encryption process?

    A. Electronic Codebook (ECB)

    B. Cipher Block Chaining (CBC)

    C. Cipher Feedback Mode (CFB)

    D. None of the above

17. What encryption standard is based upon a fixed 56-bit symmetric key encryption algorithm?

    A. RSA

    B. DES

    C. CPA

    D. DSE

18. What technology uses certificate authorities to verify that a message has not been tampered with?

    A. RSA encryption

    B. Local Security Authority

    C. Digital Signatures

    D. None of the above

19. What service is available to enable you to add encryption services directly into an application?

    A. PGP

    B. DES

    C. Uuencode

    D. CryptoAPI

20. What technology provides a secure communications channel between an internal network and a public network such as the Internet?

    A. Encryption

    B. Firewall

    C. Router

    D. None of the above

21. What kind of firewall provides a single computer with two physical network interfaces?

    A. Dual-homed firewall

    B. Screened host firewall

    C. Screening router

    D. Screened subnet firewall

22. What component(s) is included in a screened subnet firewall configuration?

    A. Single screening router

    B. Host firewall server

    C. Circuit application

    D. All of the above

23. What type of firewall is used to provide security based upon rules governing the network or transport layers?

    A. Packet level

    B. Application level

    C. Circuit level

    D. None of the above

24. What level types of firewalls can act as proxies? (Choose all that apply.)

    A. Packet level

    B. Application level

C. Circuit level

D. All of the above

25. What features are now available with firewall implementations?

A. Encryption

B. Application caching

C. Virtual Private Networks (VPN's)

D. All of the above

CERTIFICATION

Part II

Knowledge of Networking Practices

8

Network Implementation

Y ou'll find many questions concerning installing and maintaining computer networks located throughout the Knowledge of Networking Technology section of the Network+ exam. Knowing the different concepts behind computer networking is very important and provides a strong foundation for other sections of the exam. When you work with computer networks, you need to know the different components that make up the physical network as well as the theoretical terms used in computer networking as a whole.

Before you can begin connecting and shaping your network, you need to understand the concepts of computer networking. You might encounter problems with the computer network or the connection between two network segments and need to troubleshoot where the network problem is. Knowing the complete picture of how networking works and the different components involved, from the cabling technologies to networking appliances, such as routers and switches, will help you understand networking so much more.

In addition to knowing the different networking areas for this exam, you need to know and understand PC fundamentals. This includes different environmental characteristics of how PCs relate, as well as basic troubleshooting techniques. When you couple knowledge of these computer technologies with "real-world" experience, you will be a force to be reckoned with in the Information Technology industry.

CERTIFICATION OBJECTIVE 8.01

Installing the Network

Installing a computer network may seem like a mindless task of just connecting a few cables, but it's really much more complicated than that. You need to know how each independent component operates, and you need to learn many different terms. You have to think about many different aspects of your computer network other than how you are going to physically connect the network cables to your PC.

When you first decide to hook up a network, you will encounter many different things that you have probably never thought about before. Well, don't worry, because every person in the IT field has been there before. Before you can consider yourself an expert on computer networking, several important areas need your undivided attention.

First, you need to plan how to configure your network. You have a lot of choices. You have to decide how to lay out your physical location. You have to choose between several different network topologies, and some work better than others depending on the situation. As you learned in the first chapter, each topology comes with advantages and disadvantages; you have to choose which will fit your environment the best. Choosing the best networking topology and implementing that technology correctly is what separates the good network administrators from the not-so-good.

Although the physical structure of the network is very important, you also have to provide for the administrative duties that need to be performed for your network to operate. These include setting up administrative and test accounts, passwords, IP addresses, IP configurations, connectivity requirements, and the necessary software so that once you have your network working, each client can communicate with one another. Without these ingredients, all that you end up with are a lot of very expensive computer components.

When you've built the physical architecture for your network, you still have a lot of work in front of you to make sure that your network can function. As the administrator, you have total control over the layout and structure of your network, as well as how each client will communicate with other clients or servers. It's up to you to decide upon which components to throw away and which technologies to utilize to the best of your ability.

You have "administrative" control over the network, so you are in control. With the Administrator account rights for your network comes a big responsibility. You will be responsible for the security of the data, the efficiency of the network, and many other aspects that you may not have thought of yet, such as printing, sharing of files, and e-mail. These specific areas of networking are probably not what you imagined when you first thought of creating a network. However, these are all very important in the big picture of what you have before you.

Your most important duty as network administrator is to make sure that the clients on your network can communicate with one another at all times. Without this capability, your network is pretty much worthless. Besides supplying fundamental non-stop access to the network, you have to try to make sure that the people who are using the network won't be interrupted during working hours. Sounds like an easy job, right? Well, read on and see what's in store.

Communication on a computer network is accomplished by the use of protocols. You can choose from hundreds of different protocols, but one of the most widely adopted standards in the computer industry is the TCP/IP protocol. You may be familiar with this protocol if you have ever surfed the Internet or downloaded a file.

An easy way to think of protocols is to consider them as you would a language. For example, for computers to talk to one another, they have to be speaking the same language, or using the same protocol. A French-speaking person and an English-speaking person might be able to hear one another speaking, but they are not able to understand each other, and that is where the importance lies. Communication between computers is actually a little more complicated than that, but that will do for now. You'll learn more of the subtleties of the TCP/IP protocol later in this chapter.

A computer network is all about sharing data and exchanging ideas. These fundamental practices on a network, however, pose certain security problems. There are many different types of security to be concerned with on a network, such as physical security, file and directory security, and Internet security, but one core section of security that is often overlooked is password security. When you share files or printers with other users, you sometimes are asked for a password. This password is a "key" that will either admit or restrict your access to the data or peripherals on the network. Password security is the practice of making sure that the passwords are difficult to break into. Several fundamental practices are used when trying to enforce password security on a network. You'll learn more about the different practices of password security later in this chapter.

Standard Operating Procedures (SOPs) are the practices that you follow to enable your network to run smoothly and efficiently. These typically consist of backing up the data on the network, making sure everyone can communicate, and fixing any problem that may arise at a moment's notice. It doesn't get much simpler than that!

Administrative and Test Accounts

The network administrator holds the keys to the network castle. Any actions that the network administrator makes can ultimately affect those who are part of the network. The person who holds the Administrator account has complete, unrestricted access to all of the files, folders, and shares on the network. He has complete power over the security of the network.

Because the Administrator account is a sensitive issue, those with system privileges to the account should be very careful and restrict access to only those who truly need the account to complete their jobs. In no case should a person who has the capability to log in using the Administrator account use this for his day-to-day usage of the network. That is a good way to inadvertently enable a virus or an unwelcome user complete access to the network. Remember that you are dealing with the sensitive nature of your data and you should do whatever you can to protect it.

Basically, the Administrator account should be used to perform administrative duties only. All other duties should be completed when logged on with a personal user account. This practice allows for safe and restricted access to the sensitive areas of the network. The role of any network administrator is to protect the data on the network. With this role comes a lot of responsibility. As the administrator of the network, you essentially hold the data in the palm of your hand. If by some chance the Administrator account accidentally becomes compromised, you could leave the safety of your network in the hands of others. This, of course, is not what you want to do.

The administrative account is the most sensitive account on your network, so you have to be extra careful to use a password that is difficult to break. A password should consist of more than eight characters that include both upper- and lower-case letters as well as numbers or symbols. You should never use a simple phrase or word for the Administrator account.

Some operating systems, such as Windows NT Workstation and Server, allow for some flexibility with the Administrator account. For example, a good practice to follow is to immediately rename the Administrator account to something other than "Administrator." If someone is trying to break in to your computer network, they need two very important things. One, they need the name of the account and two, they need the password for that account. If a potential hacker knows the name of an administrative account, he's already half way to gaining access to your network. By renaming the Administrator account, you eliminate fifty percent of the problem right off the bat.

Another standard practice is to limit access to the Administrator account to those who have a justifiable need for the account. When the network administrator grants administrative access to too many people, there is no accountability on the network. You cannot be sure who is making changes on the network because so many different people have access.

The worst-case scenario is when people have administrative access to important files that would normally be restricted to them under their personal accounts. With administrative access, they can roam and browse any files on the network without anyone being able to do anything.

Whenever you make a change to any part of your network, you should verify that the change didn't affect any other part of your network. You can accomplish this by using a test account to make sure that your change works. A test account is an account with normal rights within the network. If you used an administrative account to make the change, then you should use a test account to test your changes. This practice is especially important when making changes to file and directory permissions. When you have administrative privileges, you have access to everything on the network, so you can't test to see your changes from the perspective of a normal user. By using a test account, you can make sure that you didn't give too much freedom on the network and that your changes went according to plan.

Consider this example of the consequences when the test account practice is not followed: A network administrator made a change to the Payroll folder and its subdirectories on one of the shares on a server. Instead of using a test account to verify that his changes went through as planned, he moved on to something else. What he didn't discover until later is that he accidentally gave everyone on the network access to the Payroll share. Anyone on the network could access the payroll files.

Table 8-1 lists the standard practices for administrative and test accounts on a network. It will help you remember the advantages and purpose of having two separate accounts on the network. Usually, a network administrator has an account with administrative privileges and one without. During the course of the day, the network administrator uses his administrative account for making any needed changes. For normal day-to-day usage, the network administrator uses his account that does not have administrative access to the entire network.

TABLE 8-1 Administrative and Test Accounts	**Administrative Account**	**Test Account**
	Maintain exclusive permissions for all files and folders on the network.	Set with sample user rights—this account should have restricted privileges on the network.
	Set and enforce tight security for anyone who has administrative rights on the network.	Set up your test account to resemble all other accounts on your network including privileges and password security.
	Assign a strong password with at least eight characters, using a mix of upper- and lowercase letters as well as numbers and symbols.	Assign a strong password.
	Restrict access to the administrative account to those few people who need access.	Assign restricted privileges to the network.
	Use this account to make any necessary changes to the network.	Use this account to test the changes that you made to the network. You are simulating a normal user with this account.

FROM THE FIELD

The Importance of Having a Backup Administrator Account

I never realized the importance of having another account with administrative rights on the Windows NT network until I found myself in a particular bind one day. While logging on to my Administrator account, I was prompted that my password was set to expire soon. I changed my password, and that's where the trouble began. I had forgotten that I was currently logged on to another server in the server room. When I changed my password, Windows NT became confused that I was logged on to the network with a username that now had two different passwords assigned to it. The result is that my account got locked out. My *administrative* account! I couldn't figure out what had happened, until I discovered that I was logged on to the server in the server room.

I had no way to unlock my Administrator account because you must have administrative rights in order to modify an account with administrative rights. Of course, I couldn't find my boss to ask him to unlock my account. When I paged my boss he told me to check the filing cabinet for a sealed envelope containing the logon information for the backup Administrator account. I used this backup account to unlock my account and enclosed the logon information in another sealed envelope. The sealed envelope is to detect whether the account information has been tampered with.

The moral of this story is to always have a backup Administrator account ready for emergencies. Another important lesson to be learned is to always log out of machines when you are done if you are using your account with administrative rights. Someone could tamper with information logged on as you, and it would appear that you were responsible. Finally, the last lesson to be learned is to never change your password on a Windows NT server or workstation if you are currently logged on to more than one machine. Your account will instantly be locked out! Be careful when you are using an account with administrative rights—it's very powerful!

—Cameron Brandon, MCSE+Internet, CNE,
A+, Network+

Passwords

Passwords are another form of computer security to ensure that those who aren't supposed to access certain files on the network don't. Passwords aren't a fail-safe method of securing your network, but if they are implemented and enforced correctly, they can impose a level of security that you should feel comfortable with.

You can think of passwords in terms of a lock-and-key system. The user account is the lock and the password associated with that account is the key. If you have both the lock and the key for the network, you can have access to any files or data that the user account has access to. It's as simple as that.

As the network administrator, it's your job to enforce strong passwords on the network and across your computing environment. A *strong password* is a password that is difficult to "crack" or break in to. With the intelligence, experience, and technology of today's hackers, it's getting easier and easier for them to gain access to our files. Your job is to keep them from doing so.

exam

ⓦatch

You should memorize what makes a secure and safe password. Make sure to eliminate the use of easily guessed words or phrases in your password!

A good way to approach password security is to think like a hacker. If I were a hacker, I'd like to break into an account with a nice and easy password that resembles a common phrase or easily guessed word or group or words. This is an absolute no-no for password security. If you want to enforce password security, you cannot, under any circumstances, allow your users to create passwords that include their names, the names of relatives, birthdays, or common phrases. Today's hackers use technology called "brute force" attacks that runs different dictionary files against the user account in question in an attempt to break into that account. They are usually successful because the user decided to utilize a commonly guessed word or phrase, such as their favorite baseball team or their spouse's birthday. Unfortunately, when you prevent users from choosing easily remembered passwords, some users are prone to compromising security even further by writing their password on a yellow sticky-note and posting it to their monitor. You must educate your users about the need for password security and institute a policy that prohibits them from posting their passwords or sharing passwords with other users.

You should require users to change their passwords frequently, such as every three to four weeks. Even the most secure and seemingly unbreakable passwords are not impervious to some high-quality hacking programs. Some hacking programs will run for a set period of time until the password is broken. On a standard Pentium 200MHz, it may take a program like this roughly three or four weeks running non-stop to break the password. If you require frequent password changes, by the time the hacker could compromise a user's password, it is time to change the password anyway, effectively stopping the hacker's progress.

on the
job

With all of the computer technology available to help secure your network, sometimes the weakest link in your network is the human factor. You can implement the strongest policies and use the latest technology available, but if your users fail to adhere to the rules and regulations regarding your network password policies, all of your work is for naught. To combat this problem, you might want to encourage your users to become better trained on the technology that they are using.

The last standard practice for enforcing password guidelines on your network is to enable password lockouts. In particular with the Microsoft Windows NT operating system, the network administrator can enable password lockout after x number of attempts to log in with an incorrect password. The network administrator specifies the duration of time that the account is locked. A reasonable amount of time is about 30 minutes. For example, if a hacker is attempting to break in to the network with a certain user account and he doesn't know the password, after three unsuccessful attempts to log in, the user account that the hacker is trying to use is disabled for 30 minutes. This practice severely limits the ability of a hacker to keep trying different passwords on the same user account.

Table 8-2 provides guidelines that will help you to enforce strong passwords on your network.

exam
⍟atch

I know it seems obvious to specify passwords with a mixture of upper- and lowercase letters and the use of at least one symbol. The exam will test your knowledge of safe password practices by having you select the most secure password from a list of choices.

IP Addresses

TCP/IP (Transmission Control Protocol/Internet Protocol) is an industry-standard suite of protocols designed for local and wide area networking. TCP/IP was developed in 1969, in a Defense Advanced

TABLE 8-2		
	Guideline	**Purpose**
Strong Password Guidelines	Password is at least eight characters long.	The more characters in a password, the more difficult it is to crack.
	Password consists of both letters and numbers.	Passwords that contain a mix of letters and numbers defeat dictionary and "brute force" attacks by disrupting the pattern that these programs look for.
	Password includes symbols (!, @, #, $, %, ^, &, *,).	The use of symbols helps complicate the password and disrupts the pattern looked for by dictionary and "brute force" programs.
	Password does not consist of common words of phrases.	A dictionary program can easily crack passwords that consist of words or phrases.
	Passwords are changed frequently.	Even a strong password can be cracked with time; changing a password frequently defeats any hacker that may have cracked the old password.
	Lock user accounts after *x* number of attempts to log in with an incorrect password.	Account lockout prevents a hacker from running a program that repeatedly tries different passwords until finding the correct one.

Research Projects Agency (DARPA) research project on network interconnection. Formerly a military network, this global area network has exploded and is now referred to as the Internet.

TCP/IP gained most of its popularity through its wide use for Internet communication. Connecting computers throughout the world, it is known for being both reliable and routable and for being able to talk to foreign networks.

Windows NT TCP/IP enables users to connect to the Internet as well as to any machine running TCP/IP and providing TCP/IP services. This includes some applications that require TCP/IP to function. The following list summarizes the advantages of the TCP/IP protocol:

- It is the backbone of the Internet. If you need to connect to the Internet, you will need TCP/IP.

- It is routable. This means that you can talk to other networks through routers.

- It is very popular. Think of all of the computers on the Internet.

- Some applications need TCP/IP to run.

- It provides connectivity across operating systems and hardware platforms. Windows NT can use an FTP client to access a UNIX workstation or server.

- It provides Simple Network Management Protocol (SNMP) support, which is used to troubleshoot problems on the network.

- It provides Dynamic Host Configuration Protocol (DHCP) support, which is used for Dynamic IP addressing.

- It provides Windows Internet Naming Service (WINS) support, which resolves Windows NetBIOS names on the network.

To configure a TCP/IP address on a computer, you need specific TCP/IP parameters. These parameters consist of a static TCP/IP address, a subnet mask, and a default gateway (router), if you are connecting to the Internet or another network. You can use either a static or DHCP-assigned TCP/IP address to connect to the Internet. If you are using a server to connect to the Internet, a static IP address makes more sense so you don't have to continue to update your DNS tables.

An IP address can be thought of as a "house" address that you might see on the side of a building. Just as every house has a street address, city, and Zip code, every computer that uses the TCP/IP protocol has an IP address. This helps identify the computer on the network so that the computers can "talk" to one another. Each IP address can be configured for a separate subnet or network so that different computers can communicate with one another. A computer uses an IP address to identify itself on the network. Just as each and every house has an address associated with it, all computers on a network that uses TCP/IP must have an IP address. An IP address is a 32-bit address that is broken up into four parts, or octets.

In order for one computer to communicate with another computer, there must be a dialog in place in the form of a network protocol. Due to its popularity on the Internet, the TCP/IP protocol has become one of the most widely adopted network communication standards within the entire computer industry. To make matters much more complicated than they need to be for this exam, I'll get into subnet masks. Because an IP address is actually a 32-bit address, a subnet mask helps separate the network from the host ID. The network ID identifies the network the computer resides on (similar to a ZIP code). The host ID identifies the specific computer (similar to a house address).

IP Configurations

The TCP/IP protocol has many different uses and many possible IP configurations. Your TCP/IP parameters determine how and what your TCP/IP configuration will be. IP configurations are ultimately determined by the network operating system that you are running on your desktop. For instance, some operating systems do not recognize Dynamic Host Configuration Protocol (DHCP). DHCP is used to automatically hand out an IP address and configuration from an open pool of TCP/IP addresses.

Table 8-3 shows examples of the many different TCP/IP parameters and the specifics of how they are used.

TCP/IP Parameters	Description
IP address	An IP address is a 32-bit network address that identifies a computer on a network. An IP address is made up of a network ID and a host ID. An IP address is a four-octet address. Example: 204.22.120.3
Subnet mask	A subnet mask separates the network ID from the host ID. This can break down an individual IP address into different and separate logical networks or subnets.
Default gateway	A default gateway is actually a router that is used to send packets to remote networks. The default gateway that is configured will receive a packet from your computer and route the packet to its correct destination. Without a default gateway configured, your computer cannot communicate with any remote networks.
Domain Name System	A DNS Service is used to map IP addresses to fully qualified domain names (FQDNs). This form of name resolution is commonly used on the Internet to map IP addresses to popular Web sites.
Windows Internet Naming Service	A WINS Service also provides name resolution for computers, but does so only for Windows computers and is normally "Microsoft centric." A WINS Service maps IP addresses to NetBIOS names.
HOST file	A HOST file is an internal computer file that maps a computer's host name to an IP address. This is commonly used when a name resolution service such as DNS or WINS is not available.
LMHOST file	An LMHOST file maps NetBIOS names to IP addresses.
MAC address	A MAC address is the physical network address of a computer's network interface card. A MAC address is a 12-letter hexadecimal address that is broken up into two segments. The first six hex letters identify the vendor of the network card; the last six hex letters are the serial number that identifies the computer.

TABLE 8-3	TCP/IP Parameters	Description
TCP/IP Configuration Options *(continued)*	Dynamic Host Configuration Protocol	DHCP is used to automatically allocate TCP/IP address information to a computer that is "DHCP enabled." This practice reduces the amount of administration necessary for large networks.
	Host name	A host name or computer name uniquely identifies the computer on the network. A host name or Fully Qualified Domain Name will uniquely identify a computer on the network or Internet, but a NetBIOS name is the computer name that is specified by the network administrator. These two names can be different, but unless changed, the Host name defaults to the NetBIOS computer name.

Name Resolution

Computers communicate with each other by using network addresses, but people tend to want to communicate by using computer names. It is much easier to remember a computer name than a set of four different numbers. A more intuitive solution has been introduced, so that people can communicate by using computer names instead of hard-to-remember network addresses. Names must be resolved to their respective network addresses. The two main options associated with name resolution on computer networks are Domain Name System (DNS) and Windows Internet Naming Service (WINS). For name resolution on Windows networks, WINS resolves NetBIOS names to TCP/IP addresses. For computers that use host names, DNS resolves fully qualified domain names (FQDNs) to TCP/IP addresses. This is what the Internet uses to keep track of all of the different names found on the Internet.

WINS

The *Windows Internet Naming Service (WINS)* was designed to eliminate the need for broadcasts to resolve NetBIOS names to IP addresses and to provide a dynamic database that maintains NetBIOS names to IP address mappings.

(The computer name is just one of many NetBIOS names.) This type of name resolution was introduced by IETF as an RFC for the use of NetBIOS Name Servers (NBNS) to resolve NetBIOS names to IP addresses. WINS is Microsoft's implementation of an RFC-compliant NBNS. The TCP/IP information is stored in a database on the WINS Service. Instead of network clients broadcasting for name resolution, the client contacts the WINS Service and the WINS Service informs the client of the correct address.

DNS

DNS (Domain Name System) maps TCP/IP addresses to computer names. Normally, computers communicate via their MAC addresses on a network. To communicate by name, the TCP/IP address must be resolved to a computer name. DNS maps TCP/IP addresses to computer host names on the network. DNS uses a distributed database over hundreds of different computers, resolving computer host names. This helps us locate computers all over the Internet. We type the DNS name of the server we want to access, and the DNS Service maps the correct TCP/IP address for us automatically. Sounds simple, right? These DNS root servers are managed by the Internet Network Information Center (InterNic). You are probably familiar with the DNS naming scheme: Microsoft.com, Cisco.com, Oracle.com, and Dell.com are all examples of DNS names.

Relevant SOPs

From network to network, many similar standard operating procedures are maintained. No matter which network you may visit, these procedures generally stay the same. The names of these procedures may change, but the duties that are involved in them are very similar. This section presents the most important standard operating procedures that you should follow on your own network.

Keep the network up and running at all times. This SOP is accomplished by many sub-procedures, such as backing up the data on the network, monitoring the performance of your servers, and performing common administration duties for the network.

Back up network data every night. This is one of the most important duties that a network administrator can perform. No matter how secure and stable your computer network is, events out of your control can bring down the network or accidentally destroy a server.

Monitor the performance of your servers and network infrastructure. This will help you to troubleshoot problems and to work proactively to prevent problems. The best way to troubleshoot a bottleneck on a server resource is to have monitored the performance of that resource so you have a "baseline" of the resource in day-to-day operation. You should also monitor the amount of traffic on the network. To do this, you can use a network *sniffer*, a network monitoring tool that analyzes the traffic on the network and can help you solve problems that are infrastructure related.

As a network administrator, you may have common duties such as securing the network, configuring network hardware, and managing users and permissions. The more comfortable you become with these daily SOPs, the more you can begin concentrating on other areas of network management, such as backing up your data and monitoring the performance of the network.

CERTIFICATION OBJECTIVE 8.02

Environmental Factors that Affect Computer Networks

Most networks have a centrally located area that can safely house all of its network appliances and servers. Within this room is a multitude of special features that can help to protect the computers and other environmentally "sensitive" equipment from failing due to extreme temperatures.

Computers, like most other electrical hardware, are affected by temperature, moisture, vibrations, and electrical interference. If the computers are exposed to

QUESTIONS AND ANSWERS

I want to connect two LAN segments that are using Ethernet and Token Ring.	Connect the two network segments with a switch. No one uses hubs anymore. Switched ports are cheap and they do a great job.
I want to connect two LAN segments in different geographical locations.	To connect LAN segments in different geographical locations, you need a router. A router can find the destination address of a packet and send the packet accordingly.
A user wants to connect his PC, which has an RJ-45 connector, with a computer that has a BNC connection.	Connect the PC with the RJ-45 connector to a hub and the BNC connection to another hub that supports both connections.
I want to connect a TCP/IP network to an IPX/SPX network.	Use a gateway to connect networks that are using two different protocols.
I have 10 PCs that all connect to one server. What do I need to support the bandwidth requirements?	All that you need is a simple hub. 10 PCs do not require too much bandwidth unless you are doing video.
My client has over 2500 computers in one geographic location. What network appliance would be right for this large a network?	With that size network you should utilize network switches and separate the computers into separate broadcast domains.
I want to connect two networks that are in the same location. Can I use a router?	A router can be used to connect networks that are in the same location, but for cost, you might want to pick a less expensive solution relative to the number of ports that are required. Generally, routers are more expensive per port than switches or hubs.

these elements, they can act irregularly and sometimes fail. Luckily, there are standards that protect computer components from these situations.

Cables

Underneath the protection of most network cables lies a fragile layer of wire (or glass, in the case of fiber optic) that carries the data from one computer to another. Like most other computer components, this wire is not resistant to moisture, heat, or other electrical interference. To protect this cable from harm, a covering is placed over the wire to protect it from breaking or accidentally becoming wet.

Cables that bring data to networks come in many different forms, from copper to fiber optic. The type of cable determines the length that it can be. When a cable exceeds the recommended distance, the signal begins to fade. Table 8-4 lists the types of cables, their characteristics, and the distance they can carry a signal.

exam
⚠ a t c h

Make sure you know the cable length limitations for each type of cable. You will be presented with scenario questions where you are to determine if the configuration is valid—you have to know whether the maximum cable length has been exceeded. These questions are challenging because of the complex scenario-based format.

The Network Operations Center

The Network Operations Center (NOC) is the home base for all of the important servers on your network. The NOC enables you to centrally manage and keep a close eye on all of your networked data.

An NOC, above all else, needs to be secure and able to house all of the data and servers. Normally in a locked room, the NOC is a secured room that is equipped with different types of fire suppression (Halon, Foam), raised floors to place the cabling, and temperature control. A price cannot be put on the value of your data, so this room should never be compromised in any way.

TABLE 8-4	Cabling Characteristics	
Type of Cable	**Characteristic**	**Length**
10BaseT	Flexible, uses RJ-45 connector.	100 meters/328 feet
10Base2	Less flexible than 10BaseT, uses a BNC connector to hook computers together. Must be terminated on one end.	185 meters/607 feet
10Base5	Rigid, does not bend well around corners. Not used too often; AUI connector.	1640 feet
Fiber optic	Does not do well in tight changes of redirection. Carries data extreme distances. Easily broken, fragile.	2 kilometers

Room Conditions

The room conditions of your NOC should be cool, dry, and temperature controlled. Computers and other electrical equipment do not like humidity, heat, or extreme cold, so you should be very careful to regulate the temperature of your NOC. When a computer overheats, there is no guarantee that the data on your servers can be saved.

Because computer equipment is very sensitive to moisture, you need to use a form of fire suppression besides water. Putting out a fire in your NOS with a sprinkler system would ruin all of your computer equipment. There are many different types of foams or Halon used to put out fires quickly and safely, while minimizing the potential damage to your computer equipment.

exam
ⓦatch

You will be asked to determine which environment is the most conducive to a server room. Just remember that servers need an environment free of dust, with plenty of ventilation, and reasonable temperature and humidity. Placing servers near a window on a sunny day or in a dusty warehouse would not create an ideal operating environment.

Minimizing Electrical Interference

Electromagnetic interference (EMI) can wreak great havoc on any type of computer equipment. You might be aware of certain types of speakers that are magnetically shielded to prevent electrical interference. However, magnets and computers don't mix, so this concept unfortunately doesn't mesh well. Your alternative to this is to keep all of your computer equipment away from any electrical device that may interrupt the computing power of your data.

exam
ⓦatch

This question is more about common sense. Make sure you don't expose your computers or network equipment to any potential environmental hazards, such as moisture or extreme heat, or to electrical interference, such as generators and televisions.

Computer Chassis

With the boom of today's technology, computers are faster than ever. Today there is more computing power on a single laptop computer than was used by NASA to place the first man on the moon. However, more computing power comes at a price. The price that we pay is heat. As processors become faster and faster, they are becoming hotter and hotter as they perform billions of calculations. The scenario is the same for disk drives as well. The larger the drives become, the more work that needs to be done to find the data on the drive. The result of this is the temperature within the PC's chassis becomes too hot for the computer to operate. When this happens, the over-heating part will fail or destroy the PC altogether.

To combat this problem, a cooling fan was placed inside the PC to circulate the air and prevent the PC from overheating. Some computer chassis are becoming more inventive every year and help circulate the air inside the PC to keep the computer cool.

Error Messages

Error messages carry a mixed blessing in the computer industry. It's great to know when you have an error, but some error messages are so vague and incomprehensible that they do nothing but confuse you further.

You will encounter many types of error messages in your day-to-day progress with computers. You will see syntax errors, general protection faults, memory dumps, Dr. Watson messages, error logs, .DLL conflicts, and several hundred others.

When using your computer, you might inadvertently generate an error message. When your computer gives you an error message, it is letting you know that it cannot understand the data input or that an unexpected error has occurred. This is what happens during the error message process.

Some of the better-written and coded programs go out of their way to let you know what exactly is happening when you generate an error message. Seeing "Error Code 12452" flash across the screen doesn't help too much unless you know exactly what "Error Code 12452" is. Chances are you don't have any idea what that cryptic error message means.

If you are lucky, sometimes you will have the capability to look into the help file to find out what a vague error message might be. It helps a lot if you can check the vendor's Web site as well, because they may have an on-line support site specifically for those types of questions.

Some error messages are user friendly and will tell you exactly what you did wrong. For instance, if you cannot print and you see the message "Incorrect Printer Driver, please Install Correct Driver," you have a good idea as to what you might have done wrong and you will know how to fix your problem.

Table 8-5 lists some common error messages and their meanings.

TABLE 8-5	Error Message	Description
Common Error Messages	Syntax error	You have entered information that your computer cannot understand. This is normally caused by a typo or an incorrect spelling of a desired command.
	General protection fault	An overlapping memory block within your computer system causes a general protection fault. This is less common with secure operating systems, such as Windows NT, because they can compensate by not enabling any software direct access to the hardware and can run processes in separate memory spaces.
	Blue Screen of Death	A common Windows NT error screen where the computer crashes, reboots, and dumps the error logs into a memory. If you are witnessing this screen, something major is not right.
	Bad command or file name	Your computer does not understand what has been entered. You should make sure that you have the correct path and that the program or file that you want to access is in the specified directory.
	File is listed as read only	You may see this error when trying to write to a file that is listed as *read only*. With this permission, you can only have *read* access to the file; you cannot change the file.
	Access denied	This error message is self-explanatory. Your permissions do not match the necessary permissions to the file or directory.

Common Peripheral Ports and Network Components

What good is a computer without all of the goodies? There are literally hundreds of peripherals and network components to choose from in today's fun-filled world of computers. Here, you will learn the basics about the ones you will likely encounter in your day-to-day experience.

All of these ports and network components are mainly used to make the experience of using a computer easier and more user-friendly. If you are going to be an expert in networking technology, you should know and understand each component in case you have to troubleshoot a problem some day.

Network Interface Card

Your network interface card (NIC) should be auto-detected during setup, but if it is not, you must enter the IRQ, the I/O address, and the base memory address. If these settings are not correct, the network fails to start when you log on, and you receive a message while booting up that a service or driver failed to load. Usually, the hardware vendor for your card provides you with a network configuration disk that tells you exactly what the settings should be. Verify these settings before you begin the setup process to save time. As you configure your card, you'll be asked whether you are wired to the network or are connecting via the Remote Access Service (RAS). Make sure you refer back to Chapter 2, on the Physical Layer, and go over the lab for installing Network Interface Cards.

Being Wired to the Network

Being part of a network is what networking is all about. Having access to thousands of files and applications that are just a click away is both convenient and efficient. In order for your web server to communicate with other computers on the network, you have to install a network interface card. This network card also has to be configured correctly with the TCP/IP protocol. The network card binds with the TCP/IP protocol to enable communication.

When you can communicate with other computers on the network, you are free to share files and information at the click of a button. This is what makes networking so special and one of the many reasons that computer networks are changing the face of business as we know it today.

Binding Different Protocols

Being wired to a network gives you connectivity to other computers and enables you to exchange information. However, each computer on a network generates a lot of traffic, and when you have a lot of computers on the network, an awful lot of traffic is generated. If you have more than one protocol installed for your NIC, your computer will try to use each protocol that is installed. For the best performance, you should have only the necessary protocols that you are going to be using on your network. Having more than one protocol installed creates extra traffic and more overhead for your network than is necessary.

Network Connection

Connecting to the Internet with a networked server requires a lot of bandwidth to provide connectivity for all users. The amount of bandwidth determines how many users can access your site at once. A fast network connection enables easy access to your Web site, whereas a slow connection sometimes prohibits users from getting to your Web site. If you are on an intranet, you probably do not have to worry about the amount of bandwidth. A normal 10MB Ethernet network card should be sufficient.

To connect straight to the Internet, you need a router or default gateway so that others outside your network can access your site. If you do not want to use a dedicated router for your Internet connection, your Windows NT 4.0 Server can perform the same duties with proper configuration.

Serial Port

In computer terminology, serial means slow. With a serial port, such as that used by your keyboard or mouse, data can flow in only one direction. This makes for slow data transfer. Your keyboard and mouse are one-way devices that require only a serial interface and line.

Parallel Port

Parallel ports are the quicker of the devices that are connected to the outside of your computer. Parallel transmission works by sending data in both directions (serial goes only one way). Your printer, for instance, uses a parallel cable to speed up the printing process.

Universal Serial Bus (USB)

Universal Serial Bus (USB) is a new innovation in computer peripheral technology that enables you to add devices such as audio players, joysticks, keyboards, telephones, and scanners without having to add an adapter card or even having to turn the computer off. Sounds like a good idea, huh? Well, USB can even transfer data up to 12 Mbps and works by using the existing power of the computer so you don't have to plug in any of your USB devices.

SCSI

Small Computer System Interface (SCSI) is a standard interface that enables personal computers to communicate with peripheral hardware, such as disk drives, tape drives, CD-ROM drives, printers, and scanners. What makes SCSI devices so special is the improvement in data transfer over parallel devices. For example, the newest Ultra-Wide SCSI 2 devices can transfer data up to 80 Mbps. Another benefit of SCSI devices is the capability to daisy chain up to 7 or 15 devices (depending on the bus width). SCSI devices are more important for high-performance computing systems, such as servers, than they are for the home PC.

Interrupts

The operating system (OS) on your machine (probably a flavor of Windows), will set up the IRQs (interrupt request) lines that enable the OS to communicate with the different devices within your system, such as graphic cards, CD-ROM drives, network cards, and printers.

Your computer communicates to the different peripherals within your computer by using the IRQs hardware lines that your computer uses to send input and output messages. These IRQs are assigned different priorities so that the microprocessor can determine which of the interrupts it's receiving is the most important.

To simplify matters, when your computer needs to use a device such as a network card, the network card signals the CPU via the IRQ so that it can use the processing power of the CPU to do its work.

Print Servers

Print servers can be either dedicated servers that are responsible for sending documents to various printer pools that can be scattered around a corporation, or they can be used in tandem with file servers. These servers are used to send documents to a server that takes care of the printing process. This makes much more sense than having a separate printer for each computer, and it gives you more control over administering the documents that are sent to each network printer.

Peripherals

With today's booming computer industry, you have many options when choosing peripherals for your computer. The standard I/O devices, such as keyboard and mouse, are the mainstays for computer peripherals, but there are many other peripherals that you can utilize to make your PC experience even better.

Along with the boom of the Internet, modems have increased in speed and have brought millions of computers into homes.

Keyboard

A *keyboard* connects to the serial port of your computer and enables you to input data. Because the keyboard is the primary input device, you rely on the keyboard more than you think. The keyboard contains certain standard function keys, such as the ESCAPE key, TAB key, cursor movement keys,

SHIFT keys, and CTRL keys, and sometimes other manufacturer- customized keys, such as the WINDOWS key.

Mouse

A *mouse* connects to the serial port of your computer and enables you to move a cursor around the GUI of your desktop operating system.

Printer

A *printer* outputs data on your computer to paper or other media, such as labels, transparencies, or envelopes.

Digital Camera

A *digital camera* is a new peripheral that enables the user to take pictures without film. The pictures are saved as digital images and can be transferred to a computer for manipulation, enhancement, and distribution through means such as e-mailing and printing.

Modem

A *modem (modulator/demodulator)* is a communications device that enables a computer to talk to another computer through a standard telephone line. The modem converts digital data from the computer to analog data for transmission over the telephone line and then back to digital data for the receiving computer.

Bridge

Bridges are intelligent devices used to connect LANs. A bridge can also forward packets of data based on MAC addresses. They can filter traffic on a LAN. They determine the source and destination involved in the transfer of packets. They read the specific physical address of a packet on one network segment and then decide to filter out the packet or forward it to another segment.

Hub (Shared)

Hubs enable you to concentrate LAN connections. You can connect devices using twisted-pair copper media to hubs to concentrate computers together. The limitation of unshielded twisted-pair (UTP) network cable is that it only has the capability to carry data one hundred meters before the signal begins to fade. To strengthen the signal, a hub is used. It also depends on what type of technology you are using. You can have either Token Ring hubs or Media Access Units (MAUs) or have standard Ethernet hubs.

Because most modern networks use UTP for installation, you need to learn the standards that an Ethernet hub is used for. If you have a network that has to cover a large physical location, you have to remember that one piece of UTP cable can only reach 100 meters. This severely limits what you can do with your network unless you use hubs.

Table 8-6 describes some benefits of using hubs in a networked environment:

TABLE 8-6

Benefits of Using Hubs in a Networked Environment

Benefit	Description
Hubs centralize monitoring and administration.	Most "managed" hubs come with special monitoring and optimization tools that can be used to let you know if you are having a problem. You can also see the performance level of the throughput of your network.
Hubs enable easy expansion, because you can daisy chain several hubs to form one large hub.	If you want to expand your hub capacity, all you have to do is daisy chain a separate hub to create one, large managed hub.
Hubs enable you to use several different ports that can connect to several different resources.	With hubs, you can utilize different ports for on-site administration and connect different media, such as a coax segment with a UTP segment of your network.
Hubs provide a high level of fault tolerance.	By having several wires coming into a hub, if one wire fails, it will not affect any of the other wires that are linked to the hub.

TABLE 8-6	Benefit	Description
Benefits of Using Hubs in a Networked Environment *(continued)*	Hubs expand the length of your network.	Due to the limitation of UTP (100 meters), you may have to use hubs to boost the strength of the signal to connect segments of your network.
	Hubs enable you to connect multiple users together to form one network.	This works with the star topology where the clients are connected to a hub in the "star."

Switch

Switches offer full-duplex dedicated bandwidth to LAN segments or desktops. You can think of a switch as an intelligent hub that guarantees that amount of bandwidth to the computer that it is connected to. This, of course, would depend on which port you are reconnected to: 10, 100 or 1000 Mbps. With a hub, you are guaranteed some of the bandwidth all of the time. This means that hubs are not intelligent enough to account for collisions on the network; you may be connected to a 10MB port, but you may only be receiving 4 megabytes of data because of the amount of traffic on the network. With a switch, you are guaranteed the entire limit of your bandwidth because the switch is intelligent and can examine the packet and send it in the right direction.

on the **job**

Today's computer networks have to support the combination of voice, video, and data, so many network administrators are beginning to favor intelligent switches over common shared hubs. Network switches enable you to have bandwidth on demand and ensure that you can use your network to the fullest capacity. If you have a switch that is capable of 100 Mbps, you are guaranteed that amount of bandwidth due to the way a switch can intelligently look at the packets. A shared hub, on the other hand, can sometimes supply only 40% of the potential bandwidth on the network.

Router

Routers route data packets across a network by opening the packet and making routing decisions based on the contents. As you learned earlier in this chapter, TCP/IP addresses enable communication between computers. Well, in order for different and remote computer networks to talk to one another, a device is needed to guide the TCP/IP network traffic to its destination. This is where routers come in and perform their duties.

Remember the OSI Model that you learned in Chapter 3? Well, to better understand the functions of routers, you should have a good understanding of the Network Layer of the OSI Model. The Network Layer, or Layer 3, is responsible for addressing messages and translating their logical addresses into an actual physical address. It is important to remember that a router is protocol dependent. That means that a TCP/IP router can connect to a TCP/IP network. In other words, this is the layer of the OSI Model that is responsible for determining where to send the TCP/IP packets to their destination. Routers essentially separate different broadcast domains from one another and route traffic based on its destination, or Layer 3, address (the Layer 2 address is the MAC address).

When you want to communicate with another computer network, your computer essentially looks within the local network first before heading out to search for a remote address. For example, when your computer needs to access a file on another computer, your computer first checks its ARP cache (Address Resolution Protocol) to see if that computer has a recognizable MAC address. If it does not, then your computer checks the local subnet by either broadcasting or asking a Name server for help.

If the address is not found on the local subnet or network, your computer checks to see if you have a default gateway or router to send the information to. Your computer sends this information to your router and the router routes the message accordingly. What happens is that the router receives the data with the address information and checks its routing tables to see where it should send your data. The type of router sometimes affects how quickly your data arrives at its destination.

Routers are either static or dynamic. Nine times out of ten, you'll only have to deal with a dynamic router—a router whose routing tables are populated automatically by receiving updates from other routers. Static routers have fixed routing tables that have to be updated manually. These static routers are at a disadvantage because they cannot communicate with any type of router in case a network route changes due to hardware failure or change to the network layout.

The main benefit of a dynamic router is that, depending on which type of routing protocol is used, it will attempt to route your network traffic to your destination as quickly as possible. An example of this would be if you have a network that is standardized on Cisco routers (dynamic) that all communicate with one another using the OSPF (Open Shortest Path First) routing protocol. All of your routers are communicating with one another via broadcasts that they send whenever there is a change in their routing. This comes in very handy and adds a layer of redundancy so that if a segment of the network fails, your routers will be able to route the network traffic to other paths so that no matter what happens to the network, your data will always arrive at its destination.

If you were using a static router and you had a segment fail on your network, your network traffic would cease until the segment was repaired or another static route was mapped on the router. This puts static routing at a severe disadvantage in a large, complex network environment.

Table 8-7 lists some of the characteristics of routers and what separates them from other network appliances.

Gateway

A *gateway* can link networks that have different protocols, such as TCP/IP to IPX/SPX. A gateway can change an entire protocol stack into another or provide protocol conversion and routing services between computer networks. Gateways examine the entire packet and then translate the incompatible protocols so that each network can understand the two different protocols. For example, protocol gateways can also be used to convert ATM cells to Frame Relay frames and vice versa.

TABLE 8-7	Router Characteristic	Explanation
Router Characteristics	Protocol dependant	Routers are usually dependent on one protocol. A TCP/IP router cannot communicate with an IPX router.
	Can communicate with other networks	A router works at the Network Layer of the OSI Model. It reads the destination of the packet and then sends the packet on its way to the destination network.
	Used to connect to the Internet	By using a router, you can communicate with various remote networks such as the ever-popular Internet.
	Can connect to different types of media, such as Ethernet and Token Ring	Some routers can connect two different networks, such as an Ethernet to a Token Ring connection or an ATM to an Ethernet. Normally, these routers work in the traditional way, but might have one or two ports to connect to different media.
	Works at the Network layer, or Level 3, of the OSI Model	Routers work at the Network Layer of the OSI Model. This means that they can identify where the packet is coming from and then send the packet off to the correct destination.
	Two different types, static and dynamic routers	Static routers have fixed routing tables that must be updated manually. Dynamic routers work by sending out broadcasts of their routing tables to other routers. This way, routers can change the path of a packet dynamically to work around a "downed" link.

CERTIFICATION OBJECTIVE 8.04

Compatibility and Cabling Issues

All network cables are not created equal. There are four different types of commonly used network cables: thicknet (10Base5), thinnet (10Base2), twisted pair, and fiber optic. For most of your networking needs, twisted pair is the cable of choice, because it is relatively inexpensive and available. It is also easy to run in tight places and many standards are adopted for its RJ-45 interface.

Twisted-pair cables come in many different types with varying degrees of reliability. They are ranked in categories based on the proven level of data they can carry.

Cable Level	Maximum Data Bandwidth
CAT 1	
CAT 3	10MB compatible
CAT 5	100MB compatible
CAT 5 Level 7	1GB compatible

Basically, if you have two different types of cables and you need to connect them, you need a hub, router, or switch to insert your cable into the correct port.

Incompatibilities with Analog Modems and a Digital Jack

An analog modem and a digital jack will not work together because they are two different technologies. An analog modem works over a standard phone line, and a digital jack for ISDN works with a digital PBX switch, not an analog phone switch.

Uses of RJ-45 Connectors with Different Cabling

An RJ-45 connector is used to connect segments of twisted-pair cabling. To connect two different types of media cable, you need either a hub or a bridge that has a specific connection for this type of cabling. For example, you can connect a 10BaseT cable that plugs into a bridge that supports connectivity with a BNC connector for 10Base2. You have to have the correct network hardware to connect the two different types of cabling media. There are no other options for connecting an RJ-45 connection to a BNC connector.

Patch Cables and Length of the Cabling Segment

A patch cable of 10BaseT is normally a couple of feet long, or however long you need. Commonly, a patch cable is used to "patch" the length it takes to get from your network card to the digital jack at the floor of your office.

CERTIFICATION SUMMARY

The information covered in this chapter is directly related to the material you will be tested on in the Knowledge of Networking Technology part of the Network+ exam. The detailed explanations in this book will make you better prepared to pass the exam. The information presented here is taken directly from the requirements listed for this exam and our approach is to explain what will be covered on the exam and to summarize the key points you'll need to understand when taking the exam.

Becoming familiar with the different networking components is one of your best ways of preparing for this exam. By understanding common networking practices, you will be better prepared to install your own network and troubleshoot problems that you might encounter in the process. Experience is the true test of knowledge and having a sound fundamental base of the networking basics is a great place to start.

Now that you have a firm grasp on networking fundamentals, you need to know more about network administration and how a network operates. Part of this process is becoming used to the standard procedures that make up most networks. Another part of networking that you should be aware of for the test is network administration. This involves making sure that you understand the day-to-day duties that a network administrator must deal with, from configuring TCP/IP to solving common network problems.

As well as understanding the different networking concepts that an administrator has to perform, you have to gain a broader perspective of networking in general. This includes understanding the different environmental factors that can affect computer performance such as temperature, moisture, and electrical interference. You should also know and understand the standard operating procedures of a Network

Operations Center (NOC) such as backup procedures, handling user accounts, and managing users and groups.

Besides having a firm grasp on the fundamentals of computers, becoming well rounded in the realm of computers is also needed. Most likely you're not going to be sitting at a desk eight hours a day, so you'll need to know the insides of a computer from IRQ settings to the different peripherals and why you need to use them.

As you gain more experience with computers and networking in general, you'll become more comfortable with the many different concepts of troubleshooting, administration, and operating procedures.

TWO-MINUTE DRILL

- ❑ You'll find many questions concerning installing and maintaining computer networks located throughout the Knowledge of Networking Technology section of the Network+ exam.

- ❑ Your most important duty as network administrator is to make sure that the clients on your network can communicate with one another at all times.

- ❑ Communication on a computer network is accomplished by the use of protocols.

- ❑ Standard Operating Procedures (SOPs) are the practices that you follow to enable your network to run smoothly and efficiently.

- ❑ The person who holds the Administrator account has complete, unrestricted access to all of the files, folders, and shares on the network.

- ❑ Passwords aren't a fail-safe method of securing your network, but if they are implemented and enforced correctly, they can impose a level of security that you should feel comfortable with.

- ❑ You should memorize what makes a secure and safe password. Make sure to eliminate the use of easily guessed words or phrases in your password!

- ❑ The exam will test your knowledge of safe password practices by having you select the most secure password from a list of choices.

❏ To configure a TCP/IP address on a computer, you need specific TCP/IP parameters. These parameters consist of a static TCP/IP address, a subnet mask, and a default gateway (router), if you are connecting to the Internet or another network.

❏ An IP address is a 32-bit address that is broken up into four parts, or octets.

❏ The TCP/IP protocol has many different uses and many possible IP configurations.

❏ The two main options associated with name resolution on computer networks are Domain Name System (DNS) and Windows Internet Naming Service (WINS).

❏ The *Windows Internet Naming Service (WINS)* was designed to eliminate the need for broadcasts to resolve NetBIOS names to IP addresses and to provide a dynamic database that maintains NetBIOS names to IP address mappings.

❏ *DNS (Domain Name System)* maps TCP/IP addresses to computer names.

❏ Keep the network up and running at all times.

❏ Back up network data every night.

❏ Monitor the performance of your servers and network infrastructure.

❏ As a network administrator, you may have common duties such as securing the network, configuring network hardware, and managing users and permissions.

❏ Computers, like most other electrical hardware, are affected by temperature, moisture, vibrations, and electrical interference.

❏ Make sure you know the cable length limitations for each type of cable. You will be presented with scenario questions where you are to determine if the configuration is valid—you have to know whether the maximum cable length has been exceeded. These questions are challenging because of the complex scenario-based format.

❏ You will be asked to determine which environment is the most conducive to a server room. Just remember that servers need an environment free of dust, with plenty of ventilation, and reasonable temperature and humidity. Placing servers near a window on a sunny day or in a dusty warehouse would not create an ideal operating environment.

❑ Make sure you don't expose your computers or network equipment to any potential environmental hazards, such as moisture or extreme heat, or to electrical interference, such as generators and televisions.

❑ Your network interface card (NIC) should be auto-detected during setup, but if it is not, you must enter the IRQ, the I/O address, and the base memory address.

❑ Connecting to the Internet with a networked server requires a lot of bandwidth to provide connectivity for all users.

❑ With a serial port, such as that used by your keyboard or mouse, data can flow in only one direction.

❑ Parallel transmission works by sending data in both directions.

❑ *Universal Serial Bus (USB),* or *fire-wire* as it is typically called, is a new innovation in computer peripheral technology that enables you to add devices such as audio players, joysticks, keyboards, telephones, and scanners without having to add an adapter card or even having to turn the computer off.

❑ *Small Computer System Interface (SCSI)* is a standard interface that enables personal computers to communicate with peripheral hardware, such as disk drives, tape drives, CD-ROM drives, printers, and scanners.

❑ *Bridges* are intelligent devices used to connect LANs. A bridge can also forward packets of data based on MAC addresses.

❑ *Hubs* enable you to concentrate LAN connections.

❑ *Switches* offer full-duplex dedicated bandwidth to LAN segments or desktops.

❑ *Routers* route data packets across a network by opening the packet and making routing decisions based on the contents.

❑ A *gateway* can link networks that have different protocols, such as TCP/IP to IPX/SPX.

❑ There are four different types of commonly used network cables: thicknet (10Base5), thinnet (10Base2), twisted pair, and fiber optic.

SELF TEST

The following Self Test questions will help you measure your understanding of the material presented in this chapter. Read all the choices carefully, as there may be more than one correct answer. Choose all correct answers for each question.

1. What hardware network components are needed when connecting two computers with a standard 8-port hub on the same subnet?

   A. Network cards

   B. Category 5 UTP cable

   C. SCSI adapter card

   D. Router

   E. Network Layer of the OSI Model

2. Susan L. wants to make some changes to her file server so that the Accounting group only has permission to the \\Payroll and \\401K shares on her network. What two accounts should Susan use to make sure that she made the necessary changes and that an ordinary user wouldn't have accidental access to the share?

   A. Account Operator

   B. Root

   C. Her "test" account

   D. Backup Operator

   E. Administrator

3. Mike K. is a new employee at a large manufacturing company and needs to set a password for his account so that he can log on to the network. He is in charge of a large group of sensitive files, so he wants to make sure that he has a safe and secure password. What is an example of a strong password?

   A. BALONEY

   B. Fuh3H3manners!

   C. ilovethemets

   D. password

   E. cheesesandwich

4. Melissa B. needs to use the Internet for work so that she can research a new product that she is interested in. When she tries to use a search engine, nothing is working. Her browser is working correctly and there is nothing wrong with the network. When she calls the help desk, they look at her IP address information and find the following. What could be wrong?

   Ethernet adapter:
   Description . . . .: 3Com 3c905XL 10/100
   Ethernet Card
   Physical Address. . . . : 00-00-86-20-45-90
   DHCP Enabled. . . . : No
   IP Address. . . . . . . : 209.116.171.105
   Subnet Mask . . . . . . : 255.255.255.192

Default Gateway . . . . . . :
Primary WINS Server . . . . :
Secondary WINS Server . . . :
Lease Obtained. . . . . . . :
Lease Expires . . . . :

A. Wrong IP address

B. Subnet mask

C. Default gateway

D. Nothing

5. Dave R. is connected to his LAN and wants to browse on his Intranet to update his 401K information. However, he cannot connect to any of the web servers on his intranet. Dave can, however, PING the computers by using their IP addresses. The IP information is listed below. What could be the problem?

Ethernet adapter:
Description . . . . : 3Com Megahertz 10/100 Ethernet +
56K PC Card
Physical Address. . . . : 00-00-86-20-45-90
DHCP Enabled. . . . . . . : No
IP Address. . . . . : 209.116.171.36
Subnet Mask . . . . : 255.255.255.192
Default Gateway . . . . . . : 209.116.171.65
Primary WINS Server . . . . :
Secondary WINS Server . . . :
Host Name . . . . : USWEBCS
DNS Servers . . . . :
Lease Obtained. . . . . . . :
Lease Expires . . . . :

A. Default gateway

B. Subnet mask

C. Name Resolution

D. DHCP

E. Host Name

6. What are three adverse environmental conditions that would affect the performance and capability of a computer network?

A. Wind

B. Humidity

C. Extreme heat

D. Barometer

E. Moisture

F. pH balance

7. What is the technical computer term for when another system's electrical interference is causing performance degradation of a computer?

A. Attenuation

B. EMI

C. Crosstalk

D. Plenum

8. Linda R. keeps getting the following error message every time she tries to start a program from the command line of her Windows 98 computer. What could the problem be?

C:\program.exe
Bad command or file name

A. Syntax error

B. Wrong path for executable

C. Typo

D. Program does not exist

9. What two things must you make sure that you do before you can use any of your external SCSI components, such as backup devices or CD-ROM devices?

A. Make sure they are turned on before your computer is.

B. Reboot them twice.

C. Terminate them.

D. Use an IDE cable.

10. Which computer peripheral is used to connect an ordinary computer to another computer by the use of an existing telephone line?

A. Network card

B. Modem

C. SCSI adapter

D. Scanner

E. Printer

11. Which network appliance is used to connect two computer networks that are separated by two different protocols?

A. Router

B. Bridge

C. ATM switch

D. Hub

E. Gateway

12. Which layer of the OSI Model does a network bridge work on that is used to connect between a TCP/IP network?

A. Physical

B. Application

C. Data Link

D. Network

E. Session

13. What are three technical characteristics of the Universal Serial Bus (USB) technology?

A. Nicknamed "Fire-Wire"

B. Daisy chains USB-supported devices

C. Must be terminated at each end

D. Requires an AC adapter

E. Works with infrared technology

F. Can support data transfer up to 12 Mbps

14. What two accounts should you use when you change an account on your network to ensure that the changes have been made?

A. Root

B. Backup Operator

C. Normal

D. Everyone

E. Test Account

F. Administrator

15. Meredith wants to increase the bandwidth capacity on her network for one geographic location that houses 2000 separate hosts. Her network is currently using shared hubs in a star topology environment. What network appliance should she use to do this?

   A. Gateway

   B. Bridge

   C. Router

   D. Switch

   E. Repeater

   F. Multiplexer

16. What type of network cable can support data speeds up to 100 Mbps on a local area network?

   A. 10BaseT (Category 1)

   B. Phone wire

   C. 10BaseT (Category 5)

   D. T.V. Cable

17. What level of the OSI Model do network switches commonly work at?

   A. Application

   B. Layer 8

   C. Network

   D. Physical

   E. Fiber-Channel

18. What environmental conditions are not recommended for housing network servers and other electrical equipment? (Choose all that apply.)

   A. Humid

   B. Wet

   C. Extreme Cold

   D. 70 Degrees.

19. Which type of NetBIOS Name resolution is used to resolve Windows computer names to TCP/IP addresses on a local area network?

   A. DNS

   B. DSN

   C. WINS

   D. HOST File

20. What is used to separate the Host ID from the Network ID in a four-octet TCP/IP address?

   A. Default gateway

   B. Router

   C. Subnet mask

   D. WINS

   E. DNS

21. In an extreme case, how long can a standard fiber-optic cable be run from one end to the other?

   A. 100 meters

B.   26.4 miles

C.   2 kilometers

D.   500 meters

22.   What port on your computer can provide the largest amount of data transfer from one peripheral to another?

A.   Serial port

B.   Parallel port

C.   Monitor

D.   Keyboard

23.   What should you not place computer equipment close to so that it will not be susceptible to different forms of electrical interference? (Choose all that apply.)

A.   Television

B.   Florescent light

C.   Generator

D.   Lead wall

24.   What account on a network server can have total control over the functionality of the server?

A.   Guest

B.   Test account

C.   Everyone

D.   Administrator

E.   Backup Operator

25.   Which type of network appliance can perform the duties of protocol conversion from either TCP/IP to IPX or ATM to Frame Relay?

A.   Router

B.   Switch

C.   Gateway

D.   Bridge

E.   MUX

26.   What protocol can be used to route to different networks and connect computers directly to the Internet?

A.   IPX/SPX

B.   NetBEUI

C.   SNA

D.   TCP/IP

E.   RIP

CERTIFICATION

9

Administering the Change Control System

CERTIFICATION OBJECTIVES

I n this chapter you will learn the techniques for managing a constantly moving network. You will learn recommended procedures for documenting current status, backing up and restoring data, and upgrading computers. You will also learn the most common user and group management issues you will encounter during your exam and in the real world when administering a network.

CERTIFICATION OBJECTIVE 9.01

Documenting Current Status

Any good network administrator will tell you that it is very important that you keep up-to-date records of the status and configuration of critical workstations and servers. Computers are in a constant state of upgrade. Usually computers are upgraded or modified on an as-needed basis, which means you will have many systems with many different hardware and software configurations. This may or may not affect the network, but it will be a factor when you need to upgrade or reconfigure a computer.

You may have established a hardware standard, requiring, for example, that every computer have a minimum of 48MB of physical memory, a 4GB hard drive, a SCSI disk controller, and a 32x CD-ROM drive. By documenting the current status and configuration of these devices, you know exactly which computers are affected when a new standard arises. For example, if you determine that Windows NT servers now require 128MB of physical memory, by keeping adequate documentation on the configuration of each computer, you will immediately know which computers need to be upgraded.

With software, you may have also established a set of applications that each workstation will have installed by default. If this standard changes, you need to quickly determine which computers are affected without having to physically touch every computer on the network to determine which applications are installed on each computer. In addition to applications, it is also very important to document service packs and software updates. Often an application requires that a certain service pack be installed on the computer. These are known as *dependencies* because the application you wish to install is dependent on these additional applications, service packs, or software updates being present on the system.

The need to document the current status and configuration of a system is recommended when you are planning to deviate from this configuration in the future. If you are planning to retrofit (a fancy term for reconfigure) a large number of computers, it is helpful to have the configuration settings and application load documented in the event you need to return to a "known good" working condition. In an extreme situation, if the computer was to completely crash and need to be rebuilt, you would have the known good working condition documented, and you could quickly install and configure the operating system and applications according to this documentation with little or no guesswork.

Returning a System to Its Original State

If you do find yourself in a situation where you must rebuild a system, the use of existing configuration settings will come in very handy. Most times when you need to rebuild a computer, you can document the operating system version, application load, software patches, hardware configuration, and user settings *before* the computer is rebuilt. However, there are times when you have to rebuild a computer without any of this information. If a user's hard disk crashes and you have not documented what was installed on the computer in three years, you will have a difficult time rebuilding the computer to the user's specifications. The user would no doubt inform you that an application is missing, a printer is not configured correctly, or a shortcut on the desktop is missing. When you finally believe you have a working rebuild, the user would once again inform you that something is not quite right still.

How can you return a system to its original state? As we indicated before, documentation is critical. Although it is impossible to document every computer on the network without third-party utilities, you should have documentation for every critical server and workstation on the network. Which computers on the network would be catastrophic if they went down suddenly? These are the computers you need to document thoroughly.

In addition to keeping documentation on these select systems on your network, you can also purchase third-party utilities that create images of these servers. If you create new, updated images every week or so, you can apply this image to a fresh rebuilt computer in a matter of minutes. You can go from a disastrous hard disk crash to being fully operational again in thirty minutes. Time is everything in these situations. In addition to creating images with third-party utilities, you can use your unattended operating system installations with a pre-defined application load to restore the system to close to its original operating state. The server will have a fresh operating system with all of the applications installed, but the data may have to be restored from a recent backup. This is not as quick as the image, but it is a viable alternative to manually installing the operating system and applications.

on the
Job

The company I work for now is in the process of migrating to Windows NT, version 4.0. The operating system installation is nearly automated with several different types of images available for servers, standard workstations, and test workstations. We could also have a standard application load, such as a Finance or Personnel load, which will install the standard application load deemed appropriate for each department. Or we could add applications individually. Each application installs with no user intervention and has been previously tested and proven error-free.

You can rebuild your own computer in thirty minutes or a little longer depending on how many applications you choose to load with the operating system. However, any data that was on the system is lost. If you were backing up your data, you will have to restore the data in order to complete the rescue process.

Microsoft recommends that you back up the Registry for each Windows computer. You must restore the Registry if you want to truly return a computer to its original operating state. The Registry contains current user and system information, which means the backup should be the most recent in order to rescue the most recent changes to the system. In the Registry, user information changes much more frequently than system information changes. The Windows NT backup program and many third-party applications, such as Ghost, are able to back up the Registry information in the image.

Another method for returning a system to its original state is to manually reinstall and configure the operating system and all applications that previously existed and then to restore the Registry and/or data from the most recent backup. This is by far the most time-consuming method so far. Many small companies are in this situation. Large companies have realized the need to engineer automated operating system installations because they can build hundreds of workstations a week for a gigantic rollout. A small company can maybe roll out ten to twenty systems a week using a manual installation method, depending on the number of technicians involved.

CERTIFICATION OBJECTIVE 9.03

Backup Techniques

I hope by now that you have realized the importance of the backup process. One of your most important tasks as a network administrator will be to guarantee the success of the backup process. It will take practice and effort to design, monitor, and test the backup process on a weekly basis.

The design process, if not already in place, will require you to develop a solution for backing up data on the network. You may have to evaluate several backup products in order to arrive at the product that is ideally suited for your organization. Features that are required for a Fortune 500 company might not be the features that are required for a small organization. The heart of the backup process is selecting which data needs to be backed up. You need to communicate with others to determine which data is important enough to back up. What would happen if you suddenly lost that data today? Would anyone care? If not, then the data should not be backed up. You can't go back in time, so make sure you are backing up the critical data from the start. It's not a pretty sight when you have to tell someone his or her project has just been lost forever.

Now that you have discovered which data needs to be backed up, you need to determine how often this data needs to be backed up. Most companies do full backups every night. If a user accidentally deletes a file, you need to go back only one day to retrieve the data.

After you have configured the initial backup process, you need to monitor it every day in order to catch errors. The backup program's error log is crucial for determining whether a backup job completed successfully or not. Some errors are not as obvious as others are. For example, if the tape was not able to load, you will get an obvious error and the backup job will fail to run. If the backup program could not attach to one user's computer because he shut his computer down at the end of the night, you will receive an error. Read through the error logs to determine where the job failed. If it fails every night trying to connect to another network server, remedy the situation before it's too late. The backup program should run successfully each night. If it does not, you must know why it did not run. I have had many managers check the backup program event logs and interrogate me as to why the backup job did not complete successfully.

When the backup process is configured and working relatively error free, you need to do test restores fairly often to ensure that the data is being backed up correctly. You may find yourself doing test restores once a week until you are very confident in the backup process. You can then start doing the test restore once a month. However, you will most likely be restoring live data for users very often, so you can substitute that for your test restores.

In addition to doing test restores of data, you should make sure you understand how to restore programs and their data, such as a Microsoft Exchange or SQL Server. These programs require more than just restoring the files from tape. Microsoft Exchange restores must be restored on a server with the same name as the computer in which they were backed up. This makes doing test restores difficult, because you cannot restore to a server with a different name.

on the Job

I remember coming in to work in the middle of the night to perform a test restore on a server where I had to down the original e-mail server and change the computer name of another server to the original server's name. After I determined the restore was successful, I brought down the test server and brought the original server online again. Microsoft SQL Server is even more difficult to restore. It requires loading the database dumps and transaction logs back into the SQL server for the test restore. This requires a good understanding of SQL Server, so we had contracted the creation of the SQL disaster recovery plan to an outside company. They developed and tested the disaster recovery plan and showed us how to do the restores ourselves.

It is a great feeling to guarantee that you can restore a file within minutes at the drop of a hat. Management will love you and so will the users when you restore the files they accidentally deleted!

Tape Backup

Backing up to tape is the most common form of backup done today, due to the availability and price. Tape backup is slower, due to the sequential access of the medium. It's like a cassette tape, where you have to fast-forward or rewind to find your favorite song. This is the opposite of *random-access*. I have found myself frustrated during the backup and restore process because the tapes take so long to initialize and restore. Just verifying the label of a new tape can take a couple of minutes. However, the price is right. For a few dollars a tape, you don't have to worry about reusing tapes. You can store every tape in an off-site storage facility. However, many companies still use tape rotation schemes to rotate tapes for reuse and permanently store a few select tapes in an off-site facility.

Multiple tape magazines are used for companies that back up large amounts of information every night. These backup jobs can even exceed a 24GB compressed tape. When one tape is full, the backup process will continue on the next available tape. The addition of more tapes makes the backup process more likely to fail and the backup process more confusing.

For example, you have one server that uses only one tape of a six-tape magazine; therefore, you can run the backup process every day for a week without reloading the tape magazine. One tape is used for the cleaning tape. You have another server that requires two tapes of a six-tape magazine. Therefore you can run the backup process every other day without reloading the tape magazine. And finally, you have another server that uses four tapes of a six-tape magazine, which needs to be reloaded on a daily basis. If this gets confusing for *you*, imagine what its like for the person who has to swap tapes for you when you are on vacation!

Replicating a Folder to a Network Drive

Replicating a folder to a network drive is a viable means of backing up data. Although extremely fast and automated, for the most part, this process does not guarantee that you have a safe copy of data stored in an off-site location in the event of an emergency. If both the workstation and the server where the data was replicated to were to fail, you would lose data, unless this data was also being backed up to tape or to another type of media. Replicating a folder to a network drive should be considered only as a temporary backup solution. To *replicate* means to copy data to another location. In the business world, duplicate data is very risky. What if Warrel and Jeff are working on the same project and they update the same document at the same time on different systems. Then Warrel goes on vacation. Which document is now the master document? You would have to merge both of their updates into one document—not a pretty sight. If you are the only one in charge of the data being replicated, you may not have these updating problems. You may know exactly which copies are being updated or not. However, if the data is important to you, it is wise to have a physical backup, such as a tape backup, of the data.

Windows NT provides a replication service to replicate data to other servers. This may sound like a means of backing up, but the service is provided to replicate commonly used items such as logon scripts to backup domain controllers. This type of information can be duplicated. For example, a logon script for the San Francisco domain is replicated to the Seattle domain, so users in Seattle do not have to contact San Francisco to run the logon script.

Removable Media

Most backup systems employ removable media for the backup process. Removable media can be removed (hence the name) and stored off site in a safe location. There are many types of removable media: floppy disks, hard disks, tape cartridges, reel tapes, and optical disks. These devices vary in price, performance, and capacity. The type of removable media you require is based on the needs of your particular network. Many companies use tape backup for nightly backups, and then use writable CD-ROMs to create images or backup sets that can be used on any machine with access to a CD-ROM. If you are in charge of developing a removable storage solution, you need to determine how much money your company is willing to spend, the amount of data that needs to be archived, and the speed at which you require the data to be archived. Table 9-1 is a summary of most removable media solutions and their descriptions.

TABLE 9-1	
Comparison of Removable Media Technology	

Device	Description
Floppy disk	Floppy disks are slow with a small capacity. Removable random-access. Some business computers have had the floppy disk drives removed for security reasons and to minimize viruses.
Disk cartridge	Disk cartridges, such as Zip and Jaz, are growing in popularity as the prices fall. Capacity is growing and the speed is increasing. Random-access.
Tape cartridge	Tape cartridges are slow, but are capable of holding large amounts of data. Sequential access.
Hard disk	Removable hard disks are dropping in price, while performance is gaining and capacity is growing. Random-access.
Reel tape	Reel tape is an older technology more commonly found on mainframe computers. Sequential-access.
Optical disk	Optical disks are high quality, have a large storage capacity, and are increasing in popularity with prices dropping. Random-access.

Multi-Generation

There are a number of different techniques used to back up data. One of the most popular is the multi-generation tape rotation scheme, known as the Grandfather – Father – Son (GFS) scheme. This scheme became popular with mainframe computer tape rotation techniques many years ago. The GFS strategy is a method of maintaining backups on a daily, weekly, and monthly basis. The GFS rotation scheme is based on a seven-day weekly schedule, beginning on any day of the week, in which you create a full backup at least once a week. All of the other days you can perform full, incremental, differential, or no backups. The daily backups are called the Son. The last full backup in the week (the weekly backup) is called the Father. The last full backup of the month (the monthly backup) is called the Grandfather.

You can reuse any of the daily tapes after six days. The weekly tapes can be overwritten five weeks after they were last written to. Monthly tapes are saved throughout the year and should be taken off-site for storage. You can change any of these rotation defaults to suit your particular organization.

The GFS scheme suggests a minimum standard for backing up the system and rotating and retiring the physical tapes.

Please understand that the GFS scheme is not the only tape rotation scheme in use. You have the freedom to do as many or few restores as required by your particular situation. You can do full backups every night, or you can do a full backup once a week, with incremental and differential backups for the remaining days of the week. The choice depends entirely on the needs of your organization. However, it's better to be safe than sorry.

CERTIFICATION OBJECTIVE 9.04

Removing Outdated or Unused Drivers After a Successful Upgrade

In any environment, computers are constantly being upgraded. The capability to upgrade is one of the most attractive features of the modern personal computer. It's simple to remove a device and replace it with a newer, faster, more powerful device. However, when people upgrade their hardware, they often forget to remove the corresponding driver that goes with it. There are a number of reasons it is recommended to remove outdated or unused drivers on a system:

- So they don't accidentally get loaded
- To conserve disk space
- To conserve memory
- To prevent interference with new drivers

When you upgrade a device, usually you replace the driver with a more current version. However, when you *remove* a device from the system, you need to remove the device driver. If you don't remove it, the driver may still be loaded on system startup. You may receive an error loading the driver because the corresponding device could not be located.

Services, like drivers, are loaded into memory on Windows NT systems. These services can be stopped and started. The chances are much greater that you will forget to stop a service when a device is removed than are the chances of forgetting to remove the unused driver.

Unused drivers, if not removed, can take up valuable hard disk space. Driver files are not very large, however, so don't worry about them too much. If you don't like the thought of anything wasting space on your hard drive, then make sure you locate these unused drivers and delete them. However, remember that Windows keeps a driver database of files on your hard disk, making it easier for you when you install a device. The corresponding driver will be loaded if it is available to you.

Physical memory is something that can't be wasted on unused drivers. In the days of DOS and optimizing memory, we needed to remove these drivers from conventional memory to have enough memory to load applications. These drivers were loaded into memory using the CONFIG.SYS file. If you don't remove these lines that load the drivers, they will continue to be loaded into memory. Having one too many drivers loaded can make or break the performance of your system.

If you forget to unload and remove the previous drivers, they may cause problems when you are loading a new driver, possibly causing the new driver to fail. If two drivers are expecting to have full control over a device, they both may fail when one tries to access the device. This was common when CD-ROM device drivers were loaded from the CONFIG.SYS file, and then Windows 95 also tried to load CD-ROM drivers later in the boot process.

exam ✦ Watch

Be sure you understand the reasons for removing unused or outdated drives from your system. The exam will present troubleshooting scenarios that will include determining the cause of a system that is not functioning correctly. When you understand how outdated drivers can affect a system, you are one step closer to answering these questions with ease during your exam.

CERTIFICATION OBJECTIVE 9.05

Effects on the Network Caused by Local Changes

Changes to a workstation or a server can have negative effects on the network. These changes include network hardware settings, protocol additions or modifications, or added or misconfigured applications or services. I wouldn't be paranoid of configuring a workstation, because the chances are very slim that you can down an entire network by misconfiguring a workstation.

However, with that in mind, make sure you use extreme caution when configuring a network adapter card. If you were going to down the network doing anything, then it would be from misconfiguring a network card. Misconfiguring the speed on a network card will confuse and lock up a hub.

Another misconfiguration that will cause some network distress is accidentally configuring a workstation as the master browser. When this workstation initializes on the network, it will broadcast a message saying it is the master browser. If another computer is configured as a master browser, an election will occur between the two devices to determine who is the rightful master browser.

When a computer with a faulty network card is on the network, it can continuously chatter on the network, eating up bandwidth. You need to use special software to analyze packets on the network to determine which computer is having problems. A Token Ring network will cease to function and the nearest active upstream neighbor (NAUN) to the failed computer will send out a beacon, alerting you to which computer is not functioning correctly.

Version Conflicts

With companies continuing to update their products at a rapid pace, it may be difficult to keep up as a consumer. You may be finding yourself with version conflicts between software applications and your operating system. In many cases, version conflicts are from software applications that are designed to run on a specific operating system type. At the very worst, the application will not run. The application may also try to run, but could fail with General Protection Faults or similar errors. Hopefully the application will still run, but will not take advantage of some features until you upgrade the affected application.

In any version conflict situation, you would like to be informed from the software that a version conflict is occurring. If you are not aware, you may have no idea of why an application is behaving erratically.

Lately we have been seeing many applications that require a certain Windows NT service pack in order to perform. This has been the case with the Y2K bug, which is said to be relieved with Microsoft's Service Pack 4 for Windows NT. A few applications require the operating system be patched with Service Pack 4 in order for the application itself to be Y2K-compliant. Other applications, such as Microsoft Office 97, require Service Pack 2 or higher be installed prior to installing Office 97.

Some versions of software will issue warnings, but will still run. Microsoft applications such as Microsoft Word can offer to save applications in a version that is compatible with all Microsoft Office versions. It is wise to save your applications in this version, in the event someone requiring access to the document does not have the version of the software that you have.

Overwritten DLLs

One of the more complex situations to track down is the condition in which one application overwrites another application's Dynamic Link Library (DLL) files. These files are used by one or more programs as libraries that contain functions that are called from the main software program. Most programs use their own DLLs, but some programs use DLLs common to the operating system and many different applications. This is a silent disaster waiting to happen. For example, you have an application that installed a DLL dated 9-12-97. This DLL happens to overwrite a newer version of the same file that is needed by another application. One of the applications may work just fine; however, the owner of the newer DLL that has just been back-leveled may not find the functions and routines within the DLL that it expects. The result can be lock-ups, General Protection Faults, or the application will refuse to run.

Overwritten DLLs become more of a problem as you add more applications to the system. It is nearly impossible to determine which applications' DLLs have been affected. You may have discovered that a DLL has been updated with a newer one, but which application was responsible? Even worse, you have an older application that has written a much older DLL over a newer DLL that was on the system. The program you installed last should have no problems, but the existing application will most likely fail with the older DLL.

Many applications are smart enough to check the date and timestamp when installing and prompt you when a file newer than the file being written is currently in use on the system. You have the opportunity to keep the existing newer file (recommended) rather than overwriting the newer file with the version on the installation program.

FROM THE FIELD

Overwritten Files Can Drive a Company Crazy

Where I am currently working, we are dealing with this very issue of overwritten DLLs. Applications and service packs are applied using a silent installation method, which means all of the files are copied to the computer without user intervention. This process is required for any large corporation that deploys applications and updates to large numbers of users. However, this type of silent install does not prompt a user to keep newer files that exist on the hard drive; therefore, the files are overwritten. If this is the most recent service pack from Microsoft, this is desired. However, what if this application is three years old and overwrites a Microsoft DLL that was just placed there with the latest service pack? This is a very serious dilemma that faces many organizations. A simple overwritten DLL can cause a problem on every computer in the field. In order to research the situation, a few of us were asked to develop a program that compares the contents of the computer before and after a software upgrade. We created a program in PERL that scans the hard disk and records the file, date, time, and size before the upgrade and saves this information to a file. After the upgrade we run the same program and produce another file. Then the contents are compared and the files that have been changed, added, or deleted are displayed. This file shows not only the name of the file, but the date, time, and size. Utilities such as Sysdiff by Microsoft only tell you the file has changed, not the actual file details. These results are then ported into a database, where they can be queried against other applications to determine which applications use the same DLLs. Once these applications are known, we can develop tests to determine which version of the DLL should be used when *both* applications are present on the system.

Not only does this affect the applications that are loaded *after* the operating system has been installed, but it can be used to determine in which order the applications can be loaded during installation. If we have determined that version X of a certain DLL will coexist with two applications peacefully, we make sure the application that installs version X of the DLL should be installed *last*, overwriting the undesired version of the DLL.

This process sounds very tedious, but is required for large corporations to deal with the blatant overwriting of existing DLLs by applications and service packs. Chances are you have dealt with incompatible DLL versions, whether you know it or not. Just be aware of this problem and the effects it could have on application installation and updates.

—*Cameron Brandon, MCSE+Internet,*
CNE, A+, Network+

CERTIFICATION OBJECTIVE 9.06

Drive Mapping

Drive mapping is the process of connecting network drives so that you may use the resources located on them. On operating systems such as Windows 95/98 and Windows NT, you have the capability of mapping network drives through a command prompt or through a GUI interface. The following illustration shows the Map Network Drive dialog box, the graphical utility for mapping network drives in Windows 95/98 and NT.

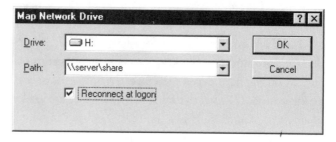

EXERCISE 9-1

Mapping a Network Drive Through the Graphical Utility with Windows 95/98 and NT

To map a network drive with the graphical utility, follow these directions:

1. Right-click on the Network Neighborhood icon on the desktop.

2. Select File | Map Network Drive. The Map Network Drive dialog box appears.

3. Select the network drive you want to map to from the Drive list. In this example we are using drive H:.

4. In the Path text box, type the Universal Naming Convention (UNC) path for the shared network drive you would like to map to. In this example we are using \\server\share. This will map to the share on the network drive called *share*, which is located on the server called *server*. You may also find the share you would like to map to in the Path drop-down list box if you have already made this mapping in the past.

5. If you want this drive mapping to remain consistent each time you log on, check the Reconnect at logon box. If you only want the drive mapping to remain for this session, leave the box unchecked.

6. Click OK to save the drive mapping.

Although using the GUI interface is easier, if you learn to use the command prompt, you can create batch files with drive mappings that connect automatically.

It is imperative that you understand the correct syntax for mapping to network shares. As indicated before, you are mapping to a specific share on a specific server. The mapping begins with two backslash characters before the server name. After the server name, a backslash precedes the share name. For example, the following command maps to the evacuation share on the safety server:

> net use S: \\safety\evacuation

Notice that we are designating the drive letter S for the mapping in the net use command. If you forget the colon after the drive designator when mapping from the command prompt in Windows NT, an error will be issued.

exam
ⓦatch

Make sure you know the correct syntax for mapping network drives. It is very likely you will receive a question on your exam asking which of the answers uses the correct syntax.

Printer Port Capturing

Just as you can connect network drives in order to use the resources located on them, you can also connect network printers in the same manner. In operating systems such as Windows 95/98 and Windows NT, you have the capability of mapping local and network printers through a command prompt or through a GUI interface. Figure 9-1 illustrates the graphical utility for mapping printers in Windows NT.

As with network drive mappings, you can use the command prompt to map network printers and place these mappings in batch files to connect automatically. You can also connect to multiple network drives and network printers, as illustrated in this example of a batch file:

```
net use S: /delete
net use S: \\finance\July1998
net use U: /delete
net use U: \\Finance\YearlyReports
Net use lpt1: \\PrintServer\HPLJ3
```

The preceding batch file commands will delete the share if it already exists and map the share again. The share is deleted before it is mapped to circumvent the error message that is received when you try to establish a drive mapping that is already in place, similar to Figure 9-2.

By deleting the share first, we ensure that we will never receive this error message. The final line in the batch file contains the network printer

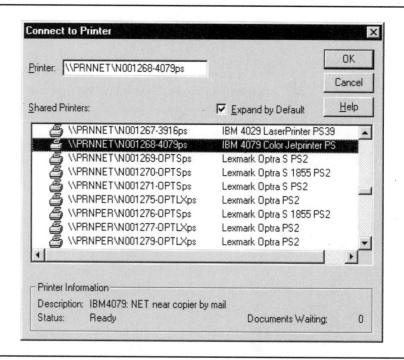

FIGURE 9-2   Deleting a share prior to mapping it

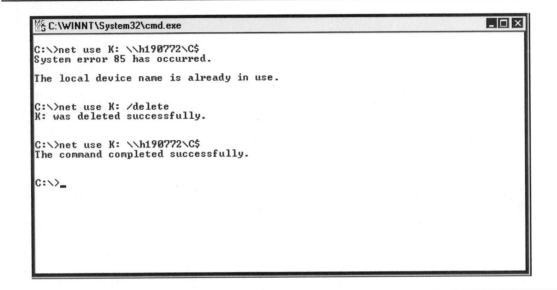

```
C:\>net use K: \\h190772\C$
System error 85 has occurred.

The local device name is already in use.

C:\>net use K: /delete
K: was deleted successfully.

C:\>net use K: \\h190772\C$
The command completed successfully.

C:\>_
```

mapping. This batch file can be executed at logon or executed anytime you want to connect all of these resources at once. Please note that when you are mapping a printer, you can omit the colon after lpt if you wish. For example, these two commands are identical in Windows NT:

```
Net use lpt1 \\printserver\printer
Net use lpt1: \\printserver\printer
```

CERTIFICATION OBJECTIVE 9.08

Changing or Moving Equipment

When you change equipment on a computer, in order to facilitate a smooth transition, you need to test the newer equipment beforehand to make sure it works correctly. For example, if you are adding a SCSI controller and two SCSI hard disks to a network server, test the SCSI cards before placing them in the new server. If you don't, and you experience hardware failure, you may have difficulty determining which is the culprit in the change: the SCSI controller, a SCSI hard drive, the SCSI cable, or the computer itself.

Moving a computer from one room to another doesn't sound like that difficult a process. However, there are hidden traps that can make this move more disruptive than it needs to be. You should test the area that you are moving the computer to before the move. Most importantly, you should test the network connection. You may also need to determine if the network outlet supports the speed of the server or workstation. If this is a high-powered server, does the network drop in the room connect to a high-speed port on a hub or a switch?

Servers contain information and resources that must be available to users. Any disruption in these resources will affect how users work. You have to care for these servers differently than you do the average workstation. You should not place a server in a dusty, hot area or in an area with little ventilation, such as a small closet. If you are moving a server to another area, make sure the area is appropriately equipped to handle a network server. Your server room should be climate controlled, well ventilated, relatively dust free, and away from windows or direct sunlight.

CERTIFICATION OBJECTIVE 9.09

Adding, Deleting, or Modifying Users

When you are graced with administrative rights on the network, you can do anything. You can delete the CEO's expense report if you wish. When given this extreme right, you have to be very responsible with it. Most problems occur when users are added, deleted, or modified without permission. I think most network administrators have been caught adding a new user without permission, or giving another user permissions they should not have. It's natural to want to be accepted as the computer techie in the organization. However, when it comes to giving other users permissions on the network that they shouldn't have, you are crossing a thin red line. If a user were to obtain information they were not supposed to have and got caught, chances are it would come right back to you, the person that granted them the permissions in the first place. For this reason, companies develop forms that users must fill out and have signed by their supervisors. These forms document the permissions required when creating or modifying a user, such as the groups this user's account will be placed in. These forms are also used to give users Internet access, dial-up permissions, and permission to take software off the premises.

When users leave the company, their accounts must be deleted or disabled. Even though it's apparent the user will not be coming back, you should obtain permission before deleting his or her account. For example, a user named Jim Sheppard has left the company. Jim was in charge of the safety department. He will be replaced soon. If you disable his account, you can rename the account to the new user that will take his place. If you delete his account immediately, you will have to re-create the account for the new hire and add the new hire to the existing shares that Jim had access to. This can be a very overwhelming task if Jim had explicit access to many files and folders.

Often the network administrator must fulfill the users' change requests, sign the documents, and submit the documents to his or her superior for approval. All this is aimed at establishing guidelines for network access and for deterring malicious behavior on the network. If you undermine this documentation process, you risk your job.

CERTIFICATION OBJECTIVE 9.10

User and Group Management

Let's face it: If not for the users, we would not have much to do on the network as administrators. Everything we do as administrators revolves around the user in some way. Next time you are having fun configuring that RAID array, remember that its purpose is to increase the performance for the user. Because everything revolves around the user, it makes sense to begin the discussion of managing resources with the user account.

The user account is what gives a user access to the network. If you do not have a user account, you aren't allowed to log on to the network. The account is based on the user, so it makes sense that a new account must be created for each user. This can be time consuming, but it is necessary. After the user account is created and configured, you don't have to do much housekeeping with it, unless the user's situation changes or he gets locked out of the system. You should place the user account in the proper groups when you create it.

Group accounts are for grouping together users who perform the same function or require access to the same resources. If it were not for group accounts, you would have to grant access to resources on a per-user basis. It is entirely possible to use group membership for resource access without having to grant access on a per-user basis, but it's nice to know you can grant or deny access down to the user level.

Your grouping should mirror the way users are logically grouped in your organization. Say you have an organization with a sales force, support engineers, and technicians. If you group the users according to their job function, it makes it easier to do such tasks as granting access to resources and sending notifications to group members. You can send a memo to the sales force informing them of sales-related information, which would not be of interest to your engineering staff. And perhaps the sales staff is the only group you would like to give Internet access to.

Although you can give rights, such as access to the Internet, to one group, it's a good idea to start a group called Internet, which will consist of users that have access to the Internet. As each user requires access to the Internet, you can place his account in this group. Even groups, such as the sales group, can be placed in this group to give every user in that group access to the Internet.

exam
ⓦatch

Make sure you understand the basics of user and group management for the exam. Placing users in groups makes assigning rights and permissions much easier. Whenever you are given a question about assigning rights to one user, consider if there is an alternative, such as creating a group and adding the user to the group.

Profiles

A user profile stores user preferences such as screen savers, last documents used, network drive mappings, and environmental settings, such as program groups. When the user logs off, the changes are saved so that the next time the user logs on, the settings are just as he left them. The profile starts as the default user and then is saved in the user's logon name in the system root, which in Windows NT is usually C:\winnt\Profiles.

Figure 9-3 shows where Windows NT stores user preferences.

This directory structure is good for administrators to know, whether they make applications and files available to everyone on the system, or just to a select few. All Users is the default that is used as a model for all users who log on to the system. Just select the user that you would like to have a program or shortcut, and then copy it to the Desktop or the Start Menu

---

FIGURE 9-3

The directory structure on a Windows NT computer for storing user preferences

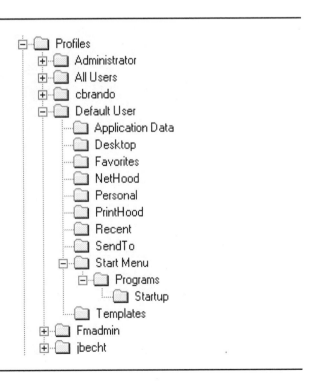

folder, whichever you prefer. Most NT administrators do this kind of thing on a daily basis when installing software, so you may want to practice it.

You have the option of making a profile a *roaming profile*, which is a profile stored on another computer, usually a server. The roaming profile enables you to keep your user preferences in one location so that any changes you make to the profile are used on any computer that you log on to. If you did not have a roaming profile, you would have a profile for each computer you log on to, and any changes you make to that profile are not accessible on other computers. It's a good idea to make your profile a roaming profile, so that you can have shortcuts to commonly used areas available regardless of the user's machine. This way you don't have to browse the network to find everything you need while the user is watching impatiently.

Rights

You may be asking yourself what the difference is between a *right* and a *permission*. Rights are given to users, much like citizens in the United States are given the right to vote at a certain age. The user's profile carries around the credentials of what objects the user has rights to. (Rights under other network operating systems are called system privileges.) Permissions are given to objects. The object itself carries around a list of who is entitled to use the object.

You can assign access to resources in one of two ways: by giving the user *rights* to access the object, or by specifying which users have *permission* to access a specific resource. Just remember from which point of view you are assigning the rights or permissions—from the user's point of view or the object's point of view.

When defining what permissions and rights a user will have on your network, it is best to make the user part of a group or groups that have the appropriate permissions to objects. In Windows NT, users should be added to global groups only. Global groups are specific to a domain. Local groups, on the other hand, are specific to a certain machine, such as a workstation or domain controller.

Very rarely do you want to give specific access to one user's account. If you find yourself giving rights to individual user accounts on a daily or weekly basis, you had better reevaluate your standards for assigning rights. It is very difficult to maintain standards when you are modifying individual user accounts.

Procedures/Policies

With your user accounts, there are account policies you can implement to help control the security of your network. Some items you can control with account policies include the minimum and maximum password age, minimum password length, and account lockout. The following is a list of the most popular policies available:

- **Maximum Password Age**   Will the password expire? If so, in how many days?

- **Minimum Password Age**   Can users change passwords immediately or do they have to wait a certain number of days?

- **Minimum Password Length**   Are blank passwords permitted? If not, how many characters does the password have to contain?

- **Password Uniqueness**   Will you keep password history? If so, how many passwords do you want the system to remember before enabling a password to be reused?

- **Account Lockout**   Will accounts be locked out for bad logon attempts? If so, how many bad logon attempts are allowed and how long before the account is reset, if at all?

- **Forcibly disconnect remote users from server when logon hours expire**   This goes hand in hand with logon hours. Logon hours can be specified for users and groups that restrict network access during a specified time period, such as 8:00PM through 6:00AM. If a user is staying late, they can continue past the logon restricting if they do not log out. Once they log off, the logon restriction will be in effect, and they will be denied access. You can use the Forcibly Disconnect

Remote Users option to log all users off when the logon hours begin. They will receive a warning a few minutes prior to the logon restriction informing them to save their data.

■ **Users must log on in order to change password**   When users get locked out, you can allow them to change their password or make them come to you as the administrator. This can depend on how network knowledgeable your users are. If you don't want them messing with username administration, you can set this up so they have to come see you to get their password back.

To set policies for user accounts, go to the Account Policy dialog box in Windows NT's User Manager for Domains by selecting Policies from the pull-down menu, and then selecting Account. Figure 9-4 illustrates the Account Policy dialog box of User Manager for Domains.

Using these policies, you can fine-tune users' access and capabilities on the network. Although system policies are very effective in what they accomplish, they can add more work for the administrator of the network. Not only must the administrator learn the various utilities for system policy, he must decide what to restrict, verify that the restrictions work, and explain to users why they have been restricted.

Most system policy restrictions are considered optional. You have to determine which settings are appropriate for your organization. The more policy restrictions you implement on your network, the angrier users get. Password restrictions, such as expiration and password uniqueness, are sure to upset users over time. For example, if your policy is that the system remembers an employee's last six passwords and passwords expire every month, you'll probably get daily complaints about the inconvenience of these restrictions. You'll just have to explain that those settings apply to everyone, from the president of the company right down to the hourly employees.

Administrative Utilities

Every network operating system has administrative utilities for managing users, groups, and resources. Microsoft Windows NT has User Manager for

FIGURE 9-4

Use the Account Policy
dialog box in User Manager
for Domains to set policies
for user accounts

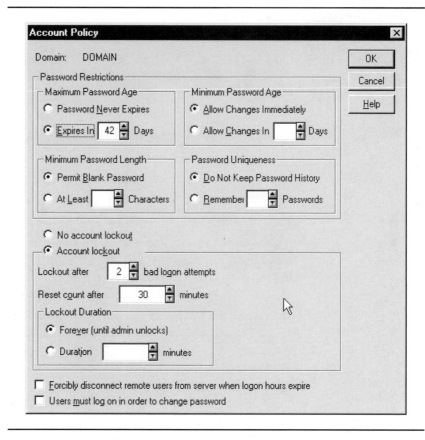

Domains; Windows NT Workstation has User Manager; Novell NetWare,
version 3.*x* has SYSCON; and Novell NetWare, version 4.*x* has the
graphical NetWare Administrator. Each of these administrative tools
enables you to add, modify, and delete users and groups. Nearly everything
you have learned about user and group management, policies, rights, and
permissions is possible within these administrative utilities. Figure 9-5
shows the main screen of User Manager on a Windows NT workstation,
which looks identical to User Manager for Domains found on Windows
NT servers.

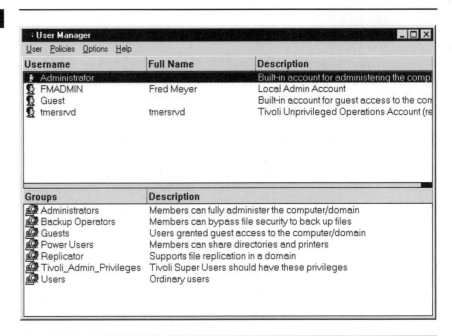

FIGURE 9-5

The User Manager utility on a Windows NT workstation enables you to manage users, groups, and resources

The User Properties dialog box enables you to configure settings for each user, as shown in Figure 9-6.

Login Accounts and Groups

Most operating systems provide two types of accounts that administrators have to manage: user accounts and group accounts. A user account is the account for an individual person on the network. A group account is for a group of users. You should place users in group accounts so that you can assign permissions and configure the users to take advantage of the features of the operating system.

When Windows NT Server is installed, there are two default user accounts that are created. These accounts are the administrator account and the guest account. The accounts that are set up during installation are the basic accounts that are needed to administer the domain. Throughout the life of the domain, users will come and go and a strong knowledge of how

FIGURE 9-6

The User Properties dialog box in Windows NT User Manager enables you to configure a user's account

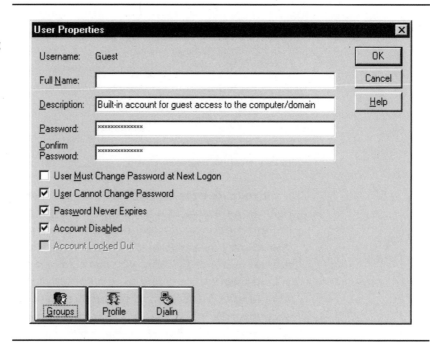

to maintain users is a must in today's networking environment. By default the guest account is disabled so that no one can access your network without being assigned a username and password. It is up to the administrator to enable this account.

The administrator account is the most important account in the domain. Administrators can complete a variety of tasks, including the following, which are not specific to one operating system:

- Creating users and groups
- Administering users and groups
- Assigning permissions and rights in the domain
- Sharing folders and printers
- Locking the server
- Formatting and managing drives on the server

It is a good idea to create a backup administrator account in the event that the administrator account's password is forgotten. This also helps if something happens to the administrator account that makes it unusable.

One other rule of thumb is to rename the administrator account. The administrator account cannot be deleted or disabled, but it can be renamed. Renaming the account makes it more difficult for someone to hack into your network. The name of the account is 50 percent of the information a hacker needs to break in; renaming the administrator account deprives the hacker of that 50 percent edge.

on the
()ob

It's a good idea for an administrator to have a second account with rights comparable to a normal user's. With this account you can't surf the Internet or test installations and applications. You don't realize how much power you have as an administrator until you log on as a normal user and find that you can't do nearly as much to the system. Where I work we are told to test the installs and applications as a normal user, in addition to testing them with our administrative accounts. We often find that shortcuts and applications we installed were only installed on the administrator's profile and did not appear for all users that logged on to the system.

When Windows NT Server is installed, a series of built-in global groups is created:

- Domain Admins
- Domain Users
- Domain Guests

A series of default (built-in) local groups is also created:

- Administrators
- Users
- Guests
- Backup operators

- Account operators (domain controller only)
- Print operators (domain controller only)
- Server operators (domain controller only)
- Power users (non-domain controllers)
- Replicators

Administrators

The Administrators local group is the most powerful of all of the groups. As you might expect, users in this group have full control of the system. For this reason, only trusted users should be members of this elite group. By default, the Domain Admins global group is a member of the local Administrators group.

Users

The Users local group has enough rights for users to get work done at their workstations, but not much else. Users don't have the right even to log on at a Windows NT Server. The Domain Users global group is a member of the Users local group by default.

Guests

The Guests group is even more limited than the Users group. It should be used for one-time or temporary access to resources. Either way, they are restricted in the tasks that they can perform. The Domain Guests global group is by default a member of the Guests local group, but you can remove it.

Server Operators

The Server Operators group is intended to relieve the burden on the administrator. Members of this group can shut down servers, format server hard disks, create and modify shares, lock and unlock the server, back up and restore files, and change the system time. The Server Operators group is only available on Domain Controllers.

Print Operators

Users in the Print Operators local group have the capability to create, delete, and modify printer shares. These will most likely be on print servers, which the members of the Print Operators group can log on to and shut down if need be. The Print Operators group exists only on a domain controller.

Backup Operators

Members of the Backup Operators local group can back up and restore on the primary and backup domain controllers. They can log on to and shut down the server, if needed.

Account Operators

Users in the Account Operators local group have permissions to add, modify, and delete most user and group accounts in User Manager for Domains. They do not have the capability to modify any of the default groups, nor can they modify any member that belongs to any of these groups. They can also use Server Manager to add computers to the domain. The Account Operators group exists only on a domain controller.

Replicators

The Replicators group contains the Replicator user account for the replication services. This group should not be used for any other purpose. In other words, users other than your Replicator service account should not be added here.

Domain Admins

The Domain Admins global group is a member of the Administrators local group on every computer in the domain by default. (Actually, this is just for computers running Windows NT, because operating systems like Windows 95 do not use groups to administer the local machine.) Having the Domain Admins global group in the Administrators local group by default gives an administrator the capability to modify computers in the domain. You can revoke this right by removing the Domain Admins group from the Administrators local group on the machine.

Domain Users

The Domain Users global group contains all subsequent accounts created in the domain. This gives users the capability to access resources in other domains. The Domain Users global group is by default a member of the Users local group on every Windows NT computer in the domain. This gives users the capability to access non-domain controller computers and workstations in the domain. If you do not wish them to have this capability, remove the Domain Users group from the Users local group on the specific machine.

Domain Guests

The Domain Guests global group is intended to provide limited and/or temporary access to the domain. By default, the Domain Guests global group is a member of the Guests local group.

The Group Memberships dialog box, shown next, shows you which groups the selected user is a member of.

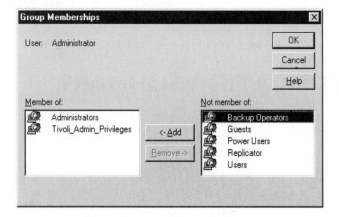

Now that you have seen the user and group management options available to you, here is a Questions and Answers session to determine which user and group methods to use in a particular scenario.

QUESTIONS AND ANSWERS

I would like to create a backup administrative account.	Copy the existing administrative account and then rename it. It is also recommended you rename the default administrator account to avoid hackers trying to guess the password.
I need another technician to help with user management.	Make them an Account Operator. They will have rights to add, modify, and delete users and groups.
I need another technician to help with the installation of operating systems.	Make them a Server Operator. They will then have the permission to add computers into the domain.
I cannot have users trying to guess another user's password.	Implement Account Lockout, which will lock the user account after a certain number of incorrect guesses.
I need to have the network as secure as possible as far as passwords are concerned.	Force the users to change their password every month, force the users to require a unique password, and force the password to contain at least six characters.
I need the system account for the backup program to never change.	Specify that this password cannot be changed, and set this account to never expire.
I need to have someone in charge of the backup routine.	Make this person a Backup Operator. They will have the permission to back up and restore files on Windows NT servers.

CERTIFICATION SUMMARY

In this chapter you learned the importance of keeping current, detailed documentation for your network. Documenting important servers and workstations makes it easier to locate, upgrade, and troubleshoot these computers. This documentation is also helpful when returning computers to their original state in the event of an emergency.

You learned the backup routine and the various tape-rotation techniques, as well as the various media on which to back up sensitive data, including tape, optical disks, floppy and hard disks, and network disks.

You learned that outdated and unused drivers can wreak havoc on a system and use up precious resources. Overwritten DLLs are also dangerous when it comes to application coexistence. One application may overwrite another application's DLLs and render the other application unstable or inoperable.

You learned about the network and printer drive mappings using the graphical and command-line utilities. It is imperative for the Network+ exam that you understand the syntax of these commands. The mapping begins with two backslash characters before the server name. After the server name, a backslash precedes the share name (\\server\share).

Finally, you learned some of the user and group management techniques that you will encounter on the exam and in real life. These include the various user and group management utilities and the settings that are configured using these programs. A big part of being a network administrator is managing users and groups effectively.

✓ TWO-MINUTE DRILL

- ❏ It is very important that you keep up-to-date records of the status and configuration of critical workstations and servers.

- ❏ In addition to keeping documentation on select systems on your network, you can also purchase third-party utilities that create images of these servers.

- ❏ Microsoft recommends that you back up the Registry for each Windows computer.

- ❏ It will take practice and effort to design, monitor, and test the backup process on a weekly basis.

- ❏ The heart of the backup process is selecting which data needs to be backed up.

- ❏ Backing up to tape is the most common form of backup done today, due to the availability and price.

- ❏ Replicating a folder to a network drive is a viable means of backing up data.

- ❏ Most backup systems employ removable media for the backup process. There are many types of removable media: floppy disks, hard disks, tape cartridges, reel tapes, and optical disks.

❏ There are a number of different techniques used to back up data. One of the most popular is the multi-generation tape rotation scheme, known as the Grandfather – Father – Son (GFS) scheme.

❏ Be sure you understand the reasons for removing unused or outdated drives from your system. The exam will present troubleshooting scenarios that will include determining the cause of a system that is not functioning correctly. When you understand how outdated drivers can affect a system, you are one step closer to answering these questions with ease during your exam.

❏ Changes to a workstation or a server can have negative effects on the network. These changes include network hardware settings, protocol additions or modifications, or added or misconfigured applications or services.

❏ Version conflicts may arise from software applications that are designed to run on a specific operating system type.

❏ One of the more complex situations to track down is the condition in which one application overwrites another application's Dynamic Link Library (DLL) files.

❏ Drive mapping is the process of connecting network drives so that you may use the resources located on them.

❏ Make sure you know the correct syntax for mapping network drives. It is very likely you will receive a question on your exam asking which of the answers uses the correct syntax.

❏ Just as you can connect network drives in order to use the resources located on them, you can also connect network printers in the same manner.

❏ When you change equipment on a computer, in order to facilitate a smooth transition, you need to test the newer equipment beforehand to make sure it works correctly.

❏ Most problems occur when users are added, deleted, or modified without permission.

❏ Group accounts are for grouping together users who perform the same function or require access to the same resources.

❑ Make sure you understand the basics of user and group management for the exam. Placing users in groups makes assigning rights and permissions much easier. Whenever you are given a question about assigning rights to one user, consider if there is an alternative, such as creating a group and adding the user to the group.

❑ A user profile stores user preferences such as screen savers, last documents used, network drive mappings, and environmental settings, such as program groups.

❑ Rights are given to users. The user's profile carries around the credentials of what objects the user has rights to.

❑ Permissions are given to objects. The object itself carries around a list of who is entitled to use the object.

❑ Some items you can control with account policies include the minimum and maximum password age, minimum password length, and account lockout.

❑ Every network operating system has administrative utilities for managing users, groups, and resources.

❑ Most operating systems provide two types of accounts that administrators have to manage: user accounts and group accounts.

SELF TEST

The following Self Test questions will help you measure your understanding of the material presented in this chapter. Read all the choices carefully, as there may be more than one correct answer. Choose all correct answers for each question.

1. Which of the following best describes the term *dependencies*?

   A. Applications that are required by another application in order to run correctly

   B. DLLs that are required by an application to run correctly

   C. Hardware resources that are required by another resource to run correctly

   D. Applications that are required for a software driver to work correctly

2. You have an e-mail server that has just lost a hard disk drive and needs to be functioning as quickly as possible. Which of the following is the fastest way to get the server running with the most current data possible?

   A. Manually install the operating system, install the e-mail program, and then restore the data from the most recent tape backup.

   B. Use a third-party disk image program to bring down an image stored on a server, and then restore the data from the most recent tape backup.

   C. Use an unattended installation of the operating system, install the e-mail program, and then restore the data from the most recent tape backup.

   D. Manually install the operating system, and then restore the e-mail program and data from the most recent tape backup.

3. Which of the following items would restore a Windows NT system as closely as possible to the original configuration before a hard disk crash?

   A. A tape restore of the operating system and the user and system database

   B. A tape restore of the operating system, the Registry, and the user profiles

   C. A tape restore of the full system, the Registry, and the most recent data

   D. A tape restore of the operating system, the Registry, the most recent data, and the user profiles

4. You came into work this morning and discovered that the tape backup did not complete successfully. The backup job usually backs up around 13GB of data, but this time the backup was around 12GB of data. This job usually fits on one tape, rarely fails, and has not been changed lately. What is most likely the cause, and how should you remedy the situation?

A. The backup server most likely could not attach to a resource to complete the backup. Check the error logs to determine where the server could not connect. If a user has turned off his computer, make sure he leaves the system on at night.

B. The backup server could not load the tape. Check the contents of the tape to verify you are not trying to overwrite a write-protected tape.

C. The backup server could not append to the tape. Check the contents of the tape to verify you are not trying to overwrite a write-protected tape.

D. The backup server most likely could not attach to a resource to complete the backup. Verify the backup server has rights to the specific share. Grant the backup server rights to attach to the share.

5. Which of the following is not true concerning tape backup?

A. It is the most expensive type of backup method.

B. It uses a sequential access method.

C. You can use multiple tapes in a tape magazine.

D. They are slower than most backup media.

6. What does Windows NT use to distribute logon scripts to multiple servers?

A. The distribution service

B. The domain controller service

C. The replication service

D. The backup process

7. You have a software development department with ten users. You need to provide everyone in the department with a way to access data that has been backed up permanently. The users will need to use this data at their computers to perform their jobs. What is the best way to accomplish this?

A. Install tape backup devices on each developer's computer and copy the nightly tape backups on tape for each user to peruse.

B. Have a tape backup server that holds the last five days worth of backups that each developer can attach to and peruse for information.

C. Archive the data on CD-ROM and copy the CD for each developer to peruse at their workstations.

D. Copy the backup data to the network, establish a share, and let the users attach to the share and peruse the information.

8. Which of the following is a large capacity, removable, magnetic medium?

A. Reel Tape

B. Floppy disk

C. Optical disk

D. Disk cartridge

9. During the GFS scheme, you begin the week by performing a full backup. For the

remaining days of the week, which type of backup could you perform? Choose all that apply.

A. Full

B. Incremental

C. Differential

D. No backup

10. Which of the following is not a good reason for removing an unused or outdated driver?

A. To conserve space

B. To conserve memory

C. So they don't accidentally get loaded

D. So they don't get corrupted

11. Which of the following workstation settings can cause the most damage on a network?

A. An improperly configured binding order

B. An improperly configured speed on the network card

C. An invalid Token Ring address

D. A workstation configured as a Master Browser

12. Which of the following computers will send out a beacon on a Token Ring network indicating a fault?

A. The most active upstream neighbor

B. The nearest upstream station

C. The most active upstream station

D. The nearest active upstream neighbor

13. You have just installed Windows NT Workstation on your machine and added a few applications. While you were trying to add Microsoft Office 97, you received an error. What will this error most likely indicate?

A. That a DLL has been overwritten by a previous application install

B. That Office 97 has not been installed correctly

C. That your system requires Service Pack 2 or later

D. That a DLL could not be copied to the destination directory

14. What is one way to determine if a DLL has been overwritten by another application?

A. Check the Event Viewer.

B. Check the install log for each application.

C. Open the sysdiff log file to determine which files have been overwritten by another application.

D. There is really no way to tell.

15. Which of the following is the correct syntax for mapping to a share called HeatherCurtis on the server called PeaceCorp with the drive designator of L?

A. net use L \\PeaceCorp\HeatherCurtis

B. net use /L: \PeaceCorp\HeatherCurtis

C. net use L: \HeatherCurtis\\PeaceCorp

D. net use L: \\PeaceCorp\HeatherCurtis

16. You have created a batch file to map network drives and printers for each user in the department. The following is your newly created batch file:

```
net use R: /delete
net use R: \\Rhapsody\March99
net use S: /delete
net use S: \\Enertia\QuarterlyReports
net use lpt1: \\Sanvoisen\HPLJ4SI
```

Which line in the batch file is invalid or incorrect?

A. The second line

B. The fourth line

C. The fifth line

D. There is no invalid or incorrect line in this batch file

17. You are planning to move the web servers from one location to another. This move is planned for later tonight. The user support database is run from the web server, so the move must be completed by the morning. What needs to be done to ensure a smooth move?

A. Migrate the user profiles to another server before the move.

B. Test the network connection in the new room.

C. Back up the data on the servers.

D. Back up the user profiles before the move.

18. Van Williams, the supervisor for the A-crew in the receiving departments, will be leaving the company. Jeff Loomis, the new supervisor, will be starting shortly in Van's position. What should happen to Van's user account?

A. It should be deleted.

B. It should be disabled.

C. It should be moved to the temporary area.

D. It should be renamed to Jeff Loomis, the new supervisor.

19. You need to give Internet access to eight users in the sales department. However, you do not want to give access to the entire sales department. How would you go about granting Internet access to these users?

A. Grant the sales group rights to access the Internet.

B. Grant each user rights to access the Internet.

C. Place each of the users into a group called Internet and give this group access to the Internet.

D. Grant the sales group rights to access the Internet, but revoke rights for those who do not need access to the Internet.

20. You are on a Windows NT workstation and would like to drop a shortcut into the personal directory of Warrel Dane, whose username is Wdane on the local computer. You are currently logged on as administrator of the local machine. Which directory do you place this shortcut in?

A. winnt\profiles\WDane\
   shortcuts\personal

B. winnt\system32\profiles\
   Wdane\personal

C. winnt\profiles\Wdane\personal

D. winnt\system\profiles\Wdane\personal

21. What is the difference between rights
    and permissions?

A. Permissions are assigned to objects,
   and rights are given to user or
   group accounts

B. Permissions are given to user or
   group accounts, and rights are
   given to objects

C. Permissions are given to user accounts,
   and rights are given to groups

D. Permissions are given to groups, and
   rights are given to user accounts

22. Tim Owens has come back this morning
    from a two-month sabbatical. He calls you
    and tells you he can't access the network.
    You haven't disabled his account. He
    believes he is typing in the right password,
    because it's written on his monitor. What
    account policy is most likely the problem?

A. Account Lockout

B. Maximum Password Age

C. Minimum Password Age

D. Lockout Duration

23. What is the user and group management
    utility provided with NetWare 3.*x*?

A. NetWare Administrator

B. SYSADMIN

C. SYSCONSOLE

D. SYSCON

24. Which of the following is not a
    recommendation for dealing with the
    administrator's account?

A. It should be deleted after you
   have used it to create your
   administrative account.

B. It should be disabled.

C. It should be copied for a backup.

D. It should be renamed.

25. Which of the following is not a built-in
    Windows NT group?

A. Domain Guests

B. Domain Admins

C. Domain Users

D. Domain Administrators

CERTIFICATION

10

Maintaining and Supporting the Network

I f there are two things you will do, they are maintain the network and support your users. These functions of a network administrator are vital to success. If you are not keeping your network up to date you are headed for constant problems and possibly network failure. If you keep all of your pieces up to date and stay on top of problems, the problems you face will be minor and the network will be a productive tool for your users.

In this chapter you will learn some of the things you have to do to ensure your network is up more than it is down and that all your applications work at their best performance. Documentation and learning are the biggest keys to success in maintaining and supporting your network. Along with the documentation come the different maintenance components. There are patches, fixes, and general upgrades. When you change something on the network you want to make sure that the network still functions. This is where documenting what you did will come in handy, especially if you have to do it again.

CERTIFICATION OBJECTIVE 10.01

Test Documentation

When it comes to maintaining software on the network, it is important to know the details of what makes or breaks an application. If there is one thing I have learned through the course of implementing and maintaining networks, it is to read the readme files. There is not a patch I've seen in the past few years that doesn't come with a readme file or a text file of some sort with installation instructions. In fact, it is usually a good idea to read through the documentation and then reread the documentation and any corresponding addendums.

It is more common today that new software installations require reading documentation from the CD or disks they come on. In order to do this you must have the appropriate viewer installed on your workstation. Usually the viewer comes on the CD with the software. Novell software has its own viewer for its documentation. Figure 10-1 shows an example of the Novell documentation viewer.

Vendor's Software Patches

Part of maintaining your network is applying patches to your existing software to make sure you have the most current release. Vendors release updates or patches to their products when bugs are found or to simply make them run better. The main software vendors for network operating systems, Microsoft and Novell, have a service pack for the core network operating system. Applying these is a must when it comes to ensuring your network

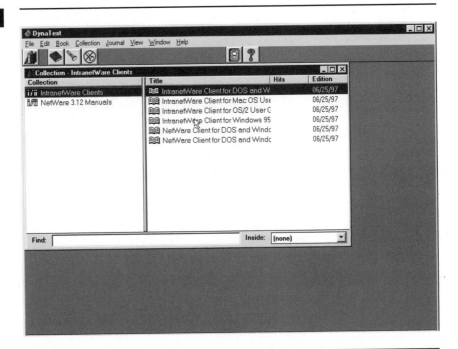

FIGURE 10-1

Novell software comes with its own viewer for reading installation documentation and readme files

functions with third-party applications. Figure 10-2 shows where you can get Novell service packs for their network operating systems.

The vendor's Web site will most likely have the patches and service packs that you need for your software. Microsoft, Computer Associates, APC, Compaq, Hewlett Packard, and other vendors all have Web sites to support their customers. These Web sites have patches along with documentation on problems. Figure 10-3 shows Microsoft's location on the Web for service packs and patches.

Sometimes it takes looking through the online support forums to figure out you need a patch. Vendors have online support where you can perform a search for a particular error or problem. These searches will lead to the appropriate patch. Figure 10-4 shows Microsoft's online support available on the Internet.

Exercise 10-1 teaches you how to search for and download patches.

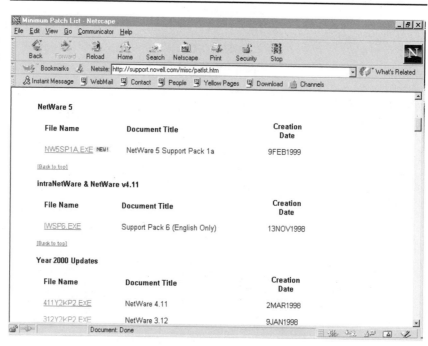

FIGURE 10-3

Go to the Microsoft Web site to download software patches and service packs

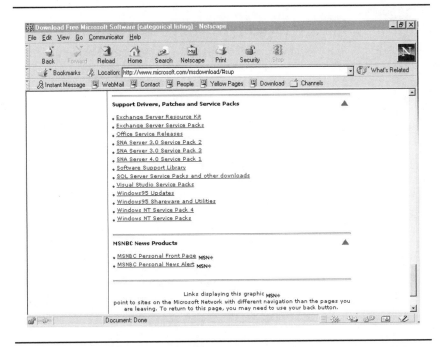

FIGURE 10-4

From the Microsoft online support page you can search for a problem you're having and find out if there's a patch available

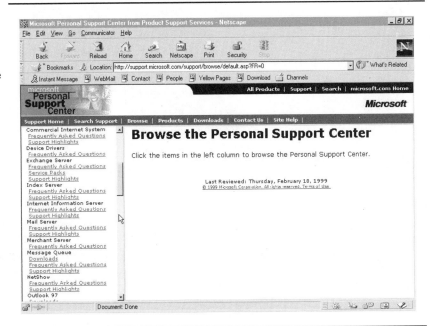

Downloading a Patch from Novell

You are upgrading a server from NetWare 3.12 to NetWare 3.2. You call tech support and you search the Web until you discover that there is one patch that you need to apply to NetWare 3.2 after the upgrade. Follow these steps to find, download, and extract a patch from Novell. (You should use Netscape in this exercise.)

1. Point your Web browser at http://support.novell.com.

2. On the Support Connection page, select the link for Minimum Patch List.

3. Scroll down to the Table of Contents and select Previous Product Versions.

4. Scroll down to the NetWare 3.12 section and find the patch named LIB312B.EXE.

5. Click the LIB312B.EXE link to go to the page where you can download the file and read about the patch.

6. Read through the Abstract, Issue, and Installation Instructions sections specifically.

7. Click on the link at the top of the page and download the file to a temporary directory.

8. After the file is downloaded, go to the DOS prompt and change to the directory where you downloaded the file.

9. Type LIB312B to execute the patch. You will be prompted to Continue Extraction? Press Y to answer yes.

10. A series of files will be extracted. One of these files is LIB312B.TXT. After the files are extracted, type **EDIT LIB312B.TXT** to open the text file.

11. Read through the text file to double-check any instructions for installation.

At this point you would apply the patch per the instructions on the Web page and in the text file; however, you probably do not actually have a NetWare 3.12 server to apply this patch to, so stop here.

Be sure to do the necessary research about the patch you are applying, so that you know what you are doing. Applying a patch incorrectly can bring down the entire network. Be sure you have a good backup in case the patch crashes the server to the point of having to restore from tape. New patches and service packs are the riskiest. The newest ones have the newest fixes, but sometimes the service pack or patch may cause other problems. A good rule of thumb is to wait a few weeks after a patch comes out and then research what other users are saying. Many vendors have forums that users can post information to. These forums are a good source of information if other users are having problems with a patch. Vendors have been known to make patches and service packs available and then have to pull them off their Web site to modify them. The first service packs for NetWare 5 and Microsoft Office 97 were released, pulled, redone, and then released again. So the point is, sometimes waiting is not a bad thing. If waiting is not an option, be sure to rename or back up the files that are being replaced. This is especially true if the files are copied manually. This gives you complete control as the network administrator.

exam
ⓦatch

The exam hits a lot of scenarios for troubleshooting and maintenance. Be sure to understand each component: patches, upgrades, virus signatures, backups, etc. This chapter is important in the role of passing the exam.

Upgrades

Software manufacturers release upgrades for their products to improve them and make them more powerful. You should always install an upgrade on a stand-alone machine before distributing it to the network. This enables you to test the application and go through the upgrade process in a non-production environment.

Many upgrades are free and require a simple download similar to a patch. Some upgrades need to be ordered from the manufacturer and are still free or at a very minimal cost if you are a registered owner and user of the older version. Again, be sure to have a good backup before you install the upgrade to prevent data loss.

Hardware Upgrades

Hardware upgrades for maintaining the network? I know this may sound wrong, but there are firmware updates for the various ROMs that exist in servers and workstations. The main ROM that controls the computer is usually programmable and can be updated. This is especially important when it comes to the year 2000. I recommend getting the latest ROM updates for all components on your entire network. If there is an update, there is a reason for it and if you can avoid the problem before it happens you are steps ahead.

Manufacturers devote an area on their Web sites to their hardware and allow you to update the components in your server and workstations. Figure 10-5 shows the Compaq Web site for downloading ROM updates for Compaq computers.

FIGURE 10-5

You can download ROM updates from this Compaq Web site

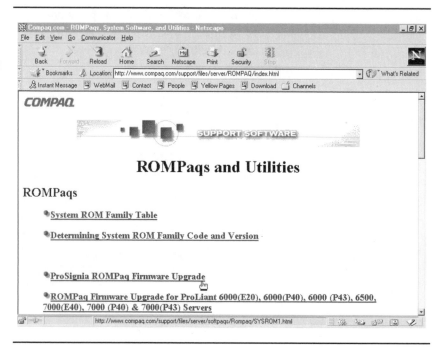

With the coming of year 2000, ROM updates are especially important. The updates include readme files or other documentation. There is usually a version number and a date associated with a ROM revision. Figure 10-6 is the Hewlett Packard Web site showing a ROM revision with the version number and a link to more information.

If you were to click on the More Info link, you would be taken to a page that shows the date of the ROM revision. This is helpful if the only thing you know is the date of your current ROM. The ROM dates are shown during the POST when the server or workstation is first turned on. Knowing only the date will usually enable you to know if your ROM needs to be updated. Figure 10-7 shows the Hewlett Packard page that appears when you click the More Info link.

The ROM date is July 31, 1998. If this is your ROM date, you have the current ROM. If your ROM date is earlier than this, you should download and apply this update.

FIGURE 10-6

This HP Web site shows a ROM revision with the version number

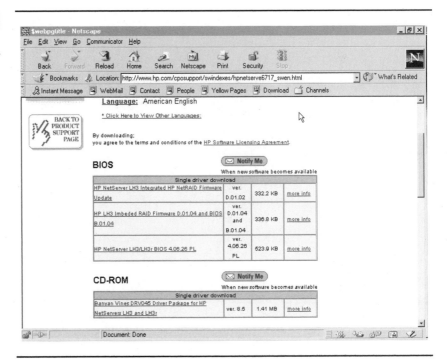

FIGURE 10-7

This HP Web site gives the date of the ROM update

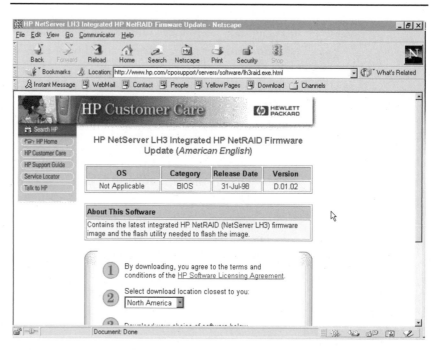

CERTIFICATION OBJECTIVE 10.02

Network Maintenance

There is more to network maintenance than patches and updates, including providing and testing a backup solution and providing and updating anti-virus software. You need to establish a routine of backing up and of applying updates of patches and virus signatures.

Standard Backup Procedures and Backup Media Storage Practices

Every network administrator should have a backup routine. Software packages are available for backing up network servers and various types of tape drives are available for storing the backup. The software and the tape drive you choose determine how fast you back up and how much you back up to the media. This is determined by the storage capacity of the tape and the compression capability of the software.

Installing Backup Software

Before you install backup software, you need to take some preliminary steps:

1. Make sure the system that you are installing to meets the hardware and software requirements.

2. Physically install the tape drive and any adapter boards that are needed. Connect the cables between the tape drive and the adapter board. Make sure that power is connected.

3. Make sure your backup software has everything in it before proceeding.

4. Refer to the instructions with your backup software for any unique pre-installation items.

This probably seems straightforward, but there are things about these steps to keep in mind. When ensuring that your system meets the hardware and software requirements, you have to know what devices are installed. Not just any tape drive or SCSI adapter will work in all cases. Also, there are things you can do with the network operating system to see what you have for available resources.

When installing the tape drive in a SCSI chain, you have to know if other devices are connected. If so, you must have a SCSI ID assigned to each device that is different. If you don't do this, your devices may not work properly.

After you install the software, you have to make sure it is loaded on the server. NetWare and Windows NT give you two distinct ways to check to see if the backup software is running. NetWare provides an NLM (NetWare Loadable Module) with a screen that you can switch to. With NetWare you can press CTRL-ESC to get a list of available screens. Windows NT enables the backup software to run as a service. Select Start | Settings | Control Panel, and then double-click the Services icon. The Services dialog box lists the services available on that server. Check to see if your backup software is listed.

NetWare and Windows NT provide two different ways to get into the administrative utility that comes with the backup software. On Windows NT, everything can be done at the server. Computer Associates ArcServeIT, for example, has a utility that is the Manager for the backup software. This utility is run at the server on Windows NT and at a workstation on NetWare. Seagate's Backup Exec also has a management utility that runs on the workstation on a Novell network.

Tape Drives

The two common types of tape drives are DAT and DLT. This section looks at each drive in some detail. The exam will not go into this much detail, but understanding the background will help you remember the information about the drives that will be on the test.

DAT (Digital Audio Tape) was developed in the mid-1980s by Sony and Philips. DAT was originally used to record music in a digital format. DAT is now very popular as a medium for computer data storage. The DAT drive uses a helical scan, which means that the read/write heads spin diagonally across the tape. DAT uses the DDS (Digital Data Storage) format. DAT uses a 4mm tape. The speed isn't as good as that of a DLT drive, but the capacity can be quite large. The two systems, audio and computer, cannot share information. There are different types of DDS formats that allow for different amounts of storage on a tape. The following table shows the breakdown of these different technologies.

Type of Format	Storage Capacity
DDS	2GB
DDS-1	2/4GB
DDS-2	4/8GB
DDS-3	12/24GB

As DDS-1 emerged, so did compression. That is why you notice that DDS-1 to DDS-3 have a second number associated with them is, which always double the base storage capacity. So standard 4mm tapes for DAT drives could hold up to 24GB of data. Other technologies have emerged with 8mm tapes, but for the exam you will not need to know these.

DLT (Digital Linear Tape) was introduced by Digital Equipment Corporation in the mid-80s. Quantum Corporation owns the technology now. The DLT tape is a half-inch magnetic tape that is reel-to-reel. The tape cartridge contains one reel and the other reel is inside the DLT drive.

The standards for DLT are shown in the following table. The main advantages are fast data transfer rates, higher storage capacity, and higher reliability. This all, of course, comes at a price to the customer.

DLT Type	Capacity
DLT2000	15/30GB
DLT4000	20/40GB
DLT7000	35/70GB

DLT drives store data on the tape differently than the DAT drives do. The data path is made up of parallel tracks recorded in a serpentine pattern. What this means is that the first track is written from one end of the tape to the other and then the heads are repositioned and the next track goes the opposite direction, again the entire length of the tape. The drive continues to go back and forth, writing until the tape is full.

Tape Automation

When it comes to maintaining the network, you need to schedule a backup job and have a routine to your backup schedule. Many companies do a tape rotation. They have daily, weekly, and monthly tapes. This rotation usually consists of 20-25 tapes. Each tape has its purposes. Sometimes this is called an autopilot rotation. The backup software keeps a database and expects a certain tape on each day of the year. The most common one is a 21-tape rotation consisting of four daily tapes for Monday through Thursday, five weekly tapes for each Friday (some months have five Fridays), and12 monthly tapes for the last weekday of the month. There are no backups on Saturday or Sunday. It is a good idea to store the monthly tapes offsite to prevent fire or other major catastrophe from ruining your data and your backups of your data.

Along with tape rotations are tape libraries and tape arrays. Tape libraries are designed to have a series of tapes in a holder that is inserted into the tape mechanism to automate the rotation of tapes throughout the week. If the amount of data is very large, the tape library may be used on a daily basis to rotate multiple tapes in and out of the various drives to make sure all data fits onto tape. Tape arrays, on the other hand, are similar to RAID technology with hard drives. Data is spread out throughout a series of drives. There can be a parity drive for fault tolerance addition. Manufacturers claim that tape arrays increase the throughput because multiple drives are writing simultaneously.

Full, Incremental, and Differential

Backup software enables you to run three different types of backups: full, incremental, and differential. These are the three you may see on the exam so we will focus on them. The key to backing up your data is to ensure you can restore the data in the event of system failure. These three types of backup will enable this if you use them together correctly.

A *full backup* backs up every file on the specified volume or volumes. Many companies run a full backup every day, no matter what. With a full backup every day, the restore process only requires the most recent tape. However, a full backup requires a large storage capacity and a lot of time. If you have a big system with a lot of data, running a daily full backup may not be practical.

An *incremental backup* backs up the files that have changed or were added since the last incremental or full backup. If you choose to run an incremental backup as your first backup, it will run as a full backup because there is not a previous one to go by. Using a combination of the full backup and incremental backup is highly effective and less time consuming than running a full backup daily. However, to restore, you will need the last full backup tape and every incremental backup tape since the last full backup.

A *differential backup* backs up the files that have changed or were added since the last full backup. This can also be very efficient when you do not want to do full backups every day. Restoring requires only two tapes: the last full backup tape and the last differential backup tape.

Differential and incremental backups can make the restoration process a little more difficult, because you have to restore from the full backup first, and then restore from the incremental or differential backups, to make sure any files that have changed since the last full backup are restored. If you have continuous full backup tapes you can restore from the most recent backup and get all files restored in one session. An important difference between differential and incremental backups is that incremental backups take less time to back up but more time to restore; differential backups take more time to back up but less time to restore.

e x a m
ⓦa t c h

You will definitely see a question or two on the exam about the different kinds of backups. Be sure to know the differences between full, incremental, and differential, especially the last two, which can be the most confusing. You may be given a scenario and have to pick the backup plan and restoration process.

QUESTIONS AND ANSWERS

I want to be able to restore from one tape and get all the data. What type of backup do I need to run?	Run a full backup on a daily basis.
I want to have the quickest possible backup of only those files that have changed or were added since the last backup. Which backup method should I use?	Run an incremental backup.
I want to run a backup that will back up all files that have changed since the last full backup. What backup do I want to use on days I am not doing a full backup?	Run a differential backup.
I want to be able to restore all my data with only two tapes. What tape backup scheme should I use?	Run a full backup with a differential backup.
If I am restoring and need to use the full backup and every tape since the full backup, which tape backup scheme am I using?	You are running a full backup with incremental backups.
If I run one full backup and then run a differential backup every day for three months, how many tapes will I need to restore the data entirely?	Two. You will need the full backup tape and the most recent differential backup tape.

FROM THE FIELD

The Importance of Network Backups

To say that having a reliable backup scheme is important is an understatement. A company can go bankrupt if all their records go up in a puff of smoke and there are not adequate backups of critical data. With this in mind, if you ever find yourself in the position of being responsible for the network backups, you had better take this seriously. I mean deadly serious, because there's more at stake than your job.

I was in charge of evaluating Seagate Backup Exec and Cheyenne ARCServe to determine which product was the most appropriate for our company. After I selected the software package, I was to identify everything that needed to be backed up on the network. This is no small task, either. How do you know something that is supposed to be backed up isn't currently getting backed up? Murphy's law states you won't know until that workstation or server's hard disk crashes. The finger will point directly to you. After I decided what was to be backed up, I had to learn every nuance of the product from tape rotation, logs, errors, alerts, and restores. I then had to prove my ability to restore successfully on a weekly basis. A disaster is not the time to discover that your backups are corrupt or that files are not backed up properly.

Here is a list of backup-related issues I have seen in the past year:

- A workstation with a single-user proprietary database with six months' worth of data lost its hard drive. This was the only workstation out of the group that wasn't being backed up. He lost everything.

- Tapes were not being taken to a safe site, and the data was continually being overwritten. Everyone assumed the other person was taking the tapes off site, but no one was. There was a one-month gap in the history of the backups.

- An administrator before me basically ignored an error log that said the backup job has exceeded the first tape. He never put a second tape in for months. When it came time to restore the Microsoft Exchange server, the restore kept asking for a tape two, which didn't exist.

- In an amazing miracle, another administrator had placed important information on the server for one night only. He assumed it would be backed up, which it was. He didn't think he needed the data until two weeks later. I told him we take the Friday tape off site, but his data was on Thursday. The tape was assumed overwritten, but upon

FROM THE FIELD

further inspection, my backup job had failed that very day, and the tape was not overwritten, and his data was intact.

These stories are not meant to scare you, but to prepare you for your backup experiences. Every situation could have been avoided if proper care was taken with the backup routines. Please, I urge you to take this seriously; you will be the hero when someone needs an emergency restore.

—Cameron Brandon, MCSE+Internet, CNE, A+, Network+

Periodic Application of Software Patches and Other Fixes to the Network

Earlier in this chapter you learned about the patching and updating software on the server. There are a couple of details you should look at a little closer. First of all, you need to patch not only the software that runs on the server itself, such as the backup software and anti-virus software, but you also need to update any applications that run from the client workstations. Some applications may be located on the server but run on the workstation. Other applications are installed on the actual workstation. It may seem time consuming to have to update applications on every workstation, but you need to have consistency throughout the network. A database application may have the client engine installed directly on the workstation and the data on the server. This is very common among database applications.

on the
job

The company I work for has a division that uses Quickbooks accounting software. The application is loaded on each workstation and the data is stored in a common directory on the server. One of the users downloaded an update from the Internet and updated his workstation. When the workstation software was updated the database also was updated, which caused a problem for the other users. When the other users tried to get into the database they would get an error because their workstations were not updated.

The other side to this piece of maintaining the network is logging the activity and documenting every change or update that is applied. If this isn't done you may start seeing inconsistencies in your network with updates and patches. This leads to problems and then things can start to snowball.

Installing Anti-Virus Software on the Server and Workstations

Anti-virus software is a must on networks and workstations today. Viruses can destroy data on a hard drive in a matter of seconds. More and more networks are connecting to the Internet. The chance of getting a virus is greater with an Internet connection. Prior to offices being on the Internet, virus infections usually started from floppy disks brought from other offices or from home.

When you install Anti-virus software in a networked environment, you must set multiple configuration items. There is usually both a workstation agent and a server application that run to constantly scan for viruses and virus-like activity. Most people think of virus software as an application you run to scan your drives and files for viruses. This is one component of virus software, but the most important one is the memory-resident piece that scans files coming into the server from the workstations or the Internet. These files are considered incoming. It also scans any files that are opened on the server. These files are considered outgoing.

The installation of anti-virus software is different on the two major platforms for network OS. We will look both at NetWare and Windows NT for installing the anti-virus software. The software that we will discuss in this section is Computer Associates' InoculateIT. Other popular virus protection suites include McAfee and Dr. Solomon's Anti-Virus Toolkit.

Installations on both platforms have similarities. The end results can be a little different. The first few steps are similar to that of the installation guidelines of just about any software.

1. Make sure that the system meets the hardware and software requirements.

2. Check the workstation or server that you are installing from for viruses locally. With NetWare you will be installing from a

workstation, but from Windows NT you will be installing at the server.

3. Install the software to your server's hard disk. The following illustration shows part of the installation procedure. If you choose custom installation, you will have the option of installing the manager software. This is the workstation component for Windows and DOS.

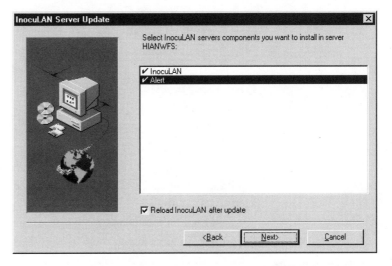

4. Apply any patches or updates from the vendor's Web site. This includes updating the virus signatures, which we will look at in the next section.

Sounds pretty easy, right? Well, the installation piece is pretty easy. It is the configuration that can be a bit challenging.

InoculateIT gives you three configuration options: Domain Manager, Local Scanner, and Critical Disk. These options are available regardless of whether you are running this on a NetWare network or a Windows NT network. The Quick Access dialog box is shown next. The Critical Disk option backs up the boot sector, BIOS information, and other important components that can be infected by viruses. This disk is used to restore this vital information in case of failure.

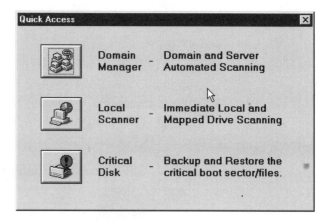

Domain Manager

The Domain Manager exists in the Windows NT version as well as the Novell NetWare version of InoculateIT. When InoculateIT is set up on a network, it is possible to configure the servers as a domain within the virus software. This keeps everything consistent throughout the network. A job can be set up and everything can be managed at the domain level, which keeps it centralized.

Click the Domain Manager button on the Quick Access dialog box to open the Domain Manager window, as shown in Figure 10-8.

FIGURE 10-8

Domain Manager window

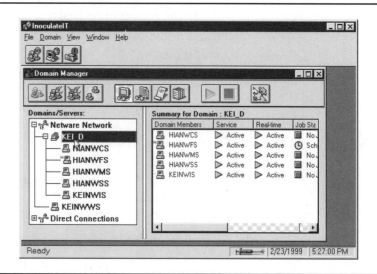

On the left is a list of possible servers or workstations to scan and on the right are the currently scheduled jobs. As you can see in Figure 10-8, there is also a listing with version number along with version and date of the virus signatures. This is very important in keeping your signatures up to date, which you will learn about in the next section.

Click the Add/Modify button to open the Job Properties dialog box, as shown in Figure 10-8. When you click this button to add or modify a job you will get a window similar to Figure 10-9. The Job Properties dialog box enables you to add a new job, modify a current job, or delete a job.

When adding or modifying a job you have plenty of options available. This is where virus protection can get tricky if you are not careful. The Targets/Schedule page is pretty straightforward. It enables you to choose what you want scanned and what you want to exclude. It also enables you to choose when you want the scan to take place.

Select the Actions/Options tab to bring it to the front, as shown in Figure 10-10. The Actions/Options page enables you to choose what you

FIGURE 10-9

Use the Job Properties dialog box to add, modify, or delete a domain job

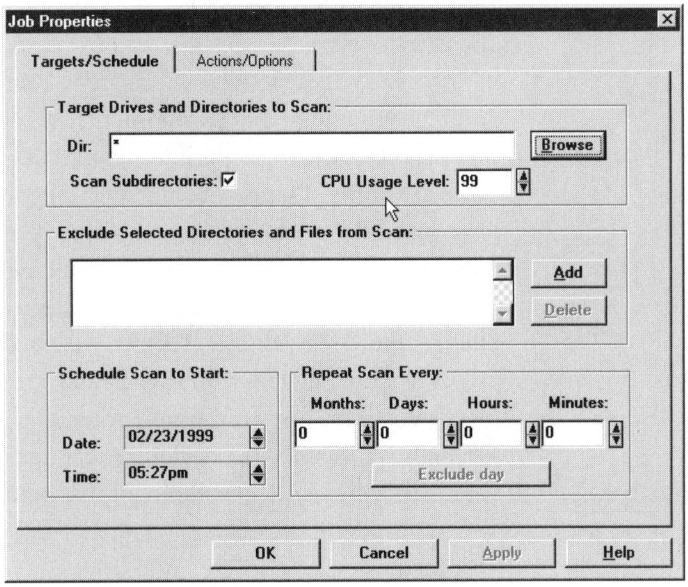

Use the Actions/Options
page in InoculateIT to
choose the types of files to
scan and what to do with
infected files

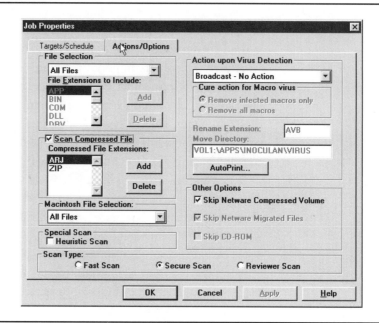

want done with infected files and what file types you want scanned based
on extension.

You can choose to have InoculateIT cure infected files, report the
problem and do nothing with the file, or report and move the file to a
special directory, or delete infected files. Moved files are renamed with a
special extension for easy recognition. If you choose the cure option, and
InoculateIT is unable to cure a file, the file will be moved and renamed with
the special extension. Other virus protection suites have similar options.

The Actions/Options page has more options for scanning compressed
files, compressed volumes, CD-ROMs, as well as the type of scan. The
types of scan available with InoculateIT are Fast Scan, Secure Scan, and
Reviewer Scan. Fast Scan simply scans the beginning of the file for faster
scanning. EXE and COM files are scanned fully with this method. This
method does risk the possibility of missing infected files, though.

Secure Scan is the preferred scan to use. Secure Scans scan every file fully. This takes more time but also is more thorough. Reviewer Scan scans every file fully and scans for virus-like activity within a file. It is possible for false alarms to be reported with this method.

Local Scanner

The local scanner option in the Quick Access dialog box is for immediate scanning of local or mapped drives. This is good to do when you may have a problem with a workstation or particular volume on a server. This is also useful for a server that may not be part of the InoculateIT domain that is scanned regularly.

Click the Local Scanner button on the Quick Access dialog box to open the InoculateIT Local Scanner window. Select the drive you want to scan with the local scanner. The Local Scanner Options dialog box appears, as shown in Figure 10-11. Use this dialog box to specify what you want scanned and how you want it scanned.

FIGURE 10-11

Use the Local Scanner Options dialog box to specify what to scan and how to scan it

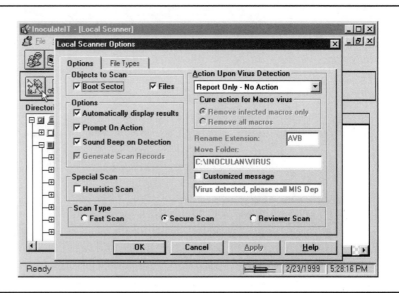

The available options are similar to those for the Domain Manager, but more concise and on one screen. Local scanning can consume network bandwidth during peak periods. It is better to do the scanning during off hours to keep from consuming the bandwidth on the network.

Log Files

When scanning is completed, the scan software writes the results to a log file, which you can review at a later time. The log file is useful when you want to determine where the viruses are originating. From time to time you may have a user who is consistently infecting the network, or at least his workstation. The log file gives date and time stamps along with the drives that were scanned. All virus activity is logged, usually with the virus name and information on whether the file or files were cured. Knowing the name of the infected files is good, so you can do a search to see if the file was copied to anywhere else on the network. Figure 10-12 shows an example of the results logged for the past few scans.

FIGURE 10-12

A virus scan results log lists the names of infected files, viruses detected, and whether the files were cured or deleted

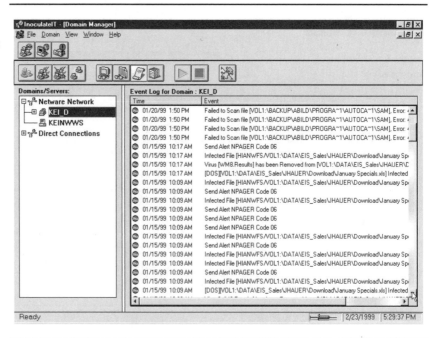

Real-Time Scanning

Virus scanning would not be very effective without real-time scanning. *Real-time* scanning scans every file that is accessed, opened, saved, or downloaded. This is especially critical when the Internet is available to users. The numerous downloads of cached information and files can bring viruses to your network.

The Real-Time Monitor page in InoculateIT gives you the option to scan files coming into the server or going out of the server. You can also specify both incoming and outgoing, which is the best scanning because it covers both angles of possible virus infection.

When you have a domain set up on the network you can configure the Real-Time monitor settings from within the InoculateIT manager. Figure 10-13 shows the Real-Time Monitor configuration options.

The options are almost the same as they are for the local scanner and domain manager. The main difference here is that the settings that are chosen take effect immediately. Real-time protection of your network is

FIGURE 10-13

Real-Time Monitor options

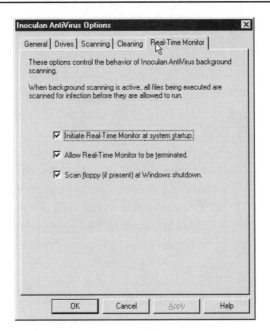

very important in keeping your network virus free on a consistent basis. If you only do regular scans, viruses have a chance of infecting your network and spreading into other areas of your network. With real-time monitoring you should notice that the viruses are caught immediately upon entering the network. This of course depends on how up-to-date your virus signatures are.

exam **Watch**

The exam will test your knowledge of client- and server-side virus scanning implementations. Remember that in order to be fully secure from viruses, you need servers that continually scan files on the network for viruses on file servers, and workstations that scan for viruses on users' workstations. Users commonly bring in viruses through floppies and e-mail.

Update Virus Signatures

To ensure the integrity of the data on your network, you must keep your virus signature files up to date. A *virus signature file* is a database of known viruses that the anti-virus software uses when scanning files to eliminate viruses. These are updated monthly by the vendor, in most cases. Usually you can download updates from the software vendor's Web site. Some vendors may mail updates to registered users. Computer Associates' InoculateIT offers a couple of options for updating virus signatures: automatic updates and manual updates.

The automatic update feature takes advantage of the fact that more and more networks are linked to the Internet. InoculateIT automatically attaches via FTP to Computer Associates and downloads the most recent virus signatures. This is a convenient feature for network administrators. The one problem with this, of course, is that after the update is done, you don't know which files were updated. If there was a problem with the download, then a file could be corrupt and therefore corrupt your live software. I personally recommend downloading and applying the updates manually. This is a much more controlled environment. You can see what files are being updated and back up those that are being updated. That way if there are problems you can revert to the previous version.

Along with updating the servers you have to update the workstations. InoculateIT comes with a feature that enables automatic synchronization of the workstations with the virus patterns off the server. This is a little more controlled, but I still recommend manually updating one workstation first each time you update to ensure that the update will go smoothly. After it is tested, you can automate the process from there. There is also a process to automatically update other servers on the network. You can automate this process after you update the first server. The documentation included with InoculateIT gives step by step instructions on how to configure and set this up, but you do not need to know this for the exam.

e x a m
ⓦ a t c h

The exam will hit on the subject of virus signatures. You need to know what they are and how to update them.

CERTIFICATION SUMMARY

Network maintenance is a never-ending process. Certain procedures and practices must be followed on a daily basis to keep the network running. It is your job as network administrator to keep everything up to date and running in top shape.

To keep the network up to date, you need to apply patches and updates from software vendors. After software is released, the vendor will usually release bug fixes and improvements, called patches and service packs, which you can download from the vendor's Web site. These patches and service packs will not necessarily jump out at you as being needed. You may need to use the vendor's Web site to search through support forums to find out that you need to install a patch.

These updates come with documentation in the form of text files, or readme files. Be sure to read these files before implementing the patch or update. There usually are certain steps to follow in order to successfully install the patch or service pack. It is a good idea to print out the readme file so you can easily refer to it during installation.

Vendors release any necessary patches and service packs in between full upgrades. Upgrades sometimes cost the customer money and other times are available for downloading from the vendor's Web site. In addition to keeping your network current with the latest software upgrades, you need to upgrade your firmware (software programmed into the hardware). Firmware updates are becoming more and more available at manufacturers' Web sites.

In addition to updating and maintaining your software and firmware, you have to perform routine daily and weekly tasks to keep your network up and running. These tasks include backup routines, anti-virus software configuration and update, and maintaining and updating non-server software.

The two common types of media used in backup tape drives are DAT (Digital Audio Tape) and DLT (Digital Linear Tape). DAT, originally used for recording audio, was ported into the computer field for storing data as a backup. DLT drives support faster performance and larger capacities than DAT drives do. Tape software has to be loaded on the server in order to run on a regular schedule. On Windows NT the tape software runs as a service, and on NetWare it is a loaded module and will be listed in the loaded list of modules when using the CTRL-ESC key sequence.

There are three main types of backup: full, differential, and incremental. A full backup backs up all data on the drive. An incremental backup backs up any files that have changed or were added since the last incremental or full backup. (This means the first incremental backup is actually a full backup.) A differential backup backs up any files that have changed or were added since the last full backup.

Another part of network maintenance is updating and patching any business-driving applications that run at the workstation. One good example of this is a database that is stored on the server but the application is resident on the workstation hard disk. Each workstation must be updated individually.

In today's networks there is a serious threat of data loss from virus infections. To protect from this, you must install anti-virus protection on the network. Installing a virus protection suite such as InoculateIT or McAfee is vital to safeguard data against loss.

Anti-virus software has different components that have to be configured properly to protect your network from serious threat. First is the component that runs at the server level doing routine scans to ensure data is not infected with a virus. Second is the workstation component that scans the workstation to ensure data is protected from infection. Third, and probably most important, is the real-time protection that can be loaded on the server and the workstation to constantly monitor all files that are opened, saved, copied, or accessed in any way. This component keeps the workstation, the server, and the entire network protected by monitoring in real time versus scanning at scheduled intervals.

To ensure that each of these components works the way you want it to, you have to choose which drives to scan, what types of files to scan, and what to do with infected files. You can choose to exclude certain types of files from scanning, and to cure an infected file or simply report on it in the activity log.

With the threat of new viruses every day, anti-virus software vendors continually update their virus signature files. A virus signature file is a database of known viruses that the anti-virus software uses to detect and cure viruses. These updates are available usually monthly from the software vendors and can be retrieved automatically by the software or implemented manually to keep from corrupting the database or any files in the live software.

TWO-MINUTE DRILL

- ❑ It is usually a good idea to read through software documentation and then reread the documentation and any corresponding addendums or readme files.

- ❑ Vendors release updates or patches to their products when bugs are found or to simply make them run better.

- ❑ Microsoft and Novell have a service pack for the core network operating system.

- ❑ The vendor's Web site will most likely have the patches and service packs that you need for your software.

- ❑ Applying a patch incorrectly can bring down the entire network.

- ❑ The exam hits a lot of scenarios for troubleshooting and maintenance. Be sure to understand each component: patches, upgrades, virus signatures, backups, etc. This chapter is important in the role of passing the exam.

- ❑ You should always install an upgrade on a stand-alone machine before distributing it to the network.

❑ There are firmware updates for the various ROMs that exist in servers and workstations.

❑ With the coming of year 2000, ROM updates are especially important.

❑ There is more to network maintenance than patches and updates, including providing and testing a backup solution and providing and updating anti-virus software.

❑ Every network administrator should have a backup routine.

❑ The two common types of tape drives are DAT and DLT.

❑ A *full backup* backs up every file on the specified volume or volumes.

❑ An *incremental backup* backs up the files that have changed or were added since the last incremental or full backup.

❑ A *differential backup* backs up the files that have changed or were added since the last full backup.

❑ You will definitely see a question or two on the exam about the different kinds of backups. Be sure to know the differences between full, incremental, and differential, especially the last two, which can be the most confusing. You may be given a scenario and have to pick the backup plan and restoration process.

❑ The other side to maintaining the network is logging the activity and documenting every change or update that is applied.

❑ When you install Anti-virus software in a networked environment, you must set multiple configuration items.

❑ The exam will test your knowledge of client- and server-side virus scanning implementations. Remember that in order to be fully secure from viruses, you need servers that continually scan files on the network for viruses on file servers, and workstations that scan for viruses on users' workstations. Users commonly bring in viruses through floppies and e-mail.

❑ To ensure the integrity of the data on your network, you must keep your virus signature files up to date.

❑ The exam will hit on the subject of virus signatures. You need to know what they are and how to update them.

SELF TEST

The following Self Test questions will help you measure your understanding of the material presented in this chapter. Read all the choices carefully, as there may be more than one correct answer. Choose all correct answers for each question.

1. What is one key component of installing an update or patch successfully on your network?

   A. Reading competitors' documentation to see whose is better, and then selecting the better package.

   B. Reading the readme files and documentation to make sure you have the information you need to install the application successfully.

   C. Reading the documentation on the server to see if the software is compatible with the server.

   D. Reading the Web site home page to see if the product is still in production.

2. To make sure you have the most up-to-date files and version of the software, you need to go to the vendor's Web site and download the most current what?

   A. Software packs

   B. Network packs

   C. Software patches

   D. Readme files

3. Network operating systems, such as NetWare and Windows NT, have these to update the specific modules within the operating system?

   A. Supdate packs

   B. Service calls

   C. Serial pack

   D. Service pack

4. Where can you go to search for information on errors you are receiving on your network to see if you need a patch or service pack?

   A. Vendor's online support forums

   B. Excite search engine

   C. Control Panel under System

   D. Help section under Start menu

5. When software vendors want to update their software in a major way and bring out a new version, this is known as a what? (Hint: This is sometimes free and sometimes costs money.)

   A. Update

   B. Upgrade

   C. Upload

   D. Patch

6. Along with updating the software, there is something dealing with the hardware that may need to be updated. What is it called?

   A. RAM

   B. ROM

   C. Formware

   D. Adapter

7. To keep a consistent approach to network maintenance, it is important to do what?

   A. Format one hard disk per month on your network to clean up hard disk space.

   B. Get into the routine of downloading patches that are not for your network just so you have a grasp of everything that is out there.

   C. Get into the routine of applying updates and patches on your network on a regular basis.

   D. Delete and reconfigure your system volumes on your servers on an annual basis.

8. What is the first thing you need to do to install backup software on your network server?

   A. Physically install the tape drive and any adapter boards that are needed. Along with this, connect the cables between the tape drive and the adapter board. Also make sure that power is connected.

   B. Make sure your backup software has everything in it before proceeding.

   C. Refer to the specific instructions for your backup software for any unique pre-installation items.

   D. Make sure the system that you are installing to meets the hardware and software requirements.

9. You are running a Windows NT Server and want to know if your backup software is running. Where do you go to get this information?

   A. Go to My Computer and select the tape drive.

   B. Go to Control Panel and select Backup.

   C. Use the CTRL-ESC sequence and select the screen for the backup software.

   D. Go to the Control Panel and select Services.

10. What are the two common types of tape drives in today's networks? (Select two.)

    A. DDS

    B. DAT

    C. DLT

    D. DET

11. Which of the following is *not* a backup job type?

    A. Full

    B. Incremental

    C. Differential

    D. Incidental

12. Along with updating your server-specific software, such as backup software and virus software, what else should you update?

    A. Application software, such as databases that are stored on the server but run the application at the workstation.

B. Cables that connect your network between the workstation and the hub.

C. Server hard disks when new ones come out.

D. User directories that contain user data should be updated with other users' data.

13. Which of the following is a component of a virus protection suite? (Choose all that apply.)

A. Real-time scanner

B. Local scanner

C. Network/Domain scanner

D. ROM scanner

14. What available options are there for taking care of viruses? (Choose all that apply.)

A. Move file

B. Cure file

C. Delete File

D. Copy file

15. If you want to scan local or mapped network drives, which of the following options should you choose?

A. Network Scanner

B. Local Scanner

C. Real-Time Scanner

D. Disk Recovery Option

16. How often are virus signatures generally updated by the vendor or manufacturer?

A. Daily

B. Weekly

C. Monthly

D. Annually

17. What are the main advantages to DLT tape drives over DAT tape drives? (Choose all that apply.)

A. Faster data transfer rates

B. Higher storage capacity

C. Higher reliability

D. Higher availability

E. More accurate

18. When DAT tapes were emerging as a popular storage media for computer data, a format was given to the storage of computer data; what is this format known as?

A. DDS

B. DDT

C. DAT

D. DLT

19. You installed a tape drive in your server. The server has an existing SCSI controller and other SCSI devices in the system. Since adding the SCSI tape drive to the SCSI chain you get errors from two devices. What is the most likely cause of this type of problem?

A. Tape drive is not compatible with system.

B. SCSI ID is unique, not enabling the tape drive to communicate in the SCSI chain.

C. SCSI ID is the same on the two devices, causing a conflict.

D. The IDE connector is not hooked up on the tape drive.

20. You have been running a full backup at the beginning of the week and incremental backups on the remaining four days. Your hard drive crashes and you have to restore from tape. What is the proper method for restoring from tape with this backup scenario?

A. Restore from the last full backup only.

B. Restore from the last full backup and the most recent incremental backup.

C. Restore from only the incremental backups.

D. Restore from the last full backup and all incremental backup tapes since the last full backup.

21. You are the network administrator for a small company. Your boss wants you to have the quickest available restoration method in the event of data loss. She also wants you to have the most up-to-date virus protection available.
Required results: Be able to restore from one tape in the event of hard disk failure. Be able to scan with most recent virus signature files.
Optional results: Have workstations and server as up to date as possible with virus software.

Proposed Solution: Implement full backup daily and update virus software signatures once a year.

A. The proposed solution produces both the required and the optional results.

B. The proposed solution produces the required but not the optional results.

C. The proposed solution produces one of the required results and the optional result.

D. The proposed solution produces one of the required results and none of the optional results.

22. What is a good rule of thumb to follow when applying patches to a network if the files need to be copied into place manually?

A. Delete original files first and then copy new files in their place.

B. Rename the original files with an extension such as OLD or BAK and then copy the new files in place.

C. Copy the new files over the old files.

D. Copy the old files over the new ones in the temporary directory.

23. When updating ROMs there are two ways to tell if the ROM you are applying is newer than what you have currently. What are the two ways?

A. ROM date

B. ROM file size

C. ROM version

D. Manufacturer file name

24. With some software there is documentation that comes on the CD or disks. In order to read through this documentation, what do you need?

 A. A printer

 B. The correct viewer

 C. A Web browser

 D. A special code

25. To ensure proper disaster recovery in the event your office is burned to the ground, what is the minimum you should do to be able to restore from tape?

 A. Store the monthly tapes in your office.

 B. Keep the monthly tapes close to the server.

 C. Store the monthly tapes offsite.

 D. Store the monthly tapes with the office supplies.

11

Identifying, Assessing, and Responding to Problems

T he Network+ exam is very good at mimicking the problems you will be faced with in the real world. Passing the Network+ exam means you are well on your way to becoming a successful network professional, which means handling and prioritizing network problems. You will need to prioritize network problems, because you will often have more than one at a time. In the real world, there is not enough time, money, or employees to fix every network problem that arises. You will need to apply "Band-Aid fixes" sometimes to temporarily fix problems until you have spent enough time researching the problems and determining solutions. This chapter will help you in the real world just as much as it will help you to ace the Network+ exam.

Handling Network Problems

It is nearly impossible for a network to run smoothly without problems. Networks are in a constant state of flux and change, and they grow bigger and more complicated as the days go by. More computers are being added to the network and the amount of available bandwidth slowly decreases. These new computers not only chew up precious bandwidth, but they require one or more network cards, more cables, ports on the hubs, and, if you are using TCP/IP, these new computers must consume another IP address. In addition to the hardware, you must make sure the network interface card has been correctly configured and that the correct network protocols have been loaded and configured. TCP/IP is the protocol that requires more planning, configuration, and troubleshooting than all other protocols combined. Incidentally, that is why you will see tons of questions on your exam regarding TCP/IP. Not only do you need the required hardware and software to get these devices functioning on the network, but you need the knowledge and experience also. This is the most important piece of the networking puzzle. Without you, the network professional, a network device such as a hub is just a useless, expensive box with wires and blinking lights. The hub needs you to make it come to life and function. You must understand how this device works and how to diagnose and resolve problems related to this device and to every other device on your network. One mistake in any of the hardware or software configurations will cause a problem. It's your job to determine what to do in the event of one of these problems.

How do you know when you are having a network problem? The symptoms can be anything from strange, reoccurring problems, to a workstation that is not able to access network resources, or even worse, an entire department unable to log in. Identifying the symptoms of the problem is the first step in diagnosing and solving the problem. This is the information-gathering phase. The more time you spend during this phase, the quicker the problem can be solved. This is also the most stressful phase for you. You will encounter problems that are mind numbing, but the more time you spend identifying the symptoms, the more the cause will be revealed. This is also where you draw on your real-life experiences. Have you ever encountered a situation such as this before? If so, how did you handle the problem? You may also draw on your studies and the books you have read during this phase. Have you read of a problem such as this before?

exam
Ⓦatch

I was surprised at the number of troubleshooting-related questions on the exam. Whenever you are faced with a troubleshooting-related question, remember that identification of the symptoms and cause is the first step in the troubleshooting process.

After you have enough information concerning the symptoms of the problem, you need to determine the nature of the action required to solve the problem. This is where the road to recovery can take several different paths. The path you take will depend on the severity of the problem and the amount of time and energy required to fix the problem. Once you are aware of a network problem, the path you take will always involve working together as a team to solve the problem, asking for help, or escalating the problem. To determine the nature of the action required, you need to understand the circumstances involved with choosing one path over another. On more severe network problems you may find yourself going down every path, searching for the answer. The good news is, no matter what the problem, you will eventually find the solution.

Information Transfer

The computer industry is built on the transfer of tons of information. This information transfer refers not only to the exchange of data from one computer to another, but also to the exchange of data between human beings. Just as in school, where the teacher is teaching the students, you may find yourself as a network professional learning from others, or you may find yourself teaching others. This communication is essential for diagnosing and resolving network problems, or any problem for that matter. The saying, "Two heads are better than one," is absolutely applicable to the process of troubleshooting a network problem. A team of professionals can distribute the load of solving network problems by assigning a different diagnostic task to each person or by every member of the team collectively investigating the problem.

Task Assignment

In attempting to resolve a network problem, you can assign each person on the team a different task for diagnosing the problem. When you distribute the load between many people, one person is not burdened with the overwhelming task of solving the problem alone. However, one person's load may still be larger than another person's load. The point of distributing the work involved with troubleshooting is to enable one person to spend quality time in one area, so that this person can thoroughly understand the complexities of the task. Bringing an entire group up to speed on a concept such as routing can be challenging. Picking one specialist to investigate the possible routing issues and report his findings to the group can be very beneficial.

Another method of assigning tasks could be to have one person phone technical support, one person read through knowledge bases and resource kits, and one or more people work with the hardware or software to determine where the problem is. Everyone can then report their findings in a team meeting.

Team Collaboration

In attempting to resolve a network problem, you can have every member of the team collectively investigate the problem. Having the entire collective experience and knowledge of a group of people will guarantee that a problem will be solved. Highly experienced professionals can quickly determine where a problem lies and the best solution for solving the problem. Chances are good that someone in your group has experienced a problem such as this in the past.

This approach, as well as the first approach, requires tremendous amounts of communication. In troubleshooting, it often takes another person to stimulate the thoughts of a person who is on the verge of discovering the problem. This method also works in reverse. One person can be banging his head against a wall trying to solve the problem, and someone who is not immersed in the problem can ask a simple question from an outsider's perspective that can shed some new light on the problem.

An essential aspect of communication, one that some technicians are lacking, is knowing when to ask for help. Many of us feel embarrassed when we have to stop to ask for help. You should feel proud of yourself that you are stopping to ask for help. Would you rather stop and ask for help, or just continue reconfiguring things until the network completely breaks? Some technicians will never ask for help. These are not the types of technicians you want on your team. You need a team that can communicate effectively.

on the
Job

At the last job I interviewed for, the manager said there was no place for hot shots on his team. He said that he has been burned by technicians who do not adhere to standards and spend time reconfiguring a workstation any way possible until it works. Rather than escalate the problem, they sit there and goof around until the problem fixes itself. This often causes more problems, especially in a tightly run ship where settings are configured for a reason.

Do not feel that you are any less of a technician because you are asking for help. You will be admired by your peers and bosses as someone who is concerned with finding the problem as a team. Another saying comes to mind: "There is no 'I' in TEAMWORK."

Handholding

It's just a matter of time before you encounter a problem that you and your team are just not knowledgeable enough to solve. This is quite common in this fast-moving computer industry. You are not expected to know

FROM THE FIELD

Everyone Can Contribute to Solving a Problem

At one of my first network jobs, my boss and I were sent out to network separate branches of a corporation to the company headquarters. My boss, who knew more than I did, was taking complete control of the situation, and I didn't feel very much a part of the process. He felt it was better for him to spend the time and work on the problem without having to explain every step to me as he went. Therefore, I felt unaware of what was going on. He had me do simple tasks to keep me busy while he focused on the much more complicated issues, such as routing and the WINS Service. It was obvious he was having problems, but he did not want to ask for help. As the hours passed, he slowly began revealing the problems he was having. "I know we are having a WINS replication problem. I can just tell." Although he didn't have the answers, he was headed down the right track. Not knowing as much about WINS as he did, I could offer little help on the technical complexities of WINS. However, I contributed in a different way. I would ask him, "How do you know it's a WINS problem?" He would then try to explain the situation, but before he could finish his explanation, a light bulb would go off in his head and he would continue down another path. "It could be routing, because we can't replicate with the WINS server on the other side of the router," he said. "How did you configure the routing?" I would ask him, and once again, before he finished his explanation, he would get another idea and investigate it. At times, I would also try talking highly technically with him, just to fuel his troubleshooting process. Eventually, we solved the problem, which was just a router that needed to be reset before changes would take effect. After feeling very happy that we fixed the problem, I admitted that I didn't really have any idea of what was going on, but I felt the more I stimulated his mental process, the further he would get, and he agreed. The more you can verbalize the problem, the clearer your mind becomes. You will find that teachers have a great understanding of concepts, because they are able to verbalize complicated issues with ease. Once you begin explaining problems to others, you will find yourself thinking of the problem in a new light and you will be further down the road to solving the problem. There is no better feeling than solving a problem that has been challenging you for hours, or even days. All it takes is working together.

—Cameron Brandon, MCSE+Internet, CNE, A+, Network+

everything; however, you are expected to know when and where to look for answers. If you and your team are not able to solve the problem, you need to find additional information and resources to solve the problem. These can take the forms of resource kits, online help, and telephone technical support.

Resource Kits

Resource kits are a valuable way of educating yourself. These are helpful for planning, implementing, configuring, and, most of all, troubleshooting. Microsoft includes the resource kits on the same TechNet CD as the Knowledge Base. The resource kits are more for reading and planning, whereas the Knowledge Base is loaded with information on symptoms, causes, and solutions to problems. If you are having a problem with a Microsoft product, you should consult the TechNet CD for more information. You should read through the resource kits and verify that you have implemented and configured the software correctly. If you are still having problems, query the Knowledge Base to see if you can find a posted solution to the same problem you are having. These solutions are often comprised of step-by-step actions that must be taken to solve the problem.

Online Help

The Internet is the most helpful resource for researching network problems. If you believe you are having a problem with a particular product or device, you should begin your search with the manufacturer's Web site. You will find information such as updated drivers and patches, detailed installation instructions, troubleshooting tips, and possibly a knowledge base of common problems. You should never feel embarrassed that you need to search on the manufacturer's Web site for answers to a problem. There is too much software with bugs and too many incompatible software drivers out there to not find updated software. You should always find the latest patches and drivers if you determine that you are experiencing problems with this software. Updated patches and drivers are there for a reason: they fix bugs and improve functionality. If the software was right the first time, there would be no need for a second version of the driver or no need for a software patch.

Telephone Technical Support

Most technicians feel that telephone tech support is the very last resort. I don't agree. Who would know more about solving a problem with a product than the people who spend eight hours a day on the phone solving problems with that particular product? They encounter every type of problem possible with their product, from small 10-node networks, to the largest companies in the world. They also troubleshoot their product on many different operating systems. These phone support personnel have a database of known problems and resolutions that they can query if they don't have the immediate answer. They can also escalate the problem to more knowledgeable engineers. I have found that almost all my problems were answered within minutes on the first call. Their response can be as simple as, "Yes, we know about that problem. Download the newest patch to fix it."

I agree that sometimes telephone support can lead down a dead-end road, but that shouldn't deter you from at least calling and seeing whether there has been a similar problem reported. These support personnel can also lead you step-by-step through installing, testing, and configuring their product. This will often reveal details that you didn't adhere to during the initial installation that was giving you problems. The support personnel can also provide you with troubleshooting steps to get at the cause of the problem quickly. When you are troubleshooting a complicated problem, don't ignore telephone technical support, because they may have a quick and easy answer.

Unfortunately, telephone technical support is not free. Some companies charge steep prices per incident, which may be out of the reach of some companies' budgets. Large corporations usually have no problems opening up phone support incidences, as long as the problem gets resolved. I have worked for companies that run the gamut of philosophies for using phone technical support. Some companies prefer you exhaust every possible resource first, such as Microsoft TechNet, resources kits, online help, and documentation, before you open up a support incident. The phone support call would be the extreme last resort, mostly because of the cost involved. Other companies do not hesitate to call phone support as the first line of defense. Many times you can save yourself hours of frustration if you just call for help beforehand. Sometimes the answer is quite simple. Sometimes the problem is as simple as downloading a new driver. However, if you have spent hours, even days on a particular problem and have involved many of your highest-level on-site support personnel, and still haven't solved the problem, you should consider calling technical support. By solving the problem more quickly, your company can save money in the long run. In this situation, the initial cost of opening up a phone support incident was outweighed by the resolution of a challenging problem.

Technical Service

Many times it is not possible to determine the cause of a network problem with conventional tools. Networks have become so complicated that you need advanced tools to determine some complex network problems. These tools happen to be very expensive, which puts them out of reach for the average network administrator. Network monitors and analyzers can inspect the packets travelling over the network and determine if any problems are occurring, such as broadcast storms.

on the
Job

One site I worked had ongoing bandwidth issues. The network seemed to be more congested than it should be. We didn't have the tools or knowledge to test for complex network problems, so we called in Bay Networks. They brought in a network analyzer and quickly determined that we had NetBEUI, AppleTalk, and IPX/SPX packets travelling the network. This was strange because we only used TCP/IP. We found some print servers were also using NetBEUI, AppleTalk, and IPX/SPX protocols in addition to TCP/IP because someone didn't uncheck these protocols during installation of the print server. Bay Networks also determined that we had a bottleneck in one area of our network that most packets had to travel. We had been unaware of this bottleneck, and armed with this information, we replaced the affected area and the network was back to running great.

Not only do you sometimes need professional equipment to monitor your network, but you also need professionals that are trained on the tools to analyze and identify possible afflicted areas based on the results. A network capture of hundreds of packets may be Greek to you, but these professionals are trained to interpret the results.

Even more common than having professionals come in to analyze the network is the need to contract the phone company for wiring issues. You do not have the tools such as Tone Generators and time domain reflectometers (TDRs) to analyze possible cable problems. Incidentally, both Tone Generators and TDRs will be discussed in more depth in Chapter 12.

At my last job, it was very common to see the phone company in the wiring closet, server room, and everywhere around the site connecting new areas. For the average administrator, this will not be your job. The lines are blurring between the phone company and network engineers, who both can be responsible for wiring. The phone company is usually subcontracted to do wiring work. This means that you should stay in close contact with them, because they may be your best allies in the event you are troubleshooting a network-related problem. Take advantage of their knowledge and tools for troubleshooting.

Documentation

In order to maintain a smoothly running network, it is imperative that you keep adequate documentation of everything from computer specifications, recent upgrades, future projects, and a list of known issues and resolved problems with each server on your network. This documentation is important for a number of reasons:

- You have something to refer to if it is determined the computer was configured incorrectly.

- You can provide instructions for the next administrator or engineer.

- You can keep accurate inventory or records for each device on the network.

- Year-end inventories are made easier with documentation.

Incorrect Configuration

Documentation is essential in the event a computer was configured incorrectly. With a large group of support personnel, it may be difficult to determine who was the last to configure a certain server that is no longer functioning or is not working to its fullest potential. Determining who is responsible is not the same thing as finding someone to blame when something goes wrong. Support personnel often configure servers and network devices in a unique way, without sharing that information with the rest of the group. By documenting the modifications to the server, you can determine what has changed and whether that change is adversely affecting the server. If the person responsible for configuring this server or network device has left, you now have the existing documentation to determine what was changed, without the need to contact the person.

The documentation must include the technician's name, as well as the date the upgrade or modification took place. This is helpful for determining the order of chronological events that can be traced in the event of an emergency.

Future Administrators or Engineers

Documentation provides a set of instructions for the next administrator or engineer. Each network administrator or engineer has countless secrets they keep inside for the network that they support. Every day they are configuring, adding, and modifying servers, workstations, printers, and devices on the network. Each one of these experiences may require custom configuration or troubleshooting in order to be installed correctly. Network support personnel can spend hours, if not days, getting something to work correctly, yet they rarely spend the time to document their findings for future use. If they leave the company, this information goes with them. The next administrator or engineer may find himself spending as much or more time than the original person trying to get the same problem resolved. If the previous person had documented his findings, it would have made the second person's job much easier.

Device Inventory

Proper documentation includes an accurate inventory or record for each device on the network. Documenting devices on the network gives you a current record of countless details about these devices. For example, you can document the amount of physical memory, the hard disk capacity, the IP address, the processor speed, the MAC address, and the serial numbers. This information can be stored in a centralized database for all computer support personnel to use. Many companies are very strict about keeping accurate, up-to-date information for their network. It is strongly recommended that you adhere to these documentation standards. If no standards currently exist, it is recommended that you start a project to inventory the network with as much information as possible. You will be surprised by how often you consult this information when it comes to locating devices, determining which devices need to be upgraded, and performing remote managing and software distribution.

Year-End Inventories

Proper documentation makes year-end inventories easier. These inventories also help for companies that have leased or bought computers from the corporation and need to report their inventory at the end of the year. I have had to visit nearly every workstation and server on a network when corporate requested an audit of all machines that were purchased from the corporate computer fund. If we had kept better documentation, I could have used this information and saved hours. If you don't currently have serial number information in your hardware inventory database, now is a good time to start.

Prioritizing Network Problems

You can expect to find yourself in a situation with more than one network problem at a time. This is not uncommon in the real world. Sometimes smaller problems are put on the back burner while the larger, more urgent problems are investigated. If you encounter more than one network problem, you need to prioritize them based on their severity. This often comes down to which problem is affecting users the most. If users are not able to do their work, then of course this becomes a major priority. You must do everything you can to get the users up and running as quickly as possible, because they could be at a standstill until you solve the network problem. When users are at a standstill, managers become impatient with the lack of work being done. Users feel the stress from management and become impatient with you to fix the problem. Performing under this stress can hamper your ability to think clearly.

Another important factor to consider when prioritizing network problems is the estimated amount of time to solve the problem. If you have a network problem that has been estimated to require 25 hours to complete by two support personnel, you may opt to rank this lower than a job that requires three hours for one person. Quick network problems, such as resetting a user's password, are often higher on the list of priorities because they can be fixed in a matter of minutes.

You should not use the estimated amount of time required to solve the problem as the only means of prioritizing network problems. For example, if you have a project that will take an estimated five hours to complete in order for the entire network to finally be up and running, this should take precedence over a 30-minute job restructuring the directories on the file server. The amount of time required to complete the job is now overshadowed by the extremely high priority of getting a failed network operational again.

When disaster strikes, you will notice how everything gets put on the back burner while all available resources are used to solve the network problem. Many projects are dependent on the network functioning correctly anyway, so it may be impossible to complete these tasks if the network is down.

High-Priority Problems

Any network problem that affects a large number of users should receive a high priority. Of course, you have to determine which network problems affect functions the users can live without for a period of time. If users cannot access important servers, you should make that a very high priority.

You will receive a lot of calls about problems that affect a large number of users. As stated before, any network problem that affects a user's ability to do his work should receive a high priority. Any problem that affects a large number of users or any of the functions listed below should be ranked high on the list of prioritized network problems:

- Logging on and becoming authenticated
- Accessing e-mail
- Printing
- Accessing a database

Obviously, if users cannot log on to the network, they have no access to network resources. Users may be able to work with local resources, such as a word processor, but will not be able to retrieve or store any information on a network server.

Users complain most about the inability to receive e-mail and the inability to print. It is becoming very common for companies and departments to share reports, orders, meeting information, and announcements via e-mail. If users cannot access e-mail, they will not be able to do their jobs. And users print everything. When they can't print, you will find out very quickly. The problem could be major, such as the downing of a print server, or it could just affect one printer, such as a hardware malfunction.

on the **Job**

At one site, the e-mail server went down for a day. I didn't realize how many users relied on e-mail until that day. One user received time-sensitive requests every day from another company for orders to be filled, and without access to e-mail, the user could not fill these orders for the company. You will be surprised how e-mail is being used in your company to exchange schedules, reports, and announcements.

Databases are why most companies use computers and networks. Databases contain critical information, such as employee records, distributor and client information, and any information related to the company's products. If users cannot access a database to add, modify, or delete records, you will know.

Low-Priority Problems

When you have more than one network problem at a time, it will be fairly evident which problem takes precedence. The problems discussed in this section are important conditions that should be resolved soon, but if you are experiencing more than one network problem, these should receive a lower priority. The following is a list of problems that affect users but do not warrant a very high priority:

- Annoying or nagging prompts
- Slow network access
- Inability to access less-used information
- Inability to print to a *desired* printer

Users will call you when they receive unusual system prompts and when printing or network access has slowed. The system prompts usually do not indicate a critical condition. It is common to see errors, or mild problems, with logon scripts that appear to the user as an error. Usually these prompts are just informational or a warning. Slow system access may be annoying to the users, but it is not a high priority if you have another problem to resolve.

If users cannot access less-used information, but can still work, you should resolve other network problems before addressing this one.

If a user cannot print to a desired printer, but can print to a different printer, or if a user cannot print to any printer and does not need to print in order to work, this problem receives a low priority.

The following items are system maintenance and do not affect users directly. They should receive a low priority when you have a high-priority network problem to resolve:

- Updating a version of software or driver
- Applying a patch to a program
- Changing or disabling a protocol

Installing updates to software or drivers is never a high priority, unless the updated version of the software fixes a critical bug. Remember that you should test the patch or version update on a test machine before implementing it in the field.

Migrating from one protocol to another, such as from NetBEUI to TCP/IP, is not a high priority, unless you have workstations that cannot access the network until the migration takes place. Some companies run NetBEUI under TCP/IP as a backup, just in case TCP/IP doesn't work correctly. This type of migration takes planning, which automatically drops it to a lower priority.

Now that you have seen some of the possible network conditions that could exist, the following is a quick reference to test your ability to prioritize conditions based on their seriousness.

exam
ⓦatch

Expect a question or two similar to the ones in the next section. The Network+ exam is trying to test your ability to determine which condition is the most serious, based on a given scenario.

QUESTIONS AND ANSWERS

Some users are experiencing problems accessing the color printer. Another department is having trouble logging on.	Logging on is more important than accessing the color printer.
One user cannot access the materials database, while a number of users are receiving a message that the database is currently busy.	Accessing a critical database is a higher priority than warning or information messages.
A few users are noticing that the network is slow this week. One user's password no longer works.	A user's inability to gain access to the network is a higher priority than a mild decrease in network performance.
A bridge is currently locking a couple times a week and needs to be replaced.	A bridge locking up can render an entire network segment useless, so this is definitely a higher priority.
A power surge has downed the messaging server, the database server, and two printers.	Although users' access to the messaging server (e-mail), the database server, and the printers is very important, the database server is most likely the more critical of the two servers, and the printers can wait until the critical servers are online.

You will find that with experience you don't even need to think about where to begin the process of prioritizing. When you receive a call from a user, you will instantly know where it ranks with your current projects.

CERTIFICATION SUMMARY

In this chapter you learned how to handle one or more network problems. You need to gather as much information as possible during the diagnosing of a network problem. You need to determine the nature of the action required to solve the problem. This involves several resources, such as communication with team members, resource kits, knowledge bases, online help, and telephone technical support. With these resources you can determine where the problem lies and how to go about solving the problem. Notice you didn't learn anything about actually solving the problem. This is for Chapter 12.

You learned about the method of prioritizing network problems when one or more conditions exist at the same time. This can be a stressful time, but with the understanding of which problems require a higher priority, you can line up tasks in your queue based on priority to efficiently manage all your tasks at once.

 # TWO-MINUTE DRILL

❑ TCP/IP is the protocol that requires more planning, configuration, and troubleshooting than all other protocols combined. That is why you will see tons of questions on your exam regarding TCP/IP.

❑ Identifying the symptoms of the problem is the first step in diagnosing and solving the problem.

❑ There are a number of troubleshooting-related questions on the exam. Whenever you are faced with a troubleshooting-related question, remember that identification of the symptoms and cause is the first step in the troubleshooting process.

❑ Communication is essential for diagnosing and resolving network problems, or any problem for that matter.

❑ A team of professionals can distribute the load of solving network problems by assigning a different diagnostic task to each person or by every member of the team collectively investigating the problem.

❑ If you and your team are not able to solve the problem, you need to find additional information and resources to solve the problem. These can take the forms of resource kits, online help, and telephone technical support.

❑ Microsoft includes the resource kits on the same TechNet CD as the Knowledge Base.

❑ The Internet is the most helpful resource for researching network problems.

❑ Network monitors and analyzers can inspect the packets travelling over the network and determine if any problems are occurring, such as broadcast storms.

❑ It is imperative that you keep adequate documentation of everything from computer specifications, recent upgrades, future projects, and a list of known issues and resolved problems with each server on your network.

❑ If you encounter more than one network problem, you need to prioritize them based on their severity.

❑ Any network problem that affects a large number of users should receive a high priority.

❑ When you have more than one network problem at a time, it will be fairly evident which problem takes precedence.

❑ The Network+ exam tries to test your ability to determine which condition is the most serious, based on a given scenario.

SELF TEST

The following Self Test questions will help you measure your understanding of the material presented in this chapter. Read all the choices carefully, as there may be more than one correct answer. Choose all correct answers for each question.

1. Which of the following is most likely not a problem when adding another workstation to the network segment?

    A. The workstation is not able to find a domain controller on the network.

    B. The bridge can no longer handle the amount of traffic on the network and begins to lock up.

    C. The workstation is not able to receive an IP address.

    D. The workstation has an error concerning the network card on boot up.

2. What is the first step to solving a problem?

    A. Replicating the problem

    B. Calling telephone technical support

    C. Gathering information

    D. Establishing a baseline

3. Why is it best to assign tasks to team members while you are troubleshooting a network problem?

    A. To keep them separated

    B. To avoid them working on the same problem

    C. To put a person in their special area of expertise

    D. To minimize duplicate information

4. Why would you want to brainstorm the problem as a group?

    A. To keep everyone interested

    B. To not isolate anyone

    C. To see if anyone has changed anything recently that you don't know about

    D. To see if anyone has experienced this problem before

5. Which of the following are reasons you should stop and ask for help if you encounter a problem that you are unable to fix? (Choose all that apply.)

    A. You may be fired if you continue further.

    B. Someone else may have the answer you are looking for.

    C. You may worsen the situation if you continue.

    D. Someone may ridicule you.

6. You are working on a user's computer that cannot access the employee database. You have tried everything on the workstation, but the user still cannot connect. What is the next logical step in arriving at a solution to the problem?

    A. Reboot the user's machine.

    B. Call the database administrator to see if anything has changed.

    C. Open up a phone incident with the manufacturer of the product.

    D. Check the resource kits for a possible solution.

7. You are not expected to know everything in your position as network administrator or engineer. However, what are you expected to know?

   A. The technical support phone numbers for every manufacturer of devices that you have on the network

   B. The version of every piece of software currently being used on the network

   C. The answer to nearly every user-related problem

   D. Where to find information

8. What is the difference between a resource kit and a knowledge base?

   A. The resource kits are free and the knowledge bases are not.

   B. The knowledge bases contain fixes to known problems.

   C. The resource kits are only for reference.

   D. The knowledge base comes with the product, and the resource kit does not.

9. Where can you go to obtain the latest driver for a device?

   A. The CD that came with the product

   B. The resource kit

   C. The manufacturer's Web site

   D. The knowledge base

10. You are having a problem with the Shiva LANRemote dial-up networking server. Which of the following will most likely not be of any help in solving the problem?

   A. The Shiva Web site

   B. TechNet

   C. The documentation that came with the product

   D. Telephone tech support

11. You are getting continual errors when you are running IBM's Personal Communications terminal emulation software. You have been in contact with IBM technical support already, and they have advised you to try their new .dll file that they e-mailed you. You are not exactly sure how to test the new bug fix. What should you do in this situation?

   A. Put the .dll in the Windows directory.

   B. Check their Web site for instructions.

   C. Call IBM technical support.

   D. Put the .dll in the Windows\system directory.

12. Which of the following resources should you consider using before you call tech support? (Choose all that apply.)

   A. Resource kits

   B. Web sites

   C. Microsoft TechNet

   D. Documentation

13. Which of the following are reasons that you may need to consult technical service professionals to analyze your network? (Choose all that apply.)

   A. They are highly trained to analyze the results.

B. Management does not trust you with the task.

C. They are very inexpensive.

D. They have expensive hardware and software for monitoring the network.

14. You have one building that has been having intermittent problems communicating with the administration building. How could you go about researching the problem?

A. Check error logs for more information.

B. Hire a company to do an analysis of your network, including capturing packets.

C. Ping the affected areas and check the response time.

D. Have the phone company check the wiring between the two buildings.

15. A company released a service pack for their product, but quickly released a notice that the service pack should not be applied. The notice instructed administrators to uninstall the service pack and wait for the newest release. You have already upgraded a few servers with this service pack. How would you determine which servers have this service pack applied and which do not?

A. Consult the documentation that is continually updated with the server.

B. Ask everyone in the department if they installed the service pack.

C. Check the event log for the date the service pack was installed.

D. Check the operating system version for the new service pack.

16. Unfortunately, your current network supervisor is moving and must quit the company. What is the best way to ensure the next administrator has enough information concerning the network configuration?

A. Have the two administrators overlap in employment for at least a month.

B. Have the new administrator call the old administrator.

C. Have the old administrator spend his last week documenting everything he can about the network.

D. Do nothing. The old administrator most likely has bad habits that you do not want to pass on to the next administrator.

17. Which of the following information is not helpful to keep in the database of network devices?

A. MAC address

B. Number of services running

C. IP address

D. Amount of physical memory installed

18. Which of the following appears to be the most important condition and should warrant the highest priority?

A. A user cannot log on.

B. One of the printers is jammed.

C. Several users are receiving a message that their hard drives are full.

D. The network is slower than normal accessing the Internet.

19. Which of the following appears to be the most important condition and should warrant the highest priority?

A. Several users are receiving a message that their hard drives are full.

B. Several users are receiving a message that their e-mail inbox limit has been exceeded.

C. The network is slower than normal accessing the Internet.

D. A printer is down in the accounting department.

20. Which of the following appears to be the most important condition and should warrant the highest priority?

A. A few users cannot access the employee time reporting database.

B. A printer is down in the accounting department.

C. Several users are receiving a message that their e-mail inbox limit has been exceeded.

D. A user cannot access his personal drive on the network.

21. The personnel department is having trouble accessing their corporate-wide database system for checking job postings. Why does this warrant a higher priority?

A. Because they are handling job postings.

B. Because they are in the personnel department.

C. Because the problem is affecting a large number of users.

D. Because they are using an older system.

22. McAfee has just announced they have a new version of their virus-checking software available on their Web site. Why should this not be the highest priority; or should it be?

A. It should be the highest priority because it is virus-scanning software.

B. It should be the highest priority because it is a new release of a program.

C. It should not be the highest priority because patches and fixes are not a priority unless they address issues that affect your network.

D. It should not be the highest priority because virus-scanning is not very important compared to other issues on the network.

23. Which of the following appears to be the least important condition and should warrant the lowest priority?

A. A printer is down in the accounting department.

B. Several users are receiving a message that their hard drives are full.

C. The network is slower than normal accessing the Internet.

D. A user cannot log on.

24. You just arrived to work this morning and you have four new voice messages. Which of the following messages appears to be the least important condition, and should warrant the lowest priority?

   A. "I'm getting an error that says I cannot access my personal drive on the network."

   B. "I'm trying to load a Web page and it says the page is outdated."

   C. "Steve and I can't print to the LaserJet over here in accounting."

   D. "It's telling me my password is expired."

25. Your boss gave you a list of things you are to accomplish in the near future. Which of the following items on the list should be done first?

   A. Migrate all workstations from NetBEUI to TCP/IP.

   B. Give Nina access to the color printer in the administration building.

   C. Upgrade the McAfee Virus Scan engine on the servers.

   D. Upgrade the hub in the development room.

CERTIFICATION

12

Troubleshooting the Network

One the most important parts of operating a network is knowing how to deal with problems on the network when they arise. Hopefully, during your tenure as a network administrator, the skills you learn here will not be applied very often. You cannot learn the resolution to every problem that exists. You can, however, learn a methodology to find and diagnose nearly every problem in a systematic and logical manner.

CERTIFICATION OBJECTIVE 12.01

Managing Network Problems

Data communication is still not bullet proof. Many things can go wrong when we are networking several different types of computers, mainframes, printers, and network devices using different operating systems, protocols, and data transfer methods. When problems occur you need to not only have an understanding of each of the devices on your network, but you need to have an understanding of the network as a whole. Learning how each device coexists and contributes to the network will provide you with a strong foundation for understanding how and why network-related problems occur and how to resolve them. If you don't understand how a router works, you will be quite overwhelmed when one segment of your network cannot communicate with another segment. If you have a very good understanding of routers and routing, and one segment of your network cannot communicate with another segment, you will immediately know that there is a problem with routing; possibly a router is malfunctioning. It is helpful to classify the types of problems you are having and to ask yourself questions concerning the problem in order to stimulate your network problem-solving abilities.

Does the Problem Exist Across the Network?

When you first encounter a problem, it is very important to determine its scope. Is this problem with this specific machine, or does the problem exist across the network? You need to narrow the problem as soon as possible. If more than one computer is having the same problem at one time, then it is obvious that you are having a network problem and not a computer-specific problem. This phase often requires you to check the status of other computers on the network to determine if they are having the same problem.

on the
!
(j)o b

Determining if a problem is computer specific or network related often entails your standing up in your cubicle and yelling, "Is anyone else having network problems?" This was the scene at least three times last week when a bridge was having problems and it caused the entire network to go down. Instantly we determined it was not the local machine, and we could then continue researching a network-related problem.

If you are having a network-related problem, the symptoms of the problem are helpful in determining the cause of the problem. In the example of one segment of the network not being able to communicate with another segment, you quickly determined you had a routing problem. Another symptom is that everyone on the coaxial-based bus network is not able to communicate. The cause of this problem is most likely a problem with the network bus backbone, which requires terminators on each end. If the network backbone becomes severed, the end points will not be terminated and the data will echo through the network and render the entire network unusable. Another symptom is that one department of the company on a twisted-pair Ethernet network can no longer communicate with the rest of the network. The cause of this problem is most likely a problem with the hub used to connect this group. Hubs are used to connect groups of computers. The hub itself is then connected to the network backbone, and in this case, the connection to the network backbone may have been severed.

As you can see, quickly determining the scope of the problem is the first step in gathering information about the nature of the problem.

Workstation, Workgroup, LAN, or WAN Problem?

To continue the discussion on determining the scope of the problem, there are even more possibilities for error on larger networks. Not only are you faced with computer-specific problems, but you can have problems within your workgroup, local area network, or even the wide area network. For example, the users of the accounting department use a terminal-based order-entry system to transfer orders to the corporate headquarters. This is through terminal sessions on their computers, across the WAN to the corporate mainframe. One day the connection on a user's computer is not working. How can you diagnose such a complicated issue as this? First of all, you need to determine whether the problem is a workstation, workgroup, LAN, or WAN problem. You continue by going over to another computer and trying the connection. You find that this computer is having the same problem. Therefore, the problem is not computer specific. Luckily, this very program can be used to acquire the monthly sales orders from another terminal session, this time at the regional headquarters. The user is able to connect to the regional headquarters mainframe with no problems. Therefore, you have proved that you can at least get out to another remote location, but you still haven't determined the true cause of the problem. As it stands now, you may be having a routing problem with the corporate headquarters, a name resolution problem, or a mainframe connectivity problem. You can test the routing problem by trying to communicate with another computer on the corporate headquarters' network. For example, you could ping another computer on this network or use a program that connects to a computer on this network. You get the IP address for another computer on this network and ping it. You receive a response from this computer. Well, this determines that you don't have a routing problem to this remote network. Next, you get the IP address of the mainframe and attempt to ping it.

```
Pinging 207.149.40.41 with 32 bytes of data:
Request timed out.
Request timed out.
Request timed out.
Request timed out.
```

Well, there's your problem. The mainframe at corporate headquarters is down. You're sure that corporate is aware of the problem, so you decide not to pester them. You can check back every so often to determine if the problem has been fixed. Luckily, it's their problem and not yours!

on the
job

I can't tell you how many times I have benefited from carrying around a list of computer and network device IP addresses. If I need to ping a server on another network, I can simply consult my table of IP addresses, rather than call someone or go back to my cube and look up the information.

See how quickly you can determine the scope of the problem? It took only a few minutes to determine whether you had a workstation, workgroup, LAN, or WAN problem. Unfortunately, all problems won't be this easy to fix, but armed with the troubleshooting methodology presented here, you are on your way to solving any network problem that occurs.

Is the Problem Consistent and Replicable?

Sometimes you are faced with weird problems that are not so easy to solve. These problems require you to gain more information than just the scope of the problem. You may already know you are having a LAN or WAN problem, but you need more information to get you down the road to solving the problem. Next, you need to ask yourself: "Is the problem consistent and replicable?" To answer this, you need to determine a way to replicate the problem. For example, when someone in the purchasing department sends a job to the printer, it takes over five minutes for the job to print. Similar to the section before this, we need to learn if more than one computer is having this problem. We sent a print job from another computer, only to discover that the print job once again takes five minutes before it is printed. Well, we have a consistent problem that is replicable. The problem is not computer specific because we were able to replicate the problem on another computer. When we take a look at the print server, we discover that there are many jobs in the print queue, including one 120MB Excel document with 340 pages that is currently being printed in the finance department. Well, there is our problem. Chances are if we attempted to print after the print queue was empty, we would not have such a problem. Once again, notice how quickly we narrowed the problem. Also, notice how we used logic when determining the cause of the problem. We went to the next logical source in our printing problem: the print server.

We didn't immediately go to the router and check to see if it was routing correctly, and we didn't go to the domain controller to check whether the user had rights to print to this printer. We used logical troubleshooting methodology to arrive at the conclusion to the problem.

Standard Troubleshooting Methods

As you learned in the previous section, it is very important to isolate the subsystem involved with the process. When you are working with a problem internal to one computer, you learned to isolate the subsystem involved. For example, the system is not detecting your primary hard drive. What subsystem do you check? You check the disk subsystem, which includes the hard disk drive, the drive controller, and the drive cable. You wouldn't begin your troubleshooting by removing the video card and CD-ROM drive.

You must apply this methodology to solving network-related problems, too. In the previous section, you knew you had a printing problem, so your troubleshooting remained on the printing subsystem. You could have been led to a problem outside the printing subsystem if you researched the problem, and found out that *everything* you did on the network took five minutes, not just printing.

CERTIFICATION OBJECTIVE 12.02

Troubleshooting Network Problems

When troubleshooting network problems, it is important to follow a logical troubleshooting methodology. Always assume that the problem will be simple. See how often the simple solution eludes you. As your experience grows, you can easily find yourself caught in a web of always assuming the problem is more complicated than it actually is. When that happens, it can result in an excessive waste of troubleshooting time. Don't forget to ask yourself three basic troubleshooting questions:

1. Did it ever work?

2. When was it last known to be working?

3. What has changed since then?

Remember this: You are a "doctor." You just have computers and networking equipment for patients. And as with any doctor, the first step to a cure is a proper diagnosis. Use logic and the scientific method and do not forget to use one variable at a time. To put it in plain English: fix one thing at a time!

exam

Ⓦatch

The four steps to becoming an effective troubleshooter are listed here. It would be wise to tape these steps to your monitor or to draw them on the white board in your office, because they are important to your success as a network professional. (Plus, they are pretty heavily tested during the exam!)

1. **Identify the exact issue.**

2. **Re-create the problem.**

3. **Isolate the cause.**

4. **Formulate a correction.**

Before we continue, let's try a quick example of determining the symptoms and causes of a problem and the process of solving the problem.

First, determine which areas of the network are affected. For example, you need to determine if the problem is with one protocol, if it is with everything on one side of a router, or if all the machines are connected to the same cable. No matter what, the affected areas will always have something in common. This could, of course, be your entire network, but that is something that they have in common.

Second, identify any differences between the affected areas and the unaffected areas. For example, if you are unable to get a network connection with all of your workstations that are connected to a thinwire coax cable, but all other workstations are functioning, more than likely your problem resides in that thinwire coax cable.

Third, restart affected hardware. This is probably the most common solution to network outages. By restarting all affected hubs, routers, and switches, you can often clear the problem up.

Fourth, segment the affected area; divide the area in half. The best example of this is in thinwire coax. Determine the midpoint of the cable and place a terminator on each end. One half of the cable should now be working and is obviously not your problem. Repeat this step until you find the problem.

Fifth, if you are still unable to find the problem, it's time to get some tools out. Later in this chapter you will learn about the various tools available for diagnosing and correcting network problems.

Identifying the Exact Issue

Troubleshooting takes skill and experience. Even the best are stumped quite often. Sometimes finding the root of the problem is next to impossible. However, the more information you gather, the closer you are to solving the problem. At first you have a wide scope of what the problem could be. As you continue investigating, this scope narrows as you eliminate causes. Often, the exact issue is not so obvious, but after you have collected enough information, the cause could be staring you right in the face. Having others troubleshoot the problem as a team will give you many different perspectives and theories as to the cause of the problem. Having a diversified group of people to bounce ideas off also helps when you are trying to determine if the problem is hardware or software specific.

on the
job

When you do realize the exact cause of the problem, it is strongly recommended that you document your findings and share the results with others. It is quite common for errors to surface again, so why waste time troubleshooting the exact same problem six months down the road?

Re-creating the Problem

Sometimes it is possible to re-create the problem, learning exactly why and how the problem occurred. Other times you just want the problem fixed and do not need to re-create the problem. For example, if your hub goes down and needs a network interface card replaced, you want to fix the problem because re-creating the problem, in this instance, doesn't do any good for future reference. However, you should understand the symptoms of the problem, because this will enable you to pinpoint the problem much quicker when it happens again.

When dealing with software issues, it is very common to re-create the problem. If you can continually re-create the problem, you are that much closer to solving it.

on the **Job**

Once we had a problem with a communications program locking up, and we had no idea where to start troubleshooting the program. After we successfully re-created the problem, we determined when and where it happened, which gave us more insight into the cause of the problem. We opened up a technical support incident and provided the support engineers with our test information and they were able to quickly determine the cause of the problem, which was buggy code—something we could not have fixed ourselves.

Isolating the Cause

If you haven't figured it out yet, the most important step of network troubleshooting is isolating the problem. This is for two different reasons. First, by isolating the problem to the fewest possible workstations, you enable the most people to continue working, no matter what the status of the entire network is. This is just economically sensible. Second, it is easier to diagnose a problem that is occurring on five computers rather than 500. If there are some machines that you can definitely be sure are not causing the problem, there is no need to do further tests on them.

Same Line, Different Computer

One method to isolate the network problem is to put a workstation that is known to be good in place of the workstation that is having problems. If the workstation that is known to be good has difficulties, then the problem cannot be isolated to the original workstation. You should then begin troubleshooting network components such as the cable, hub, repeater, or network backbone, because the problem is not computer specific.

Same Computer, Different Line

Another similar method is "Same Computer, Different Line." In this method, the workstation having difficulties is moved to another line. If the workstation is able to function correctly in the new line, the problem is on the original line, not with the workstation itself.

Swapping Components

Swap the components that are between the failing workstations. This includes hubs, cables, terminators—anything that can possibly go bad. This is a quick way to return the network to a functioning state. After the network is functioning, you can test the components that were replaced to determine which component failed. A lightning strike, or some other type of electrical problem, can sometimes cause a NIC to behave unpredictably. By swapping components, this problem can be solved quickly and efficiently.

Isolating Segments of the Network with Terminators

If you are using a thinwire coax network, isolating your network is easy. Simply choose a workstation to be the dividing line for the isolation. Next, unplug the network cable from the T-connector and replace it with a terminator. You have now quickly isolated the network trouble.

Steps for Problem Isolation

Table 12-1 shows the steps you should take to isolate network problems.

Formulating a Correction

After you have an idea of what the problem could be, you may find that it's not the easiest problem to correct. This is especially the case when a problem has extended beyond one computer and is affecting the entire network. You need to begin formulating a correction by discussing the methods available to correct the problem. Many times there is more than

TABLE 12-1	Step	Action
Techniques for Problem Isolation	Determine which workstations are and are not experiencing symptoms.	Separate the working and non-working workstations from each other using a hub or terminator.
	Rule out simple problems.	Reset all major components that are affected by unplugging the devices and plugging them back in.
	Further determine which workstations are and are not experiencing symptoms.	Divide the non-working network segment in half and determine which half is not working properly.
	Eliminate simple cable problems.	Examine cable for any physical damage.
	Eliminate complicated cable problems.	Examine cables with a TDR to find any problems.
	Get more help.	Consult TechNet, resource kits, or vendor Web sites for further information.

one way to correct a problem, each with its own set of related issues and consequences. By determining the various methods of correcting the problem, you can choose the method that most effectively resolves the problem with minimal amount of work and consequences. However, there are times when a problem can be patched temporarily. In these cases, you need to evaluate the effects of temporarily fixing a problem or expanding the effort to permanently fix the problem. You also need to be aware that the process of correcting one problem may spawn a problem in a related area. This can hopefully be avoided by careful foresight during your discussing of the different ways to solve a problem.

CERTIFICATION OBJECTIVE 12.03

System or Operator Problems

In some cases, it is very apparent whether a system or operator error has occurred. A system error can be classified as an error on the part of a computer or network device or process that was not associated with a user's direct actions. This can be hardware failure or errors involved in the process of transferring or manipulating data. An operator problem will be a result of a user's action, such as not logging on correctly, connecting to the wrong server, printing to the wrong printer, etc. Most of these operator-related problems are obvious. However, operator problems can stem from misconfiguration of a device, program, or service by the initial operator: the network administrator. If a device is misconfigured, it may not be apparent until the device is promoted to a production area and fails in the process. For the Network+ exam, you need to understand the various ways a system or network device error occurs, what the symptoms are, and how to go about resolving the problem. First, you need to learn the areas that will provide you with a clue as to the nature of the problem.

CERTIFICATION OBJECTIVE 12.04

Checking Physical and Logical Indicators

When you begin troubleshooting a network-related problem, you have several indicators available that will help you determine the problem. These are a combination of physical and logical indicators that a problem has occurred. From a physical level, you can determine many things about the nature of the problem from the device in question.

Link Lights

Link lights are invaluable in determining if a network connection is present. A link light will be a green or amber LED that will shine if the networking device has detected a network connection. Many network devices, such as routers, hubs, and network cards are equipped with link lights for this very reason. Most network cards have two lights—a link light, which will remain on for the duration of the network connection, and a light that displays the current activity of the network card, which pulses as data is transferred to and from the computer or device. This can be an obvious indicator that the device is functioning on the network. If you are troubleshooting a network-related problem, it is best to start with examining the link light on the device to determine if a network connection is detected.

Power Lights

Even more rudimentary in the network troubleshooting area than the link light is the power light. Simply put, absence of a power light means no power is present in the device, or the power light is burned out. If the power light is not present, check that the device is receiving proper power. If it is not, you should check the power supply, power cable, or the wall connector. If you have verified all these to be correct, the device may literally be dead. In this case, you will have to replace the device.

Error Displays

An error display is a means of alerting you to a malfunction or failure in a device. This can be from a visual error dialog box on a computer, or an LED error display on a network device. This error should describe the problem that is occurring; however, it may not provide the necessary course of action required to solve the problem. The error display may refer to an error code that you must look up in order to determine the cause of the problem and the ways to resolve the problem. Referring documentation for the device is very helpful when troubleshooting a network device, because each manufacturer has its own special procedure to resolve a physical or logical problem with the device.

Error Logs and Displays

Similar to the error display is the error log, which maintains a listing of errors encountered. This error log should contain the time the problem occurred, the nature of the problem, and quite possibly the procedure for resolving the problem. Unfortunately, error logs usually don't contain enough information to solve a problem, and documentation must be consulted to diagnose and resolve the problem. However, error logging is very important, because you can determine when the problem occurred, what may have cause the problem, and what other processes are affected by this problem. Often, error displays signal a visual alert of the problem and also log the error into the error log for future reference. Many entries in the error log are not critical stop errors. Some entries are warnings that do not currently indicate a problem but are worthy of your attention. Other entries are purely informative, such as when the computer was restarted or when a service started or stopped.

Microsoft Windows NT Server and Workstation have an error log that is critical to the diagnosis and resolution of problems called Event Viewer. It is recommended that you consult Event Viewer during the troubleshooting process, being cognizant of critical red-stop error entries that have occurred.

The Event Viewer is an application that reads the binary log files. The log you open depends upon the type of items you need to view.

- The *System Log* contains events that are provided by the Windows NT internal services and drivers.

- The *Security Log* contains all security-related events when auditing has been enabled.

- The *Application Log* contains events that have been generated by applications.

Performance Monitors

The Network Monitor is an outstanding tool for monitoring the network performance of your system. The Network Monitor that comes with Windows NT Server only displays the frames that are sent to or from your system. It does not monitor your entire network segment. To monitor the entire segment, you need to use the Network Monitor that comes with Systems Management Server (SMS).

Another useful tool is the Performance Monitor. The Performance Monitor tracks the usage of resources by the system components and applications. Tracking different components of your system can help you to see what is degrading the performance. The Performance Monitor can be used for a variety of reasons including the following:

- Identifying bottlenecks in CPU, memory, disk I/O, or network I/O
- Identifying trends over a period of time
- Monitoring real-time system performance
- Monitoring system performance history
- Determining the capacity the system can handle
- Monitoring system configuration changes

CERTIFICATION OBJECTIVE 12.05

Network Troubleshooting Resources

Once you have determined exactly what the cause of your network problems it, the battle is only half over. You still have to figure out how to fix the problem. In many cases, the solution may be obvious, such as replacing a bad cable. But in other cases, additional solutions may be required. There are some resources available to help in your search for the solution to your problems.

TechNet

TechNet is a product of Microsoft that is distributed on a monthly basis. TechNet is a searchable database of all of Microsoft's articles and documentation on nearly all of the products they produce. You would be amazed, but there is a really good chance that someone else has actually already had the same problem that you are having, and TechNet is likely to contain some documentation about how they solved the problem. Figure 12-1 shows the TechNet main screen.

| FIGURE 12-1 | Using Microsoft TechNet for troubleshooting |

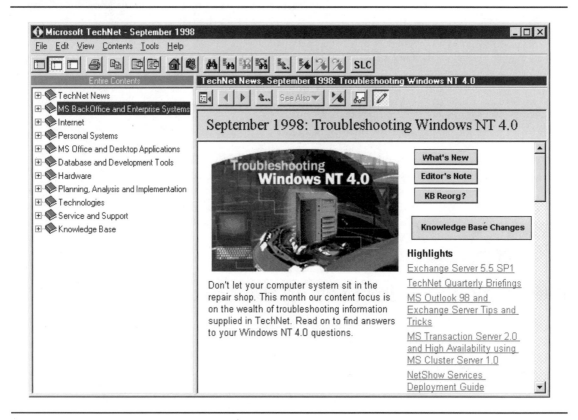

Manufacturer Web Sites

The World Wide Web has simplified network troubleshooting tenfold. The Web enables us to find up-to-the-minute information on both hardware and software. If you are having a problem with a network interface card (NIC) not communicating on the network properly, a good place to start is the Web site of the NIC's manufacturer. Most sites provide troubleshooting information, suggested steps to resolve common problems, phone numbers with which to contact technical support, and the latest updated drivers. Figure 12-2 illustrates the Microsoft Technical Support Web site.

FIGURE 12-2   Microsoft Technical Support Web site

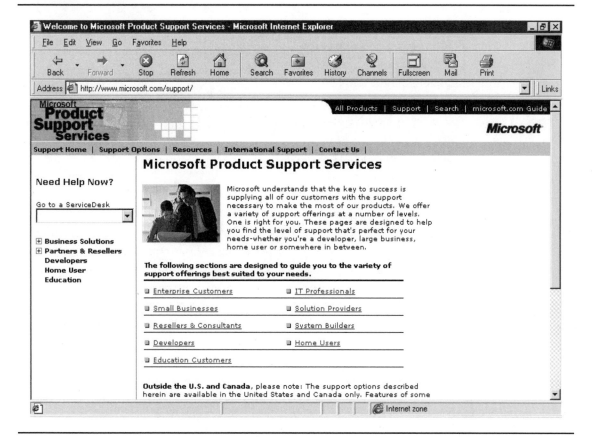

FROM THE FIELD

A Little TechNet Advice

One thing I cannot stress enough is to consult Microsoft's TechNet if you are a Windows NT network administrator or you support Windows-based clients. The TechNet CD contains an unbelievable amount of information for planning, maintaining, and troubleshooting Windows-based networks. I use TechNet almost daily as my first line of defense for solving problems. I also found TechNet to be a wonderful tool for studying for Microsoft exams. If you are not an expert TechNet user, you may not have discovered some quick ways to make researching information easier. The following are some helpful hints that save time and effort when you are in need of answers:

- Select Tools | Options. In the Full-Text Search box, select the Jump to First Highlight in Topic check box. TechNet will immediately jump to the hit within a document so you don't have to scroll around looking for the exact hit.

- Select Tools | Options. In the General box, select the Save History List check box. TechNet will save your query history so you can see which queries you've already used to narrow information.

- Select Contents | Define Subset. You can create a custom subset of information for narrowing information even more. I like

to define a subset that doesn't include all of Microsoft's sales information. You can also create a subset for Windows NT Server 4.0, and not include hits from Windows NT Server 3.51.

- If you would like to find two words that are in close proximity to each other, use the *near* keyword when you query. For example, to search for NetBIOS and resolution, use the following query string: NetBIOS near resolution.

- If you get thousands of hits on a query, click Book at the top of the query results screen to sort the query results by topic.

You will be amazed at just how many problems you solve with TechNet. I remember encountering a very strange fax problem and I felt embarrassed in front of the user because I had no idea what the problem was. I left his office with the problem unresolved and went to search through TechNet. Within a minute of entering my search criteria I found an article with a fix to the *exact* problem we were having! I surprised the user by showing up ten minutes later and eventually leaving with the fax service working. Remember, no one knows all the answers, but everyone should know where to go to research problems.

—Cameron Brandon, MCSE+Internet, CNE,
A+, Network+

Resource Kits and Documentation

Resource kits are a wealth of information about your operating system that provide technical information that is not available anywhere else. Resource kits contain additional documentation on your operating system that was too comprehensive to cover in the standard documentation. Whenever you are faced with a problem that you cannot solve, check the resource kit— your problem may already have been solved.

Trade Publications and White Papers

Other excellent sources of information are trade publications and white papers. These documents provide valuable information on current techniques and new practices that cannot be acquired anywhere else. In the event of actual network problems, these publications will probably be of little direct use to you, but the information you have absorbed over time will be one of your greatest tools.

Telephone Technical Support

Often, after you have exhausted your resources, such as vendor Web sites, resource kits, and documentation, it is common to open up a technical support incident with the vendor to solve the problem. Who better to solve your problem then highly skilled technicians that work for the company and field similar requests on a daily basis? Chances are the support personnel have already encountered the specific problem with their own software/hardware and have documented fixes available. A problem that boggles you may be a very common tech support call for these professionals. To improve the speed and accuracy of your technical support incident, make sure you have the following ready to assist the support technician:

- Hardware and software environment, such as the operating system you are running
- Version numbers of affected hardware or software
- Serial numbers
- Detailed account of the problem
- Troubleshooting steps taken so far, and their results

Vendor CDs

Vendor-provided CDs that come with hardware and software are very important references for installation, configuration, and troubleshooting. Many technicians overlook these CDs and spend countless hours troubleshooting on their own, or head straight to the phone for technical support. These CDs should be the first consultation, even before the product is installed, because usually the CD provides pre-installation tips and warnings that are critical for a smooth installation. The vendor-provided CDs also can have a technical information base, similar to Microsoft's TechNet, with a number of problems and their resolutions. Other CDs have tutorials, documentation, and software patches. Whatever these CDs contain, they should not be overlooked, whether you are planning to implement, support, or troubleshoot the product.

CERTIFICATION OBJECTIVE 12.06

Other Symptoms and Causes of Network Problems

It sounds obvious, but you need to closely examine the symptoms of a network problem in order to determine what the cause is. Now that you have seen the various causes for network problems, on the next page is a quick reference of network-related problem scenarios and the appropriate answers. It outlines some examples of the most common problems you will encounter in your networking professional journey. You should begin to see that the same problems will continue to arise, but the causes may be a bit different.

exam
⚙atch

Out of this entire chapter, you can expect most of your exam questions regarding troubleshooting the network to come out of the preceding area. You will be presented with a scenario, much like we presented above, but the exam will be more elaborate. You are to determine the cause of the problem. They will throw in tons of information, but it usually comes down to one sentence that gives the problem away, much like we demonstrated above.

QUESTIONS AND ANSWERS

I cannot connect to a computer on a remote network.	This sounds like a routing issue. Check to see if you can connect to a computer on your local network. If so, then try to ping the router or another host on the remote network. You need to determine whether the host is down or the link to the host is down.
No one can communicate on the entire network.	If this is a coax-based network, make sure the bus has not been accidentally segmented, meaning a connection came loose somewhere. If this is a twisted-pair network, ensure the hub is operational. If this is a Token Ring network, make sure a computer is not beaconing, indicating a problem.
It takes way too long to connect to a network resource.	Make sure the network is not being overloaded. Most network devices like hubs and routers display a percentage of bandwidth being used; check this to determine if the network is not being saturated. You can also use network monitor software to do the same thing. You should also determine who and what is being affected. Maybe you are experiencing a broadcast storm on one segment and not another.
A domain controller cannot be found.	Is anyone else receiving this error? This is most commonly a local workstation issue, either with an incorrect TCP/IP configuration or a problem with the network adapter or cable. Ensure that the network card has a link light and the cable is firmly plugged in. You should also try replacing the cable to the workstation.
A device in my system is not functioning and I can't connect to the network.	This sounds like a network card configuration error. Make sure the NIC is configured correctly. Be sure to use a free IRQ and I/O address when configuring the card. Also, the driver may not have loaded correctly. What has changed since this adapter worked correctly?
No one is this department can communicate, but other departments can.	Make sure the hub is not locked up. Resetting the hub will usually fix this problem. Sometimes an incorrectly configured network adapter causes it. The speed of the network card is usually set different from other cards on the network. For example, a Token Ring network can use speeds of 4 Mbps or 16 Mbps. If a workstation is set to 4 Mbps and the entire network is set to 16 Mbps, the network may go down. On an Ethernet network, setting a NIC to 10 Mbps on a 100 Mbps network may cause the network to lock up.

QUESTIONS AND ANSWERS

No one can get out to the Internet.	This can be many things, but make sure there is not a problem with the Internet gateway if you are using one, which is a computer acting as an intermediary between the Internet and your local intranet. This also may be a routing issue if you are using a dedicated connection to the Internet. Verify that the router or gateway is functional and try pinging key computers on remote networks and the Internet.
I can't reach the mainframe using its host name.	Make sure you are not having a name resolution problem. Did this problem just start occurring? Test for connectivity by pinging the host. If you can connect to the host using an IP address instead, then you definitely have a name resolution problem. If you can't connect with an IP address, try pinging another computer on that network. Maybe you are having routing problems.
Our Token Ring network just locked up all of the sudden.	Someone on the network is beaconing. Therefore, the nearest active upstream neighbor (NAUN) is having a problem. The network cannot continue until the problem is fixed. Sometimes the problem is because a bridge locks up too.

Recognizing Abnormal Physical Conditions

The key to recognizing abnormal physical conditions on the network revolves around knowing what is a *normal* physical condition. This may be different from one network to another. For example, it may take your network only three seconds to spool up a print document, but it may take another network one minute to spool up a document of the same size. This doesn't mean the second network has a problem. This could be a normal physical condition for their network. The following are things to look for when determining if an abnormal condition is occurring on your network:

- Printing takes longer.
- Authentication takes longer.
- You are receiving more errors than usual.

- Connecting to remote resources takes longer, if you can connect at all.

- You are losing connections to resources.

- Network applications are not running.

To determine if these are abnormal occurrences on your network, you need to ask yourself a few questions:

- How many users are affected by this problem?

- Is the problem consistent?

- Is the problem replicable?

- Was there a recent upgrade to the network or computer?

- Has any of the equipment been moved?

- Have we encountered this problem before?

- Has anyone else attempted to fix the problem?

- How many applications is this problem affecting?

- Are there new users or computers on the network?

- Is this a busy or congested time of day?

- Which products are involved?

Your mind should be going frantically thinking of what could have contributed to the problem. With knowledge of what constitutes a normal network environment, you can determine rather quickly what is not normal.

Isolating and Correcting Problems in the Physical Media (Patch Cable)

Experienced network administrators know that cabling is one of the most common causes of network failure. For this reason, you should check cabling first during your network troubleshooting process. Most often the cable that is damaged is the cable from the workstation to the wall jack. This cable receives the most abuse. Sometimes you may fix the problem by simply plugging the cable back in if it has fallen out.

If you have determined that a cable may be the culprit of a network-related problem, the most logical step is to test your hypothesis by replacing the cable with a known good cable. The results are simple: if you can communicate once again, then the old cable was bad. If you cannot communicate again, you need to continue troubleshooting or find another cable to test.

There are devices you can use to determine whether cables have gone bad, but these devices can be expensive. Most of the time you can swap out the cables to determine if cables are bad.

The following table lists of some of the more common cable-related problems and their solutions:

Cable Problem	Likely Solution
None of the workstations on the network are able to communicate with each other. They use a thinwire coax Ethernet to connect to each other.	The backbone has been severed. Find the point at which the bus became severed and reconnect it.
You have a brand new UTP cable, but the workstation is still not able to communicate on the network. The workstation worked with your test cable.	The brand new UTP cable may be a crossover cable. Obtain a regular UTP cable.
A workstation was just moved to a new location and is no longer able to communicate on the network. There is nothing wrong with the workstation's configuration.	Cables were damaged in the move. Replace each cable one at a time to find the problematic cable.

exam
ⓦatch

The preceding section will be important for the exam. Make sure you know what the symptoms of cable problems are and how to correct them.

Checking the Status of Servers

A lot of network administrators don't take enough time to check the status of the servers. This is critical because servers can be plagued with ongoing problems that are not so obvious, and if not corrected, can become worse. There are many ways to continually monitor the status of your servers, and each is operating-system specific. Some general monitoring tasks are listed below:

- Check error logs.
- Check services.
- Verify connectivity.
- Monitor the performance and the network.
- Verify backup logs, including test restores.
- Test alerts.

The error logs can give you an indication of a failed device or service and can give you a good idea of how to fix the problem. The errors listed will vary from critical to informational. Some errors, such as a service failing to start, warrant immediate action. A service failing to start can be critical, and often the service has dependencies that require the running of another service in order for the services themselves to be running.

on the

J o b

At one job I had, every Monday I had to check the Event Viewer logs on the Windows NT servers for possible errors that we were not aware of. It was a tedious task, but you would not believe how many problems we uncovered by inspecting the error logs. I recommend you do the same.

You can test for connectivity with a server with utilities such as ping to determine if the server is responding to network requests.

Performance and network monitoring can determine if the server is overloaded or if the server is broadcasting unnecessarily. An overloaded server can increase the length of time needed to fulfill network requests.

If you are backing up a server, which is always recommended, you need to verify the backups have finished successfully. This is imperative, because in the event of an emergency you will need to recover data from the backup tapes. You must also do test restores to make sure the data can be restored correctly and that you understand the restore process. A disaster is the worst time to discover that your backup routine hasn't been working correctly.

on the *Job*

I will never forget my first day on the job at one particular company. At 8:00 AM when I arrived, two of the administrators were looking at a Windows NT blue screen of death on one of the servers. This was the Microsoft Exchange server, which is responsible for e-mail. Users have a habit of complaining when e-mail goes down. Well, we all continued troubleshooting the problem, which appeared to be a failed hard disk drive. No problem, just restore from tape backup. Well, that's when the trouble began. We learned that the size of the nightly backup had grown larger than the one tape they had been using. The other administrators thought it was no big deal when they received errors from the backup software every day. We could not restore from the tape backup and the information was lost. It was too late to find out our backup routine wasn't working correctly. Now we had to face the users and tell them the e-mail they had been saving was gone.

And finally, you can configure your server to send alerts to specific computers or users in the event of emergencies, or when the system encounters thresholds that you have predefined. Setting thresholds includes baselining your system so you know the normal rate of activity. A threshold is a peak in the rate of activity in which you would like to be notified so you can correct the situation.

Checking for Configuration Problems

When you are bringing a new server online, or configuring a server with a new service, such as DNS or WINS, it is imperative you begin on the right foot by verifying that the configuration is correct. Many times you will incorrectly configure a server and it will continually deteriorate the server, or many times the server will not work at all. You will have to make sure the base operating system is configured correctly, such as TCP/IP, networking, error logs, and memory allocation. You will also have to correctly configure the additional services that will be running on top of the operating system. Many times you will have an application or database server that also runs a backup service, such as ARCserve or Backup Exec. When you are configuring the backup server, you may have to reboot the machine in order for changes to take effect. This means downing a critical server for a few minutes, which will break connections with all users and services that are currently using that machine. You may have to do this during off-hours, so be very careful about configuring services for mission-critical machines during business hours.

It is very important that the following services be correctly configured, because they have the capability to affect the entire network, not just the local server, which is a catastrophe waiting to happen.

DNS

Configuring the DNS Service requires planning. You need to gather the following information prior to the installation of the service:

- Your domain name
- The IP address of each server for which you wish to provide name resolution
- The host names of each of the servers

This information must be correct, or else your network will experience ongoing name-resolution problems that will be difficult to diagnose. This is especially the case with host name to IP address mappings. DNS entries are entered manually, so you must be very careful to not enter a wrong IP address or host name. You will not be prompted with an error message informing you that you have entered an incorrect IP address.

WINS

The WINS Service is another service that can run over the base operating system. The WINS Service is much like a DNS Service that provides name resolution; however, the DNS Service resolves host names to IP addresses and the WINS Service resolves NetBIOS names to IP addresses. Unlike DNS, WINS does not require you to manually enter mappings before you begin. This is because WINS is a dynamic service that can add, modify, and delete mappings dynamically, saving valuable time for the network administrator. There are times when you would like to add a static mapping for important clients or servers.

WINS, like DNS, also has many configuration possibilities, but most of the WINS configuration parameters will not be covered on your Network+

exam. A few of the WINS configuration settings are the duration of the client renewal and extinction of names, and the replication partners with which this WINS server will replicate. You can strategically replicate with other WINS servers based on frequency and location.

Expect many client-based configuration questions on your exam, but not WINS Service-related configuration questions.

HOSTS File

As you learned with DNS, you have to manually add host-name-to-IP-address mappings in order to resolve host names when you are using the DNS Service. With the HOSTS file, you also have to manually configure a database with these exact mappings. Unlike DNS, which uses a centrally located database of host name mappings, the HOSTS file resides on every computer. This makes updating the HOSTS file very difficult.

All the same rules apply with DNS: you must be very careful that you are entering the correct host-name-to-IP-address mappings. A helpful tip when configuring the HOSTS file is to copy to the remaining hosts the newly created file that you have guaranteed to be accurate. This will ensure you don't make any more clerical errors on each of the remaining machines.

exam
Ⓦatch

Make sure you know the definition of WINS, DNS, the HOSTS file, and the LMHOSTS file. You won't be expected to know any in-depth information about each, just the purpose for each. For more information, review Chapter 4 on TCP/IP fundamentals.

Checking for Viruses

If you have ever been a network administrator in the midst of a virus attack, you know how frustrating it can be. Once the virus gets in from the outside, whether by the Internet, a user's home computer, or from the local Intranet, it poses a much greater problem. But how can you get the viruses before they come into the network? A server running a virus-scanning program can make all the difference.

Many companies engage in a multi-pronged attack against viruses, including continually scanning for viruses on the file and messaging servers, and installing virus-scanning software on every workstation. Both are critical for stopping the spread of viruses. The server can catch viruses coming in from the messaging servers, such as Microsoft Exchange, and from files being stored on the file servers. The workstation virus-scanning programs can catch viruses on users' machines before they get a chance to replicate to the servers and to other users' computers on the network. In any case, the virus-definition files must be updated on a continual basis. Many virus-scanning utilities will enable the workstations to automatically update the virus definition files from a central server, which means you, the network administrator, do not have to visit every workstation once a month to apply the new definition files.

Checking the Validity of the Account Name and Password

Usually you configure services or applications to log on with a certain account in order to perform their functions. The services usually use the built-in system account, but if the service requires logging in to a remote computer, it will require an account name and password to do this. Some services require administrative privileges or membership in certain groups on the network to accomplish their tasks. You must document these special system and service accounts and remember to not delete or tamper with their accounts in any way. If you mistakenly disable, delete, or affect the account details, you may find yourself with a service that fails to start. This is often very difficult to diagnose. I have seen network administrators install applications and specify their own administrator account for the service to use. When the network administrator leaves the company, his account is disabled or deleted, and, mysteriously, some of the programs fail. If the other members of the department were not aware of this configuration, they could be scratching their heads for days wondering why this program or service will not work anymore.

Rechecking Operator Logon Procedures

The most obvious problems often involve logging on. The ordinary user is not nearly as computer savvy as you are, and even the process of logging on can boggle them. You usually have a number of domains you can log on to.

If a user mistakenly tries to log on to a domain in which he doesn't have an account, he will be denied, and you, the network administrator, will be called. Users often forget their passwords or neglect the fact that the password is case sensitive. After three strikes (or however many times you have configured the system to accept guesses) the user will be locked out and you will receive a call from a disgruntled user.

Sometimes users return from vacation to find that their accounts have been disabled or their passwords have expired. You will need to intervene to correct the situation.

The following illustration shows the user password information in Windows NT.

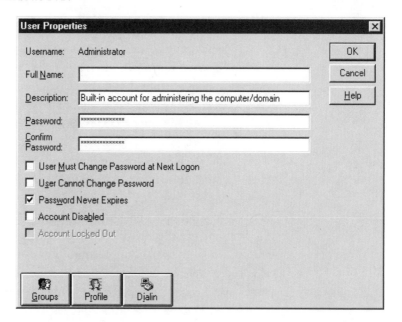

Selecting and Running Appropriate Diagnostics

To build a strong network you will need to run diagnostics to determine bottlenecks or problematic situations. These diagnostics may reveal problems or limitations that you can fix before they get too bad.

You will need to choose diagnostic programs that correlate to your specific network needs. For example, you can purchase extensive protocol-analyzing and packet-sniffing products, but they would be overkill for a twenty-node network. Often the free diagnostic products such as Performance Monitor and Network Monitor are capable of determining computer and network problems.

Whichever tool you choose, you must spend plenty of time with the product to determine the most effective way to deploy it. You must also be trained to analyze the results and determine what needs to be adjusted in order to remedy the situation. It will take more than one trial to establish a reliable baseline of activity for your testing. For example, running the diagnostics at 8:00 A.M. when all the users are logging on will give entirely different results from running the diagnostics at noon, when everyone is at lunch. Taking snapshots of activity from various periods of the day, week, and month will give you the most accurate assessment of your network. The longer you spend baselining your network, the more accurate the results will be. From there, you can begin assigning thresholds to chart and alert for abnormal activity. Also, you are training yourself to read the various diagnostics so you can quickly determine how, why, and where a problem is occurring. The following section gives you more examples of devices that can help you troubleshoot your network.

CERTIFICATION OBJECTIVE 12.07

Network Tools

In most network troubleshooting sessions, there is a time where a simple isolation of problems is just not feasible. In that situation, it's time to use some electronic tools to determine what and where your problem is. This section discusses the most common network tools and how they are used.

Crossover Cable

A *crossover cable* appears to be just another twisted-pair cable, but two wires are crossed, which makes the cable not fit for plugging into a computer and a hub for normal use. The crossover cable is used to connect two computers to each other directly, without the use of a hub. To connect the two computers, you have to use a small, inexpensive hub that both computers plug into, or go directly through the crossover cable to each computer.

A crossover cable is also used to connect hubs in the event you need to cascade hubs. If you were to substitute a crossover cable for a regular twisted-pair cable to connect two hubs, it would not work correctly. Therefore, it is important that you mark your crossover cables or use a different color cable to designate a crossover cable. Many companies use yellow or black cables for regular cables and blue for crossover cables. You will not need many crossover cables, and they are possible to make yourself if you have the correct pinout.

Hardware Loopback

A hardware loopback adapter is a way to test the ports on a system without having to connect to an external device. For example, you can use a serial loopback adapter to verify that a transmitted signal is leaving your serial port and returning through the loopback adapter, ensuring that your serial port is working correctly.

Tone Generator (Fox and Hound)

The *Tone Generator* is used to perform tests on phone and network lines by clipping to a wire, terminal panel, or standard modular jack and will aid in the identification of wires during the wire-tracing process. You begin by attaching the Fox to the cable, jack, or panel that you would like to trace, and you continue with the Hound on the other end of the cable to find the Fox's tone. When you find the tone, you will know that you have correctly tracked the cable. This is very helpful for determining which cable in a group of many cables, such as a wiring closet, has gone bad and needs to be replaced.

TDR

A *time domain reflectometer (TDR)* sends a signal down the cable, where it is reflected at some point. The TDR then calculates the distance down the cable that the signal traveled before being reflected by measuring the amount of time it took for the signal to be returned. If this distance is less than your overall cable length, a cable problem exists that distance from your location. (Yes, this means that it is in the most inconvenient location possible. It is a law of networking that when something breaks, it will be in the worst possible place to fix it.)

exam
ⓦatch
A TDR is a device that sends out an electronic pulse down the cable. The pulse then travels until it is reflected back, and the distance traveled can be calculated. This is similar to how sonar works.

Oscilloscope

An *oscilloscope* can determine when there are shorts, crimps, or attenuation in the cable. An oscilloscope formats its output in a graphical format. Oscilloscopes are commonly used to test cables that have been recently run through walls to ensure there are no problems with the cable prior to using it.

Network Monitors and Protocol Analyzers

Network monitors and protocol analyzers monitor traffic on the network and display the packets that have been transmitted across the network. If a particular type of packet is not being transmitted across the network, your problem may lie with that particular packet type. Note that a network monitor enables you to view the contents of *all* packets on the network. In many cases, viewing the contents of these packets is considered unethical or even illegal. Figure 12-3 shows some data using the Microsoft Network Monitor utility.

| FIGURE 12-3 | Capturing network data with Microsoft's Network Monitor |

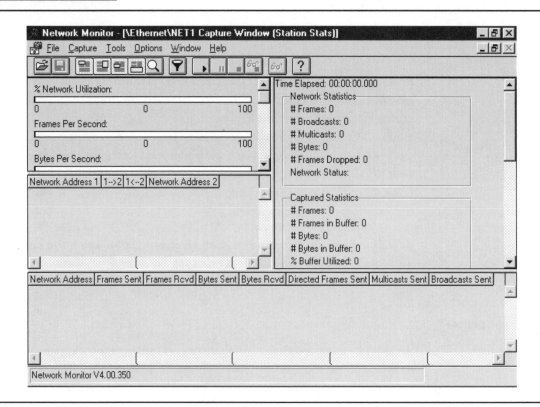

Selecting Appropriate Tools to Resolve Network Problems

You have seen the tools available for troubleshooting a network; now you'll learn the appropriate time to use each tool. The following quick reference describes a symptom of a network problem, and then gives

QUESTIONS AND ANSWERS

I need to create a baseline of network performance.	This is a job for Network Monitor, or a similar product that can trend the network and determine the average utilization to provide a baseline of network activity. Use this baseline to determine if an abnormal network situation is occurring.
I have a cable that appears to be broken somewhere.	Use a TDR or an oscilloscope to find the exact spot where the cable is broken. If you don't have access to one, you may be able to replace the cable without determining the exact area of breakage. However, it may be helpful to call in a networking company with access to a TDR or oscilloscope if the cable is long and the network is complex.
I need to find one end of a wire in a giant bundle of wires.	Definitely use a Tone Generator. Without it, it's virtually impossible to know which cable is the cable that you have singled out on the other end of a bundle of cables.
I need to look at the packets as they travel the network.	Use Network Monitor. It has the capability to capture packets so that you may analyze them.
I need to add another hub to increase the number of ports.	You can use a crossover cable to connect two hubs to each other. This is often helpful when you are adding a hub to a zone to increase the number of available ports.
I need to determine a baseline for my computer.	Use Performance Monitor. This tool is perfect for trending activity on your local computer. It can also be used to determine network-related information, such as the number of bytes sent and received, etc.

the likely tool to use to solve the problem or to help gather additional information about the problem.

exam

ⓦatch

Expect a couple questions on your exam similar to the ones presented in the Questions and Answers section. With that in mind, you need to know what each network tool is, and how it can be used in troubleshooting the network.

CERTIFICATION SUMMARY

You learned quite a lot in this chapter that will not only help you on the Network+ exam, but has given you a troubleshooting methodology that you will use for the rest of your career. You learned the general model for troubleshooting, which involves identifying the exact issue, re-creating the problem, isolating the cause, and formulating a correction.

You learned to ask yourself questions such as these:

- Does the problem exist across the network?
- Is this a workstation, workgroup, LAN, or WAN problem?
- Is the problem consistent and replicable?

You learned the physical and logical indicators of network problems, such as link and power lights, and error messages and error logs, which give you a good indication of the problem that is occurring.

You discovered network troubleshooting resources, such as TechNet, manufacturers' Web sites, and vendor CDs. Each of these resources is invaluable for solving network problems and is highly recommended.

And finally, you learned about the various network tools that are available to you to obtain more information about the problem, to solve the problem, or just to make your networking life a little bit easier.

With the lessons you have learned here, you should be on your way to becoming an invaluable network troubleshooting resource for your company. With experience in solving network problems, you will add more and more to your network troubleshooting repertoire, and you will be appreciated and sought out by your peers to help them with their network problems!

TWO-MINUTE DRILL

❑ Learning how each device coexists and contributes to the network will provide you with a strong foundation for understanding how and why network-related problems occur and how to resolve them.

❑ When you first encounter a problem, it is very important to determine its scope.

❑ You need to determine whether the problem is a workstation, workgroup, LAN, or WAN problem.

❑ Determine if the problem is consistent and replicable.

❑ It is very important to isolate the subsystem involved with the process.

❑ When troubleshooting network problems, it is important to follow a logical troubleshooting methodology.

❑ The four steps to becoming an effective troubleshooter are listed here. It would be wise to tape these steps to your monitor or to draw them on the white board in your office, because they are important to your success as a network professional. (Plus, they are pretty heavily tested during the exam!)

  ❑ Identify the exact issue.

  ❑ Re-create the problem.

  ❑ Isolate the cause.

  ❑ Formulate a correction.

❑ Having others troubleshoot the problem as a team will give you many different perspectives and theories as to the cause of the problem.

❑ Sometimes it is possible to re-create the problem, learning exactly why and how the problem occurred.

❑ The most important step of network troubleshooting is isolating the problem.

❑ Many times there is more than one way to correct a problem, each with its own set of related issues and consequences.

❑ In some cases, it is very apparent whether a system or operator error has occurred.

❑ When you begin troubleshooting a network-related problem, you have several indicators available that will help you determine the problem.

❑ Link lights are invaluable in determining if a network connection is present.

- ❑ Even more rudimentary in the network troubleshooting area than the link light is the power light.

- ❑ An error display is a means of alerting you to a malfunction or failure in a device.

- ❑ Similar to the error display is the error log, which maintains a listing of errors encountered.

- ❑ The Network Monitor is an outstanding tool for monitoring the network performance of your system.

- ❑ The Performance Monitor tracks the usage of resources by the system components and applications.

- ❑ There are some resources available to help in your search for the solution to your problems.

- ❑ TechNet is a searchable database of all of Microsoft's articles and documentation on nearly all of the products they produce.

- ❑ The Web enables us to find up-to-the-minute information on both hardware and software.

- ❑ Resource kits are a wealth of information about your operating system that provide technical information that is not available anywhere else.

- ❑ Other excellent sources of information are trade publications and white papers.

- ❑ It is common to open up a technical support incident with the vendor to solve the problem.

- ❑ Vendor-provided CDs that come with hardware and software are very important references for installation, configuration, and troubleshooting.

- ❑ Review the Q & A scenario sections. Out of this entire chapter, you can expect most of your exam questions regarding troubleshooting the network to come out of what was presented in these sections. On the exam, you will be presented with elaborate scenarios. You are to determine the cause of the problem. The exam will throw in tons of information, but it usually comes down to one sentence that gives the problem away.

❑ Experienced network administrators know that cabling is one of the most common causes of network failure.

❑ Make sure you know what the symptoms of cable problems are and how to correct them.

❑ There are many ways to continually monitor the status of your servers, and each is operating-system specific.

❑ When you are bringing a new server online, or configuring a server with a new service, such as DNS or WINS, it is imperative you begin on the right foot by verifying that the configuration is correct.

❑ Make sure you know the definition of WINS, DNS, the HOSTS file, and the LMHOSTS file. You won't be expected to know any in-depth information about each, just the purpose for each. For more information, review Chapter 4 on TCP/IP fundamentals.

❑ A server running a virus-scanning program can make all the difference.

❑ To build a strong network you will need to run diagnostics to determine bottlenecks or problematic situations.

❑ A hardware loopback adapter is a way to test the ports on a system without having to connect to an external device.

❑ A TDR is a device that sends out an electronic pulse down the cable. The pulse then travels until it is reflected back, and the distance traveled can be calculated. This is similar to how sonar works.

❑ An *oscilloscope* can determine when there are shorts, crimps, or attenuation in the cable.

❑ Network monitors and protocol analyzers monitor traffic on the network and display the packets that have been transmitted across the network.

❑ You need to know what each network tool is, and how it can be used in troubleshooting the network.

SELF TEST

The following Self Test questions will help you measure your understanding of the material presented in this chapter. Read all the choices carefully, as there may be more than one correct answer. Choose all correct answers for each question.

1. A few computers on the engineering segment are having problems reaching the AutoCAD design segment on the network. What is your initial prognosis of the problem?

   A. It's a default gateway issue.

   B. It's a routing issue.

   C. The computers are having cable problems.

   D. A hub is locked up.

2. Every user on a bus topology network has suddenly complained that the network is not functioning and they can no longer access resources on remote networks. What is your initial prognosis of the problem?

   A. It's a routing issue.

   B. It's a default gateway issue.

   C. The network is no longer terminated.

   D. A hub is locked up.

3. You think you are having problems with the UNIX server in another region. Two users have already complained this morning. What would be the next logical step in your troubleshooting methodology?

   A. Check the router.

   B. Check the hub.

   C. Ping the UNIX server by name.

   D. Ping the UNIX server by IP address.

4. Someone in the graphics department is complaining that it takes too long to open his renderings, which wasn't the case yesterday. What is the next logical step in your troubleshooting methodology?

   A. Run Performance Monitor.

   B. Ping the server that holds the renderings.

   C. Try opening a rendering on another computer.

   D. Restart the affected computer.

5. You are called down to look at a user's computer. He says it takes way too long to print a simple document. What is the next step in your troubleshooting methodology?

   A. Check the print server.

   B. Restart the affected computer.

   C. Run diagnostics.

   D. Try opening a few files on the affected computer.

6. You are experiencing problems on a coax bus network. How can you quickly determine where the problem is occurring?

   A. Divide the network in half, terminate it, and find which side is still not functioning. That is the affected area.

Continue this process until the break is found.

B. Use a network packet sniffer to determine where the packets eventually stop responding. This will tell you which computer is the closest to the break.

C. Use a Fox and Hound process to determine where the break is in the network backbone.

D. Use Network Monitor to determine what is causing the broadcast storm. One computer's faulty network card is the likely culprit, and must be found.

7. How can you eliminate complicated cable problems in your troubleshooting process?

A. Visually inspect the cables.

B. Use a Fox and Hound to find cables in a tangled mess.

C. Examine cables with TDR to find any problems.

D. Swap suspect cables with known good cables.

8. What is a quick way to determine if your computer is communicating on the network?

A. Run diagnostics.

B. Check the Network applet in the Control Panel.

C. Check the physical link light.

D. Ping the loopback adapter (127.0.0.1).

9. You came back to work on Monday morning only to notice that you are having network problems. Your domain controller, which also functions as a database server, appears to be having problems. How can you further investigate the problem?

A. Check the error log.

B. Ping the server to see if it responds.

C. Run diagnostics on the server.

D. Restart the computer and then begin troubleshooting.

10. You have made system configuration changes to one of your servers. How can you tell if the changes have made a difference?

A. Watch the server closely for a few hours, especially during peak usage.

B. Run Network Monitor to perform an assessment of the current system activity and compare that with your previous baseline before the configuration change took place.

C. Run Performance Monitor to perform an assessment of the current system activity and compare that with your previous baseline before the configuration change took place.

D. Check the Event Viewer for errors, warnings, or any indicators that system degradation has occurred.

11. You feel you are having driver incompatibility problems with your network adapter. What is the best resource for finding another network adapter driver?

A. TechNet

B. Resource Kit

C. Vendor Web site

D. Documentation CD

12. You are instructed to migrate the DHCP service from a Windows NT 3.51 server to Windows NT 4.0 server. What is the best resource to begin preparing for the migration?

A. Windows NT magazine

B. Telephone tech support

C. Vendor CDs

D. Resource kits

13. You are experiencing lockup problems with a new version of the virus-scanning utility that you just implemented. Which of the following is probably not needed when you open a technical support incident?

A. The version of affected software or hardware

B. Number of users on the network

C. Troubleshooting steps taken so far, and their results

D. Current operating system

14. You have a user receiving the error: "A domain controller cannot be found." Assuming no one else has called you with this error, which of the following is not likely the problem?

A. The TCP/IP configuration is not correct on the computer.

B. The domain controller could be down.

C. The network card is not functioning correctly.

D. A cable may be faulty or not plugged in.

15. Which of the following is not likely an abnormal condition on a network?

A. It takes a long time to print a large document with images.

B. It takes longer to become authenticated.

C. Users are having problems connecting to the SQL database.

D. You continually lose connection to the mainframe.

16. You have a workstation that you moved from one cubicle to another. Nothing on the workstation was changed; however, the computer refuses to connect to the network. Which of the following is not likely the cause?

A. The network drop has not been activated in the wiring closet.

B. The cable was damaged in the move.

C. The TCP/IP configuration is incorrect.

D. The network adapter was damaged in the move.

17. Which of the following is the most reliable indicator that a network server may be overloaded?

A. The activity light on the network card is constantly lit.

B. Performance Monitor shows network requests are backing up in the queue.

C. Network Monitor shows too many packets are leaving this server.

D. The computer is very slow to respond when you log on.

18. Which of the following will you not need prior to the installation of the DNS Service?

A. The DNS address scope

B. Your domain name

C. The host names of each of the servers

D. The IP address of each server for which you wish to provide name resolution

19. Which of the following is not true regarding the WINS service?

A. It resolves NetBIOS names to IP addresses.

B. You can replicate with other WINS servers.

C. You have to manually enter the address mappings.

D. The WINS Service dynamically updates the WINS database.

20. Which of the following is not true concerning the HOSTS file?

A. You have the capability to use a centrally located HOSTS file.

B. The HOSTS file is not case-sensitive.

C. The HOSTS file resolves host names to IP addresses.

D. The HOSTS file can have more than one host name per line.

21. Which of the following is not a good recommendation when implementing virus-scanning utilities?

A. Using a live update to download new virus definition files

B. Scanning file server hard drives once a month

C. Using scanning utilities on every workstation

D. Scanning messaging servers, such as Microsoft Exchange

22. Steve just got back from a two-week vacation. He calls you first thing Monday morning. Which of the following is most likely not the reason for Steve's call?

A. He forgot his password.

B. His account has been disabled.

C. His password has expired.

D. He forgot the domain he is supposed to log on to.

23. Which of the following is *not* a good recommendation when it comes to performing a baseline of your network?

A. Monitor traffic at different times of the day.

B. Configure the snapshots to take place at midnight each night.

C. Monitor traffic for days, even weeks.

D. Take as many traffic snapshots as possible.

24. Which of the following network situations require a crossover cable?

    A. Connecting the patch panel to the workstation

    B. Connecting a workstation to a hub

    C. Connecting a transceiver to a hub

    D. Connecting a hub to another hub

25. What is the best tool to determine where a break has occurred in a cable?

    A. A Tone Generator

    B. A Spectrum Division Analyzer

    C. A time domain reflectometer

    D. A Fox and Hound

Network+

CERTIFICATION

Part III

Appendixes

Network+
CERTIFICATION

A

Self Test
Answers

Chapter 1 Answers

1. Which of the following is an example of a network?

   A. A computer attached to a printer and a scanner to input and output information.

   B. A computer sharing a communication medium to communicate with peripherals or other computers to share information.

   C. Several printers connected to a switch box going to a single terminal.

   D. Several floppy disks holding information for one workstation.
   B. A network is made up of multiple entities connected to share information and resources.

2. The physical layout of computers, cables, and other components on a network is known as what?

   A. Segment

   B. Backbone

   C. Topology

   D. Protocol
   C. The topology is the physical layout of computers, cables, and other components on a network.

3. Which topology uses one long cable segment and must terminate at each end to prevent signal bounce?

   A. Bus

   B. Start

   C. Mesh

   D. Ring
   A. The Bus topology has one cable segment and must have terminators so the signal doesn't bounce causing communication problems.

4. Which topology has a centralized location where all the cables come together to a central point, similar to a mainframe, and if this point fails, it will bring down the entire network?

   A. Bus

   B. Star

   C. Mesh

   D. Ring
   B. The Star topology has a central point, a hub or switch, where all the various cables come together. If this point fails the entire network comes down.

5. Which topology has a layout where every workstation or peripheral has a direct connection to every other workstation or peripheral on the network?

   A. Bus

   B. Star

   C. Mesh

   D. Ring
   C. A mesh topology has a physical connection between every device on the network.

6. Which topology is like a circle with a continuous loop connecting all computers without termination?

A. Bus

B. Star

C. Mesh

D. Ring
D. The ring topology has a circle of workstations which each have an equal chance of communicating on the network.

7. Which of the following are two logical segments of a computer network?

A. Two computers joined by a cable within the same IP subnet.

B. Several computers joined by several cables in a star topology within the same IP subnet.

C. Several computers joined by several cables in a star topology within different IP subnets.

D. Several computers joined by a backbone in a bus topology on or within the same IP subnet.
C. A logical segment is based on network address. Multiple physical segments can make up a logical segment. The key here is different IP subnets making up different logical segments.

8. Which network operating system was developed from the VMS platform?

A. NetWare

B. UNIX

C. Windows 95

D. Windows NT

D. Windows NT was developed from the VMS system to become what it is today.

9. Which network operating system was developed originally as a college project and uses a popular directory services structure to organize the network management?

A. UNIX

B. NetWare

C. Windows NT

D. OS/3.90
B. NetWare was originally developed as a college project and uses the very popular Novell NDS, or directory services.

10. Which operating system was originally developed at U.C. Berkeley and has multitasking, multiuser, and built-in networking?

A. UNIX

B. Windows NT

C. Windows 95

D. NetWare
A. UNIX was developed at U. C. Berkeley and has three main features of multitasking, multiuser, and built in networking.

11. What do networks use to communicate with each other that is sometimes known as a language that networked computers use?

A. NICs

B. Segment

C. Protocol

D. Cable

C. A protocol is what networked computers need to communicate and understand each other. Protocols are like languages to humans.

12. Which network protocol was developed by Novell for use in their network operating systems?

A. IPX

B. TCP/IP

C. NetBEUI

D. DLC

A. IPX is the protocol of choice in the various versions of NetWare until NetWare 5, which uses pure IP.

13. Which protocol is used on the Internet to give each computer a unique address?

A. IPX

B. TCP/IP

C. NetBEUI

D. DLC

B. TCP/IP is a 32-bit addressing protocol that is used on the Internet.

14. Which of the following is not a routable protocol and cannot be used on the Internet?

A. IPX

B. TCP/IP

C. NetBEUI

D. DECnet

C. NetBEUI is not a routable protocol and cannot be used in a WAN or on the Internet.

15. Which of the following are methods of ensuring fault tolerance with data on a network? (Choose all that apply.)

A. Disk mirroring

B. Disk striping without parity

C. Disk striping with parity

D. Tape backup

E. Disk duplexing

A, C, D, E. All but disk striping without parity are fault tolerant and help to ensure that data is not lost.

16. Which of the following is not a layer in the OSI Model?

A. Physical

B. Transport

C. Network

D. Data Transmission

D. The Data Link Layer is a layer in the OSI model but the Data Transmission Layer is not.

17. Which of the following is not a common type of media used in networking?

A. coaxial

B. twisted-pair

C. fiber-optic

D. RJ-45

D. RJ-45 is a type of connector, not a cable type. The other three are the common media used in networking.

18. What is the distance limitation on 10Base2 or Thinnet?

A. 100 meters

B. 185 meters

C. 250 meters

D. 500 meters
   B. 185 meters is the limitation on 10Base2. 10Base5 is 500 meters and 10BaseT is 100 meters.

19. When data is able to travel in both directions on a cable this is known as what?

   A. Fault Tolerance

   B. Half Duplex

   C. Bi-Duplex

   D. Full Duplex
      D. Full Duplex communication is the type of communication where data transmission can occur simultaneously in both directions on the cable.

20. In what type of network is there no dedicated server and each node on the network is an equal resource for sharing and receiving information?

   A. Client/Server

   B. Peer-to-Peer

   C. Windows NT Server 4.0

   D. Novell IntraNetWare 4.*x*
      B. Peer-to-peer networking has no dedicated servers and each node is equal in terms of sharing and receiving information on the network.

21. In order for differing networks to communicate with each other we need to use a _____ to translate between the networks.

   A. Protocol

   B. Medium

   C. Gateway

   D. Bridge
      C. A gateway translates between two differing networks.

22. When troubleshooting your network you know the following: the topology is a bus network, the entire network is down, and there is no cable break through the backbone. What could be a possible cause of the network being down?

   A. A bad network card

   B. Terminators missing from cable segment ends

   C. One PC turned off and not logged in

   D. User error with workstation that worked previously.
      B. Out of the choices, B makes the most sense in terms of the information in the question. A bus network needs termination at both ends.

23. In which topology does each device on the network have equal access to communicate on the network?

   A. Bus

   B. Star

   C. Ring

   D. Mesh
      C. A ring is the type of topology that Token Ring runs on, which gives each device equal access to communicate on the network.

24. Which of the following are network operating systems and not just operating systems that will communicate on a network? (Choose all that apply.)

    A. Novell NetWare
    B. Microsoft Windows 3.1
    C. Microsoft Windows 9x
    D. Microsoft Windows NT
       A, D are examples of network operating systems. B, C are operating systems that with the appropriate client and network components installed will be a client on a network.

25. When multiple disk controllers are used in a drive mirroring scenario it is known as what?

    A. Disk multiplexing
    B. Disk duplobuilding
    C. Bidirectional disking
    D. Disk Duplexing
       D. Disk duplexing is the process of using two disk controllers for added redundancy in the drives and the controllers.

Chapter 2 Answers

1. What does a network interface card add to a computer functionality?

    A. It provides faster communication between the CPU and the hard disk.
    B. It provides the capability to communicate across a phone line to another computer.
    C. It provides the capability to communicate with other computers across a medium like a CAT5 cable, with an RJ-45 connector connecting the computer to a hub.
    D. It provides the capability to save more information on a floppy than normal.
       C. It provides the capability to communicate with other computers across a medium like a CAT5 cable, with an RJ-45 connector connecting the computer to a hub. A network interface card enables a computer to communicate across a network on a medium such as CAT5 with an RJ-45 connector.

2. In order for a network interface card to interact with the computer, what needs to be installed?

    A. The appropriate documentation for the user to take advantage of the features of the interface card.
    B. A driver, which is software that enables the network interface card and the computer to communicate with each other.
    C. A bus, which enables the interface card to communicate through the various topologies of the Internet.
    D. Nothing.
       B. A driver, which is software that enables the network interface card and the computer to communicate with each other. All components must have drivers installed. Drivers are usually included on a disk from the .

manufacturer and can be downloaded from their Web site.

3. Which of the following is NOT a function of a network interface card?

   A. To translate data from the parallel data bus to a serial bit stream for transmission across the network

   B. To format packets of data in accordance with protocol

   C. To transmit and receive data based on the hardware address of the card

   D. To send data from the CPU to the various expansion slots within the computer

   D. To format packets of data in accordance with protocol. The network interface card does not send data from the CPU to the various expansion slots. This is more related to the computer bus. The network card is what handles translation and communication between the computer bus and the network medium.

4. Which of the following is a 16-bit computer bus?

   A. ISA

   B. EISA

   C. PCI

   D. MCA

   A. ISA. ISA is the 16-bit bus that was introduced in the IBM AT/XT models. The slots are longer than PCI and are still used today in many IBM compatible PCs. ISA stands for Industry Standard Architecture.

5. Which of the following is a 32-bit computer bus? (Choose all that apply.)

   A. ISA

   B. EISA

   C. PCI

   D. MCA

   B, C, D. EISA, PCI, and MCA are all 32-bit computer buses. EISA was brought about by companies like Hewlett Packard and Compaq. The PCI bus was introduced by Intel and the MCA Bus was introduced by Compaq. All have different slot sizes so each bus type has a specific connector on the card. For the exam you will not need to know the specific sizes.

6. Which of the following is a 64-bit computer bus?

   A. ISA

   B. EISA

   C. PCI

   D. MCA

   C. PCI. PCI, or Peripheral Components Interconnect, is a 32-bit bus introduced by Intel. The Bus is actually a 64-bit bus that is implemented as a 32-bit bus. The connector slots for PCI are shorter than ISA slots.

7. Which of the following are methods that you can use to prevent electrostatic discharge when installing a network interface card? (Choose all that apply.)

   A. Wear an anti-static wrist strap.

B. Wear an anti-static ankle strap.

C. Use anti-static spray on all components.

D. Use an anti-static floor mat.
A, B, D. Wearing an anti-static wrist strap, ankle strap, or using an anti-static floor mat are the methods that can be used to prevent electrostatic discharge when installing components. Electrostatic Discharge can damage the components inside the computer.

8. If the network interface card is not software configurable, what is the most likely method of configuring the NIC with the appropriate IRQ?

A. Diagnostics supplied by manufacturer

B. Jumpers on the interface card itself

C. Setup utility by manufacturer

D. Plug and Play will automatically set the IRQ
B. Jumpers on the interface card itself. The card will most likely have jumpers to set the IRQ. If the card is not software configurable, then neither diagnostics nor a setup utility will work. Plug and Play will not set the IRQ because the card is not software configurable.

9. What determines that a device can interrupt the process and request service?

A. I/O Address

B. DMA

C. IRC

D. IRQ
D. IRQ. The IRQ enables the device to interrupt the process and request service. No two devices can share the same IRQ. IRQ addresses range from 1 to 15. IRQ stands for Interrupt Request because the device interrupts the processor with a request for service.

10. What has to be set to enable a device to directly access memory on the system without the intervention of the CPU?

A. I/O Address

B. DMA

C. IRC

D. IRQ
B. DMA. The DMA (Direct Memory Address) enables a device to directly access system memory without the intervention of the CPU. No two devices can share the same DMA. If this happens, it is almost guaranteed to lock up the computer due to a hardware conflict.

11. In addition to the IRQ, what other configuration setting must not conflict with other devices?

A. IRA

B. I/O base address

C. IDE

D. PCI
B. I/O base address. The I/O base address refers to the starting address for a series of registers used to control the interface. These cannot be the same for two devices.

12. If a card has the capability to connect to more than one kind of media, you may have to set which of the following in order to ensure connectivity?

    A. IRQ setting

    B. Link light on/off setting

    C. Transceiver type setting

    D. PCI setting
       C. Transceiver type setting. The Transceiver type determines which media the network card connects to if it has multiple media capabilities. Setting the wrong transceiver can be a cause of no network communication.

13. Which of the following is not a network component that connects multiple computers on a network?

    A. Bus

    B. Hub

    C. Switch

    D. MAU
       A. Bus. The bus is the internal communication channel where devices communicate with the CPU, not a network connectivity device. The network card communicates between the computer bus and the network medium.

14. Which of the following types of hubs does not regenerate the signal and therefore is not a repeater?

    A. Active

    B. Hybrid

    C. Passive

    D. Switching Hub
       C. Passive. A passive hub does not regenerate the signal and is not a repeater. Ordinarily a passive hub has no power source. Passive hubs are not widely used in today's networks.

15. What network component is used to extend the distance of the signal when transmitting over the normal specified distance?

    A. Passive Hub

    B. NIC

    C. IRQ

    D. Repeater
       D. Repeater. A repeater takes a signal and regenerates it to enable the media to reach beyond normal distance specifications. With large networks this can be a necessity with very large offices. All active hubs are repeaters.

16. Which types of transceivers are built into the network interface card?

    A. External

    B. Internal

    C. On-board

    D. T-connector
       C. On-board. On-board transceivers are built into the network card. External transceivers connect to the medium outside the computer. The on-board transceiver is part of the network adapter where other types may actually be a physically different component.

17. What is the fourth step in troubleshooting, using the logical step-by-step plan presented in this chapter?

    A. Restart affected hardware.

    B. Segment the affected area.

    C. Identify any differences between affected and unaffected areas.

    D. Get additional tools out, such as technical databases or diagnostics.
    B. Segment the affected area. This will help to pinpoint the exact location of the problem. If you cannot isolate the problem the troubleshooting process may go on for days or even weeks.

18. What does EPROM stand for?

    A. Enhanced Programmable Read Only Memory

    B. Erasable Programmable Read Out Memory

    C. Enhanced Permanent Read Only Memory

    D. Erasable Programmable Read Only Memory
    D. Erasable Programmable Read Only Memory. EPROM is a set of instructions written to give the interface card its capabilities. The EPROM is the written software instructions or brains of the device that make it work.

19. If you are configuring a network interface card in DOS, what is the most likely extension for the file that determines the settings for the interface card?

    A. INF

    B. CON

    C. CFG

    D. DOS
    C. CFG. CFG is the extension that the DOS-level drivers use to set configuration items. INF files are driver configuration installation files. The CON and DOS extensions are not used for configuration files

20. If you have a workstation that has no floppy drive or hard drive and you want to put it on your network, what do you have to do?

    A. Simply add any network card.

    B. Add a network card that has a mini-hard disk on it.

    C. Add a network card that has an external connector for a floppy disk drive.

    D. Add a network card that has a remote boot prom chip.
    D. Add a network card that has a remote boot prom chip. The remote boot prom is the only option here that makes sense. The remote boot prom connects the workstation to the network, and then the system files reside on the server.

21. What type of connector does a twisted-pair cable use?

    A. RJ-45

    B. T-connector

    C. RJ-11

D. BNC connector

A. RJ-45. Twisted-pair cabling uses an RJ-45 cable to connect to the network adapter's transceiver. The RJ-45 connector looks like a phone connector, only wider, and has eight pins instead of four.

22. What is an AUI connector?

A. A 9-pin DB male connector

B. A 15-pin D female connector

C. A 25-pin D female connector

D. Same as an RJ-45 connector

B. A 15-pin D female connector. An AUI or DIX connector is a 15-pin D connector that is female and looks like a joystick port. Many times this connects the workstation to a drop cable connecting to the backbone of the network.

23. What type of network component enables each device to have the full bandwidth of the medium when transmitting?

A. Hub

B. Repeater

C. Switching Hub

D. Transceiver

C. Switching Hub. A switching hub enables a workstation to utilize the full bandwidth of the transmission medium. The hub switches between ports giving the connected workstation the full medium for a split second.

24. What does MAU stand for?

A. Multisensing Action Unit

B. Multistation Access Unit

C. Multisplit Addtransmission Unit

D. Multistation Action Unit

B. Multistation Access Unit. MAU is a device that multiple workstations connect to in a Token Ring network. The MAU can be powered or not powered. Connectors in newer MAUs are RJ-45 as in the standard patch cable for Ethernet

25. What type of hub enables more than one type of cable or medium to connect to it?

A. Passive

B. Active

C. Hybrid

D. Multi-station access unit

C. Hybrid. A hybrid hub is a hub that enables more than one type of cable to connect to it joining different types of cable segments. This is especially useful in mixed environments where cabling cannot be easily changed.

Chapter 3 Answers

1. Which network layer has the important job of addressing?

A. Network Layer

B. Physical Layer

C. Data Link Layer

D. Transport Layer

C. Data Link Layer. The MAC sublayer maintains *physical device addresses* for communicating with

Appendix A: Self Test Answers

other devices (commonly referred to as *MAC addresses*).

2. What happens when a server you are trying to reach is located on another segment of the network?

   A. You don't need the MAC address of this server.

   B. You still need the MAC address of this server.

   C. You need the MAC address of the nearest bridge.

   D. You need the MAC address of the nearest router.
   D. You need the MAC address of the nearest router. After you have the MAC address of the nearest router, it is up to the router to determine the MAC address for the destination server, or the MAC address of the next router that can reach the destination server.

3. Which of the following is not displayed when you issue the WINIPCFG command on a Windows 98 machine?

   A. MAC address

   B. Default gateway

   C. DNS server

   D. Subnet mask
   C. DNS server. When you issue the WINIPCFG command, all that is listed is the adapter address (MAC address), the IP address, subnet mask, and default gateway. Clicking the More Info button will display more information, including the IP address

of the DNS server, if DNS is being used.

4. What layer of the OSI model does a bridge function in?

   A. Data Link Layer

   B. Network Layer

   C. Transport Layer

   D. Physical Layer
   A. Data Link Layer. Unlike a router, a bridge cannot discriminate whether a packet is destined for a remote network by the IP address. Bridges segment the network by MAC addresses, and are used little in comparison to routers in today's networks.

5. Which IEEE 802 category uses *Carrier Sense Multiple Access with Collision Detection (CSMA/CD)* for access to the physical medium?

   A. 802

   B. 802.2

   C. 802.3

   D. 802.5
   C. 802.3. Because Ethernet is the more popular network implementation, CSMA/CD has become the most widely used method for access to the network medium. Not to be confused with CSMA/CA, which broadcasts an intent to transmit, thus using Collision Avoidance.

6. Which network topology does the IEEE 802 standard 802.5 map to?

A. ARCnet

B. Token Ring

C. Ethernet

D. Twisted Pair

B. Token Ring. The IEEE standard for a Token Passing network is 802.5. The Ethernet standard is 802.3, and the ARCnet standard is 802.4, which represents a Token Bus network, which uses a bus backbone to pass a token around, similar to a Token Ring network which passes the token around a logical ring.

7. In order to operate on an internetwork, each network that participates must be assigned what?

A. An IP address

B. A network address

C. An IPX address

D. A default gateway

B. A network address. A network address must be unique, which is what enables packets to be sent across many different networks. A packet soon finds the proper network address, and the next step is to locate the destination computer located on the network.

8. What is a bridging protocol designed to do?

A. Combine several networks into one virtual network

B. Combine several protocols into one distinct protocol

C. Separate a physical network into multiple virtual networks

D. Separate a number of physical networks into smaller subnetworks

A. Combine several networks into one virtual network. Although bridges function at a higher level in the OSI model then repeaters, they are still at a lower layer than routers and are unable to intelligently route packets. Bridges are used to consolidate several networks into one larger network; however, most companies require just the opposite: separating a physical network into multiple virtual networks, which is the job of the router.

9. When should you use a brouter?

A. When you are only using one protocol on the network

B. When you are using a routable and non-routable protocol

C. When you have to subnet the network with the TCP/IP protocol

D. When you need to make other network segments visible to the entire network with a non-routable protocol such as NetBEUI

B. When you are using a routable and non-routable protocol. A brouter combines the features of a bridge and a router; it will bridge the non-routable protocols such as NetBEUI and route the other protocols, such as TCP/IP and IPX/SPX/NWLink.

10. You have just migrated your small company from Novell NetWare to Windows NT. Since you are very familiar

with the IPX/SPX protocol, you decide to use this protocol on your Windows NT network and not TCP/IP. What limitations will you have as your company network grows larger and requires access to the Internet?

A. You will not be able to route the IPX/SPX protocol.

B. Your network will become saturated due to the large broadcast traffic associated with the IPX/SPX protocol.

C. You will have to eventually install TCP/IP for access to the Internet or use an Internet gateway.

D. None. IPX/SPX is a very logical choice for ease of configuration, speed, routing, and access to the Internet.
   C. You will have to eventually install TCP/IP for access to the Internet, or use an Internet gateway. The Internet is comprised of the TCP/IP protocol. To access the Internet, you need TCP/IP installed on the machine or you need to go through a *proxy server* that will accept IPX/SPX traffic from the network and repackage this information in the TCP/IP protocol as it speeds out to the Internet. This proxy server will also need to repackage the incoming TCP/IP packets into IPX/SPX as they pass through the firewall and into the network.

11. What will happen if we have a routing table with the same route to the same destination network?

A. You cannot have the same route listed twice.

B. You cannot have the same destination listed twice.

C. The route with the closest router will be used.

D. The route with the fewest number of hops will be used.
   D. The route with the fewest number of hops will be used. The router will select the best possible path to send the packet based on the number of hops, which is the most efficient path to the destination.

12. Which of the following is not true regarding a dynamic router?

A. It can choose the most efficient path to a destination network

B. It can communicate and share information with neighboring routers

C. It cannot be configured with static routes

D. It can communicate with other routers using RIP and OSPF.
   C. It cannot be configured with static routes. It is possible, and sometimes a good idea, to configure a router with a static route that includes a specific path you want a packet to take in order to reach the destination network. This is common for routers at each end of a slow WAN link.

13. What will happen if the default gateway is not specified on your computer and you are trying to reach another network?

A. The packet will ask every router if they know the path to reach the destination.

B. The packet will broadcast for the IP address of the nearest router.

C. The packet will be forwarded to the DNS server.

D. The packet will not be sent.
D. The packet will not be sent. Unless you are using a static route that will override the default gateway, the packet will not be sent because the default gateway entry is not present. The default gateway is used to route packets to remote networks. The default gateway should be thought of as a router, which is the gateway to another network.

14. Which of the following is not true of the Transport Layer of the OSI model?

A. It is responsible for error control.

B. It is responsible for encrypting session information.

C. It interacts with the Network Layer.

D. It is responsible for segment sequencing.
B. It is responsible for encrypting session information. Encrypting session information is not one of the tasks of the Transport Layer. Encryption occurs higher in the OSI model. The key to remembering the purpose of the Transport Layer is in the name: this layer is responsible for transporting data to its destination.

15. Virtual circuits are examples of what?

A. Mailslots

B. Connectionless-oriented delivery

C. Datagrams

D. Connection-oriented delivery
D. Connection-oriented delivery. Virtual circuits provide a link between two computers using a well-defined path. This is an example of connection-oriented data delivery, because error correction and flow control are provided at various points from the source to the destination.

16. What of the following is not a characteristic of connection-oriented communication?

A. Datagrams

B. Handshaking

C. Virtual Circuits

D. Sessions
A. Datagrams. Datagrams are not connection-oriented because they contain everything they need to get from the source to the destination, such as the source and destination address. These are like pieces of mail that fly all across the country, but magically arrive intact.

17. Why is connection-oriented data delivery faster?

A. Because a session between the two computers is maintained for the entire duration of the transfer of data.

B. Because you can quickly resend data if it becomes lost or corrupt.

C. Because the packets already know where they are going and don't have to find alternate routes.

D. Connection-oriented data transfer is not quicker than connectionless-oriented data transfer.
D. Connection-oriented data transfer is not quicker than connectionless-oriented data transfer is. When you are communicating via a connectionless-oriented session, the sending computer does not need to wait for a reply from the destination computer that the data arrived error-free; the source computer just sends the data out as fast as it can. That is why connectionless-oriented data transfer is not reliable.

18. Which is the best example of a mailslot?

   A. A two-way telephone conversation

   B. A bulletin board

   C. An answering machine

   D. A specific port on a computer used for sending and receiving mail
   B. A bulletin board. A mailslot is a way to send a message where no one person or 100 persons can receive the message. The purpose is that you are sending information to many clients and do not require a response that every single person has read the message.

19. The LMHOSTS file is a static file to resolve what types of names?

   A. UNIX

   B. NetBEUI

   C. Host

   D. NetBIOS
   D. NetBIOS. NetBIOS names are resolved using a static text file called LMHOSTS. LMHOSTS is being replaced by WINS, which is a dynamic means of registering and releasing NetBIOS names that doesn't involve manual intervention from an administrator.

20. What does DNS stand for?

   A. Directory Name Structure

   B. Domain Name System

   C. Domain Naming System

   D. Directory Naming System
   B. Domain Name System. DNS is the centralized database that contains a large amount of host name to IP address mappings. Clients configured to use the DNS server will query the server in the event they require host name resolution. DNS is still not dynamic at this time; an administrator needs to manually enter the host name-to-IP address mappings in the DNS database.

21. What will happen on a Windows NT Workstation if a duplicate IP address is detected during the boot process?

   A. An error will be issued and you can continue; just don't forget to fix the problem before it gets worse.

   B. An error will be generated and TCP/IP will not be working on your machine.

C. You will be prompted to change your IP address to avoid an address conflict.

D. Nothing will happen, at least until the first computer attempts to access the network.

B. An error will be generated and TCP/IP will not be working on your machine. If a duplicate IP address is detected on the network, the second machine will not be able to function on the network. The first machine will also receive an error indicating a duplicate address has been detected. Having TCP/IP not initialize on the second computer eliminates the condition in which duplicate IP addresses on the network can cause lingering problems that are difficult to isolate.

22. Which of the following is a valid IPX internal network address?

A. 00EE2210FF

B. 112233ZZ

C. ABACAB

D. 1EF332001

C. ABACAB. The IPX internal network address is a one- to eight-digit hexadecimal address. Remember that hexadecimal numbers include the letters A-F. The other addresses listed contained too many digits or invalid characters, such as Z.

23. Which two protocols are located in the Network Layer?

A. IPX and NetBEUI

B. IP and SPX

C. IPX and SPX

D. IP and IPX

D. IP and IPX. As you discovered in the Network Layer discussion, IP and IPX are located in the Network Layer, and the other components of these protocols, TCP and SPX, are located within the Transport Layer. The protocols in this layer provide for communications sessions between computers to move data reliably.

24. In which layer of the OSI model is the SPX protocol present?

A. Network

B. Internet

C. Data Link

D. Transport

D. Transport. The SPX protocol, a portion of the IPX/SPX protocol, resides in the Transport Layer. SPX is an acronym for Sequential Packet Exchange, which describes the purpose of the SPX protocol: to sequence the data.

25. NetBEUI is considered a protocol at what layer of the OSI model?

A. Network

B. Data Link

C. Transport

D. Physical

C. Transport. NetBEUI is considered a Transport protocol because it establishes sessions between computers with the use of NetBIOS, and also provides the data transport services.

Chapter 4 Answers

1. TCP/IP's unique addressing mechanism provides for more than how many IP addresses?

   A. 3.5 billion addresses
   B. 5.2 billion addresses
   C. 4.2 billion addresses
   D. 6.6 billion addresses
   C. 4.2 billion addresses. TCP/IP's unique addressing mechanism provides for more than 4.2 billion addresses. Don't try counting for yourself, just trust us! Although 4.2 billion unique IP addresses seems like a lot, we are running out and are currently working on a plan called IPv6 for the next generation of IP addresses, which will remain backwards compatible with the current TCP/IP addressing scheme.

2. What if the default gateway is not configured in the DHCP server for a client that is configured to use DHCP?

   A. An error will be issued.
   B. The default gateway defaults to 0.0.0.0.
   C. The default gateway defaults to 255.255.255.255.
   D. You must specify the IP address, subnet mask, and default gateway as a minimum for DHCP configured clients.
   B. The default gateway defaults to 0.0.0.0. If the default gateway is not configured in the DHCP server, it defaults to 0.0.0.0. The default gateway does not have to be supplied to a DHCP-enabled client; however, the IP address and subnet mask must be present for DHCP to work correctly.

3. Which of the following is not true regarding DNS servers?

   A. Any machine can provide this DNS domain service for one or more zones.
   B. The DNS server and the domain are not necessarily one machine.
   C. The DNS server for the domain must be indicated by the top-level domain server.
   D. The actual DNS server machine is not indicated within the DNS hierarchy.
   C. The DNS server for the domain must be indicated by the top-level domain server. The actual DNS server machine never has to be specified within the DNS hierarchy; any machine can provide the DNS domain service for one or more zones.

4. Which of the following is not true regarding DNS root servers?

   A. DNS root servers are not required.
   B. The root DNS database is maintained locally by a specific authority.
   C. The root servers are used to route the request to the next correct server.
   D. The root servers provide addresses to the domain servers associated with that root.

A. DNS root servers are not required. DNS root servers are essential for the name resolution process because the root server looks up the domain name in question in its database and sends the packet on to that specific domain name service. This specific domain name then provides an answer, or an error if nothing was found.

5. Where is DNS information stored?

   A. unix/bin/etc/DNS

   B. %systemroot%\system32\DNS

   C. unix/etc/bin

   D. %systemroot%\system32\etc\DNS
   B. %systemroot%\system32\DNS. Although DNS information can be supplied in the Registry, it can also be supplied in the following directory: %systemroot%\system32\DNS on a Windows NT machine.

6. How are name registration and replication implemented in WINS?

   A. Name resolution is static, and replication is done manually.

   B. Name resolution is dynamic, and the whole database is replicated.

   C. Name resolution is static, and changes are replicated.

   D. Name resolution is dynamic, and changes are replicated.
   D. Name resolution is dynamic, and changes are replicated. You must remember that WINS is dynamic and DNS is static. Another major difference between WINS and DNS is that with WINS, changes to the database are replicated, whereas with DNS, the entire database is replicated.

7. How can you stop name resolution packets from looping around the network endlessly?

   A. Specify a lower TTL value.

   B. Specify a maximum number of hops in the HOSTS file.

   C. Specify a higher TTL in the HOSTS file.

   D. Specify a lower TTL in the DNS cache file.
   A. Specify a lower TTL value. The Time-To-Live (TTL) value for a TCP/IP packet is the maximum number of hops, usually around 30, that a packet can travel in the course of the packet's lifetime. "Hopping" over a router designates a hop. This TTL value is not specified in the HOSTS or DNS cache file.

8. What does ICMP stand for?

   A. Internal Control Message Protocol

   B. Internet Control Mail Protocol

   C. Internet Control Message Protocol

   D. Internal Control Mail Protocol
   C. Internet Control Message Protocol. The ICMP protocol is used to share status and error information about the TCP/IP protocol. Ping and tracert utilities use ICMP packets to report their status on the destination status and route progress.

9. Which of the following is not associated with the SNMP implementation?

   A. Network protocol identification and statistics

   B. Management system

   C. Packet routing

   D. Management Information Base

   C. Packet routing. Simple Network Management Protocol (SNMP) enables you to monitor the status of devices on your network. The Management system queries network devices' Management Information Bases for configuring and status information. Packet routing is not associated with SNMP.

10. Which of the following is true regarding the IP protocol?

    A. The IP protocol guarantees timely and error-free delivery.

    B. The TCP protocol can be used to send information if the IP protocol is not configured correctly.

    C. The IP protocol is a connectionless delivery system.

    D. The IP protocol requires that the TCP protocol provide routing information.

    C. The IP protocol is a connectionless delivery system. TCP provides a reliable, connection-based delivery service, but IP is a connectionless delivery system that makes a "best-effort" attempt to deliver the packets to the correct destination. The IP protocol provides packet delivery for all other protocols within the TCP/IP suite.

11. Which network address class supports more than 70,000 hosts?

    A. Class A

    B. Class B

    C. Class C

    D. Class D

    B. Class B. In the Class B range there is the possibility of having 16,384 networks, with each network having the capability of 65,534 unique hosts when using the default subnet mask.

12. The Class C address range is from 192.0.1.0 to what?

    A. 221.255.255.0

    B. 223.255.255.0

    C. 223.255.0.0

    D. 225.255.255.0

    B. 223.255.255.0. Class C addresses range from 192.0.1.0 to 223.255.255.0. Class D addresses range from 224.0.0.0 to 239.255.255.255. In the Class C range there is the possibility of having 2,097,152 networks, with each network having the capability of 254 unique hosts when using the default subnet mask.

13. What is the default subnet mask for a Class C network?

    A. 255.255.0.0

    B. 225.225.225.0

    C. 255.255.255.0

D. 225.255.255.0

C. 255.255.255.0. The default subnet mask for a Class C network is 255.255.255.0, or in binary representation, 11111111 11111111 11111111 00000000. You can see how the first three octets of the IP address are masked by binary 1s to display the three octet, or 24-bit network address.

14. Which host is normally used in a BOOTP process?

A. The local host

B. The DHCP server

C. 255.255.255.255

D. 0.0.0.0

D. 0.0.0.0. this is a special address that has all 0s in the host ID, which signifies "this host" and is normally used in a BOOTP (another name for DHCP) process when a host doesn't yet know its IP address. The second special address is an address that has all 1s in the host ID, which signifies a broadcast address.

15. Which address is reserved for internal loopback functions?

A. 0.0.0.0

B. 1.0.0.0

C. 121.0.0.0

D. 127.0.0.0

D. 127.0.0.0. Network IDs cannot start with 127, because this address is reserved for loopback and is used mainly for testing TCP/IP and internal loopback functions on the local system. For example, pinging the address of 127.0.0.1 on your TCP/IP-based machine, if properly configured, will cause a response from the loopback adapter, namely your network interface card. This is a testing procedure to make sure TCP/IP has initialized on your interface.

16. What is the well-known port number for the HTTP service?

A. 20

B. 21

C. 80

D. 70

C. 80. The HTTP service uses a well-known port of 80 on the server. A client is not forced into using port 80 to contact the web server with HTTP traffic; it will use any port number.

17. Which of the following methods would not be helpful when you are trying to stop the assignment of duplicate IP addresses on your network?

A. Using two DHCP servers on the same network

B. Using a spreadsheet to track in-use IP addresses

C. Using ping to test for connectivity before you assign an IP address

D. Using a DHCP server

A. Using two DHCP servers on the same network. It is not advisable to use two DHCP servers on one network, unless the network is separated by routers. The second DHCP can provide backup for the first DHCP server, but the IP address scope should *not* contain the same IP addresses.

18. On a Windows 98 machine, which page of the TCP/IP properties dialog box would you use to configure your workstation to use a DHCP server?

   A. Identification

   B. DHCP

   C. IP Address

   D. WINS

   C. IP Address. On a Windows 98 machine, the IP address can be used to specify the use of a DHCP server for obtaining an IP address automatically, or you can manually assign the workstation a valid IP address and subnet mask.

19. Which of the following is not on the DNS page of the TCP/IP Properties dialog box?

   A. DNS Service Search Order

   B. Domain Suffix Search Order

   C. Use WINS for DNS Resolution

   D. Domain name

   C. Use WINS for DNS Resolution. In Windows 95, 98, and NT, there is no option on the DNS page of the TCP/IP Properties dialog box to use WINS for DNS resolution. The only other options on the DNS page that

are not listed here are Host name, Enable DNS, and Disable DNS.

20. Where can you specify a second DNS Service for faster host and domain name resolution?

   A. DNS Service Search Order

   B. Domain Suffix Search Order

   C. Domain Name

   D. You can't specify a second DNS Service for faster host and domain name resolution.

   D. You can't specify a second DNS Service for faster host and domain name resolution. The DNS Service Search Order is a fail-over list, not an additional location. Only if the first one fails to respond after a nominal timeout period, is the next DNS Service list tried with the same request, and so on.

21. You are having problems communicating with a remote network via the default gateway. Which of the following will not ensure fault tolerance if you have specified an incorrect default gateway on a client computer?

   A. Obtain the default gateway entry from a DHCP Service.

   B. Configure the workstation to use the WINS Service instead.

   C. Implement a route table, which can be used to route packets to known networks before the default gateway entry is used.

D. Specify multiple gateways.
B. Configure the workstation to use the WINS Service instead. Each of the above selections, with the exception of B, can be used to specify a correct default gateway entry, or to work around the problem of an unresponsive default gateway entry.

22. Which tab would you click on a Windows 98 machine to configure the gateway?

    A. IP Address

    B. NetBIOS

    C. Advanced

    D. Gateway
    D. Gateway. No trick here. To specify the default gateway on a Windows 98 machine, click the Gateway tab on the TCP/IP Properties dialog box. You have the option of specifying more than one gateway on this page.

23. Which is not an available option on the WINS Configuration page of the TCP/IP Properties dialog box on a Windows 98 machine?

    A. WINS Suffix Search Order

    B. Scope ID

    C. Use DHCP For WINS Resolution

    D. WINS Server Search Order
    A. WINS Suffix Search Order. DNS uses a suffix search order, but the WINS Service uses a server search order. The DNS Service also uses a DNS Service search order, so don't let all these services get you confused.

24. How do you automatically configure a Windows 98 client to point to a specific WINS server?

    A. Enter the IP address on the WINS Configuration page of TCP/IP Properties dialog box.

    B. Select the Enable WINS Lookup option button on the WINS Configuration page of the TCP/IP Properties dialog box.

    C. Select the Use DHCP for WINS Resolution option button on the WINS Configuration page of the TCP/IP Properties dialog box.

    D. Enter the NetBIOS name of the WINS server on the WINS Configuration page of the TCP/IP Properties dialog box.
    C. Select the Use DHCP for WINS Resolution option button on the WINS Configuration page of the TCP/IP Properties dialog box. You can automatically obtain the IP address of the WINS server through use of DHCP. Be warned that entering any address manually while your workstation is configured to obtain the IP address automatically will override the DHCP WINS server address.

25. Where can you specify a new computer name on a Windows 95 machine?

    A. The TCP/IP Properties dialog box

    B. The IP Address page

    C. The Identification page

D. The DNS page

C. The Identification page. The Identification page of the Network applet in the Control Panel is where you assign your computer a new NetBIOS name. To assign your computer a new host name, enter the host name on the DNS page of the TCP/IP Properties dialog box.

Chapter 5 Answers

1. Which utility can be used to display and modify the table that maintains the TCP/IP address to MAC address translation?

A. NBTSTAT

B. TELNET

C. ARP

D. SNMP

C. ARP. The Address Resolution Protocol is responsible for translating IP addresses to MAC addresses. The utility with the same name is used to display and modify the entries contained within its table.

2. Which format types are not valid for ARP? (Choose all that apply.)

A. ARP reply

B. ARP decline

C. ARP response

D. ARP request

B, C. ARP decline and ARP response. The only valid formats for ARP are the reply and the request. ARP decline and ARP response are not valid formats.

3. Which command uses the proper syntax for adding a static entry to the ARP cache?

A. ARP -s 137.21.19.211 00-1A-0B-1C-32-11

B. ARP –add 137.21.19.211

C. ARP –s 00-1A-0B-1C-32-11 137.21.19.211

D. ARP –s 137.21.19.211

A. ARP -s 137.21.19.211 00-1A-0B-1C-32-11. To add a static entry to the ARP cache, you must specify the IP address and then the MAC address. Entries will not be added if the entries are not in order. The –add is not a valid option.

4. How long will a dynamic ARP entry remain in cache if it is not in use?

A. 10 minutes

B. 5 minutes

C. 2 minutes

D. None of the above

C. 2 minutes. Dynamic entries are cleaned out of cache periodically. The default settings for this interval are two minutes if they are not in use. If the entries are being used, they will time out after ten minutes.

5. Which utility enables you to execute console commands remotely at a virtual terminal?

A. FTP

B. Ping

C. Telnet

D. NBTSTAT

C. Telnet. Telnet is used to execute console commands remotely. This functionality is used for remote administration and troubleshooting.

6. Which protocol is defined to use TCP port 23?

A. Telnet

B. FTP

C. HTTP

D. SMTP

A. Telnet. Telnet uses TCP port 23.

7. What is the default terminal emulation type for Telnet?

A. DEC

B. ANSI

C. VT52

D. VT100

D. VT100. Although multiple emulation types are available with Telnet, VT100 is the default terminal emulation type.

8. Which protocol uses a 16-character name with the last digit reserved as a resource identifier?

A. TCP/IP

B. IPX

C. NetBT

D. NBTSTAT

C. NetBT. The NetBIOS over TCP/IP, or NetBT protocol, uses this naming convention.

9. Which utility can be used to troubleshoot NetBIOS over TCP/IP connectivity issues?

A. NetBT

B. NetBEUI

C. NBTSTAT

D. NetBIOS

C. NBTSTAT. NBTSTAT is used to troubleshoot NetBT connectivity problems. It can also be used to display statistics relating to this protocol.

10. Which NBTSTAT switch enables you to display the computer's local NetBT name cache?

A. –R

B. –c

C. –a

D. –A

B. –c. The -c switch can be used while troubleshooting to list the computer's local NetBT name cache.

11. In what ways can a computer with a NetBIOS name register its services on the network?

A. Broadcast

B. HOSTS file

C. WINS server

D. Both A and C

D. Both A and C. NetBIOS names can be registered both via broadcast and by a WINS server. The HOSTS file contains only IP host name to IP address mappings.

12. Which NBTSTAT option will display statistics such as number of bytes inbound?

A. −s

B. −r

C. −n

D. −a

A. -s. The −s switch is used to display these types of statistics. It can also display outbound bytes and connection states.

13. Which utility is used to determine the path data is taking during transport to a remote host?

A. NBTSTAT

B. ARP

C. FTP

D. Tracert

D. Tracert. The tracert utility uses ICMP to monitor a data's route and report statistics.

14. What is the default HOP count used by tracert?

A. 5

B. 16

C. 30

D. 32

C. 30. You must use the −h option to specify a different value.

15. Which utility is used to display TCP/IP specific protocol and interface statistics?

A. NBTSTAT

B. ARP

C. Netstat

D. None of the above

C. Netstat. Information such as the specific transport protocol being used and the connection state can be obtained with this utility.

16. Which netstat option continually updates the displayed output based upon a time interval?

A. −p

B. −r

C. <interval>

D. −e

C. <interval>. By appending a numeric interval after the command, you can specify a time frame in seconds that the command uses to update the display.

17. Which option is used with netstat to display server-based connections and listening ports?

A. −r

B. −k

C. −s

D. None of the above

D. None of the above. By default, server connections are not displayed. The −a option is used to display these statistics.

18. Which protocols do not have statistics available with the netstat utility?

A. TCP

B. ICMP

C. ARP

D. IP

C. ARP. Statistics for the Address Resolution Protocol are not available through the netstat utility. The ARP utility must be used to obtain this information.

19. Which utility is used to display TCP/IP address information in Windows 95?

A. IPCONFIG

B. NBTSTAT

C. WINIPCFG

D. None of the above

C. WINIPCFG. WINIPCFG is used in Windows 95 and Windows NT uses IPCONFIG.

20. Which items are not available for display in IPCONFIG?

A. TCP/IP address

B. MAC address

C. DHCP Lease information

D. None of the above

D. None of the above. All of the options listed can be displayed in IPCONFIG by using the /ALL option.

21. Which option listed is not available with WINIPCFG?

A. /ALL

B. /Release

C. /Obtain

D. /Renew

C. /Obtain. There is not a parameter for /Obtain.

22. Which utility is used to facilitate file transfers between two remote hosts?

A. FTP

B. Telnet

C. Ping

D. None of the above

A. FTP. File Transfer Protocol is used for transferring files between two computers.

23. What TCP ports are used by FTP services?

A. TCP port 20

B. TCP port 25

C. TPC port 21

D. Both A and C

D. Both A and C. FTP uses TCP port 20 for data transfer and TCP port 21 for commands.

24. Which FTP command line option is used to turn on debugging?

A. –r

B. –d

C. –debug

D. –v

B. –d. The –d switch turns on debugging when used with the FTP command..

25. Which utility is used to verify network connectivity of a remote host?

A. Route

B. ARP

C. Ping

D. None of the above
C. Ping. The ping command is used to contact a remote host to verify connectivity.

Chapter 6 Answers

1. Which network layer protocols can the Serial Line Internet Protocol use during a dial-up session?

A. TCP/IP

B. IPX

C. SLP

D. None of the above
A. TCP/IP. The Serial Line Internet Protocol (SLIP) was designed for remote access on UNIX servers. IPX and SLP are not valid with SLIP as it only supports TCP/IP.

2. Which protocol supports multiple Network Layer protocols over a serial link?

A. SLIP

B. PPP

C. IPX

D. NetBEUI
B. PPP. Point-to-Point Protocol supports multiple network layer protocols, such as TCP/IP, IPX, and NetBEUI. SLIP only supports TCP/IP while IPX and NetBEUI do not support multiple network layers at all.

3. Which components are part of the Point-to-Point Protocol?

A. Network Control Protocol

B. Link Control Protocol

C. Internet Protocol

D. Internet Packet eXchange Protocol
A, B. Network Control Protocol and Link Control Protocol. NCP facilitates different network layer protocols through PPP. The LCP tests and configures the connection. The Internet Protocol (IP) and Internet Packet eXchange Protocol (IPX) are network layer protocols that can be used to connect to remote resources once a PPP connection has been established.

4. Which Network Control Protocol is used in PPP to facilitate the transport of TCP/IP?

A. IPNP

B. IPCP

C. IPXCP

D. None of the above
B. IPCP. IPCP (Internet Protocol Control Protocol) is the NCP used to pass TCP/IP data through a PPP dial-up link. IPCP does not exist for PPP and IPXCP is the NCP used for the IPX protocol.

5. Which forms of validation can PPP use to authenticate users against a remote server? (Choose all that apply.)

A. CHAP

B. Domain Account

C. PAP

D. KPA

A, C. CHAP and PAP. CHAP (Challenge Handshake Authentication Protocol) and PAP (Password Authentication Protocol) are valid forms of authentication used by PPP services. A Domain Account is not an authentication method used by PPP and KPA does not exist.

6. Where is the connection information for a PPP dial-up session stored?

A. C:\Windows\ppp\PPPLOG.TXT

B. C:\Windows\PPP.LOG

C. C:\Windows\PPPLOG.TXT

D. C:\PPP.TXT

C. C:\Windows\PPPLOG.TXT. By default, the information logged during a PPP dial-up session is stored in C:\Windows\PPPLOG.TXT. A PPP directory does not exist by default in C:\Windows and PPP.TXT is not the name used for the log file by default.

7. What technology does Virtual Private Networks (VPNs) offer to provide a more secure communications channel?

A. IP header compression

B. Tunneling

C. Multiple network protocol support

D. None of the above

B. Tunneling. Tunneling enables a user to cross a public TCP/IP network, such as the Internet, to a private network, using a secure connection. IP header compression is used to speed up the connection and multiple network protocol support is provided by the PPP protocol.

8. Virtual Private Networks use what kind of devices as if they were modems inside the computer?

A. Network Interface Cards

B. Virtual Devices

C. Non-Virtual Devices

D. Modems

B. Virtual Devices. VPNs set up virtual devices to act as a modem in the transfer of data through a PPTP link. Network Interface Cards are actual physical devices and modems are used for serial based connections. Non-Virtual Devices do not exist.

9. What is the process called for setting up a "tunnel" for the PPTP protocol?

A. PPP Connection and Communication

B. PPTP Control Connection

C. PPTP Data Tunneling

D. PPTP Data Transfer

B. PPTP Control Connection. The process for actually setting up the tunnel is PPTP Control Connection.

10. What is the maximum number of virtual devices a Windows NT 4.0 server can have set up?

A. 10

B. 50

C. 256

D. 1024

C. 256. By default, Windows NT Server can accommodate up to 256 VPNs. Workstations will require only 1 VPN while servers require as many connections as users attaching to it.

11. What was the first Integrated Services Digital Network standard to be published by the ITU?

A. ISDN-1

B. ISDN-NI

C. NI

D. NI-1

D. NI-1. The ITU first recognized NI-1 (National ISDN 1) as the official standard. ISDN-1, ISDN-NI, and NI are not valid standards for ISDN.

12. What is the standard bandwidth that is available with an ISDN B channel?

A. 4 Kbps

B. 64 Kbps

C. 64 Mbps

D. 128 Kbps

B. 64 Kbps. The standard bandwidth available in an ISDN B channel is 64 Kbps. A typical ISDN line contains 144 Kbps, 128 Kbps for data, and 16 Kbps for line administration.

13. How many B channels are available in a typical ISDN PRI?

A. 2

B. 20

C. 23

D. 30

C. 23. In a standard ISDN PRI, 23 B channels are included. While 2 and 20 are not valid, 30 channels are available in the European implementation of an ISDN PRI.

14. What category of ISDN devices would peripherals such as a standard telephone, a fax machine, or a personal computer fit into?

A. TE1

B. I1

C. NT1

D. None of the above

D. None of the above. Peripherals such as a standard telephone or PC fall in the ISDN device category of TE2. TE1 devices include ISDN specific items such as ISDN fax machines and connect to an NT1 or NT2 device. I1 is not a valid device type and NT1 devices connect directly to the central office switch.

15. What ISDN identifier includes the directory number plus additional numbers used to identify an ISDN channel?

A. Bearer ID

B. SPID

C. SAPI

D. None of the above

B. SPID. The Service Profile Identifier identifies an ISDN channel and includes the directory number plus additional numbers. A Bearer ID and SAPI do not exist as identifiers for ISDN.

16. What network did wide area network technologies originate from?

    A. ISDN

    B. PSTN

    C. PKB

    D. None of the above
    B. PSTN. WAN technologies originated from the PSTN. ISDN came about because of this progression while PKB is not a WAN technology.

17. What is the maximum speed current analog modems can reach?

    A. 33.6 Kbps

    B. 56 Kbps

    C. 128 Kbps

    D. 1.5 mbps
    B. 56 Kbps. The maximum speed available using an analog modem is 56 Kbps. Some existing modems can only speak 33.6 Kbps while 128 Kbps and 1.5 Mbps are not valid speeds for a standard analog modem.

18. Which modem type is not a valid category for the Public Switched Telephone Network?

    A. Single internal modem

    B. Single external modem

    C. Multiline rack mount modems

    D. None of the above
    D. None of the above. All three of these entries are valid categories for the PSTN. Each type of modem option provides its own advantages and disadvantages.

19. What line protocols are available with Microsoft's dial-up networking?

    A. NetWare Connect

    B. Point-to-Point Protocol

    C. Serial Line Internet Protocol

    D. All of the above
    D. All of the above. NetWare Connect, PPP, and SLIP are all valid line protocols with Microsoft's dial-up networking. NetWare Connect only supports IPX, PPP support multiple network protocols, and Slip only supports TCP/IP.

20. What serial standard is typically used to connect a modem to a computer?

    A. IRQ

    B. EIA/TIA-232

    C. 232

    D. None of the above
    D. EIA/TIA-232. The EIA/TIA-232 standard is generally used when connecting a modem to a computer via a serial interface. An IRQ is a computer resource type and 232 is not a serial standard.

21. What COM port is used by default when setting up a modem?

    A. 2

    B. 4

    C. 1

    D. 3
    C. 1. Although each of these COM ports is available, COM1 is used by default. COM2 is used for a second

modem and COM3 and COM4 are
not usually used.

22. What is the default IRQ setting
    for COM2?

    A. 2

    B. 14

    C. 4

    D. 3
       D. 3. The default IRQ setting for
       COM2 is 3. COM 1 uses a default
       IRQ of 4. IRQ's 2 and 14 are usually
       taken by the system for other resources

23. Which modem standard defines
    error-checking standards?

    A. V.42

    B. V.34

    C. V.52

    D. V.100
       A. V.42. The V.42 modem standard
       defines error-checking standards. The
       V.34 standard defines the standard for
       communications at the speed of 28
       Kbps. V.52 and V.100 are not valid
       modem standards.

24. Which application programming interface
    is used to include features such as call
    monitoring and multiple localities?

    A. Unimodem

    B. COMM

    C. TAPI

    D. None of the above
       C. TAPI. TAPI (Telephony API)
       enables the use of features such as
       call monitoring and multiple

localities. Unimodem is used to
provide a single interface to
applications for accessing the modem
while COMM does not exist.

25. Which items listed are required for a
    dial-up connection to a remote host?

    A. Modem device

    B. Line protocol setup

    C. Valid user ID and password

    D. All of the above
       D. All of the above. A modem device,
       a line protocol, and a valid user ID
       and password are all required to
       connect to a remote host.

Chapter 7 Answers

1. What portion of the Windows NT
   security subsystem handles local security
   policies and user authentication and
   generates audit log messages?

   A. Local Security Authority (LSA)

   B. Security Accounts Manager (SAM)

   C. Security Reference Monitor

   D. None of the above
      A. Local Security Authority (LSA).
      The LSA handles these functions
      above the Security Accounts Manager
      and Security Reference Monitor. They
      are used to provide specific functions
      for the LSA.

2. What portion of the security reference
   model maintains the database used for
   storing user and group account
   information?

A. Local Security Authority (LSA)

B. Logon Process

C. Security Reference Monitor

D. Security Accounts Manager (SAM)
   D. Security Accounts Manager (SAM).
   The SAM maintains the database that
   users and groups are stored in. The
   LSA authenticates the logon processes
   and the Security Reference Monitor
   generates audit logs.

3. When an access token is created for a user,
   which information is included?

   A. User Security Identifier (SID)

   B. Primary Group Security Identifier

   C. Group Security Identifier

   D. All of the above.
      D. All of the above. An access token
      includes the User Security Identifier, a
      Primary Group Security Identifier,
      and a Group Security Identifier. In
      addition, an access token also includes
      access permissions.

4. What access control list object determines
   what users and groups have permissions to
   this object?

   A. System Access-Control List (SACL)

   B. Discretionary Access-Control
      List (DACL)

   C. Owner

   D. User
      B. Discretionary Access-Control List
      (DACL). The DACL determines the
      permissions associated and the SACL

controls security auditing. The owner
maintains ownership of the object and
a user is not a valid ACL object type.

5. Which of the following are valid,
   predefined file permission types? (Choose
   all that apply.)

   A. No access

   B. List

   C. Add

   D. Change
      A, C, D. No access, Add, and Change.
      No access, Add, and Change are file
      and directory attributes, but List is
      used only in directory permissions.

6. Which groups are created by default for a
   standalone Windows NT server and
   workstation? (Choose all that apply.)

   A. Administrators

   B. Account Operators

   C. Backup Operators

   D. Print Operators
      A, C. Administrators and Backup
      Operators. These two groups are
      created on both member servers and
      domain controllers. Account
      Operators and Print Operators are
      only created on domain controllers.

7. What identifier is used in conjunction
   with a share name to make them hidden?

   A. #<share name>

   B. <share name>#

   C. <share name>$

D. None of the above.
C. <share name>$. Appending the $ to the end of a share name keeps the share name from appearing in the browse list of available resources.

8. Which of these is a common rule for creating a secure password?

A. Do not use a familiar name such as your child's name, your spouse's name, or your pet's name.

B. Do not use your first, middle, or last name or nickname.

C. Do not use a password of all single digits or the same letter. For example: 1111111 or AAAAAAA.

D. All of the above.
D. All of the above. Each one of these is a good rule of thumb when creating passwords. Other rules include using non-alphanumeric characters, randomly changing the capitalization, and using more than six characters in your password.

9. Which of the following is a common mechanism for creating passwords? (Choose all that apply.)

A. Create a password that uses a myriad of intermingled alphanumeric characters.

B. Take several words and use different portions of each, separated by a non-alphanumeric character.

C. Uses a four-character password of non-alphanumeric characters.

D. All of the above.
A, B. Create a password that uses a myriad of intermingled alphanumeric characters and take several words and use different portions of each, separated by a non-alphanumeric character. Both of these make an effective password, but using a four-character password is not recommended.

10. What policies are not available from within User Manager for Windows NT?

A. Minimum password length

B. Maximum password length

C. Minimum password age

D. Maximum password age
B. Maximum password length. Windows NT does provide a maximum number of characters usable in a password; however, this cannot be modified through User Manager.

11. Within User Manager, what menu option lists additional user rights that can be added?

A. Policies | Audit

B. Users | Audit

C. Policies | User Rights

D. Users | User Rights
C. Policies | User Rights. The Policies | Audit option only supports auditing. The Users tab does not have an Audit or User Rights option on its menu.

12. Which of the following options are available when setting up auditing?

A. Interactive Logon

B. Remote Resource Access

C. Logon and Logoff

D. System Process
   C. Logon and Logoff. This option is used to monitor the logon and logoff activity by users. Interactive Logon, Remote Resource Access, and System Process are not valid options.

13. After auditing has been set up, what utility is used to monitor the activity and the events generated?

   A. User Manager

   B. Server Manager

   C. Event Viewer

   D. Performance Monitor
      C. Event Viewer. When events trigger a log entry, they will appear in the security event logs. User Manager is used to create the audit policy. Server Manager does not list security events, and Performance Monitor can monitor activity but is not where the logs are sent.

14. What is the symmetric encryption algorithm better known as?

   A. Digital Encryption Standard (DES)

   B. RSA standard

   C. Private-key algorithm

   D. Public-key algorithm
      C. Private-key algorithm. The symmetric algorithm is known as the private-key algorithm because both parties use the same key to encode and decode the encrypted data.

15. Which of the following is classified as an encryption method? (Choose all that apply.)

   A. Stream Cipher

   B. Data Cipher

   C. Byte Cipher

   D. Block Cipher
      A, D. Stream Cipher and Block Cipher. Both are valid encryption methods. Data Cipher and Byte Cipher do not exist.

16. What Block Cipher Mode encrypts each block individually during the encryption process?

   A. Electronic Codebook (ECB)

   B. Cipher Block Chaining (CBC)

   C. Cipher Feedback Mode (CFB)

   D. None of the above
      A. Electronic Codebook (ECB). The Electronic Codebook mode encrypts each block individually, but the Cipher Block Chaining and Cipher Feedback Modes do not.

17. What encryption standard is based upon a fixed 56-bit symmetric key encryption algorithm?

   A. RSA

   B. DES

   C. CPA

   D. DSE
      B. DES. The Data Encryption Standard uses this algorithm. The RSA uses a different type of algorithm

and CPA and DSE are not valid encryption standards.

18. What technology uses certificate authorities to verify that a message has not been tampered with?

A. RSA encryption

B. Local Security Authority

C. Digital Signatures

D. None of the above
   C. Digital Signatures. This technology does not encrypt the message; it only verifies that it arrived without being tampered with. RSA is an encryption standard and the Local Security Authority is a Windows NT subsystem.

19. What service is available to enable you to add encryption services directly into an application?

A. PGP

B. DES

C. Uuencode

D. CryptoAPI
   D. CryptoAPI. Microsoft has provided the CryptoAPI to interface encryption services into applications. PGP cannot support services at this level and DES is only an encryption standard. Uuencode does not provide encryption but is used to convert binary e-mail attachments to ASCII so they can be transported using SMTP.

20. What technology provides a secure communications channel between an internal network and a public network such as the Internet?

A. Encryption

B. Firewall

C. Router

D. None of the above
   B. Firewall. Firewall is used to provide the secure communications channel. Encryption service provides secure data. A router is used to provide a normal channel. Special types of router configurations are available for providing a secure channel.

21. What kind of firewall provides a single computer with two physical network interfaces?

A. Dual-homed firewall

B. Screened host firewall

C. Screening router

D. Screened subnet firewall
   A. Dual-homed firewall. A dual-homed firewall contains two internal physical interfaces. A screened host firewall passes data through a screening router first. A screening router is a secure configuration for a router; a screened subnet firewall provides two screening routers.

22. What component(s) is included in a screened subnet firewall configuration?

A. Single screening router

B. Host firewall server

C. Circuit application

D. All of the above
B. Host firewall server. However, this configuration requires two screening routers.

23. What type of firewall is used to provide security based upon rules governing the network or transport layers?

A. Packet level

B. Application level

C. Circuit level

D. None of the above
A. Packet level. The packet level controls the network or transport layer within packets. The application level type controls the layers above the transport level. The circuit level type works at the transport layer.

24. What level types of firewalls can act as proxies? (Choose all that apply.)

A. Packet level

B. Application level

C. Circuit level

D. All of the above
B, C. Application level and circuit level. Both of these types of firewalls can be used to proxy information, but the packet level firewall cannot work at this level of the OSI reference model.

25. What features are now available with firewall implementations?

A. Encryption

B. Application caching

C. Virtual Private Networks (VPN's)

D. All of the above.
D. All of the above. All three of these features are now included in some firewall implementations.

Chapter 8 Answers

1. What hardware network components are needed when connecting two computers with a standard 8-port hub on the same subnet?

A. Network cards

B. Category 5 UTP cable

C. SCSI adapter card

D. Router

E. Network Layer of the OSI Model
A, B. Network cards and Category 5 UTP cable. If you are going to be using a hub, all that you need to connect the two computers are a network card and the necessary cable (unshielded twisted pair). A SCSI adapter card is normally used to connect SCSI components, so you wouldn't use it. A router is used to connect two different networks, and the Network Layer of the OSI Model is a logical layer that is used to help explain the concept of networking.

2. Susan L. wants to make some changes to her file server so that the Accounting group only has permission to the \\Payroll and \\401K shares on her network. What two accounts should Susan use to make

sure that she made the necessary changes and that an ordinary user wouldn't have accidental access to the share?

A. Account Operator

B. Root

C. Her "test" account

D. Backup Operator

E. Administrator

C, E. Her "test" account and Administrator. Whenever making changes to your network in any capacity, from changing permissions on a file server to implementing a new network policy, you should always make the changes with an Administrator account and then verify that you made the correct changes with a test account. With a test account that has "normal" privileges on the network, you can simulate an ordinary user. By not going back over your changes, you cannot guarantee that you made the correct changes. Account Operator, Root, and Backup Operator are all different accounts that wouldn't have full access to the network.

3. Mike K. is a new employee at a large manufacturing company and needs to set a password for his account so that he can log on to the network. He is in charge of a large group of sensitive files, so he wants to make sure that he has a safe and secure password. What is an example of a strong password?

A. BALONEY

B. Fuh3H3manners!

C. ilovethemets

D. password

E. cheesesandwich

B. Fuh3H3manners! Remember that when choosing a strong password, it should be more than eight characters and consist of both letters and numbers. To increase the strength of your password, you might even consider using the various keys such as !,@,#,$,%,^,&,*,(,). You should never consider using easily remembered passwords such as phrases, words, or birthdays. And please do not place any passwords on any yellow sticky notes stuck to your monitor!!!!

4. Melissa B. needs to use the Internet for work so that she can research a new product that she is interested in. When she tries to use a search engine, nothing is working. Her browser is working correctly and there is nothing wrong with the network. When she calls the help desk, they look at her IP address information and find the following. What could be wrong?

```
Ethernet adapter:
Description . . . . . . . . :
  3Com 3c905XL 10/100 Ethernet Card
Physical Address. . . . . . :
00-00-86-20-45-90
DHCP Enabled. . . . . . . . : No
IP Address. . . . . . . . . : 209.116.171.105
Subnet Mask . . . . . . . . : 255.255.255.192
Default Gateway . . . . . . :
Primary WINS Server . . . . :
Secondary WINS Server . . . :
```

Lease Obtained. . . . . . . :

Lease Expires . . . . :

A. Wrong IP address

B. Subnet mask

C. Default gateway

D. Nothing

    C. Default gateway. For a computer with a TCP/IP address to reach another network, the computer must be able to reach a router or default gateway. A router is a device that looks at the Network Layer of the OSI Model and "routes" or sends packets to foreign networks. Without this device configured, Melissa's computer cannot send her IP information to any network other than her own.

5. Dave R. is connected to his LAN and wants to browse on his Intranet to update his 401K information. However, he cannot connect to any of the web servers on his intranet. Dave can, however, PING the computers by using their IP addresses. The IP information is listed below. What could be the problem?

Ethernet adapter:

Description . . . . :

   3Com Megahertz 10/100 Ethernet +

   56K PC Card

Physical Address. . . . . . :

00-00-86-20-45-90

DHCP Enabled. . . . . : No

IP Address. . . . . : 209.116.171.36

Subnet Mask . . . . : 255.255.255.192

Default Gateway . . . . . . : 209.116.171.65

Primary WINS Server . . . . :

Secondary WINS Server . . . :

Host Name . . . . : USWEBCS

DNS Servers . . . . :

Lease Obtained. . . . . . . :

Lease Expires . . . . :

A. Default gateway

B. Subnet mask

C. Name Resolution

D. DHCP

E. Host Name

    C. Name Resolution. Name resolution enables computers with TCP/IP addresses to be mapped to logical names on a network. Two common name resolution means are WINS or DNS servers that will automatically map these IP addresses to computer names. If he does not have any form of name resolution, Dave will not be able to map his computer to any computers by using their names.

6. What are three adverse environmental conditions that would affect the performance and capability of a computer network?

A. Wind

B. Humidity

C. Extreme heat

D. Barometer

E. Moisture

F. pH balance

    B, C, E. Humidity, Extreme heat, and Moisture. At optimal conditions, your computer room should be air-conditioned, dry, well lit, and have fire suppression. Extreme heat and moisture are detrimental to your computer. Air conditioning circulates the air and keeps it cool. Of course, this room should be locked at all times.

7. What is the technical computer term for when another system's electrical interference is causing performance degradation of a computer?

A. Attenuation

B. EMI

C. Crosstalk

D. Plenum

   B. EMI. EMI, or electromagnetic interference, occurs when an electrical device interferes with your computer's normal performance. To fix this problem, you should move all of your computer cables away from fluorescent lighting and other electrical appliances.

8. Linda R. keeps getting the following error message every time she tries to start a program from the command line of her Windows 98 computer. What could the problem be?

   C:\program.exe
   Bad command or file name

A. Syntax error

B. Wrong path for executable

C. Typo

D. Program does not exist

   A. Syntax error. Normally, if you see a "Bad command or file name" message, you are not in the right path of your executable or program. You should make sure that you are in the correct directory and make sure that your program exists before calling tech support for this problem.

9. What two things must you make sure that you do before you can use any of your external SCSI components, such as backup devices or CD-ROM devices?

A. Make sure they are turned on before your computer is.

B. Reboot them twice.

C. Terminate them.

D. Use an IDE cable.

   A, C. Make sure they are turned on before your computer is and terminate them. Whenever using external SCSI devices, you need to make sure of a couple things before you can use them effectively. First of all, all SCSI devices must be turned on prior to starting your computer. Secondly, you need to make sure that you terminate the end of your SCSI adapter that is located on your adapter card. Once you have these areas ironed out, you shouldn't have any problems with your SCSI devices.

10. Which computer peripheral is used to connect an ordinary computer to another computer by the use of an existing telephone line?

A. Network card

B. Modem

C. SCSI adapter

D. Scanner

E. Printer

B. Modem. A modem (modulator/demodulator) is a communications device that enables a computer to talk to another computer through a standard telephone line. The modem converts digital data from the computer to analog data for transmission over the telephone line and then back to digital data for the receiving computer.

11. Which network appliance is used to connect two computer networks that are separated by two different protocols?

A. Router

B. Bridge

C. ATM switch

D. Hub

E. Gateway

E. Gateway. A gateway is used to connect two networks that are separated by two different protocols, such as TCP/IP and IPX/SPX. A gateway differentiates itself from a router in the sense that a router can connect two different networks that are separated by the *same* protocol and a gateway can take a look at the packet and rebuild the protocol stack to the desired network.

12. Which layer of the OSI Model does a network bridge work on that is used to connect between a TCP/IP network?

A. Physical

B. Application

C. Data Link

D. Network

E. Session

C. Data Link. A bridge works at Layer 2, or the Data Link layer, of the OSI Model by forwarding packets of data based on MAC addresses. A bridge can be used to filter traffic on a LAN by determining the source and destination involved in the transfer of packets. A bridge reads the physical address of a packet on one network segment and then decides to filter out the packet or forward it to another segment on the network.

13. What are three technical characteristics of the Universal Serial Bus (USB) technology?

A. Nicknamed "fire-wire"

B. Daisy chains USB-supported devices

C. Must be terminated at each end

D. Requires an AC adapter

E. Works with infrared technology

F. Can support data transfer up to 12 Mbps

A, B, F. Nicknamed "fire-wire," Daisy chains USB-supported devices, and Can support data transfer up to 12 Mbps. USB, or fire-wire, is a new technology that enables you to daisy chain devices from your computer. Because USB relies on the existing power supply of your computer, each device does not require any further power. The most remarkable feature about USB technology is the amazing amount of data that can be shared—up to 12 Mbps.

14. What two accounts should you use when you change an account on your network to ensure that the changes have been made?

A. Root

B. Backup Operator

C. Normal

D. Everyone

E. Test Account

F. Administrator

E, F. Test Account and Administrator. To make any changes on your network, you need an administrative account. To ensure that your changes are working under normal operating conditions, you should verify that your changes are working by using a test account.

15. Meredith wants to increase the bandwidth capacity on her network for one geographic location that houses 2000 separate hosts. Her network is currently using shared hubs in a star topology environment. What network appliance should she use to do this?

A. Gateway

B. Bridge

C. Router

D. Switch

E. Repeater

F. Multiplexer

D. Switch. For a network the size of Meredith's, she should implement network switches to increase the amount of bandwidth for her network. Switches are intelligent and can ensure the amount of bandwidth for each port. You can also create VLANs and create collision domains to help route traffic.

16. What type of network cable can support data speeds up to 100 Mbps on a local area network?

A. 10BaseT (Category 1)

B. Phone wire

C. 10bT (Category 5)

D. T.V. Cable

C. 10BaseT (Category 5). 10BaseT network cabling that has been certified as "Category 5" can support data transfer up to 100 Mbps for distances up to 100 meters.

17. What level of the OSI Model do network switches commonly work at?

A. Application

B. Layer 8

C. Network

D. Physical

E. Fiber-Channel

C. Network. Network switches commonly work at Layer 3, or the Network Layer, of the OSI Model. Switches have the capability to look into the header of the packet and examine its contents and transmit the packet according to its destination.

18. What environmental conditions are not recommended for housing network servers and other electrical equipment? (Choose all that apply.)

A. Humid

B. Wet

C. Extreme Cold

D. 70 Degrees.
A, B, C. Humid, Wet, and Extreme Cold. You should keep your servers and other electrical equipment away from extreme temperature, moisture, vibrations, and electrical interference. If computers are exposed to these conditions they can act irregularly and sometimes fail.

19. Which type of NetBIOS Name resolution is used to resolve Windows computer names to TCP/IP addresses on a local area network?

A. DNS

B. DSN

C. WINS

D. HOST File
C. WINS. A WINS, or Windows Internet Naming Service, server is used to resolve Windows Computer names to TCP/IP addresses. Whenever a computer wants to communicate with another computer, it will check its local name cache and

then contact a configured WINS server to resolve the IP address.

20. What is used to separate the Host ID from the Network ID in a four-octet TCP/IP address?

A. Default gateway

B. Router

C. Subnet mask

D. WINS

E. DNS
C. Subnet mask. A subnet mask is used to separate the Host ID from the Network ID in a TCP/IP address. This enables you there to split up an IP address into more than one configuration to scale to a new environment.

21. In an extreme case, how long can a standard fiber-optic cable be run from one end to the other?

A. 100 meters

B. 26.4 miles

C. 2 kilometers

D. 500 meters
C. 2 kilometers. The maximum length a fiber-optic cable can be run is 2 kilometers. When that distance has been achieved, a device must be in place to boost the signal of the cable to continue.

22. What port on your computer can provide the largest amount of data transfer from one peripheral to another?

A. Serial port

B. Parallel port

C. Monitor

D. Keyboard

B. Parallel port. A parallel port can transfer data in both directions and offers more data transfer between the computer and the peripheral.

23. What should you not place computer equipment close to so that it will not be susceptible to different forms of electrical interference? (Choose all that apply.)

A. Television

B. Florescent light

C. Generator

D. Lead wall

A, B, C. Television, florescent light, and generator. All three of these devices can disrupt computer equipment by causing a disturbance in the electrical field.

24. What account on a network server can have total control over the functionality of the server?

A. Guest

B. Test account

C. Everyone

D. Administrator

E. Backup Operator

D. Administrator. Only the person who uses the Administrator account can manage and control the network to its fullest extent. The administrator is responsible for all changes to the network and should test all changes when finished.

25. Which type of network appliance can perform the duties of protocol conversion from either TCP/IP to IPX or ATM to Frame Relay?

A. Router

B. Switch

C. Gateway

D. Bridge

E. MUX

C. Gateway. A gateway can perform protocol conversion and routing services from one protocol to another. A router can route packets and data, but cannot perform protocol conversion from one type to another.

26. What protocol can be used to route to different networks and connect computers directly to the Internet?

A. IPX/SPX

B. NetBEUI

C. SNA

D. TCP/IP

E. RIP

D. TCP/IP is used to connect computers directly to the Internet, and is also routable. IPX/SPX is a routable protocol, but is not used to connect computers to the Internet.

Chapter 9 Answers

1. Which of the following best describes the term *dependencies*?

   A. Applications that are required by another application in order to run correctly

   B. DLLs that are required by an application to run correctly

   C. Hardware resources that are required by another resource to run correctly

   D. Applications that are required for a software driver to work correctly
   A. Applications that are required by another application in order to run correctly. Many times an application requires that a certain service pack be installed on the computer. These are known as *dependencies* because the application you wish to install is dependent on these additional applications, service packs, or software updates being present on the system.

2. You have an e-mail server that has just lost a hard disk drive and needs to be functioning as quickly as possible. Which of the following is the fastest way to get the server running with the most current data possible?

   A. Manually install the operating system, install the e-mail program, and then restore the data from the most recent tape backup.

   B. Use a third-party disk image program to bring down an image stored on a server, and then restore the data from the most recent tape backup.

   C. Use an unattended installation of the operating system, install the e-mail program, and then restore the data from the most recent tape backup.

   D. Manually install the operating system, and then restore the e-mail program and data from the most recent tape backup.
   B. Use a third-party disk image program to bring down an image stored on a server, and then restore the data from the most recent tape backup. In addition to keeping documentation on these select systems on your network, you can also purchase third-party utilities that create images of these servers. If you create new, updated images every week or so, you can apply this image to a fresh rebuilt computer in a matter of minutes. You can go from a disastrous hard disk crash to being fully operational again in thirty minutes.

3. Which of the following items would restore a Windows NT system as closely as possible to the original configuration before a hard disk crash?

   A. A tape restore of the operating system and the user and system database

   B. A tape restore of the operating system, the Registry, and the user profiles

C. A tape restore of the full system, the Registry, and the most recent data

D. A tape restore of the operating system, the Registry, the most recent data, and the user profiles

C. A tape restore of the full system, the Registry, and the most recent data. Microsoft recommends backing up and restoring the Registry for each Windows computer if you truly want to return a computer to its original operating state. The Registry contains current user and system information, which means the backup should be the most recent in order to rescue the most recent changes to the system. The most recent data will most likely come from the tape backup done the night before.

4. You came into work this morning and discovered that the tape backup did not complete successfully. The backup job usually backs up around 13GB of data, but this time the backup was around 12GB of data. This job usually fits on one tape, rarely fails, and has not been changed lately. What is most likely the cause, and how should you remedy the situation?

A. The backup server most likely could not attach to a resource to complete the backup. Check the error logs to determine where the server could not connect. If a user has turned off his computer, make sure he leaves the system on at night.

B. The backup server could not load the tape. Check the contents of the tape to verify you are not trying to overwrite a write-protected tape.

C. The backup server could not append to the tape. Check the contents of the tape to verify you are not trying to overwrite a write-protected tape.

D. The backup server most likely could not attach to a resource to complete the backup. Verify the backup server has rights to the specific share. Grant the backup server rights to attach to the share.

A. The backup server most likely could not attach to a resource to complete the backup. Check the error logs to determine where the server could not connect. If a user has turned off his computer, make sure he leaves the system on at night. If the backup program could not attach to one user's computer because he shut his computer down at the end of the night, you will receive an error. Read through the error logs to determine where the job failed. If it fails every night trying to connect to another network server, remedy the situation before it's too late.

5. Which of the following is not true concerning tape backup?

A. It is the most expensive type of backup method.

B. It uses a sequential access method.

C. You can use multiple tapes in a tape magazine.

D. They are slower than most backup media.

A. It is the most expensive type of backup method. Backing up to tape is the most common form of backup done today, because of the availability and price. Tape backup is slower, due to the sequential access of the medium. It works like a cassette tape does, where you have to fast-forward or rewind to find your favorite song. This is the opposite of *random-access.* Multiple tape magazines are used for companies that back up large amounts of information every night. These backup jobs can even exceed a 24GB compressed tape. When one tape is full, the backup process will continue on the next available tape.

6. What does Windows NT use to distribute logon scripts to multiple servers?

   A. The distribution service

   B. The domain controller service

   C. The replication service

   D. The backup process
      C. The replication service. Windows NT provides a replication service to replicate data to other servers. This may sound like a means of backing up, but the service is provided to replicate commonly used items such as logon scripts to back up domain controllers.

7. You have a software development department with ten users. You need to provide everyone in the department with a way to access data that has been backed up permanently. The users will need to use

this data at their computers to perform their jobs. What is the best way to accomplish this?

   A. Install tape backup devices on each developer's computer and copy the nightly tape backups on tape for each user to peruse.

   B. Have a tape backup server that holds the last five days worth of backups that each developer can attach to and peruse for information.

   C. Archive the data on CD-ROM and copy the CD for each developer to peruse at their workstations.

   D. Copy the backup data to the network, establish a share, and let the users attach to the share and peruse the information.
      C. Archive the data on CD-ROM and copy the CD for each developer to peruse at their workstations. The type of removable media you require is based on the needs of your particular network. Many companies use tape backup for nightly backups and then use writable CD-ROMs to create images or backup sets that can be used on any machine with access to a CD-ROM.

8. Which of the following is a large capacity, removable, magnetic medium?

   A. Reel Tape

   B. Floppy disk

   C. Optical disk

D. Disk cartridge

D. Disk cartridge. The disk cartridge, such as a Zip or Jaz drive, is growing in popularity as the price falls. The capacity is growing and the speed is increasing. The disk cartridge is a random-access device, which makes it faster than sequential-access devices.

9. During the GFS scheme, you begin the week by performing a full backup. For the remaining days of the week, which type of backup could you perform? (Choose all that apply.)

A. Full

B. Incremental

C. Differential

D. No backup

A, B, C, D. The GFS (Grandfather – Father – Son) strategy is a method of maintaining backups on a daily, weekly, and monthly basis. The GFS rotation scheme is based on a seven-day weekly schedule, beginning on any day of the week, in which you create a full backup at least once a week. On the other days you can perform full, incremental, differential, or no backups.

10. Which of the following is not a good reason for removing an unused or outdated driver?

A. To conserve space

B. To conserve memory

C. So they don't accidentally get loaded

D. So they don't get corrupted

D. So they don't get corrupted. There are a number of reasons why it is recommended to remove outdated or unused drivers on a system: so they don't accidentally get loaded, to conserve disk space, because loaded drivers consume memory, and they can interfere with a new driver.

11. Which of the following workstation settings can cause the most damage on a network?

A. An improperly configured binding order

B. An improperly configured speed on the network card

C. An invalid Token Ring address

D. A workstation configured as a Master Browser

B. An improperly configured speed on the network card. However, with that in mind, make sure you use extreme caution when configuring a network adapter card. If you are going to down the network doing anything, it will be from misconfiguring a network card. Misconfiguring the speed on a network card will confuse and lock up a hub.

12. Which of the following computers will send out a beacon on a Token Ring network indicating a fault?

A. The most active upstream neighbor

B. The nearest upstream station

C. The most active upstream station

D. The nearest active upstream neighbor
D. The Nearest Active Upstream Neighbor. When a computer with a faulty network card is on the network, it can continuously chatter on the network, eating up bandwidth. Usually you will need to use special software to analyze packets on the network to determine which computer is having problems. A Token Ring network will cease to function and the nearest active upstream neighbor (NAUN) to the failed computer will send out a beacon, alerting you to which computer is not functioning correctly.

13. You have just installed Windows NT Workstation on your machine and added a few applications. While you were trying to add Microsoft Office 97, you received an error. What will this error most likely indicate?

    A. That a DLL has been overwritten by a previous application install

    B. That Office 97 has not been installed correctly

    C. That your system requires Service Pack 2 or later

    D. That a DLL could not be copied to the destination directory
    C. That your system requires Service Pack 2 or later. Lately we have been seeing many applications that require a certain Windows NT service pack in order to perform. This has been the case with the Y2K bug, which is said

to be relieved with Microsoft's Service Pack 4 for Windows NT. A few applications require that the operating system be patched with Service Pack 4 in order for the application itself to be Y2K-compliant. Other applications, such as Microsoft Office 97, require that Service Pack 2 or later be installed prior to installing Office 97.

14. What is one way to determine if a DLL has been overwritten by another application?

    A. Check the Event Viewer.

    B. Check the install log for each application.

    C. Open the sysdiff log file to determine which files have been overwritten by another application.

    D. There is really no way to tell.
    D. There is really no way to tell. Overwritten DLLs become more of a problem as you add more applications to the system. It is nearly impossible to determine which applications' DLLs have been affected. You may have discovered that a DLL has been updated with a newer one, but which application was responsible? Even worse, you have an older application that has written a much older DLL over a newer DLL. The last program installed should have no problems, but the existing application will most likely fail with the older DLL.

15. Which of the following is the correct syntax for mapping to a share called

HeatherCurtis on the server called PeaceCorp with the drive designator of L?

A. net use L \\PeaceCorp\HeatherCurtis

B. net use /L: \PeaceCorp\HeatherCurtis

C. net use L: \HeatherCurtis\\PeaceCorp

D. net use L: \\PeaceCorp\HeatherCurtis

D. net use L: \\PeaceCorp\ HeatherCurtis. The mapping begins with two backslash characters before the server name. After the server name, a backslash precedes the share name.

16. You have created a batch file to map network drives and printers for each user in the department. The following is your newly created batch file:

```
net use R: /delete
net use R: \\Rhapsody\March99
net use S: /delete
net use S: \\Enertia\QuarterlyReports
net use lpt1: \\Sanvoisen\HPLJ4SI
```

Which line in the batch file is invalid or incorrect?

A. The second line

B. The fourth line

C. The fifth line

D. There is no invalid or incorrect line in this batch file

D. There is no invalid or incorrect line in this batch file. The preceding batch file commands will delete the share if it already exists and map the share again. The share is deleted before it is mapped to circumvent the error

message that is received when you try to establish a drive mapping that is already in place. The last line in the batch file will map a printer to the local lpt1 port.

17. You are planning to move the web servers from one location to another. This move is planned for later tonight. The user support database is run from the web server, so the move must be completed by the morning. What needs to be done to ensure a smooth move?

A. Migrate the user profiles to another server before the move.

B. Test the network connection in the new room.

C. Back up the data on the servers.

D. Back up the user profiles before the move.

B. Test the network connection in the new room. Moving a computer from one room to another doesn't sound like that difficult a process. However, there are hidden traps that can make this move more disruptive than it needs to be. In order to complete a move without incident, you should test the area you are moving the computer to before the move. Most importantly, you should test the network connection.

18. Van Williams, the supervisor for the A-crew in the receiving department, will be leaving the company. Jeff Loomis, the new supervisor, will be starting shortly in

Van's position. What should happen to Van's user account?

A. It should be deleted.

B. It should be disabled.

C. It should be moved to the temporary area.

D. It should be renamed to Jeff Loomis, the new supervisor.

D. It should be renamed to Jeff Loomis, the new supervisor. You know the user name of the new supervisor, so you should rename the account to his name. If you didn't know the name of the new user, you could have disabled Van's account and renamed the account when the new user arrived. If you delete his account immediately, you will have to re-create the account for the new hire and add the new hire to the existing shares that Jim had access to. This can be a very overwhelming task if Jim had explicit access to many files and folders.

19. You need to give Internet access to eight users in the sales department. However, you do not want to give access to the entire sales department. How would you go about granting Internet access to these users?

A. Grant the sales group rights to access the Internet.

B. Grant each user rights to access the Internet.

C. Place each of the users into a group called Internet and give this group access to the Internet.

D. Grant the sales group rights to access the Internet, but revoke rights for those who do not need access to the Internet.

C. Place each of the users into a group called Internet and give this group access to the Internet. Although you can give rights, such as access to the Internet, to one group, it's a good idea to start a group called Internet, which will consist of users that have access to the Internet. As each user requires access to the Internet, you can place his account in this group. Even groups, such as the sales group, can be placed in this group to give every user in that group access to the Internet.

20. You are on a Windows NT workstation and would like to drop a shortcut into the personal directory of Warrel Dane, whose username is Wdane on the local computer. You are currently logged on as administrator of the local machine. Which directory do you place this shortcut in?

A. winnt\profiles\WDane\shortcuts\personal

B. winnt\system32\profiles\Wdane\personal

C. winnt\profiles\Wdane\personal

D. winnt\system\profiles\Wdane\personal

C. winnt\profiles\Wdane\personal. A user profile stores user preferences such as screen savers, last documents used, network drive mappings, and environmental settings, such as program groups. When the user logs off, the changes are saved so that the next time the user logs on, the settings are just as he left them. The profile starts as the default user and then is saved in the user's logon name in the system root, which in Windows NT is usually C:\winnt\Profiles.

21. What is the difference between rights and permissions?

   A. Permissions are assigned to objects, and rights are given to user or group accounts

   B. Permissions are given to user or group accounts, and rights are given to objects

   C. Permissions are given to user accounts, and rights are given to groups

   D. Permissions are given to groups, and rights are given to user accounts
   A. Permissions are assigned to objects, and rights are given to user or group accounts. The user account carries around the credentials of what objects the user has rights to. Permissions are given to objects. The object itself carries around a list of who is entitled to use the object.

22. Tim Owens has come back this morning from a two-month sabbatical. He calls you and tells you he can't access the network. You haven't disabled his account. He believes he is typing in the right password, because it's written on his monitor. What account policy is most likely the problem?

   A. Account Lockout

   B. Maximum Password Age

   C. Minimum Password Age

   D. Lockout Duration
   B. Maximum Password Age. Some networks have a policy that passwords expire after a certain number of days. With your user accounts, there are account policies you can implement to help control the security of your network. Some of the items you can control with account policies include the minimum and maximum password age, minimum password length, and account lockout.

23. What is the user and group management utility provided with NetWare 3.*x*?

   A. NetWare Administrator

   B. SYSADMIN

   C. SYSCONSOLE

   D. SYSCON
   D. SYSCON. Microsoft Windows NT 4.0 Server has User Manager for Domains; Windows NT Workstation has User Manager; Novell NetWare, version 3.*x* has SYSCON; and Novell NetWare, version 4.*x* has the graphical NetWare Administrator. Each of these administrative tools enables you to add, modify, and delete users and groups.

24. Which of the following is not a recommendation for dealing with the administrator's account?

A. It should be deleted after you have used it to create your administrative account.

B. It should be disabled.

C. It should be copied for a backup.

D. It should be renamed.
   A. It should be deleted after you have used it to create your administrative account. It is a good idea to create a backup administrator account in the event that the administrator account's password is forgotten. This also helps if something happens to the administrator account that makes it unusable. It's also a good idea to rename the administrator account. Renaming the account makes it more difficult for someone to hack into your network. The administrator account cannot be deleted or disabled.

25. Which of the following is not a built-in Windows NT group?

A. Domain Guests

B. Domain Admins

C. Domain Users

D. Domain Administrators
   D. Domain Administrators. When Windows NT Server is installed, a series of built-in global groups are created:
   - Domain Admins
   - Domain Users
   - Domain Guests

The Domain Admins global group is a member of the Administrators local group on every computer in the domain by default. The Domain Users global group contains all subsequent accounts created in the domain. The Domain Guests global group is intended to provide limited and/or temporary access to the domain.

Chapter 10 Answers

1. What is one key component of installing an update or patch successfully on your network?

   A. Reading competitors' documentation to see whose is better, and then selecting the better package.

   B. Reading the readme files and documentation to make sure you have the information you need to install the application successfully.

   C. Reading the documentation on the server to see if the software is compatible with the server.

   D. Reading the Web site home page to see if the product is still in production.
      B. Reading the readme files and documentation to make sure you have the information you need to install the application successfully. The key point here is that the readme files and the documentation are vital to successful installation on the network. Missing a step or doing things in the wrong

order can result in network problems or even bringing the network down.

2. To make sure you have the most up-to-date files and version of the software, you need to go to the vendor's Web site and download the most current what?

   A. Software packs

   B. Network packs

   C. Software patches

   D. Readme files

   C. Software patches. The latest patches are vital to successful implementation of software. Service packs and patches update the software and take care of known bugs that result in workstation, server, or network problems.

3. Network operating systems, such as NetWare and Windows NT, have these to update the specific modules within the operating system?

   A. Supdate packs

   B. Service calls

   C. Serial pack

   D. Service pack

   D. Service pack. Vendors release service packs from time to time to do an overall update to the components that may have bugs in them or need improvements for performance purposes. These are available from Microsoft's and Novell's Web sites.

4. Where can you go to search for information on errors you are receiving on your network to see if you need a patch or service pack?

   A. Vendor's online support forums

   B. Excite search engine

   C. Control Panel under System

   D. Help section under Start menu

   A. Vendor's online support forums. The vendor's Web site usually has a support forum you can either search through or read posts from other users for common problems and patches and service packs that are available.

5. When software vendors want to update their software in a major way and bring out a new version, this is known as a what? (Hint: This is sometimes free and sometimes costs money.)

   A. Update

   B. Upgrade

   C. Upload

   D. Patch

   B. Upgrade. An upgrade is a major release update and change to the software. Vendors do this to make their software more powerful and better for the end user.

6. Along with updating the software, there is something dealing with the hardware that may need to be updated. What is it called?

   A. RAM

   B. ROM

   C. Formware

D. Adapter

B. ROM. The ROM update is a firmware update that updates the software within a hardware component, such as an adapter.

7. To keep a consistent approach to network maintenance, it is important to do what?

   A. Format one hard disk per month on your network to clean up hard disk space.

   B. Get into the routine of downloading patches that are not for your network just so you have a grasp of everything that is out there.

   C. Get into the routine of applying updates and patches on your network on a regular basis.

   D. Delete and reconfigure your system volumes on your servers on an annual basis.
   C. Get into the routine of applying updates and patches on your network on a regular basis. Establishing a routine is important to keep your network up to date across all platforms and applications. Consistency and keeping everything up to date is important to successful network administration.

8. What is the first thing you need to do to install backup software on your network server?

   A. Physically install the tape drive and any adapter boards that are needed. Along with this, connect the cables between the tape drive and the adapter board. Also make sure that power is connected.

   B. Make sure your backup software has everything in it before proceeding.

   C. Refer to the specific instructions for your backup software for any unique pre-installation items.

   D. Make sure the system that you are installing to meets the hardware and software requirements.
   D. Make sure the system that you are installing to meets the hardware and software requirements. The first thing to do is make sure that your system will run the software you are installing. If this step isn't successful, none of the other steps matter. Checking compatibility is the first step in installing any software on any system, stand alone or networked.

9. You are running a Windows NT Server and want to know if your backup software is running. Where do you go to get this information?

   A. Go to My Computer and select the tape drive.

   B. Go to Control Panel and select Backup.

   C. Use the CTRL-ESC sequence and select the screen for the backup software.

   D. Go to the Control Panel and select Services.
   D. Go to the Control Panel and select Services. Windows NT runs the backup software as a service. To view

the services, go into the Control Panel and select Services. Then you can scroll through the list and see if the service for the backup is started.

10. What are the two common types of tape drives in today's networks? (Select two.)

   A. DDS

   B. DAT

   C. DLT

   D. DET
      B, C. DAT and DLT. The DAT and DLT tape drives are the most common tape drives in today's networks. The DAT drive uses small Digital Audio Tapes with helical scanning. The DLT drive uses large tapes that are faster and have more capacity. The DLT system is similar to the old reel-to-reel tape system.

11. Which of the following is *not* a backup job type?

   A. Full

   B. Incremental

   C. Differential

   D. Incidental
      D. Incidental. The three backup job types are full, incremental, and differential. The full backup is a full backup. The incremental backup backs up the files that were added or changed since the last incremental or full backup. The differential backup backs up those files that were added or changed since the last full backup.

12. Along with updating your server-specific software, such as backup software and virus software, what else should you update?

   A. Application software, such as databases that are stored on the server but run the application at the workstation.

   B. Cables that connect your network between the workstation and the hub.

   C. Server hard disks when new ones come out.

   D. User directories that contain user data should be updated with other users' data.
      A. Application software, such as databases that are stored on the server but run the application at the workstation. Updating applications that run at the workstation but store data on the server is also vital to network success. A good example of this is a database that resides on the server but the application runs on the workstation and needs to be updated at each workstation.

13. Which of the following is a component of a virus protection suite? (Choose all that apply.)

   A. Real-time scanner

   B. Local scanner

   C. Network/Domain scanner

   D. ROM scanner
      A, B, C. Real-time scanner, Local scanner, and Network/Domain scanner. The real-time scanner

monitors for viruses in real time; the local scanner can scan local drives or mapped drives on a workstation; and the Network/Domain scanner scans the entire network for viruses to protect you from getting infected.

14. What available options are there for taking care of viruses? (Choose all that apply.)

    A. Move file

    B. Cure file

    C. Delete File

    D. Copy file

    A, B, C. Move file, Cure file, and Delete File. The options when dealing with virus-infected files include moving the file, deleting the file, curing the file, and also reporting the virus with no activity. These options give network administrators some flexibility regarding how viruses are handled on their network.

15. If you want to scan local or mapped network drives, which of the following options should you choose?

    A. Network Scanner

    B. Local Scanner

    C. Real-Time Scanner

    D. Disk Recovery Option

    B. Local Scanner. The Local Scanner gives the option of scanning local and mapped network drives. This is good for doing manual scans of drives that have not been scanned recently; it is done from a workstation.

16. How often are virus signatures generally updated by the vendor or manufacturer?

    A. Daily

    B. Weekly

    C. Monthly

    D. Annually

    C. Monthly. The updates on virus signatures are generally on a monthly basis. Virus signatures should be updated on a monthly basis to ensure that your virus software is as up to date as possible and ready to detect the latest viruses.

17. What are the main advantages to DLT tape drives over DAT tape drives? (Choose all that apply.)

    A. Faster data transfer rates

    B. Higher storage capacity

    C. Higher reliability

    D. Higher availability

    E. More accurate

    A, B, C. Fast data transfer rates, Higher storage capacity, and High reliability. Along with the advantages of faster data transfer rates, higher storage capacity, and higher reliability, comes a higher cost. The DLT technology is more expensive. The DAT drive uses the old reel-to-reel system where the tape cartridge holds one reel and the other reel is contained in the tape drive.

18. When DAT tapes were emerging as a popular storage media for computer data,

a format was given to the storage of computer data; what is this format known as?

A. DDS

B. DDT

C. DAT

D. DLT

A. DDS. DDS format stands for Digital Data Storage. This is a little different from the original storage methods of storing audio. Most DAT drives use a 4mm tape. A helical scan is used and the read/write heads spin diagonally across the tape.

19. You installed a tape drive in your server. The server has an existing SCSI controller and other SCSI devices in the system. Since adding the SCSI tape drive to the SCSI chain you get errors from two devices. What is the most likely cause of this type of problem?

A. Tape drive is not compatible with system.

B. SCSI ID is unique, not enabling the tape drive to communicate in the SCSI chain.

C. SCSI ID is the same on the two devices, causing a conflict.

D. The IDE connector is not hooked up on the tape drive.

C. SCSI ID is the same on the two devices, causing a conflict. The SCSI ID has to be unique between devices in a SCSI chain. If they are not unique, there will be a conflict with the other SCSI device that shares the SCSI ID.

20. You have been running a full backup at the beginning of the week and incremental backups on the remaining four days. Your hard drive crashes and you have to restore from tape. What is the proper method for restoring from tape with this backup scenario?

A. Restore from the last full backup only.

B. Restore from the last full backup and the most recent incremental backup.

C. Restore from only the incremental backups.

D. Restore from the last full backup and all incremental backup tapes since the last full backup.

D. Restore from the last full backup and all incremental backup tapes since the last full backup. You need to use the full backup and all incremental backups because the incremental backup backs up only those files that were added or changed since the last incremental backup. Each incremental tape will have only those files that are new or different. You also have to be sure to restore in order from oldest to newest backup tape. Restore from the last full backup tape first, and then restore from each incremental backup tape in order from the one after the full backup to the most recent.

21. You are the network administrator for a small company. Your boss wants you to have the quickest available restoration method in the event of data loss. She also wants you to have the most up-to-date virus protection available.
Required results: Be able to restore from one tape in the event of hard disk failure. Be able to scan with most recent virus signature files.
Optional results: Have workstations and server as up to date as possible with virus software.
Proposed Solution: Implement full backup daily and update virus software signatures once a year.

    A. The proposed solution produces both the required and the optional results.

    B. The proposed solution produces both the required but not the optional results.

    C. The proposed solution produces one of the required results and the optional result.

    D. The proposed solution produces one of the required results and none of the optional results.
    D. The proposed solution produces one of the required results and none of the optional results. The proposed solution satisfies the backup needs but not the virus protection needs of your boss. The virus signatures need to be updated on a monthly basis in order for them to be as up to date as possible on both the server and the workstations.

22. What is a good rule of thumb to follow when applying patches to a network if the files need to be copied into place manually?

    A. Delete original files first and then copy new files in their place.

    B. Rename the original files with an extension such as OLD or BAK and then copy the new files in place.

    C. Copy the new files over the old files.

    D. Copy the old files over the new ones in the temporary directory.
    B. Rename the original files with an extension such as OLD or BAK and then copy the new files in place. It is always good to rename the old files to have them available in case the patch causes problems. Yes, this does happen from time to time. Being able to roll back from a patch isn't necessarily a bad thing.

23. When updating ROMs there are two ways to tell if the ROM you are applying is newer than what you have currently. What are the two ways?

    A. ROM date

    B. ROM file size

    C. ROM version

    D. Manufacturer file name
    A, C. ROM date, ROM version. You can tell by the ROM date and version number whether the ROM on your system can be updated to a newer one. Updates take care of any known issues with the common network operating

systems and will sometimes simply increase performance.

24. With some software there is documentation that comes on the CD or disks. In order to read through this documentation, what do you need?

   A. A printer

   B. The correct viewer

   C. A Web browser

   D. A special code

   B. The correct viewer. The documentation requires that a special viewer be installed. A common one used today is Adobe Acrobat. We looked at the Dynatext Viewer that Novell uses for their documentation. The viewer generally comes with the documentation and can be installed prior to reading the documentation.

25. To ensure proper disaster recovery in the event your office is burned to the ground, what is the minimum you should do to be able to restore from tape?

   A. Store the monthly tapes in your office.

   B. Keep the monthly tapes close to the server.

   C. Store the monthly tapes offsite.

   D. Store the monthly tapes with the office supplies.

   C. Store the monthly tapes offsite. Storing the monthly tapes offsite will help ensure you have a somewhat recent tape backup to go back to if the office and servers and tapes are burned up in a fire or destroyed in a tornado

or something similar. Offsite storage is a good rule of thumb for any business.

Chapter 11 Answers

1. Which of the following is most likely not a problem when adding another workstation to the network segment?

   A. The workstation is not able to find a domain controller on the network.

   B. The bridge can no longer handle the amount of traffic on the network and begins to lock up.

   C. The workstation is not able to receive an IP address.

   D. The workstation has an error concerning the network card on boot up.

   B. The bridge can no longer handle the amount of traffic on the network and begins to lock up. These new computers not only chew up precious bandwidth, but they require one or more network cards, more cables, ports on the hubs, and, if you are using TCP/IP, these new computers must consume another IP address. In addition to the hardware, you must make sure the network interface card has been correctly configured and the correct network protocols have been loaded and configured.

2. What is the first step to solving a problem?

   A. Replicating the problem

   B. Calling telephone technical support

C. Gathering information

D. Establishing a baseline

C. Gathering information.
Identifying the symptoms of the problem is the first step in diagnosing and solving the problem. This is the information-gathering phase. The more time you spend during this phase, the quicker the problem can be solved.

3. Why is it best to assign tasks to team members while you are troubleshooting a network problem?

A. To keep them separated

B. To avoid them working on the same problem

C. To put a person in their special area of expertise

D. To minimize duplicate information
C. To put a person in their special area of expertise. The point of distributing the work involved with troubleshooting is that one person can spend quality time in one area, and this person can thoroughly understand the complexities of his task. Getting an entire group up to speed on a concept such as routing can be challenging. Picking one specialist to investigate the possible routing issues and report his findings to the group can be very beneficial.

4. Why would you want to brainstorm the problem as a group?

A. To keep everyone interested

B. To not isolate anyone

C. To see if anyone has changed anything recently that you don't know about

D. To see if anyone has experienced this problem before
D. To see if anyone has experienced this problem before in the past. Although it would be nice to know if anyone has changed anything recently, the most appropriate answer is to see if anyone has experienced this problem before. Having the entire collective experience and knowledge of a group of people will guarantee that a problem will be solved. Highly experienced professionals can quickly determine where a problem lies and the best solution for solving the problem. Chances are someone in your group has experienced a problem such as this in the past.

5. Which of the following are reasons you should stop and ask for help if you encounter a problem that you are unable to fix? (Choose all that apply.)

A. You may be fired if you continue further.

B. Someone else may have the answer you are looking for.

C. You may worsen the situation if you continue.

D. Someone may ridicule you.
B, C. Someone else may have the answer you are looking for, and you may worsen the situation if you

continue. Many of us feel embarrassed when we have to stop and ask for help. You should feel proud of yourself that you are stopping to ask for help. Would you rather stop and ask for help, or just continue reconfiguring things until the network completely breaks? You may find the answer very quickly if you get other technicians involved in the troubleshooting process.

6. You are working on a user's computer that cannot access the employee database. You have tried everything on the workstation, but the user still cannot connect. What is the next logical step in arriving at a solution to the problem?

    A. Reboot the user's machine.
    B. Call the database administrator to see if anything has changed.
    C. Open up a phone incident with the manufacturer of the product.
    D. Check the resource kits for a possible solution.
    B. Call the database administrator to see if anything has changed. Maybe something has changed that you are not aware of yet. Would you rather stop and ask for help, or just continue reconfiguring things until the network completely breaks? Some technicians will never ask for help. This is not the type of technician you want on your team. You need a team that can communicate effectively.

7. You are not expected to know everything in your position as network administrator or engineer. However, what are you expected to know?

    A. The technical support phone numbers for every manufacturer of devices that you have on the network
    B. The version of every piece of software currently being used on the network
    C. The answer to nearly every user-related problem
    D. Where to find information
    D. Where to find information. You are not expected to know everything; however, you are expected to know when and where to look for answers. If you and your team are not able to solve the problem, you need to find additional information and resources to solve the problem. These can take the form of resource kits, online help, and telephone technical support.

8. What is the difference between a resource kit and a knowledge base?

    A. The resource kits are free and the knowledge bases are not.
    B. The knowledge bases contain fixes to known problems.
    C. The resource kits are only for reference.
    D. The knowledge base comes with the product, and the resource kit does not.
    B. The knowledge bases contain fixes to known problems. Resource kits are a valuable way of educating yourself.

These are helpful for planning, implementing, configuring, and, most of all, troubleshooting. Microsoft includes the resource kits on the same TechNet CD as the knowledge base. The resource kits are more for reading and planning, whereas the knowledge base is loaded with information on symptoms, causes, and solutions to problems.

9. Where can you go to obtain the latest driver for a device?

A. The CD that came with the product

B. The resource kit

C. The manufacturer's Web site

D. The knowledge base
C. The manufacturer's Web site. If you believe you are having a problem with a particular product or device, you should begin your search with the manufacturer's Web site. You will find information such as updated drivers and patches, detailed installation instructions, troubleshooting tips, and possibly a knowledge base of common problems.

10. You are having a problem with the Shiva LANRemote dial-up networking server. Which of the following will most likely not be of any help in solving the problem?

A. The Shiva Web site

B. TechNet

C. The documentation that came with the product

D. Telephone tech support
B. TechNet. TechNet is Microsoft's technical information database. Phone support personnel have a database of known problems and resolutions that they can query if they don't have the immediate answer. The Web site, in addition to the product documentation, will also have information such as updated drivers and patches, detailed installation instructions, troubleshooting tips, and possibly a knowledge base of common problems.

11. You are getting continual errors when you are running IBM's Personal Communications terminal emulation software. You have been in contact with IBM technical support already, and they have advised you to try their new .dll file that they e-mailed you. You are not exactly sure how to test the new bug fix. What should you do in this situation?

A. Put the .dll in the Windows directory.

B. Check their Web site for instructions.

C. Call IBM technical support.

D. Put the .dll in the Windows\system directory.
C. Call IBM technical support. These support personnel can also lead you step-by-step to installing, testing, and configuring their product. This will often reveal details that you didn't adhere to during the initial installation that was giving you problems. The

support personnel can also provide you with troubleshooting steps to get at the cause of the problem quickly. When you are troubleshooting a complicated problem, don't ignore telephone technical support, because they may have a quick and easy answer to the problem.

12. Which of the following resources should you consider using before you call tech support? (Choose all that apply.)

A. Resource kits

B. Web sites

C. Microsoft TechNet

D. Documentation
A, B, C, D. Resource kits, Web sites, Microsoft TechNet, and documentation. Some companies would prefer you exhaust every possible resource first, such as Microsoft TechNet, resources kits, online help, and documentation before you open up a support incident. The phone support call would be the last resort, mostly because of the cost involved. Other companies do not hesitate to call phone support as the first line of defense.

13. Which of the following are reasons that you may need to consult technical service professionals to analyze your network? (Choose all that apply.)

A. They are highly trained to analyze the results.

B. Management does not trust you with the task.

C. They are very inexpensive.

D. They have expensive hardware and software for monitoring the network.
A, D. They are highly trained to analyze the results, and they have expensive hardware and software for monitoring the network. Not only do you sometimes need professional equipment to monitor your network, but you also need professionals that are trained on the tools to analyze and identify possible afflicted areas based on the results. A network capture of hundreds of packets may be Greek to you, but these professionals are trained to interpret the results.

14. You have one building that has been having intermittent problems communicating with the administration building. How could you go about researching the problem?

A. Check error logs for more information.

B. Hire a company to do an analysis of your network, including capturing packets.

C. Ping the affected areas and check the response time.

D. Have the phone company check the wiring between the two buildings.
D. Have the phone company check the wiring between the two buildings. Even more common than having professionals come in to analyze the network, is the need to contract the phone company for wiring issues. You

do not have the tools such as Tone Generators and time domain reflectometers (TDRs) to analyze possible cable problems.

15. A company released a service pack for their product, but quickly released a notice that the service pack should not be applied. The notice instructed administrators to uninstall the service pack and wait for the newest release. You have already upgraded a few servers with this service pack. How would you determine which servers have this service pack applied and which do not?

 A. Consult the documentation that is continually updated with the server.

 B. Ask everyone in the department if they installed the service pack.

 C. Check the event log for the date the service pack was installed.

 D. Check the operating system version for the new service pack.
 A. Consult the documentation that is continually updated with the server. Determining who is responsible is not the same thing as finding someone to blame when something goes wrong. Support personnel often configure servers and network devices in a unique way, without sharing that information with the rest of the group. By documenting the modifications to the server, you can determine what has changed, and whether that change is adversely affecting the server.

16. Unfortunately, your current network supervisor is moving and must quit the company. What is the best way to ensure the next administrator has enough information concerning the network configuration?

 A. Have the two administrators overlap in employment for at least a month.

 B. Have the new administrator call the old administrator.

 C. Have the old administrator spend his last week documenting everything he can about the network.

 D. Do nothing. The old administrator most likely has bad habits that you do not want to pass on to the next administrator.
 C. Have the old administrator spend his last week documenting everything he can about the network. Network support personnel can spend hours, if not days, getting something to work correctly, yet they rarely spend the time to document their findings for future use. If they leave the company, this information goes with them. The next administrator or engineer may find himself spending as much or more time than the original person trying to get the same problem resolved. If the previous person had documented his findings, it would have made the second person's job much easier.

17. Which of the following information is not helpful to keep in the database of network devices?

    A. MAC address

    B. Number of services running

    C. IP address

    D. Amount of physical memory installed

    B. Number of services running. By documenting devices on the network, you have a current record of countless details about these devices. For example, you can document the amount of physical memory, hard disk capacity, IP address, processor speed, MAC address, and serial numbers. This information can be stored in a centralized database for all computer support personnel to use.

18. Which of the following appears to be the most important condition and should warrant the highest priority?

    A. A user cannot log on.

    B. One of the printers is jammed.

    C. Several users are receiving a message that their hard drives are full.

    D. The network is slower than normal accessing the Internet.

    A. A user cannot log on. Any problem that affects a user's capability to log on and become authenticated should be a high priority. This means a user will not be able to log on to gain access to the network resources. The user may be able to work with local resources, such as a word processor, but will not be able to retrieve or store any information on a network server.

19. Which of the following appears to be the most important condition and should warrant the highest priority?

    A. Several users are receiving a message that their hard drives are full.

    B. Several users are receiving a message that their e-mail inbox limit has been exceeded.

    C. The network is slower than normal accessing the Internet.

    D. A printer is down in the accounting department.

    D. A printer is down in the accounting department. Users complain most about the inability to receive e-mail and the inability to print. Users print everything. When they can't print, you will find out very quickly. The problem could be major, such as the downing of a print server, or it could just affect one printer, such as a hardware malfunction.

20. Which of the following appears to be the most important condition and should warrant the highest priority?

    A. A few users cannot access the employee time reporting database.

    B. A printer is down in the accounting department.

    C. Several users are receiving a message that their e-mail inbox limit has been exceeded.

D. A user cannot access his personal drive on the network.
A. A few users cannot access the employee time reporting database. Whenever a database issue arises, it usually takes precedence over anything else, especially if it is the employee time reporting database. After that, you would begin working on the printer in the accounting department.

21. The personnel department is having trouble accessing their corporate-wide database system for checking job postings. Why does this warrant a higher priority?

    A. Because they are handling job postings.

    B. Because they are in the personnel department.

    C. Because the problem is affecting a large number of users.

    D. Because they are using an older system.
    C. Because the problem is affecting a large number of users. Although some problems affect a large number of users, you have to prioritize which functions the users can live without for a period of time. Problems such as access to important servers that are affecting many users should be very high priority.

22. McAfee has just announced they have a new version of their virus-checking software available on their Web site. Why should this not be the highest priority; or should it be?

    A. It should be the highest priority because it is virus-scanning software.

    B. It should be the highest priority because it is a new release of a program.

    C. It should not be the highest priority because patches and fixes are not a priority unless they address issues that affect your network.

    D. It should not be the highest priority because virus-scanning is not very important compared to other issues on the network.
    C. It should not be the highest priority because patches and fixes are not a priority unless they address issues that affect your network. Unless the updated version of the software fixes a critical bug, this condition does not warrant a high priority. You should test the patch or version update on a test machine before implementing it in the field.

23. Which of the following appears to be the least important condition and should warrant the lowest priority?

    A. A printer is down in the accounting department.

    B. Several users are receiving a message that their hard drives are full.

    C. The network is slower than normal accessing the Internet.

    D. A user cannot log on.
    C. The network is slower than normal accessing the Internet. Conditions in which the network is slower than usual do not warrant a high priority, unless the network is significantly slower. This can be expected in most

networks at certain times of the day, such as in the morning when users are logging on to the network, or at lunch time, when some users are browsing on the Internet.

24. You just arrived to work this morning and you have four new voice messages. Which of the following messages appears to be the least important condition, and should warrant the lowest priority?

   A. "I'm getting an error that says I cannot access my personal drive on the network."

   B. "I'm trying to load a Web page and it says the page is outdated."

   C. "Steve and I can't print to the LaserJet over here in accounting."

   D. "It's telling me my password is expired."
   B. "I'm trying to load a Web page and it says the page is outdated." The message most likely refers to a user having problems accessing a page on the Internet. Since this condition is not highly critical, it can be set to a lower priority if you have more than one problem you are working on. This user is probably just surfing on the Internet anyway.

25. Your boss gave you a list of things you are to accomplish in the near future. Which of the following items on the list should be done first?

   A. Migrate all workstations from NetBEUI to TCP/IP.

   B. Give Nina access to the color printer in the administration building.

   C. Upgrade the McAfee Virus Scan engine on the servers.

   D. Upgrade the hub in the development room.
   B. Give Nina access to the color printer in the administration building. All the items on the list are basically low-priority tasks, which introduces another aspect of prioritizing: when all tasks are the same priority, you should do the quickest one first. It would only take a couple minutes to give Nina access to the color printer.

Chapter 12 Answers

1. A few computers on the engineering segment are having problems reaching the AutoCAD design segment on the network. What is your initial prognosis of the problem?

   A. It's a default gateway issue.

   B. It's a routing issue.

   C. The computers are having cable problems.

   D. A hub is locked up.
   B. It's a routing issue. If you have a very good understanding of routers and routing, and one segment of your network cannot communicate with another segment, you will immediately know that there is a problem with routing—possibly a router is malfunctioning.

2. Every user on a bus topology network has suddenly complained that the network is not functioning and they can no longer access resources on remote networks. What is your initial prognosis of the problem?

   A. It's a routing issue.

   B. It's a default gateway issue.

   C. The network is no longer terminated.

   D. A hub is locked up.
   C. The network is no longer terminated. One segment of the network is not able to communicate with another segment; therefore, you should quickly determine that you have a routing problem. Another symptom is everyone on the coaxial-based bus network not being able to communicate. The cause of this problem is most likely a problem with the network bus backbone, which requires terminators on each end.

3. You think you are having problems with the UNIX server in another region. Two users have already complained this morning. What would be the next logical step in your troubleshooting methodology?

   A. Check the router.

   B. Check the hub.

   C. Ping the UNIX server by name.

   D. Ping the UNIX server by IP address.
   D. Ping the UNIX server by IP address. You can test the routing problem by trying to communicate with another computer on the corporate headquarters' network. For example, you can ping another computer on this network or use a program that connects to a computer on this network.

4. Someone in the graphics department is complaining that it takes too long to open his renderings, which wasn't the case yesterday. What is the next logical step in your troubleshooting methodology?

   A. Run Performance Monitor.

   B. Ping the server that holds the renderings.

   C. Try opening a rendering on another computer.

   D. Restart the affected computer.
   C. Try opening a rendering on another computer. You need to learn if more than one computer is having this problem. For example, when someone in the purchasing department sends a job to the printer, it takes over five minutes for the job to print. You send a print job from another computer, only to discover that the print job once again takes five minutes before it is printed. Well, now you have a consistent problem that is replicable.

5. You are called down to look at a user's computer. He says it takes way too long to print a simple document. What is the next step in your troubleshooting methodology?

   A. Check the print server.

   B. Restart the affected computer.

   C. Run diagnostics.

D. Try opening a few files on the affected computer.
D. Try opening a few files on the affected computer. You need to determine whether the problem is printing related or network related. If *everything* you do on the network takes five minutes, not just printing, then you know the problem is network related.

6. You are experiencing problems on a coax bus network. How can you quickly determine where the problem is occurring?

A. Divide the network in half, terminate it, and find which side is still not functioning. That is the affected area. Continue this process until the break is found.

B. Use a network packet sniffer to determine where the packets eventually stop responding. This will tell you which computer is the closest to the break.

C. Use a Fox and Hound process to determine where the break is in the network backbone.

D. Use Network Monitor to determine what is causing the broadcast storm. One computer's faulty network card is the likely culprit, and must be found.
A. Divide the network in half, terminate it, and find which side is still not functioning. The best example of this is in thinwire coax. Determine the midpoint of the cable and place a terminator on each end. One half of

the cable should now be working and is obviously not your problem. Repeat this step until you find the problem.

7. How can you eliminate complicated cable problems in your troubleshooting process?

A. Visually inspect the cables.

B. Use a Fox and Hound to find cables in a tangled mess.

C. Examine cables with TDR to find any problems.

D. Swap suspect cables with known good cables.
C. Examine cables with TDR to find any problems. Eliminate complicated cable problems by examining cables with a TDR to find any problems. Visually inspecting a cable cannot determine if the cable is faulty. You need more advanced tools to determine if a cable is faulty. This will save time and money if you catch a potentially faulty cable now before it is put into production.

8. What is a quick way to determine if your computer is communicating on the network?

A. Run diagnostics.

B. Check the Network applet in the Control Panel.

C. Check the physical link light.

D. Ping the loopback adapter (127.0.0.1).
C. Check the physical link light. Most network cards have two lights: a link

light, which will remain on for the duration of the network connection, and a light that displays the current activity of the network card and pulses as data is transferred to and from the computer or device. This can be an obvious indicator that the device is functioning on the network.

9. You came back to work on Monday morning only to notice that you are having network problems. Your domain controller, which also functions as a database server, appears to be having problems. How can you further investigate the problem?

    A. Check the error log.

    B. Ping the server to see if it responds.

    C. Run diagnostics on the server.

    D. Restart the computer and then begin troubleshooting.
    A. Check the error log. Error logs usually don't contain enough information to solve a problem, and documentation must be consulted to diagnose and resolve the problem. However, error logging is very important because you can determine when the problem occurred, what may have caused the problem, and what other processes are affected by this problem.

10. You have made system configuration changes to one of your servers. How can you tell if the changes have made a difference?

    A. Watch the server closely for a few hours, especially during peak usage.

    B. Run Network Monitor to perform an assessment of the current system activity and compare that with your previous baseline before the configuration change took place.

    C. Run Performance Monitor to perform an assessment of the current system activity and compare that with your previous baseline before the configuration change took place.

    D. Check the Event Viewer for errors, warnings, or any indicators that system degradation has occurred.
    C. Run Performance Monitor to perform an assessment of the current system activity and compare that with your previous baseline before the configuration change took place. The Performance Monitor can be used for a variety of reasons including the following:

    ■ Identifying bottlenecks in CPU, memory, disk I/O, or network I/O

    ■ Identifying trends over a period of time

    ■ Monitoring real-time system performance

    ■ Monitoring system performance history

    ■ Determining the capacity the system can handle

    ■ Monitoring system configuration changes

11. You feel you are having driver incompatibility problems with your network adapter. What is the best resource for finding another network adapter driver?

    A. TechNet

    B. Resource Kit

    C. Vendor Web site

    D. Documentation CD

    C. Vendor Web site. If you are having a problem with a network interface card (NIC) not communicating on the network properly, a good place to start is the Web site of the NIC's manufacturer. Most sites provide troubleshooting information, suggested steps to resolve common problems, phone numbers with which to contact technical support, and the latest updated drivers.

12. You are instructed to migrate the DHCP service from a Windows NT 3.51 server to Windows NT 4.0 server. What is the best resource to begin preparing for the migration?

    A. Windows NT magazine

    B. Telephone tech support

    C. Vendor CDs

    D. Resource kits

    D. Resource kits. Resource kits contain additional documentation on your operating system that was too comprehensive to cover in the standard documentation. Whenever you are faced with a problem that you cannot solve, check the resource kit—your problem may already have been solved.

13. You are experiencing lockup problems with a new version of the virus-scanning utility that you just implemented. Which of the following is probably not needed when you open a technical support incident?

    A. The version of affected software or hardware

    B. Number of users on the network

    C. Troubleshooting steps taken so far, and their results

    D. Current operating system

    B. Number of users on the network. To improve the speed and accuracy of your technical support incident, make sure you have the following ready to assist the support technician:

    ■ Hardware and software environment, such as the operating system you are running

    ■ Version numbers of affected hardware or software

    ■ Serial Numbers

    ■ Detailed account of the problem

    ■ Troubleshooting steps taken so far, and their results

14. You have a user receiving the error: "A domain controller cannot be found." Assuming no one else has called you with

this error, which of the following is not likely the problem?

A. The TCP/IP configuration is not correct on the computer.

B. The domain controller could be down.

C. The network card is not functioning correctly.

D. A cable may be faulty or not plugged in.

B. The domain controller could be down. If no one else is receiving this error, it is most commonly a local workstation issue, either with an incorrect TCP/IP configuration, or a problem with the network adapter or cable. Ensure that the network card has a link light and the cable is firmly plugged in. You should also try replacing the cable to the workstation.

15. Which of the following is not likely an abnormal condition on a network?

A. It takes a long time to print a large document with images.

B. It takes longer to become authenticated.

C. Users are having problems connecting to the SQL database.

D. You continually lose connection to the mainframe.

A. It takes a long time to print a large document with images. For example, it may take your network only three seconds to spool up a print document, but it may take another network one minute to spool up a document of the same size. This doesn't mean the second network has a problem. This could be a normal physical condition for their network.

16. You have a workstation that you moved from one cubicle to another. Nothing on the workstation was changed; however, the computer refuses to connect to the network. Which of the following is not likely the cause?

A. The network drop has not been activated in the wiring closet.

B. The cable was damaged in the move.

C. The TCP/IP configuration is incorrect.

D. The network adapter was damaged in the move.

D. The network adapter was damaged in the move. A workstation was just moved to a new location and is no longer able to communicate on the network. There is nothing wrong with the workstation's configuration. Cables have been damaged in the move. Replace each cable one at a time to find the problematic cable.

17. Which of the following is the most reliable indicator that a network server may be overloaded?

A. The activity light on the network card is constantly lit.

B. Performance Monitor shows network requests are backing up in the queue.

C. Network Monitor shows too many packets are leaving this server.

D. The computer is very slow to respond when you log on.
   B. Performance Monitor shows network requests are backing up in the queue. Performance and network monitoring can determine if the server is overloaded or if the server is broadcasting unnecessarily. An overloaded server can increase the length of time needed to fulfill network requests.

18. Which of the following will you not need prior to the installation of the DNS Service?

   A. The DNS address scope

   B. Your domain name

   C. The host names of each of the servers

   D. The IP address of each server for which you wish to provide name resolution
   A. The DNS address scope. You will need to gather information prior to the installation of the service, such as:

   ■ Your domain name

   ■ The IP address of each server for which you wish to provide name resolution

   ■ The host names of each of the servers

19. Which of the following is not true regarding the WINS service?

   A. It resolves NetBIOS names to IP addresses.

   B. You can replicate with other WINS servers.

   C. You have to manually enter the address mappings.

   D. The WINS Service dynamically updates the WINS database.
   C. You have to manually enter the address mappings. A few of the WINS configuration settings are the duration of the client renewal and extinction of names and the replication partners with which this WINS server will replicate. You can strategically replicate with other WINS servers based on frequency and location.

20. Which of the following is not true concerning the HOSTS file?

   A. You have the capability to use a centrally located HOSTS file.

   B. The HOSTS file is not case-sensitive.

   C. The HOSTS file resolves host names to IP addresses.

   D. The HOSTS file can have more than one host name per line.
   A. You have the ability to use a centrally located HOSTS file. Unlike DNS, which uses a centrally located database of host name mappings, the

HOSTS file resides on every computer. This makes updating the HOSTS file very difficult.

21. Which of the following is not a good recommendation when implementing virus-scanning utilities?

    A. Using a live update to download new virus definition files

    B. Scanning file server hard drives once a month

    C. Using scanning utilities on every workstation

    D. Scanning messaging servers, such as Microsoft Exchange
       B. Scanning file server hard drives once a month. Many virus-scanning utilities will enable the workstations to automatically update the virus definition files from a central server, which means you, the network administrator, do not have to visit every workstation once a month to apply the new definition files.

22. Steve just got back from a two-week vacation. He calls you first thing Monday morning. Which of the following is most likely not the reason for Steve's call?

    A. He forgot his password.

    B. His account has been disabled.

    C. His password has expired.

    D. He forgot the domain he is supposed to log on to.

    D. He forgot the domain he is supposed to logon to. It's common for a user to return from vacation to find that his account has been disabled or his password has expired. You will need to intervene to correct the situation.

23. Which of the following is *not* a good recommendation when it comes to performing a baseline of your network?

    A. Monitor traffic at different times of the day.

    B. Configure the snapshots to take place at midnight each night.

    C. Monitor traffic for days, even weeks.

    D. Take as many traffic snapshots as possible.
       B. Configure the snapshots to take place at midnight each night. Taking snapshots of activity from various periods of the day, week, and month will give you the most accurate assessment of your network. The longer you spend baselining your network, the more accurate the results will be. If you are taking network activity snapshots at midnight, you are not getting an accurate assessment of the normal network activity that occurs throughout the day.

24. Which of the following network situations require a crossover cable?

    A. Connecting the patch panel to the workstation

B. Connecting a workstation to a hub

C. Connecting a transceiver to a hub

D. Connecting a hub to another hub

    D. Connecting a hub to another hub. A crossover cable is also used to connect hubs in the event you need to cascade hubs. If you were to substitute a crossover cable for a regular twisted-pair cable to connect two hubs, it would not work correctly.

25. What is the best tool to determine where a break has occurred in a cable?

A. A Tone Generator

B. A Spectrum Division Analyzer

C. A time domain reflectometer

D. A Fox and Hound

    C. A time domain reflectometer. Use a TDR or an oscilloscope to find the exact spot where the cable is broken. If you don't have access to one, you may be able to replace the cable without determining the exact area of breakage.

B

About the CD

T his CD-ROM contains a browser-based testing product, the *Personal Testing Center.* The *Personal Testing Center* is easy to install on any Windows 95/98/NT computer.

Installing the Personal Testing Center

Double clicking on the Setup.html file on the CD will cycle you through an introductory page on the *Test Yourself* software. On the second page, you will have to read and accept the license agreement. Once you have read the agreement, click on the Agree icon and you will be brought to the *Personal Testing Center's* main page.

On the main page, you will find links to the *Personal Testing Center,* to the electronic version of the book, and to other resources you may find helpful. Click on the first link to the *Personal Testing Center* and you will be brought to the Quick Start page. Here you can choose to run the Personal Testing Center from the CD or install it to your hard drive.

Installing the *Personal Testing Center* to your hard drive is an easy process. Click on the Install to Hard Drive icon and the procedure will start for you. An instructional box will appear and walk you through the remainder of the installation. If installed to the hard drive, the "Personal Testing Center" program group will be created in the Start Programs folder.

Should you wish to run the software from the CD-ROM, the steps are the same as above until you reach the point where you would select the Install to Hard Drive icon. Here, select Run from CD icon and the exam will automatically begin.

To uninstall the program from your hard disk, use the add/remove programs feature in your Windows Control Panel. InstallShield will run uninstall.

Test Type Choices

With the *Personal Testing Center,* you have three options in which to run the program: Live, Practice, and Review. Each test type will draw from a pool of over 300 potential questions. Your choice of test type will depend on whether you would like to simulate an actual Network+ exam, receive instant feedback on your answer choices, or review concepts using the testing simulator. Note that selecting the Full Screen icon on Internet Explorer's standard toolbar gives you the best display of the *Personal Testing Center*.

Live

The Live timed test type is meant to reflect the actual exam as closely as possible. You will have 90 minutes in which to complete the exam. You will have the option to skip questions and return to them later, move to the previous question, or end the exam. Once the timer has expired, you will automatically go to the scoring page to review your test results.

Managing Windows

The testing application runs inside an Internet Explorer 4.0 or 5.0 browser window. We recommend that you use the full-screen view to minimize the amount of text scrolling you need to do. However, the application will initiate a second iteration of the browser when you link to an Answer in Depth or a Review Graphic. If you are running in full-screen view, the second iteration of the browser will be covered by the first. You can toggle between the two windows with ALT-TAB, you can click your task bar to maximize the second window, or you can get out of full-screen mode and arrange the two windows so they are both visible on the screen at the same time. The application will not initiate more than two browser windows, so you aren't left with hundreds of open windows for each Answer in Depth or Review Graphic that you view.

Saving Scores as Cookies

Your exam score is stored as a browser cookie. If you've configured your browser to accept cookies, your score will be stored in a cookie named History. If you don't accept cookies, you cannot permanently save your scores. If you delete the History cookie, the scores will be deleted permanently.

Using the Browser Buttons

The test application runs inside the Internet Explorer 4.0 browser. You should navigate from screen to screen by using the application's buttons, not the browser's buttons.

JavaScript Errors

If you encounter a JavaScript error, you should be able to proceed within the application. If you cannot, shut down your Internet Explorer 4.0 browser session and re-launch the testing application.

Practice

When choosing the Practice exam type, you have the option of receiving instant feedback as to whether your selected answer is correct. The questions will be presented to you in numerical order, and you will see every question in the available question pool for each section you chose to be tested on.

As with the Live exam type, you have the option of continuing through the entire exam without seeing the correct answer for each question. The number of questions you answered correctly, along with the percentage of correct answers, will be displayed during the post-exam summary report. Once you have answered a question, click the Answer icon to display the correct answer.

You have the option of ending the Practice exam at any time, but your post-exam summary screen may reflect an incorrect percentage based on the number of questions you failed to answer. Questions that are skipped are counted as incorrect answers on the post-exam summary screen.

Review

During the Review exam type, you will be presented with questions similar to both the Live and Practice exam types. However, the Answer icon is not present, as every question will have the correct answer posted near the bottom of the screen. You have the option of answering the question without looking at the correct answer. In the Review exam type, you can also return to previous questions and skip to the next question, as well as ending the exam by clicking the Stop icon.

The Review exam type is recommended when you have already completed the Live exam type once or twice, and would now like to determine which questions you answered correctly.

Questions with Answers

For the Practice and Review exam types, you will have the option of clicking a hyperlink titled Answers in Depth, which will present relevant study material aimed at exposing the logic behind the answer in a separate browser window. By having two browsers open (one for the test engine and one for the review information), you can quickly alternate between the two windows while keeping your place in the exam. You will find that additional windows are not generated as you follow hyperlinks throughout the test engine.

Scoring

The *Personal Testing Center* post-exam summary screen, called Benchmark Yourself, displays the results for each section you chose to be tested on, including a bar graph similar to the real exam, which displays the percentage of correct answers. You can compare your percentage to the actual passing percentage for each section. The percentage displayed on the post-exam summary screen is not the actual percentage required to pass the exam. You'll see the number of questions you answered correctly compared to the total number of questions you were tested on. If you choose to skip a question, it will be marked as incorrect. Ending the exam by clicking the End button with questions still unanswered lowers your percentage, as these questions will be marked as incorrect.

Clicking the End button and then the Home button allows you to choose another exam type, or test yourself on another section.

C

About the Web Site

Access Global Knowledge

As you know by now, Global Knowledge is the largest independent IT training company in the world. Just by purchasing this book, you have also secured a free subscription to the Global Knowledge Web site and its many resources. You can find it at: http://access.globalknowledge.com.

You can log on directly at the Global Knowledge site, and you will be e-mailed a new, secure password immediately upon registering.

What You'll Find There. . .

The wealth of useful information at the Global Knowledge site falls into three categories.

Skills Gap Analysis

Global Knowledge offers several ways for you to analyze your networking skills and discover where they may be lacking. Using Global Knowledge's trademarked Competence Key Tool, you can do a skills gap analysis and get recommendations for where you may need to do some more studying. (Sorry, it just might not end with this book!)

Networking

You'll also gain valuable access to another asset: people. At the Access Global site, you'll find threaded discussions, as well as live discussions. Talk to other certification candidates, get advice from folks who have already taken the exams, and get access to instructors.

Product Offerings

Of course, Global Knowledge also offers its products here, and you may find some valuable items for purchase—CBTs, books, or courses. Browse freely and see if there's something that could help you take that next step in career enhancement.

Network+

CERTIFICATION

Glossary

10Base2 An Ethernet topology using thin Ethernet coaxial cable, also known as Thin Ethernet or thinnet. The maximum distance per segment is 185 meters.

10Base5 An Ethernet topology using thick Ethernet coaxial cable, also known as Thick Ethernet or thicknet. 10Base5 was once commonly used for backbones in Ethernet networks. It is now being replaced by 10BaseT. The maximum distance per segment is 500 meters.

10BaseT An Ethernet topology using unshielded twisted-pair cable, also known as twisted pair. 10BaseT has become the most popular Ethernet cable; because many buildings are already wired for 10BaseT, it is inexpensive and easy to work with, and if the cable specifications are CAT5, it can transmit data at 100 Mbps. The maximum distance per segment is 100 meters.

100BaseT An Ethernet topology using CAT5 twisted-pair cable to transmit at 100 Mbps, also known as Fast Ethernet. The maximum distance per segment is 100 meters.

Access Control Entries (ACE) Specify auditing and access permissions to a given object, for a specific user, or for a group of users.

Access Control List (ACL) Checked by each resource's file and print servers before they enable a user to access a file or use a printer. If the user, or a group to which the user belongs, is not listed in the ACL, the user is not allowed to use the resource.

access methods The rules governing the use of the physical network by various devices.

access permissions Access permissions are types of access to an object on Windows NT. Windows NT includes six individual permissions: read, write, execute, delete, take ownership, and change permission.

account   An account, or user account, provides access to the network. It contains the information enabling a person to use the network, including user name and logon specifications, password, and rights to directories and resources.

account lockout   Part of the Windows NT account policy that can be set to lock out an account after a certain number of unsuccessful logon attempts. (Three bad attempts are a common choice.) This helps to prevent hackers from breaking into accounts.

account policies   Set from the User Manager to control rules for password usage and account lockout. The Account policy will help in preventing your system from being broken into by some unauthorized user.

account restrictions   Restrictions on an account determine when and how a user gains access to the network.

acknowledgment (ACK)   A packet of information sent from the recipient computer to the sending computer, for the purpose of verifying that a transmission has been received and confirming that it was or was not a successful transmission. Similar to a return receipt.

   An unsuccessful transmission will generate a negative acknowledgment (NACK).

active hub   A hub device used in a star topology to regenerate and redistribute data across the LAN. Unlike a passive hub, the active hub requires electricity. *See also* **hub**, and **passive hub**.

active partition   On an Intel based computer the active partition is the system partition. It contains the files needed to boot.

adapter   A network adapter card, also called a network interface card, transmits data from the workstation to the cable that connects the machine to the LAN. It provides the communication link between the computer and the network. *See also* **network interface card**.

adapter unit interface (AUI)   Enables a network card to be used with multiple types of media. The AUI connector is a female 15-pin D connector that looks very much like a joystick port. Also called a DIX (Digital-Intel-Xerox) connector.

address resolution   The process of finding the address of a host within a network.

administrator account   The account used to administer the settings on an NT Server and network. This account is created during install and has unlimited access to the server. Care must be taken when logged on to a server as an administrator, because administrator access rights include the capability to shut down the server and erase critical data.

alias   A name used for a person or group on a computer system. Mail aliases are a common use of the alias feature. When an alias is used, the computer system still recognizes a person by a user name, but an alias can be set so that people can send mail or other information using the alias name instead of the user name.

analog   A continuous, non-digital data transmission usually associated with telephone communications.

AppleTalk   The protocol designed for communicating with Macintosh computers.

Application Layer   (1) OSI layer that provides a consistent way for an application to save files to the network file server or to print to a network printer. (2) TCP/IP layer that is the highest layer in the TCP/IP model. It is used by applications to access services across a TCP/IP network. Examples of applications that operate at this layer are a Web browser, file transfer program (FTP), and a remote logon program.

archiving   A process that enables you to move old files off the file server to preserve disk space for new files. If the old files are later needed, they can be unarchived and retrieved. Archived data can be saved to CD-ROM, WORM, or tape.

ARCnet (Attached Resource Computer Network)   A bus network topology that is similar to token ring, in that it uses a token to transmit data across the network. ARCnet transmits data at 2.5 Mbps and can run on coaxial, twisted-pair, and fiber-optic cable.

ARP (Address Resolution Protocol)   Used to determine a host's MAC address from its IP address. This utility is also used to view and make changes to IP address-to-MAC address translation tables. *See also* **MAC**.

ARPANET (Advanced Research Project Agency Network)
Funded as a research project by the Department of Defense, ARPANET was created to enable remote installations to communicate with each other and to provide redundancy in case of war. The first truly remote network, ARPANET was the precursor to the Internet.

ASCII (American Standard Code for Information Interchange)
A representation of standard alphabetic and other keyboard characters in a computer-readable, binary format.

asynchronous communication   Sending all data separately and relying upon the node on the other end to translate the packet order.

Asynchronous Transfer Mode (ATM)   A packet-switching network technology for LANs and WANs that can handle voice, video, and data transmissions simultaneously.

Attached Resource Computer Network (ArcNet)   A networking standard that was very common, but has lost popularity due to its limited transmission speeds.

attributes   A file can be designated with different attributes: Read Only, System, Hidden, and Archived. On an NTFS partition there is one additional attribute: Compressed.

backbone   The main cable that connects file servers, routers, and bridges to the network.

back door   Used by system administrators to access the network at an administrator's level, if something happens to the network administrator's home account. This provides a means to rebuild the administrator's account or otherwise fix the network.

backup   The process of saving files to a separate location, usually an offline storage location, such as tape.

backup domain controller (BDC)   A computer that contains a backup of a domain's security policy and domain database, maintained by the Primary Domain Controller. Serves as a backup to the primary domain controller. A BDC is not required but is recommended.

bad sector   A damaged or non-working area of a hard disk. If data has been saved to that area, it cannot be accessed.

bandwidth   The amount of data that the media can transfer. Bandwidth is usually measured in bits per second (bps).

base I/O address   The memory address that identifies where data will flow to and from the hardware device on the computer.

baseband transmission   Technique used to transmit encoded signals over cable using digital signaling. *See also* **broadband transmission**.

baseline   A snapshot of your system that is established by the Performance Monitor under normal operating conditions and used as a yardstick to measure future abnormalities.

bearer code (BC)   An identifier made up of the combination of TEI and SAPI. It is used as the call reference and is dynamic, like the two identifiers included within it.

binary representation   Any value represented with just zeros and ones.

binding   The linking of network components on different levels to enable communication between those components. For example, binding links protocols to network adapters.

bit order   The order in which computers transmit binary numbers across a network. Computers can start at either end of a binary number when transmitting it across a network.

Blue Screen of Death   Text-mode STOP messages that identify hardware and software problems that have occurred while running Windows NT Server.

BNC (British Naval Connector)   Also known as a barrel connector, the connector type used in 10Base2 (Thin Ethernet) networks to connect two cable segments, creating a longer segment.

BOOT.INI file   BOOT.INI is created when NT is installed and is used to build the Operating System Selection menu to display the operating systems currently installed on the computer.

boot partition   The boot partition in Windows NT is the partition containing the operating system files.

boot prom   Boots the workstation if there is not a hard drive or disk to boot from.

bootup   The process a computer executes when powered up. Bootup includes the files that initialize the hardware and the starting of the operating system.

bottleneck   (1) Indicates that a component within your system has limitations that impede the system as a whole from operating at its maximum potential. (2) The resource that consumes the most time while a task is executing.

bridge   A hardware device that connects two LAN segments of either the same or different topologies. Bridges look at the destination and source addresses of a network packet and decide whether to pass that packet on to the LAN segment. A bridge can be used to filter out traffic for a local subnet and prevent it from being passed on to an unnecessary LAN segment.

broadband transmission   Techniques used to transmit encoded signals over cable using analog signaling. *See also* **baseband transmission**.

broadcast   Data packets sent without a specific destination address, intended for all the computers it can reach.

broadcast storm   Occurs when there are so many broadcast packets on the network that the capacity of the network bandwidth approaches or reaches saturation.

browser   (1) Web application that uses HTTP to access URLs and to download and display Web pages (documents that are usually written in HTML). (2) A computer that maintains a centralized list of network servers.

browser election   The process to guarantee one and only one master browser in a workgroup or a domain subnet.

browsing   A process that enables computers on a network to find each other.

buffer space   A reserved portion of RAM that provides room for the storage of incoming and outgoing data.

bulk encryption key   *See* **secret key cryptography**.

bus topology   A network topology that connects all computers to a single, shared cable. In a bus topology, if one computer fails, the network fails. *See also* **star topology** and **ring topology**.

byte order   The order in which computers transmit larger binary numbers, consisting of two or more bytes, across a network. Computers can start at either end of a group of bytes when transmitting the group across a network. *See also* **bit order**.

cable modem   A device that uses a cable system (such as cable TV) to connect to a network or ISP.

cache   *See* **disk caching**.

callback security   Security feature implemented within RAS. When a user is configured to use callback and dials in to a RAS server, the server disconnects the session and then calls the client back at a preset telephone number or at a number provided during the initial call.

carrier service   Provides the transmission media. Carrier services are traditionally telephone companies.

carrier signal   An analog signal whose characteristics—the frequency, the amplitude, and/or the phase—have been modulated to represent data.

CDFS   Read-only CD-ROM file system. On a CDFS volume, the files are burned into the volume or marked read only.

CD-ROM   A device, similar to a musical compact disc, that stores data.

Challenge Handshake Authentication Protocol (CHAP)   An authentication protocol that uses an encryption algorithm to pass the authentication data to protect it from hackers. Because CHAP is so much more secure than PAP, it is used widely today on the Internet.

Character-Based Setup   The first part of a Windows NT Server installation. During this phase Windows NT Server performs an in-depth examination of your system.

checksum   A form of error checking that simply counts the number of bits sent and sends this count along. On the receiving end, the bits are once again counted and compared with the original count. If the two counts match, it is assumed the data was received correctly.

Class A IP address   Assigned to networks with a very large number of hosts. A Class A IP address has a 0 in the Most Significant Bit location of the first octet. The network ID is the first octet. Class A addresses range from 0.1.0.0 to 126.0.0.0.

Class B IP address   Assigned to medium-sized networks. A Class B IP address has a 1 0 in the two Most Significant Bit locations of the first octet. The network ID is the first and second octet. Class B addresses range from 128.0.0.0 to 191.255.0.0.

Class C IP address   Usually assigned to small local area networks (LANs). A Class C IP address has a 1 1 0 in the three Most Significant Bit locations of the first octet. The network ID is comprised of the first three octets. Class C addresses range from 192.0.1.0 to 223.255.255.0.

Class D IP address   Used for multicasting to a number of different hosts. Data is passed to one, two, three, or more users on a network. Only those hosts registered for the multicast address will receive the data. A Class D IP address has a 1 1 1 0 in the four Most Significant Bit locations of the first octet. Class D addresses range from 224.0.0.0 to 239.255.255.255.

Class E IP address   An experimental address block that is reserved for future use. A Class E IP address has a 1 1 1 1 0 in the five Most Significant Bit locations of the first octet. Class E addresses range from 240.0.0.0 to 247.255.255.255.

client   (1) The workstation accessing the resources in a client/server model. *See also* **client/server model.** (2) The software that enables communications for various network services. (3) A computer that accesses resources on servers via the network.

client/server messaging   One program on one computer communicating with another program (usually on another computer).

client/server model   Model in which processing is requested by the client on the server. The server fulfills this request and sends the result back to the client. The client requests the server to do the processing, for instance, number crunching.

client/server network   A network architecture, based on distributed processing, in which a client performs functions by requesting services from a server.

coaxial (or coax) cable   One of the three types of physical media that can be used at the OSI Physical Layer. A coaxial has one strand (a solid-core wire) that runs down the middle of the cable. Around that strand is insulation. There are two different types of commonly used Ethernet coaxial cables: thickwire and thinwire. *See also* **twisted-pair cable** and **fiber-optic cable.**

command line   A character-mode interface for computer applications that relies on commands instead of a graphical interface to process information.

Complex Instruction Set Computing (CISC)   Computers with processors that require large sets of processor instructions. Such processors (including Intel 80xxx processors and most other processors on the market) use expanded instruction sets that require several execution cycles to complete. *See also* **Reduced Instruction Set Computing**.

compression　A mathematical technique that analyzes computer files in order to compress them to a smaller size. Most backup systems, and many file servers, compress files to provide increased storage capacity.

computer virus　A computer program built to sabotage or destroy a computer or network.

concentrator　A device that connects workstations to the path of the file server. Concentrators typically have 8 – 12 ports to which workstations are attached.

container object　A container object can contain other objects and can inherit permissions from its parent container. *See also* **noncontainer object** and **object**.

conventional memory　The memory below 640K. If you have room, your LAN drivers are loaded in conventional memory.

cryptography　*See* **public key cryptography**, **secret key cryptography**, and **symmetric cryptography**.

CSNW (Client Services for NetWare)　CSNW is the client redirector that enables Microsoft workstations to interact with NetWare networks. *See also* **NWLink**.

CSU/DSU (Channel Service Unit/Data Service Unit)　A piece of hardware that sits between a network and a digital telephone line to translate data between the two formats. CSU/DSUs are most commonly used to attach a network router to a T1 or other digital telephone line.

cyclical redundancy check (CRC)   Form of error checking that involves running a byte or group of bytes through a mathematical algorithm to produce a single bit or byte to represent the data (a CRC). The CRC value is transmitted with the data. When the data reaches its destination, the receiver runs it through the same mathematical algorithm. The results are compared with the original CRC, and if they match, the receiving computer assumes the data is correct. If they do not match, the receiver must discard the data and try again.

DAT (Digital Audio Tape)   A hardware option for tape backup. DATs can be 4mm or 8mm.

database management system (DBMS)   A software application that manages a database, including the organization, storage, security, retrieval, and integrity of data in a database.

data bus   Pathway that carries data between the hardware components.

Data Link Control (DLC)   A protocol for communication and connectivity with IBM Mainframes, as well as Hewlett-Packard's network-attached printers.

Data Link Layer   OSI layer that handles the disassembling and the reassembling of frames on a network.

DBMS   *See* database management system (DBMS).

demand paging   The process of bringing information from disk or memory into a working set on an as-needed basis.

device drivers   Small programs called upon when the system needs to communicate with the various hardware components in the system.

Device Manager   A configuration tool that manages devices within Windows 98. New devices can be automatically detected and installed (if they are Plug and Play) or manually added (if they are not Plug and Play).

device sharing   Prevents inbound calls from going to anything but the specified device. Device sharing is particularly useful in the small home office where there is usually only one phone line but multiple phone-enabled devices such as phones, fax machines, or modems.

DHCP (Dynamic Host Configuration Protocol)   A dependable, flexible alternative to manual TCP/IP configuration that provides PCs with automatic configuration of the three necessary TCP/IP parameters: IP address, subnet mask, and default gateway.

dial-up networking (DUN)   Dialing-out service that is made available when RAS is installed as a service. DUN enables you to connect to any dial-up server using the Point-to-Point Protocol (PPP) as a transport mechanism, enabling TCP/IP, NetBEUI, or IPX/SPX network access over your analog modem, ISDN, or X.25 Pad device.

dial-up networking server   Enables Windows 98 to host a single dial-up network connection. Any client with support for PPP can dial in using IP, IPX, or NetBEUI as the connection protocol. Windows 98 can then act as a server sharing its files and printers, just as it does on a LAN, or it can act as a gateway for an IPX or NetBEUI network.

differential backup   Backs up only the files that have changed since the last full or differential backup and does not modify the archive bit. *See also* **full backup.**

Digital Access Cross-Connect System (DACCS)   The combination of all of the T1 and T3 lines.

digital voltage meter (DVM)   Used to test the continuity of a connection cable to see if there are any shorts in it.

directory number (DN)   The ten-digit phone number or address the telephone company assigns to any ISDN line. Unlike with an analog line where a one-to-one relationship exists, the DN is only a logical mapping.

directory path   The path to a directory on a file system which could include the server, volume, and other names leading to the directory.

Directory Replication   A Windows NT service that makes an exact copy of a folder and places it on another server.

Directory Service   One of the four core components of Exchange Server. The Directory Service contains addresses, public folders, mailboxes, distribution lists, and site configuration.

directory synchronization   (1) The Windows NT process of synchronizing the BDCs with the PDC on a periodic basis. (2) In the Microsoft Exchange Server, directory synchronization is the exchange of addresses between a Microsoft Exchange Organization and a foreign mail system, such as Microsoft Mail and cc:Mail.

directory tree   The file structure, including directory and subdirectory layout below the root directory.

discovery   Process that occurs when a non-domain controller computer starts up and looks across the network for a domain controller in its domain and in all trusted domains.

discretionary access   Access control when the person who created the file or folder is the owner and is responsible for securing that file or folder.

Disk Administrator   A program that creates and manages partitions.

Disk Cache Manager   Manages disk caching that results in reducing the amount of I/O traffic to the hard disk. It does this by storing frequently used data in physical memory so that it doesn't have to be read each time from the hard disk.

disk caching   Storing frequently used data in physical memory so that it doesn't have to be read each time from the hard disk.

disk duplexing   Exactly like disk mirroring except that it uses two disk controller cards—one card for each drive in the mirror set. This provides redundancy in case one of the controllers fails. *See also* **disk mirroring**.

disk mirroring   Provides redundancy by mirroring data from one hard drive to another. If a crash or other problem occurs on the active drive, Windows NT automatically begins to use the backup drive and notifies you of the switch.

distributed applications   Applications that split processing between computers on a network, such as a client/server application, in which processing is divided between the client computer and a more powerful server computer. Normally, the part that runs on the client computer is called the front end, and the part that runs on the server computer is called the back end.

DLC (Data Link Control)   A method that enables workstations to connect to IBM mainframes and minicomputers in an NT environment. DLC has also been adopted by printer manufacturers to connect remote print devices to print servers, which is a second way that Windows NT uses DLC.

DLL   *See* Dynamic Link Library (DLL).

DLT (Digital Linear Tape)   A hardware solution for tape backup and storage that enables multiple tapes to be loaded into the system, providing unattended backups and easy access for keeping data in online storage.

DMA (Direct Memory Access)   A process whereby some devices can directly access memory on the system without the intervention of the CPU.

DNS zone file   The database file that will contain all records created in the defined zone.

domain   A group of computers containing domain controllers that share account information and have one centralized accounts database. (Not to be confused with Internet domains, such as microsoft.com.)

Domain model   A model in which a Windows NT Server acts as a domain controller. The domain controller authenticates users into the domain before they can access resources that are a part of the domain.

Domain Name System (DNS)   A protocol and system for mapping IP addresses to user-friendly names. It resolves host names to IP addresses, and vice versa (with reverse lookups).

dotted-decimal representation   Consists of four 8-bit fields written in base 10, with dots (periods) separating the fields. Each 8-bit field is represented by a number ranging from 0 to 255.

driver   A small application that coordinates the communications between hardware and the computer. For example, a driver enables a LAN adapter or other card to work.

DriveSpace   A Windows 98 disk drive compression software package. With DriveSpace, you can take all or part of a hard disk and create a new compressed drive. All data stored on the compressed drive is automatically compressed, giving you more free space.

DTE (data terminal equipment)   Any device that converts information into digital signals for transmission and vice versa.

Dynamic Host Configuration Protocol (DHCP)   Defined by the Internet community to handle IP address ranges through temporary assignments of addresses. DHCP provides automatic IP address allocation to specific workstations.

Dynamic Link Library (DLL)   A module of executable code that is loaded on demand. DLL is used in Microsoft Windows products.

dynamic routing   Protocols that advertise the routes they are familiar with and pass on the metrics, number of other routers, or hops required to get from their host to another network, either directly or indirectly through another router.

edge connector   The portion of an expansion board inserted into an expansion slot when the card is seated in the computer. The number of pins, and the width and depth of the lines, differ depending on the various types of interfaces (e.g., ISA, EISA, PCI, Micro Channel).

EIDE (Enhanced IDE)   EIDE is a disk drive interface that can support up to four 8.4GB drives.

EISA (Extended Industry Standard Architecture)   A standard for the PC bus that extends the 16-bit ISA bus (AT bus) to 32 bits EISA; also provides bus mastering. Designed to be backward compatible with ISA devices, EISA is the data bus of choice for PC servers in non-IBM environments for high performance and throughput.

election datagram   A packet that includes that system's election criteria. All current browsers and potential browsers receive the datagram. If a browser has better election criteria than it receives, it sends out its own election datagram and enters an election in progress.

electronic mail (e-mail)   Mail messages transmitted electronically from one network user to another, or across the Internet.

Emergency Repair Disk (ERD)   Disk that can repair missing Windows NT files and restore the Registry to include disk configuration and security information.

emergency startup disk   Provides a bootup option for Windows 95/98 if the server will not boot from its hard disk.

encapsulation   The process of encoding data for transmission across the network.

encrypted authentication   Methods for secure network transmission that include the simple Password Authentication Protocol (PAP), which permits clear-text passwords, and the Shiva Password Authentication Protocol (SPAP), used by Windows NT workstations when connecting to a Shiva LAN Rover.

encryption   An algorithm that hides the contents of a message, or other file or communication, by deliberately scrambling the elements that compose the item. The item must then be decrypted to its original form before it can be read.

end-to-end communication   Communication on networks that are concerned only with the two ends of the conversation dealing with each other directly (for example, a telephone call).

environment subsystem   Provides support for the various application types that can be run, such as POSIX, Win32, and OS/2. It mimics the original environment the application expects to see.

EPROM (Erasable Programmable Read-Only Memory)   A set of software instructions built into the interface card to perform its functions. The software in the EPROM can sometimes be upgraded.

error checking   Used when sending data across a network to ensure that the data received is identical to the data that was sent originally. *See also* **parity bit, checksum**, and **cyclical redundancy check**.

Ethernet   A networking technology defined by the Institute for Electrical and Electronic Engineers (IEEE) as IEEE standard 802.3. This Physical Layer technology is the most popular Data Link Layer protocol because of its speed, low cost, and worldwide acceptance.

event logs   Log files containing the system, security, and application events.

Executive Services   Windows NT Executive Services (also called System Services) acts as an interface between the Kernel and the environmental subsystems. It is comprised of the following components: Object Manager, Security Reference Monitor, Process Manager, Local Procedure Call Facility, Virtual Memory Manager, and I/O Manager.

Explorer   The file system navigation tool for Microsoft Windows 95 and Microsoft Windows NT 4.0 operating systems.

export server   The computer that provides the directories to be replicated. These directories are kept in the export directory located by default at %systemroot%SYSTEM32\REPL\EXPORT.

Extended Capabilities Port (ECP)   Windows 98 port that provides high-speed printing and support for ECP-compliant devices.

FAQs (Frequently Asked Questions)   Appear in specific areas of bulletin boards and Web sites, and contain answers to frequently asked questions about a product or service. FAQs are used in newsgroups to cover questions that have appeared often.

Fast Ethernet   *See* 100BaseT.

FAT (File Allocation Table)   A file system predominantly used for operating systems such as Windows 3.*x* and Windows 95. FAT is universally accepted and accessible through other operating systems. To support backward compatibility, Windows NT fully supports the FAT file system.

FAT32   The Windows 98 32-bit upgrade to the FAT file system that originally came from DOS. The benefits of FAT32 include optimal use of disk space and larger partition sizes than the maximum 2GB size enabled by FAT. Note: Windows 98 supports only FAT and FAT32 files systems; Windows NT does not support FAT32.

fault tolerance   The capability of a computer to ensure that data and resources remain functional in an emergency.

FDDI (Fiber Distributed Data Interface)   A high-speed token-passing network architecture that is much faster and more fault tolerant, and can cover more distance, than Token Ring. This technology uses fiber-optic cabling to reach speeds of 100 Mbps. FDDI is an alternative to standard Ethernet implementations, often used as a high-speed backbone to connecting LANs.

fiber-optic cable   One of three types of physical media that can be used at the Physical Layer to carry digital data signals in the form of modulated pulses of light. An optical fiber consists of an extremely thin cylinder of glass, called the core, surrounded by a concentric layer of glass, known as the cladding. For most fiber-optic cables, the conductive element is most likely a form of special glass fiber, rather than copper or some other conductive metal. The beauty of fiber-optic cable is that it is immune to electronic and magnetic interference and has much more bandwidth than most electrical cable types. There are two fibers per cable—one to transmit and one to receive. *See also* **coaxial cable** and **twisted-pair cable**.

FIFO (First In, First Out)   The first data in the buffer will be the first out when the buffer becomes full.

file server   A network computer that runs the network operating system and services requests from the workstations.

file system   The network operating system's rules for handling and storing files.

File Transfer Protocol (FTP)   A protocol designed primarily for transferring data across a network. FTP denotes both a protocol and a utility used for this purpose. It was created to quickly and efficiently transfer data files from one host to another without impacting the remote hosts' resources.

Finite-State Automation (FSA)   Processes status messages between each layer to coordinate communications.

firewall   Software that prevents unauthorized traffic between two networks by examining the IP packets that travel on both networks. Firewalls look at the IP address and type of access the packet requires (such as FTP or HTTP) and then determine if that type of traffic is allowed.

Firewire   In Windows 98, an external connection standard geared more toward higher-speed devices than USB is. Capable of supporting videodisc players and external storage boxes, it is a very promising addition to future computers. *See also* USB.

four-octet address   The 32-bit IP address is broken into four octets that can be represented in binary (11010100 00001111 10000100 01110101) or decimal (212.15.132.117) format.

fragmentation   (1) Occurs when there is unused space within contiguous pages. (2) The process in which networks chop or fragment large pieces of data into more manageable units before transmission. When data is fragmented, it is important to ensure that all the pieces make it to the other end in the right sequence. If they are not in order, it is sometimes possible to resequence the data into the right order.

frame relay   A packet-switched protocol.

full backup   Backs up every file on the specified volume or volumes. Full backups should be run frequently, and at least one current copy should be stored off-site.

full-duplex dialogs   Used by OSI Session Layer to enable data to flow in both directions simultaneously.

full synchronization   In a full synchronization, the PDC sends a copy of the entire directory service database to a BDC.

fully qualified domain name (FQDN)   The complete DNS namespace path to a computer is known as a FQDN.

gateway   A device or service that translates communication protocols. Gateways enable two dissimilar systems that have similar functions to communicate with each other. Gateways can be electronic or software devices and are becoming more common as the need for cross-platform communications increases.

GB (gigabyte)   The equivalent of a billion bytes.

global groups   Created on domain controllers and used to organize the users.

Graphics Device Interface (GDI)   Graphics engine that controls the display of graphics on the monitor and printers. It is responsible for communication between applications and the graphics devices.

group accounts   Accounts used for grouping users who perform the same function or require access to the same resources. If it were not for group accounts, you would have to grant access to resources on a per-user basis.

groupware   Any software that enhances a group's capability to collaborate in the performance of a task.

guest account   Used for limited access for remote users or users from other domains. Disabled by default, the guest account provides low-level access to the computer for users who do not have a user account of their own.

half-duplex dialogs   Used by OSI Session Layer to enable data to flow in two directions, but only one direction at a time. With half-duplex dialogs, replies and acknowledgments are possible.

Hardware Compatibility List (HCL)   A compilation of computer systems and hardware that have been tested for compatibility with a given operating system.

hardware profile   An alternate configuration you can select from a startup to specify various options. Laptop users employ one hardware profile for the docked configuration and another for the undocked, or travel, configuration.

HDLC (High-Level Data-Link Control)   Protocol used to encapsulate the data stream as it passes through the PPP connection.

heterogeneous   A mixed network operating environment involving different operating systems like NT, UNIX, and Novell.

home directory   An option for a user account that can give the user an accessible place to store files from anywhere in the domain.

host   A server that is accessed by clients. In a TCP/IP network, any computer connected to the network is considered a host.

host ID   The portion of the 32-bit address that identifies the device on a TCP/IP network.

HOSTS file   Contains mappings of remote host names to IP addresses.

hot-swappable parts   Parts that can be replaced without shutting down the system.

HTTP (Hypertext Transfer Protocol)   The protocol used to connect to the Internet to view Web pages.

hub   The device used in a star topology that connects the computers to the LAN. Hubs can be passive or active. *See also* **passive hub** and **active hub**.

I/O addresses (Input/Output addresses)   Spaces in memory designated for a device's own use.

I/O Manager   Part of the Windows NT Executive Services, responsible for all input and output for the operating system.

IDE (Integrated Drive Electronics)   One of two common interface types in a tape drive. IDE is mainly used in the slower and lower-capacity QIC-style tape drives. *See also* SCSI.

IEEE (Institute of Electrical and Electronics Engineers)   A large and respected professional organization that is also active in defining standards.

impersonation   Technique for a server process to access objects that it doesn't have permissions to. If the client process has proper access permissions, the server process impersonates the client process in order to access the object.

import computer   Systems that receive the replicated files and directories from the export server. The directories are kept in an import directory located by default at systemroot%SYSTEM32\REPL\IMPORT.

incremental backup   Backs up all the files that have been changed since the last backup and modifies the archive bit.

Information Store   One of the four core components of Exchange Server. The Information Store consists of two databases, the public Information Store (PUB.EDB) and the private Information Store (PRIV.EDB). This is where all electronic messages are stored.

inherited permission   Permissions inherited from the parent folder for a file or folder.

Integrated Services Digital Network (ISDN)   Connections that take place over digital lines and provide faster and more reliable connectivity. The primary benefit of ISDN is its speed and reliability. ISDN is commonly found in two speeds: 64 Kbps and 128 Kbps.

interference   Noise that disturbs the electrical signals sent across network cables.

Internet Control Message Protocol (ICMP)   Enables systems on a TCP/IP network to share status and error information. Two of the most common uses of ICMP messages are ping and tracert.

Internet Engineering Task Force (IETF)   Group responsible for the operation, management, and evolution of the Internet. The steering committee of the IETF is known as the Internet Engineering Steering Group (IESG).

Internet Explorer   *See* **Microsoft Internet Explorer.**

Internet Information Service (IIS)   Provides FTP, Gopher, and Web services in Windows NT. (As of IIS 4.0 there is no longer Gopher support.)

Internet Layer   TCP/IP layer that is responsible for handling the communication from one computer to another computer. It accepts a request to send data from the Transport Layer. The Internet Layer consists of two protocols, the Internet Protocol (IP) and the Internet Control Message Protocol (ICMP).

Internet Network Information Center (InterNIC)   The central authority responsible for issuing all network IDs that will be used on the Internet. InterNIC operates under contract with the National Science Foundation (NSF).

Internet News Service   Enables an Exchange Organization to participate in USENET newsgroups.

Internet Protocol (IP)   Provides packet delivery for all other protocols within the TCP/IP suite.

internetworks   A network of networks, such as the Internet. Repeaters, bridges, and routers are devices used to link individual LANs together to form larger internetworks. *See also* **repeater**, **bridge**, and **router**.

interprocess communications (IPC)   Methods of communication between one program and another. Depending on the IPC method being used, this communication can even be across a network. IPC is often used in the client/server environment as a means of communication between the server and the client across the network.

intersite communication   Communication that uses messaging connectors to connect two sites. Messaging connectors include the simple-to-implement Site Connector, the complex but extensible X.400 Connector, the Dynamic RAS Connector, and the Internet Mail Service.

intrasite communication   Communication that takes place among servers in the same Exchange Server site. Intrasite server communication uses Remote Procedure Calls. RPCs can be used over several protocols, including IPX/SPX, TCP/IP, and NetBEUI.

IP (Internet Protocol)   A common protocol that sets up the mechanism for transferring data across the network. Usually seen in TCP/IP.

IP address   Uniquely identifies a computer on the network. It is 32 bits long, with four octets separated by dots. This number is then converted to binary and used as a unique identifier.

IPCONFIG   The command-line based Windows NT utility used to display the current TCP/IP configurations on the local computer and to modify the DHCP addresses assigned to each interface. *See also* **WINIPCFG**.

IPX   The native transport protocol for Novell's NetWare. IPX is also available in the Windows NT environment.

IPX/SPX (Internetwork Packet Exchange/Sequenced Packet Exchange)   Protocol that is primarily used by Novell NetWare networks, but which can be used by other networks (such as Microsoft networks) as a routable protocol or to connect to Novell networks.

IRQ (interrupt request)   Used by the device to interrupt the processor and request service.

IRQ lines   Hardware lines over which devices send interrupt signals to the microprocessor.

ISA (Industry Standard Architecture)   The bus used in most PCs since it was introduced in 1985.

Jetpack   Windows NT Server utility that can be used to compact a WINS or DHCP database.

Kbps (kilobits per second)   A data transfer speed of 1024 bits per second.

Kernel   Also called Microkernel, refers to the core of code in an operating system. This is the most important part of the operating system and is responsible for all functions on the system, such as creating, managing, and scheduling threads.

Kernel Mode   Also called Privileged Mode, the Kernel Mode has direct access to the hardware. Some components of NT that used to run as User Mode components now run as Kernel Mode components. These are the Window Manager, GDI, and graphics device drivers.

Key Management Server   An integrated component within Exchange Server. It is used to provide advanced security to an Exchange Server organization. The Key Management Server uses **public key cryptography** and **secret key cryptography**.

lag   The slowing of network performance usually caused by increased demand for available bandwidth.

LAN (local area network)   Consists of any two or more computers joined to communicate within a small area, usually not larger than a single building.

LAN driver   Provides the information to enable the NIC to communicate with the network.

LastKnownGood   The configuration that was saved to a special control set in the Registry after the last successful logon to Windows NT.

LCP (Link Control Protocol)   Used by PPP to establish, test, and configure the data link connection.

least significant bit   When a computer starts reading at the last digit of a binary number, it is using the least significant digit. When a computer starts with the first digit, it is using the most significant digit.

legacy system   An existing system that either needs updating or is no longer capable of maintaining required performance.

LMHOSTS file   A special text file that helps map NetBIOS names to IP addresses.

load   The amount of data present on the network. Also known as network traffic.

local groups   Groups that access resources on a single domain.

Local Procedure Call Facility   Responsible for passing information between processes.

Local Security Authority The heart of the Windows NT security subsystem. It creates security access tokens, authenticates users, and manages the local security policy.

log off (or log out) The procedure for exiting the network.

log on (or log in) The procedure for checking on to the network so that you can access files and other network information. When you have access to the network, you are said to be logged on.

logon scripts Used to start applications or set environment variables for a computer at startup.

long file name capability Frees you from the restrictive 8.3-naming scheme that was a part of previous versions of Windows. With longer file names, you can adopt a more descriptive naming scheme.

loopback test A test that verifies that the TCP/IP stack was installed correctly and is working.

MAC (media access control) A networked computer's unique address for its network interface card (NIC). Data is transported over networks in packets that always contain the source and destination MAC addresses. A bridge reads this information off the packets it receives to fill its routing table.

mail client Software application that retrieves the messages from the mailbox, and then in most cases, deletes them from the mailbox. In addition, most mail clients enable you to send outgoing e-mail, and have some type of message decoding built in. Some popular mail clients include Microsoft Outlook, Eudora, and Pegasus.

mail routing Mail transfer from one location to another.

Management Information Base (MIB) Defines management objects for a network device.

mandatory logon   Windows NT uses mandatory logon to force everyone to log on before it grants access to the system.

Master Domain Model   All user accounts are located in a single domain called the master domain. Resources, such as printers and files, are shared in other domains called resource domains. This model allows for central administration.

maximum port speed   Defined by the kilobytes per second that the modem can support. Maximum rates are defined primarily by the modem hardware; however, the current public telephone network has an upper limit of 56 Kbps through an analog modem.

Mbps (megabits per second)   Used to measure throughput or communication speed. Mbps is a communications rate of 1,048,576 bits per second.

MCA (Microchannel Architecture)   The 32-bit data bus released by IBM in 1988 with IBM's PS/2 product line. MCA was a totally new architecture that was not backward compatible with ISA cards. MCA adapters are more expensive and offer higher performance than the ISA adapters.

media filter   Used on Token Ring networks to change the type of media from Type 1 (shielded twisted pair) to Type 3 (unshielded twisted pair) or vice versa.

memory   Physical memory is RAM (random-access memory); virtual memory is hard disk space acting as though it is additional RAM.

member server   Any Windows NT Server computer in a domain that is not acting as a domain controller.

Message Transfer Agent (MTA)   One of the four core components of the Exchange server. The MTA is responsible for delivering messages between Exchange servers by means such as Exchange Site Connectors, other X.400 MTAs, Microsoft Mail Connectors, and the Lotus Notes Connector.

Microsoft Backup Microsoft utility for backing up and restoring files from your hard disk to both removable and non-removable disks or tapes.

Microsoft Batch 98 The program created by Microsoft to help create the files required for Windows 98 automated setup. Microsoft Batch 98 is included in the Windows 98 Resource Kit.

Microsoft Exchange Server A powerful messaging, communication, and collaboration server. The Exchange Server architecture is component based. There have always been four core components: System Attendant, Directory Services, Message Transfer Agent, and the Information Store.

Microsoft Infrared In Windows 98, a wireless transmission used for network connectivity and for printing to infrared-ready printers. Infrared devices can now be used in Windows 98 just like devices that are normally connected directly with a cable.

Microsoft Internet Explorer (IE) Microsoft's Web browser. Windows 98 integrates IE into the desktop.

Microsoft Proxy Server Proxy Server enables a single connection to the Internet to be shared by many users, enabling outbound FTP and Web access (and other supported TCP/IP ports). Proxy Server accomplishes this by making requests for Internet resources on behalf of users so that only a single TCP/IP address appears to be initiating Internet access.

Microsoft System Information (MSI) A utility that provides easy read-only access to detailed information regarding the Windows 98 operating system, computer hardware, and even third-party software.

MIME attachment A type of Internet message. MIME messages are made up of headers and bodies. MIME is the preferred way to send and receive messages, because a MIME message's content is categorized by a richer set of type.

mirroring   Duplicating information to another hard disk. If one hard drive fails, the other hard drive is immediately available with the very same information.

modem (modulator/demodulator)   A device used to translate digital signals from the computer into analog signals that can travel across a telephone line.

modularity   (1) In the TCP/IP protocol stack, each layer can communicate with only the layer above or below it. (2) In hardware and software design, a program that has been broken down into modules (small units), each providing a certain service or task. These modules can then be installed or removed, depending on the software's requirements. Windows NT and Windows 98 are modular operating systems.

most significant bit   When a computer starts reading the first digit of a binary number, on the far left, it is using the most significant bit. When a computer starts reading the last digit, on the far right, it is using the least significant digit.

MS-CHAP   A Microsoft adaptation of CHAP. It uses the same type of encryption methodology but is slightly more secure. The server sends a challenge to the originating host, which must return the user name and an MD-4 hash of the challenge string, the session ID, and the MD-4 hashed password.

multi-homed system   When a computer is configured with more than one IP address.

Multilink Channel Aggregation   Feature of Windows 98 that multiplies the total bandwidth between the remote PC and the host by combining two or more modem or ISDN lines. The only issue with using this technology is that there must be a separate telephone or ISDN line for each modem or ISDN device that is used.

Multi-Modem Adapters with NT Server (Multilink)   Combines two or more physical links, most commonly analog modems, into a logical bundle, which acts as a single connection to increase the available bandwidth/speed of the link.

Multiple Master Domain model   Managed much like the master domain model, except it can handle more users. The multiple master domain is actually two or more master domain models joined by a two-way trust.

multiprocessing   Capability of the system to increase processing power by adding more processors. *See also* **symmetric multiprocessing** (SMP).

multistation access units (MAUs)   The central hubs in a Token Ring LAN.

multitasking   The capability to run several applications at once using one processor. There are two kinds of multitasking: *Preemptive* multitasking gives the operating system the capability to take control of the processor without the consent of the application. This is the most common type of multitasking in Windows NT. *Cooperative* multitasking, or non-preemptive multitasking, requires an application to check the queue for other waiting applications and relinquish control to those applications.

multi-vendor gateways   Provide a translation method between one type of mailbox server to another type of mail client. The gateway enables clients such as Microsoft Outlook to read data from hosts that are not the same as Outlook.

NBTSTAT   A utility used to troubleshoot connectivity between two computers trying to communicate via NetBT.

NDIS (Network Driver Interface Specification)   A network device driver specification, NDIS provides hardware and protocol independence for network drivers. A benefit of NDIS is that it offers protocol multiplexing, which enables multiple protocol stacks to coexist in the same host.

near-line backups   These backups differ from offline backups, in that they are kept on devices connected to the network for faster restoration of files. They require more effort to restore than accessing a file from a hard disk, but less effort than restoring a file from an offline backup.

NetBEUI (NetBIOS Extended User Interface)   A Transport Layer driver that is the Extended User Interface to NetBIOS. Windows NT and other operating systems use it to deliver information across a network. NetBEUI cannot be routed.

NetBIOS (Network Basic Input/Output System)   A networked extension to PC BIOS. NetBIOS enables I/O requests to be sent and received from a remote computer. Commonly called an application program interface (API).

NetBT   A software standard and naming convention.

NETSTAT   A utility is for relating protocol statistics and current active connections utilizing TCP/IP.

NetWare   Novell's network operating system.

NetWare Connect (NRN)   Used to connect to NetWare services via IPX/SPX.

NetWare Directory Services (NDS)   In Windows 98, a database that catalogs all NetWare resources, including the user IDs, printers, servers, volumes, and any other network resources.

network   Two or more computers linked so that they can communicate. Any type of interactive information-carrying system.

network adapter   *See* network interface card.

Network Client Administrator   Tool that gives the administrator a way to create installation startup disk and installation disk sets.

Network Dynamic Data Exchange (NetDDE)   Enables two applications to communicate, with a link always maintained.

network infrastructure   The physical equipment that hooks computers into a network. This includes the cables, hubs, routers, and software used to control a network.

network interface card (NIC)   Also called an adapter card or interface card, it is installed in a computer to enable it to communicate with other computers over a network. A NIC changes the parallel signals inside the computer into serial signals that go over the network cable.

Network Interface Layer   The lowest level in the TCP/IP model. It accepts the datagram from the Internet layer and transmits it over the network.

Network Layer   OSI layer that manages addressing and delivering packets on a complex internetwork such as the Internet. Internetworks are joined by devices known as routers, which utilize routing tables and routing algorithms to determine how to send data from one network to another.

network map   A detailed map of information about what's on the network. Includes an inventory of machines and other hardware, a map of cable layout, and other information to document the network.

Network Monitor   A tool that "sniffs out" packets on the network and helps diagnose any problems concerning protocols. It is a very helpful tool when you are trying to diagnose network traffic, Windows Internet Naming Service (WINS), Domain Name System (DNS), or name resolution issues on your network.

Network Neighborhood   An application available from the Windows 95, 98, and NT desktops that enables you to view computers in a workgroup or domain and to access the resources they are sharing. In Windows 98, Network Neighborhood enables a user to browse the resources available on the NetWare network.

network operating system (NOS) An operating system that permits and facilitates the networking of computers. Manages and controls other file systems, other printers connected to workstations, or input or output to network devices. Windows NT is a network operating system.

Network Terminator 1 (NT1) Device located at the end-user side of the ISDN connection.

Network Terminator 2 (NT2) Placed between an NT1 device and any adapters or terminal equipment.

newsfeeds *See* **push feed** and **pull feed**

New Technology File System (NTFS) A secure file system developed for Windows NT. NTFS is transaction orientated, enables permissions to be assigned to both files and directories, and has the capability to compress files. It can only be read by NT operating systems, and therefore cannot be used on computers with single hard disks that dual boot with other operating systems.

NFS (Network File System) A protocol for file sharing that enables a user to use network disks as if they were connected to the local machine.

node Each device on a network is an individual node. It can be a workstation, a printer, or the file server.

noncontainer object A noncontainer object doesn't contain other objects. *See also* **container object** and **object**.

non-MIME A type of Internet message usually encoded as BINHEX or UUENCODE. These are both older standards used to send binary images over the Internet. They still are the method of choice with Internet POP clients such as Eudora and most Macintosh mail readers.

NOS *See* **network operating system**.

NSLOOKUP Used to examine information from DNS servers.

NTDETECT The hardware recognition program used by Windows NT.

NT File System (NTFS) The file system used by Windows NT. It supports large storage media and file system recovery, in addition to other advantages.

NTHQ A Windows NT utility that identifies what hardware is installed on your computer, including PCI, EISA, ISA, and MCA devices.

NTVDM (Virtual DOS Machine) A 32-bit application run in a separate memory space that is capable of being multitasked with other applications (thereby increasing performance). This process will run DOS applications and Windows applications that require DOS.

NWLink Microsoft's implementation of Novell's IPX/SPX protocol suite. NWLink is a routable transport protocol for Microsoft networks and for connecting to NetWare networks through CSNW or GSNW. *See also* **CSNW**.

object In Windows NT, just about everything is an object. A file is an object and so is a window. Objects have a type, various attributes, and a set of operations. They can be physical devices (such as a COM port) or they can be abstract (such as a thread). NT controls access to objects. *See also* **container object** and **noncontainer object**.

Object Manager Responsible for the creation and use of objects, including the naming, managing, and security for objects.

offline backups Backups that are kept offline. They are removed from the operation of the server and require the medium, usually tape, to be loaded in order to restore.

off-site storage A place in a separate location from the file server, used to store backup tapes. A complete backup should always be kept off-site.

online backups   Backups that are stored online so that they are immediately available.

open protocol standards   Non-proprietary. For example, because TCP/IP is not tied to an operating system, any vendor developing a new operating system with a network component can refer to the RFCs to build a TCP/IP component.

Open Systems Interconnect (OSI)   The most common network model used in PC networks. Consists of seven layers: Application, Presentation, Session, Transport, Network, Data Link, and Physical.

OS/2 subsystem   The most limited of the subsystems provided with Windows NT. There is less need to create a fully functional OS/2 subsystem, because support for the OS/2 environment has dwindled.

Outlook Web Access client   A Web browser that supports JavaScript and frames accessing an IIS server with the proper active server pages loaded.

overhead   The control attached to packets transmitted across a network. Overhead data includes routing and error-checking information. Overhead also refers to the bandwidth used to sustain network communications.

packet   Small, manageable pieces of data that are transmitted over the network as a whole. The packet must include a header section, a data section, and, in most cases, a cyclic redundancy check (CRC) section, also called a trailer.

packet burst   Used in IPX when a packet burst-enabled source sends multiple packets across a network without waiting for an acknowledgment for each packet. Instead, one acknowledgment is sent for the group of packets.

page   The size of the smallest portion of memory that can be managed, which is 4KB.

paging file   A file used by Windows NT to move an unused portion of memory to the hard disk and to retrieve the data when it is needed. The paging file is actually a file called PAGEFILE.SYS, and by default is located in the root directory of the drive you specify in the Virtual Memory dialog box.

parity bit   A basic method of checking for errors with transmitted data. Before sending data, the number of individual bits that make up the data is counted. If there is an even number of bits, a parity bit is set to one and added to the end of the data so that the total of the bits being sent is odd. If there is an odd number of bits, the parity bit is set to zero and added to the end. The receiving computer adds up the bits received, and if there is an even number of bits, the computer assumes that an error has occurred. The parity method is not foolproof, because if an even number of bits is corrupted, they will offset each other in the total.

partial synchronization   The automatic, timed replication to all domain BDCs of only those directory database changes that have occurred since the last synchronization.

partition   A logical division of a physical disk that is treated as though it were a separate hard disk. After partitioning the hard disk, you need to decide which partition will be the system partition and which will be the active partition. *See also* **active partition** and **system partition**.

passive hub   A hub device used in a star topology that connects machines to the network and organizes the cables, but does not regenerate or redistribute data.

pass-through authentication   Occurs when your creditials are not in the local directory service database.

password   The key to access the network during logon.

Password Authentication Protocol (PAP)   An authentication protocol in which the client authenticates itself to a server by passing the username and password to it. The server then compares this information to its password store. Because the password is passed in clear text, this is not recommended in an environment where security concerns are an issue.

PC card bus   Formerly known as PCMCIA. An architecture designed primarily for laptops and other portable computers.

PCI (Peripheral Component Interconnect)   A PC local bus that provides high-speed data transmission between the CPU and a peripheral device.

Peer Resource Sharing   In Windows 98, the capability to simulate a server by sharing its files, drives, and printers across a network.

peer-to-peer network   A network in which any machine can serve as the server and any machine can serve as the client. There are no hierarchical differences between the workstations in the network. These networks are used to enable small groups to share files and resources, including CD-ROM drives, printers, and hard drives.

Peer Web Services   A scaled-down version of the Internet Information Server (IIS) that enables you to publish Web pages on your company's intranet.

Performance Monitor   A utility that tracks the usage of resources by the system components and applications and provides performance information about the network to help locate bottlenecks, determine which resources are too taxed, and plan upgrades to the system's capacity.

performance tuning   The art of maximizing the performance of an existing configuration to achieve the optimal outcome.

permissions   Permissions regulate the capability of users to access objects such as files and directories. Depending on the permissions, a user can have full access, limited access, or no access to an object. Permissions are types of access used in creating ACEs.

phonebook entry   Stores the configuation information required to connect to a remote network. Entries are stored as individual dial-up connections in a phonebook file.

Physical Layer   Bottom OSI layer that is only concerned with moving bits of data on and off the network medium. The Physical Layer does not define what that medium is, but it must define how to access it.

ping (Packet InterNet Groper)   Utility for verifying IP-level connectivity.

platform   A type of computer system. For example, Intel x86 and UNIX are platforms.

Point-to-Point Protocol (PPP)   A serial protocol used for sending information over a dial-up connection. This protocol enables the sending of IP packets, supports compression, enables IP address negotiation, and is the successor to the older SLIP protocol.

Point-to-Point Protocol Multi-link Protocol (PPP-MP)   Protocol used to enable multiple ISDN devices or multiple modems using separate phone lines to aggregate their bandwidth. By using two or more devices for a single dial-up link, the bandwidth of the devices is combined, thereby increasing the total bandwidth.

Point-to-Point Transmission (PPT)   Many computer networks use point-to-point transmission methods, where there may be one to dozens of points between the source and the destination of a message. (E-mail is a good example of this.) Each point is only concerned with transferring data to the next point downstream.

Point-to-Point Tunneling Protocol (PPTP)   An Internet standard enabling multiple protocols, such as NetBEUI and IPX, to be encapsulated within IP datagrams and transmitted over public backbones such as the Internet. PPTP enables the secure transfer of data from a remote client to a private server by creating a multi-protocol virtual private network (VPN).

POP   *See* Post Office Protocol.

portability   The capability of a system, such as Windows NT, to be ported to other architectures.

port numbers   Pre-assigned TCP/IP port numbers on the server that do not change (although they can be changed). They are pre-assigned so they can expect traffic on a corresponding port relating to the service that is using that port. Values less than 1026 are known as "well-known ports."

POSIX (Portable Operating System Interface)   A standard developed by the Institute of Electrical and Electronic Engineers (IEEE) for file naming and identification based on UNIX. In order to be POSIX-compliant, the software must fulfill certain requirements, such as case-sensitive filenames, hard links (which can be compared to Windows NT shortcuts, in which many entries can point to the same file), and additional time stamping. POSIX is supported by Windows NT.

Post Office Protocol (POP)   Designed to overcome the problem encountered with SMTP, in which workstations were not confined to permanent terminal-based connections to a mainframe. A POP3 mail server holds the mail in a maildrop until the workstation is ready to receive the mail.

POTS (Plain Old Telephone Service)   The standard analog telephone system, such as the one used in most houses.

preemptive multitasking   A method of multitasking that has the capability to prioritize the order of process execution and preempt one process with another.

Presentation Layer   OSI layer that ensures that data sent by the Application Layer and received by the Session Layer is in a standard format. If it is not, the Presentation Layer converts the data.

Primary Domain Controller (PDC)   The NT Server maintaining the master copy of the directory service database for the domain. It handles synchronization with the Backup Domain Controllers.

print device   The actual hardware that prints the document. The three basic types of print devices are raster, PostScript, and plotter.

print driver   The software that enables an application to communicate with printing devices. Print drivers are composed of three files that act together as a printing unit: printer graphics driver, printer interface driver, and characterization data file.

printer pooling   An efficient way to streamline the printing process. One software interface can send print jobs to a pool of printing devices, of which only one printing device actually prints the document.

printing software   Considered the printer. A printer is software that manages a specific printing device (or devices, in case of printer pooling). The printer determines how the print job gets to the printing device—via parallel port, serial port, or the network.

print job   Source code consisting of both data and commands for print processing. All print jobs are classified into data types. The data type tells the spooler what modifications need to be made to the print job so it can print correctly on the printing device.

print monitor   Controls access to the printing device, monitors the status of the device, and communicates with the spooler, which relays this information via the user interface. Controls the data going to a printer port by opening, closing, configuring, writing, reading, and releasing the port.

print processor   Completes the rendering process. *See also* **rendering**.

print queue   The line that handles printing requests and supplies files to the printing device in their proper order.

print router   Routes the print job from the spooler to the appropriate print processor.

print server   Controls network printing and services printing requests. Print servers can be hardware devices or a software solution.

print spooler   A service that intercepts print jobs to the printer and redirects them to disk or memory until the print device is ready for them.

process   A program that has its own set of resources.

Process Manager   Responsible for process and thread objects, including deleting, creating, and managing these objects. A process is a program, or a part of a program, that has an address space, contains objects, and spawns threads that need to be processed.

properties   Object descriptors set in the Windows NT naming system or Registry, depending on the type of object.

protocol   A set of rules governing formatting and interaction that enables machines to communicate across a network. Networking software usually supports multiple levels of protocols. Windows NT supports several protocols, including TCP/IP and DLC.

protocol stacks   Protocols are grouped together to form protocol stacks, which are capable of doing everything from receiving data from an application, to putting the data onto the network cable.

proxy server   A local server between the client workstation and the Internet. A proxy server provides security, remedies the need for each workstation to have a direct connection to the Internet, and enables several computers to use a single Internet connection.

public folders   Used by the Exchange Server to facilitate collaborative workflow processes.

public key cryptography   Consists of a public key and a private key. The public key is given freely to anyone who needs it, and the private key is kept secret by the key's owner and is stored in the user's security file.

Public Switched Telephone Network (PSTN)   The technical name for the medium you use every day to make phone calls and send faxes. The Remote Access Service enables connections across several media. The most common of these is PSTN.

Public Wireless Networks   Public data networks operated by third parties that receive a monthly fee from users in exchange for providing wireless data service.

pull feed   A newsfeed that occurs when the local host initiates the communication to start the replication of messages.

pull partner   All WINS replication is a pull activity. A pull partner is a WINS server configured to make a request for database updates at a given time interval to other WINS servers.

push feed   A newsfeed that occurs when the service provider configures its servers to send news messages to your server.

push partner   A WINS Service that sends update notification messages to its partner when its WINS database has changed.

QIC (Quarter Inch Cartridge)   A tape cartridge format common for backup tapes.

RAID (Redundant Array of Inexpensive Disks)   Designed to provide disk based operating systems with increase I/O performance and fault tolerance through data redundancy.

RAM (Random Access Memory)   Short-term storage memory, physically residing in the computer on memory chips. Because computer applications use RAM in their processing, the amount of RAM in a computer is a major determinant of how well the computer works.

real-time scanning   An option on virus-protection software that scans every file that is accessed, opened, saved, or downloaded.

redirector   Also called a requester, a redirector is software that accept I/O requests for files and then sends the request to a network service on another computer.

Reduced Instruction Set Computing (RISC)   Enables fast, efficient processing of a small number of instructions. Processors such as DEC Alpha, MIPS, CISC, and PowerPC are all based on the RISC design.

Registry   (1) In Windows NT, a central repository that contains the system's hardware and software configuration. (2) In Windows 98, the Registry is a set of two files: SYSTEM.DAT and USER.DAT. SYSTEM.DAT contains hardware and global settings. USER.DAT contains user settings and can also be located in each user profile directory.

Registry Editor   A Microsoft tool to view and modify the Registry. Both the new tool, REGEDT32.EXE, and the traditional Registry editor, REGEDIT.EXE, are included with the Windows NT 4.0 operating system.

Remote Access Service   The dial-up service in Windows NT that enables users to access the network remotely by telephone lines.

Remote Procedure Call (RPC)   An IPC mechanism used by programmers to create an application consisting of multiple procedures—some run on the local computer, and others run on remote computers over a network.

rendering   The process of translating print data into a form that a printing device can read.

repeater   Connects network cables by regenerating signals so they can travel on additional cable lengths.

reservation   An IP address that is reserved for a specific DHCP client.

resource domains   A domain in the Master Domain model (Multiple Master Domain and the Complete Trust models) that has control of its own resources. The master domain controls account information, and resource domains control resources, such as printers and files, within their domain.

Reverse Address Resolution Protocol (RARP)   Enables a machine to learn its own IP address by broadcasting to resolve its own MAC address.

RFC (Request for Comments)   Documents that publish the standards for TCP/IP.

rights   Authorizes users to perform specific actions on a network. Similar to permissions.

ring topology   A network topology that connects the computers in a circular fashion. If one computer fails, the entire network fails, so this topology is rarely used. *See also* **bus topology** and **star topology**.

roaming profile The roaming profile enables you to keep your user preferences in one location so that any changes you make to the profile are used on any computer that you log on to. Gives the user the same desktop environment on any workstation he logs on to.

roaming user A user who logs on to the network at different times from different computers.

root The top level of a directory structure, above which no references can be made.

ROUTE Command that can be used to add, modify, delete, and display route information for one or all interfaces. Used to configure network routing tables.

router A device that connects more than one physical network, or segments of a network, using IP routing software. As packets reach the router, the router reads them and forwards them to their destination, or to another router.

routing The process of forwarding a packet from one segment to another segment until it arrives at its final destination. A router makes decisions as to where to send network packets by looking at the network addresses of the packets it receives before passing them on.

routing table Used by routers to determine whether data is destined for the local network.

RPC (Remote Procedure Call) A request sent to a computer on the network by a program, requesting the computer to perform a task.

RS-232C Null Modem Cable Null modem cables, or LapLink cables, can be used to connect the RAS server serial port directly to the serial port of the client machine.

SAM (Security Access Manager) Database   A database that maintains all user, group, and workstation accounts in a secure database along with their passwords and other attributes.

satellite   A communication satellite functions as an overhead wireless repeater station that provides a microwave communications link between two geographically remote sites.

scaleable   The capacity to change with the network. As requirements change, a scaleable network can grow or shrink to fit the requirements.

script   Used to describe programs, usually those written in an interpreted language, as opposed to a compiled language, because the instructions are formatted similarly to a script for actors.

SCSI (Small Computer System Interface)   A high-speed interface used to connect peripherals such as hard disks, scanners, and CD-ROM drives. SCSI enables up to seven devices to be lined in a single chain.

secret key cryptography   Encrypts and decrypts messages using a single secret key called a bulk encryption key in the Key Management Server. Two examples of secret key cryptography are DES and CAST. The Key Management Server supports CAST 40 and CAST 64. DES and CAST 64 are available only in North America.

Security Accounts Manager (SAM)   A set of routines responsible for managing the directory service database.

security descriptors   Describe the security attributes for an object and have the following parts: Owner security ID (identifies the owner of the object, which enables that person to change the permissions for the object); Security ID of the primary group (only used by the POSIX subsystem); Discretionary access control list (identifies the groups and users who are allowed and denied access); and the System access control list (specifies which events get logged into the security log file).

Security ID (SID) Uniquely identifies each user, workstation, and server on the network.

Security Reference Monitor Component of the Windows NT operating system that is responsible for checking access on objects, manipulating rights, and generating audit messages.

server A computer that provides shared resources to network users.

server alert Used to send notification messages to users or computers. Server alerts are generated by the system and relate to server and resource use. They warn about security and access problems, user session problems, printer problems, and server shutdown because of power loss, when the UPS service is available.

Server Manager A utility not only for managing servers, but also for managing workstations and the domain.

server mirroring Duplicating a complete server to reduce the demand on the main server.

Service Address Point Identifier (SAPI) Identifies the particular interface on the switch that devices are connected to.

service pack A program that provides new functionality, adds more capability, or corrects a bug in an earlier release. Service packs provide software updates in between full releases of the program.

Service Profile Identifier (SPID) An alphanumeric string that identifies the ISDN terminal capabilities by pointing to a memory location that stores details about the device.

services   Options loaded on computers enabling them to help each other. Services include the capability to send and receive files or messages, talk to printers, manage remote access, and look up information.

Session Layer   OSI layer that manages dialogs between computers. It does this by establishing, managing, and terminating communications between the two computers. *See also* **simplex dialogs**, **half-duplex dialogs**, and **full-duplex dialogs**.

share   A setting to make resources such as printers, CD-ROM drives, and directories available to users on the network.

shared processing   When the processing for a task is not done on only the client, or only the server, but on a combination of both the client and the server.

share-level security   Used to give other users access to your hard disk via the network. The four types of share permissions are No Access, Read, Change, and Full Control.

shell   A program that provides communication between a server and a client or a user and an operating system.

shielded twisted pair   A twisted-pair cable that has foil wrap shielding between the conducting strands and the outer insulation.

Simple Mail Transfer Protocol (SMTP)   Protocol used to send and receive mail over the Internet.

Simple Network Management Protocol (SNMP)   An Internet standard for monitoring and configuring network devices. An SNMP network is composed of management systems and agents.

simplex dialogs   Used by the OSI Session Layer to enable data to flow in only one direction. Because the dialog is one way, information can be sent, but not responded to, or even acknowledged.

single instance storage   A message is sent to more than one recipient on a server, and the message is stored only once on the server. The Exchange Server's Information Store uses single instance storage.

SLIP (Serial Line Internet Protocol)   A TCP/IP protocol that provides the capability to transmit IP packets over a serial link, such as a dial-up connection over a phone line.

SMTP Service Extensions (ESMTP)   A standard that permits the receiving host to tell the sending computer of the extensions it supports.

SNA (Systems Network Architecture)   The basic protocol suite for IBM's AS/400 and mainframe computers.

sniffer   Network monitoring tool that analyzes the traffic on the network and can help solve problems that are infrastructure related.

SNMP (Simple Network Management Protocol)   An Internet standard that provides a simple method for remotely managing virtually any network device.

star bus topology   If you replace the computers in a bus topology with the hubs from star topology networks, you get a star bus topology.

star ring topology   Also called star wired ring, the smaller hubs are internally wired like a ring and connected to the main hub in a star topology.

star topology   All computers are directly cabled to a hub. *See also* **bus topology** and **ring topology**.

stateless   The most efficient type of network communication, a protocol that needs no information about communications between sender and receiver.

static routing   Configuration method used by early routers. It required programming exactly which networks could be routed between which interfaces, especially if there were many network interfaces.

stripe sets without parity   Like volume sets, except they provide performance gains. They can combine 2 – 32 areas of free space as a single volume. However, the free space must be on different hard disks, and each hard disk must contain the same amount of free space that you want to use for the size of the stripe set.

striping data   RAID 5 uses a method of striping data across several hard disks, with parity information also included. This parity information is striped across the drives, rather than being stored on a single hard disk.

subnet mask   Used in TCP/IP communications, the subnet mask enables the recipient of IP packets to distinguish the Network ID portion of the IP address from the Host ID portion of the address.

swap file   File used by Windows 95/98 to create virtual memory. When physical memory becomes used up, pages are written to the swapfile to free physical memory.

switch   A common solution to traffic problems, a switch calculates which devices are connected to each port.

Switched Megabit Data Service (SMDS)   SMDS technology transports data in 53-byte calls at data rates of 1.544 to 45 Mbps.

symmetric cryptography   Both the sender and receiver use a single key.

symmetric multiprocessing (SMP)   A multiprocessor operating system in which there is no master processor in that all threads, including system threads, can be scheduled to run on any processor.

synchronous communication   Sends all data in a steady stream and uses a clock signal to interpret the beginning and end of a packet.

Synchronous Optical Network (SONET)   A fiber-optic network communications link. SONET supports rates up to 13.22 Gbps.

system administrator   Manages the network. It is this person's responsibility to ensure that network functions are running smoothly: for example, that backups are complete, network traffic is running smoothly, and drive space is available when needed.

System Attendant   One of the four core components of Exchange Server. System Attendant performs the following functions: When a new recipient is created in the directory, it generates an e-mail address for that user. It builds the routing tables for the site where the server is a member. It maintains message-tracking logs and manages server and link monitors. It sets up advanced security for the clients. It reclaims space made available by deleted directory objects.

System File Checker (SFC)   Windows 98 tool for automatically checking that all system files are in order and that none are corrupt.

system partition   In Windows NT where the hardware specific files needed to boot are located. The active partition is the system partition on Intel-based computers.

System Policy Editor   Tool used to create policies that restrict users, groups, or computers on the local domain.

T1   A widely used digital transmission link that uses a point-to-point transmission technology with two-wire pairs. One pair is used to send and one to receive. T1 can transmit digital, voice, data, and video signals at 1.544 Mbps.

T3   Similar to T1 but designed for transporting large amounts of data at high speeds. T3 is a leased line that can transmit data at 45 Mbps.

Task Manager   Tool for observing and deleting processes; also provides a more granular level of detail when looking at processes and threads, including the option of removing or setting the priority of individual processes.

T-connector   A T shaped device used in Thin Ethernet cabling to connect the Thinnet cable to the NIC.

TCP/IP (Transmission Control Protocol/Internet Protocol)
An industry standard suite of protocols designed for local- and wide-area networking, including the Internet. TCP/IP is the most widely used networking protocol and can be used to connect many different types of computers for cross-platform communication.

TechNet   A technical support CD-ROM published by Microsoft. TechNet is a searchable database of all of Microsoft's articles and documentation on nearly all Microsoft products.

Telephony Advanced Programming Interface (TAPI)   TAPI enables communication applications on a computer to control functions of the telephone and manages all signaling between the computer and a telephone network.

Telnet   A TCP/IP network service that enables a computer to connect to a host computer over the network and run a terminal session. It's used for terminal emulation for character-based communicating.

template   A template is a partially completed object, designed to help you start a task. Windows NT Server provides templates to help the new administrator configure objects and complete other tasks.

terminal adapter (TA)   Connects TE2 devices to an ISDN network. TA connects through the R interface to the TE2 device and through the S interface to the ISDN network.

Terminal Endpoint Identifier (TEI)   Identifies the particular ISDN device to the switch. This identifier changes each time a device is connected to the ISDN network.

Terminal Equipment 1 (TE1)   Any ISD ready device that can connect directly to ISDN.

Terminal Equipment 2 (TE2)   Any non-ISDN ready device that requires a terminal adapter to work with ISDN.

Thick Ethernet   *See* 10Base5.

Thin Ethernet   *See* 10Base2.

thrashing   Occurs when information is being swapped in and out of memory, to and from the paging file, at a tremendous rate. It's caused by a deficiency of RAM.

thread   The smallest unit of code in a process.

throughput   A measure of the rate at which data is transferred across a network measured in bits per second (bps).

thunking   Process used by Windows NT to translate 16-bit calls into 32-bit calls and vice versa.

time domain reflectometer (TDR)   A device that sends an electronic pulse down the network cable. The pulse is reflected when it reaches a flaw or the end of the cable.

token   An electronic marker packet, used in ArcNet and FDDI networks, that indicates which workstation is able to send data on a Token Ring topology.

Token Ring   A networking topology that is configured in a circular pattern and circulates an electronic token on the ring to pass data. A Token Ring network has great reliability, but it is costly compared to other network architectures.

Tone Generator   Used to perform tests on phone and network lines by clipping to a wire, terminal panel, or standard modular jack. Aids in the identification of wires during the wire-tracing process.

topology   The physical configuration of a network, including the types of cable used. Common topologies include bus, ring, and star.

TRACERT   Utility commonly used to locate failures along a TCP/IP communications path by tracing the route from origin to destination. Each router interface encountered is echoed to the screen along with some statistical information about the path timing.

transceiver   The portion of the network interface that actually transmits and receives electrical signals across the transmission media. It is also the part of the interface that actually connects to the media.

Transport Layer   (1) The OSI layer that ensures reliable delivery of data to its destination. The Transport Layer consists of two protocols: the Transmission Control Protocol (TCP) and the User Datagram Protocol (UDP). (2) TCP/IP layer that is located at layer 3 of the TCP/IP model. The main responsibility of the Transport Layer is to provide communication from one application to another application.

Trivial File Transfer Protocol (TFTP)   Similar to the file transfer protocol, but does not require user authentication.

trusted domain   The domain that contains the directory service database thereby containing the user accounts. A user logging in to one domain can be authenticated by another domain if a trust relationship was previously established.

trust relationship   A trust is a relationship between two and only two domains. Once a trust is established users from one domain can be given permission to access resources on another domain.

tunneling   When a PPP session is established, PPTP creates a control connection between the client and the remote PPTP server.

twisted-pair cable   A cable type in which conductive wires are twisted to help reduce interference. There are two types of twisted-pair: shielded and unshielded. *See also* **coaxial cable** and **fiber-optic cable**.

UARTs (Universal Asynchronous Receiver/Transmitters)   The hardware pieces designed for the computer to send information to a serial device.

unattended backup   The backup program launches at a scheduled time, does the specified backup, then terminates.

UNC (Universal Naming Convention)   A standardized way of specifying a shared resource on a computer. The syntax is always *\\computername\sharename*

unshielded twisted pair (UTP)   A twisted-pair cable that does not have any shielding between the conducting strands and the outer insulation.

UPS (Uninterruptible Power Supply)   A battery backup system commonly used on file servers to protect in times of power outages.

URL (Uniform Resource Locator)   Provides the address to a document on the World Wide Web.

USB (Universal Serial Bus)   In Windows 98, an external bus standard that enables devices to be added and automatically installed and configured without the need for user intervention or rebooting. USB enables up to 127 simultaneous connections, with connection speeds up to 12 Mbps. This slower speed makes USB suitable for devices such as keyboards, mice, and joysticks.

user   Any person who accesses the network.

user account   Represents a user who accesses the resources on a computer or network. User accounts do not have to represent individuals; they can also be accounts for services, such as an SQL Server account.

User Datagram Protocol (UDP)   Offers a connectionless datagram service that is an unreliable "best effort" delivery.

User Environment Profile   Enables you to control the system environment according to which user is logged on.

User Manager   The administrative tool used to manage user accounts, groups, and policies. You can create, rename, or delete user accounts with User Manager.

User Mode   Also called non-privileged processor mode. This is where applications and the various subsystems are run. User Mode is designed to prevent applications from bringing down the operating system.

username   A name used by a user to log on to a computer system.

user profile   Stores user preferences, such as screen savers and last documents used, and environmental settings, such as program groups and network connections. The user profile is the set of stored characteristics that set the default desktop configuration for each individual user account.

User Profile Editor   The administrative tool used to set user options.

user right   Enables the user to perform specific operations on the computer. You set user rights to control which operations a user or group performs. Some vendors may use the term "system privileges."

verify operation   Used to compare files on the hard disk to files that have been backed up to tape.

Virtual File Allocation Table (VFAT)   Enables the use of long filenames, while maintaining the 8.3 naming convention for older applications viewing the same file. Released with the Windows 95 operating system.

virtual memory   Created by Windows NT to simulate RAM on a computer when more memory is needed. It does this by using the computer's hard disk as needed.

Virtual Memory Manager (VMM)   Responsible for the use of virtual memory and the paging file in the system.

Virtual Private Networks (VPNs)   Provide tunneling through a public network with a secure communications channel. VPNs use PPTP or other protocols for secure connections to a remote network. By using PPTP or a similar tunneling protocol, you are able to tunnel through an Internet or LAN connection without compromising security.

virus signature file   A database of known viruses that the anti-virus software uses when scanning files to eliminate viruses. The virus signature file must be kept current.

volume   A logical division of space on a physical drive that is treated as a single unit.

volume sets   The combining of different-sized areas of free space as a single volume (drive letter) from any type of hard disk (IDE, SCSI, or ESDI). Volume sets don't provide any fault tolerance or performance gains. They are simply used to combine multiple areas of free space as one single volume.

WAN (wide area network)   Multiple local area networks (LANs) linked over a broad physical distance, ranging from a few miles to across the world. TCP/IP is the primary WAN protocol and was developed to provide reliable, secure data transmissions over long distances.

Win32   The primary subsystem for NT, it is responsible for all user input and output. The Win32 subsystem is also responsible for receiving requests from the other environment subsystems.

Windows 98 Hardware Compatibility List   This list is updated with hardware components that have been tested and found to meet the Windows 98 requirements.

Windows Scripting Host   Windows 98 shell that enables an administrator to use more robust, language-independent commands in logon scripts through ActiveX scripting.

Windows Update   Windows 98 principal Internet-based troubleshooting tool that automatically compares your system configuration to the most recent available from Microsoft and enables you to easily download and install any updates and fixes.

WINIPCFG   The Windows 95/98-based graphical utility used to display the current TCP/IP configurations on the local workstations and to modify the DHCP addresses assigned to each interface. *See also* **IPCONFIG**.

WINS (Windows Internet Naming Service)   The Windows NT Service that provides a map between NetBIOS computer names and IP addresses. This permits NT networks to use either computer names or IP addresses to request access to network resources.

wireless bridge   Provides wireless connectivity of remote Ethernet networks and is fully transparent to network protocol and applications.

wireless connectivity   Connectivity is achieved without cable connections.

wireless networking   A network configured to use communication techniques such as infrared, cellular, or microwave, so that cable connections are not required.

workgroup   A group of computers that are each individually managed.

workstation   The client machine used to access a network.

WORM (Write Once, Read Many)   An optical storage medium that permits you to write to it only once but enables you to read from it many times. CD-ROM drives are basically WORM devices.

X.25   A protocol that runs on a worldwide network of packet-forwarding nodes that deliver X.25 packets to their designated X.121 addresses. X.25 networks transmit data with a packet-switching protocol, bypassing noisy telephone lines.

INDEX

P

R

S

U

Custom Corporate Network Training

Train on Cutting Edge Technology   We can bring the best in skill-based training to your facility to create a real-world hands-on training experience. Global Knowledge has invested millions of dollars in network hardware and software to train our students on the same equipment they will work with on the job. Our relationships with vendors allow us to incorporate the latest equipment and platforms into your on-site labs.

Maximize Your Training Budget   Global Knowledge provides experienced instructors, comprehensive course materials, and all the networking equipment needed to deliver high quality training. You provide the students; we provide the knowledge.

Avoid Travel Expenses   On-site courses allow you to schedule technical training at your convenience, saving time, expense, and the opportunity cost of travel away from the workplace.

Discuss Confidential Topics   Private on-site training permits the open discussion of sensitive issues such as security, access, and network design. We can work with your existing network's proprietary files while demonstrating the latest technologies.

Customize Course Content   Global Knowledge can tailor your courses to include the technologies and the topics which have the greatest impact on your business. We can complement your internal training efforts or provide a total solution to your training needs.

Corporate Pass   The Corporate Pass Discount Program rewards our best network training customers with preferred pricing on public courses, discounts on multimedia training packages, and an array of career planning services.

Global Knowledge Training Lifecycle   Supporting the Dynamic and Specialized Training Requirements of Information Technology Professionals

- Define Profile
- Assess Skills
- Design Training
- Deliver Training
- Test Knowledge
- Update Profile
- Use New Skills

College Credit Recommendation Program   The American Council on Education's CREDIT program recommends 53 Global Knowledge courses for college credit. Now our network training can help you earn your college degree while you learn the technical skills needed for your job. When you attend an ACE-certified Global Knowledge course and pass the associated exam, you earn college credit recommendations for that course. Global Knowledge can establish a transcript record for you with ACE, which you can use to gain credit at a college or as a written record of your professional training that you can attach to your resume.

Registration Information

COURSE FEE: The fee covers course tuition, refreshments, and all course materials. Any parking expenses that may be incurred are not included. Payment or government training form must be received six business days prior to the course date. We will also accept Visa/MasterCard and American Express. For non-U.S. credit card users, charges will be in U.S. funds and will be converted by your credit card company. Checks drawn on Canadian banks in Canadian funds are acceptable.

COURSE SCHEDULE: Registration is at 8:00 a.m. on the first day. The program begins at 8:30 a.m. and concludes at 4:30 p.m. each day.

CANCELLATION POLICY: Cancellation and full refund will be allowed if written cancellation is received in our office at least six business days prior to the course start date. Registrants who do not attend the course or do not cancel more than six business days in advance are responsible for the full registration fee; you may transfer to a later date provided the course fee has been paid in full. Substitutions may be made at any time. If Global Knowledge must cancel a course for any reason, liability is limited to the registration fee only.

GLOBAL KNOWLEDGE: Global Knowledge programs are developed and presented by industry professionals with "real-world" experience. Designed to help professionals meet today's interconnectivity and interoperability challenges, most of our programs feature hands-on labs that incorporate state-of-the-art communication components and equipment.

ON-SITE TEAM TRAINING: Bring Global Knowledge's powerful training programs to your company. At Global Knowledge, we will custom design courses to meet your specific network requirements. Call 1 (919) 461-8686 for more information.

YOUR GUARANTEE: Global Knowledge believes its courses offer the best possible training in this field. If during the first day you are not satisfied and wish to withdraw from the course, simply notify the instructor, return all course materials, and receive a 100% refund.

In the US:

CALL: 1 (888) 762-4442

FAX: 1 (919) 469-7070

VISIT OUR WEBSITE:

www.globalknowledge.com

MAIL CHECK AND THIS FORM TO:

Global Knowledge

Suite 200

114 Edinburgh South

P.O. Box 1187

Cary, NC 27512

In Canada:

CALL: 1 (800) 465-2226

FAX: 1 (613) 567-3899

VISIT OUR WEBSITE:

www.globalknowledge.com.ca

MAIL CHECK AND THIS FORM TO:

Global Knowledge

Suite 1601

393 University Ave.

Toronto, ON M5G 1E6

REGISTRATION INFORMATION:

Course title ————————————————————————————

Course location ———————————————————— Course date ——————

Name/title ———————————————————————— Company——————

Name/title ———————————————————————— Company——————

Name/title ———————————————————————— Company——————

Address ———————————— Telephone —————— Fax ——————————

City ———————————— State/Province ———— Zip/Postal Code————

Credit card —————— Card # ———————————— Expiration date ————

Signature ————————————————————————————————

1999 COMPTIA OFFICIAL NETWORK+ EXAM OBJECTIVES
TO GET NETWORK+ CERTIFIED, YOU MUST DEMONSTRATE MASTERY OF:

1. KNOWLEDGE OF NETWORKING TEHCNOLOGY

BASIC KNOWLEDGE
- **Demonstrate understanding of basic network structure, including:**
  - The characteristics of star, bus, mesh, and ring topologies, their advantages and disadvantages
  - The characteristics of segments and backbones
- **Identify the following:**
  - The major network operating systems, including Microsoft Windows NT, Novell NetWare, and Unix
  - The clients that best serve specific network operating systems and their resources
  - The directory services of the major network operating systems
- **Associate IPX, IP, and NetBEUI with their functions.**
- **Define the following terms and explain how each relates to fault tolerance or high availability:**
  - Mirroring, duplexing, striping (with and without parity), volumes, tape backup
- **Define the layers of the OSI model and identify the protocols, services, and functions that pertain to each layer.**
- **Recognize and describe the following characteristics of networking media and connectors:**
  - The advantages and disadvantages of coax, Cat 3, Cat 5, fiber optic, UTP, and STP, and the conditions under which they are appropriate
  - The length and speed of 10Base2, 10BaseT, and 100BaseT
  - The length and speed of 10Base5, 100Base VGAnyLan, 100BaseTX
  - The visual appearance of RJ-24 and BNC and how they are crimped
- **Identify the basic attributes, purpose, and function of the following network elements:**
  - Full- and half-duplexing
  - WAN and LAN
  - Server, workstation, and host
  - Server-based networking and peer-to-peer networking
  - Cable, NIC, and router
  - Broadband and baseband
  - Gateway, as both a default IP router and as a method to connect dissimilar systems or protocols

PHYSICAL LAYER
- **Given an installation, configuration, or troubleshooting scenario, select an appropriate course of action if a client** workstation does not connect to the network after installing or replacing a network interface card. Explain why a given action is warranted. The following issues may be covered:
  - Knowledge of how the network card is usually configured, including EPROM, jumpers, and plug-and-play software
  - Use of network card diagnostics, including the loopback test and vendor-supplied diagnostics
  - The ability to resolve hardware resource conflicts, including IRQ, DMA, and I/O Base Address
- **Identify the use of the following network components and the differences between them:**
  - Hubs, MAUs, switching hubs, repeaters. transceivers

DATA LINK LAYER
- **Describe the following data link layer concepts:**
  - Bridges, what they are and why they are used
  - The 802 specs, including the topics covered in 802.2, 802.3, and 802.5
  - The function and characteristics of MAC addresses

NETWORK LAYER
- **Explain the following routing and network layer concepts, including:**
  - The fact that routing occurs at the network layer
  - The difference between a router and a brouter
  - The difference between routable and nonroutable protocols
  - The concept of default gateways and subnetworks
  - The reason for employing unique network IDs
  - The difference between static and dynamic routing

TRANSPORT LAYER
- **Explain the following transport layer concepts:**
  - The distinction between connectionless and connection transport
  - The purpose of name resolution, either to an IP/IPX address or a network protocol

TCP/IP FUNDAMENTALS
- **Demonstrate knowledge of the following TCP/IP fundamentals:**
  - The concept of IP default gateways
  - The purpose and use of DHCP, DNS, WINS, and host files
  - The identity of the main protocols that make up the TCP/IP suite, including TCP, UDP, POP3, SMTP, SNMP, FTP, HTTP, and IP
  - The idea that TCP/IP is supported by every operating system and millions of hosts worldwide
  - The purpose and function of Internet domain name server hierarchies (how email arrives in another country)
- **Demonstrate knowledge of the fundamental concepts of TCP/IP addressing, including:**
  - The A, B, and C classes of IP addresses and their default subnet mask numbers
  - The use of port number (HTTP, FTP, SMTP) and port numbers commonly assigned to a given service
- **Demonstrate knowledge of TCP/IP configuration concepts, including:**
  - The definition of IP proxy and why it is used
  - The identity of the normal configuration parameters for a workstation, including IP address, DNS, default gateway, IP proxy configuration, WINS, DHCP, host name, and Internet domain name

TCP/IP SUITE: UTILITIES
- **Explain how and when to use the following TCP/IP utilities to test, validate, and troubleshoot IP connectivity:**
  - ARP, Telnet, NBTSTAT, Tracert, NETSTAT, ipconfig/winipcfg, FTP, ping

REMOTE CONNECTIVITY
- **Explain the following remote connectivity concepts:**
  - The distinction between PPP and SLIP
  - The purpose and function of PPTP and the conditions under which it is useful
  - The attributes, advantages, and disadvantages of ISDN and PSTN (POTS)
- **Specify the following elements of dial-up networking:**
  - The modem configuration parameters that must be set, including serial port IRQ, I/O address and maximum port speed
  - The requirements for a remote connection

SECURITY
- **Identify good practices to ensure network security, including:**
  - Selection of a security model (user and share level)
  - Standard password practices and procedures
  - The need to employ data encryption to protect network data
  - The use of a firewall